Re-Awakening and Shaping Africa's Future in a Globalised World

Re-Awakening and Shaping Africa's Future in a Globalised World

Editors:
Vusi Gumede,
Alinah Segobye,
Shadrack Gutto &
Serges Djoyou Kamga

AFRICA WORLD PRESS
TRENTON | LONDON | CAPE TOWN | NAIROBI | ADDIS ABABA | ASMARA | IBADAN | NEW DELHI

AFRICA WORLD PRESS
541 West Ingham Avenue | Suite B
Trenton, New Jersey 08638

Book design: Dawid Kahts
Cover design: Ashraful Haque

Cataloging-in-Publication Data may be obtained form the Library of Congress.

ISBNs: 978-1-56902-651-9 HB
978-1-56902-652-6 PB

Dedication:

The book is dedicated to the late Professor Sam Moyo for his role and mentorship.

Table of Contents

Acknowledgements

Book projects involve many hands and eyes. For a book that has taken as long as this one to finalize, there are inevitably many people who have played some role in it. In a book series of the Thabo Mbeki African Leadership Institute (TMALI), this is the third book coming out of the symposium that was convened at the University of South Africa (where TMALI is based) in August 2013. TMALI is a partnership project between the University of South Africa (UNISA) and the Thabo Mbeki Foundation (TMF).

The 2010 Inaugural Conference formally launched TMALI and the first book was published in 2013. This book owes many people for its publication, after many years. TMALI deliberately brought on board younger researchers/scholars and by implication the finalization of chapters took long. And the symposium also involved very senior scholars who presented but took long to finalize papers into quality book chapters. The editorial team also had some challenges that further delayed the publication of the book.

First and foremost, we are very grateful to the anonymous reviewers and copy editors. Secondly, we thank Professor Vusi Gumede, former TMALI Head, who started the book series that this book is part of and also for ensuring that the book is finally published. We are very grateful to the publisher also for patience and also ensuring that this book became reality. I worked with many others in ensuring that the book was finalized. I would like to particularly thank Moorosi Leshoele (TMALI Researcher & Doctoral Candidate at UNISA), Dr Richard Iraonya (who was a Postdoctoral Fellow at TMALI) and Mahlolo Makgati (who was a Research Assistant at TMALI). We are also grateful for cover design ideas from Sammy Mafu of Amafu Marketing in South Africa.

We would like to thank all those who played roles in the symposium, including TMALI and UNISA colleagues. We thank the editors and the contributors to this book. We acknowledge the role that the late Dr Roseline Achieng (who was a Senior Lecturer at TMALI) played in mentoring the younger researchers/scholars who also contributed in this book after reworking their papers after reviews.

We dedicate this book to the late Professor Sam Moyo who played a big role in the symposium and acted as our mentor until his tragic passing. We are also grateful to the TMALI Patron, H.E. Thabo Mbeki, who also participated in the symposium.

Victoria Qhobosheane
Research Coordinator: Thabo Mbeki African Leadership Institute, UNISA

Foreword

by
Prof Shadrack B. O. Gutto

Universities, research institutions and think tanks in Africa are slowly realising that the peoples of Africa are questioning the relevance of the knowledge they are generating and what they are teaching. Academics, scholars and intellectuals are expected to inform and influence Africa's governance and developmental paths. They have to fertilise the acceleration of transforming the continent and reposition it in the cruel, fiercely competitive, and globalised world. Africans and Africa need to determine their own destiny as was declared in the New Partnership for Africa's Development (NEPAD) "....We will determine our own destiny and call on the rest of the world to complement our efforts..." (OAU: 2001 paragraph 7). However, even the concept of 'partnership' conceived in NEPAD needs critical rethinking, precisely because those who enslaved Africans and later colonised us keep changing their colours but not the manner they relate with us. For a long time since the independence of many African countries, the imperialists whose development used the labour of Africans as slaves and the colonised (Williams: 1944, 1994) and plundered Africa's resources for their development (Rodney: 1972) have masqueraded as 'donors' and later changed the language to that of 'development partners'(Chang: 2007).

Progressive African and internationalist academics, scholars and intellectuals across institutional locations are beginning to rethink purposively and reconceptualise knowledge paradigms with a view to challenge Eurocentric knowledge systems embedded in universities in the former colonised societies in the global South. Decolonising universities and knowledge is the current flag of this struggle of ideas (Alvares and Faruqi (editors): 2012). This publication is contributing to this discourse, amongst others, with the aim of contributing to the search for Africa's development. What needs to be appreciated is that this is taking place within a historical context. Critical academics and activist students in many newly independent African countries were repressed and terrorised from the 1970s to 1990s by coercing state apparatuses, with the complicity of compromised judiciaries (CODESRIA: 1995; Africa Watch: 1991). Students and academics were sent to jail and were tortured, some were killed, and many were pushed into exile in some African countries, Europe and the Americas. I was among those who were forced to seek asylum and refuge abroad. The impact of this was the taming and silencing of critical thinking and robust scholarship in the universities. The current and apparent resurgence of critical thinking, scholarship and activism that is seeking the re-awakening of Africa and propelling Africa's development should be welcome, but with knowledge that some African countries are still led by tyrants who do not adhere to constitutionalism and the rule of law. They will pounce on those who expose the rottenness of their leadership.

This book is the third in the TMALI book series. The first book (*Perspectives on Thought Leadership for Africa's Renewal*) was edited by Kwandiwe Kondlo (published by AISA Press in 2013) while the second one (*Perspectives on African Renewal*) was edited by Chris Landsberg (published by Real African Publishers Press in 2018). This book is published at a time when there are powerful global forces (mainly neo-imperialistic in nature) that are pushing the agenda of a 'new scramble for Africa' (French: 2005; Stephan and Power (editors): 2012; Carmody: 2011; Southall and Melber (editors: 2009). It is not just a scramble for raw material resources such as minerals, oil and agricultural land; it is also the illegal and corrupt channeling of Africa's financial capital to the so-called developed economies (AU/ECA: 2015).

African academics, scholars and intellectuals should be prepared and ready to engage with African peoples and states to ensure that poverty and endemic desceases are eradicated. They should ensure that neo-colonialism and underdevelopment are countered vigorously to move Africa forward and aspire to be a strong global power politically, economically, technologically, militarily, culturally and socially. This book series is aligned to the Pan-African and African Renaissance perspectives with the hope that it will broaden its scope by attracting contributions from the African Diaspora, wherever they may be in the world. This sixth region of Africa, as the African Union has formally acknowledged, is essential to the Africa of today and the future.

REFERENCES

Africa Watch. 1991. *Academic Freedom & Human Rights Abuses in Africa.* London: Africa Watch.

African Union and The Economic Commission for Africa. 2015. *Illicit Financial Flows: Track it! Stop it! – Report of the High Level Panel on Illicit Financial Flows from Africa.* Addis Ababa: AU/ECA.

Alvares, C. and Faruqi, S.S., eds. 2012. *Decolonising The University – The Emerging Quest for Non-Eurocentric Paradigms.* Pulau Pinang: Penerbit Universiti Sains

Carmody, P. 2011. *The Scramble for Africa.* Cambridge: Polity Press.

Chang, H.J. 2007, 2008. *Bad Samaritans: The guilty secrets of rich nations & the threat to global philosophy.* London: Random House Business Books.

Churchill, W. 2002. *White Studies: The Intellectual Imperialism of Higher Education.* Penang: Citizens International.

Council for the Development of Social Science Research in Africa. 1995. *The State of Academic Freedom in Africa.* Dakar: CODESRIA.

French, H. W. 2005. *A Continent for the Taking – The Tragedy and Hope of Africa.* New York: Vintage Books.

Organisation of African Unity. 2001. *New Partnership for Africa's Renaissance.* Lusaka: NEPAD

Rodney, W. 1972. *How Europe Underdeveloped Africa.* Nairobi: East African Educational Publishers.

Southall, R and Melber, H., eds. 2009. *The New Scramble for Africa? Imperialism, Investment and Development.* Durban: University of KwaZulu Natal.

Stephan, H., and Power, M. eds. 2012. *The Scramble for Africa in the 21st Century – From the Old World to the New.* Cape Town: Renaissance Press.

Williams, E. 1944, 1994. *Capitalism & Slavery.* Chapel Hill: The University of North Carolina Press.

Introduction

Engaging the African Academy for Africa's Development

Vusi Gumede, Alinah Segobye,
Shadrack Gutto & Serges Djoyou

The Thabo Mbeki African Leadership Institute (TMALI) at the University of South Africa (UNISA) hosted a symposium in August 2013 titled: *Finding Solutions for Africa's Development*. The symposium was held as a follow up event to initiatives by TMALI, which was established in 2010 as an institute of the Thabo Mbeki Foundation in partnership with UNISA. The symposium brought together leading minds in Africa's research and development landscape and provided a vibrant space to interrogate the idea of African solutions for Africa's problems. The symposium came at a time when leading African intellectuals and other development practitioners were reflecting on a recently published report by *The Economist,* declaring Africa a hopeful continent[1]. This article caused palpable consternation and indignation among African researchers and development practitioners who observed that only a decade earlier, that the same publication had declared the continent a hopeless continent[2].

African leaders reacted to the Afro-pessimism spewed by the 2000 article in different ways. Leaders on the continent refuted this negative portrayal of an entire continent by championing the idea of African solutions for Africa's problems. In fact, the process towards realizing this position had begun much earlier in the 1990s, inspired by the democratic dispensation in South Africa and the celebration of the continent and indeed the world on the demise of a brutal and violent regime – apartheid. The peaceful transition to democracy with the leadership of freedom struggle icon Nelson Mandela had given buoyance to the continent to take full leadership of its development agenda and future. Africa's triumphant moment was in the dispelling of the myth that a Black led government in South Africa, on ascension to power, would seek revenge on the minority white population. Former President Thabo Mbeki underscored this stance of a leadership with dignity with his seminal *I am an African* speech delivered on the occasion of the inauguration of South Africa's Constitution on the 8th May 1996.

When South Africa became a member of the OAU, a leadership groundswell calling for greater African ownership of Africa's development agenda grew and the next few years witnessed momentous changes to Africa's institutional landscape. Some of the milestones include the transformation of the Organisation of African Unity (OAU) to the African Union (AU), which subsequently included the establishment of New Partnership for Africa's Development (NEPAD) and the African Peer Review Mechanism; the establishment of the Pan African Parliament and a commitment towards Africa's integration. The AU Commission took the development priorities enshrined in the founding principles of these African institutions as its cue and set about developing institutional frameworks to address priority issues including good governance, human rights and democratization on the continent. Peace, security and greater regional cooperation on the continent were also prioritized. The vibrancy of the AU Commission further saw it lead a groundbreaking initiative to host a conference in 2004 called the Conference of Intellectuals of Africa and the Diaspora. Africa's leaders, intellectuals, activists, cultural practitioners and civil society converged at this groundbreaking event to articulate the idea of African solutions for Africa's problems. The success of this conference spurred the hosting of the second conference in 2006 in Salvador de Bahia, Brazil which highlighted the importance of the African Diaspora as a key region of the continent and the significance of co-operation in the global South to realize Africa's development agenda. More importantly, the conference participants from the African continent were able to hear first-hand the lived experiences of liberation heroes such as Abdias do Nascimento and Afro-centric scholars including Molefi Kete Asante. Leaders of the global South, Africa-based intellectuals and Africans in the Diaspora, by showing solidarity with the Afro-Brazilians, were able to commit a strong solidarity, which has since been realized by many bilateral and multilateral cooperation and partnership agreements particularly in the African academy (see for instance Paul Zeleza and Tade Aina's initiatives in this regard). Follow-up of such conferences were held in London in the United Kingdom of Britain and in Kingston in Jamaica.

It is against this background that TMALI hosted an event proudly to continue conversations and come up with practical ideas on how the African academy can contribute meaningfully to discourses on Africa's development. Such a call has been made on a number of occasions by TMALI Patron H.E. Thabo Mbeki[3]. The symposium resulted with this book project, which is about realizing the aspiration of TMALI to develop knowledge products in addition to producing thought leaders. The chapters in this book have been peer reviewed and the book has undergone a rigorous process to select some of the best papers from the symposium. The book covers four thematic areas namely: coloniality; good governance; peace and security; African political economy, regional integration, trade and development and land, human rights and justice for Africa's development.

The first part of this book focuses on the coloniality theme. It comprises chapters that highlight the ill-fated nature of development in Africa against the backdrop of a relentless onslaught of imperial overtures from the global North. The chapters focus on what some of the authors characterise as the structural violence of imperial domination and its negation of an African development agenda. In this perspective, Ndlovu-Gatsheni embarks on 'unsmaking development's political economy of thrught' by 'taking stock of fifty years of African struggles for decolonization and development. Although development can be defined in numerous ways, the author favours historical and political perspectives in which development is a highly controversial idea and discourse as well as 'a terrain of hegemony and counter-hegemony' (Pieterse 2010: 9). This is linked to the post-1945 Truman version of development which portrays Europe and America as the saviour of the developing world. The chapter demonstrates that this version was pushed back by the 1955 Bandung decolonial version of development which verbalized development as liberation and a human right that has to be fought for (Mkandawire 2011). Ultimately, the author finds that the roadmap to global democracy in which Africa can develop goes through voluntary decolonization of the world system by Europe and North America.

Building on the coloniality discourse, Sithole through the lense of Chinweizu's 'critique and the 'scandal of Africa's maldevelopment' argues that the idea of development is based on the need to fix the ruins which result in 'maldevelopment' by the global North that relies on colonial infrastructure after the departure of the colonial masters. Sithole highlight the need to decolonise the mind of the Africans by showing them how colonial infrastructure still subdues them in time of freedom. In line with

Chinweizu's critique of development, Sithole calls for decolonisation of 'decolonisation' which has resulted in maldevelopment.

Adding his voice to the decolonial critical discourse, Mpofu underlines the need to decolonize power and knowledge in Africa by moving 'beyond imperial designs of interventionism and Eurocentrism'. The author argues that after instigating wars and conflicts on the continent and hiding behind the concepts of "the responsibility to protect," human rights, democracy and development, the former colonial masters loot African resources. They also penetrate the continent through Eurocentric epistemologies that are now the norm in African Universities. Mpofu therefore urges Africans to avoid reliance on 'coloniality library' that casts black people as non-beings and has defended the colonial and slavery projects. Ultimately, he calls for resistance to all types of Euro-American imperial designs that hinder Africa's development.

Zondi revisits Diop's perspectives on the future of African integration and its modalities as a contribution to on-going discussions initiated by Dr Nkosazana Dlamini-Zuma (when she was the chairperson of the African Union Commission) on Africa's second jubilee after independence. Zondi demonstrates the extent to which ideas proffered at the beginning of the independent period remain relevant today, and that in fact they are similar to ideas being put forward to define Africa's second jubilee today. In this sense, the chapter argues for the centrality of historical memory in enriching debates about Africa's futures today, so as to avoid either silencing the voices from the past that have not been heeded anyway or merely borrowing from experiences of others to respond to Africa's predicament today. The chapter suggests that two conditions are important when re-discovering the agency of African thought in history: firstly, it highlights the need to recognise the persistence of coloniality in general characterised by three vectors - coloniality of being, coloniality of power and coloniality of knowledge. This expresses itself in the connection of Africa with lack - lack of history, lack of civilisation, lack of development, lack of science and even lack of heritage of ideas necessary for defining its future. This coloniality of knowledge thrives on the erasure of historical memory in order to cement the place and dominance of exogenous ideas, policies and sciences in policy discourses and scholarly work today. Consequently, the contribution of Diop in the regional integration discourse must begin with an epistemic disobedience to Eurocentrism. Secondly, such disobedience requires that one adopts decolonial methodological options like Afrocentric thought. It is impossible to be authentic in thought without looking beyond the blinkers of Eurocentric thought for lenses and tools of analysis.

In her chapter 'Building Critical Consciousness for Advancing African Renaissance: Case Study from Pan-African and Afrocentric Institutions', Nkenkana argues that the relevance of the African renaissance will be questioned if it cannot motivate its beneficiaries who are the Africans. She is of the view that without a particular type of education or an empowering education marked by critical consciousness, the African renaissance will not be relevant. Unfortunately, most African institutions are the bridge to critical consciousness, but are the drivers of coloniality projects. Nevertheless, the author argues that there are solid Afrocentric institutions. To make her case, she provides a case study analysis of the Thabo Mbeki African Leadership Institute, the Molefi Kete Asante Institute in United State of America and African Leadership Academy in Kenya where she found that education is informed by Afrocentric paradigm and African epistemologies. She, however, highlights the need to infuse such transformative paradigms in mainstream education. Fotoyi, similarly, makes case for a specific type of education if the renaissance of Africa is to be achieved. She acknowledges the importance of education for the transformation of Africa, decries the current perspective, which studies Africa from a Eurocentric perspective. The latter cannot tell the true story of Africa and cannot do justice to African knowledge system perceived as inexistent under this paradigm. Fotoyi calls for the abandonment of a Eurocentric education system crafted in the coloniality of power aiming to subjugate Africans. She argues for a departure from an education which echoes coloniality towards Afrocentric paradigm, which would capture African tradition and culture and therefore be relevant and significant for the African renaissance.

The second theme, constituting Part 2, focuses on democratic governance, peace and security and Africa's development. The intertwined nature of these is tackled by the authors who highlight the way in which Africa's resource abundance has not always translated to positive development. If anything, resources have created the conditions for extreme impoverishment in many countries with the complicity of Africans. Many African states failed their citizenry by not providing good governance and oversight for resources, leading to protracted conflicts and war. The African state too often became the violator with citizens lacking both peace and security, often for long periods. Politics of patronage and 'Big man' syndrome continue to plague many countries, which should be demonstrating better development indicators given their natural resources endowment (Kwengwere; Shilaho in this volume).

In his chapter "Redefining Good Governance for Africa's Development: Going beyond Mediocrity", Kwengwere interrogates the concept of good governance and its relevance for Africa's development. To this end he examines the challenges of governance in Africa. He focuses on how the positive relationship between governance and development seems to work in some countries but fails to work in others. It is argued that in countries such as Botswana and Mauritius where governance policies are implemented, development follows. Nevertheless, where little attention is paid to the implementation of these policies, in countries such as DRC for example, development remains a dream. Therefore, Kwengwere calls on African countries to implement adopted policies, enable the civil society to play its role of watchdog, empower to private sector and the media to become of the equation, as well as relying on homegrown solutions and not exclusively to the "one size fits all approach" generally imported. In the same perspective, he urges development partners to respect homegrown governance solutions which are likely to be more responsive to the local context.

The implementation of governance policies goes through strong institutions. In this perspective, Alemazung in his chapter argues that African "Constitutional Democratic Governance [is] in Need of Checks and Balances of Powers in Africa". These checks and balances should be established through a strong separation of powers where no institutions or branch of government is above the law. The effectiveness of the separation of powers will foster institutions and destroy "strong men" who abused power in Africa. For this to happen it is imperative to enshrine the notion of separation of powers in the constitutions to prevent gross abuse of power and manipulation of electoral processes by ruling parties and leaders as leaders have to be reviewed continually and compelled to enforce healthy democracies. Therefore, promoting constitutionalism and the rule of law will certainly improve governance for Africa's development. The author adds his voice to the call for the establishment of constitutionalism as the backbone of strong institutions,

Shilaho advocates for the reformation of the post-colonial state in Africa to deepen democratic principles and meaningful participation of citizenry. Shilaho makes his point through his chapter 'Africa's Third Wave of Democracy: Reform Indispensable to Democratic Consolidation'. The author argues that the entrenchment of the rule of law and constitutionalism will assist in checking excesses of informalisation of politics and guarantee credible elections. This will not only improve transparency in the process of elections and people-centric democracy, but will also unseat "Big Men". Ultimately, entrenching the rule of law and constitutionalism will ensure sustained economic growth, and equitable distribution of its benefits through development to secure stability and pre-empt conflicts related to contestation over scarce resources.

In her chapter 'Enhancing Governance in Public-Private Partnerships in Africa: Some Lessons Learned from South Africa', Fombad presents an assessment of the extent to which governance has been achieved in Public-Private Partnerships (PPPs) in South Africa given that it is the leading sub–Saharan African country in PPPs, and critically examined the lessons learned for other African countries. A creative solution is proposed by Fombad who observes the potential PPPs as an avenue for bringing private sector management and governance principles to the public sector domain. This said, the author notes that PPPs are also prone to inherent maladies including lack of transparency and inclusiveness. The author proposes people-centric PPPs, which one would assume was already embodied in the formulation of such entities. One can only note that Africa's experience with PPPs has given rise to very interesting if not sometimes bizarre institutional formations, which have not escaped the taint of corrupt practice or undue influence from those with vested interests. It can be said that the capacity to deliver a different era of good leadership and governance may lie far beyond the current models of PPPs in African private and public sector partnerships (see also Adekilekun and Gan in this volume). Ultimately, Fombad is of the view that attaining the promises of development through PPP rests on enhancing the following key governance factors: the need for sound procurement procedures, the importance of participatory involvement, firm political will and commitments towards PPPs, frameworks built on transparency techniques, and clarity on risk sharing strategy. She submits that poor governance in PPPs will lead to a lack of appeal of PPPs as a new policy alternative for development in Africa.

The third thematic area – Part 3 – addresses issues of the African political economy, regional integration, trade and development. A number of chapters in this pillar pointed at the intertwined nature of these sectors in Africa's development trajectories. This section opens with a chapter 'Towards Building an Institutional Infrastructure for Africa's Development and Economic Self-Determination' by Ajoku and Magashi. The authors call for a more radical transformation of Africa's development agenda through self-determination of Africa's economies by using the vehicle of regional cooperation and infrastructure development and strengthening both public and private institutional frameworks. Their call is based on the sad reality that so far Africa's development model is borrowed from the West that has 'vested interest' in the model. Ajoku and and Megashi call for a revolution in Africa. This entails moving away from the free market economy which is an extension and consolidation of neo-colonialist strategies. The authors urge African countries to build an effective infrastructure to create an attractive and secure operative atmosphere for growth and economic self-determination. While they welcome reliance on foreign direct investment (FDI), the latter should be embraced on the bases of fairness and equity. In the same perspective, Africans should invest regionally thereby promoting regional integration through acquisition of home grown technology. There is a strong need for effective regulatory mechanisms that shall pervade sectoral investments that support and encourage intra-regional investments. Ajoku and Megashi simply argue that without economic self-determination to be developed through regional integration, Africa will not develop.

In his chapter 'the Integrative Functions of the African Union Commission: Reconsidering the Operational Context' Fagbayibo challenges the AU Commission to provide more robust leadership to drive the process of regional and continental integration. He argues that in spite of the widespread recognition of the role of regional integration as a solution to Africa's development, little has been done to create durable and effective regional institutions to drive the integration process. The AU Commission is simply unable to discharge its integration functions. This inability is caused by the operational context that is intergovernmental in a rigid manner, an operational framework that is not articulated clearly and a defective internal administration system in the Commission. Therefore, it is essential to strengthen the Commission. This would entail enhancing resources allocation for the AU commission and support for the work of the Commission and its institutions by member states. This point was made cogently during the plenary of the symposium. The observation that the AU Commission cannot provide leadership for an Africa-centric development agenda whilst it is heavily dependent on external donor funding for its operational budget is disquieting. Numerous platforms both at AU summits and beyond have called for African leaders to commit resources to the AU but sadly this has not happened. As a result, the AU's decade has not translated into a developmental opportunity harnessed by the continent's leaders. The interests of states continue to take precedence above well intentioned aspirations of the regional economic communities and the continental body.

Furthermore, there is a need to include the Commission in the implementation structures of the AU and Regional Economic Communities (RECs); ensure the flexibility arrangements with respect to some of the functions of the Commission, enhancing the visibility of the Commission in critical aspects of the integration process and a comprehensive evaluation framework.

Adekilekun and Gan in their chapter on infrastructure development through Public Private Partnerships (PPPs) deplore the lack of infrastructure on the continent. In fact, they are of the view that current infrastructure challenges hinder Africa's development. The situation is exacerbated by the inefficiencies, corruption, lack of skills and technical know-how that have characterized the provisions of public infrastructure through the traditional public procurement model. Adekilekun and Gan therefore propose PPPs approach to infrastructure development in Africa. For this to happen effectively, governments should work with the private sector and tap into its capital to fund and maintain infrastructure projects and rely on skills and technological know-how from the private sector among other initiatives. In addition, African governments should adopt a uniform legal and regulatory regime to address PPPs transactions in the continent, review outdated policies carefully, build mutual trust with the private sector and develop the capacity to deal with PPP projects at the national state/provincial and the local government levels. Failure to establish a credible PPPs for infrastructure building would definitely cripple Africa's development initiatives.

Olowu examines some of the quandaries facing the continent in reflecting on the impact of aid on Africa and future outlook. He explores how best aid can achieve development results in a cost-effective manner and how this should be measured in human terms in Africa. Through this interrogation, Olowu echoes what has been cogently articulated by other scholars in noting that development aid weakens Africa's capacity to lead its own development agenda and more critically its capacity to innovate in the development arena. In Olowu's view, aid will not make a significant difference unless there is development cooperation accountability framework between recipient governments and their donors, especially in light of planned monitoring and follow-up by autonomous social agents. In addition, it is essential to have a framework for improving country-level mutual accountability between developing countries, donors and stakeholders; and measures to enhance accountability for development results produced by aid.

The chapter by Qhobosheane examines 'the potential impact of Economic Partnership Agreements (EPAs) with Europe on Africa's development.' The EPAs which seeks to replace the Lomé and Cotonou Agreement between the EU and African Caribbean and Pacific (ACP) countries are not compatible with the World Trade Organisation agreement as they offer preferential treatment for developing countries. It calls for reciprocity in trade between the EU and ACP countries. Qhobosheane argues that the EPAs will under-develop Africa, which is not yet able the compete with the EU as equal partners. In making her case she highlights the need for regional integration to be finalized first before the implementation of EPAs and not the other way round as claimed by proponents of EPAs. In addition, opening the playing field to full reciprocity without the exports of interest to Sub-Saharan Africa (SSA) countries being considered in the liberalization would frustrate SSA existing industries. Moreover, EPAs would lead to a huge loss in revenue collections in the ACP countries due to elimination of tariffs under the agreement. In addressing these shortcomings, Qhobosheane urges the engineers of EPAs to deepen regional integration with a view to boosting intra-Africa trade. This should be given sufficient lead time to allow the African countries to build requisite competitiveness accompanied with significant developmental and industrial programmes to complement the larger markets with increased supply and diversified capacities. Opening African markets for entry of the EU's goods without tariff should take place gradually for the sake of allowing industrial upgrading and export diversification in the continent among other measures. Ultimately, it is found that the EPAs through full reciprocity will be detrimental to Africa's economic advancement, both through loss of the revenue and loss of industrial development.

Given the unavoidable role of the BRICS (the consortium made of Brazil, Russia, India, China and South Africa) in the contemporary development discourse, Saurombe assesses the opportunities the BRICS brings to Africa and urges African countries not to miss the opportunities to enhance South-South cooperation through the BRICS. In reality all BRICS countries are investing in Africa. While Saurombe appreciates the availability of foreign direct investment through the BRICS, he is also worried about BRICS countries' interest in African natural resources. He not only wishes South Africa represents the entire continent's interest in the BRICS, he also calls on African leaders to be open minded and deal with the BRICS countries through bilateral relations between countries and less as a group. He calls on African leaders to avoid turning the BRICS Africa relations into a relationship based on natural resources to one that promotes Africa's long terms economic growth and development trajectory.

The last theme in this book deals with land, human rights and justice. Clearly, discourses of land in the context of Africa's development remain as complex and vexing as they were on the eve of independence for many African states. When freedom fighters took to arms in the quest for liberation land was the uniting force, it remains so today and will inform realities in the future. The continually changing game of Russian roulette that is the subject of land and who owns it in Africa has to take into account climate change when taking a long term perspective to Africa's development agenda. Clearly Africa is not short of productive land, however the governance of land resources has been a major challenge leading to some of the worst humanitarian crises affecting millions of citizens. Dlamini writes on 'The Link Between Governance and Land Grabs in Sub-Saharan Africa'. To this end, he unpacks the links between governance, land grabs and illegal land alienation in Africa by pointing out the global scenarios which drive this phenomenon. In this analysis, the continued loss of land by citizens in the post-independence state highlights the abdication of accountable leadership and greed by corporates and colluding Africans in disenfranchising citizenry. This phenomena, often linked to self-aggrandizing tendencies of corrupt leaders has also been the cause and source of poverty and conflicts on the continent. It is argued that, any desire for peace and security and or healthy developmental indicators for the continent's masses will remain an elusive dream whilst the appetite for quick and illicit rewards remain key drivers for those who wield power and leadership positions.

For Africa, he underlines a strong need of 'leadership for Land governance in Africa'. According to him, the concept of 'land governance' captures the legal and bureaucratic system for managing social relationships in land, and is receiving increasing attention from the international development community. In the modern nation-state, it involves a wide array of agencies, professions and bureaucracies, requiring significant resources. The so-called professions of the land include lawyers, land surveyors, planners and valuers. Yet not only these groups have been deeply compromised by their associations with past colonial structures of power and knowledge, the technical complexities of their work can be used to obscure issues, hide the power relationships underlying law, and confuse the public. Therefore, a transformative leadership is needed for land governance to avoid land-grabbing for example. Essentially, for the achievement of pro-poor land governance, it is necessary to rely on more participatory local strategies, the management of land and ensure that most basic resource of the state meet the needs of 'the poor'.

Odusola examines 'Economic and institutional determinants of foreign land acquisition in Africa' based on 'an empirical analysis'. He shows that the appetite for land is informed by the need to secure food, raw materials for industrial production and residences. In addition, availability of inland water is also a defining factor for land acquisition as those who need such turn to Africa to satisfy the thirst. The acquisition of land is also exacerbated by weak governance and corruption. Foreign land acquisition in Africa is indeed rampant. Odusola address the issue by calling for the adoption of clear policies to ensure that foreign land acquisition does not compromise water use for domestic and industrial purposes. He also identifies a critical role for the political class and the civil society organisations (CSOs) that should champion land reforms and serve as vanguard of the poor. In the same perspective, governments should be more active in investing in land related documentations and processes such as titling, registration and certification of land and broadly adopt a continent-wide strategy for land acquisition. Governments should capacitate local chiefs and landlords to ensure that they participate meaningfully in land deals, their consent should be considered and adequate compensation should be provided when their land is acquired.

The chapter by Molebatsi cogently highlights the tensions between state and citizens on the subject of land. He argues that the development project in Botswana has been accompanied by systematic land dispossession and marginalization of the poor, particularly San communities. The chapter draws attention to impoverishment, which often affects vulnerable indigenous minorities when their land is expropriated under the guise of national development. The chapter highlights how citizen agency through civic society mobilization can challenge the state and in some cases provide alternative routes for inclusion for minority groups. This has indeed been one of the ways in which solutions for Africa's development challenges have been realized when groups reorganized themselves to form development-oriented institutions such as community based and not for profit institutions, which benefited citizenry. Ultimately it is argued that these sites of resistance are important pointers towards more inclusive social transformation in Botswana.

With regards to human rights and justice for Africa's development, the chapters highlight the importance of a human rights and justice for Africa's development agenda. Jegede makes a case for linking climate change and its adverse impacts and protection of human rights. He highlights the need to rethink the climate change debate by giving more attention to its impact on human rights and not only on the environment and meteorology. In making his case, Jegede demonstrates how climate change implicates a range of human rights guaranteed under the African Charter on Human and Peoples' Rights and the prospects in the functions of the African Commission on Human and Peoples' Rights as a response to threats posed by climate change in Africa. According to the author, climate change constitutes a threat to a range of human rights such as rights to food, water, housing, peace, health and environment which are guaranteed either expressly or impliedly under the African Charter. In the same vein, Jegede shows that through its promotional, protective, interpretive and assembly-entrusted mandate, the African Commission has the potential to address threats to human rights posed by climate change on the continent.

Still on human rights, Kamga is of the view that the re-awakening of Africa will not happen if Africans are not welcome in other African countries. He examines what can be done to develop a positive attitude for the reduction of xenophobia and the realisation of human rights of migrants and refugees' communities in South Africa. Kamga found that while there is a need to address socio economic inequality broadly, xenophobia will not be defeated without education of the host communities on the need to respect human dignity of all South Africans and those from outside South Africa who live within the country, a clear and practical implementation of the Bill of Rights to the benefit of refugees and migrants and securing their cultural integration. The author is of the view that if politicians keep foreign nationals at the margins trough policies and practices, xenophobia cannot be defeated and as a result migrant's rights will be tempered with. Ultimately, Kamga calls for a human rights based approach to migration to address xenophobia in Africa and in South Africa in particular.

Indeed, if Africa is to own its development agenda, one of the critical conditions is to minimize if not completely eliminate internal sources of conflict, strengthen state capability and empower citizenry. Africa needs strong, democratic and effective institutions fostering a healthy, active and meaningfully participating citizenry in a context where human rights are respected. This collection of chapters highlight how the African continent needs to have the disposition of a healthy and organic body from mental, physiological to psychosocial realms to resist and repel direct and indirect attacks, which will continually probe and prod in search of new lines of weakness through which to invade and attack from within as many have argued. This book calls for a unity of purpose, consciousness and voice for Africa's leadership, academy, citizenry and development practitioners to realize a truly united and capable continent. As it is taken for granted at TMALI, thought leadership, critical consciousness and thought liberation are the three key ingredients that can truly take Africa forward.

PART 1:

Questioning Coloniality

Unmasking Development's Political Economy of Truth:

Taking Stock of more than Fifty Years of African Struggles for Decolonization and Development

Sabelo J. Ndlovu-Gatsheni

Introduction

> The genuine implementation of the principle of autocentric development implies very different reasoning that has the nerve to challenge the criteria of economic rationality observed by conventional economics (Amin 1990: 58).

As noted by James Ferguson, 'Development' in our time is such a central value. Wars are fought and coups launched in its name. The entire systems of government and philosophy are evaluated according to their ability to promote development. Indeed, it seems difficult to find any way to talk about large parts of the world except in these terms (Ferguson 1990: xiii). Inevitably, African leaders were so enchanted by the post-1945 developmental promise to the extent that they strongly believed that decolonization would not only result in taking over of the colonially-crafted colonial state, but that they would achieve full sovereignty. This would enable them to launch autonomous developmental trajectories aimed not only at reducing the inequality gap between economies of ex-colonies and those of erstwhile colonial powers but also at improving the socio-economic conditions of the formerly colonised peoples. However, more than fifty years since the dawn of decolonization, 'the promised land of development remained an illusion' (Grosfoguel & Cervantes-Rodriguez 2002: xxvi). This study seeks to explain why development has remained an illusion through an analysis of development's political economy of truth and its implications for the fifty-years of African struggles for deepening decolonization and achievement of socio-economic development.

The chapter commences with a definition of development from two vantage points informed by post-1945 Truman imperial version of development. The first point is premised on the ideas of Europe and North American imposing development on Africa. The second point is on the post-1955 Bandung decolonial version of development that privileged the ability of Africans to advance their own development in a decolonised and democratised global environment. It proceeds to articulate the nationalist, decolonial and humanist philosophical basis informing African development thought. The third section is a critical assessment of development initiatives by Africa and how they locked horns with imperial development initiatives for Africa cascading from the Breton Woods paradigm. The last section is the conclusion.

Development can be understood from two vantage points. The first is ahistorical and apolitical technicist-liberal approach. In this perspective, development is understood in three ways. Firstly, development is understood as a vision, description or measure of the state of being of a desirable society. Secondly, development is understood as a process of social change in which societies are transformed over long periods. Finally, development is conceived to be consisting of deliberate efforts aimed at improvement of human life (Thomas 2000: 773-787). The problem with the ahistorical and apolitical approach is that it does not take into account the realities of world power and global interests as well as colonial matrices of power that constitute the discursive context within which the notions of development emerge, are defined and articulated, contested and questioned (Ndlovu-Gatsheni 2013a; Ndlovu-Gatsheni 2013b). For Africa, the longstanding challenge has been how to democratize the racially hierarchized and Euro-North American-centric world system that is informed by power politics and coercion (Grosfoguel & Cervantes-Rodriguez 2002: xi-xxix).

This chapter favours historical and political perspectives where development is understood as a highly contested idea and discourse as well as 'a terrain of hegemony and counter-hegemony' (Pieterse 2010: 9). This is a more appealing approach because modern conceptions of development as an idea and discourse are commonly traced to a modernity that privileged Euro-North American regime of truth about human progress as cascading from Europe and North America as a global centre of power. The popularization and globalization of development as a human aspiration, unfolded as a form of theorization, ideologization as well as imposition of Europe and North America's own path of development on other parts of the world (Escobar 2012). This culminated into the post-1945 Truman version of development whereby Europe and North America claimed to have been entrusted by modern history with the task of developing the Third World in its image (Truman 1949). At the centre of Truman version of development is what Fantu Cheru termed 'the imperial project' that is informed by geopolitical considerations and global North's power calculations as well as consistent rhetoric of humanitarianism that conceals coloniality (Cheru 2009: 275-278).

The Truman version of development is deeply situated in the long history of the making of the modern world system and the invention of Africa that was accompanied by what Valentin Y. Mudimbe terms the 'paradigm of difference' (Mudimbe 1988; Mudimbe 1994). It is traceable to what became known as 'voyages of discovery' that opened the way for mercantilism, the slave trade, imperialism and colonialism. These processes were articulated from a colonial perspective as entailing the spreading of civilization, modernity, commerce and Christianity to those places like Africa that were described as the 'heart of darkness' (Conrad 1902). Consequently, development as an offspring of enlightenment and modernity became entangled in a complex and long history of the logic of coloniality informed by domination, oppression, and exploitation on the one hand, and the rhetoric of modernity that promised a brave modern society where salvation, civilization, progress, economic growth, freedom and democracy would be the order of life (Mignolo 2005).

The Truman version of development became contested by the Bandung decolonial version of development cascading from Bandung Conference of 1955. The Bandung version articulated development as liberation and a human right that has to be fought for (Mkandawire 2011). African struggles for decolonization and development have remained trapped within the hegemonic Truman version of development which is backed up by what Adebayo Adedeji termed the 'development merchant system' (DMS) driven by the Breton Woods Institutions (BWI) which finances the implementation of exogenous development agenda (Adedeji 2002: 4). At the centre of the DMS is what David Slater termed 'imperiality of knowledge' constituted by 'interweaving of geopolitical power, knowledge and subordinating representation of the other' (Slater 2004: 223). DMS maintains coloniality long after the dismantlement of administrative colonialism. It still approaches Africa as a space inhabited by a people 'shorn of the legitimate symbols of independent identity and authority' as well as a 'space ready to be penetrated, worked over, restructured and transformed' from outside (Slater 2004: 223). DMS exist as a consortium of International Monetary Fund (IMF), World Bank (WB), World Trade Organization (WTO), International Non-Governmental Organizations (IGOs) and Multinational Corporations (MCs). They advance a 'Bretton Woods Paradigm' of development as part of continuation of the Truman version (Therien 1999: 723-742).

At another level, the Bandung decolonial version of development continues to contest the Truman imperial version of development through enabling the crafting of counter-hegemonic development initiatives and strategies that included the formation of the Organization of African Unity (OAU); the demand for a New Economic International Order (NIEO); the crafting of the African Declaration on Cooperation, Development and Economic Independence of 1973; the Revised Framework of the Principles for the Implementation of New International Economic Order in Africa of 1976; the Lagos Plan of Action for the Economic Development of Africa 1980; the African Priority Programme for Economic Recovery of 1986; the African Alternative Framework to Structural Adjustment Programme for Social Economic Recovery and Transformation of 1989; the African Charter for Popular Participation for Development of 1990; United Nations New Agenda for Development of Africa of 1991; right up to the current New Partnership for African Development (NEPAD) of 2001 (Adesina et al 2006).

The Bandung version shared some commonalities with the 'United Nations Paradigm' and its emphasis on human development. The Bandung Conference was informed by the spirit of decolonization, South-South solidarity and principle of non-alignment. The conference laid the basis for the struggle to decolonize and democratize the international society so as to achieve equitable representation in global decision-making bodies as it called for a new International Economic Order (NIEO) (Kahin 1956). Development was articulated in terms of transcending colonialism and coloniality as well as in terms of freedom, self-determination and self-reliance under state mediation and direction (Berger 2004). The Bandung Conference also endorsed the right of governments to freely choose their own political and economic systems (Abdulgani 1964). For all the states that emerged from colonialism, nationalism and development were articulated as inseparable processes simply because colonialism denied Africans both development and freedom. Therefore, in Africa and other ex-colonised parts of the world, nationalism and developmentalism constituted efforts at 're-membering' those dismembered societies and peoples so as to regain their lost ontological density.

Re-membering Africa: Philosophical drive to transcend colonialism and capitalism

In the language of Ngugi wa Thiong'o African development initiatives constituted efforts aimed at 're-membering' Africans after centuries of being 'dismembered from the land, from labour, from power, and from memory' (Ngugi wa Thiong'o 2009: 22). Thus development conceived in decolonial historical and political-Africa-centred terms can be defined as a long-term struggle for 're-membering of Africa' that encapsulates such initiatives as Ethiopianism, Garveyism, Negritude, Pan-Africanism(s), African Personality, Afrocentricity, Concienscism, African humanism, African socialism(s), Black Consciousness Movement, and African Renaissance. This point was well captured by Nigerian novelist Chinua Achebe when he said:

> You have all heard of African personality; of African democracy; of an African way to socialism; of Negritude, and so on. They are all props we have fashioned at different times to help us get on our feet again. Once we are up we shall not need any of them anymore. But for the moment it is in the nature of things that we need to counter racism with what Jean-Paul Satre has called an anti-racist racism, to announce not just that we are good as the next man but that we are better (Achebe 1997: 179).

Re-membering Africa entailed building unity inside individual states, aspiring for pan-African unity at the continental level and fighting for deracialization, decolonization and democratization of the racially hierarchized and Western-centric modern world system that came into being in 1492. Inevitably the discourse of development in Africa commenced with a new presentation of African history since the encounter between Africa and Europe resulted in partial usurpation of African history if not its displacement and silencing (Depelchin 2005). This is why Paul Tiyambe Zeleza posed the question: 'Is autonomy of African history possible, can this history be written without European referents, is it possible to liberate African history from the epistemological traps of Eurocentrism, the traps of the 'colonial library?' (Zeleza 2005:1). This is also why Kwame Nkrumah emphasised the need to re-write the history of Africa as part of 're-membering' the continent and centring of African personality (Nkrumah 1964). His concept of philosophical consciencism articulated African development as embracing traditional Africa, Islamic Africa and Euro-Christian Africa as constituent elements of a new emergent ideology for the harmonious growth and development of society. This is how he put it:

> The philosophy that must stand behind this social revolution is that which I have once referred to as philosophical consciencism: consciencism is the map in intellectual terms of the disposition of forces which will enable African society to digest the Western and the Islamic and the Euro-Christian elements in Africa, and develop them in such a way that they fit into the African personality. The African personality is itself defined by the cluster of humanist principles which underlie the traditional African society. Philosophical consciencism is that philosophical standpoint which, taking its start from the present content of the African conscience indicates the way in which progress is forged out of the conflict in that conscience (Nkrumah 1964: 79).

If development to African nationalist thinkers and theorists, meant moving from one state of being that is no longer adequate towards another that is more desirable, then that state of being was that of slavery, imperialism, colonialism, apartheid and capitalism. Such African leaders and theorists as Frantz Fanon, Leopold Sedar Senghor, Kenneth Kaunda, Julius Nyerere and Nelson Mandela emphasised the importance of humanism that was denied by the slave trade, imperialism, colonialism, apartheid and neo-colonialism. There was a strong feeling that slavery, imperialism, colonialism, capitalism, apartheid and neo-colonialism were antithesis of humanism and resulted in denial of humanity to black people. Independence and development had to culminate in restoration of lost African ontological density as part of 're-membering' process. Kenneth Kaunda defined humanism as a 'philosophy of life' and noted that colonialism 'devalued man' (Kaunda & Morris 1966: 19-21). Kaunda posited that:

> It was nationalism, of course, which restored our self-confidence, for it taught us what we could do together as men [and women], and only as men [and women]—at no stage in the freedom struggle had we the material power or military might of colonialists. It was humanity in revolt that won us freedom. [...] It was the triumph of a Man-centred society over a Power-centred society. This intense belief in the possibility of Man is a discovery which Africa appears to be making long after the West has discarded it (Kaunda & Morris 1966: 21).

In his 'meditations on man', Kaunda expressed his conviction that 'only the recovery of a sense of the centrality of Man will get politics back on the right track' and he posed the question: "How can we humanise our politics in Zambia so that the humblest and least endowed of our citizens occupy a central place in Government's concerns?" (Kaunda & Morris 1966: 41) The dominance of humanist nationalism resulted in various experimentations with African socialism, the most well-known example being that of 'Ujamaa' (family-hood) of Tanzania under Julius Nyerere, which sought to provide an escape route from capitalism's idea of happiness based on 'exploitation of man by man' (Nyerere 1967).

Nationalist developmentalism was informed by a realisation that colonial domination was imposed on Africa successfully because of 'guns and steel' (Mkandawire 2005: 13). Therefore, for Africa to survive domination and humiliation there was a need to develop and modernize. Another important element of nationalist developmentalism was the desire to eradicate what Thandika Mkandawire termed the 'unholy trinity of ignorance, poverty and disease' (Mkandawire 2005: 13). It is therefore important to take stock of African nationalist-inspired development initiatives since the dawn of decolonization, beginning with the implications of the Bandung spirit for the demand of a New Economic International Order (NEIO).

The Bandung Spirit and the demand for a New Economic International Order

The Asian-African Conference that was held in April 1955 in Bandung in Indonesia constituted the highest point of the Afro-Asian solidarity and movement that was informed by Afro-Asian decolonial nationalism. When the Afro-Asian movement was formed, its specific aim was to hasten the process of decolonization (Kimche 1973). The focus of the Bandung Conference by 1955 was how to create conditions for global peaceful co-existence within a post-1945 dispensation that was troubled by ideological rivalry between the West and the East, which became known as the Cold War. The focus was also on consolidation of solidarity and cooperation among newly independent states in the face of a 'mixture of wooing, bullying, flattery, threats and "presents" coming from superpowers (Jansen 1966: 309).

At another level, a 12-point economic cooperation agenda of the Bandung Conference identified development as an urgent priority for Afro-Asian states. It is clear that at Bandung the African and Asian leader realised that the development they urgently wanted could not be attained within a modern world system that was racially hierarchized and Euro-North American-centric. Decolonization needed to be expanded to grapple with a global system that remained asymmetrical in its power configuration—a world where the newly independent African states had no voice in global decision-making. This is why the participants at the Bandung Conference were deeply troubled by their lack of participation in the international institutions that had been established to govern world affairs (Abdulgani 1964).

One can safely argue that the Bandung conference correctly identified 'global coloniality' as a major hindrance to the achievement of development in Africa and Asia (Ndlovu-Gatsheni 2013). This argument is amplified by the fact that three objectives drove the Bandung spirit namely non-alignment in the Cold War; elimination of all forms of colonialism and racism and finally, modernization and economic development (Mayall 1990). The idea of non-alignment spoke to an aspiration for a new international norm that gave states the right to develop and orchestrate an autonomous, freely chosen trajectory in the international system without being compelled to follow the imperial-hegemonic dictates of the superpowers. The issue of equality of states was stressed including raising concerns about under-representation of African and Asian states on the United Nations Security Council. The Bandung spirit also articulated the problem of international economic injustices (Krasner 1981).

What is also important about the Bandung worldview was to introduce new and alternative principles for international society informed by international engagement based on dialogue and cooperation; justice, fairness and peaceful co-existence. These principles indicated the desire of those states emerging from colonialism to make a paradigm shift from imperial and colonial principles that were informed by the spirit of domination and coercion as international mode of interaction that has been in place since 1492.

The Bandung spirit laid a strong basis to the crystallization of a Third World coalition in the United Nations, which in 1964 constituted the United Nations Conference on Trade and Development (UNCTAD) and informed the ideas that produced the Non-Alignment Movement, which was formerly constituted at a summit in Algiers in 1971. NAM included Latin American states, which had gained political independence far earlier than Asian and African colonies. The Latin American states had been active within the United Nations in pushing the agenda of reforming the international economic and political system. At the Cairo Economic Conference of 1962, the Afro-Asian and Latin American states had already pointed out that the more dangerous division of the world was the North-South divide, which is taking the form of the 'haves' and the 'have nots' rather than the ideologically informed East-West divide that pre-occupied the western powers (Nesadurai 2005: 12).

The resolutions of first NAM Summit held in Belgrade in Yugoslavia in 1961 and the Cairo Summit of 1962 are credited for putting pressure of the United Nations to establish UNCTAD as an agency to address Third World development issues. The problem is that UCTAD played a marginal role in global economic governance as the United States of America and other industrial powers rejected any role for the body in trade negotiations (Taylor 2003). At the time of the launch of UCTAD the Latin American economist Raul Prebisch was pushing forward the dependency thesis to explain the problem of development in the Third World. He was appointed UCTAD's first Secretary General. Informed by dependency ideas UCTAD's demands included greater access to industrial countries' markets; greater self-reliance amongst the Third World countries; right to nationalise assets and democratization of all binding international decision-making based on the principle of 'one-nation, one vote' (Gosovic 1972). These demands were informed by Prebisch's decolonial diagnosis of Third World underdevelopment in terms of its structural dependency on a capitalist core that controlled all levers of international decision-making and profitable economic activity. The proposals were rejected by industrial powers.

Third World leaders did not give up the fight for a reformed international system. The period from 1973 to 1980 were dominated by the demand for NIEO. It was following the oil crises of 1971 and 1973 that the Third World coalition united to push further for NIEO. They pushed for this through the G77—a coalition of developing countries. NIEO was informed by the dependency ideas which emphasised decolonization of global coloniality that favoured the industrial powers and disadvantaged those countries that emerged from colonialism. NIEO called for restructuring of global structural regimes informing unequal trade and other economic interactions (Cox 1979: 257). The more radical members of the G77 demanded restitution based on the notion that the industrialised powers owed something to the South as compensation for slavery and colonialism (Cox 1979). In the spirit of NIEO, the African leaders adopted the *African Declaration on Cooperation, Development and Economic Independence* in 1973, which articulated Africa's strategy for gradual disengagement from the world economy through escalation of national and continental self-reliance. This was followed by the production of *The Revised Framework of the Principles for the Implementation of New International Economic Order in Africa* of 1976. It was produced by the United Nations Economic Commission for Africa (UNECA) and became the intellectual and theoretical foundation for the drafting of *Monrovia Strategy for the Economic Development of Africa* of 1979. The Monrovia Declaration emphasised collective self-reliance and economic integration of African economies; investment in science and technology as the backbone of Africa's development process; ensuring Africa's self-reliance in food production and a commitment to achieve modern African economies by the year 2000 (Baah 2003).

The African demand for NIEO was resisted by the industrial powers as part of communist conspiracy, as irrational and as too revolutionary. Consequently, very little headway was made simply because the powerful and the dominant want to stay powerful and dominant. The little concession made was the adoption in 1975 of the Charter of Economic Rights and Duties of States at the United Nations General Assembly, which to a minor included 'rights and duties of all states to aid the economic development of others states along the path chosen by its government' (Murphy 2005).

But the overall picture is that proposals and demands from the Global South suffered rejection by the powerful industrialised nations of Europe and North America. The lack of strong unity within the Third World coalition also contributed to the failure and collapse of NIEO. Samir Amin had this to say about the demise of NIEO:

> So, in the end, the battle for the NIEO was lost. As well as the failure being noted, the causes have to be studied. Are they purely circumstantial (in the economic crisis)? Can they be attributed to 'tactical errors' by the Third World (its own divisions and weaknesses)? Or do these circumstances and weaknesses show the impossibility of autocentric development at the periphery of capitalist system? (Amin 1990: 56-57)

NIEO was soon eclipsed by the era of hegemonic neoliberalism that was ushered in by the Anglo-American leaders Margaret Thatcher and Ronald Reagan in the late 1970s. But African leaders continue to try and forge ahead with African development initiatives even with a context dominated by development merchant system that carried imperiality and coloniality.

The Lagos Plan of Action: the search for autonomous development trajectory

Over the years since the dawn of decolonization it became increasingly clear to many Africans that Africa's development could not be merely a philanthropic gift from the industrialised powers of the West. It had to be planned for and fought for as part of deepening decolonization. This is why the OAU working closely with UNECA produced a consciously inward looking pan-African development plan which sought to articulate a comprehensive and unified strategy to reduce dependence on external powers and to replace it with self-reliance. This initiative became known as Lagos Plan of Action (LPA) of 1980. At the centre of the plan was not complete de-linking but strategic disengagement from those features of the international economic system that were keeping Africa dependent, underdeveloped, weak and poor (Ikome 2007).

The LPA was a comprehensive initiative consisting of thirteen chapters covering all sectors of the African economy and informed by detailed objectives that included alleviation of poverty among Africans, diversification of productive economic capabilities, internalization of forces of supply and demand, and mobilization of Africans for production. Just like the Bandung Conference, the LPA identified Africa's development as structural and exacerbated by a hostile external environment. The LPA was informed by both dependency ideas and the spirit of pan-Africanism.

The LPA of action has been criticised for articulating a one-sided cause of the development crisis in Africa. It identified hostile external environment without paying too much attention to internal problems, which are equally important in understanding the problems of Africa's development. The emphasis on hostile external environment led the LPA to focus too much on trade and ignored such internal constraints as lack of serious commitment of African leadership to the development of the African continent and its people (Onimonde et al 2004). Corruption and authoritarianism were not clearly identified as internal constraints to development. The LPA is said to have been conceived as a top-down project that ignored other important sectors that are capable of driving Africa's development. More importantly, the LPA identified the problems and offered some solutions but without committing financial resources to the implementation of the initiative (Ikome 2007). But more importantly the LPA document, 'demonstrated both a disturbing lack of imagination and a low level of consciousness of the character of the option of self-reliance' (Amin 1999: 59).

What must be emphasised is that if the LPA was an authentically African development initiative, it was destined to suffer lack of financial support and delegitimization. Thus when one assesses the failure of African development initiatives, it is important to broaden the critique to the level of global discursive terrain within which Africans fought for development. What Adedeji identified as development merchant system worked actively to destabilise any African development initiative so as to push in an exogenous initiative that does not threaten the hegemony of the West. The LPA, despite its declared self-reliance paradigm and its robust criticism of the colonial and neo-colonial heritage, 'could not escape the conventional methodology closely associated with the conventional strategy of peripheral capitalist development' (Amin 1990: 59). Amin posed the question:

> Should development be conceived in accordance with the demand of the international order, or conversely, is it necessarily in conflict with it. Can the international order be transformed and 'adjusted' to the priority demands for Third World development, or conversely can the latter only be the result of the reverse 'adjustment'? (Amin 1990: 60).

It is important to realise that the LPA was launched in the midst of the rise of neoliberalism and the Washington Consensus.

Development merchant system, neoliberalism and Washington Consensus

According to Adebayo Adedeji 'the overarching objective of the Development merchant system (DMS) is for the African canoe to be firmly tied to the North's neo-liberal ship on the waters of globalization' (Adedeji 2002: 4). The DMS actively work to make sure African development initiatives do not operate outside the grip of Euro-North American development orthodoxy and coloniality. If we understand this reality, it is clear that we are where we are because the powerful industrial powers of the North have consistently rejected demands for reforming the modern world system and actively made sure that no alternative development paradigms, alternatives and agendas are entertained. It is within this context that the *Lagos Plan of Action (1980-2000)*, the *African Priority for Economic Recovery (1986-1990)*; the *African Alternative Framework to Structural Adjustment Programmes for Socio-Economic Recovery and Transformation*; the *African Charter for Popular Participation for Development (1990)* and the *United Nations New Agenda for the Development of Africa in the 1990s*, were not well received by the donor community and the Breton Woods institutions.

The 1980s and 1990s witnessed the ascendance and consolidation of the neoliberal model of development informed by the post-Keynesianism. This post-Keynesianism became known as the Washington Consensus that carried anti-state philosophies and strong belief in free reign of markets, privatization and deregulation. The *Berg Report of 1981* introduced the philosophy and practice of Structural Adjustment Programmes (SAPs). As a result of implementation of SAPs, African states lost the little that was remaining of control over development policy. African development became driven from outside with devastating consequences on the African people and their leaders. Thandika Mkandawire argued that:

> For Africa the 1980s and 1990s was a period of wanton destruction of institutions and untrammelled experimentation with half-baked institutional ideas. The result was 'unconstructive destruction' in its most institutionally debilitating form (Mkandawire 2003: 10).

The consequences of SAPs included removal of state from driving development; exacerbation of internal inequalities and worsening poverty; rehabilitation of coloniality and loss of policy space by African leaders. Instead of the Bretton Woods Institutions accepting responsibility for drawing Africa deeper into crisis through introduction of SAPs, the World Bank produced the document entitled *From Crisis to Sustainable Growth* of 1989 in which they blamed lack of good governance and policy reform as the cause of economic crisis and lack of development in Africa in the 1980s. In 1994 the World Bank produced another report entitled *Adjustment in Africa* in which the issue of sound macroeconomic and structural management were defended as prerequisites for growth and poverty reduction in Africa. Lack of development and economic growth in Africa was explained in terms of poor policy choices by African leaders, inefficiency and corruption. Structural barriers in the international political economy were not identified as a cause of underdevelopment. The Africa postcolonial state was identified as the major culprit inhibiting development in Africa (Fukuyama 2004).

An African consensus emerged that SAPs were a disaster for the development of the continent. By late 1980s through UNECA an alternative to SAPs was being sought and these efforts culminated in the production and adoption of *African Alternative Framework to Structural Adjustment Programmes for Socio-Economic Recovery and Transformation of 1989.* Through this document, Africans rejected SAPs and offered well reasoned arguments for the rejection (Tomori and Tomori 2004). This African initiative was not taken seriously; its recommendations fell on deaf ears.

The dawn of the Third Millennium witnessed the rise of the so-called new African leaders who were less corrupt and fully committed to the economic renewal of the continent. The new leaders committed themselves to enabling Africa to claim the 21st century as the African century for development. The philosophy of African Renaissance that was increasingly associated with President Thabo Mbeki of South Africa provided the discursive framework for re-launching African development. The flagship project for the new leaders of Africa became the *New Partnership for African Development (NEPAD)* that was adopted in 2002. NEPAD was informed by positive millenarian thinking. There was an optimistic mood that the 21st century will indeed be an African century where Africa will be allowed to drive its own development with the positive support of the developed countries of the North. This optimistic mood made some Africans to be oblivious of coloniality as an obstacle to African development. Inevitably, unlike the LPA that focused mainly on external structural barriers as responsible to African development failures, NEPAD highlighted such factors as bad governance, corruption and conflicts as responsible for African underdevelopment. What is distinctive about NEPAD has been its strong conviction on the possibilities of mutual beneficial partnership between the poor African countries and the industrialised and rich countries of the North. Coloniality as a global power structure that sustains asymmetrical economic power relations between the underdeveloped South and the developed North remains a destabilizing and inhibiting force.

If one took the political rhetoric of the leaders of the industrialised countries of the North, one would be misled to believe that there was a paradigm shift and a new international order that was favourable to African development that was emerging. The G8 pledged to fully support NEPAD. The question that developed in many African scholars was why the G8 was openly supporting NEPAD when throughout the postcolonial period the industrialised countries from the North opposed African development initiatives. Was NEPAD really an African initiative? Is NEPAD not part of those spurious neo-colonial partnerships that hide the realities of structural inequalities? Is NEPAD part of Africa's indigenous development agenda or is it a project cascading from the DMS but masquerading as an African development initiative?

It would seem NEPAD falls neatly within the discourse of partnerships that commenced with such initiatives as the Lome Conventions rather than the Bandung decolonial version of development. Lome Conventions were part of sustenance of coloniality long after the end of direct colonial administrations. It also falls neatly within the discourse of 'our common interest' contained in Tony Blair's Commission for Africa (Hurt 2007: 355-368). Does Africa need the external world to develop development initiatives and plans for it or does it need a just economic order that does not torpedo its development initiatives and plans?

Conclusion

The reality about the African struggle for development is that it is taking place within a modern world system that is resistant to decolonization and an international order that consistently works towards disciplining anti-systemic movements and forces so as to give the world system a new lease on life. The world system and its shifting international orders continue to subject African development initiatives and plans to the logic of classical economic thought and the dominant logic of capitalist accumulation that created Africa as a periphery. This is why the Bandung spirit was consistently frustrated and the African demand for a new international economic order was vehemently resisted. The acceptable model of development for Africa in the eyes of those in the global North is one whereby African economies are adjusted and aligned to the imperatives and demands of the international division of labour. Africa has never run short of development initiatives and plans but what has been lacking is imagination of autocentric development outside the template cascading from classical economic thought and capitalist imperatives. The DMS work actively to prevent and destroy any development initiative that threatens to subvert the modern world system and its international order. As indicated by Samir Amin in the epigraph at the beginning of this chapter, Africa has been fighting for a space to originate new economic ideas and imagine new development alternatives suitable for the African reality and experience. Such a space is denied. But Africa continues to work in cohort with other developing countries for space and economic justice. To achieve the objective of building a new international economic order, there is need for Europe and North America to embark on voluntary decolonization of the world system which they built through embracing what we call deimperialization. Only a combination of voluntary deimperialization on a world scale and decolonization would result in global democracy in which Africa would be afforded space to develop.

References

Abdulgani, R. 1964. *Bandung Spirit: Moving on the Tide of History.* Jakarta: Prapanga Publishers.

Achebe, C. in Moore-Gilbert, B. 1997. *Postcolonial Theory: Contexts, Practices, Politics*. London: Verso.

Adedeji, A. 2002. 'From the Lagos Plan of Action to the New Partnership for African Development and from the Final Act of Lagos to the Constitutive Act: Wither Africa? (Unpublished Keynote Address Delivered at the African Forum for Envisioning Africa, Nairobi, Kenya, 26-29 April).

Adesina, J. O., Graham, Y. And Olukoshi, A. (eds.). 2006. *Africa and Development Challenges in the New Millennium: The NEPAD Debate*. Dakar & London: CODESRIA and Zed Books.

Amin, S. 1990. *Maldevelopment: Anatomy of a Global Failure*. Tokyo and London: United Nations University Press and Zed Books.

Baah, A. 2003. 'History of African Development Initiatives.' Paper presented at the African Labour Research Network, Johannesburg, South Africa.

Berger, M. T. 2004. *The Battle for Asia: From Decolonization to Globalization*. London and New York: Routledge.

Cheru, F. 2009. 'Development in Africa: The Imperial Project versus the National Project and the Need for Policy Space.' *Review of African Political Economy*, 120, pp. 275-278.

Conrad, J. 1902. *Heart of Darkness and Other Stories*. London: Wordsworth Editions Ltd.

Cox, R. 1979. 'Ideologies and the New International Economic Order: Reflections on Some Recent Literature.' *International Organization*, 33(2), pp. 257-308.

Depelchin, J. 2005. *Silences in African History: Between the Syndromes of Discovery and Abolition*. Dar es Salaam: Mkuki Na Nyota Publishers.

Escobar, A. 2012. *Encountering Development: The Making and Unmaking of the Third World: With a New Preface by the Author.* Princeton and Oxford: Princeton University Press.

Ferguson, J. 1990. *The Anti-Politics Machine: 'Development',' Depoliticization, and Bureaucratic Power in Lesotho*. Cambridge: Cambridge University Press.

Fukuyama, F. 2004. *State Building: Governance and World Order in the Twenty-First Century*. London: Profile Books.

Gosovic, B. 1972. *UCTAD: Conflict and Compromise*. Leiden: A. W. Sifthoff.

Grosfoguel, R. and Cervantes-Rodriguez, A. M. 2002. 'Introduction: Unthinking Twentieth-Century Eurocentric Mythologies: Universalist Knowledges, Decolonization, and Developmentalism.' In R. Grosfoguel and A. M. Cervantes-Rodriguez (eds.), *The Modern/Colonial/Capitalist World-System in the Twentieth Century: Global Processes, Antisystemic Movements, and Geopolitics of Knowledge*. Westport, CT: Praeger Publishers.

Hurt, S. R. 2007. 'Mission Impossible: A Critique of the Commission for Africa.' *Journal of Contemporary African Studies*, 25(3), pp. 355-368.

Ikome, F. N. 2007. *From LPA to NEPAD: The Political Economy of African Regional Initiatives*. Midrand: Institute for Global Dialogue.

Jansen, G. H. 1966. *Afro-Asia and Non-Alignment*. London: Faber and Faber.

Kahin, G. M. 1956. *The Asia-African Conference: Bandung, Indonesia, April 1955*. Ithaca: NY: Cornell University Press.

Kaunda, K. D. And Morris, C. M. 1966. *A Humanist in Africa: Letters to Colin M. Morris from Kenneth D. Kaunda President of Zambia*. Nashville and New York: Abingdon Press.

Kimche, D. 1973. *The Afro-Asian Movement: Ideology and Foreign Policy of the Third World*. Jerusalem: Israel University Press.

Krasner, S. 1981. 'Transforming International Relations: What the Third World Wants and Why.' *International Studies Quarterly*, 25 (2), pp. 119-148.

Mayall, J. 1990. *Nationalism and International Society*. Cambridge: Cambridge University Press.

Mignolo, W. D. 2005. 'Prophets Facing Sidewise: The Geopolitics of Knowledge and the Colonial Difference.' *Social Epistemology*, 19(1), January-March, pp. 111-127.

Mkandawire, T. 2003. 'Institutions and Development in Africa.' In Cambridge Journal of Economics Conference: Economics for the Future. UNRISD

Mkandawire, T. 2005. 'African Intellectuals and Nationalism.' In T. Mkandawire (ed.), *African Intellectuals: Rethinking Politics,*

Language, Gender and Development. Dakar and London: CODESRIA Books and Zed Books.

Mkandawire, T. 2011. 'Running While Others Walk: Knowledge and the Challenge of Africa's Development.' *Africa Development*, XXVI (2), pp. 1-36.

Mudimbe, V. Y. 1988. *The Invention of Africa: Gnosis, Philosophy, and the Order of Knowledge*. Bloomington and Indianapolis: Indiana University Press.

Mudimbe, V. Y. 1994. *The Idea of Africa*. Bloomington and Indianapolis; Indiana University Press.

Murphy, C. N. 2005. *Global Institutions, Marginalization and Development*. London and New York: Routledge.

Ndlovu-Gatsheni, S. J. 2013a. *Coloniality of Power in Postcolonial Africa: Myths of Decolonization*. Dakar: CODESRIA Book Series

Ndlovu-Gatsheni, S. J. 2013b. *Empire, Global Coloniality and African Subjectivity*. New York and Oxford: Berghahn Books.

Nesadurai, H. E. S. 2005. 'Bandung and the Political Economy of North-South Relations: Sowing the Seeds for Re-visioning International Society.' *Working Paper No. 95*, Singapore: Institute of Defence and Strategic Studies. December.

Ngugi wa Thiong'o. 2009. *Re-membering Africa*. Nairobi: east African Educational Publishers Ltd.

Nkrumah, K. 1964. *Consciencism: Philosophy and Ideology for De-Colonization*. New York: Monthly Review Press.

Nyerere, J. K. 1967. *Freedom and Unity*. Dar es Salaam: Oxford University Press.

Onimonde, I. et al. 2004. *African Development and Governance Strategies in the 21st Century*. London and New York: Zed Books.

Pieterse, J. N. 2010. *Development Theory; Deconstructions/ Reconstructions: Second Edition*. Los Angeles: SAGE.

Slater, D. 2004. *Geopolitics and the Post-Colonial: Rethinking North-South Relations*. Malden, MA: Blackwell Publishing.

Taylor, I. 2003. 'The United Nations Conference in Trade and Development.' *New Political Economy*, 8(3), pp. 409-418.

Therien, J. P. 1999. 'Beyond the North-South Divide: Two Tales of World Poverty.' *Third World Quarterly*, 20(4), pp. 723-742.

Thomas, A. 2000. 'Development as Practice in a Liberal Capitalist World.' *Journal of International Development,* 12 (6), pp. 773-787.

Tomori, S. O. and Tomori, O. W. 2004. 'Revisiting African Alternative Framework to Structural Adjustment Programme for Socio-Economic Recovery and Transformation in Contemporary Nigeria.' In I. Onimonde et al (eds.), *African Development and Governance Strategies in the 21st Century*. London: Zed Books.

Truman, H. [1949] 1964. *Public Papers of the Presidents of the United States: Harry S. Truman.* Washington, D.C.: Unites States Government Printing Office.

Zeleza, P. T. 2005. 'Banishing the Silences: Towards the Globalization of African History' (Unpublished Paper Presented at the 11th CODESRIA General Assembly Conference, Maputo, Mozambique, 6-10 December.

Decolonising 'decolonisation':

Chinweizu's Critique and the Scandal of Africa's Maldevelopment

Tendayi Sithole

Introduction

Development in Africa is predicated on the virtuous, the ideal and the fix of ruins, and yet, it is still a scandal as it is infected by coloniality. Essentially, development in Africa is coloniality and it is its antithesis – maldevelopment. Coloniality refers to long standing patterns of the colonial infrastructure continuing long after the departure of the colonial administration where in which Africa is still operating in the logic that is the antithesis unto itself. It is essential to bring what is hidden to exposure through Chinweizu's critique of maldevelopment, which exposes how development is a scandal. Chinweizu's critique is necessary as it is the effort to combat coloniality. His articulation of decolonising the African mind enforces awareness that was supposed to be ignorance that it is made not to see coloniality.

Chinweizu takes decoloniality *sensu stricto* as a radical point of critique for Africa's development simply because coloniality is a tragedy of maldevelopment. Thus, coloniality *qua* maldevelopment cannot be *ad infinitum* as decoloniality exposes its scandal. What is central here is that Chinweizu's critique is decoloniality and this will be expounded in six ways. Firstly, Chinweizu's critique impels development to be a priority through decolonisation of 'decolonisation'. Secondly, it takes cognisance of the colonial wound and the phenomenology of the cry explicates how the long colonial night of maldevelopment continues to afflict its colonial victims. Thirdly, it positions development as an epistemological project that combats the criminalisation of Africa's criticism to maldevelopment. Fourthly, it problematises cargo development and shows how development has been institutionalised, naturalised and normalised as something which is tantamount to being 'manna from heaven'—where it should, in all times, come from the Euro-North American empire and Africa to be at the receiving end. Fifthly, Chinweizu's critique of black colonialists puts them at interlocked the register of tyranny and the register of puppetry. Last and not least, it deploys the concept of de-linking from maldevelopment and to suggest new horisons for Africa's development.

Decolonising 'decolonisation': where art thou Africa's development?

The question posed by Chinweizu three decades ago is still a spectre that haunts. Chinweizu (1975: 187) asks: "[h]aving won independence, what were we to do with it?" In where Africa is today, the frenzy of fête euphoria of the celebratory of the more than 50 years of independence in some African countries puts 'decolonisation' as something in need of decolonisation for there to be Africa's development. It seems that this 50th celebration still avoids Chinweizu's question. It means that the 'decolonisation' that occurred at the departure of colonialism, the one which is marked to have been the new beginning, was the epochal break which is emancipation and not a radical break which is liberation. So then, the avoiding of Chinweizu's question is a scandal since this was supposed to be the moment of contemplating such a question. Decolonisation as emancipation is what Africa is caught in at this moment. 'Being liberated and/or emancipated were subsumed under the rubric of decolonization to mean a single state of being' (Ndlovu-Gatsheni 2013: 66).

What is decolonisation today is the form of constitutional guilt that haunted Europe's colonial administration and which saw it necessary to *give* freedom to the natives, who were to celebrate what their masters had given them. Decolonisation which plagues Africa, to emphasise Chinweizu's critique, is based on emancipation and not liberation. Emancipation is a product of European modernity, not African liberation, and is only about the attainment of civil and political rights which, of course, do not take African existential conditions seriously but reducing Africa to the appendage of Europe. It is in emancipation that what is deemed fit for Europe, so it is for Africa. Taking development into account and for it to coincide with the euphoria of the arrested decolonization, fundamental conditions necessary for liberation, which will yield Africa's development proper are erased, distorted and even denied. So then, it is very clear why emancipation does not clarify how maldevelopment will be done away with; it only presents a set of projects, programmes and propaganda on the need for development and, of course, within the institutional apparatus of the Euro-North American empire. These are political projects that are born out of the bourgeois revolution, and the only end is reformism, and reformism does not resolve the existential predicament of maldevelopment. This is the very imaginary which is necessary to decolonise in order to chart development so that it coincides with Africa's liberation and not emancipation with its arrested decolonisation.

What is noted well by Ndlovu-Gatsheni (2013) is that decolonisation as liberation is the action that aims to undo the complex colonial matrices of power, which hampers Africa's development. Decolonisation is informed by political imagination and seeks to uncover, uproot and remove all forces that put the African subject into subjection whether psychologically, bodily, materially and existentially. The decolonisation that Chinweizu agitates is different from the one that is popularised by means of anniversaries, constitutions, carnivals, flags, national anthems and Independence Day fiascos, which have nothing concrete to offer on Africa's development, but only the rhetoric overloaded with repetitive, banal and mystique promises. These are the acts of emancipation, meaning that they are decolonisation without liberation—the very antithesis of Africa's development.

The trajectory that Africa is caught in in so far as the rhetoric of development is concerned is ritualistic, symbolic and at worse, cosmetic as what is celebrated is a modicum. This is the trajectory that serves as an indictment that indeed it is necessary to decolonise 'decolonisation', and such a political and epistemological practice of development should be in many ways, the one that deepens itself since it will not be celebrated but challenged, if not completely destroyed. This is taking into account the extent to which the colonial project and in its very continued mode puts Africa outside development to perpetuate maldevelopment. To decolonise 'decolonisation' will be to start taking the trajectory that Africa is in seriously by not erasing the genealogy of the colonial archive of development (which of course was not the development of Africa) and to re-assert Africa's development in its own terms and by African subjects *themselves* and *for themselves* in service of the broader interests of the continent. This might sound sentimental if the political imagination is hesitant to consider seriously the horisons and futures that Africa's development should be – the very political possibility to bring Africa to itself. Africa is alienated in the sense that it is just a satellite and non-existent continent as it was colonised and yet still in the clutches of coloniality. This should be a tragedy in the imagination of those discourses that continue to celebrate 'decolonisation', which of course, if there were no such, there would have been a project to decolonise the very same trajectory of coloniality that Africa is still in. For the mere fact that this is taken out of the picture, it means that serious problems that Africa faces and development being the focal point here, do make the political imagination of unthinking, re-articulation and re-emergence of development.

Political imagination is the very seriousness of asking where is Africa's development and the very form of asking will start, as the act of decolonisation to account to the ways in which what is missing is searched and ultimately to make the concerted effort to find it. Africa first needs to find itself, and this is only possible through decolonising itself from the decolonisation it is trapped in, since this is not the decolonisation that is brought by Africans themselves but their colonial masters. It then follows that if decolonisation is given, it needs to be decolonised. What should necessarily prevail is that decolonisation should prevail as critical consciousness to African subjects and they must be fully in charge of it as the epistemological and political project.

Towards developing the epistemological and political project of decolonising it is first to admit that decolonisation was given to Africa and this is *mala fide* as there are conditions attached to it. That is why the 'decolonisation' that Africa continues to celebrate is the 'arrested decolonisation'. At the level of development *qua* political and epistemic project, this is very clear as Africa is still dependent on its former colonial metropole in order for development to be realised. To decolonise the arrested decolonisation is to, among other things, take decolonisation as a matter of struggle where in which the coloniser cannot be expected *to give* since the sole intention is *to take*. So what is refused to be given must, as it reasonably applies, taken by force and the antagonisms being at the epicentre of such a struggle. These antagonisms mean, Africa will face resistence develops itself, but it should by all necessary means, forcibly develop itself in order to avoid being dominated. What is given in the struggle of antagonisms should not be accepted, the moment of giving should not be waited upon, and it should be ceased at time knowing that no oppressor can give liberation to the oppressed since this would mean the end of the oppressor. So then, Africa's development in relation to Chinweizu's critique should be understood in this register—that is, Africa needs to develop itself and to admit that it is still colonised by virtue of being in the trajectory of arrested decolonisation.

The starting point that is central to Chinweizu is that there is no Africa's development. It is then necessary to ask, "Where art thou Africa's development?" This question is fundamental in the sense that Africa was and still is conquered and that maldevelopment still persists to conquer and dispossess Africa's development. Africa cannot be its own if this question does not propel it to be the enforcer of its development, something that will emerge at the point of decolonisation. As Chinweizu points out, arrested decolonisation exists because African subjects were divided, deceived and incapacitated. Therefore, they became ultimate losers because what could have been a leverage to launch the decolonisation was liquidated into a mere arrested decolonisation, which is a defeated disguised as triumphed. Thus, there cannot be any Africa's development under such conditions, and where it is, is yet to be found by starting decolonisation of the arrested decolonisation.

The colonial wound and the phenomenology of the cry

What is Africa today is still what it was if it were to mean Africa that is free from the tentacles of the colonial night. Africa is still yet to become and it is the one that is wanted by those who are concerned with it in making it better rather than taking the two extreme poles of its comfort—that is, Afro-pessimism and Afro-optimism. Afro-pessimism on one hand is simply the stigmatisation of Africa and Afro-optimism on the other hand is the celebratory of Africa—both being faulty—the necessity being that of collapsing these two extreme poles to start unthinking. The intellectual critique of Chinweizu is positioned in what Maldonado-Torres (2008) refers to as the phenomenology of the cry precisely because the agony is that of the colonial wound. Phenomenology of the cry emerges at the moment of existential predicament, which of course inflicts the colonial wound that alienates the African subject. It is in Africa's development where the colonial wound is evident and this calls for the phenomenology of the cry to be at the centre. Chinweizu articulates the colonial wound thus:

> It is too late for us, the imperiali[s]ed, to weep upon the shoulders of those who have brought about our oppression for sympathy toward our plight. We need, rather, to understand our past defeats if we want to avoid the deadly shocks our future seems to be holding in ambush for us. (Chinweizu 1975: xi).

What is taken by Chinweizu here is positionality – that is, the composure of articulating the grammar of existence to marshal demands of the African subject. In so doing, Chinweizu's colonial wound puts him at the pedestal for advocacy of agency to heal the colonial wound. The manner in which this is done is not his plight, as he highlighted, being something that must evoke sympathy from the coloniser, but where he would move in his own dictates since the sympathy of the coloniser is not sincere at all, and as stated early, it is *mala fide*. It is well noted that '[t] he phenomenology of the cry is the revelation of someone who has been forgotten or wronged' (Maldonado-Torres 2008: 133). It is the cry at the moment of the re-emergence, re-existence and also, the resurrection of the African subject from the colonial wound. Taking this in the context of development suggests that the ways in which the political effort and the epistemological one is made in order to challenge maldevelopment. So then, the phenomenology of the cry is not to mourn or grieve the colonial wound, but to start the political project of breaking the silence that is brought by the colonial experience and its remnants.

Who is wounded if not those who are at the receiving end of the colonial experience, the pain which is still felt through the existential conditions of Africans? This question is essential to ask in that it centres on the very fundamental issue of having been trapped in the colonial night. This night did not dawn with the coming of independence, which, of course, is a supposed decolonisation. It is the night of the colonial laughter since the place of the native is still that of the victim of the colonial experience, its remnants having to remain for the long time to come if there is no wakening that can come through the phenomenology of the cry. What needs to be introduced at the same time is the notion of colonial laughter that is happening at the times where the colonial misery is still continuing and, of course, the departure of colonialism assumes the omnipotent presence seen as stated, in maldevelopment. Those who are existentially wronged by the colonial night are bound to cry out since they have inflicted the colonial wound and those who are laughing cannot in any way understand the plight of those who are crying, let alone understand the pain of the colonial wound. The colonial wound is what affects Chinweizu and his decolonial critique centres on the ways in which the wound is excruciating and him screaming not for help but as the scream of combat against the remnants of colonisation. In no way has the colonial wound been treated, it is instead, avoided. Chinweizu is blamed for pointing out to the colonial wound, and he is one of those who are labelled by Appiah (1992) as suffering from victimology and being pre-occupied by the discourse of colonialism. What is not asked by Appiah is why Chinweizu rails against colonisation, and part of the answer lies in the fact that colonisation is still present as a project managed by the African leaders whom Chinweizu refers to as black colonialists. Simply, if there was no colonial experience and its remnants, there would be no need to rail against colonisation.

It is the colonial wound that is still deep-seated in the mind and soul of the African subject. Colonisation is the encounter of dehumanisation and the project masquerading as humanisation of the African subject. There is no way that those who are wounded can engage in a systematic attempt to 'therapeutic politics' without them being pontificated to by those who oppress them. The scandal of therapeutic politics is that it perpetuates silence in those who are suffering from the colonial wound and to render them tolerant enough in order not to express the phenomenology of the cry. Therapeutic politics mean avoiding the colonial wound and the silence of not being able to critique colonisation in its guises. For Chinweizu's subject position is indifferent to therapeutic politics, it is to reveal the scandal behind them and determining how the African subject should engage its existential predicament, which in fact is not regarded as a predicament but a symptom of some sort. The interest for Chinweizu is not only to rail against the West, but also to rail against Africans who are native assistants in the colonial project. The phenomenology of the cry will never cease to exist if the presence of the colonial wound persists. It is expected that Chinweizu's continued decolonial critique is the rise and revolt against the injustices meted against the African project of liberation, and maldevelopment continue to exist.

The epistemological project of development

Development as the epistemological project is not only at the level of discourse, but the political project that informs it. The political project being that of control and manipulation by the Euro-North American empire, which dictates the terms of engagement in relation to development. It does this by projecting the epistemology of development as the apolitical project whereas, in fact, it is a politicised project. So then, development is packaged as the betterment of the existential condition of Africa and to put it in progress if it were stagnant. The knowledge constitution and practice of development is the exercise of fulfilling interests and it is fundamental to ask: whose interest is development serving anyway? This question is imperative in that in many cases, and particularly to Africa, development has been a promise and a dream whose realisation is just a mirage. The development that comes from the Euro-North American empire is not development at all, but maldevelopment. The case in point is that it is development for the sole interest of the Euro-North American itself, and not that of Africa, which is said to be the recipient of development. The domain of African development has been left to the foreign experts, and those who belong to the Euro-North American empire and the African leaders have and continue to fall victim to what Chinweizu (1975) refers to as the foreign expert misadvice. This is the misadvice which appears sound but which in reality is costly and misleading. Although this has been a repeated historical offense, Africans seem not to learn since the foreign experts continue to dictate the discourse of development.

The epistemological project of development means that development thrives on what Mignolo (2009) refers to as coloniality of knowledge. Coloniality of knowledge is the authorising of the Euro-North American knowledge while erasing, distorting and denying other knowledges. Development in this context should be understood through coloniality of knowledge since it is a project that thrives on epistemic violence. To expose epistemic violence is not only to understand Africa as a region, but an epistemic space violated at the level of all its spaces of existence. It is in these epistemic spaces where decolonial critique emerges and asserts itself to question the very basis of modernity and the concealment of its darker side. 'The definition of violence carries with it the definition of power' (Depelchin 2005: 64). It is the practices of violence that ensure that development should be seen from the perspective of the Euro-North American empire and this, of course, suggests the ways in which violence is practiced. Also, this suggests that no development can occur from Africans, thus, Africa must be developed.

Santos (2007) submits that knowledge is not conceived in abstractions but practices and interventions—that is, knowledge is a political project. In this case, the epistemological project of development is politically proper and it is the one that is serving the very purposes of how the world system works. This is to say, it serves as to perpetuate the dominance and hegemony of the Euro-American empire while at the same time, subjecting Africa to the clutches of coloniality. Knowledge is not created, produced and socialised for its own interest sake as it is likely to appear, but to reach particular ends, and with the political project of modernity—to organise the world through the world system and to ratify subjection of the African into maldevelopment. As Santos (2007: 37) posits, knowledge is '[e] mbedded in different Western and non-western cultures, such experiences used not only different categories, symbolic universes, and aspirations of a better life'.

Coloniality of knowledge creates mechanistic narratives of development which are informed by dominant tendencies informed by Euro-North American dominance and hegemony, which discards other subjectivities differing from its own. As Walsh (2007: 225) points out, '[t]o speak of the geopolitics of knowledge and geopolitical locations of critical thought is to recogni[s]e the persistence of a Western hegemony, that positions Eurocentric thought as 'universal', while localising other forms of thought as at best folklore'. So, the deployment of coloniality of knowledge is essential to account for ways in which knowledge is used to erase other knowledges which might be essential for the project of development by Africans themselves. The erasure serves the purposes of denial, distortions, deception, and at worse, extinction which essentially translates into the failed development or its realisation being just an illusion. What then remains is development as a monolithic project where the interests, needs and wants of African subjects are known and they must be fulfilled without African subjects themselves. In short, it is known what is good for Africans in so far as development is concern. The development of Africa means that Africa is developed and it does not develop itself. The justification being that the Euro-North American empire serves as the only blue print and something that moves outside its template not being development at all.

The epistemological project of development has been that of Euro-North American canon, which is in need of transplants and appendages that reproduce such knowledge, and of course, development turning into the decadence of maldevelopment. This canon, in its epistemological project of development, 'has created an efficient apparatus for producing knowledge about, and the exercise of power over, the Third World' (Escobar 1995: 9). 'Knowledge-making in the modern/colonial world is at once knowledge in which the very concept of 'modernity' rests and the judge and warrantor of legitimate and sustainable knowledge' (Mignolo 2009). For Mignolo, knowledge-making of development is entrenched in modernity with its imperialist purposes largely informed by maldevelopment. The epistemic decolonial shift of development, which is the movement of the geography of reason clearly indicates that knowledge about Africa's development should be looked through the locus of enunciation of Africa and not that of the Euro-North American empire, which is in control of imperial global designs that are the constitutive parts of modernity. Modernity is informed by the expansionism of western civilisation, which is seen as the absolute civilisation that is the only process than other forms of civilisations, hence there is a colonialist argument that Africa is not developed due to its absence of civilisation and modernity.

Development as identity can be understood in relation to what Escobar (1995) regards as the regime of representation. This means that the geography is laid out in which parts of the worlds are considered developed and those who are said to be developing—and the very regime of representation being the manner in which the Euro-North American empire constructs other parts of the worlds, and of course, writing them off from worldliness. They are, in effect, the other, that is, that which needs development from the Euro-North American empire. This regime of representation, as Escobar points out, forms itself in the form of order and truth where in which the paternalistic attitude towards the other parts of the world remain so profound, and for them to come into worldliness they will need the assistance and dependence of the Euro-North American empire.

> Development has only relied exclusively on one knowledge system, namely, the modern Western one. The dominance of this knowledge system has dictated the marginalisation and disqualification of non-Western knowledge systems (Escobar 1995: 13).

The knowledge system propagates itself as rational and objective. It serves as a blue-print of development which does not take differences of contexts into account. There is no contextual reflection, and the project of development in Africa is the transplant from the Euro-North American context. The criticism of development is criminalised, more so if it comes from Africans themselves. It means then that there should be silence. The very criticism of Chinweizu is criminalised from the basis that it does not originate from the epicentre of knowledge—that is, the Euro-American empire. And not only that, it is criminalised for exposing a scandal where in which such a knowledge is the same as the colonial project in relation to Africa's development. Coloniality of knowledge *qua* development is at the epicentre of Chinweizu's critique; hence the concept of maldevelopment which still puts Africa at the position of subjection. The epistemological project of development should be enunciated from Africans for their own development and in their own terms. It is from this criminalised positionality that the rearticulation of Africa's development should emerge and to get rid of what Chinweizu (1987) refers to as cargo development.

On cargo cult maldevelopment

The conception of development is in Africa, the very thing that must be authorised from the Euro-North America, if not coming from there. It means that Africans must always be hopeful that development should come from that centre and in no way can they initiate development themselves. Ultimately, development then resonates with the notion of paradise, to suggest the end of social ills and the inauguration of the new African continent with the grace of Euro-North American heaven. This is where development comes from in a packaged form and it must be accepted as such.

> The cargo cult believed that gods and their spirit agents were packing manufactured goods in crates, labelling them with Melanesian names and addresses, and loading them into the holds of ships and planes. (Chinweizu 1987: 15)

This has been the political ontology of development and the forms of imaginations and thinking in terms of the ways in which Africa's development has become. Further, it is not only the belief system of most of the African subjects in general, the one which Africa elites are taking a huge role in. The African elite might not want to be seen as fatalistic, but their political imagination and political practices are to a higher degree, that of the cargo cult mentality. The difference is that unlike the African subjects in general, they do not endure the brunt of having to wait and wait since they can loot from the state for their own personalised and stylised development. It is also essential to note that the cargo cult mentality is still pious in the ways that it is very hard to make it dispensable. The cargo cult mentality is, of course, the manna from heaven and it is the very mentality that is deceptive and obliterates the capacity of political imagination and action, and has assumed the easier route of development, and which means being developed. As Chinweizu (1987: 23) warns, '[c]argo [c]ult maldevelopment has failed, and shall continue to fail, to create industrial culture and society'.

Chinweizu here suggest that the conception of development has been that of waiting for manna from heaven and largely based on the tried and tested failed models, but which are still reinforced nevertheless. It has been something inherent in the development discourse that Africa should be at the receiving end and this obviously incapacities for development to be self-generated and driven by Africans themselves. It has been a normality that Africa should be developed and not to develop itself. In so doing, it has to be acted upon and this is the colonial virus that is deeply inherent in the minds of the African elites who, in many ways do not act as the agents of change but agents of decadence and stagnation, and what is perceived as change is the consumerist culture which sees change in their accumulative excess and display. While they continue with this mode of life of accumulation and excess, the citizens must wait. To wait has been something akin to development discourse itself since what is perceived or propagated as development comes from outside, and this, of course, suggesting that external tutelage and control is necessary from the Euro-North American empire. This is the centre of power which can dictate the terms of engagement in relation to development and the erasure of Africans as their own custodians of development is in the face of total erasure.

Fatalism has taken the centre stage and as such it has rendered the imagination of development devoid of any form of intent in realising development. What often preoccupies the African elite is that whatever form of development that is about to take place or planned is something that must be externally funded, and this has been the repeated model of failure, but the one which continues to be advocated nevertheless. Africans as people in waiting of development are said to be redeemed by the very same development. Their current condition warranting development is basically that they are in a way, figures of subjects who must be humanised by the external order to make the material conditions humanised. As they are the interiority, they cannot change themselves and there is need for exteriority to redeem them. So then, there is no interiority without exteriority—the very logic of development—that is, manna from heaven is not only voluntary, it is compulsory. The state of idleness and that of perpetual waiting is the existential crisis which cannot generate development in the condition of interiority.

How is it possible that those who loot Africa are the very ones developing it? This question is fundamental in that it gets to the crux of the matter and that is the scandal of development. It is essential to point out that there cannot be development in the existential scale where there are asymmetrical power relations. The psyche of manna from heaven should be exorcised by all means necessary if development is to take place in Africa. There has never been development in Africa and there will never be for as long as coloniality is still intact and no political imagination of decoloniality exists. To suggest that there has been development in Africa is to say something scandalous at best, since there has been no development in Africa itself. If it happens it gets frustrated since dependency is emphasised.

It is not only the prevention of development that appears in maldevelopment, but the guise of development with a limited gaze. To understand maldevelopment it is essential to look not only at the outcome of development, but to unmask its rhetoric and reality. What Africa can be positioned at is the state of maldevelopment and the case will be made in reference to the World Bank and the International Monetary Fund as institutional practices and structures of maldevelopment. It is the very maldevelopment that must be combated before the construction of development. In the light of these two institutions it is essential to ask then why Africa is still colonised by them, and in particular indebted to them to the point where the development of Africa needs to confirm to the dictates of such institutions. The African elite do not rule in the interests of the African people who are in need of development, but maldevelopment being the agenda. This means that the African elites are still entrapped in the condition where they fail to engage in political imagination.

Black colonialists: on tyranny and puppetry

Chinweizu is scathing on African elites and he even goes to the extent of referring to them as black colonialists. They are black colonialists on the basis that their only aim was to replace white colonialists (Chinweizu 2009). Decolonisation needs to be decolonised, and black colonialists believe in 'decoloni[s]ation as mere transfer of power from white colonialists to black nationalists' (Ndlovu-Gatsheni 2013: 32). Chinweizu also accuses them of being the problem in Africa's development and them perpetuating maldevelopment. African elites are the agents of the colonial structure and they serve such a structure at the expense of their own Africa. The nature of African elites is just to consume while they are preaching the rhetoric of development and they will fight at all costs to be the beneficiaries of the development of their own personal lives and not that of Africa and their countries in particular. What pervades Africa and something which stalls development is what Chinweizu calls the fear of political experimentation. There will rather be the maintenance of the status quo (maldevelopment) rather than engage in the domestic grown development initiatives. What perpetuates the fear of political experimentation of mimicry, which blocks all sites of imagination. What exists in the discourse of development as Chinweizu points out is the assumption that what derives from the West works, since it has worked there, and added to that, having the Western experts as advisors. African realities even if they contradict the very advice of the West are likely not to be taken into account on the basis that what the west represents is virtue.

The comfort zones of being in the state of fear which sees rethinking and redefinition of development as the obstacle to development, and African elites would rather as a result stick to maldevelopment. This is the very nature of development practice which is informed by the models that are out of context and the African elites will not make any effort in engaging the development project that is their own innovation, incubation and realisation. Due to this state of perpetual paralysis, they will stick to maldevelpment which is informed by mimicry. So, mimicry is the way development is done by external actors in the models that will not succeed at all, but which are models that are applied and of course, with the advice of the foreign experts. It is very much clear that what African elites want is not development but maldevelopment. They are in a way, a disservice to what they were supposed to serve.

For black colonialists, 'wanting development became virtually the same thing as wanting to be like the West' (Ake 1981: 142). For Ake, this is the very same conception of development (being like the West) that is still prevalent in Africa. It is the one that borders on mimicry and prone to accept whatever form of development project that is from the West. This is what has led to the African petite-bourgeoisie to inherit the development project rather than revolutionalise it. African elites do not make an effort to liberate Africa from the clutches of maldevelopment, but they keep it in the perpetual condition of oppression. They also do not ensure that no sense of agency exists that might agitate development. The African elite will not withstand criticism or opposition to their idealistic forms of development no matter how good they might sound. Development assumes, as Ake (1981) elaborates, some form of ideology in the sense that it is made into the political project, which constitutes the utopian vision to visualise the condition of a better society and which all the people must rally behind. According to Ake, the obsession with development is such that they do not want to revolutionise it but to inherit it in the way it has been packaged by the Euro-North American empire.

The Western notion of development does not encourage attention to the revolutionising of existing social relations of production as a likely or even possible stimulation for development. It does not encourage the disengagement of African economies from the exploitative structural links with Western capitalist economies. It encourages the perception of the process of development as the gradual solution of limited and technical problems within the context of the existing order. The organising principle of racialisation makes the discourse of development to fit the very logic of maldevelopment. Putting modernity at the centre, the development discourse of the Euro-North American empire suggests that those who are racially otherised should gravitate towards modernity in order to move out of the mould of backwardness. This even shows that development *qua* modernity is the very same practice, just like the colonial project – that is, the civilising mission.

Development is packaged here as the treatment of the universal problem which needs universal solutions. That is the sense in which the notion of development under review limits the scale of change of African economies as they still embrace the exploitative structures that still do not serve Africa (Ake 1981). African elites as Chinweizu states, were quick to concede power right after gaining independence. It means that independence is not what they have wanted but to still remain under the tutelage of their colonial masters, whom they still continue to serve. How can there be African development under such conditions? How can the former colonial masters stop maldevelopment if they have black colonialists who continue to serve them to fulfil that role? For the mere fact that there is a presence of African leaders who are black colonialists, then there is no problem in relation to Africa being continued to be plundered. This reality is still present and it can be understood by engaging both the tyranny and puppetry of black colonialists – the form of political practice that operates in tandem.

Tyranny and puppetry have been, and continue to be the political reality of Africa in the sense that the discourse of order and disorder is the form of justification in political practice. It is in both tyranny and puppetry alike that African development will be propagated and it has to be believed as if it is something real whereas it is not. In the context of tyranny, the political disorder is blatant and its maldevelopment practices are legitimised. Tyranny creates a condition where political oppression is used as a basis to discipline and as means to serve the colonial masters. Puppetry cannot be de-linked from tyranny in that it is the political practice that allows disorder to prevail, and its acts of complicity removing it from the responsibility. It is nevertheless a form of maldevelopment in itself in that puppets are controlled in order to perpetuate injustice. This is affirmed by Chinweizu who states:

> One trouble with colonies is that they are, by the deliberate design of their owners, deprived of all indigenous political power; they are not motivated toward an internally integrated development. Independence,

> if it was to have much value other than the sentimental, had to enable us to redesign the African economies, to make the self-directed and internally coherent, to shift them away from foreign-oriented to domestic motivated productivity, and thereby produce prosperity for the people of the continent. Such integrative development requires that political power be employed to remove all stumbling blocks put in its way... (Chinweizu 1975: 247).

Chinweizu paints a clear picture on what the problem of African development is and how political imagination is needed to gear into action in order to deal with the very problem of maldevelopment. Black colonialists did not want to revolutionise the colonial infrastructure, they wanted to inherit it and continue with its practices. Neither the structure of antagonism existed at the economic level, nor the new *imaginaire* of African development. The interests of African development were dispensed by the African bourgeoisie class, since to them what mattered most was access to political power without understanding the logic and structure of colonisation that perpetuates maldevelopment in the imperialist logic.

Self-reliant development and de-linking from maldevelopment

The way African development operates, it is something that is disciplined and controlled in that it is not in the control of Africans themselves. So, it essentially means that whatever posture of development programme there is, it is not African development but maldevelopment. African development can be regarded as the dream that has been progressively turned into a nightmare (Escobar 1995). The World Bank and IMF are the hegemons of development in that they provide intellectual and financial hegemony. So, whatever form of development there is, it is subjected to the dictates of these institutions which have shown not to have the interests of African development at heart, and they should, of course, not expected to have Africa's interests. Their hegemonic position still maintains the colonial relations. The World Bank and IMF as development apparatus dictate the nature, form and content of development, and African development is made to operate under the capture and gaze of this apparatus. The reality of development is the institutionally created one – safe to say the least, it is the rhetoric of development. As Escobar (1995: 222) warns, 'there are no grand alternatives that can be applied to all places or all situations'.

The contention of Chinweizu (1987) is that development can only emerge if self-reliance is reinforced and this will create new ways of thinking and the new developmental model. Development thought and practices should be rooted in the theoretical frameworks of Africa properly and they should, as Chinweizu states, say a lot about self-reliance. Chinweizu, however, warns that the concept of self-reliance is also used as a rhetoric and not reality to serve the interests of the African elites in order to mask maldevelopment. This is done through the logic of perpetuating the non-existence of development as if it is existence. What is clear is that no development can come from the Euro-North American empire and African elites alike since both do not have the interests of Africa. Chinweizu's quotes below are essential as a testimony to this:

> Left to their own devices, discarded countries would have no choice but to embark upon self-reliant development if they want any development at all. They would have to redefine their problem of development, not in terms of global system or world market relations, but in local and regional terms (Chinweizu 1987: 66).

> Since the structure of the world economy works against the prosperity of the poor economies, it seems clear that, in order to prevent their further pauperi[s]ation, they must be detached from the empire economies of the rich lands (Chinweizu 1975: 263).

It is important to note that this is a call for development in reality and not rhetoric where in which development is maldevelopment. This will be informed by what Mignolo (2007) calls de-linking, which is what Maldonado-Torres (2004) regards as a radical dislocation from the Euro-American empire and its roots. De-linking is the new discourse of development and it cannot be done by African elites as they have no political imagination. De-linking is the very good starting point for self-reliant development and this is the development that has Africa as its fulcrum and with the strong emphasis on decolonisation. This will also inculcate the remaking of Africa and fracturing the maldevelopment practice which is institutionalised, normalised and naturalised. What is urgent and necessary is to get rid of maldevelopment, and this will lead to self-reliant development.

There cannot be de-linking if the current discourse of development is at the centre, since it does not inform the existential realities of Africa and also reducing them to a mere symptom which can be dealt with intechnicist forms of development. De-linking from the current mould of development is to open new vistas of political imagination and innovating new practices. And then again, self-reliance is the new political practice. For Chinweizu (1987), the decolonisation of the African mind is the starting point and this will expand the horisons of political imagination—the very act of rethinking and redefining Africa's development. Also, this will mean to bring into existence what has not been in existence in Africa and that is development. Chinweizu makes it clear that this comes at the greater cost, since it is the very risk that the African elites fear to take. This is to make such political formations visible and to re-exists in order to centre the discourse of development. These are the processes, which Escobar (1995) refers to as that of 'unmaking development', which come at the greater costs of being long and painful. Nevertheless, the cost, the very fear of political imagination is maldevelopment itself, and to get rid of this fear, there should be ways to engage in self-reliant development as the very entry point to decolonised development. Self-reliant through the very political act of de-linking is a necessity.

Conclusion

African development has not been realised and it is non-existent in the very fact of it not being the project carried out by Africans themselves. What has been development in Africa has been the transplant development carried out by Euro-American empire and African elites as rubber stamping intermediaries. Development in Africa has been a scandal of maldevelopment. In relation to Africa's development, Chinweizu's decolonial critique poses a series of political question that seeks to move development to the lived experience of African subjects concerned about the legitimate change of the social arrangements and practices, which development must speak to as opposed to maldevelopment. This comes into being through the unravelling of the rhetoric of development and to reveal the reality of maldevelopment, which is a scandal. It is important to understand development as an epistemological and political project predicated on political identity. From this political identity is Africa's development, and Africa here is the geo-political arrangement and also as the epistemic location – both which suggests Africa's alienation from development. It is this very same development discourse that provides a posture of the apolitical project whereas it is political, and the problems that are peculiar to development become depoliticised. Chinweizu's decolonial critique to the trajectory of Africa's development is still necessary in that the political questions he posed and the call for political imagination is still the spectre that haunts. This spectre will continue to haunt if Africa is still caught in maldevelopment. The only way out, though with a greater cost is decolonisation, which will give birth to self-reliant development and not development as maldevelopment.

References

Ake, C. 1981. *A political economy of Africa*. Harlow: Longman.

Appiah, K.A. 1992. *In my father's house: Africa in the philosophy of culture*. New York: Oxford University Press.

Chinweizu. 2009. *Black colonialists: the root of the trouble with Africa*. The New Frank Talk: Critical Essays on the Black Condition. Issue 5.

________. 1987. *Decolonising the African mind*. Lagos: Pero Press.

________. 1975. *The west and the rest of us: white predators, black slavers and the African elite*. New York: Vintage Books.

Depelchin, Jacques. 2005. *Silences in African history: between the syndromes of discovery and abolition*. Dar Es Salaam: Mkuki na Nyota Publishers.

Escobar, Arturo. 1995. *Encountering development: the making and unmaking of the third World*. Princeton: Princeton University Press.

Maldonado-Torres, N. 2008. *Against war: views from the underside of modernity*. Durham and London: Duke University Press.

________. 'The topology of being and the geopolitics of knowledge: modernity, empire and coloniality'. *City*, 8 (1): 29-56.

Mignolo, W. D. 2009. 'Epistemic disobedience, independent thought and de-colonial freedom'. *Theory, Culture and Society*, 26 (7-8): 1-23.

________. 2007. 'Delinking'. *Cultural Studies*, 21 (2-3): 449-514.

Ndlovu-Gatsheni, S. J. 2013. *Coloniality of power in postcolonial Africa: the myths of decolonization*. Dakar: CODESRIA.

Santos, B. S. 2007. 'Beyond abyssal thinking: from global lines to ecology of knowledges'. *Review* 30 (1): 1-33.

Walsh, C. 2007. 'Shifting the geopolitics of critical knowledges: decolonial thought and cultural studies 'others' in the Andes'. *Cultural Studies*, 21 (2-3): 224-239.

Decolonising Power and Knowledge in Africa

Beyond Imperial Designs of Interventionism and Eurocentricism

William J. Mpofu

> *Yet, the colonial matrix of power is not going away. Coloniality will remain as long as the final horizon of human life is guided by the desire to accumulate capital. The control of authority will continue, disguised by rhetoric of progress, happiness, development and the end of poverty, and will justify the huge amounts of energy and money spent on the conflicts between the centres ruled by the capitalist economy.*
>
> **(Tlostanova and Mignolo 2009: 139)**

Introduction

The eve of the American Revolution in March 1776 saw the publication of a classic of Western capitalist economics. *The Wealth of Nations*, written by Adam Smith (2002:1-307) was to be one of the most influential books in world history and in the history of thought. Praising the publication as an epochal treatise, Joseph Schumpeter (1954:181) observed that it was 'the most successful, not only of all books on economics, but with the possible exception of *Darwin's Origin of Species*, of all scientific books' ever published under the sun. In this celebrated manifesto of the violence and opportunism of capital, Adam

Smith argues that the 'invisible hand' of providence guides the march of Western powers in their 'progress toward opulence' and that the wealth of nations comes from the maximum exploitation of labour.

One of Adam Smith's students and celebrants of his contribution to the spirit of capitalism, John Millar (1895:55) exclaimed that observance of 'expediency' and 'self-interest' rather than 'justice' in pursuit of the wealth of Western nations had been adequately vindicated by Smith. In Smith's fundamental observation about the need for cheap slavish labour and easy profits 'the demand for men, like that for any other commodity necessarily regulates the production of men' by any means necessary. In reaction to this predatory economics in *Capitalism and Slavery,* Eric Williams (1964:1-284) had to observe that European civilisation was built with bricks that were cemented with the sweat and blood of slaves who were kidnapped from Africa and the larger global South. In the logic of Williams, Europe owes its magnificence and 'opulence' to slave labour and the siphoning of raw materials and other resources from the colonies. For that reason, Aime Cesaire (1972:01) charges that 'Europe is indefensible' and that 'it is unable to justify itself either before the bar of reason or before the bar of conscience' leading to its refuge in 'hypocrisy' and deception.

In the same tone as Williams and Cesaire, in Africa, in the long colonial 1970s, Walter Rodney (2012: 1-313) published, *How Europe Underdeveloped Africa*, giving a solid account of exactly how Africa had 'developed' itself 'before the coming of the Europeans' who came and 'underdeveloped" the continent by turning it into a source of slaves, raw materials, cheap labour, and a ready constituency for Eurocentric education and cultural imperialism. Through political violence and the muscular economics of 'expediency' and disregard for 'justice' Europe transformed itself into a centre of the world, her knowledge became the knowledge of the world, and her interest became universal interests. While Europe basked in the glory of her Renaissance and the light of her Enlightenment on the one hand, on the other hand she literally darkened the world with slavery and colonialism.

The present chapter, using a decolonial critical prism of observation and analysis, posits to give an account of the enduring continuation of Europe's pursuit of imperial and colonial projects in Africa. The sponsorship of *coup d'états* disguised as assisted regime change projects for the democratisation of African countries, the illegal Western sponsorship of civil wars in Africa and promotion of conflicts to open markets for the sale of arms are but some of the projects of political and economic 'expediency' that so called developed countries in the North continue to visit upon Africa. African tyrants who secure European imperial and colonial projects in their countries are cushioned from censure and dethronement, while those that resist, safeguarding the independence and interests of their countries, are toppled through guile and force. Using the mantra of United Nations' 'responsibility to protect' the North Atlantic Treaty Organisation (NATO), as demonstrated in the invasion of Libya and the murder of Colonel Muammar Gaddaffi, are prepared to ignore all standing international protocols to eliminate leaders who threaten their access to African resources. This imperial and colonial interventionism, which is imbricated in keeping Africa and the global South in entirety open to the Western siphoning of cheap resources and the deposition of slavish and colonial knowledge is so ably described by Michel Chossudovsky (1998:1-280) as the predatory project of 'globalisation of poverty' and internationalisation of suffering.

From here, the present chapter intends an explication of decolonial critical thought as a theoretical and conceptual tool of reading the African condition of coloniality that is underpinned by tyranny, the puppetry of some African leaders to Western capitalist and imperial powers and the hegemony of Eurocentric knowledge. Pursuant to that, the chapter will explore some anecdotal spectacles of the manifestation of colonial and imperial designs of Europe in Africa, while in the main observing that African political and economic challenges will not be solved using Eurocentric epistemologies and methods that are imbricated in coloniality and imperiality. Finally, the chapter will achieve its terminus in the argument that proposes a decolonial turn toward the reading and knowing of the African condition from an African locus of enunciation that is not mediated by colonial and imperial epistemologies of the West.

Decolonial Critical Analysis

Perhaps part of the reason why thinkers and scholars in the global South have still to arrive at finding effective tools to disrupt Western colonial and imperial designs of coloniality, is that European theories and conceptual tools remain the dominant means of seeing the world and interpreting Africa. There seems to be doubt that coloniality and the dominance of Eurocentric knowledge in the world can be dethroned or at least disturbed using colonial and Eurocentric thoughts. In electing to use decolonial thought as a critical lens, this chapter seeks to participate in unmasking the presences of coloniality and its various manifestations in tyranny, puppetry and the installation of Eurocentric knowledge as a mode of knowing Africa. For that to happen, coloniality as a global power structure must be understood. Not only that, but this chapter must enunciate the difference that exists between juridical colonialism and coloniality. About coloniality, Peruvian sociologist, Anibal Quijano (2000:342) says:

> Coloniality is one of the specific and constitutive elements of the global model of capitalist power. It is based on the imposition of a racial/ethnic classification of the global population as the cornerstone of that model of power, and it operates on every level, in every arena and dimension (both material and subjective) of everyday social existence, and does so on a societal scale (Quijano 2000:342).

From Quijano's definition of coloniality we can draw that it is a power structure that is entwined with global capitalism and its attendant habits of imperialism, slavery, expansionism and colonialism. It is also implicated in the classifications of humanity according to lines of race and ethnicity, lines which are locatable in such African maladies as apartheid and the multiplicity of civil wars. Racism and tribalism, the underside of identity politics have emphatic imbrications in most conflicts and wars in the African continent. Coloniality, in the argument of this chapter, defines the effects of the inequality, imperiality and relations of domination by Europe of other parts of the world today.

There is a forgivable though disabling tendency among some students in the Social Sciences and the Humanities to mistake coloniality for colonialism. This justifies the need for this chapter to flesh out the difference between the two concepts and phenomenon. While decolonisation is the antidote of colonialism as a system, decoloniality which this chapter prefers as a project and prescribes as a way out of the condition of coloniality in Africa, is the antidote of coloniality. Nelson Maldonado-Torres (2007: 240) says:

> Coloniality is different from colonialism. Colonialism denotes a political and economic relation in which the sovereignty of a nation or a people rests on the power of another nation, which makes such a nation an empire. Coloniality, instead, refers to long-standing patterns of power that emerged as a result of colonialism, but that define culture, labour, intersubjectivity relations, and knowledge production well beyond the strict limits of colonial administrations. Thus, Coloniality survives colonialism.

The key departure of coloniality from juridical colonialism is its ability to survive decolonisation and remain as a technology of control of the minds of the former subjects of colonialism and to remain incarnated in the 'culture' and 'relations' of those who are supposed to have been freed in decolonisation. Torres' understanding of coloniality sits so centrally to the objects of this chapter in that he emphasises how coloniality infects the 'knowledge production' in former colonial settings of which Africa is a large part. It is one of the key projections of this chapter to discover how the knowledge of Africa in Africa remains annexed to the Eurocentric archive, where Africa remains being studied and analysed in colonial terms. The tendency continues where African countries still continue, even in the African academy, being judged down against the Western political, economic and intellectual standard.

Decolonial thought or decolonial analysis as a way of seeing and knowing the world seeks to dethrone the pretensions of post-colonial thinking that gesture to the effect that decolonisation exhausts every article of colonialism, hence the arrival of a post-colonial epoch. To decolonial thinkers and decolonial philosophers alike, post-coloniality is mythical and participates in misleading falsehoods in so far as it celebrates the pending and not the arrived epoch of liberation from coloniality and imperiality.

Achille Mbembe (1992:01), a contractor to post-colonial thinking and its mistakes, describes the 'post-colony' as 'specifically given historical trajectory - that of societies recently emerging from the experience of colonialism and the violence which the colonial relationship *par-excellence*, involves.' Mbembe is convinced that there is an 'emerging' from the 'colonial relationship' and its 'violence,' whereas decolonial thinkers such as Ramon Grosfoguel espouses that the colonial conditions continue in form of what this chapter describes as coloniality which perpetuates the sins of colonialism in Africa after the departure of formal colonial structures. In a vehement contest to post-colonial thought and its fantasies of a post-colony, Ramon Grosfoguel (2007:219) notes that:

> One of the most powerful myths of the twentieth century was the notion that the elimination of colonial administrations amounted to the decolonisation of the world. This led to the myth of a post-colonial world. The heterogeneous and multiple global structures put in place over a period of 450 years did not evaporate with the juridical political decolonisation of the periphery over the past 50 years.

To Grosfoguel and perhaps to most decolonial thinkers, coloniality was not exhausted in the events of decolonisation and its illusory spectacles in the erection of post-independence governments in Africa, or the installation of liberation war cadres as the new rulers. It provides for monumental mythmaking and fantasising to imagine that there was ever a departure of coloniality as a global systemic power that has governed relations between the North and the South since 1492, through colonial encounters to date. It is a crowning project of the present chapter to observe how imperiality and coloniality endure in the economic, political and social landscape of the current African condition.

Bewitched in his imagination of the mythical post-colony and antagonism to what he condemns as 'Afro-radicalism' and 'nativism' in Marxist and nationalist readings of the African condition, Mbembe conducts an analysis that collapses to a mockery of African efforts at liberation. While decolonial thought observes the limited resources of Marxism and African nationalism in reading post-independence settings in the global South, given that the two currents of thought have their roots in the same modernity/coloniality that they seek to dethrone, decolonial thinkers are still careful not to slide towards pessimism and contempt of the agency of activists in Africa and the global South. It is Achille Mbembe's (2002:01) charge against nationalism and Marxism that:

> Fundamental to both currents of thought are three historical events, broadly construed: slavery, colonization, and apartheid. A particular set of canonical meanings has been attributed to these three events. First, on the level of individual subjectivities, there is the idea that through the processes of slavery, colonization, and apartheid, the African self has become alienated from itself (*selfdivision*). This separation is supposed to result in a loss of familiarity with the self, to the point that the subject, having become estranged from him - or herself, has been relegated to a lifeless form of identity (*objecthood*). Not only is the self no longer recognized by the 'Other'; the self no longer recognizes itself. The second canonical meaning has to do with property. According to the dominant narrative, the three events have led to dispossession, a process in which juridical and economic procedures have led to material expropriation. This was followed by a unique experience of subjection characterized by the falsification of Africa's history by the 'Other', which resulted in a state of maximal exteriority (*estrangement*) and deracination. These two phases—the violence of falsification and material expropriation—are said to be the main components of African history's uniqueness and of the tragedy that is at its foundation. Finally, there is the idea of historical degradation: slavery, colonization, and apartheid are supposed to have plunged the African subject not only into humiliation, debasement, and nameless suffering but also into a zone of nonbeing and social death characterized by the denial of dignity, heavy psychic damage, and the torment of exile. These three fundamental elements of slavery, colonization, and apartheid are said to serve as a unifying

> center of Africans' desire to know themselves, to recapture their destiny (*sovereignty*), and to belong to themselves in the world (*autonomy*)

What Mbembe mocks as what was 'supposed' to be Africa's challenges in the post-independence context are actually presences and not absences of the 'colonial wound' that Mbembe seeks to pretend evaporated with decolonisation, ushering in a 'post-colony.' The sponsored coups as in Equatorial Gunea in 2004, carefully choreographed 'revolutions' as in Libya 2011, and machinated genocides such as the one in Rwanda 1994 and Zimbabwe 1982 to 1987, in their imbrications in coloniality and implication of global colonial designs, offer a loud denial of post-coloniality but a compelling case of a marching presence of coloniality as this chapter will argue.

The purchase of decolonial thought, and the relevance that it has to a clear understanding of the African condition is that it refuses the allure of 'illusions of decolonisation' as Sabelo Ndlovu-Gatsheni (2013) describes the fantasies of a post-coloniality. In the tyrannies, genocides and toxic knowledges that continue to zone Africa as 'hellish' and portray it as the colonial 'heart of darkness,' decolonial thinkers and philosophers are able to diagnose coloniality as the global systematic causality that orders the historical and political chaos that marks the African post-independence setting. Boaventura de Sousa Santos (2002:11) maintains that:

> The conditions that brought about the crisis of modernity have not yet become the conditions to overcome the crisis beyond modernity. Hence the complexity of our transitional period, portrayed by oppositional postmodern theory: we are facing modern problems, for which there are no modern solutions. The search for a postmodern solution is what I call oppositional postmodernism...what is necessary is to start from the disjunction between the modernity of the problems and the post-modernity of the possible solutions, and to turn such disjunctions into the urge to ground theories and practices capable of reinventing social emancipation out of the wrecked emancipatory promises of modernity.

Santos equips this chapter with the view that since coloniality itself is the 'underside' and the 'darker side' of a modernity that envelops the global South that includes Africa, and occasions the historical and political challenges that find expression in African events of tragedy and disaster, there is need to go beyond modernity for 'possible solutions'. There is a need to see beyond the 'wrecked promises' that include the myth that the invasion of Libya and the murder of Gaddafi were for the good of Libyans. Such other promises as that the attempted toppling of Obiang Nguema by Western sponsored mercenaries was for democracy and not for the siphoning of oil need to be debunked. Arturo Escobar (2007:8) argues that in the pervasive presence of 'imperial globality' and the assault of 'global coloniality' there is need to imagine 'worlds and knowledges otherwise' where a 'decolonial turn' and 'epistemic disobedience' can be achieved. The emphatic gesture of Escobar's argument is that there is need in such sites as Africa for decolonial thinkers to abandon the attempt to solve African political and economic challenges using received Eurocentric knowledges that are the source of the challenges in the first place. From here the present chapter proceeds to examines some of the spectacles of coloniality in Africa.

Africa: The spectacles of coloniality

The present section of this chapter posits to point to some of the spectacular evidence that confirms how much Africa remains arrested in the grips of coloniality and imperiality that is visited by the West in pursuit of the 'opulence" that prophets of capitalism and imperialism such as Adam Smith defined. Just how economic 'expediency' and the 'self-interest' of Western powers takes primacy over 'justice' in non-European parts of the world such as Africa describes conditions of coloniality and imperiality.

In *Cry Havoc*, British soldier of fortune and former Special Air Services officer, Simon Mann (2011,) reveals how the failed Equatorial Guinea coupd'état in 2004 was organised by a former British Prime Minister and financed by 'investors' in shape of oil barons in the West and Asia. The coup 'was about oil' according to Mann, but it had to be dressed up in the beautiful grammar of a humanitarian intervention. The coup was embellished as a benevolent attempt to free the suffering people of Guinea from the venal tyranny of Obiang Nguema Mbasongo and to install a 'good leader,' Severo Moto who had, for years, been living under the palatial hospitality of the 'investors' in his exile in Spain. Away from the narrative of a mercenary to that of a scholar, Horace Campbell (2012) in *NATO's failure in Libya: Lessons for Africa*, gives an account of how the financial depression in Europe, and the hunger for more oil, led to the invasion of Libya and the murder of Muammar Gaddafi, again the action was cloaked in the noble language of 'the responsibility to protect' the civilians of Libya from the genocidal Gaddafi establishment. What the majority of the people of Libya and the world saw as humanitarian United Nations (UN) intervention was actually the Smithian economic "expediency" of Europe towards African oil resources, this chapter will argue.

This chapter, as stated above, departs from the argument that Africa is still enveloped in imperial and colonial matrices of power, where from the centres of economic and political power in Europe and in Asia, African politics and economics are still decided, dictated and manipulated. Where Africa has beautiful and colourful flags and her people sing melodious anthems, saluting black presidents and Prime Ministers but her economies remain subject to the siphoning of resources for the benefit of Europe and Asia, in typical *How Europe Underdeveloped Africa* fashion as argued by Walter Rodney (2012). Years after colonialism and apartheid are declared over, the lives of the people remain hellish and enmeshed in poverty and disease. Attempts to revive African polities and economies always get hindered by that scholars and political activists in Africa continue to rely on colonial and Eurocentric blueprints.

In *The Shadow World: inside the Global Arms the Global Arms Trade*, Andrew Feinstein (2011), details how European and Asian gun runners and dealers, outside the perimeters of international law and the confines of standing embargoes and controls, supply weapons to the parties in African civil wars, sometimes supplying both warring camps with arms, in pursuit of profit. Such spectacles as the genocide of 1994 in Rwanda, the civil war of Sierra Leone in 1999 and the Gukurahundi genocide in Zimbabwe 1982 to 1987, have their causalities and imbrications in Western economic and political interests.

This 'darker side' of Western 'modernity' that sees the same patrons of democracy and human rights in Europe funding terror and sponsoring wars in other corners of the world, in pursuit of resources and profits is vividly described by John Pilger (2002) in *The New Rulers of the World.* In Pilger's account, as Saddam Hussein 'ordered the gassing of the Kurds in the town of Halabja,' in his palace he hosted 'Margaret Thatcher's Trade Secretary, who, within a month of the gassing of the Kurds' was back 'offering Saddam Hussein 340 million pounds' in 'export credits' together with an assortment of weapons and armaments. The same Saddam Hussein was to be hunted down later on as a developer and keeper of weapons of mass destruction that were never found. In the habit of economic and political 'expediency' that neglects the importance of truth and 'justice' the imperial powers of the world are willing to fight terror and tyranny with the right hand, while with the left they sponsor the same pathologies as long as capital marches 'toward opulence' as in the prescriptions of Adam Smith and other engineers of the capitalist and imperialist ethics.

Clearly, there is 'the increasing realisation that there are modern problems for which there are no modern solutions' as Arturo Escobar (2007:01) argues. This modern civilisation that permits in Europe democracy, human rights and peace with the right hand, while with the left hand in the Global South it visits financing of civil wars, the irrigation of tyrants and dumping of weapons to fuel conflicts is described as the 'underside of modernity' and 'global coloniality'. It is a long living global power structure that sentences Africa and the Global South to a zone of nonbeing that is populated by people whose lives are punctuated with 'lacks' and 'deficits' of values and knowledges that have to be forced upon them by the prefects of the world in the West. Ramon Grosfoguel (2011: 28) observes that:

> During the last 510 years of the 'Capitalist/Patriarchal Western-centric/ Christian-centric modern/Colonial World-System', we went from the 16th Century 'Christanize or I shoot you', to the 19th Century 'civilize or I shoot you', to 20th Century 'develop or I shoot you', to late 20th Century 'neo-liberalise or I shoot you', and to the early 21st Century 'democratize or I shoot you'.

From the period of slavery to date, African countries and those other countries in the Global South have had Western values and knowledge forced upon them with the threat or application of various kinds of violence and forceful persuasion. The encounters of Africa with the West, either in slavery, colonialism, neo-colonialism or the financial advice of the Bretton Woods Institutions and the Humanitarian military interventions of NATO have been violent encounters that involve the force of arms, the enticements with money with strings attached to it and other untoward impositions.

Mahmood Mamdani (2008:01) observed correctly in that "..it is hard to think of a figure more reviled in the West than Robert Mugabe." For grabbing white owned land, committing genocide in Matabeleland and unleashing political violence while literally refusing to concede electoral defeat, Mugabe has attracted very unkind world attention. Mamdani is also correct in that an investment of too much attention on Mugabe, as an offending individual "does little to illuminate the socio-historical issues involved." Even as George Bush named Mugabe's Zimbabwe as part of the global 'axis of evil' there is need to go beyond naming and descriptions to locate the imbrications and entanglements of coloniality in the tyranny and puppetry of Mugabe and the political violence that climaxed into a genocide in Zimbabwe.

While the political violence, economic meltdown and the genocide that perished more than 20 000 civilians and exiled many more thousands are part of the ignoble political order that Mugabe has represented, they are at the same time bitter fruitions of a global system that irrigates tyranny and cultivates chaos for its survival. Arturo Escobar (2009:11) describes the capitalist global Euro-American empire as an:

> Empire that increasingly operates through management of asymmetrical and spatialised violence, territorial control, subcontracted massacres, and cruel little wars, all of which are aimed at imposing the neo-liberal capitalist project. At stake is a type of regulation that operates through the creation of a new horizon of global violence. The empire regulates disorder through financial and military means, pushing chaos to the extent possible to the outskirts of empire, creating a predatory peace to the benefit of a global noble caste and leaving untold poverty and suffering in its path. It is an empire that does not take responsibility for the wellbeing of those over whom it rules.

Escobar portrays a monster. The Euro-American Empire in its capitalist pursuits and haste for the control of the globe has no iota of conscience or does it suffer any sense of irony or paradox that it keeps for itself the fruits of modernity in democracy, human rights and peace, while in the peripheries in the global South it exports death and hellish conditions. Proving that this empire is willing, for a profit, to be both fireman and arsonist, the prefects of the world wage a 'war against terror' and 'tyranny' with the right hand, and with the left, they sponsor terrorism and irrigate tyrants who scatter mass-graves and much suffering under the sun.

Talking about the Zimbabwean genocide in particular, Timothy Scarnecchia (2011:01) begins his important paper by disclosing how world powers were imbricated in the genocide that the Mugabe regime committed in Zimbabwe:

> Based on a preliminary reading of South African Department of Foreign Affairs files for 1983, Cold War relations between Zimbabwe and the United Kingdom helped to provide cover for the Zimbabwe National Army's Fifth Brigade's campaign of terror. Similarly, American support for Mugabe's claims to be a pro-Western leader committed to non-racialism helped provide international cover for the atrocities. At the same time evidence shows high ranking ZANU-PF officials negotiated with the South African Defence Forces in 1983 to co-operate in their efforts to keep ZANU-PF from supporting South African ANC operations in Zimbabwe. The 5th Brigade's campaign therefore served the purposes of South Africa, even as ZANU-PF officials rationalised the Gukurahundi

> violence in international and anti-apartheid circles as a campaign against South African destabilisation.

Such powers as America, in their national interests maintained relations with the Mugabe regime even as the regime committed crimes against humanity. In the same way in which Saddam Hussein received American and British support even when he committed despicable atrocities in some parts of Iraq, the Mugabe establishment at the time it committed a large scale genocide in Zimbabwe, was not censured or condemned in any way by the powers that have installed themselves as captains of human rights and democracy in the prevailing world system and global order.

While it might appear that American and British support for the Mugabe regime might as well have been a genuine error of judgement in international relations, it does not look that innocent when Scarnecchia quotes Geoff Hill, who discloses that the British Commissioner to Zimbabwe at the time of the genocide said the official policy of Britain at the time was to treat the Matabeleland massacres as a 'side issue' and support Mugabe. Geoff Hill (2011:08) says:

> Sir Martin Evans, High Commissioner in Harare at the time, admitted on camera his instructions from London were to 'steer clear of it' when speaking to Mugabe. 'I think Matabeleland was a side issue,' he said. 'The real issues were much bigger. We were extremely interested that Zimbabwe should be a success story, and we were doing our best to help Mugabe and his people bring that about.

It did not end there with the activity to 'steer clear' of the topic of the genocide but in 1994, freshly after the genocide, the Queen of England knighted Mugabe under the venerated Order of Bath. Mugabe's commander, Perence Shiri who was the kingpin during the massacres was invited to study at the exclusive British Royal College as an esteemed candidate. Clearly, to the British and the American establishment, the self appointed prophets of human rights, the Mugabe regime could slaughter their political enemies, the Ndebele people with impunity, as long as Western business interests were secure in Zimbabwe. Coloniality operates in such paradoxes where terrorism is a fight for freedom if it is advancing the interests of Empire, and freedom fighting is terrorism if it challenges capital and the interests of Empire.

The Mugabe, who is reviled as a genocidal tyrant, has been venerated as a Knight in shining armour, and a willing puppet, by the same global centres of power. For that reason, the observation is in order that the genocide in Zimbabwe, while it was supervised by Mugabe, as a crime against humanity, it implicates and indicts the global superpowers who benefit from the condition of coloniality under whose grip of the octopus the entire global South is held. That Mugabe who has grown so huge in tyranny is a joint creature of his ambitions and the promotion of the West, that have permitted him to be dismissive and contemptuous of his country and his people to the extent of telling them off about elections and political change. Before the elections of 2008 that were mired in violence Mugabe told the nation that:

> The war veterans came to me and said, "President, we can never accept that our country which we won through the barrel of the gun can be taken merely by an 'x' made by a ball-pen. Will the pen fight the AK rifle? Is there going to be a struggle between the two? Do not argue with a gun" (Mugabe 2008).

That impunity and arrogance of a tyrant has developed under support and promotion by the imperial powers of the world that have previously financed, armed and even 'knighted' the leadership of Mugabe in pursuit of their own economic and political interests in the African region. In the malady of tyranny in Africa is incarnated and embedded western puppetry where African tyrants are used to perpetuate agendas of the imperial West at the expense of the interests of their people. Africa has produced such a catalogue of fiery characters who chant Pan-African slogans by the light of day, and by night sentence the African people they lead to mass-graves, jails and much suffering. Joseph Mobutu of Zaire was the champion of African authenticity; while Idi Amin of Uganda was the architect of black empowerment, and Kamuzu Banda the 'ingwazi', an African warrior, yet in practice they sent thousands of Africans to early deaths and above all, conspired with Western imperialism in the looting and exploitation of African resources.

The 'puppetisation' and then the condemnation and 'tyrannisation' of Mugabe in the Euro-American political dictionary, under the logic of coloniality that is camouflaged behind the rhetoric of human rights, development and peace is not an isolated event. Tony Blair (2011), former British Prime Minister admits in his book that the British and American powers armed Saddam Hussein at some point, however, that did not stop them from hanging him at another point. Observing the same tendency of Empire to use and then abuse their clients and agents when it suits them, Andrew Feinstein (2011:43) invokes that screaming example of the unhygienic politics of empire when he says:

> The US arming of the *Mujahideen* in Afghanistan armed and trained to drive the Soviet Union out of the country, the same trained fighters, with the same weapons, formed the core of the Taliban and the adumbral Al-Qaida network that today constitute America's greatest enemy.

Such anecdotal examples of the 'underside' of the modernity that is represented by super powers of the North, and their visitation of violence and disorder in the world, especially in the global South testify to continuing coloniality and subjection of the peripheries to suffering. For the pursuit of profits and wealth by giant countries of Europe and Asia, places like Africa will remain very dangerous places as the Nuclear powers do not only participate in building weapons of mass destruction but also champion mass deception as they declare themselves to be global and universal standards of democracy when they literally manufacture and export wars, and proliferate weapons in African conflict spots.

In his important study of the 1994 genocide in Rwanda, Mahmood Mamdani (2001:14) advances an artisanal explication of the colonial roots of the genocide, and for that reason, the coloniality factor that fertilised the historical and political landscape for the genocide. To Mamdani, the colonial relations and classifications of people as 'settlers' and some as 'natives' gave birth to the genocide. The 'settler' and 'native' binaries were later inherited as relations of difference and sources of conflict by the indigenous people after the dethronement of formal colonialism in Rwanda. Mamdani argues that:

> The crime of colonialism went beyond expropriating the native, the name it gave to the indigenous population. The greater crime was to politicise indigeneity in the first place: first negatively as a settler libel of the native; but then positively, as a native response, as self-assertion. The dialectic of the settler and the native did not end with colonialism and political independence. To understand the logic of genocide, I argue, it is necessary to think through the political world that colonialism set into motion. This was the world of the settler and the native, a world organised around a binary preoccupation that was as compelling as it was confining. It is in this context that Tutsi, a group with a privileged relationship to power before colonialism, got constructed as a privileged alien settler presence...by Hutu power propaganda in 1990.

Colonial relations of 'settler' and 'native' got reconstructed and reproduced among the 'natives' after independence. In the Rwandan case, the Tutsi were named 'settlers' and aliens who became candidates for death in the genocide of 1994. Massive propaganda was deployed by the Hutu Power movement to define the Tutsi as pollutants and 'settlers' who needed to be removed from the land. Mamdani continues to say:

> I argue that the Rwanda genocide needs to be understood as a native's genocide. It was a genocide by those who saw themselves as sons—and daughters—of the soil, and their mission as one of clearing the soil of a threatening alien presence...not a violence against one who is seen as a neighbhour, but against one who is seen as a foreigner...one that seeks to eliminate a foreign presence from home soil (Mamdani 2001:14).

By manufacturing differences in classifying indigenous people as primitive 'natives' in colonial Rwanda, with the colonists fitting the definition of conquerors and 'settlers,' colonialism planted the seeds of genocide in post-independence Rwanda. The power structure of hated and privileged 'settlers' versus backward and poor 'natives' did not evaporate with the dethronement of administrative colonialism but remained to haunt the country after independence as those who believed themselves to be 'natives' sought to cleanse the land of those they believed to be 'settlers,' the Tutsi. Colonialism as a system and coloniality as the power structure that 'survives' colonialism cannot be exonerated from the crime against humanity as played out in the Rwandan genocide.

In what he ably describes as the 'silence of geography' Mahmood Mamdani (2001: 7-8) enunciates how the Rwanda genocide must not be read simplistically as a Rwandan misfortune and event, but a human event with regional and international causalities. This thesis of expanded geographies of genocide by Mamdani is in accord with decolonial analysis that identifies coloniality as having links with 'imperial globality' and 'global coloniality' at the same time. It is Mamdani's compelling view that:

> Since the genocide happened within the boundaries of Rwanda, there is wide spread tendency to assume that it must also be an outcome of processes that unfolded within the same boundaries. A focus confined to Rwanda state boundaries inevitably translates into a silence about regional processes that fed the dynamic leading to genocide.

The deployment of puppets and agents, the sponsorship of militias by shadowy international groupings and the supply of weapons by arms manufacturers to conflict zones in Africa as described by Andrew Feinstein (2011:42), cancels any imaginable innocence of Western powers in the genocide of Rwanda and other armed conflicts in Africa. Feinstein notes that:

> China and Russia sell weapons to many of the world's despots, including Sudan, Syria, Burma, Iran, North Korea and Zimbabwe. Their small arms proliferate in conflict zones from Darfur to Mullaitivu. The Chinese were willing suppliers of weapons to Hosni Mubarak's Egypt, along with Russia, France, the UK and the United States. The NATO powers, in their attacks on Libya's Muammar Gaddafi, have had to destroy not only Russian weapons, but also those sold to the dictator by France, Germany, Italy and the UK.

By the wisdom of an African proverb which holds that "to root out murder in the village" the villagers have to "go for the man who manufactures the Machete," the mass murder of Africans by tyrants and sponsored militias can be largely blamed on those who supply the weapons and the money that oils the conflicts and fuels genocides. Added to that, is the rude irony that the same suppliers of weapons that are used to commit crimes against humanity are the same who crusade about "war on terror"; and pretend to wage war against tyranny in the globe. The loud rhetoric of peace and human rights, democracy and development, in the mantra of the West, conceals under it the enduring logic of coloniality. The Euro-American Empire and its intervening economic interests in Africa is an absence that is always a presence in so far as the hidden agendas of imperialism and coloniality are always locatable in African conflicts.

Willie Esterhuyse (2012), a University of Stellenbosch Professor of philosophy, in a revealing book, *Endgame: Secret Talks and the End of Apartheid,* tells how in 1987 he was enlisted by the apartheid South African intelligence to negotiate the end of apartheid with ANC leaders that included Thabo Mbeki and Nelson Mandela. The talks were kept 'secret' and the sticking issues were 'white fears' that had to be settled before any headway could be made. Big International businesses 'funded' the talks in which the ANC had to make the now well known 'historic compromises'. The agreements that were made and which permitted the transition of South Africa from apartheid to democracy were greeted with euphoria and understandable jubilation. Paul Tiyambe Zeleza (2007 & 1997) describes the euphoria thus:

> Relief, and indeed Euphoria greeted the transformation, and the fact that the bloodbath predicted by both the foes and friends of apartheid had not materialized. In a world wrecked by ethnic or racial hatreds, gross social inequalities, moral corruption and despair, the demise of apartheid in South Africa marked a rare moment of joy and hope, of faith in the human capacity to transcend the yawning divisions and miseries bequeathed by history.

As large an anti-apartheid icon as Desmond Tutu, at the swearing in of the National Assembly of South Africa in 1994 said, in excitement, "we of many cultures, languages and races have become one nation, we are the rainbow people of God." Neville Alexander (2002:76). The metaphor of a rainbow nation went viral as the world celebrated the South African 'miracle of reconciliation', which was soon to be exposed as an illusion of biblical proportions as soon as the realities of continuing coloniality set in.

Thabo Mbeki (1999:88) who features in Esterhuyse's book as the point man of the negotiations alongside Nelson Mandela was to quickly complain about the 'rainbow nation' being 'two unequal nations'. As the then deputy president, Mbeki decried the increasing poverty of blacks in the face of mounting white wealth. Before the National Assembly, Mbeki said South Africa urgently needed:

> A commitment to confront the economic challenges facing our country, in a manner that simultaneously addresses issues of high and sustained growth and raising the living standards of especially the black poor, an all-embracing effort to build a sense of common nationhood and a shared destiny, as a result of which we can entrench into the minds of all our people the understanding that however varied their skin complexions, cultures and life conditions, the success of each nevertheless depends on the effort the other will make to turn into reality the percept that each is his or her brother's keeper; and a united view of our country's relations with the rest of the world.

As Neville Alexander (2002:76) argues, the celebrations of South Africa as one happy 'rainbow nation' of 'God' were somewhat dramatically premature and may be as a result of "a justifiable fit of euphoria" that was soon to be dampened by social and political conditions on the ground. For the majority black and poor of South Africans, it was still "not yet Uhuru" as the fruits of democracy and reconciliation were long in coming. John Pilger (2006) after a tour of South Africa, wrote a spirited book, *Freedom Next Time* in which he provides evidence of continuing dispossession of black people and their peripherisation from the mainstream South African economy. Pilger's damning conclusion was that "apartheid did not die."

The metaphor of South Africans as the 'rainbow people of God' remains an emphatic symbol that together with the venerated image of Nelson Mandela as a messianic and saintly liberator provides a stubborn myth of a free democratic South Africa. However strong this myth is, its beautiful symbolisms and imagery are contradicted by the daily experiences of the poor black people in the shanty towns and locations. Continuing with his sobering speech, Thabo Mbeki said:

> We therefore make bold to say that South Africa is a country of two nations. One of these nations is white, relatively prosperous, regardless of gender or geographical dispersal. It has a ready access to a developed economic, physical, educational, communication and other infrastructure. This enables it to argue that, except for the persistence of gender discrimination against women; all members of this nation have the possibility to exercise their right to equal opportunity, the development opportunities to which the constitution of 1993 committed our country. The second and larger nation of South Africa is black and poor, with the worst affected being women in the rural areas (Mbeki, pers. comm. 1999:88)

Reading Thabo Mbeki thus, confirms that the glossy South Africa that represents God's 'rainbow' and portrays a happy people remains an elusive pie in the sky. The South Africans who live in Sandton do not have the same experience of South Africa as those across the street in Alexandra and Tembisa. Other South Africans of the white and black elite nation swim in obscene prosperity, while the others of the poor mainly black nation drown in hellish poverty in one country. This gulf between the rich and the poor bespeaks the 'two nations' that Mbeki describes, and these nations are a stubborn refusal of the rainbowism that Tutu dreamt of.

For that loud manifestation of inequalities and dearth of hope in a post-apartheid setting that was supposed to project miraculous emergence from racism and tyranny but did not, South Africa fits the definition of what Arturo Escobar (2009:12) calls 'social fascism'. This social fascism describes:

> The structural predominance of exclusion over inclusion. Either because of the exclusion of many of those formerly included, or because those who in the past were candidates for inclusion are now prevented from being so, the problematic of exclusion has become terribly accentuated, with ever growing numbers of people thrown into a 'veritable state of nature'. The size of the excluded class varies of course with the centrality of the country in the world system, but is particularly staggering in Asia, Africa and Latin America (Escobar 2009:12)

In accord with Thabo Mbeki, the crisis that confronts most black people in South Africa is that of 'exclusion' from what has been called 'the first economy'. The promises of liberty and equality that the end of formal apartheid held have been wrecked by the reality of poverty and unfulfilled dreams of independence. Escobar says "this fascism may operate in various modes: in terms of 'spatial exclusion' and sometimes 'financial fascism'. Such pathologies in South Africa as violent crime, xenophobia and social death are bitter fruitions of exclusion and the dog eat dog scramble for limited resources. It dawns therefore, as John Pilger concludes that "apartheid did not die" in South Africa, it only negotiated away its vulgar and formal qualities of overt racism; otherwise its technologies of exclusion and marginalization remain intact.

The Libyan case provides theatres of violent coloniality that must jolt scholarly conscience to more research. While Muammar Gaddafi's efforts at improving the lives of Libyans cannot be denied by most honest observers, his haughty nature and roughshod approach to the will of his people is equally prominent. This is the same leader and revolutionary who described himself as he said, "I am an international leader, the dean of the Arab rulers, the king of kings of Africa" who is also "the Imam of Muslims, and my international status does not allow me to descend to a lower level" of listening to commoners.

Not only that, but Gaddafi did say that "Those who do not love me do not deserve to live," all of which are words that define excess and imprudence in a leader who requires consent from his people and who must submit to accountability. It is the same haughtiness of Gaddafi that projected itself when he called the militant protesters against his rule in February 2011--- 'rats'. Under the cover of the United Nations Security Council's mantra of "the responsibility to protect," the NATO countries bombarded Libya, armed the militants that ironically included Al-Qaida Jihadists, and eventually got Gaddafi captured and killed. In his artisanal study of the Libyan scenario, Horace Campbell (2012:4) advances telling observations that testify to 'imperial globality' and 'global coloniality' that became the hidden hand in the military and political spectacle that ensured in the oil rich country. Campbell notes that:

> African petroleum resources are caught up in a new transitional period, where the future of the top Western oil corporations is on the line. Even before the complete fall of Gaddafi's regime, one British scholar, David Anderson, had opined on the "fight for Libya's oil". Waxing on the 'significant pickings' in Libya, Anderson reflected on the opportunities for Europe's oil giants-Eni, Total, Bp and Repsol YPF- who are 'perfectly positioned' to take advantage of these commercial opportunities.

From Campbell's compelling observations that emanated from his rigorous research, the scramble for access to Libya's oil became a prominent motive in the NATO invasion and bombardment of Libya. The 'responsibility to protect' the Libyans from the 'tyrant' became a convenient cover for the scramble for African resources, just as the 'civilising mission' and the 'christianising agenda' became a cover for colonialism. Campbell reminds us of a United States 'former Congressman William Jefferson' who had the temerity to publicly say "African oil should be treated as a priority for US national security post 9/11, its occurred to all of us that traditional oil sources are not as secure as we thought they were," words that gesture to an increasing imperial appetite for African resources. An appetite that saw America and NATO teaming up with Al-Qaida to oust Gaddafi.

Veiled behind NATO's 'responsibility to protect' mantra are damning manifestations of coloniality and imperiality that include the persecution of black Africans in Libya. Campbell records that:

> The more chilling aspect of this persecution is the racist attacks on those who are supposed to be black Africans. There are reports from numerous sources that, in addition to black Africans being detained enmasse on the suspicion that they were mercenaries for Gaddafi, the town of Tawergha, previously a black African community, has been completely emptied and declared a 'closed military zone' by the NATO-supported militia forces (Campbell 2012:8).

The NATO-supported uprising in Libya did not fail to display the racism that has always accompanied 'global coloniality' and all the imperial workings of empire that include slavery and colonialism, which were based on doubting the humanity of the black person and seeing him or her as a beast of burden in the service of capital and empire. Campbell emphsises again that whenever the West are squeezed for resources, they expand to 'pickings' in Africa, "this attack on Africans in the midst of a depression is not new."

Even during the 'great depression' the 'European powers failed to intervene to halt the Italian invasion of Abyssinia.' Conclusions that such Western military escapades as the invasion of Libya under the pretext of 'the responsibility to protect' are modes of re-colonisation are not far-fetched. The present chapter moves on from here to examine how Eurocentric and colonial knowledge continues to exercise hegemony in Africa and hinders efforts at finding home-grown solutions for African challenges.

Africa: Coloniality of knowledge and Eurocentricism

At this stage, the present chapter seeks to give account to Eurocentric knowledge that provides sustenance to the global power structure of coloniality that has such an impact on African affairs as described above. Such ideas on capitalist economics as provided by Adam Smith

(2012) became the oxygen that gave impetus to imperialism, slavery and colonialism as projects of Euro-American capital (Muzlish 2012:3) confirms that Smith among other thinkers across generations had monumental influence on European thought and policy, 'what he had to say on the East Indian Company was heeded. His comments on war and the financial basis of the military operations had their effect' as he became a foremost 'policy advisor' to imperial Europe. In line with such influential Western thinkers such Plato, Aristotle and Machiavelli among many others Adam Smith produced knowledge that equips Western imperial and colonial projects in such settings as Africa to date. It is one of the aims of this chapter to observe how this colonial and Eurocentric knowledge on politics and economics continues in Africa to impede progress in areas of decolonisation, development and democratisation.

In arguing how Africa was not looked at by colonists as a reality but as a colonial invention, (Mudimbe 1988) insists that the colonising forces had their own Africa in the mind that suited their imperial interests, they did not need to understand Africa as it really is. The argument that this chapter seeks to advance is that even some apparently Afrocentric scholars and activists, continue to read Africa using colonial inventions and imaginations. Mudimbe calls this habit the unfortunate reliance on the 'colonial library' by the colonised that ought to rely on their own knowledges for survival. Ramon Grosfoguel (2013:79) provides an account of how conquering colonist invaders in the Americas in the 16th century burnt libraries of the colonised, and forced the indigenous people to convert to their own religions as part of what he calls 'epistemicides' and erasures of the knowledges of the indigenous peoples. In Africa too, colonist did enough imperial homework to convert Africans through religion and education into Eurocentric ways of thinking and knowing which ways continue to impede African development and democratisation.

At the heart of African Eurocentricism of knowledge and coloniality of reading and understanding Africa is the African university and the education systems that remain rooted in the 'colonial library' and European episteme. Because of this coloniality of the African university and the archive that it sustains, Sabelo Ndlovu-Gatsheni (2013) notes that it is "the university in Africa, not an African University," gesturing that the institutions of higher learning might be in Africa physically and geographically, but they contain European sense and sensibility and discharge European understanding of Africa. In accord with Ndlovu-Gatsheni, Claude Ake (1979) laments that the social sciences diet dished in the African academy continues to feed African minds with "noxious values, false hopes, to make us pursue policies which undermine our competitive strength and guarantee our permanent underdevelopment and dependence." It is Ake's considered conclusion that 'social science' happens in Africa 'as imperialism' in its form and content.

This ongoing infection of African sensibility and culture by Eurocentricism produces colonised minds which Ngugi wa Thiongo (1997:16) has emphatically, in his writings about 'the language of African literature' challenged by calling for 'decolonising' the African 'mind.' Mahmood Mamdani (2011) who has done research on how African 'scholars' exist as labourers in the intellectual 'market place' has also decried the intrusion of 'consultancy cultures' into the African academy where scholars have declined to short and sharp 'power point' experts who are bereft of large scale researches and explications of knowledge. Issa G. Shivji (2003:11), regretting the corporatization of the African academy and the decline of the intellectual said:

> The metamorphosis of the African intellectual from a revolutionary to an activist, from a critical political economist to a post-modernist, from a social analyst to a constitutionalist liberal, from an anti-imperialist to a cultural atavist, from a radical economics professor to a neo-liberal World Bank spokesperson, from an intellectual to a consultant is blatant, unrepentant and mercenary.

Shivji vividly captures the collapse of the revolutionary African intellectual from that of the calibre of Walter Rodney and Frantz Fanon to paid up consultants of today who relish in contracts and projects that drive researches whose output is to endorse colonial knowledge and sustain 'global coloniality.' The other contributory factor to this is the availability in huge numbers of scholars from Europe most of whom fall into the category of those that Paul Tiyambe Zeleza (1997) describes as 'academic tourists' who still advance 'imperialist historiography' of Africa, and study the continent as if it were a zoo and historical experimental laboratory of the world and not a peopled continent.

The colonised condition of the corporatized African academy calls for a decolonial turn. This turn constitutes not what is called 'epistemic breaks' but 'epistemic ruptures' that occasion an 'insurrection of previously subjugated' African knowledges that emanate from the locus of enunciation of the Global South, and espouse Afrocentric understanding of Africa while erecting 'ecologies of knowledge' that imagine a world of cognitive justice and pluriversality, 'where other worlds are possible,' not the suffocating tyranny of one Eurocentric epistemic universe that fetishises Europe as the centre of all that is good for humanity. Decoloniality as the anti-thesis of coloniality becomes the option for African thinkers and scholars who wish to contribute to the liberation of Africa from the imbrications of coloniality in its various manifestations by producing knowledge about Africa that is from decolonial African *loci* of enunciation.

Conclusion

This chapter has participated in the decolonial practice of unmasking coloniality that lies incarnated in African polities and economies. In such seemingly 'post-colonial' African tragedies and misfortunes as tyranny and puppetry that occasion political violence, genocide and civil wars, manifests coloniality as a presence of 'imperial globality' and 'global imperialism.' The Euro-American empire hides behind innocent and even humane vocabularies of "the responsibility to protect," human rights, democracy and development, while the true logic behind their false rhetoric is access to African resources. The potency of decolonial analysis, against the destitution of postcolonial thought in reading the African condition has been defended.

The shadowy and lawless global arms trade and coups that crowd the continent are some of the dramatisations of the workings of empire in Africa where chaos and political violence are sponsored to fertilise historical and political landscapes for the entrance of empire and its colonial technologies and designs. Even the Eurocentric knowledge and impotent scholarship that marks the large part of the African academy, and shapes the colonial content of the African archive constitutes a projection of empire. The emphatic suggestion of the present chapter is that the Africans should desist from reliance on the 'colonial library' that projects the same knowledge that defended slavery and colonialism. Adam Smith's *The Wealth of Nations* for example, might be a brilliant work of economic philosophy, buts its brilliance was of benefit to the Euro-American enterprise and not the African project of decolonisation and development. Decoloniality suggests a refusal of and resistance to the Euro-American project of coloniality and imperiality, which besides interfering in African affairs through invasions, coups and other imperial designs, also sustains colonial and Eurocentric knowledge that continues to muddy the way of Africa towards development.

References

Ake, C. 1979. *Social Science as Imperialism: The theory of Political Development*, Second Edition, Ibadan University Press

Alexandra, N. 2002. *An Ordinary Country: Issues in the transition from South Apartheid to Democracy in South Africa,* Pietermaritzburg, University of Natal Press.

Boron, A. 2005. *Empire and Imperialism: A Critical Reading of Michael Hardt and Antonio Negri*. London and New York: Zed Books.

Blair, T. 2011. *The Journey*, London. Arrow Books. UK

Chossudovsky, M. 1998 *The Globalisation of Poverty: Impacts of IMF and World Bank reforms*. London and New Jersey: Zed Books

Campbell. H. 2012. *NATO's failure in Libya: Lessons for Africa*, Pretoria, Africa Institute of South Africa, RSA

David, A. 2011. 'The fight for Libya's Oil,' Sustainable Security, http://sustainablesecurity.org/article/fight-libya-oil (accessed June 2013)

Escobar, A. 2007. 'Worlds and Knowledges Otherwise' *Cultural Studies*, (21)2, pp.179-210

Esterhuyse, W. 2012. *Endgame: The secret Talks and the end of Apartheid.* Cape Town: NB Publishers.

Feinstein, A. 2011.*The Shadow World: Inside the global arms Trade*, Johannesburg and Cape Town, Jonathan Ball Publishers. http://www.brainyquote.com/quotes/authors/m/muammar_algaddafi.html#xJPrcKiqswiPfzw7.99

Grosfoguel, R. 2011. 'Decolonizing Post-Colonial Studies and Paradigms of Political Economy: Transmodernity, Decolonial Thinking, and Global Coloniality'. *Modernity: Journal of Peripheral Cultural Production of the Luso-Hispanic World*, 1(1), pp. 1–39.

Grosfoguel, R. 2013. 'The structure of knowledge in Westernised Universities: Epistemic Racism/ Sexism and the four Genocides/ Epistemicides of the long 16th Century' *Humana Architecture: Journal of the Sociology of Self-Knowing*, 1 (1) pp. 73-90.

Hill G. 2003. *The Battle for Zimbabwe*. Cape Town: Zebra Press.

Mamdani. M. 2008. 'Lesson of Zimbabwe: Mugabe in context' Oxford Review of books, 30, n 23

Mamdani Mahmood. 2001. *When Victims become Killers*. London & Princeton: Princeton University Press.

Mann, S. 2011 *Cry Havoc*, Johannesburg and Cape Town: Jonathan Ball Publishers.

Maldonado-Torres, N. 2007. 'On the Coloniality of Being: Contributions to the Development of a Concept'. *Cultural Studies,* 21(2–3), pp. 240–270.

Mbembe, A. 2002a. 'African Modes of Self-Writing'. *Public Culture*, 14(1), pp. 239–273.

Mbembe, A. (1992). "Provisional notes on the postcolony". *Africa*, 62, pp 3-37. Doi: 10.2307/1160062.

Mbeki, T. 1999 "South Africa: Two Nations" In Adrian Hadland and Jovial Rantao, *The life and the times of Thabo Mbeki,* Cape Town: Struik Book Distributors.

Miller, J. 1895. In Rae, J. *Life of Adam Smith*, London, Dover Publications, UK

Mugabe, R: *The Herald* (23 June 2008).

Mudimbe, V. Y. 1988. *The Invention of Africa: Gnosis, Philosophy, and the order of knowledge*, Oxford: James Currey.

Muzlish, B. 2012. In Smith, A. *The Wealth of Nations*, New York: Dover Publications.

Ndlovu-Gatsheni, S. J. 2013. *Empire, Global Coloniality and African Subjectivity*. New York and Oxford: Berghahn Books

Pilger. J. 2006. *Freedom Next Time*, London: Transworld Publishers

Pilger. J. 2002. *The New Rulers of the World*, London: Verso Publishers

Quijano, A. 2000a. 'The Coloniality of Power and Social Classification'. *Journal of World Systems*, 6(2) pp. 342–386.

Tlostanova, M.V. and Mignolo, W.D. 2009. 'Global Coloniality and the Decolonial Option'. Kult 6 – Special Issue: *Epistemologies of Transformation: The Latin American Decolonial Option and Its Ramifications*, pp. 130–147.

Rodney. W. 2012. *How Europe Underdeveloped Africa*, Dakar: CODESRIA

Santos, B. de S. 2002. *Towards a New Legal Common Sense.* London: Butterworth.

Smith, A. 2012. *The Wealth of Nations*, New York: Dover Publications.

Scarnecchia T. 2011. "Rationalising Gukurahundi: Cold war and South African Foreign Relations with Zimbabwe, 1981-1983." *Kronos* (37) pp. 20-31

Schumpeter, J. 1954. *History of Economic Analysis*, New York, Dover Publications, USA

Zeleza P. T. 1997. *Manufacturing African Studies and crises*. Dakar, CODESRIA, Senegal

Wathiongo, N.1994. *Decolonising the Mind: The politics of Language in African Literature*, Harare, Zimbabwe Publishing House

Williams, E. 1964. *Capitalism and Slavery*, London: Andre Deutsch Publishers.

Shivji, I. G. 2003. "The rise, the fall and the insurrection of nationalism in Africa. "Keynote Address to CODESRIA Conference, Addis Ababa, Ethiopia.

The Future of Africa's Development:

A Diopan Perspective

Siphamandla Zondi

Introduction

The late Cheikh Anta Diop is a towering figure in African thought, best known for what Ntongela Masilela (2009) describes in an essay paying homage to Diop after his passing as "demystifying a contentious zone of African history by giving it to the African peoples." This, he suggests, is the reason why Diop's ground-breaking works on African antiquity is conspicuous by its absence in neocolonial African historiography and literature. Diop has also been a figure of fun and scorn among European intellectuals who disagree with his argument that the Egyptian civilisation was essentially African and black. Masilela (2009) ventures further to explain that this obscurity of Diopan perspectives in social science about Africa is to do with the fact that "contemporary European liberal historiography on Africa, at least large portions of it, is merely a continuation, though subtle and hidden, of imperial colonial historiography on Africa."

Diop came from a tradition of scholarship that sought to challenge the basic tenets of this imperial or, now, neo-imperial canon of scholarship on Africa. This is the tradition that Joseph Ki-Zerbo (2005: 2-3) suggests is both pan-Africanist and liberationist in essence because it acts in disobedience of the imperial designs of western-centric knowledge and science in much the same way that the liberationist political movements challenged the colonial state and its imperial power. Diop belongs to the generation of African intellectuals including Frantz Fanon, Aime Cessaire, Allioune Diop, WEB du Bois, C.L.R. James and others that rebelled against imperial and colonial domination including intellectual subordination.

They engaged in what C.L.R James (1969) termed a Pan-African revolt to claim Africa's past and destiny from the terrible hand of colonial and imperial designs.

Diop's work on the future of Africa's unity, integration and development is the least analysed or known of his large intellectual heritage; and it is subject to even worse silencing than the more prominent work on African agency in their own history. Diop concerned himself with the state of Africa in the post-1960s period as he observed how newly independent states were managed and how they responded to the historical imperative to decolonise Africa for real, and the task of giving birth to a free and prosperous Africa. Out of this, he thought deeply about what the state and political leaders in charge of it might consider as options to practically realise this historical goal. It could be argued that even in his writings on the ancient Egyptian civilisation, Diop sought to look back in order to imagine an African future in which Africans are not assumed to be automatically inferior and to be a people without history. After reviewing controversies that followed Diop's publications on antiquity, Masilela (2009) concluded that it is evident in Diop's work that he envisaged a "world when the great historical writings of Cheikh Anta Diop will no longer be necessary, that is a world beyond class oppression, free of all forms of oppression and racism." "The works of Diop," he surmised, "bring that era much closer to us." In his collection of essays first published in 1960 (and re-published in 1974 under the title *Black Africa: The Economic and Cultural Basis for a Federated State*), Diop reflected deeply on the basis of the terrible experience of post-colony in South America – especially disunity, ubiquity of violence and poverty – on necessary conditions for African unity as essential for completing the decolonisation of Africa including getting rid of the demons of disunity, violence, and poverty. This was the basis on which he took time to consider in detail the desired future for Africa and how might Africa get there.

This chapter revisits Diop's perspectives on the future of African integration and its modalities as a contribution to on-going discussions initiated by the chairperson of the African Union Commission, Dr Nkosazana Dlamini-Zuma, on Africa's second jubilee after independence. It demonstrates the extent to which ideas proffered at the beginning of the independent period remain relevant today, and that in fact they are similar to ideas being put forward to define Africa's second jubilee today. In this sense, the chapter argues for the centrality of historical memory in enriching debates about Africa's futures today, so as to avoid either silencing the voices from the past that have not been heeded anyway or merely borrowing from experiences of others to respond to Africa's predicament today. The chapter suggests that two conditions are important when re-discovering the agency of African thought in history: first is to recognise the persistence of coloniality in general marked by three vectors - coloniality of being, coloniality of power and coloniality of knowledge. This expresses itself in the association of Africa with lack - lack of history, lack of civilisation, lack of development, lack of science and even lack of heritage of ideas necessary for defining its future. This coloniality of knowledge thrives on the erasure of historical memory in order to cement the place and dominance of exogenous ideas, policies and sciences in policy discourses and scholarly work today.

Therefore, the contribution of Diop in the regional integration discourse must begin with an epistemic disobedience to Eurocentrism. The second condition is that such disobedience requires that one adopts decolonial methodological options like Afrocentric thought. It is impossible to be authentic in thought without looking beyond the blinkers of Eurocentric thought for lenses and tools of analysis.

Cheikh Anta Diop, Coloniality and Africanity

Cheikh Anta Diop was a situated African intellectual in the sense that he took a position in the continued struggle to subordinate Africa by falsifying its history and other forms of academic charlatanism. He stood for reclaiming African historical memory against the myths of Africa without history, an Africa that only had legends. Thus, Diop stood opposed to the coloniality of knowledge, which in the African setting sought to perpetuate the subordination of Africa and its peoples in a Euro-American world. In this sense, Diop stood for epistemic liberation or his vocation could be described as epistemic disobedience against Eurocentrism. To the extent that Diop sought to demonstrate African agency both in his reinterpretation of the available and largely distorted records of history and by showing that Africans were subjects rather than objects of their ancient history, he advocated Afrocentric analysis of Africa and the understanding of Africanity from within and from below. This locates Diop firmly in the canon of knowledge to which belongs many shades of decolonial thought.

Decolonial thought is associated with recent renaissance of epistemic disobedience dominated by South American scholars that have sought to unmask the coloniality of power, knowledge and being in the South American experience, especially after the end of colonial rule. Decolonial thought is born out of the convergence of critical thinking from various parts of the former colonial territories, commonly known as the global south or third world, on the need to find analytics of the limits of Eurocentrism as a hegemonic structure of knowledge and beliefs. While this was thought to be necessary, but it was generally also considered insufficient for epistemic liberation of the subordinated without epistemic de-linking or disobedience, which became known as decoloniality. Thus, decoloniality came to embody the analysis of conditions that limit the expression of subalternity, the rise of the subject from below or the birth of true epistemic plurality – the structure of hegemonic power from political power through economic power to the structure of knowledge. It also embodied the acceptance that there was no way out of coloniality from within itself or western traditions of thought, but could only be experienced by de-linking or disobeying the structures of hegemonic power. It was also a rejection of the Foucaultan idea of 'newness' by which it was contemplated that coloniality could renew itself by shedding its darker side. These are assumptions embedded in the currency of post-modernism, the idea that certain conceptual devices were 'better' merely because they were new. Decolonial analysis offers the possibility of starting the thinking somewhere other than Greece.

This leads us to the idea and system of modernity, which was supposed to denote progressive improvement in the lives of peoples, but which in Eurocentric thought denotes the incorporation of the 'other' in the system whose logic is oppression and whose effect on the 'other' is wretchedness, to use Frantz Fanon's concept. Decolonial thought makes it possible to see modernity as a double-headed hydra that uses the rhetoric of salvation and progress to mask the logic of oppression and subordination. It conceals coloniality, its other face that is manifest in oppression, structural poverty, stereotyping, under-development and so forth. The same system that parades its charity in the form of aid and investment in Africa is also responsible for wretchedness of Africa; it speaks about partnership, but operates on the basis of paternalism; it trumpets its intensions to build more equal relations with Africa, but in practice it perpetuates dependency; and while it publicly commits to Africa's unity, it does everything to fragment the continent. This led to the idea of a darker side of modernity, which is concealed, under-stated and hidden, only visible in the evident wretchedness of the subalterns in Africa and other parts of the global south.

This argument is extended further to the very nature of global power, system and order. It is argued that global modernities (that underpin the global discourse on development, progress and partnerships) are again an essentially Eurocentric narrative that also implies global colonialities, which is partly why the discourse is disputed, challenged and disowned by many especially among the excluded, the wretched of the earth. Just there cannot be modernity without coloniality, Walter Mignolo (undated) argues, there can be no global modernity without global coloniality. This, he contends, undergirds the polycentric capitalist world system and order today. In this sense, globalisation and the largely positive narratives about it represent the same order of things or a similar power matrix as the one that held sway under global imperialism and colonialism. It is a new version, an improvement upon rather than a break away from the former. The crimes committed, violence unleashed and harm caused in the name of modernity sums up coloniality as a consequence of modernity. This is what weaves together the implications of the international order, international law, international political economy, international governance, international military power, and even international cultural power on the subalterns. It undergirds the irresponsible use of military power to forcibly remove governments that the west dislikes, the western control over international finance institutions whose power to subvert national sovereignty is well known, the selective use of international law to punish those that are on the global periphery, and the skilful use of so-called soft power (in the form of control or influence over the media, arts and cultural artefacts) to project coloniality in a bright light.

In the case of Africa again, coloniality as an analytic weaves together various critical narratives that decry the continued fragmentation of the continent (including such as being perpetuated by the EU's negotiating strategy in negotiations with African, Caribbean and Pacific countries on Economic Partnership Agreements); the paternalistic relations with the west, especially; the aid dependency syndrome; constricted national sovereignty; neo-colonial relationships with former colonial powers; the scramble for Africa's land and natural resources; the failure to transform economies by stimulating endogenous development and industry; the ubiquity of structural poverty; weak regional institutions and poor intra-Africa trade as compared to external trade; a neocolonial African elite that is unpopular at home and embraced in the west; and other major criticisms of the African condition today. Discourses of development, progress, happiness and partnership represent a modernity narrative that conceals the intention to keep Africa divided, dependent and demoralised.

The Negritude paradigm that Diop is associated with sought first and foremost to unmask the tendency of the colonial system, even after the end of colonial rule, to negate African contributions to humanity and civilisation. It was thus also focused on uncovering the darker side of colonial and post-colonial modernity. It focused quite strongly on how coloniality had battered the African's ego in order to kill his agency in service of humanity. This is the reason why negritude had a lot to do with reclaiming this ego and agency in order to enable Africans to escape their wretchedness. This is why Leopold Senghor, who would later become the first president of independent Cote d'Ivoire, described negritude as a weapon of defence, attack and inspiration. Defence was necessitated by the fact that it was accepted that African identity (ego), power and knowledge were under attack from coloniality in its various forms including Eurocentrism. Diop (1981:302) described the various layers of this onslaught, bringing together western science and politics, economics and culture in pursuit of coloniality as follows:

> [T]he line of ill-intentional Egyptologist, equipped with a ferocious erudition, have committed their well known crime against science, by becoming guilty of a deliberate falsification of the history of humanity. Supported by the governing powers of all the Western countries, this ideology, based on a moral and intellectual swindle, easily won out over the true scientific current developed by a parallel group of Egyptologist of good will, whose intellectual uprightness and even courage cannot be stressed strongly enough.
>
> The new Egyptological ideology, born at the opportune moment, reinforced the theoretical bases of imperialist ideology. That is why it easily drowned out the voice of science, by throwing the veil of falsification over historical truth. This ideology was spread with the help of considerable publicity and taught the world over, because it alone had the material and financial means for its own propagation.

If one removes the reference to Egyptiology as just site of imperial designs that negritude and other examples of African thought and movements that had decolonial motives were born to resist and undo, the observation applies to a wide spectrum of matters relating to Africa' political economy, culture and science/knowledge today. Like Archie Mafeje, Diop sought to unmask the alterity that underpins Eurocentrism or western modernity, which tended to consign Africans into what has been called the zone of social death. This is what Diop calls cultural murder in the quotation above. Diop identified tendency of coloniality of knowledge (or what he called imperialist ideology in science) to use Africa's objective reality (data) to validate western thought about itself and about Africa; what Hountondji (1987) calls extroversion. He thus would be among the first to uncover in detail the imperialist nature of mainstream social science as would be further elucidated by Claude Ake (1982) later. There are many other examples demonstrating the interest in unmasking the coloniality of the modernity narrative in the form of intellectual work on Egyptian history and civilisation. Diop understood that unmasking the darker side of Eurocentric knowledge was a form of counter-attack, which is why he described one of the tasks of negritude as attacking negations.

Diop saw the task of negritude - the thought and practice - as being also redemptive, restoring back to Africans the lost identity, the vanquished ontological density and the suppressed agency over their present and destiny. He took the view shared by many subalternists and decolonial thinkers that a necessary part of the making of coloniality is the transformation of a people into objects rather than subjects of their story. Slavery, colonisation and apartheid did not only humiliate, degrade and debase Africans, but it also plunged them into what is called "the zone of nonbeing and social death characterized by the denial of dignity, heavy psychic damage, and the torment of exile" (quoted in Mbembe, 2002:242).

In *Civilisation or Barbarism*, Diop (1981:302) described this loss of ontological density in this way: "Thus imperialism, like the prehistoric hunter, first killed the being spiritually and culturally, before trying to eliminate it physically." The negation of history, cultural heritage, intellectual accomplishments and independent identity of Africans was, in his view, "cultural and mental murder" that paved the way for actual physical genocide in some cases, otherwise harassment. In this sense, evidence of physical humiliation is not all there is to demonstrate the coloniality of modernity, for cultural and psychological debasement is also an important element of it.

This fact is in Afrocentric paradigm and decolonial thought the reason for Africans' yearning for self-knowledge, the recapture of control over their destiny (sovereignty) and for a rightful place in the world (autonomy). This necessitated a response, which is called negritude, subalternity, endogenuity, Afrocentricity, epistemic disobedience, unthinking, and many other versions of decolonial thought. This response is to a large measure an attempt by the 'other' to reclaim their ontological significance for, as Archie Mafeje (2011:32) put it, "we would not proclaim Africanity, if it has not been denied or degraded; we would not insist on Afrocentrism, if it has not been for Eurocentric negations." In this sense, self-writing or decolonial thought generally is regarded as negation of negations. Mafeje (2011:33) continues to suggest that this kind of epistemic disobedience "is nothing more than a legitimate demand that African scholars study their society from inside and cease to be purveyors of alienated intellectual discourse."

With regard to epistemological implications of his work, Diop (1981:348) saw his entire intellectual entreprise as being about reclaiming Africa's pride of place at the centre of the common intellectual heritage of humanity, guided only by notions of what is useful and efficacious in this heritage for addressing today's problems. Thus, he did not see epistemic disobedience as intended to replace Eurocentric hegemony with the hegemony of subalterns, a new form of alterity. In keeping with decolonial thought and strands of Afrocentric thinking, Diop sought to realise epistemic plurality.

But there is also an overtly political motive in Diop's writings. He stated boldly that, "The African who has understood us is one who, after the reading of our works, would have felt a birth of another person in himself, impelled by a historical conscience, a true creator, a Promethean carrier of a new civilisation and perfectly aware of what the whole earth owes to his ancestral genius in all the domains of science, culture, and religion." Thus, he sums about the utility of Afrocentric decolonial thought for the purposes of a renaissance of Africa; giving birth to conscious African agents of renewal, the renaissance activists. He takes this further, arguing that this should extend further to an 'atavistic, but vigilant, African optimism' and a willingness to position Africa strategically in a collective international effort "to build a planetary civilisation instead of sinking down to barbarism." This brings us to the discussion of the Diopan perspective on the making of a continental Africa best suited for this dialogic global cosmopolitanism.

Diop on a Prosperous African Future

One of the neglected works of Cheikh Anta Diop even in scholarship on African integration and development as well as futuristic studies that it made profound propositions on is entitled, *Black Africa: The Economic and Cultural Basis for a Federated State*, first published by Présence Africaine in 1974 roughly within the first decade of independence. While space does not permit a full exploration of the rich tapestry of ideas and policy proposals that Diop put forward, this chapter provides those that relate to current debates on the continent regarding the continent of African integration towards 2063. This is the debate first stimulated by the continent-wide dialogue started by the proposal in 2007 by Libya's Muamar Qadaffi for the immediate establishment of the Union Government of Africa. This caused many to discuss the meaning of African integration, the route it should take and, most importantly, the developmental implications of this.

This debate led to the conduct of the audit of the African Union as an institutional driver of integration to identify ways in which it could improve its efficacy with regard to accelerating African integration and development. The Audit Report provided useful insights into the state of the African Union and more importantly the plight of African integration and development, a decolonial project initiated by Africa's leaders at independence. Many of these insights and recommendations made, both in the Audit Report, and the Union Government debate, as well as is in general scholarship on African integration echo, probably unwittingly, the ideas that Diop presented over three decades earlier (Zondi 2012: 25-41).

The discussion that follows replicates the Diopan methodology in that it deploys historical memory to make sense of the current state of African integration and development, an attempt to bring the past back to the arena of the present. It is also an attempt to deploy memory (the forgotten Diopan propositions) to imagine a future. This intention is influenced by Bernard Lategan's idea (2010:145-61) of future-oriented look at the past; that historical memory can provide some orientation to the future. This, Lategan suggests, has a potential to make history-making in the present possible. We are thus remembering the past with the future in mind. This enables the discussion that follows to bring the dead Diop alive in conversations with the living in the present about the future of African integration and development.

Diop's diagnosis of the slow pace of integration remains relevant, being echoed in today's dialogues. In the foreword to the book, Diop offers courageous propositions about the state of African integration when it would have been too early to pass judgement on what was still in infancy. Firstly, he proposed that African unity had only made small progress in certain specific domains and that even in those cases unity was hardly anything more than the establishment of regional and continental organisations. The substitution of the profound agenda for unity as a decolonial project would, indeed, be substituted by the creation of institutions without any profound power to bring about substantive political, economic and social integration in Africa.

Diop took this criticism further by arguing that the regional organisations were of limited value, not because of matters of institutional or organisational efficiency or financial resources as it is often argued, but because they lacked sovereignty to drive a common political, economic and social agenda. He castigated African leaders for being willing to launch regional and continental groupings than ceding an iota of national sovereignty to enable these organisations to pursue pan-African integration and development. Diop's proposition preceded Julius Nyerere's chastisement of his counterparts about the demon of nationalism on the continent that was anachronistic in the main and, therefore, ill-suited for the pursuit of pan-Africanism and continental renewal.

It is for this reason that Diop likened these organisations to "giants with feet made of clay engaged in trying to square the circle." This extended to his next proposition, which was the pursuit of economic cooperation or integration without political union, which he thought was as ill-advised as impractical. His thesis was simply that African states were hoping for benefits of economic integration that they knew about without sacrificing "the self interests of their governing groups on the altar of African unity." On this basis, he opined, the regional and continental organisations had lofty goals without the wherewithal and power to turn them into lived realities.

Under these conditions, Diop argued, there was no prospect of real economic integration as this would have required much stronger action to transform the fragmentated economies inherited from colonial rule. As a result, he observed, western multinational companies with the backing of western powers were not perturbed by intensions of the regional groupings to enact and enforce laws to protect local industries, boost economic diversification and promote trade within groupings as they were able to circumvent this to manufacture cheaply and export to the rest of Africa, thus perpetuating the logic of colonial economies. Given the fact that the countries at the forefront of the economic integration discourse had not even attempted serious transformation of the national economy, Diop found it absurd that they could undertake sacrificial actions needed to build regional markets and enable intra-regional trade and investment.

All of these points are echoed in most analyses of African integration and development today including the AU Audit Report referred to above. Hardly any work I have come across in this canon have acknowledged Diop's foresight in anticipating many of the key messages they make. If this fact has not reached scholars as it appears, then the possibility that Diop's diagnosis of the slow pace of integration seems not to have been revealed to the political class with the power to act on the simple points that Diop made.

Diop's Proposed African Energy Initiative

Diop also offered proposals on what might be key engines for a more successful and developmental African integration. These are not necessarily proposals on how to directly solve the problems pointed out above, for he thought the solutions to these were too straightforward to need elaboration. They identify what might be key drivers of developmental continental integration through a set of continent-wide policy initiatives on sectors that were generally considered among Africanists as essential for a prosperous Africa.

For Diop the first consideration is to decide on a single continental state, which he argued, 'enlightened self-interest' required. Such a state, he thought, would be federal in form because it would be ideal for "a rational formula covering the development of our countries with their infinitely varied potentials to be put into effect." This would, of course, require a surrender of sovereignty, which could not happen under what he described as 'transitory' Organisation of African Unity and regional groupings that had been established for economic cooperation and integration. He averred that under the transitory institutional arrangements, Africa was unable to even resolve conflicts between Chad and Libya, Ghana and Togo, Mali and Burkina Faso (Upper Volta then), and Ethiopia and Somalia. Of course, there would be many more devastative inter-state conflicts that the institutions would be unable to resolve speedily. These institutions were also unable, in his view, to help small and vulnerable states contend with powerful neo-colonial economic interests of big multinationals and western powers in a scramble for Africa's mineral resources.

The first proposal is on a continental energy initiative that would not only power internal economic development, but would enable Africa to be a pre-eminent source of the global energy prosperity. Diop's ideas on this preceded the global energy crisis of the early 1970s as they were actually developed and written in an essay in 1960. He first proposed the ideas through the *L'Organisation pour la Mise en Valeur du Fleuve Sénégal*, a regional scheme on the development of the River Senegal, arguing for a schema of continent-wide energy development that took into account renewable and non-renewable energy resources, ecological diversity and anticipated technological advances. In this sense, Diop was well ahead of his time as ideas of energy pluralism/mix, balance between renewables and non-renewables, balance between environmental and economic concerns and so forth would really only gain currency in global discourses in the aftermath of the energy crisis and become firmed up at the United Nations' Rio Earth Summit of 1992 (Miller 1992:710-13).

Diop contended that it was in Africa's interest to find an efficient formula that builds energy pluralism combining the use of hydro-electric, solar, nuclear, geothermal, hydrocarbons and thermonuclear energy sources in a harmonious energy doctrine. The rational was in four parts. The first was that Africa had latent potential for generating these kinds of energy at the time when the world needed greater volumes and a variety of energy sources. The second was the view that such an initiative would divert Africa's focus away from environmentally damaging and economically short-sighted export of raw materials and natural resources for cash injection (foreign direct investment), which he thought sacrificed the future to meet short-term immediate need for cash. The third was that energy pluralism could be Africa's comparative advantage in a fast changing global economy, thus enabling it to reverse its marginalisation. The fourth justification, in Diop's perspective, was that the energy doctrine would encourage investment in imported and endogenous technologies and science needed to power Africa's prosperity over a long period of time. He (something is missing here) actually it was a plan for the forty years between 1960 and year 2000, enabling Africa to end the millennium on a high note (Diop 1974:104-14).

To give effect to this, Diop thought that working on the basis of a continent-wide perspective, African leaders needed to establish what could in today's language be called centres of excellence generating the practical strategies and tactics for the roll out of the energy mix programme. On account of this, the most important energy source for Africa – being both in abundant supply and least harmful to environment and health – was hydro-energy and the Inga site on the Congo River (then Zaire River) was the epicentre of the African energy doctrine. It was already known then, as it is also often repeated today, that the Inga has the capacity to adequately supply economical electricity to the whole continent and South America together. There were several other water resources capable of generating further hydropower including the Aawan and Kabora Bassa. Africa holds two-thirds of the world's hydropower reserves.

With regard to thermonuclear energy, he thought (to establish?) a pilot fusion centre in an appropriate African country working with qualified African researchers. On solar energy, Africa needed to build energy banks in many parts of Africa where there is sufficient sunshine throughout the year. Geothermal energy, he thought, required the establishment of energy centres in volcanic regions of East Africa. Diop proposed that African scientists already knew regions of Africa most optimal for wind and tidal energy generators.

Diop proposed that while Africa had a huge and growing potential in the harnessing of petroleum and hydrocarbons, these should be systematically and gradually reduced in the energy mix because of their harm to the environment. So, he foresaw a formula that enhanced energy capacity without harming the natural environment. He argued that there were indications already in the 1960s that hydrocarbons should be considered only as raw materials for the synthetic chemical industry, which he thought was a potentially significant source of economic development on a continental state.

Diop understood that while nuclear energy was already considered bad for the environment, it was an important catalyst for technological development that could be used for other areas of development as the continent phased nuclear energy out after two generations or so. He suggested that anyway the technological advancements would of necessity lead to less polluting ways of generating nuclear energy. Diop agonised a lot about what the continent was to do with the stockpiles of atomic/nuclear waste produced during energy generation, especially if this generation was expanded to continental scales. He conceded that this was a huge moral dilemma until more efficient methods of waste disposal were found, methods better than the controversial embedding of waste in rocks or sinking it into the ocean bed via pipelines, which major western powers were doing.

Diop saw the federal state architecture as crucial in this regard in facilitating the continent-wide rejuvenation of existing energy projects, the initiation of new ones as needs of a changing society and opportunities in the global market required, and for creating dynamic linkages between all these initiatives, thus giving effect to the desire to have a continental energy grid. This, he argued, would create a continent-wide energy market to finance further developments, while powering the economic renaissance of Africa through its ripple effects. Only on this basis, Diop thought, could Africans' energy needs be met economically and without sacrificing other essentials in the game of re-allocation of budgets as the needs become more pressing in the period between the 1980s and 1990s. Diop thought that this was the way to go about driving self-driven and endogenous development, while enhancing African institutional governance and improving Africa's respectable role in the global economy.

Space does not permit a detailed analysis showing the coincidence between Diop's energy proposal and the continental policy initiatives on energy, while also noting that the continent had not engaged with Diop's proposals because they were not widely distributed and because the continent has relied on western advisors for most of its policy ideas. Suffice it to make three points here: the first is that while the Conference of African Ministers of Energy (successor to OAU's Pan-African Energy Ministers' Conference of African Ministers Responsible for the Development and Utilisation of Mineral and Energy Resources established in 1995) has become a regular statutory meeting, making sound pronouncements about Africa's energy interests and what ought to be done, it remains an informal committee without any power to implement its decisions. It is useful only for generating a common view, exchange of national strategies and for advocacy within the AU, but it is not optimal for generating an Africa-wide energy grip. National interests, lack of a secretariat of its own, lack of a single uniting vision on energy and weak linkages between it and the AU and the Regional Economic Communities limits the body's ability to turn energy into a catalyst to power continental integration as Diop envisaged.

The second point is that while it should be commended that the AU has a commissioner dedicated to coordinating continental efforts in the area of energy, the commissioner can only persuade or cajole nation-states to achieve continent-wide ambitions that all policy sovereignty rests with nation-states under current arrangements. The ministerial conference counts on the commissioner to champion the consensus generated in difficult negotiations designed to find points of convergence between 54 national paradigms, but the commissioner is only mandated to coordinate such implementation. For instance, since about 2005, energy ministers have generated consensus about the importance of solar energy from the Sahara desert, have asked for a pilot study and called for acquisition of technologies necessary for harnessing this power. There has not been a movement on these resolutions because the AU does not have sovereign power to ensure the implementation of these, even though they are a product of consensus involving all AU member states. Its most recent meeting in Maputo, Mozambique in 2010, African energy ministers were still re-iterating the resolutions mentioned above and urging the commission to conclude the energy study (Maputo Declaration, 2010). Of course, there is also the African Energy Commission decided on in 2006 as an AU agency whose board would include all member states, with the mandate to coordinate the actions of individual African countries to develop energy resources and deal with common problems encountered. It has been useful in promoting research highlighting the continent's energy potential, assessing the role and function of existing energy resources, generating counselon how to enhance intra-African energy trade and infrastructure development. It was supposed to derive its impact from its advisory role to the ministerial conference, but then the conference itself has an advisory and coordinating function.

The third is that where opportunities are presented to Africa to place energy at the centre of its global diplomacy such as in discussions in the G20, discussions with the G8, strategic partnerships that Africa has developed with the likes of the EU, China, India and Japan, the continent is yet to present a really mega-energy project that realises its potential for a positive ripple effect on the economy and development. There are energy projects on the agenda, but they tend to be specific and limited in geographical location, suggesting that they are not seen as part of a gradual or staggered process of building a continent-wide energy platform marked by plurality of sources and types.

In remembering the past in order to envisage the future suggests that Diop's ideas are worth recalling as the African citizenry and the political class discuss where Africa might be by 2063. Not only are Diopan ideas on energy aligned to a general political consensus on the continent as recorded in the discussions of the ministerial conference since 1975, the Abuja Treaty establishing the African Economic Community in 1991 and the AU Summit dedicated to energy and infrastructure on 20-24 March 2006, but they are germane to any thinking about accelerating continental integration and development. The idea of a continent-wide energy doctrine with the development of a mixed energy grid connected to specialised energy centres in various regions is worth exploring for implementation. The idea of an environment-sensitive doctrine that allows for a gradual shift in the balance of the energy mix in favour of renewables and other ecology-friendly energy sources is also in keeping with the paradigm of humanistic development and the concept of sustainable development. The proposal for a self-funded and self-driven energy development inextricably linked to acceleration of integration and development broadly would find very few opponents on the continent today. The need to link Africa's doctrine on energy to changing dynamics in the global environment, especially using energy to move Africa from the periphery to the centre of global power with a view to recast this order to the benefit of all of humanity, is a noble idealism in keeping with dimensions of African renaissance and pan-Africanism that have been in vogue since the beginning of the 20th century.

Conclusion

When read from within and on the basis of what is in the best interest of Africa and Africans, the Diopan perspective on the future of African integration (1960s-2000), which is now our past, is worth remembering with an orientation of our own future towards 2063. It is a useful reminder of what have been points of consensus among decolonial thinkers on the African continent about how to transform the African landscape that is still scarred by the mapping pens of Berlin into a united, integrated and prosperous continent. The specific proposal on the African energy doctrine, as he put it, offers useful insights into how Diop and perhaps those who belonged to his epistemic network thought about the kind of statehood Africa needed to develop in order to achieve real integration, one that is accompanied by concrete development. The general point being made is that as the continent begins discussions and reflections on what might be scenarios that Africa should pursue to become successful by 2063, it would be wise to remember that the present is the making of what was done or not done in the past. Therefore, there are some ideas that may have to be exhumed from the tomb of the past because having not been tried, they have not failed and therefore they are not dead, though buried. There will be many ideas on economic integration, cultural emancipation, scientific renaissance and so forth that needed unearthing to provide a sound perspective to the present discourses about Africa's future. In this sense, Africa's future is contained also in its past.

References

Ake, C. 1982. *Social Science as Imperialism*, Lagos: Ibadan University.

Diop, C.A. 1974. *Black Africa: The Economic and Cultural Basis for a Federated State*, Paris: Présence Africaine.

Diop, C.A. 1974. *Black Africa: The Economic and Cultural Basis for a Federated State*, Paris: Présence Africaine (kindle book).

Diop, C.A. 1981. *Civilisation or Barbarism: An Authentic Anthropology*, Paris: Présence Africaine.

Diop, C.A. 1981. *Civilisation or Barbarism: An Authentic Anthropology*, Paris: Présence Africaine, Kindle Location no. 302.

Hountondji, P. (ed.) 1997. *Endogenous Knowledge: research trails*. Dakar: CODESRIA Books.

James, C.L.R., 1969. *A History of Pan-African Revolt*, Washington: Drum and Spear.

Ki-Zerbo, J., 2005. 'African Intellectuals, nationalism and pan-Africanism: a testimony', in Mkandawire, T. (ed.) *African Intellectuals: Rethinking Politics, Language, Gender and Development.* Dakar: CODESRIA Books, p. 4.

Lategan, B. 2010. 'Remembering with the Future in Mind', in Diawara, M., Lategan, B. and Rusen, J. (eds.), *Historical Memory in Africa: Dealing with the Past, Reaching for the Future in an Intercultural Context*, New York: Berghahn Books, pp. 145-161.

Lategan, B.2010. 'Remembering with the Future in Mind', in Diawara, M., Lategan, B. and Rusen, J. (eds.), *Historical Memory in Africa: Dealing with the Past, Reaching for the Future in an Intercultural Context*, New York: Berghahn Books, pp. 145-161.

Mafeje, A. 2011. 'A Combative Ontology', in Devisch, R. and Nyamnjoh, F. B. (eds.) *Postcolonial Turn: Imagining Anthropology and Africa*, Bamenda and Leiden: Langaa, p. 32.

Maputo Declaration Adopted by the African Union Conference of Ministers in charge of Energy, 1-5 November 2010, Maputo, Mozambique, Africa Union Library, AU/MIN/Energy/Decl.

Maputo Declaration Adopted by the African Union Conference of Ministers in charge of Energy, 1-5 November 2010, Maputo, Mozambique, Africa Union Library, AU/MIN/Energy/Decl.

Masilela, N. 'In Memoriam: Cheikh Anta Diop'. No Page Numbers. Available at pzacad.pitzer.edu/nam/general/essay/diop.pdf (accessed on 3 May 2010).

Mbembe, A. 2002. 'African Modes of Self-Writing', *Public Culture*, 14 (1), p. 242.

Mignolo, W. 'Coloniality: the Darker Side of Modernity', Available at http://www.macba.cat/PDFs/walter_mignolo_modernologies_eng.pdf (accessed on 2 August 2012).

Miller S., 1992. "The Road from Rio," *Environment, Science and Technology*, 26 (9), pp. 710-1713.

Zondi, S. 2012. 'The African Union Audit and the State of Continental Integration: An Analysis', *Africa Insight*, 42 (3), pp. 25-41.

Zerbo, J. 1981. 'General Introduction'. In Ki-Zerbo, J. (ed.), *Methodology and African History: the UNSECO General History of Africa*, California: UNESCO, pp. 2-3.

Building Critical Consciousness for Advancing African Renaissance

Case Study from Pan-African and Afrocentric Institutions

Akhona Nkenkana

Introduction

The major historical challenge as echoed by a number of scholars from Africa such as Mphahlele (2002); Xulu (2004); Banda (2010) has been how to infuse effectively the cardinal ideology of Pan Africanism and the African Renaissance into popular consciousness and translating them to the motor driving the action of Africans as a global community. That evidently is the challenge of moving Pan Africanism and the African Renaissance from rhetoric to positive activism. This challenge is in mobilizing the will to begin a fundamental realignment in all facets of the life of Africans and black humanity in particular. This requires the will to forge new beginnings that would lead to a radical restructuring of our African firmament, states from the messy circumstances of Africa in the last half-century (Alalade, 2013:2).

This chapter asserts that if the idea of an African Renaissance is to be of any significance on the African continent, it has to address and motivate the very people it is supposed to re-awaken and re-energize, namely the African masses. Its importance lies in the assertion that the renewal of the continent will come to possibility through an adoption and embracing of a particular type of knowledge and education by Africans. This knowledge and education ought to bring about the critical consciousness in its citizens. This consciousness should emancipate and empower the African citizen to deal critically with social problems they encounter and chart an independent future for them.

Education institutions that produce the consciousness of the masses of the continent are charged with a great responsibility of answering to questions such as, what kind of consciousness is required for Africa to advance her development and how is this consciousness built and by what kind of knowledge should it be built. However, these are the questions that are not explored critically by traditional institutions, instead they are victims of the colonial project given the kind of product it produces that remains with entrenched forms of coloniality through its thinking and reasoning.

In arguing that there exists this particular type of education Africa requires, a case study of institutions whose premise stems from Afrocentric, Pan-African and African Renaissance paradigms was conducted. Institutions such as the Thabo Mbeki African Leadership Institute in South Africa, Molefi Kete Asante Institute in United State of America and African Leadership Academy in Kenya were interviewed together with experts whose work in one way or the other contribute to the advancement of African Renaissance. Findings from the in-depth interviews pointed out to a need of a different type of education to the one offered in traditional mainstream education systems.

Education offered in the traditional mainstream education system remains within the confines of coloniality as it remains with limitations of producing critical consciousness that is able to advance African Renaissance. Be that as it may, according to findings from the institutions interviewed there exists this particular type of education that is required for building critical consciousness. Its major challenge is that it is not found in the mainstream education and so it is unable to reach African masses in large scales.

The conceptual framework

Arguably, African Renaissance, implanted in the broader concept of Pan-Africanism as a conceptual framework with which this critical consciousness of African masses should be built for a possible renewal of Africa, must provide the necessary clarity on the ambiguity of the originality of the term (African Renaissance).

Mabogo More (2002) finds the premise of African Renaissance under two conceptions. The first conception is an Afro-pessimistic conception that constitutes the return as a regression to something similar to the

Hobbesian 'state of nature' and thus retrogressive and oppressive. The second and opposite conception interprets the return as necessary, and thus progressive, liberatory politics. This chapter argues that African Renaissance is an inevitable process that Africa must undergo to achieve her ultimate liberation. Furthermore, Mabogo More asks a number of questions that must be taken into cognizance when understanding the African Renaissance. He asks these questions in the context of the originality of the renaissance as known from the Italians. In summing up all his questions he asks if Africa's renewal is to be authentic and ensuring that it breaks away from coloniality which is Eurocentric, would it not be a contradiction if then Africa adopts the term 'Renaissance' in rediscovering herself. Ramose (2000) augments Mabogo More's argument that African Renaissance is a North bound gaze. Ramose argues that the concept Renaissance is deeply rooted in Europe and has its primary reference point and other parts of the world are its secondary reference point.

If an argument of the concept of Renaissance, particularly its historical originality, is to be made, it would be important to analyse critically the limitations of Ramose's argument for reasons that the originality of the concept of Renaissance in the broader context of knowledge cannot be rejected on the basis of history and geography, for relevance by definition it requires more than that. When Italy was re-discovering herself it was not doing so in the context of what is known as Europe or European Renaissance. The Renaissance that Europe talks about is not the same as the Renaissance that Italy initially and authentically discovered. Therefore, modern history which Ramose's argument is remains a limitation in how it conceptualizes and defines terms as it disregards the medieval historians who wrote histories from the early ages and provide a rather critical understanding of the evolution of Renaissance from Italy than other parts of what is later, in modern histories known as Europe.

Cossa, (2009:8) argues that one way to address the conceptual question of African Renaissance is to deal with the individual terms, i.e. African and Renaissance, within the main concept of African Renaissance. He points out that the term African has been used to define those things that are indigenous to Africa. Terms such as traditional African values and return to aspects of Africa's indigenous civilization imply that there are such things as traditional values and indigenous civilization that are unique to Africa. Assuming that traditional stands for things related to Africa prior to imperial occupation, it follows that African values (past and present) are distinct from other continents. The conceptual analysis of the term Renaissance as discussed by (Cossa 2009:11) hinges on the model case of what constitutes a Renaissance in Europe, and then assesses the legitimacy of using such a term in Africa. The European Renaissance was triggered by social and political conditions during Europe's dark ages. Peasants, subjected to the rule of aristocrats, lived throughout Europe. Pillage, high and random taxation, and terrorism found its epitome in the role of the Catholic popes who not only supported the aristocracy, but also had long ceased being servants of God. The popes had become aristocrats living in a charmed existence barely distinguishable from that of the aristocracy. It was due to such critical state that the Renaissance has become unavoidable in Europe. Estep (1986) in Cossa (2009) describes the Renaissance as a return to classical excellence in the social, political, and religious realms. Some important features of its background were (1) the rise of a pan-European culture; (2) emergent individual thinking; (3) the rise of capitalism opposed to the church's prohibition of loans for interest, as well as the Church's later compromise with capitalism; and (4) the nation-states in Europe with the consequent division of territory.

Having given the analysis of the two terms (African and Renaissance), Cossa concludes his arguments that in view of what constituted Renaissance for Europe, Africans do have a fair case for comparing the two phenomena, and although they are not exactly the same and do not occur under the same circumstances, Africans do have a rebirth of some sort. Renaissance is a French term for rebirth; thus, to use such term to mean only that which it means is fair.

Arguably, Renaissance is an inevitable process that any nation must undergo. And each nation's journey to its own discovery and re-discovery is what constitutes the authentic renaissance not the mere concept as Cossa has also alluded to. Africa's journey to her renaissance was disturbed by the history that defines her today. This does not mean that renaissance should not take place; it simply means moving beyond the history that disturbed Africa's development to the ultimate rediscovery and renewal of the continent. In fact, what would be secondary Renaissance is what is currently taking place in as far as Africa's development discourse is concerned. The pressure for Africa to catch up with the world results in Africa mimicking the development of Europe and North America, this way Africa is trying to achieve European Renaissance in Africa, and not to achieve authentic African Renaissance.

The greater task for Africa's Renaissance is a challenging one, unlike the Renaissance of other nations especially the one of Europe. Africa's Renaissance must begin with a difficult process of renewing the African who is a product of slavery, colonialism and now coloniality. The renewal must be driven from the context of Decoloniality, grounded in Afrocentricity and Pan-Africanism and what is fundamental in the process primarily must be to build an alternative consciousness of an African that is critical of any coloniality element in the psycho-socio-economic condition that Africa finds herself in today.

Thabo Mbeki (Mbeki 2014:12) argues that the principal task we face is to answer a critical question, "what must be done to achieve the objectives which all Africans and progressive humanity accepts as being of fundamental importance to the renewal and renaissance of Africa". The objective that defines African Renaissance and how Africa arrives at those objectives should be what authentically defines African Renaissance.

The fault line – Education entrapped in coloniality, impossibility for building critical consciousness

Metzler (2009) asserts that in the early 1960s at the beginning of the post colonial era in Africa there was consensus regarding the role of formal education in Africa's political, economic, and social development and the achievement of human 'progress'. This consensus was shared by external actors such as the former European colonial powers, and the US through their bilateral and programmes, and the United Nations (UN), the United Nations Development Programmes (UNDP), the United Nations Educational, Scientific and Cultural Organization (UNESCO), and the United Nations Children's Fund (UNICEF), the World Bank, and western academic 'experts', on the one hand, and leaders of the nascent (postcolonial) nation-states on the other (Metzler, 2009:277-278). Metzler argues further that the consensus asserted that formal education was an essential and some policy actors augmented the consensus as the most powerful/effective instrument in the struggle for economic, social development, political unity. This to a large extent allows a capacitation of the nascent postcolonial states, generating modernity, creating the 'new-man', broken of his primordial, traditional, worldview, interpreting the world and acting in the post colonial era as modern men (disregarding women until the 1990s).

What has been a consequence of this education and its consensus? Metzler goes further and argues that the result is a number of African countries as evident from the UNDP and MDG reports becoming impressive in terms of increased access to all levels of formal education, but are not as impressive when examined against the 'promise' held out for schooling 50 years ago at the dawn of the post colonial era in Africa.

The fault line this chapter asserts emanates from the limitations if not lack thereof of the education in Africa to fundamentally address or appropriate the education and knowledge that should build the critical consciousness of African citizens, thereby renewing their mind and continent to fulfil the 'promise' as highlighted by Metzler. Arguably, the current education in Africa does not build the kind of consciousness that is required for the renewal of its citizens and the continent at large to advance her development. Instead the contemporary education in Africa perpetuates what is known as coloniality, in that it continues to produce a consciousness that perpetuates a mindset found in the relations of inferiority-superiority complexes. This argument is found on the broad understanding of the role colonialism played especially through education in Africa. Frantz Fanon, notes that colonialism was never simply contented with imposing of its grammar and logic upon the "present and the future of a dominated country". Colonialism was also not simply satisfied with merely holding the colonized people in its grip and emptying "the native's brain of all form and content. Rather, by a kind of pervasive logic, it turns to the past of the oppressed people, and distorts it, disfigures and destroys it" (Fanon, 1961:67). The kind of education therefore Africa needs must first appropriate the distortions that have been crafted by colonialism and still lives on through coloniality.

Augmenting the argument by Fanon, Mphahlele (2002) argues that Education in Africa does not strengthen the learner to enable him/her to understand the life one goes back to outside the walls of the school. This is the contradiction of the education as an instrument for renewal of Africa on one hand and as an instrument to alienate Africans from their own realities in their communities.

Maldonado-Torres, (2007:243) provides a critical difference between colonialism and coloniality. This was in understanding his assertion of what coloniality is, in the context with which colonial education in Africa is found.

He asserts that;

> Colonialism denotes a political and economic relation in which the sovereignty of a nation or a people rests on the power of another nation, which makes such a nation an empire. Coloniality, instead, refers to long-standing patterns of power that emerged as a result of colonialism, but that define culture, labour, intersubjective relations, and knowledge production well beyond the strict limits of colonial administrations.

> Thus coloniality survives colonialism. It is maintained alive in books, in common sense, in the self-image of people, in aspirations of self and so many other aspects of our modern experience. In a way, as modern subjects we breathe coloniality all the time and every day.

With what Torres has defined as coloniality, arguably, the education and education system in Africa is subject to coloniality. This is evident in the kind of education that produces a graduate that is alienated from his/her community and rather attuned to structures and systems that perpetuates coloniality instead of the transformation in the community that one comes from.

Dei, (2012) reiterates that in the current epoch of globalization and advanced capitalism, schooling and education have become discursively configured to meet the needs of modernization from the context of Euro modernity. Dei argues further that from curricula to pedagogies, dominant knowledge systems have been organized and inscribed through governing Eurocentric paradigms historically augured within colonial specificities. Education systems and processes, as well as ideas about what counts as education, have been entrenched in the reproduction of colonial ways of knowing which concomitantly limit possibilities for many learners.

Dei further provides his own personal experience in augmenting the colonial education that persists in Africa today. He states that;

> I have written how colonial education in Ghana taught me less about my own communities than other distant places, which made it difficult to relate education to my lived experiences. Cultural community knowledges were not affirmed in my education and it has taken many years of struggle to shed the Eurocentric gaze and interpretations that have been ingrained in my thinking. Many of us, whether as indigenous, colonized or racially minoritised scholars/learners, continue to struggle to convey liberatory ways of understanding for/in different socio-cultural, economical and political spaces.

Morgan Ndlovu (2013) argues that colonization experience of the indigenous communities in the continent of Africa did not only take place in the political and economic spheres of their lives but it also impacted on other crucial aspects of life such as patterns of knowing, imagination of development, conception of truth, representation of own identities and other various subjectivities; all which today complicate the meaning of both pan-African education and development in African in the colonial era. He augments the notion that education is central to development. He argues that this notion is in fact fundamental and foundational. What

Ndlovu argues is the state of Africa's education system, he states that the manner in which the education system in the post-colonial Africa is conceived and/or implemented needs decolonization in order to contribute positively to the development of the continent (Morgan Ndlovu 2013: unpublished monograph).

Dei and Morgan's argument on education in Africa advancing the needs of modernity and/or perpetuating coloniality is augmented in (Rodney, 1973:263) when he discusses the role of education in producing Africans to serve the colonial system and subscribe to its values. He notes that class stratification, which leads to neo-colonialism, begins with the linking of colonial education to material gain.

Rodney points out that;

> education is crucial in any type of society for the preservation of the lives of its members and the maintenance of the social structure . . . The most crucial aspect of pre-colonial African education was its relevance to Africans in sharp contrast with that which was later introduced (that is, under colonialism). . . . [T]he main purpose of colonial school system was to train Africans to participate in the domination and exploitation of the continent as a whole . . . Colonial education was education for subordination, exploitation, the creation of mental confusion and the development of underdevelopment.

In interviews conducted through a case study, which will be discussed in detail later in this chapter, one of the interviewees, Prof Sabelo J Ndlovu-Gatsheni, in responding to a question on education as a means for facilitating critical consciousness from the perspective of African Renaissance asserts that the kind of education Africa has is driven by the kind of institutions that make us see our societies from the outside. He states that African Renaissance must be driven by African genius; however, this remains a challenging task because African genius has and continues to be alienated from the systems and structures of education. African genius has been a victim of colonialism and now coloniality in that it remains inferiorised as knowledge that should embrace our education and therefore build the critical consciousness.

Beyond Colonial Education – The pedagogy for building critical consciousness

Arguably, at the core of critical intervention is a practice of liberation which starts with an educational process of cultivating people's critical consciousness with an overall aim of changing the world (Keqi Liu, 2012:23), a possible way Africa can move beyond colonial education through building critical consciousness that must advance the renewal of the conscious of its masses. Furthermore, an argument augmenting Liu (2012) is that for education to facilitate rather than limit learning possibilities and educational transformation, it is crucial that a development and application of liberatory conceptual frameworks that are accessible to learners must be explored (Dei 2012:103).

Dei, (2012: 108) providing analysis of Dubois, Fanon and the question of black education argues that, "We have to recognize that we cannot simply add new floor/structures to the currently crumbling building that is education until we address the cracks in the foundation. To ensure Black/African educational success, we must seriously consider and begin working on creating new educational systems and alternatives that hold the promise of excellence for all. Secondly, we cannot expect success while reproducing an unsatisfactory status quo or while continuing to do the same things that are failing us".

Ndlovu (2013) augments Liu and Dei's argument in the context of Africa's education discourse by asking what should fundamentally be Pan-African education. Responses (which are not exhaustive Liu's practice of liberation through education processes nor to Dei's liberatory conceptual framework) to Morgan Ndlovu's question must be found on the fundamental need to re-educate an African and exploration of processes such as the critical intervention that Liu (2012) is basing his argument on. Morgan's question of Pan-African education emanates from his argument that if the purpose of education as a means of knowledge production is to advance development of the people in any particular context across the world, then the process of decolonizing education in Africa needs to be accompanied by that of decolonizing development so that there is no mismatch between education that is imparted on the peoples of Africa and the manner in which they conceive development *and education for that matter.* The need for this re-education is founded on the premise that African education does not respond to the needs of any dimensions of development in Africa especially the renewal of its masses. This need of re-education of an African departs from the fundamental challenge posed by colonial education, which has been explored earlier as well as by an argument made by Alex Kwapong (1998) that there is a need for an integrated, culturally coherent educational system to produce the kind of results that Africa ought to produce. Essentially the challenge for education is how to produce an African who responds to the internal, spiritual and human needs of the African on the one hand and on the other to the challenge of living in a global community (without the global imperialists impositions on Africa) where science and technology have reached a level of profundity with which one should be familiar (Alex Kwapong, 1998).

Kwapong (1998) argues that the challenge of education in Africa indeed needs to be reassessed. The reassessment must take into cognizance the challenge of education is to develop the human resources that will ensure accelerated development without compromising Africa's cultural identity. Education must expand the knowledge base of Africans that will allow us to undertake the socio-economic, cultural, and political transformation necessary to achieve development. The argument on the forum goes further to pose the question of philosophy of education to say one of the major problems in educational effort in the continent has been concerned with literacy in its different forms up to university level and this has been what is referred to as Education in Africa. A question remained central to the discussions that "what is the philosophy of African education?" This question is asked in the context where equipment, through education, to deal with the problems of life has become increasingly externalized, and that reservoir of knowledge that had to do with the practical realities of communities and the world at large which Africans live in has been undermined (Alex Kwapong 1998:2-4).

Alex Kwapong (1998) argues further that to absorb external ill-digested ideas without reflecting, adapting or evolving from our own circumstances has limitations. An education that fits the cultural identity of an individual has to be approached in different layers: at the basic of level of primary education; the education and the training of the person should be made to fit in with his environment, to make a living. Without the knowledge of his/her own history, the geography of his country, the social dynamics of his/her own culture, he/she may be a skilled technician but would not be a very useful *one in advancing the renewal of his/her country and continent.* Education is a dynamic process that must begin from within and these philosophic reflections should come from within the institutions of learning in the continent and not, for example, from the Institution of Education in London.

Mphahlele (2002) augments Kwapong's argument on the reassessment of African Education. This argument is important as it provides the context of African Education as embedded in what defines African Renaissance, an important aspect for building critical consciousness that should advance the renewal of Africa. This contention is made on the fundamental premise that defines the purpose of education as Mphahlele argues that knowledge is power and if so, when the people receive the appropriate education, they will eventually be able to build the resilient moral fibre of a society (Mphahlele 2002:7).

Furthermore, the cultural purpose of an education system rightly belongs in a statement about its philosophical foundations argues Mphahlele (2002). Therefore, this type of education that should build critical consciousness for Africa's renewal must cut across the dividing lines that have fragmented and alienated African communities from one another and importantly from its African roots.

Here, this chapter asserts that Paulo Freire's theory of liberating education as a framework for the kind of education to building critical consciousness is the kind of framework that is required for education in Africa. This assertion is found in how Freire defines the process of conscientization, that as a cultivation of critical consciousness and conscience, it not only provides a stimulus for better understanding of the root causes of human suffering and dehumanization or the loss of humanity but also brings full effect to humanization, an effective approach to address dehumanization problems. Augmented by (Michele Lewis & Anna Lee 2009:51), a process of critical consciousness development must be measured by focusing on action and reflection components. The action component of critical consciousness involves the degree to which persons move from being objects of oppression to being subjects that act upon their socio-political environment. The reflection component measures thought during the process of developing critical consciousness. Specifically, this aspect of critical consciousness represents the capacity for questioning inequities.

From Paulo Freire's framework for a need to build critical consciousness, it is evident that for Africa to move beyond colonial education an alternative education that produces a different kind of thinker is required. Coloniality suggests that we have been entrapped in deceptive thinking that produces no progress in as far as our general development and renewal in particular are concerned.

Arguably, building critical consciousness through education must not be a process understood within the parameters of how traditional curriculum is defined. Liu (2012) argues that Freire's notion of education includes schooling but goes beyond the limit of schooling. Because any individual is conditioned by specific historical and social conditions and cultural norms, the dynamic of Freire's education is forged in the dialectical relation between individuals and structural constraints. (Giroux 1985 in

Liu, 2012:29) points out certain contradictions and struggles caused by certain structural constraints and ideologies define and mark off human lived realities and the development of history in various societies. It is in this dialectics that power and politics find education as the terrain to give a fundamental expression of desire, language, meaning, and values. Therefore, education, for Freire, relates to the deeper beliefs about the very nature of what it means to be human.

Paulo Freire's framework for building critical consciousness is important for Africa to consider as they continue to view the type of education they have, which brings minimal progress in as far as conscientization of African masses is concerned.

Given the crisis of education as alluded earlier, this is not however to say efforts have not been made to bring to realization this particular type of education that builds this critical consciousness that is required for Africa's renewal.

An Alternative Education: Evidence from Case studies

It is agreeable, that the model of western education, which Africa seems to have adopted has proved completely unsuitable for Africa's needs. This statement is qualified by the mainstream education that is at the pre-disposal of the majority of the masses of Africa from their elementary through secondary right up to tertiary education.

However, Africa's liberation today, even though it has its limitations, while it is owed to education, arguably the type of education that has liberated Africa thus far has more to do with the education that is not on the mainstream but rather the education for conscientization that remains with a challenge of being mainstreamed and fully recognized today. The education that built the critical consciousness of Africa, as history has proven that while it did not take place in mainstream education, it was however very instrumental to facilitate the progress of liberation we observe today in Africa and in the Diaspora.

This education is defined according to (Shadrack Gutto, 2006:306) as the education that should entail among other things, focusing on confronting, with a view to correcting and departing from, hegemonic knowledge and knowledge systems that are predicated on racist paradigms that have deliberately and otherwise distorted and continue to distort the realities of Africa. Gutto (2006) argues that the primary purpose of education, both formal and non-formal, is the development of interrelated and interdependent sets of human capacity to think, to know and to act by honing social consciousness or awareness, values and skills and this purpose makes it more important to invest in education, relevant education.

In what Gutto (2006) defines as fundamentals of education, in Africa, it has been experienced, while not necessarily through formal institutions of education, the movements such as Pan-African movements have been and continue to be amongst sources who have knowledge that produces the critical consciousness that is required for appropriation of Africa's development discourse. Even the Black Consciousness Movement could be argued for the same reason. These two movements, even though not exhaustive, have played a critical role to bringing about the consciousness that is possible to drive the process of the renewal of Africa.

Pan-Africanism and Black Consciousness have and continue to represent the complexities of black political and intellectual thought over a number of years.

In search for validation of the hypothesis that the institutions not in the mainstream traditional education system have and continue to contribute to education that is better suited for building critical consciousness. This hypothesis was validated by a conduct of in-depth interview in three different institutions namely; Thabo Mbeki African Leadership Institute (TMALI) in South Africa where an interview was conducted with the Head of the Institute (Prof Vusi Gumede), Molefi Kete Asante Institute (MKA) for Afrocentric studies in the Unites States of America where an interview was conducted with the Head of the Institute (Prof Molefi Kete Asante) and African Leadership Centre (ALC) in Kenya where an interview was conducted with its Head (Dr Funmi Olonisakin).

A brief background of these Institutes; TMALI's principal purpose is to train Africans for the political, economic, social and cultural renewal of the African continent and its people. Its courses are designed on a number of areas that are of relevance for the further advancement of the renewal of the African continent. Worth noting, these courses offered in TMALI are regarded as short courses and therefore not qualifying as formal qualification. Similarly, to MKA, which promotes a healthy cultural agency-oriented dimension to research that rejects particularly the marginalization, peripheralisation, and dislocation of African people. While MKA does not offer a full teaching programme, the institute conducts training sessions for urban teachers, social workers and community leaders engaged in African American studies, African history, innovative leadership strategies and social and economic development programmes. Africa Leadership Centre is a Pan-African centre of excellence on peace, security and development in Africa. Its training programmes offer a distinctly African perspective to the challenges that plague the continent, and utilize a methodology that encourages participants to use their specific contexts and realities to begin to respond to these challenges.

These institutes are grounded by paradigms that centralize Africa and Africans, offering education, training and research that are grounded on Pan-African and Afrocentric paradigms. Having gone through three of the programmes in TMALI, one could say if a need for building critical consciousness requires a particular type of education, the education received in TMALI and its similar institutions is precisely that education.

In understanding in-depth the knowledge and education that should be offered by these types of institutions that were interviewed, another set of interviews to individuals regarded as experts in paradigms that affirm Africa and its Africans, either epistemologically or ideologically were conducted. These experts have directly and indirectly unpacked in their works the need for the building of critical consciousness that should bring about the renewal required for the African continent from the perspective of Decoloniality, Pan-Africanism, and Feminism.

The experts for these in-depth interviews were Prof Patricia McFadden from TMALI, Prof Amina Mama from Africa Gender Institute, Dr Siphamandla Zondi from Institute of Global Dialogue, and Prof Sabelo J. Ndlovu-Gatsheni from the Archie Mafeje Institute.

Interviews were conducted using two different data collection techniques, Questionnaire self-completion and face-to-face interviews. Telephone, Skype and emails were used for follow up and clarity seeking questions and data was collected over a period of three months (December 2013, January-February 2013).

Summary of institution interviews

Four themes were derived from data that was analyzed from the institutions and they are; the need for establishment of institutions driving African Renaissance, the kind of knowledge offered and whether it is building critical consciousness, ideology driving the knowledge and curriculum of the institutions, and the delivery method of teaching to those institutions who teach. Worth noting on the institutions that were sampled for the study, TMALI and ALC have a full teaching programme.

1. The need for establishment of institutions driving African Renaissance

While interviews were different, responses pointed out to a need for the establishment of these institutions if Africa and Africans are to build a different type of cadre that should advance her renewal. A summary of responses varied from; a need to generate a transformation in the thinking of a critical mass of young Africans as well as the institutions in which they live and work was key to sustaining the agenda to transform Africa into a peaceful, stable and secure continent. At the heart of this cluster of challenges confronting Africa, is the lack of a sound knowledge base on peace and security among the next generation of scholars and policy analysts and within academic institutions. It is these institutions that should normally lead the discourse to guide change. While Africa boasts of more than 300 Universities, with approximately 5 million students annually, much of the knowledge that provides the framework for addressing Africa's security and development challenges is produced outside of Africa. This is despite the abundance of local knowledge and African ideas for achieving security and development on the continent; a need for closing the gap emanating from poor or weak thought leadership in Africa – thought leadership is understood as an ability to decipher challenges confronting a phenomenon and being able to devise potential solutions. A creation of thought leaders for the further advancement of Africa's renewal by training Africans for the political, economic, social and cultural renewal of the African continent and its people, from the Pan-African paradigm and influenced by Afrocentricity, African renaissance and African-centred epistemologies and methodologies as well as informed by Africa-wide policies agreed through the Organisation for African Unity (OAU) and the African Union (AU).

2. The kind of knowledge offered whether it is building critical consciousness

The institutions agreed that indeed their teaching programmes offer a kind of knowledge that builds critical consciousness to advance Africa's Renaissance. Responses varied from; "The need for independent thinking and the pursuit of excellence is seen as a way to build the confidence of young African scholars and analysts in ways that they can effectively respond to the needs of their continent while transforming their spaces and being globally competitive", to "the kind of knowledge offered in the institution is specifically geared to strengthen critical consciousness for Africa's renewal. The packaging of the curricula and pedagogy ensures that students are engaged with the issues in a way that makes them critically conscious. The knowledge and research in these institutions is guided by themes such as combating all forms of oppression, establishing the basis of an African Renaissance on the African continent and in the African Diaspora, and promoting efforts for national and international peace and harmony. This is done through maintenance of a diverse group of experts with various points of view on themes and topics of the institute as it seeks to promote a healthy cultural agency-oriented dimension to research which rejects particularly the marginalization, peripherization, and dislocation of the African people.

3. Ideology driving curriculum and knowledge

Responses had a consensus of the point of departure of the knowledge that Africa should be educating its citizens on, that the overall research and teaching must be shaped by a pan-African paradigm and influenced by Afrocentric philosophy, African renaissance and African-centred epistemologies and methodologies. Education that is informed by ideologies and philosophies that is essentially pan-African. This way, African narratives are privileged over those that are non-African – for instance, African scholars are extensively used. The institutes showed a devotion to generating knowledges in all issues from the standpoint of African people as agents and subjects of human experience, not as on the margins of any other culture.

4. Delivery and methods for teaching

The manner in which the curricula is designed and packaged for those institutions that teach allows students to engage, almost if not completely independently, with materials. Teachers facilitate and challenge students to unthink, rethink and or deconstruct and reconstruct. This is informed by the desire to produce future leaders that are change agents in the African continent. Pan-Africanism, Afrocentricity and African Renaissance inform the approach.

5. Summary of the individual interviews

Similar to institution interviews, themes were derived from data analyzed from the individual questionnaires. The two themes for individual questionnaire analysis are; the critical analysis of knowledge discourse as a means of facilitating education building critical consciousness for African Renaissance and the kind of knowledge that is required for building critical consciousness.

6. The critical analysis of knowledge discourse as a means of facilitating education building critical consciousness for African Renaissance

Respondents deliberated on the basis of limitation of the current state of knowledge, highlighting that there is sufficient evidence to suggest that far from being decolonized the current formal knowledge and educational curriculum is an offspring of colonial ways of knowing, designed to buttress the systematic subordination of others under the western modernity therefore, for this reason it becomes a fundamental challenge to rely on such education as it is embedded in our systems to build critical consciousness that will advance African Renaissance.

A quote from one of the respondent's response in providing the analysis stated;

> "This kind of knowledge system is an important layer in the construction of a global power system that we call coloniality or imperiality. It cannot be adequate for the purposes of decolonizing the mind, time and space because of necessity such decoloniality cannot be born within coloniality. Therefore, an education and knowledges system that is fundamentally heterogeneous, diverse and pluralistic is necessary for allowing African ways of knowing and others to interface for the benefit of the new global man, the decolonial being."

Therefore, the respondents highlighted that, it is knowledges rather than knowledge that is needed. It is a knowledges system that permits epistemic disobedience, diversion, subversion, difference, undisciplined thinking, located and situated ways of knowing. It is a system that does not replace one hierarchy of knowledges with a new one, but that disrupts this pecking order of knowledges by levelling the playing ground enabling learners to know African, Latino, Western, Asian, Pacific ways of knowing, truly arming them for an effective role in shaping the world order. This is what curriculum transformation rather than reform means, it is to disrupt the 'normal', the 'usual', the 'common' and the 'universal', for these are normalizing just one way of knowing with its claims to superiority, thus perpetuating coloniality of knowledge, of being and power in the world.

Lastly, other responses stated that to develop critical consciousness it requires expertise in radical pedagogy. This is a field that has developed globally, building on the decolonizing pedagogic legacies of the likes of Paulo Freire. It would involve bringing together and deploying the energies of the radical teachers/intellectuals among us (too many of whom are scattered around the world or pouring energy into moribund, conservative, often-corrupt and bureaucratic university structures). "Mass public education is the only way to generate the critical consciousness we need," said one of the respondents.

We have many highly developed, educated and conscious individuals, but are failing to make this part of daily life in the manner that continental renewal will require. Not everything African deserves to be renewed as many of our cultures are/were feudal and patriarchal and need to be radically interrogated and thus advanced, culture (and psychology) being the dynamic product of human interaction with the material world.

7. Education as a means of facilitating critical consciousness

Responses that fed to this theme varied from understanding African Renaissance within a context of education so that the critical consciousness built departs from a fundamental understanding of the Africa, Renaissance discourse.

The summary points of the interviews are:

The notion and discourses around the African Renaissance as currently conceptualized must be intrinsically embedded in a strategy that uses education as one of the means by which a critical African consciousness can be generated and spread across the continent infusing the learning and thinking process of all young and older Africans with a comprehensive and inclusive discourse that encompasses all the traditions of resistance, celebration, expression and visioning that make up the total legacy of what Africa is. The notions and discourses that infuse the idea of an African Renaissance will have to be re-located within a wider and more inclusive epistemic paradigm; one that recognizes, integrates and celebrates the ideas and perspectives of feminists and gender activists as key players in the imagination of a new type of Africa.

Secondly, there has to be a radical economic and structural shift in the modes through which life is produced, shared, utilized and protected in all the societies of the continent. The given western education that is part of affirming western modernity is intended to maintain structural global inequality and cultural inequality between the western man is assumed to be rational and logical (thinking) and others who are assumed not to be rational and logical (not thinking, but mimicking and copycats). So, the education system would need to be transformed in order for it to enable the majority of students to be psychically and morally liberated to think creatively and progressively.

Conclusion

A need for reassessment of education in Africa must take into cognizance the challenge of education in developing the human resources that will ensure accelerated development without compromising Africa's cultural identity. Education must expand the knowledge base of Africans that will allow us to undertake the socio-economic, cultural, and political transformation necessary to achieve development.

However, the knowledge for building critical consciousness required for advancing African Renaissance is not evident in the traditional mainstream education in Africa. The education found in the traditional mainstream education systems remain colonized and does not produce the critical consciousness required for advancing African Renaissance.

Critical consciousness for advancing African Renaissance requires a particular type of knowledge/education with pedagogy different to the one existing in traditional institutions.

There exist decolonized institutions with knowledge that is based on Pan-African and Afrocentric paradigms whose education is appropriate for the advancement of the African Renaissance. Even as these institutions may not be found in the mainstream education systems, their knowledge which is grounded from African perspectives in approaching challenges and solutions of the continent, have proved to be better positioned to build critical consciousness for advancing African Renaissance. The ideologies which these institutions are found are ideologies which authentic African liberation can be found.

References

Alalade, O. 2013. Beyond Rhetoric: Pan Africanism and the African Renaissance. *Africa Peace and Security Monitor* 3, (1)

Banda, Z.J. 2010. African Renaissance and Missiology: A perspective from mission praxis, Thesis submitted in partial fulfilment of the requirements for the degree of Doctor of Theology, University of South Africa.

Cossa, J. A. 2009. African Renaissance and Globalization: A conceptual analysis. *UFAMU: A Journal of African Studies* 36(1)

Dei, G.S. 2012. Indigenous anti-colonial knowledge as 'heritage knowledge' for promoting Black/African education in diasporic contexts. *Decolonization: Indigenity, Education & Society*, 1, 102-119

Fanon, F. 1961. *The Wretched of the Earth.* New York: Grove Press.

Freire, P. 2000. *The pedagogy of the oppressed.* New York: The Continuum International Publishing group Inc.,

Gutto, S. B. O. 2006. Towards a new paradigm for pan-African knowledge production and application in the context of the African Renaissance. *International Journal of African Renaissance Studies* 1 (2) 306-323

Kwapong, A.A. 1998. The challenge of Education in Africa, Discussions of the Inaugural programme of the Africa Leadership Forum, Ota, Nigeria, 24 October to 1 November 1998

Lewis, M. K. & Lee, A. K. 2009. Critical consciousness in Introductory Psychology: A historically black university context. *Pedagogy and the Human Sciences*, 1, (1) 50-60

Liu, K.D. 2012. Conscientization and the Cultivation of conscience. A thesis submitted in partial fulfilment of Doctor of Philosophy in Education, University of Canterbury 2012

Maldonado-Torres, N. 2007. On the Coloniality of Being. *Cultural Studies* 21 (2) 240-270

Mbeki, T. 2014. Tasks of an African Progressive Movement. *The Thinker* 59 12 – 18

Metzler, J. 2009. The Developing States and Education: Africa. *Springer International Handbooks of Education* 22 277-294

More, M.P. 2002. African Renaissance: The politics of Return. *Africa Journal of Political Science* 7 (2) 61-80

Mphahlele, E. 2002. "*Eskia*" *Down Second Avenue.* Stainbank & Associates (Pty) Ltd

Ndlovu, M. 2013. *What fundamentally is Pan-African Education? A De-colonial Epistemic perspective on Education and Development in Post-colonial Africa.* Pretoria: Archie Mafeje Institute, UNISA (Unpublished Monograph).

Ramose, M.B. 2000. African Renaissance: a northbound gaze. *Politeia* 19 (3) 47-63

Rodney, W. 1973. *How Europe underdeveloped Africa.* Dar es Salaam: Bogle-LÓuverture Publication

Xulu, V.S. 2004. The Place of African Renaissance in the South African Education, Thesis submitted in partial fulfilment of the requirements for the degree of Doctor of Education, University of Zululand

Education for Africa's renaissance:

A Case of Curriculum Ideology

Asanda Fotoyi

Introduction

As asserted by Xulu (2004), the synthesis of the two concepts African Renaissance and education, by implication suggests educational reform. Central in the educational reforms proposed by African scholars who have looked at education in Africa is decoloniality and the adoption of an Afrocentric paradigm. Maldonado-Torres (2006: 114) explains that by decoloniality it is meant the dismantling of relations of power and conceptions of knowledge that foment the reproduction of racial, gender, and geo-political hierarchies that came into being or found new and more powerful forms of expression in the modern/colonial world. Thus Gutto (2006: 306), for instance, argues that the educational reforms must focus on confronting, with a view to correcting and departing from hegemonic knowledge and knowledge systems that are predicated on racist paradigms that have deliberately and otherwise distorted, and continue to distort, the reality of who Africans really are. According to Ndlovu (2014: 134) it is because of this existence of coloniality as a power structure that, in the African context, was introduced by imperialism and colonialism, that decoloniality becomes an epistemic project that seeks to destroy various colonial situations, in order to bring about a pluriversal world where all knowledge has the right to influence the world in every corner of its location. Similarly, the adoption of an Afrocentric paradigm in education is critical because Africans have been educated away from their own culture and traditions and attached to the fringes of European culture; thus dislocated from themselves (Asante 1991: 170). That is why African scholars such as Mphahlela (1982), Mugo (1999) and Xulu (2004) have called for the enhancement of African culture in African learners. By African culture it is meant, the sum total of African philosophy, behaviour, ideas and artefacts (Asante 1985: 4). According to Asante (1991: 171), Afrocentricity is a frame of reference wherein phenomena are viewed from the perspective of the African person. The Afrocentric approach seeks in every situation the appropriate centrality of the African person. In education this means that teachers provide students the opportunity to study the world and its people, concepts and history from an African world view (Asante 1991: 171). Essentially Afrocentricity in African education arises from awareness that the overall character of much of educational theory and practice in Africa is overwhelmingly Eurocentric. Samir Amin describes Eurocentrism as a culturalist phenomenon that;

> "assumes the existence of irreducibly distinct cultural invariants that shape the historical paths of different people. Eurocentrism is therefore anti-universalist...but it does present itself as universalist, for it claims that imitation of the Western model by all people is the only solution to the challenges of our time...Eurocentrism is a specifically modern phenomenon, the roots of which go back to only the (European) Renaissance...In this sense, it constitutes one dimension of the culture and ideology of the modern capitalist world...Eurocentrism is a distortion from which the majority of dominant social theories and ideologies suffer...Eurocentrism is a paradigm...For this reason, it manifests itself in a variety of ways, as much as in the expression of received ideas, popularized by the media, as in the erudite formulations of specialists in different areas of social science" (see, Amin 1988).

Therefore, as a point of departure this chapter echoes the call for the reform of Africa's education systems through decoloniality and the adoption of an Afrocentric paradigm. This chapter, because education has a significant role to play in the advancement of the agenda for Africa's political, economic, social and cultural renewal, calls for an education for Africa's renaissance. The need for an education for Africa's renaissance arises because the colonialist Eurocentric education that had been imposed on Africans has, for a very long time distorted the reality of Africans and marginalised their existence. Moreover, the colonialist Eurocentric neutralised the Africans from taking part in their self-development, the development of their communities and their continent. At this point it is also important to indicate that for the purpose of this chapter African Renaissance is viewed as a reconstruction agenda that is based on two major understandings. Firstly, that the African continent is faced with adverse political, economic, social and cultural challenges. Secondly, that Africans have the ability to be masters of their own destiny and trounce over these social ills that have ensured, the marginalisation of the continent in world affairs and development processes. Also throughout the chapter African(s) is used in reference to the indigenous person and people. Coloniser or colonialist is used in reference to those who through slavery, racism and oppression formed or established colonies in the African continent.

This chapter is structured as follows:

Firstly, the African renaissance agenda is presented as the conceptual framework of this chapter. This is followed by a discussion on an education for Africa's renaissance - arguing a case of curriculum ideology. Lastly, the chapter presents a case study of the curriculum ideology of South Africa's grade 10-12 economics Curriculum and Assessment Policy Statement (CAPS). As will be later discussed the economics subject is chosen as an important subject of concern because, whereas a great part of the 21st century has seen advancement in Africa's political, social and cultural emancipation; Africa's economic emancipation is lagging behind.

The conceptual framework: African Renaissance Agenda

The year 2002 saw the disbanding of the Organisation of African Unity (OAU) a pan-African organisation that had served Africa from the early years of the continent's liberation in 1963, and in 1994 saw the abolishment of the racially discriminatory colonial apartheid regime in South Africa. The disbanding of the OAU was making way for the formation of the African Union (AU). This shift from OAU to AU is what Bujra (2004) refers to as a move from the Lagos Plan of Action (LPA) to the New Partnership for Africa's Development (NEPAD). The establishment of the AU in 2002 was motivated by the desire to advance Africa's political, economic, social and cultural renewal. This vision and agenda has been conceptualised as the African Renaissance. In 2001 the former president of South Africa, Thabo Mbeki declared that;

> "We speak about the need for the African Renaissance in part so that we, ourselves, and not another, determine who we are, what we stand for, what our vision and hopes are, how we do things, what programs we adopt to make our lives worth living, who we relate to and how" (Mbeki 2001).

In his 1996 speech at the launch of the African Renaissance Institute at the University of South Africa (UNISA), the former president Thabo Mbeki outlines the tasks of the African Renaissance, to include:

- the establishment of democratic political systems to ensure the accomplishment of the goal that 'the people shall govern';
- ensuring that these systems take into account African specifics so that, while being truly democratic and protecting human rights, they are nevertheless designed in ways which really ensure that political and, therefore, peaceful means can be used to address the competing interests of different social groups in each country;
- establishing the institutions and procedures which would enable the continent collectively to deal with questions of democracy, peace and stability;
- achieving sustainable economic development that results in the continuous improvement of the standards of living and the quality of life of the masses of the people;
- qualitatively changing Africa's place in the world economy so that it is free of the yoke of the international debt burden and no longer a supplier of raw materials and an importer of manufactured goods;
- ensuring the emancipation of the women of Africa;
- successfully confronting the scourge of HIV/AIDS;
- the rediscovery of Africa's creative past to recapture the peoples' cultures, encourage artistic creativity and restore popular involvement in both accessing and advancing science and technology;
- strengthening the genuine independence of African countries and continent in their relations with the major powers and enhancing their role in the determination of the global system of governance in all fields, including politics, the economy, security, information and intellectual property, the environment and science and technology.

The first to ask the question of when we can talk of an African Renaissance was Cheikh Anta Diop in 1948. In his collection of essays titled *Towards the African Renaissance: Essays in Culture and Development, 1946-1960;* Diop (1960) argues that we can speak of an African renaissance, when:

- African writers write for the African public and not when their aim is to impress Europeans while incidentally defending an African cause. This can be achieved by the use of indigenous languages and not when an African writer is, for example, mainly trying to express himself correctly in French, to demonstrate an unexpected literary talent or to exhibit his mastery of grammatical subtleties rather than expressing ideas that can be useful to his community (Diop 1996: 34);

- Indigenous culture is established based on African languages. This can be achieved if teaching were done in the African languages as quite often this faulty pedagogical procedure - the use of European language - leads to a complete break with reality and subsequent contact is only established at a very slow rate, a situation that would not have occurred if teaching were done in Wolof (language spoken in Senegal), because not only is there something natural and ordinary in that reality when expressed in his mother tongue that makes the African master and dominate any reality, but also the chances of his not understanding the meanings of words are negligible. Also through the study of African languages because, by studying how this language gave birth to another and how this happened, we would succeed in building a sort of linguistic chain going from the earliest to the latest and thus get to know about a very important period in our history. Also the study of the origin of African languages is another way of enriching indigenous languages and from there can develop new words to suit our needs (Diop 1996: 35-36);
- Greater cultural awareness is achieved amongst the grassroots of Africa, because culture does not consist of literary expression only, it is also made up of plastic expression. This can be achieved if centers like Dakar, for example, should rather have museums where one could see side by side with an authentic indigenous collection, if possible, from all parts of Africa, some reproductions of European classical sculpture and contemporary paintings which can still be purchased (Diop 1996: 40-41);
- Architecture is developed in accordance with African styles in order to vivify art forms that are our own or that have become so adapted to our needs that we claim them as ours. Architecture is of great importance, it possesses this interesting characteristic of having age-long forms that are susceptible to new adaption and which, besides, can serve for religious and civil constructions (Diop 1996: 43); and
- African music expresses the song of the forest, the power of darkness and nature, the mobility of suffering, with all human dignity. Music is also part of culture and that Africa is a very rich continent in terms of rhythm (Diop 1996: 43-44).

- In 1968 the first president of Nigeria, Nnamdi Azikiwe, pronounced that the notion of a 'Renascent Africa' exists in a transitional stage between the Old and New African. According to Azikiwe (1968), in this context, Old Africa - refers to the Africa of yesterday; Renascent Africa refers to the Africa of today; and New Africa refers to the Africa of tomorrow. Azikiwe (1968: 24-24) argued that the philosophy of the New Africa hinges itself on the following five bases which are indispensable to its realisation.
- Spiritual Balance: respect for the opinion of others; and conceding to others the right to state their opinion whilst admitting one's right to state one's opinion. Thus Renascent Africa must cultivate respect for the views of others (Azikiwe 1968: 24).
- Social Regeneration: discarding all forms of prejudice be they racial, national, tribal, societal, religious, political, economic, or ethical; and the realization that an African is an African no matter where he was born, the breaking down of all barriers of tribal prejudice, be they inter-tribal or intra-tribal, which, so far, has postponed social unity of African peoples. Thus Renascent Africa that must take the burden of looking at a fellow African as a man, nothing more, nothing less (Azikiwe 1968: 24).
- Economic Determinism: the realisation that economic self-sufficiency on a sane basis is the ultimate means to the salvation of the Renascent Africa. Renascent Africa cannot create a new social order without an economic foundation. Therefore, the Renascent African must make tomorrow secure for posterity and a milestone is reached towards African economic interdependence with the rest of the world (Azikiwe 1968: 24-25).
- Mental Emancipation: emancipation is essential because for the African to cultivate an inferiority complex that he is inferior to other races is to sign the death warrant of Africans. Thus Renascent Africa must rid of the inferiority complex and all the trappings of 'hat-in-hand Uncle Tom-ism'. This includes education of the sort which should teach African youth to have faith in his ability, to believe that he is equal of the people of other races of mankind, mentally and physically and to look at no man as his superior simply because that man comes from the Antarctic or Arctic regions (Azikiwe 1968: 25).
- National Risorgimento/Political Resurgence: If the Renascent Africa has cultivated spiritual balance, had experienced social regeneration,

> had realized economic determinism, had experienced mental emancipation, the expectation of political risorgimento is not far-fetched. Renascent African must then usher in a New Africa, and Africans of tomorrow need not continue to be political servitude. This right of self-determination is a phenomenon which defies human ingenuity (Azikiwe 1968: 24-25).

The African Renaissance agenda fosters renewed pride in their identity, new dreams and hope, new consciousness, and restoration to a people who have been subjected to centuries of slavery, colonialism, and racism. Thus the vision has been received with excitement and enthusiasm by many Africans both in the continent and in the Diaspora. On the other hand, the African Renaissance discourse has also been received with criticism. Ramose (2000: 48) for instance, criticises the use of the word 'Renaissance' to conceptualise Africa's reconstruction agenda. According to Ramose (2000: 48) 'Renaissance' is a historical concept signifying a specific period in the history of Europe and is specifically a European historical movement that originated in Italty and spread through other parts of Europe and therefore as a historical concept the Renaissance is deeply rooted in Europe and has Europe as its primary reference point. Ramose (2000:49) asks why this borrowing which creates lack of conceptual clarity and sows confusion as if there is something unnatural about the natural environment of Africa such that the history of Africa cannot be described and defined by concepts originating from Africa? Moreover, Ramose (2000: 58) suggests that this borrowing is a fixation of the African gaze to the North and in that way Africa concedes prominence and leadership to the North. Maloka (n.d) on the other hand critiques that there is consistent failure to historicise the renaissance discourse to recognise works such as those by Nnamdi Azikiwe and Cheik Anta Diop. Maloka (n.d) also critiques how the concept of renaissance has been conceptualised suggesting that it would be useful if the debate would recognise renaissances (in plural) rather than renaissance with a capital 'R'. In contrast to Ramose (2000), Maloka (n.d) however does not question the 'borrowing' of the concept instead asserts that renaissance is a universal phenomenon in terms of its spatial and temporal distribution across the universe and not peculiar to the 'Renaissance' period itself.

In response to such criticism Gutto (2006: 313) suggests that since the concept 'Renaissance' is historically associated with the European 'Renaissance' of the fourteenth to the seventeenth centuries, it is important to take account of the motivating forces that propelled the European Renaissance and its manifestations, products and consequences, and then to appreciate what makes the quest for an African Renaissance different. According to Gutto (2006: 313-314) one differentiating feature of the past European Renaissance and the African Renaissance that is under construction is that the former was labelled as such by intellectuals only after the event, while the African Renaissance is, from the beginning, proactively driven by a vision and mission. African Renaissance, Gutto (2006: 314) says, is a deliberate conscious commitment of what is desired because of objective and subjective factors. Although the African Renaissance will share some generic attributes with the European Renaissance, however the African Renaissance;

> "will not enslave non-Africans and use them as providers of free labour for the purposes of accumulating capital for a successor global capitalist mode of production, starting with the so-called industrial revolution, as the European Renaissance did. It, the African Renaissance, will also not have the luxury of benefiting from colonial conquests, often involving committing genocide against the indigenous peoples as occurred in the Americas, Australia and Africa, perpetuating systemic sexism against women, including institutionalized rape of enslaved and colonized women and girls, and plundering and pillaging of natural and people-made resources all over the world, as the European Renaissance did. The African Renaissance will also not off-load its poor, including common social criminals, by assisting them in colonizing and settling in other parts of the world, as the European Renaissance did" (Gutto 2006: 314).

Mbeki (1999) responds by saying that all of us know the word 'renaissance' means rebirth, renewal, springing up anew, and therefore, when we speak of an African Renaissance, we speak of the rebirth and renewal of our continent, and acknowledges that;

> "this idea is not new to the struggles of the peoples of our continent for genuine emancipation. It has been propagated before by other activists for liberation, drawn from many countries. But it has been suggested that when this perspective was advanced in earlier periods, the conditions did not exist for its realisation. Accordingly, what is new about it today is that the conditions exist for the process to be enhanced, throughout the continent, leading to the transformation of the idea from a dream dreamt by visionaries to a practical programme of action for revolutionaries" (Mbeki, 1999).

According to Mbeki (1999) these conditions are:

- the completion of the continental process of the liquidation of the colonial system in Africa, attained as a result of the liberation of South Africa;
- the recognition of the bankruptcy of neo-colonialism by the masses of the people throughout the continent, including the majority of the middle strata;
- the weakening of the struggle among the major powers for spheres of influence on our continent, as a consequence of the end of the Cold War; and
- the acceleration of the process of globalisation.

Education for Africa's Renaissance

That education is central to development is both fundamental and foundational (Ndlovu 2014: 131). According to Ndlovu (n.d.), the manner in which education (as a system of knowledge production) contributes to development is dependent on various considerations – and, its relevance is one of the most important considerations. This is because what a particular kind of education system can do in one context is not necessarily the case in a different context.

Pre-colonialization, traditional African education existed but the many years of colonialization had marginalised and disregarded these indigenous knowledge systems by the introduction of colonial Eurocentric education systems. Rodney (1973: 374) says the colonisers did not introduce education into Africa, they introduced a new set of formal educational institutions which partly supplemented and partly replaced those which were there before. Rodney (1973: 372) says the most crucial aspect of pre-colonial African education was its relevance to Africans, and that the following features of indigenous African education can be considered outstanding:

- its close links with social life, both in a material and spiritual sense;
- its collective nature;
- its many-sidedness; and
- its progressive development in conformity with the successive stages of physical, emotional and mental development of the child.

According to Rodney (1973: 372), there was no separation of education and productive activity or any division between manual and intellectual education. Altogether, through mainly informal means, pre-colonial African education matched the realities of pre-colonial African society and produced well-rounded personalities to fit into that society. Some aspects of African education were formal, that is to say, there was a specific programme and a conscious division between teachers and pupils and that formal education in pre-colonial Africa was also directly connected with the purposes of the society, just like informal education. Rodney (1973: 374-375) articulates that this is in contrast to what was later introduced, as the main purpose of the colonial school was;

> "to train Africans to help man the local administration at the lowest ranks and to staff the private capitalist firms owned by Europeans. In effect, that meant selecting a few Africans to participate in the domination and exploitation of the continent as a whole. It was not an educational system that grew out of the African environment or one that was designed to promote the most rational use of material and social resources. It was not an educational system designed to give young people confidence and pride as members of African societies, but one which sought to instil a sense of deference towards all that was European and capitalist. Education in Europe was dominated by the capitalist class. The same class bias was automatically transferred to Africa; and to make matters worse the racism and cultural boastfulness harboured by capitalism were also included in the package of colonial education. Colonial schooling was education for subordination, exploitation, the creation of mental confusion and the development of underdevelopment."

The African Renaissance as a reconstruction agenda is viewed to be based on two major understandings. Firstly, that the African continent is faced with adverse political, economic, social and cultural challenges. Secondly, that Africans have the ability to be masters of their own destiny and trounce over these social ills that have ensured, the marginalisation of the continent in world affairs and development processes. As NEPAD (Article 53) appeals, Africans in spite of their present difficulties must regain confidence in their genius and their capacity to face obstacles and be involved in the building of a new Africa (see, NEPAD 2001). Therefore, for education in Africa to be relevant, it would concern itself with developing the learner to actively champion, urgently engage and be involved in achieving Africa's political, economic, social and cultural renewal. This therefore requires for the education systems in Africa to be organised with the vision of the African Renaissance motivated by the achievement of its tasks – that is an education for Africa's renaissance.

Dr Reuel Khoza, in his speech to university of Limpopo at inauguration as chancellor titled '*Education for an African Renaissance: Providing Solutions for Africa*' articulates that:

> "education for an African Renaissance is about how to visualise and create a future for Africa and her people..., for what is an African renaissance but the realisation of a (African) people that they can be masters of their own destiny" (Khoza 2007).

As should be the starting point of any education system, this chapter aims to focus on arguing a case of curriculum ideology - that is beliefs about the aim of the subjects; content knowledge; instructional/learning process; role of students; teaching and the purpose of assessment. According to Mnguni (2013: 2) curriculum ideology is defined as beliefs about what should be taught, what the outcomes should be and what the purpose for teaching should be. Curriculum ideology therefore outlines the vision of education by clarifying the process and outcomes of student development (Mnguni n.d.). An essential question therefore is of what curriculum ideology should inform an education for Africa's renaissance. To assist in responding to this question a comparison of four curriculum ideologies - Scholar Academic Ideology, Social Efficiency Ideology, Learner Centered Ideology and Social Reconstruction Ideology - is presented in Table 1.

According to Mnguni (2013: 2) the;

- Scholar Academic ideology ensures that students develop a discipline-specific thinking ability reflecting the disciplines they specialise in;
- Social efficiency ideology's objective is to prepare students for particular roles in society as adults;
- Student-centered ideology facilitates the growth of students by helping them develop their skills and abilities further; and
- Social reconstruction ideology believes that humans have the ability to influence their world by using intelligence, knowledge and skills to solve social problems.

Of the four curriculum ideologies, the social reconstruction ideology resonates greatest with the Africa's renaissance agenda as both hold a social perspective with a vision of a better society. The social reconstruction ideology as does the African Renaissance agenda assumes that society is threatened by many problems. Underlying many of these problems, which include among others racism, war, sexism, poverty, pollution, worker exploitation, global warming, crime, political corruption, population explosion, energy shortage, illiteracy, inadequate health care, and unemployment; are deep social structures many based in Eurocentric conceptions of knowledge, culture, and values. The social reconstruction ideology as the African Renaissance agenda nonetheless believes that an improved society is achievable, by first developing a vision of a better society then the people reconstruct their society into the envisioned one. According to Schiro (2008: 134) promoters of the social reconstruction curriculum ideology believe, education provides the means by which society is to be reconstructed. For the social reconstructionist education has the power to educate people to analyse and understand social problems, envision a world in which those problems do not exist, and act so as to bring that vision into existence (Schiro 2008: 134). This chapter therefore argues that curriculum ideology adopted for an education for Africa's renaissance must be guided by the social reconstruction praxis.

Table 1: A comparison of curriculum ideologies (Adopted from Mguni, 2013)

Curriculum features		Scholar academic ideology	Social efficiency ideology	Student-centred ideology	Social reconstruction ideology
Aim of the subject	Purpose of knowledge	Understanding	Doing/Action	Actualizing oneself	Interpret and reconstruct society
Content knowledge	Nature of knowledge	Didactic statements	Capabilities for action	Personal meaning	Intelligence and moral stance
	Source of knowledge	Objective reality as interpreted by academic discipline	Normative objective reality as socially interpreted	Individual's personal creative response to experience	Individual's interpretation of society's past, present and future

Instructional process	Learning viewed from	Transmitter	Transmitter	Receiver	Transmitter
	Primary function of learning	Social transmission	Social transmission	Growth	Social transmission
	Results of learning	Changed mindset	Changed behaivor	Changed mindset	Changed behavior
	Primary actor during learning	Agent	Agent/student	Student	Agent/student
	Students readiness	Simplification of difficult topics	Providing prerequisite behavioral capabilities	Stages of growth	Gestalt of prior experience
The student	Role during learning	Passive	Active	Active	Active
	Teacher focuses on	Child's mind	Child's behavior	Child's mind	Child's behavior
	Teachers concerned with children	As they ought to be	As they ought to be	As they are	As they ought to be
	Viewing children	In relation to standardized norms	In relation to standardized norms	As individuals	In relation to standardized norms
Teaching	Role of teacher	Transmitter	Supervisor	Facilitator	Colleague
	Standards used to measure teacher effectiveness	Accurate presentation of discipline	Efficiency of student learning	Facilitation of growth	Effective transference of the vision
	Teachers stimulate	Uniformity	Uniformity	Diversity	Uniformity
	Teachers	Directly implement curriculum	Directly implement curriculum	Adapt curriculum (according to children's needs)	Adopt curriculum (according to social concerns)
	Media used during learning	Didactic discourse	Programmed instruction	Child-environment interaction	Group dynamics
	Intent of teaching	To advance students in a discipline	To prepare students to perform skills	To stimulate child growth	To acculturate students into educators vision

Assessment	Purpose of evaluation to the evaluator	Rank students for a future in the discipline	Certify that student have the skill	Diagnose student's abilities to facilitate growth	Measure student progress with respect to ability
	Nature of assessment tools	Norm reinforced	Criterion reinforced	Informal subjective diagnosis	Informal subjective diagnosis
	Assessments are	Objective	Objective	Subjective	Subjective
	Point of assessment	After instruction	After instruction	During instruction	During instruction

In line with the social reconstruction praxis and adopting an Afrocentric paradigm (refer to, Asante 1991, Mazama 2001 and Mazama 2003) the following is thus proposed:

a.) Aim of subjects

African societies are plagued by dire social ills. These include endemic poverty, crime and wars, unemployment and inequality, illiteracy to mention a few. It is therefore imperative that the aim of subjects be is to resolve the current societal problems and create better ones by developing leaners who will be agents and leaders and actively and urgently be involved in transforming their societies.

b.) Content knowledge

The colonialist Eurocentric content knowledge that has been presented to Africans had disconnected learners from the lived life experiences of Africans. This has been the result of the extent by which the realities of Africans have been marginalized. Thus content knowledge must in its interdisciplinary integrate the lived life experiences of Africans. The curriculum content suggested by Gutto (2006) is indispensable and can facilitate the reconnection of learners to the lived life experiences of Africans. Gutto (2006: 306) views this content knowledge as that which Africans and peoples of African descent need to possess as basic and shared common knowledge about Africa, the Diaspora and the world. The content (see Gutto 2006: 319-320) takes account of:

- Africa as the cradle of all humanity.

- Africa's leadership and contributions to human civilization.
- Africa's indigenous knowledge systems, cultural diversity and spiritual traditions.
- The transformation of modern Africa since the fifteenth century: slavery and slave trade, colonialism, neo-colonialism.
- Africa's contributions to Western industrialization, wealth accumulation, science, technology and cultures.
- African Diaspora in the Americas, the Caribbean, Europe and Asia.
- The era of decolonization, nation formation and nation building and the movement from the OAU to the AU.
- AU principles, objectives, organs and institutions and the Regional Economic Communities (RECs).
- NEPAD, Africa's industrialization, intra-African trade and investments.
- The African environment and ecosystems.
- In-depth understanding of each country.
- Understanding and enhancing the role of the youth, women and the elderly in society.
- Basic Kiswahili.
- The future of Africa and the Diaspora: The African Renaissance.
- Reclaiming of Africa's islands that are still under colonial occupation.
- Africa, the Diaspora and transformation of the unjust globalized world order, etc.
- The development of teachers overall but with particular focus on the revamped African Renaissance curricula.

The next three curriculum features look at the teacher-learner relationship.

c.) Instructional/learning process

The learning process has to move away from what Paulo Freire (1970) calls the 'banking concept of education'. In which the scope of action allowed to the student extends only as far as receiving, filing, and storing the deposits (Freire 1970: 72). Freire (1970: 72) says that in this misguided system, at best; it is the people themselves who are filed away through the lack of creativity, transformation and knowledge. Therefore, the learning process has to encourage what Paulo Freire refers to as *conscientizaçáo*; which means learning to perceive social, political and economic contradictions and to take action against the oppressive elements of reality (Freire 1970: 35). The learning process must therefore be group-oriented, closely connected to the society and driven by current social context. Where the critical consciousness required from learners to enable identify problems in their societies, initiate action and engage to transform their societies is not restricted or limited, but rather encouraged.

d. The student

African learners must be seen full-of-potential to transform society for the better, and must be lead to advance Africa's renaissance. This is complete divergence from how the African child has been perceived and taught by the colonialist Eurocentric education. The student must reject any passive role imposed to them of storing deposits entrusted to them, thus develop critical consciousness and assume an active role in transforming of their world.

e. The Teacher

The teacher must not, as Freire (1970: 72) puts it, present himself to the students as their necessary opposite or consider himself as knowledgeable upon those whom they consider to know nothing, but rather present himself as a colleague who upholds the vision of the African Renaissance and in dialogue communicates this vision with the learners. The fundamental goal of dialogue teaching is to create a process of learning and knowing that invariably involves theorizing about the experiences shared in the dialogue process (Freire 1970: 17). According to Freire (1970: 92) only dialogue which requires critical thinking, is also capable of generating critical thinking.

f. Assessment

Assessment must be for the purpose of facilitating learners to develop the critical consciousness necessary in order to reconstruct their societies. Thus for assessment purposes circumstance is key, and evaluation must be subjective. Assessment must take into account social context and the learner's ability to perform at the point of evaluation.

CASE STUDY: South Africa's Grade 10-12 Economics Curriculum and Assessment Policy Statement

Historical context

This section begins by giving a historical background of the curricula that had been presented to Africans in the South African context. Firstly, it is important to state that, as in the rest of Africa, an education did exist in South Africa long before the arrival of the Dutch colonists in 1652. According to Jansen (1990: 195) this traditional African education was led by community elders through an oral tradition based on cultural transmission and was closely integrated with life experience. This education system was however disregarded and interrupted by the colonists' education that was imposed to the African people.

Jansen (1990) provides a pre-1994 history of the curriculum in South African Black education:

- Evangelical Curriculum: The first colonial curriculum presented was the Evangelical Curriculum and the purpose of this schooling of African slaves in the mid-17th century was religious confirmation leading to full church membership rather than secular education (Jansen 1990: 196).
- Academic Curriculum: The Academic Curriculum which included the subjects of history, geography, Italian book keeping, and the French language, and later subjects such as drawing, needlework, woodwork and nature studies was introduced late in the 18th century. This curriculum led to university entrance by Africans, and this resulted in intensified White opposition to 'Black' education (Jansen 1990: 198).
- Industrial Training Curriculum: Also presented to Africans was the Industrial Training Curriculum and although this curriculum was aimed at providing Africans with skills for manual labour, George Grey, appointed governor of the Cape in 1854, defined the purpose of education as social control through peaceful subjugation (Jensen 1990: 198).
- Differential Curriculum: As the socioeconomic conditions of the 1880s worsened these intensified racist calls for an education system that could afford Afrikaners an economic and political status superior to that of 'Blacks'. This resulted to the Differential Curriculum that

provided a separate and inferior curriculum for Africans. The main purpose of this curriculum was to handicap African children with the introduction of an inferior syllabus (Jansen 1990: 199).

- Apartheid Curriculum: In 1948 the formalisation and systemisation of racist apartheid system led to the development of a racially intensified Apartheid Curriculum that was introduced based on Bantu Education under the Bantu Education Act of 1953 (Jansen 1990:120). The Bantu education, as pronounced by Isaac B. Tabata (1979), was:

> "calculated to serve as an instrument for creating and ensuring the continuance of a vote-less, right-less and ignorant community whose main purpose in life, apart from reproducing their kind (for there is not yet a specific law against that aspect of their life) is to minister to the Whites. The invoking of a dead tribalism and of Bantu Communities wherein 'education will find its expression' is cynical political claptrap. The plain fact is that Bantu Education is to rob the African of education, cut him off from the main stream of modern culture and shut him into a spiritual and intellectual ghetto" (Tabata 1979: 35).

As a result, the first South African democratically elected government has since 1994 taken significant advances in reforming the education system by adopting new education policies (see, Jansen and Taylor 2003, Sayed and Kanjee 2013 and Gumede 2013b), with the aim of a non-racial, non-sexist, inclusive and more democratic education that is effective and efficient. For instance, in 1997 the post-Apartheid South Africa saw the introduction of Curriculum 2005 that was introduced based on Outcome-based education (OBE). Challenges in implementation of OBE led to reviews of the curriculum, first in 2000 and then in 2009 (see, www.education.gov.za). These reviews led to the current National Curriculum Statement for Grades R-12 that is based on the - Curriculum and Assessment Policy Statements (CAPS), National policy pertaining to the programme and promotion requirements of the National Curriculum Statement Grades R-12 and National Protocol for Assessment Grades R-12, (see Department of Basic Education).

Aims of the case study

This case study examines which ideology - Scholar Academic, Social Efficiency, Learner Centered or Social Reconstruction – is adopted by South Africa's grade 10-12 economics CAPS. The economics subject is chosen as an important subject of concern because, whereas a great part of the 21st century has seen advancement in Africa's political, social and cultural emancipation; Africa's economic emancipation is lagging behind. This is evident in the major economic development challenges that Africa faces. According to Gumede (2013a) these challenges include:

- celebrated gross domestic product (GDP) growth rates that have not translated into improved quality of life (many of these economies are still with high levels of hardship, endemic poverty, inequality, etc.);
- deteriorating welfare (with over 500 million Africans expected to fall into poverty by 2015);
- human development which remains very low (on average, in Africa the Human Development Index (HDI) that is below 0, 5);
- the delivery on many of the Millennium Development Goals (MDG) that remains off track;
- challenges in the availability of decent jobs (those available majorities are in the informal sector with low incomes); and
- low productivity and poor working conditions.

It is important that a distinction, for instance between economic development and economic growth is made. Economic growth, measured as the rate of change or growth rate in real GDP, refers to the steady process by which the productive capacity of the economy is increased over time to increase the levels of national output and income (Schoeman, 2011: 216). Economic development on the other hand is economic growth accompanied by changes in, output distribution and economic structures. These changes may include improvements in the material well-being of the poor, an increase in the services and industry's share in gross national product (GNP), an increase in the education and skills of the labour force, and substantial technical advances originating within the economy (Nafziger, 2012: 14). Thus we can see that it is possible for output to be growing and yet the mass of the people may be becoming poorer. For example, Todaro and Smith (2009: 15) tell us that in the 1950s and 1960s many developing countries reached their economic growth targets of 5 per cent and above but the levels of living of the masses of the people remained for the most part unchanged, and this resulted in an increasing number of economists and policymakers who clamored for more direct attacks on widespread absolute poverty, increasingly inequitable income distributions, and rising unemployment. In December 2011 *The Economist* popularised an African rising narrative when it published an article titled "The hopeful continent: Africa rising", celebrating that over the past decade six of the world's ten fastest-growing countries were in Africa. The article also highlighted that Africa had grown faster than East Asia including Japan. However, as Gumede (2013a: 486) points out that the celebrated GDP growth rates averaging at 5 per cent a year with some countries registering annual growth rates of between 7 and 11 per cent have not translated to significant improvements in the wellbeing of peoples of the continent.

Mnguni (2013:2) states that for education to effectively lead to social transformation requires the adoption of the social reconstruction curriculum ideology. The study thus also seeks to determine to what extent the curriculum reflects characteristics of the social reconstruction ideology. Thereby the study aims to conclude on whether the curriculum facilitates economics learners and graduates to perceive Africa's economic development challenges, and act urgently to bring Africa's economic renaissance into existence.

Approach to the case study

The approached used in this study mirrors that in Mguni (2013). In the cited study the researcher examines features of the curriculum guided by six open-ended questions: What is the aim of the subject? What kind of knowledge is prescribed? How is the learning supposed to take place? What is the role of the students in the learning process? What is the role of teachers during instruction? What is the purpose of assessment? Responses are then formulated inductively by the researcher using verbatim and narrated extract from the document being analysed.

The results section of this chapter presents the outcome of the above process. Extracts from South Africa's grade 10-12 economics CAPS are indicated in the left-hand column of tables 2-5. Then based on the characteristics of the curriculum ideologies presented in Table 1. The formulated extracts are then used to make inferences regarding the curriculum ideology that is best represented, this is presented on the right-hand column of the tables 2-5.

Results

1. What is the aim of the subject?

Purpose of economics [4]	Curriculum ideology
understand the concept of monetary and real flows in an open economy within the confines of production, consumption and exchange understand reconstruction, growth and development, as well as a critical approach to initiatives for a fair distribution of income and wealth, human rights, and responsibilities acquire an advanced Economics vocabulary that will allow them to debate and communicate the essentials of the subject	Scholar academic ideology
use resources efficiently to satisfy the competing needs and wants of individuals and of society develop skills to apply demand and supply, and cost and revenue analyses to explain prices and production levels apply, in a responsible and accountable manner, principles that underlie basic economic processes and practices explore a variety of methods and strategies to analyze and explain the dynamics of markets analyze and assess the impact of local and global institutions on the South African economy explain economic events and forecast their consequences or predict likely future outcomes	Social efficiency ideology

collect, analyze and interpret production, consumption, and exchange data as well as other information in order to solve problems and make informed decisions understand human rights concerns, reflect on the wealth creation process, and engage in poverty alleviation	Social reconstruction ideology

[4] Source: Department of Basic Education Grade 10-12 Economics CAPS (2001:9).

2. What kind of knowledge is prescribed?

Main topics [5]	**Corresponding topics 5**	**Curriculum ideology**
Macroeconomics	Economic: basic concepts Basic economic problems Curricular flow Quantitative elements Economic systems Business cycles	Scholar academic ideology
Microeconomics	Dynamics of markets Public sector intervention and composition of the RSA economy	
Economic pursuits	Economic growth and development Money and banking Population and labour force Labour market Redress since 1994	Social efficiency ideology

Contemporary economic issues	Unemployment Labour relations Globalization Inflation Tourism Poverty Other economic issues and quantitative elements of economics	Social reconstruction ideology

[5] Source: Department of Basic Education Grade 10-12 Economics CAPS (2001: 8).

3. How is the learning supposed to take place?

Requirements to offer economics as a subject [6]	Curriculum ideology
For each learner: a textbook and stationary	Scholar academic Ideology

The teacher Variety of textbooks for referencing Statistics SA and SARB Quarterly Bulletin SA Yearbook SARS brochures Legislation, for example, the Labour Relations Act Business, financial and economics magazines and newspapers A television set (TV) and a radio Internet (those with access to the internet)	Social reconstruction Ideology

[6]Source: Department of Basic Education Grade 10-12 Economics CAPS (2001: 9-10)

4. What is the role of the students in the learning process?

The curriculum is not specific with regards to the role of the grades 10-12 economics students in the learning process.

5. What is the role of teachers during instruction?

The curriculum is not specific with regards to the role of the grades 10-12 economics teachers during instruction.

6. What is the purpose of assessment?

Assessment in economics focuses on 7	Curriculum ideology
knowledge of activities of production, consumption and exchange	Scholar academic ideology
skills in the activities of production, consumption and exchange	Social efficiency ideology

values inherent in the activities of production, consumption and exchange	Social reconstruction ideology

[7]Source: Department of Basic Education Grade 10-12 Economics CAPS (2001: 39).

From the case study

The results show that each of the curriculum features of the South African grades 10-12 economics CAPS adopts a multi-curriculum approach in relation to scholar academic ideology, social efficiency ideology and social reconstruction ideology. This makes the curriculum confusing in terms of its curriculum ideology and its processes, intended outcomes, student development as well as the envisioned graduate. Although the curriculum has shown some relation to the social reconstruction ideology it is minimal and thus may not be able to develop learners who will perceive and act urgently to address current socio-economic challenges in their societies. This suggests a dearth of agency from South Africa's economics leaners to address the socioeconomic challenges of high GPD rates that do improve standards of living, endemic poverty, low education levels, high unemployment, and inequalities that plague their communities etc. This imposes a hindrance in the realization of Africa's economic renaissance in the country.

In light of these results, again adopting the social reconstruction praxis and an Afrocentric paradigm, features of the economics curriculum that would advance Africa's economic renaissance above all propose that:

- The aim of the economics subjects must intentionally be to resolve current socioeconomic challenges that plague African societies.
- The content knowledge in order to assist learners to perceive Africa's economic development challenges critically integrate as main topics:
  - *African Economic History*. To highlight the pre-colonial history of African economies and the advantages of pre-colonial traditions.
  - *Africa's Economic Development*. To inform on the state of the African economies (whether developing or stagnation) pre-slavery, in colonial times and recent times. This is also to enable learners to understand what has influenced the various successes and trajectories of Africa's development and growth.

- *African Economic Renaissance.* To convey the vision for African economies and economic development tasks of the African Renaissance agenda. This includes teachings on the various OAU economic pursuits and programs of actions highlighting shortcomings and successes, and teachings on the AU's economic development objectives.

- The learning process must assist learners to develop the critical consciousness required to enable them to identify economic challenges in their societies, initiate action and engage in transforming their societies.
- Economics student should be seen and should also see themselves as agents whose roles are to advance Africa's economic renaissance.
- The teacher upholds the vision of an African Economic Renaissance and in dialogue communicates this vision of better African societies with the learners as well as the tasks of the African Renaissance.
- For assessment purposes societal economic circumstance is crucial, and evaluation must be for the purpose of assisting learners in the reconstruction of their economies.

Conclusion

As the African continent trounces over the ills introduced by the many years of imperialism and colonialism the chapter recommends a sensible consideration of the role of the education system. Essentially the need for decoloniality and the adoption of an Afrocentric paradigm in African education is critical. Furthermore, for education in Africa to be relevant, it would concern itself with developing the learner to actively champion, urgently engage and be involved in achieving Africa's political, economic, social and cultural renewal. This therefore requires for the education systems in Africa to be organised with the vision of the African Renaissance motivated by the achievement of its tasks – that is an education for Africa's renaissance. In a case of curriculum ideology, it is argued that the education for Africa's renaissance must adopt the social reconstruction praxis.

References

Amin, S. 1988. *Eurocentrism*. United Kingdom: Zed Books.

Asante, M. K. 1985. Afrocentricity and Culture. In Asante, MK and Asante, KW (eds) *African Culture: The Rhythms of Unity.* United States of America: Greenwood Press. Pp 3-12.

Asante, M. K. 1991. The Afrocentric Idea in Education. *The Journal of Negro Education, 60 (2): 170-180.*

Azikiwe, A. 1968. *Renascent Africa*. London: Frank Cass & Co Ltd.

Bujra, A. (2004). 'Pan-African Political and Economic Visions of Development from the OAU to the AU: From the Lagos Plan of Action (LPA) to the New Partnership for African Development (NEPAD)', DPMF Occasional Paper, No.13, Addis Ababa: DPMF.

Department of Basic Education (2011). Curriculum and Assessment Policy Statement Grades 10-12 Economics.http://www.education.gov.za/LinkClick.aspx?fileticket=2rUGjrK%2freQ%3d&tabid=420&mid=1216. (Accessed October 2011).

Diop, C. A. 1996. *Towards the African Renaissance: Essays in Culture and Development* 1946-1960. London: Karnak House.

Freire, P. 1970. *Pedagogy of the Oppressed*. New York: The Continuum International Publishing Group Inc.

Gumede, V. 2013a. African Economic Renaissance as a Paradigm for Africa's Socio-Economic Development. In Kondlo, K (ed) *Perspectives in Thought Leadership for Africa's Renewal*, Pretoria: AISA Press. Pp 484-507.

Gumede, V. (2013b). Public Sector Reforms and Policy-making: A Case of Education in an Emerging Developmental South Africa. In A. Kanjee, M. Nkomo and Y. Sayed (eds) *The Search for Quality Education in Post-apartheid South Africa.* Pretoria: HSRC Press. Pp 61-80.

Gutto, SBO. 2006. Towards a New Paradigm for pan African Knowledge Production and Application in the Context of the African Renaissance. *International Journal of African Renaissance Studies, 1(2): 306-323.*

Higgs, P. 2003. African Philosophy and the Transformation of Educational Discourse in South Africa. *Journal of Education, 30: 5-22.*

Jansen, JD. 1990. Curriculum as Political Phenomenon: Historical Reflections on Black South African education. *The Journal of Negro Education 59(2):195-206.*

Jansen, JD., and Taylor, N. 2003. Educational Change in South Africa 1994–2003: Case studies in large scale education reform. Country Studies: Education and Management Publication Series of the World

Bank. http://www.jet.org.za/publications/research/Jansen%20and%20 Taylor_World%20Bank%20report.pdf. (Accessed April 2011).

Khoza, R. 2007. Speech to University of Limpopo at Inauguration. http:// www.ul.ac.za/application/downloads/SPEECH_TO_UNIVERSITY_ OF_LIMPOPO_AT.pdf. (Accessed April 2011).

Lewis, WA. 1955. *The Theory of Economic Growth*. London: George Allen & Unmwin Ltd.

Maloka, E.T. (n.d.). The South African 'African Renaissance' Debate: A Critique. http://www.polis.sciencespobordeaux.fr/vol8ns/maloka.pdf. (Accessed April 2011).

Mazama, A. 2001. The Afrocentric Paradigm: Contours and Definitions. *Journal of Black Studies, 31(4): 387-405.*

Mazama, A. 2003. *The Afrocentric Paradigm*. New Jersey: Africa World Press Inc,

Mbeki, T. 1999. Speech at the Launch of the African Renaissance Institute. Education for an African Renaissance: Providing Solutions for Africa. http://www.unisa.ac.za/contents/colleges/docs/tm1999/tm101109. pdf. (Accessed April 2018).

Mbeki, T. 2001. Address at the University of Havana, Cuba. http://www. unisa.ac.za/contents/colleges/docs/2001/tm2001/tm032801.pdf. (Accessed, May 2011).

Mnguni, L. (2013). The Curriculum Ideology of the South African Secondary Biology. *South African Journal of Education, 33(2):1-11.*

Mohr, P. 2005. *Economic Indicators 3rd Edition*. Pretoria: University of South Africa Press.

Mphahlela, E. 2002. *Es'kia. South Africa*: Stainbank & Associates (Pty) Ltd.

Mugo, MG. 1999. African Culture in Education for Sustainable Development. In Makgoba, Mw (ed) African Renaissance. Johannesburg: Mafube Publishing (Pty) Ltd and Tafelberg Publishers Ltd.

Nafziger, E.W. 2012. *Economic Development, 5th Edition.* New York: Cambridge University Press.

Ndlovu, M. 2014. What, Fundamentally, is pan-African Education? A De-colonial Epistemic Perspective on Education and Development in Post-colonial Africa. In Muchie, M., Gumede, V. Olukhele-Olorunju,

P. and Demissie, HT.(eds) *Unite or Perish: Africa, Fifty Years after the Founding of the Organisation of for African Unity.* Pretoria: AISA Press

New Partnership for Africa's Development. 2001. Available at: http://www.nepad.org/system/files/framework_0.pdf. (Accessed November, 2011).

Ramose, MB. 2000. 'African Renaissance' A Northbound Gaze. *Politeia, 19 (3): 47-61.*

Rodney, W. (1973). *How Europe Underdeveloped Africa.* Washington, DC: Howard University Press

Sayed, Y and Kanjee, A (2013). An Overview of Education Policy Change in post-Apartheid South Africa. In A. Kanjee, M. Nkomo and Y. Sayed (eds) *The Search for Quality Education in Post-apartheid South Africa.* Pretoria: HSRC Press.

Schiro MS. 2008. *Curriculum Theory: Conflicting Visions and Enduring Concerns.* Los Angeles, CA: Sage Publications.

Schoeman, M. 2011. The Political Economy of South Africa in a global context. In Venter, A. and Landsberg, C. (eds) *Government and politics in South Africa 4th edition.* Pretoria: Van Schaick Publishers.

Tabata, I. B. (1979). Education for Barbarism. http://www.sahistory.org.za/archive/education-barbarism-ib-tabata-october-1979. (Accessed April 2011).

The Economist. (2011). The hopeful continent: Africa rising. http://www.economist.com/node/21541015. (Accessed April 2011)

Todaro, M.P and Smith, S.C. 2009. *Economic Development 10th Edition.* England: Addison-Wesley.

Xulu, V. S. 2004). *The Place of the African Renaissance in the South African Education.* http://uzspace.uzulu.ac.za/handle/10530/562 (Accessed May 2011).

PART 2:

Democratic Governance, Peace, Security and Africa's Development

Redefining Good Governance for Africa's Development

Going beyond Mediocrity

Paul Kwengwere

Introduction

Over the past two decades, governance has become one of the most popular terms used in the development arena. It is now generally believed that there cannot be proper development without good governance (Rodrik 2008). Using governance indicators, it has been shown that most of the countries that are the worst in governance, are also performing poorly in development. With such knowledge and information, one would think that the solution to development has been found since by concentrating on governance, it would be easy to attain development. However, this hypothesis seems not to have worked for most of African countries, therefore raising the question of "what is really good governance for Africa?" This is now another major debate in development studies.

A number of western countries and international financial institutions, such as the International Monetary Fund (IMF) and the World Bank have used different initiatives to improve governance in Africa to help countries move out of poverty (Adejumobi 2006). Unfortunately, little change has taken place in most of the countries targeted[1], and some of them still appear almost in the bottom 20 of the list (for example, Chad, Ethiopia, Niger, Malawi). While this chapter analyses some of the challenges of governance in Africa, it concentrates on how the positive relationship between governance and development seems to work in some countries but fails to work in others. Using that knowledge some suggestions are made for the benefit of countries that have failed in development. The chapter also provides some suggestions to the international community, especially those dealing with aid, on how they can best utilise the situation and hence minimise the mistakes they have been making.

Why Africa?

One may ask the question "why Africa?" for this chapter. The analysis between governance and development would have been done more broadly for any group of countries in the world. However, most of the countries that are listed as poor and least developed are in Africa. Africa therefore presents a very good case, in that it is one of the heavily resourced continents but has the largest number of countries that do not perform well. At the start of the 21st Century, except for a few countries, like Mauritius, Botswana and Namibia – most of the countries in the Sub-Saharan African region were caught in a serious poverty trap. While poverty rates in East Asia declined from 77.2 percent in 1981 to 12.5 percent in 2010, and in South Asia, from 61.1 percent in 1981 to 31.0 percent in 2010; in Sub-Saharan Africa, it only reduced the $1.25-a-day per person poverty level measurement to 48.5 percent in 2010 from 51.5 percent in 1981 (World Bank 2013). Further, 22 out of the 25 poorest countries in the world are in Africa, with a population of about half a billion in extreme poverty.

The socio-economic indicators like infant mortality, life expectancy and school enrolments in Africa are equally appalling. In Sub-Saharan Africa 157 children out of 1000 die before the age of 5, and 90 out of 1000 die before the age of one. Gross primary school enrolment rate is 74%, one of the lowest in the world, and life expectancy stands at an average of 52 years. Among the ten countries with high infant mortality rates between 1995 and 2010, nine were African countries (Sierra Leone, Chad, Ginnea-Bissau, Democratic Republic of Congo, Liberia, Angola, Somalia and Niger) [2]. Over 250 million people in Africa lack access to safe drinking water and over 200 million people have no access to basic health care services (World Bank 2003).

After the introduction, this chapter looks at good governance in general terms as well as how it is perceived in Africa. It proceeds to look broadly at issues of development in Africa and how Africa has been fairing on the world map. Several indicators are used to determine where most countries in Africa are, followed by an attempt to give reasons for the general poor or good performance of some of the countries. This is followed by a look at whether good governance is the solution to Africa's problems by examining a few cases. The last section suggests some ways forward for Africa before concluding.

Good Governance

Governance is not a new phenomenon. It originated from early theories of democracy discussing the relationship between the rulers and the ruled (Golding, 1992, 84). For example, in the 19th century Woodrow Wilson defined a government that practices good governance as "a government that can properly and successfully implement a given policy…with the utmost possible efficiency and at least possible cost of either money or of energy" (Laporte 2002:3).

Overall, governance has been considered as a multidimensional concept, which consists of political, economic and socio-cultural variables that determine whether public policy designed by the government can achieve its intended goals and improve the welfare of its people (Chigbu 2010). African scholars have also been involved in developing the concept at different stages and sometimes with African perspectives. However, the qualification of the term 'good' gave birth to a whole new concept of – good governance. It is popularly asserted that the term, *good governance*, was initially articulated in a 1989 World Bank publication which identified it as a structural necessity for market reform (Chigbu 2010 :6).

In the World Bank's report 1989, *Sub-Saharan Africa: from Crisis to Sustainable Growth. A long-term perspective study*, (World Bank 1989: xii) asserted that the major cause of poor economic performance in Africa was 'the failure of public institutions' and noted that 'private sector initiative and market mechanisms are important, but must go hand-in-hand with good governance…' (World Bank 1989: xii). The main concern of authors such as Claude Ake, Waheed Oshikoya, and Gladson Kayira was that state-society relations in Africa should be developmental, democratic, and socially inclusive (Chigbu 2010 and Mkandawire 2007).

It is worth discussing, albeit briefly, Africa's history in terms of governance. Most of the countries in Africa gained independence in the late 1950 and early 1960's. Following independence most politicians were interested in 'national integration', and then, 'modernization' (Ayittey 1998). Both national integration and modernisation were not easy for the leaders as the countries were largely rural, and basically agricultural societies, governed by the new states in contradictory relations with traditional authorities who were often deemed decadent and reactionary. Between the 1960s and early 1990s a number of countries moved from the supposedly formal democratic states, which they adopted when gaining independence to autocratic and dictatorial; several went through coup d'états consequently becoming military governments. In 1990 only 4 of the 54 African countries were democratic (Ayittey 1998). By 1996, this number had grown to 14 (Botswana, Benin, Cape Verde, Central African Republic, Madagascar, Malawi, Mali, Mauritius, Namibia, Sao Tome and Principe, Senegal, Seychelles, South Africa and Zambia (Ayittey 1998).

By 2000, despite several countries practicing electoral democracy, it was clear that Africa was facing a lot of development challenges as most of the people were still trapped in poverty (Fosu 2012). This was further exacerbated by policy interventions advice from international financial institutions that felt the situation would be easily solved the way it was solved in other parts of the world (like Latin America). The road to democracy still continues to be bumpy for most African nations as they continue facing challenges. In such a situation, good governance, as politicised as it may be, requires to be understood in terms of its contribution to development.

People's perception plays an important role in defining and constructing good governance because the term can be interpreted in so many different ways, some of them vague. The Least Developing Countries (LDC) Report by United Nations Conference on Trade and Development (UNCTAD) (2009), for example, looks at 'good governance' as inevitably contestable because the goodness of governance rests on values and ethical judgment. Some of the principles mentioned include participation, fairness, decency, accountability, transparency and efficiency.

Consequently, the past two decades have seen great interest in good and quality governance. The drivers of this growth of interest are people who variously seek to monitor conditions in and/or assess prospects for diverse developing countries in terms of local political stability, investor friendliness, economic growth or effective market size, poverty reduction, respect for human rights and long term development (Arndt and Oman, 2006). This has led to overwhelming supply of indicators to measure governance.

The World Bank alone has two sets of indicators, one published bi-annually since 1996 by Daniel Kaufmann and his colleagues at the World Bank Institute, usually known as KKZ, and the other called Country Policy Institute Assessments (CPIAs), which are produced annually by the Bank's own staff. Freedom House, a private liberal advocacy organisation in the United States of America, also produces governance indicators that are widely used by journalists, analysts and academics. International investors mostly use International Country Risk Guide (ICRG) rating system, done by a privately owned firm, PRS Group, which was formed in 1980 (Howell 2001). Perhaps more important is the Ibrahim Index of

African Governance (IIAG) measure, which provides annual assessment of governance performance specifically for Africa. This is the case because Mo Ibrahim is a Sudanese-British who is genuinely connected to Africa.

The IIAG is funded and led by Mo Ibrahim Foundation. It statistically monitors African governance levels in all the countries of Africa. It basically measures governance outcomes, looking at both country and regional performances across four major categories–Safety & Rule of Law, Participation & Human Rights, Sustainable Economic Opportunity and Human Development–and 88 component indicators. The index was designed to reflect accurately the nature of governance. The idea is to be able to compare increases or declines in governance year on year. This serves two purposes: firstly, to show that Africa is not always badly governed and should not be judged by the standards only those countries experiencing severe problems. Secondly, to allow citizens of individual countries and civil society institutions to monitor accurately how well their government is doing.

Apart from targeting only African countries, IIAG has a comprehensive set of indicators under each of the four categories. For example, the safety and rule of law has four sub-categories (rule of law, accountability, personal safety and national security). Under each of the sub-categories there are at least five indicators. When we take one of the sub-categories – accountability, for example–the indicators under it are: 1) accountability, transparency and corruption in the public sector; 2) accountability, transparency and corruption in rural areas; 3) corruption and bureaucracy; 4) accountability of public officials; 5) corruption in government and public officials; and 6) prosecution of abuse of office. A comprehensive structure is in annex 2.

Although the mode of calculating indicators is different among the various institutions presented, the basics are similar. The KKZ defines governance broadly as the traditions and institutions by which authority in a country is exercised. These include the processes by which governments are selected, monitored and replaced; the capacity of the government to effectively formulate and implement sound policies; and the respect of citizens and the state for the institutions that govern economic and social interactions among them. The uses of the indicators are varied depending on the purpose of the institution. Those that look at Africa in terms of investment have tended to use specific indicators while public and aid organisations seem inclined towards World Bank's indicators.

Development in Africa

Development is a broad scholarly and enterprise discipline that became very significant in the period immediately after World War II (Rapley 2007: 1). Initially, development was largely associated with industrialisation, with the ultimate goal to raise incomes and in the process give poor people access to a range of goods and services. Over time the concept has been broadened and it covers many issues. Rios (2001) define development as an endogenous, self-managed and sustainable process. Development, according to the author, strives to improve the quality of life – material, intellectual, cultural and emotional – of the whole humanity and in particular, of those who cannot even attain the basics of biological survival due to hunger, disease and lack of nutrition and health. He mentions sustainability, as one condition of development that must exist at four levels: economic, ecological, energetic and social (or equity). One point emphasised by Rios is that "nobody is better placed than the subject of development themselves to take charge of its management in a way that is autonomous" (Rios 2001).

Africa, which is endowed with immense natural resources and human resources as well as great cultural, ecological and economic diversity, is regarded as underdeveloped. Several reasons have been put forward as causes of poverty in Africa. While it has been assumed that all parts of the world have the same prospects for economic growth and long-term development and those differences in performance are the result of differences in institutions, recent findings have suggested otherwise. There is strong evidence that geography plays an important role in shaping the distribution of world income and economic growth (Sachs et al 2001: 71-74). Africa, with 55 independent countries is the main victim of this. A good example is the analysis that looks at accessibility to sea, and the availability of mineral resources in different countries in Africa.

With about 16 landlocked countries, most African countries tend to have many challenges in transportation. This is coupled with poor infrastructure development. It was noted in 2000 that shipping a six-meter-long container from Rotterdam, the Netherlands, to Dar-es-Salaam, Tanzania—an air distance of 7,300 kilometres—was about $1,400. But transporting the same container overland from Dar-es-Salaam to Kigali, Rwanda - a distance of 1,280 kilometers by road - cost about $2,500 or nearly twice as much (Sachs 2001: 72).

Fig 1: Map of Land-Locked Countries in Africa

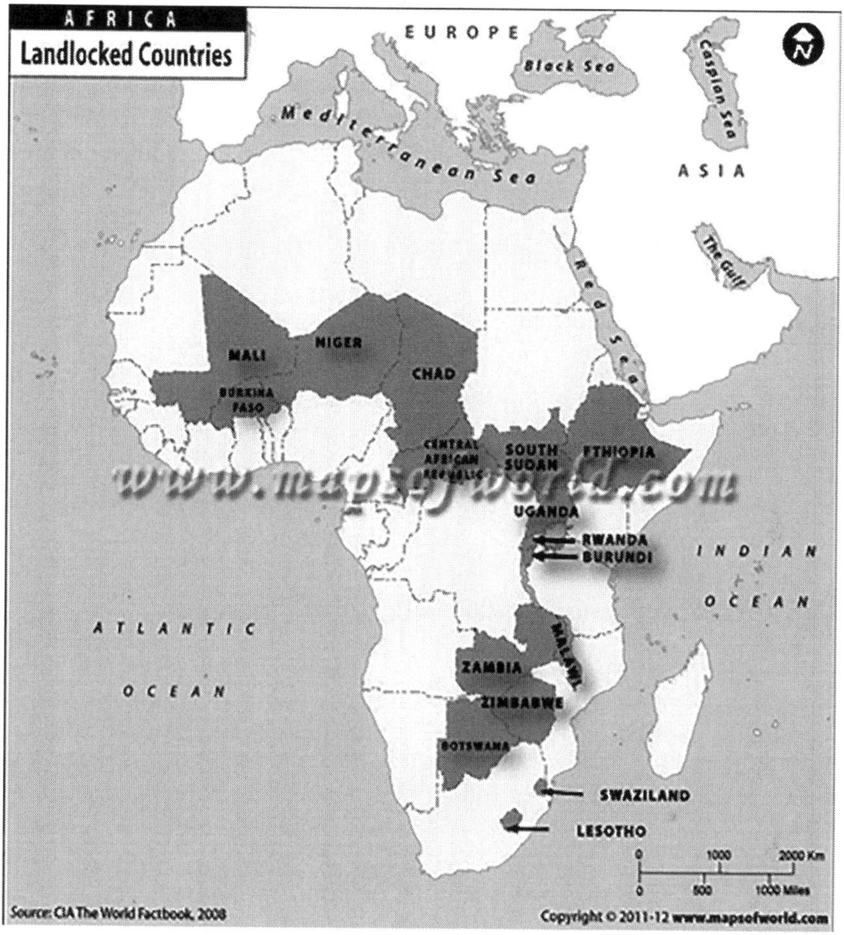

Source: CIA, The World Factbook. www.mapsofworld.com

Using the above characteristics, Collier (2010) has categorised the African countries into three main groups: resource-rich, resource-scarce but coastal, and resource-scarce and landlocked. Using the subgroups, a more detailed analysis has been done to show that economic growth for countries will depend more on whether the country is located along the coast, or it is resource rich (Collier 2007). The best-performing category globally has been the coastal resource-scarce countries of which there are many Asian examples and the worst performing category globally has been the landlocked and resource-scarce. With the unevenly distribution resources in Africa, and about a third of the countries landlocked, the development indicators seem to agree with the geographical argument.

Other scholars have expressed different views from the above explanation, and termed it 'resource curse' approach, which attempts to explain the dilemma countries like DRC, Sudan, Nigeria and Somalia are in, despite the massive resources or good geographical location. It has been argued that natural resources, while desirable in terms of the income they could bring into the country, they actually become a curse (Richard Aunty 1993). Irrespective of the fact that Africa is well endowed with resources, without peace and security there can be no economic growth. Greed among the elites is another problem.

This approach seems controversial because the results are mixed, with some countries that heavily rely on minerals not affected. Paul Collier (2010B) clarified the 'curse' to be interplay between politics and natural resources. The interplay is potentially in both directions: politics can affect the exploitation of natural assets, and natural assets can affect politics. A simple illustration is similar to a basic supply and demand curve.

Fig 2: Natural resource Effects on Political System

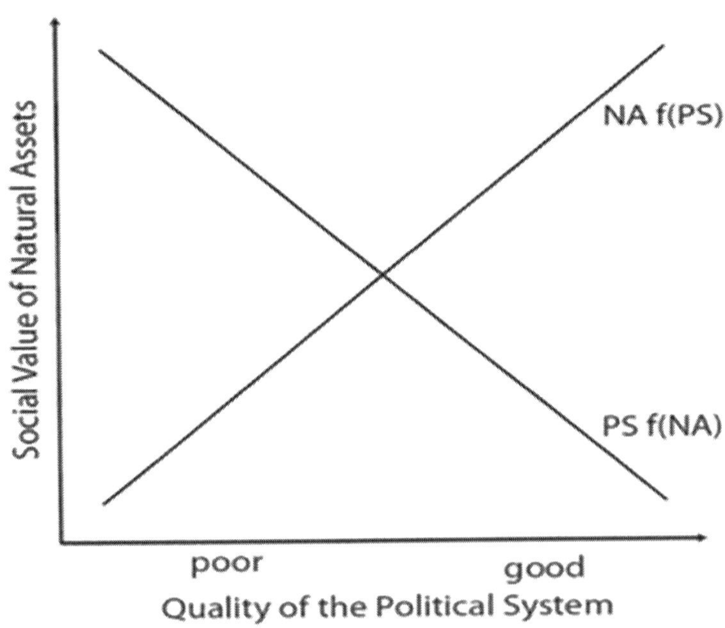

Source: Paul Coullier (2010B)

The vertical axis shows the social value of the national endowment of natural assets and the horizontal axis measures the quality of the political system, from poor to good. The graph shows that the better the system, the more able is the society to harness the potential value of its natural assets. The PS locus depicts the political system as a function of the endowment of natural assets. Needless to say, the larger the endowment present in the country, the worse the political system. In general, as with any interdependent system, in equilibrium the two relationships are resolved simultaneously.

Even though some resource rich countries like Brazil seem not to be affected by this notion, the resources available in most of the countries in Africa that are classified as less developed countries (LDCs), support the hypothesis. Out of the 49 LDCs countries in the world, over 60% are endowed with good natural resources and tend to export such resources. United Nations Conference on Trade and Development (UNCTAD) has classified the LDCs into six export specialisation categories, according to which type of exports accounted for at least 45 per cent of total exports of goods and services in 2009–2011 (shown below). The exceptions to this criterion are Bhutan, Madagascar, Mozambique, Sierra Leone and Uganda, for which a threshold of 40 per cent was used (UNCTAD 2009).

Agricultural and Food exporters: Benin, Burkina Faso, Guinea-Bissau, Kiribati, Malawi, Somalia, Uganda.
Fuel exporters: Angola, Chad, Equatorial Guinea, Sudan.
Manufactures exporters: Lesotho.
Mineral exporters: Democratic Republic of the Congo, Guinea, Mali, Mauritania, Mozambique, Sierra Leone, Zambia, Angola.
Mixed exporters: Burundi, Central African Republic, Niger, Senegal, Togo, United Republic of Tanzania.
Services exporters: Djibouti, Eritrea, Ethiopia, Gambia, Liberia, Madagascar, Nepal, Rwanda, Sao Tome and Príncipe.

Is Good Governance the Panacea to Africa's Development?

The introduction of Poverty Reduction Strategy Papers (PRSP) seem to be the major starting point when governance institutions (though mostly based in the North[3]) felt good governance is the solution to the development problems by poor countries (Adejumobi 2007). However, prior to PRSP the Brandt report (Mesbahi 2006) and the introduction of

Structural Adjustment Programmes (SAPs) played major roles in ushering in the discourse on good governance. The PRSP came in after general failure[4] of the SAPs prescribed to the majority of African countries after the oil crisis which hit most developing world in the 1980s. The SAPs main intention was reduction of state control with the emphasis being on private enterprises as drivers of economic growth. SAPs had severe negative effects on people's livelihoods in many African countries; they ended up increasing the rate of unemployment, deteriorated income levels, undermined the provision of social services, promoted inflation, and exacerbated income inequalities – neither the rural poor nor the urban working class benefited from SAPs (Mkandawire and Olukoshi 1995; Adejumobi 2007).

Despite the fact that most countries targeted for PRSPs were having poverty and development problems, the unique feature of PRSP was not so much focusing on poverty reduction, but the process by which it sought to achieve it. This was through the participatory element of PRSPs, considered to have far reaching implications for governance. PRSPs emphasised stakeholders' participation especially of the civil society in defining the poverty agenda. They sought to create national consensus, giving voice and power to the people on how their lives could be improved. PRSPs developed a procedure intended to lead African governments into democratic patterns of behaviour, through deliberation, negotiation, and participative enquiry. By 2004, 22 African countries had full PRSP[5].

After over a decade since the PRSPs were introduced, there is some doubt whether they really achieved the ultimate goal of improving development in most of the African countries. The main point of the chapter is to seek to understand what Africa is missing. If governance is considered the solution to development, how come most African countries that seem to have good governance are still characterised with poverty and underdevelopment?

How have some countries (Botswana, Mauritius, Democratic Republic of Congo(DRC) and Zambia) faired?

The popular success stories often cited among African countries include Botswana, Cape Verde, Namibia, and Mauritius. Understanding how some of these countries moved from low income countries can give proper insight about development tips in relation to governance if indeed governance played a major role. And what makes them so different from those countries that are not doing well like DRC or Somalia? Is it basically the 'resource curse' playing its role? But what about countries like Malawi, Zambia and Tanzania that seem to be doing fairly well in terms of governance but remain in the lower half of the human development index? The focus below is on Botswana, Mauritius, DRC and Zambia.

Botswana

Botswana is taken as one of the super success stories of Africa. When Botswana achieved self-rule in 1965 and independence in 1966 its social indicators were appalling. It had around 22 university graduates, 13 kilometres of paved road and its per capita income was estimated at US$ 60 or at most US$80 (Sebudubudu 2010). Today Botswana's per capita is in excess of $5,700, graduated from Least Developed Countries and boasts of a stable democracy. Several countries in Africa boast of stable democracy and are no different from Botswana in terms of resources but are not anywhere near Botswana's prosperity.

There are a number of things Botswana put in place to reach the current status. It has used its valuable resources quite well. Apart from that, the government has put in place strong institutions to deal with accountability and transparency. According to Sebudubudu (2010) Botswana has a broad framework of third generation or what has been dubbed 'watchdog institutions' in the form of the anti-corruption body, the ombudsman, the independent electoral commission and the relatively elaborate and independent media. The constitution also empowers the auditor general, accountant general and the parliamentary committees to inspect and report on the state and use of public accounts in all government departments and parastatal organizations.

Undeniably, the production of diamonds in Botswana has had a remarkable impact on the economy. Leadership qualities, a reasonable human rights record and other democratic achievements have prevented natural resource abundance from turning into a curse for Botswana. However, a few contradictions still exist – inequality (the gini coefficient at 0.54 at the beginning of the 21st century) and there are still pockets of poverty in some places (Mokhawa 2005). Nevertheless, the situation is better than most nations in Africa.

Mauritius

Similar to Botswana, Mauritius is one of the countries that is both on top of most governance index lists as well as doing well economically. Unlike Botswana, its success has mainly been due to trade and tourism and partly due to geographical location.

Good and strong institutions supported by a vibrant civil society have also helped Mauritius maintain positive growth and prosperity. The country has been holding regular multiparty elections since independence; made sure that the basic freedoms, rights of individuals, rule of law, and independent media are maintained. Elections are organized in a transparent manner, and have been accepted as free and fair by all, winners and losers. Elections are done through an independent electoral commission, managed by an electoral commissioner who is appointed by the Judicial and Legal Service Commission. Mechanisms of accountability and transparency are provided for in the constitution, including provisions for the functioning of parliament. The office of Director of Audit is independent of the executive and is answerable only to parliament. The department of the Director of Audit scrutinises the accounts of government and the Director gives his/her report, more often critical than not, to the parliament. The Auditor General's report is laid in parliament. It is given wide publicity by the press, and is generally an instrument of action for the opposition.

Most countries in Africa have failed to maintain independence of such positions and institutions, where the head of state appoints most critical positions, thereby making the President's office and all cabinet members (or most senior party members) immune from scrutiny.

DRC

In terms of valuable mineral resources, DRC is one of the richest countries in the world, far more than Botswana. DRC has been assessed as one of the top five countries in the world with minerals. Furthermore, it has huge arable land, next to Brazil, and is geographically located in an area where water resources are not a problem. The DRC's water resources alone could solve Africa's energy challenges through hydroelectric power; and the agricultural prospects, if realized, could feed the whole of African continent[6]. However, DRC ranks at the bottom (or almost occasionally) of the list in every indicator.

Unlike Botswana, DRC has been going through many problems since colonial times. Overexploitation of resources, mainly by foreign capital, worst dictatorship and continuous armed conflicts are some of the problems.

Even though, arguably, DRC's political system may be representative there is a lot of uncertainties in the country such that investors (local or foreign) tend to be hesitant to invest. The major lesson here about putting in place proper institutions can be emphasised. Despite a good political system on paper, the country is now rated one of the worst in terms of governance (Shekhawat 2009). Where there is constant civil unrest, little is done to address these problems effectively. Civil society operates in a state of fear because the government can decide to silence the activists or groups who are in the forefront criticising it.

Recently (August 2013), a member of the Congolese National Assembly was sentenced to three years in prison by the country's Supreme Court for allegedly 'scandalising' the President of the Republic and 'demoralising' government troops fighting rebels in the eastern DRC battlefront. MP Muhindo Nzangi, member of the Social Movement for Renewal (*Mouvement Social pour le Renouveau*–MSR), which is part of President Joseph Kabila's ruling coalition, was arrested following his participation in an interactive radio programme broadcast in Goma[7]. Mr Nzangi is an elected representative of the city of Goma, the capital of North Kivu province. If freedom of speech is not entertained for an MP who is part of the government's coalition in his constituency, it would be even harder for civil society or members of the opposition to criticise the government and live freely. The 2011 results of President Joseph Kabila's election have been questioned.

Zambia

Zambia, though with a stable political system and with good copper deposits seems to be far away from Botswana, even though it has equally enjoyed stability. However, the liberalisation of the economy in the 1980s and massive corruption after the multiparty dispensation brought down the momentum of growth. Zambia's second president and the first in the multiparty era, died while being tried for corruption – he also tried to change the constitution to extend his term in office beyond what the constitution provided for[8] . Nevertheless, with recent developments, the passing on power peacefully to an opposition party/president after a legacy of one-party rule may increase investor confidence. IHS Global Insight's Country Risk Ratings[9], downgraded Zambia's risk score from 'significant' for over a decade to the improved rating of 'medium' in late 2011. So, while political uncertainty is a negative for foreign investors, when industry analysts see evidence that political plurality can be expressed in a smooth leadership transition, the result is a net positive (GGA 2013).

Unlike Botswana that has heavily benefited from diamonds, Zambia (and even DRC) suffers from a serious inability to collect taxes. In Zambia, for instance, the mining industry accounts for about 80% of the country's export earnings but only 2% of the government's annual revenue. According to GGA (2013), the situation is suspected to be as severe in the DRC, if not worse. There is a dearth of legitimate governmental authority in the provinces as well as low technical knowledge of the mining sector. This translates into a government that cannot adequately assess the levels of production within the sector and therefore has no benchmark for determining what to tax.

While little is being done to rectify the situation in DRC, Zambia is now participating in the Extractive Industries Transparency Initiative (EITI), a voluntary programme in which countries and companies publish their payments and revenues. As a result, it has discovered how large the gap is between what is collected and what should be collected, motivating the government to act. More tax revenue means more money to spend on infrastructure such as roads, rail and power distribution. It is an example of good governance promoting a better business environment for investors and a better quality of life for citizens.

General Overview

Cases of mismanagement of funds, corruption, and clinging on to power by presidents are not uncommon in Africa. Transparency International (TI) estimates that corruption in Africa siphons off 20 to 30 per cent of finances earmarked for basic services. Many newspapers and studies have reported that African leaders appropriate billions of dollars every year from their economically strapped countries. In 1991, United Nations estimated that the ruling elites drained more than $200 billion out of Africa annually. The past president of Malawi (a neighbouring country to Zambia), Dr Bingu Wa Mutharika is accused of amassing over $170m during the 7 years he ruled the country, approximately 10% of country's overall annual budget[10]. Another previous president's case for a similar charge has been on-going for over 10 years.

The 'Resource Curse' as noted earlier has played a role in most of the African countries. However, in Botswana, the resources have had an opposite effect, or the expected proper effect – rather than leading to rent seeking, the resources have led to quality leadership, prudence management and good negotiation skills. The 50-50% shareholding between De Beers and the government of Botswana has been rated to be one of the best ever secured between a developing country government and a major multinational mining company. This has been because the country has used the resources effectively in the development of the country through good prudent macro-economic management: good planning, adjustment policies that affect exchange rate, and dealing with inflation. Most of the policies have been locally owned and less reliant on external advice. While most countries in Sub-Saharan Africa were going through the World Bank/IMF SAPs and Poverty Reduction Strategy Papers, Botswana concentrated on their own planning, improving key sectors like education and productivity, much similar to the East Asian Nearly Industrialised Countries (NICs).

Civil Society and media independence have not tended to work in most of the African countries. Prior to change of power, there tends to be good voices of civil society, but in most cases, these voices are silenced thereafter. For example, in Benin the movement challenging the human rights abuses slowed down considerably when President Boni Yayi's cabinet included no less than three ministers from civil society coalition that campaigned against the amendment of the Constitution to ensure that the candidate did not compete against Benin's other political formations (Adjolohoun 2013). The consequence of this debacle is the weakening of independent critical voices in society. Just a few years after campaigning strongly against any revision, civil society leaders turned into proponents of such revision.

Some lessons from East Asian Newly Industrialised Countries (NICs)

The NICs under consideration here are China, Singapore and Taiwan.

With the huge influence China and a few other Asian countries have on Africa, we would be missing the point if we looked at Africa's governance and development without looking at some of the effects from these Asian countries. It is quite clear that examples of East Asian NICs and that of the People's Republic of China do not really demonstrate that democracy or governance as advocated by the Western countries is a precondition for economic development. Some of these Asian countries have moved to middle income and/or industrialised levels with record speeds.

In China and the other East Asian NICs most of the policies adopted were production focused. The emphasis was on expanding employment opportunities and labour productivity, thereby increasing living standards. Policies further encouraged structural transformation, a process in which the relative importance of agriculture and primary commodity extraction declined within the economy while that of manufacturing industries increased, and in which production processes progressed from less to more skill-, technology- and capital-intensive activities. Contrary to western perception of some complex measures in order to grow, most of these countries used deliberate strategy approach. In a cross country analysis of the NICs, Rodrik found a relationship between institutions and growth and that "large-scale institutional transformation is hardly a prerequisite for getting growth going. The initial spurt in growth can be achieved with minimal changes in institutional arrangements. Countries do not need an extensive set of institutional reforms in order to start growing" (Rodrik 2007: 191).

The success story in China rests in making sure any reforms fit their situation before adopting them. For example, when the IMF introduced liberalisation as one way of improving the economies, instead of liberalising interest rates over two or three years (like what many other countries did), Chinese officials are still busy with reforms today. They have used the time to learn about common mistakes, experiment with different options, and fit new solutions into the particular context (Andrews 2012). That way the country's financial sector was able to weather the financial crisis well.

Way Forward for Africa

On its own, good governance without practical commitment from the people in power may not be the ultimate solution to development. So many countries could claim good governance but if there is little commitment by general leadership and no proper institutions put in place, the chances of improvement in development are minimal. The case of Botswana presents an interesting scenario, because, just like most African countries a lot can be said about its governance flaws.

Sebudubudu (2010) cites some corruption scandals in Botswana; some of these include failure to implement the declaration of assets and liabilities by the leaders, and autocratic tendencies within the ruling party where some members are suspended because of having or expressing publicly different views from the leader. When in 2005 the then Botswana-based Professor Kenneth Good described governance in the country as controlled by an elite that manipulated state media and largely ignored rural development, he was (tellingly) kicked out of the country (GGA 2013). All these would have been highly featured areas of criticism and reasons for failure if the country had not been doing well. However, the presence of established institutions and the rule of law, good education system that has improved the literacy rates [to over 90%] compared to 25% in the 60s – all these have helped the country to move forward.

Governance reforms are always high on the political agenda, but making them work for the reduction of poverty and development requires specific actions. Overcoming the political economic challenges of governance reforms is often the most difficult task, because even if promising reform options are identified, they are often considered too costly or too contentious. Birner (2011) summarises some of the experiences that can help improve pro-poor governance. Even though her thesis has more emphasis on governance to improve hunger and poverty, these discussed below are the main pillars when we talk about development in most African countries.

- *Moving from 'one-size-fits-all' to 'good-fit' approaches.* Governance reforms work only if they are tailored to country- and sector-specific conditions.
- *Promoting experimentation and learning.* Because reforming governance is complex, it is useful to provide scope for experimentation and learning and to use approaches that are flexible enough to allow for adjustments over time.
- *Combining demand-and supply-side approaches.* Various strategies to reform governance can reinforce each other. Particularly promising is combining demand-side approaches that give the poor more voice with supply-side approaches that give public administration the capacity and incentive to respond to the needs of the poor.
- *Creating an enabling environment.* Both demand-side and supply-side approaches to governance reform depend on an enabling policy environment.
- *Strengthening leadership.* Governance reforms require leadership from political decision makers, members of public administration (supply side), and civil society (demand side).
- *Coordinating and aligning donors.* Although governance reforms, as political and social processes, are ultimately driven by a country's citizens and their leaders, donors can play an important role. Coordination of donor activities and alignment with country-owned strategies and programmes, as expressed in the 'Paris Declaration on Aid Effectiveness', is particularly important in promoting governance reforms.

- *Mainstreaming poverty in all governance reforms.* Mainstreaming a focus on poverty in all types of governance reforms is necessary to prevent the poor from losing out in the reform process.

From the aid point of view, similar factors have been pointed out in order to make good governance effective in development. Carothers and Gramont (2011) have looked at the evolution of governance and aid. They acknowledge that improved governance is not as straight forward in providing development progress, as many aid practitioners would wish. Eight insights proposed for governance and aid include:

- Governance deficiencies are often primarily political and cannot be resolved through technical assistance alone.
- Fostering citizen demand for better governance is as important as top down efforts aimed at improving the 'supply' of governance.
- Governance of aid may be more effective at the local level than at the national level.
- Despite the intuitive appeal of governance best practices, concentrating on locally determined 'best fit' may be more productive.
- Informal institutions are a central part of the governance puzzle and cannot be treated as developmental marginalia.
- Governance concerns should be integrated into the full range of assistance programming.
- Donor countries should address international drivers of poor governance.
- Aiding governance effectively requires development agencies to rethink their own internal governance.

Carothers and Gramont (2011) have termed this as the second generation set of governance is drawn from formal research findings, but most emerged directly from the accumulated experiences, especially the frustrations, of practitioners. This new generation of governance aid seeks to be more politically attuned in conception and implementation, to address demand for governance alongside supply, to reach the local level as much as or more than the national level, to push for institutional change that best fits local circumstances, to take into account informal institutions, to integrate a governance focus into traditional aid sectors, to address international causes of poor governance alongside domestic ones, and to modify internal donor governance to allow for the positive adaptation to these new principles.

Table 1: Evolutionary Path of Governance Assistance

First Generation	Second Generation
Technocratic Assistance	Politically informed assistance
Focus on Supply	Incorporate demand side approaches
Central institutions	Add local focus
Best practices	Best fit streaming from best practices
Formal institutions	Incorporate informal institutions
Standalone programs	Integrated programs
Focus on domestic determinants	Include international factors
Existing aid mechanisms	Renovated aid mechanisms

In looking at the way forward for Africa, the solution lies more within Africa than imported agendas. A key lesson of many decades of donor assistance has been that if interventions are not domestically owned, they will not have much impact. Each African country or group of African countries has unique features depending on many factors, including location, resource availability, historical background, cultural issues, colonisation experience etc. What may work in some countries may not necessarily work in others. However, there are some common denominators that are important and it would be necessary that when talking about good governance, these should not be compromised. As already shown in this analysis most African countries are failing to develop not because they have not put proper institutions in place but because those in power tend to be the first ones not to abide by the principles of those institutions. Corruption, accountability and the rule of law tend to be phrases that do not apply to most African leaders and the lieutenants surrounding them. Some of the specific areas that need to be considered seriously for Africa are in three-fold (national, regional and from development partners' point of view) as summarised below:

National Levels

Recognition of different players in development is very vital for the country to make progress in development. Most of the countries in Africa have good institutions that relate to good governance (good constitution, great policies), but do not make the effort to follow what is in such constitutions and policies. Furthermore, other key players in development, like civil society, private sector and the media are given little space.

The question of how the civil society can play this role has been a major debate. Being independent and the ability to give constructive criticism is most usually the best. However, many times governments tend to silence the critical views of civil society by offering the critical members of the civil society positions in the government. Once civil society is getting good funding from government, it becomes less critical because its sustainability is at stake should the government suddenly stop funding. It is important for civil society and media to build resilience and rely on the private sector, at the same time governments should provide the necessary environment and space.

The countries also need to look back at the history, and consider home grown solutions that have been in existence before. For example, most of the countries have thrived over time through informal institutions, but now tend to neglect such a sector which can play a role in solving the unemployment problem. In some countries, the roles of the chiefs that played major roles in governance are completely neglected, sometimes leading to internal conflicts (Bujra 2002). The governments' failures to deal with such conflicts have led to the derailment of most development projects, thereby reducing the overall progress. The countries need to take special care in respecting cultures in relation to good governance.

Areas that need to special attention at country level include:

- Make the institutions as Anti-corruption bureaus, ombudsman, and auditor general be independent from the government of the day in order to have maximum accountability;
- There should be respect of human rights and full participation by the countries' citizens in different initiatives that promote development such as free and fair elections, freedom of association etc;
- Provide an environment that gives citizens economic opportunities to prosper, especially in the rural areas where the majority of Africans live and have problems making ends meet; and
- Access to social services should be uniform to all citizens regardless of location or political affiliation – this will help in human development, one of the major ingredients to development.

Sub-Regional and Regional Levels

The sub-regional groupings should be effective in following up on countries that are slack in governance. In most cases, these groupings have tended to be talk shows, with little or no action when the member countries are going astray. Many good initiatives are introduced but no proper efforts are made to see them work effectively. Charters (like the SADC Charter of fundamental social rights) could help improve governance and lead to development for some countries. The African Peer Review Mechanism (APRM), African Governance Architecture, all seem to have good intentions but there is no effective mechanism in place to initiated compliance.

Development Partners

The development partners should respect home grown solutions in governance rather than impose solutions. While good governance should be integrated into the assistance programmes, the local involvement should be paramount in defining the parameters of good governance. All the areas identified earlier on should be taken into consideration, including having politically informed assistance; incorporating demand side of approaches, and most important, have a local focus.

Conclusion

Governance remains one of the important ingredients to Africa's development. Only a few countries out of the 55 African countries, are effectively utilising good governance and having good results. In the countries where good governance is functional, proper reforms have taken place and most of the principles of governance are respected and practiced. The cases of Botswana and Mauritius as have been discussed as indicative examples. Furthermore, the countries have come up with their own plans adapting to the local conditions. In the other countries where development is lagging, on the other hand, even though they have most of the institutions that define good governance in place, they have hardly adopted proper mechanisms to enhance practice. Corruption is rampart, the rule of law is not respected, and national planning is mostly imported. The author has posited that as much as good governance is a solution to development, most African countries seem to be missing the point by expecting that by putting mere institutions in place alone will change the situation. There is need for practical policy implementation and willingness from the leadership to adopt reforms/ recommendations for good governance to be effective.

Notes and References

1 Several countries went through the Poverty Reduction Strategy process in Africa. According to Adejumobi (2006) by October 2004 about 22 countries had full PRSP – see section 4 below (endnote 5).

2 This is using United Nations Population Division Infant mortality rate (deaths/1000 births). Countries are ranked based on 1995-2010 average calculated in order to make the rank more independent from fluctuations in any single (most recent) column. See http://data.worldbank.org/indicator/SP.DYN.IMRT.IN.

3 Here the North implies the countries in the North hemisphere, which are mostly developed countries, a contrast to countries in the South that are mainly underdeveloped.

4 The general consensus among most scholars in Africa is that SAPs were a failure even though few have attributed economic growth in the 1980s to SAPs. See Fosu, 2012.

5 The 22 countries included: Burkina Faso, The Ghambia, Guinea, Malawi, Mauritania, Mozambique, Niger, Rwanda, Tanzania, Uganda, Zambia, Benin, Cameroon, Chad, Ethiopia, Ghana, Mali, Senegal, Djibouti, Madagastcar and Kenya. see Adejumobi S 2006. Governance and Poverty Reduction in Africa: A critique of the Poverty Reduction Strategy Papers (PRSP). ECOWAS.

6 See Global governance Africa. http://gga.org/analysis/prospecting-for-better-governance-in-the-democratic-republic-of-congo.

7 See http://www.africareview.com/News/DRC+MP+jailed+for+scandalising+Kabila/-/979180/1956106/-/a2ywcaz/-/index.

8 The Constitution provides for a maximum of two terms for the president.

9 IHS Global Insight is a country intelligence group that provides constantly updated analysis of business conditions, economic prospects and risks in over 200 countries. See www.ihs.com.

10 See Nyasatimes: http://www.nyasatimes.com/2013/07/02/probe-discovers-bingus-worth-more-than-k61bn-property-accounts-in-singapore-australia-and-isle-of-man/

Adejumobi, S. 2006. *Governance and poverty reduction in Africa: a critique of the poverty reduction strategy papers (PRSP).* Lagos, Nigeria: ECOWAS

Adjolohoun, H. S. 2013. Between presidentialism and a human rights approach to constitutionalism: twenty years of practice and the dilemma of revising the 1990 constitution of Benin. In Mbondeyi, M.K

& Ojienda, T. 2013. *Constitutionalism and Democratic Governance in Africa: Contemporary Perspectives from Sub-Saharan Africa. RSA*: Pretoria University Law Press. (Pages 245-288)

Andrews, M. 2013. *The limits of institutional reform in development: changing rules for realistic solutions.* New York: Cambridge University Press

Arndt, C & Oman, C. 2006. *Uses and abuses of governance indicators.* Paris: OECD Development Centre.

Ayittey, G. 1998. *Africa in chaos*. New York: St Martin"s Press.

Birner, R. 2007. *Improving governance to eradicate hunger and poverty.* No BB33 Special Edition. 2020 focus brief the world's poor and hungry people. Washington DC. International Food Policy Research Institute (IFPRI).

Booth, D. 2011. *Governance for development in Africa: Building on what works.* Policy Brief 1. London: Overseas Development Institute, Africa Power and Politics Program.

Bujra, A. 2002. *African conflicts: their causes and their political and social environment.* Occasional paper No 4. Nairobi: Development Policy Management Forum (DPMF).

Carothers, T & Gramont D. 2011. *Aiding governance in developing countries: progress amid uncertainties.* Washington DC: Carnergie Endowment for Peace.

Chigbu, UE. 2010. *Addressing good governance in Africa.* AGGN Research and Publication Committee. www.aggn.org

Collier, P. 2010A. *Poverty reduction in Africa. CSAE.* Oxford

Collier, P. 2010B. The political economy of natural resources. *Social Research* 77 (4)

Collier, P. & Goderis B. 2007. Commodity prices, growth and the natural resource curse: reconciling a conundrum. Oxford. *CSAE.*

Fosu, A. K. 2012. The African economic growth record, and the role of policy syndromes and governance. In Noman, A, Botchwey, K, Stein, H & Stiglitz J E (ed) 2012. *Good growth and governance in Africa.* Oxford: Oxford University Press. Pp 175-220.

GGA. 2013. Good governance Africa analysis. http://gga.org/analysis/prospecting-for-better-governance-in-the-democratic-republic-of-congo

Golding. S 1992. *Gramsci's democratic theory: contributions to a post-liberal democracy.* Toronto: University of Toronto Press.

Howell, L.D. 2001. *The handbook of country and political risk analysis. Third Edition*. New York: The PRS Group.

Kaufmann, D, Kraay, A, & Mastruzzi, M. 2009. Governance matters VIII: aggregate and individual governance indicators, 1996-2008. Washington DC: *World Bank Policy Research.* Working Paper No. 4978.

Kwengwere, P. 2010. Inequality in Malawi. In Jauch, H & Muchena, D (eds.), *Tearing us apart: Inequalities in Southern Africa.* Windhoek: Labour Resource and Learning Institute, pp 123-172.

LaPorte, Robert, Jr. 2002. *Governance: a global perspective.* Paper presented at the South Asia Regional Conference of the Herbert H. Humphrey Fellowship Program, Kathmandu, Nepal, February 20, 2002. http://www.fulbrightnepal.org.np. Retrieved on 20th June 2013.

Mesbahi, H. 2006. The Brandt Report. http://www.sharing.org/information-centre/articles/brandt-report

Mkandawire, T & Olukoshi A. 1995. *Between liberalisation and oppression: the politics of structural adjustment in Africa.* Dakar: Council for Development of Social Science Research in Africa (CODESRIA).

Mkandawire, T. 2007. Good governance: the itinerary of an idea. *Development in Practice* 17. (4 & 5) 679 – 681.

Mokhawa, G. 2005. All that glitters is not diamond: the politics of diamond dependence and abundance in Botswana. In Basedau, Matthias; Mehler, Andreas (eds.), *Resource politics in Sub-Saharan Africa.* Hamburg: Institute of African Affairs, pp. 105-120.

Noman, A, Botchwey, K, Stein, H & Stiglitz J E (ed) 2012. *Good growth and governance in Africa*. Oxford: Oxford University Press.

Rapley, D 2007. *Understanding development: theory and practice in the third world.* Colorado: Lynne Rienner Publishers

Rios, J M C 2001. *Development, communication, information and training.* Research Institute for Development Communication (Runa). http://www.asociacionmapu.org/index.php?option=com_content&view=article&id=6%3Adesarrollo-bien-entendido&catid=2%3Aquienes-somos&Itemid=35&lang=en.

Rodrik, D. 2008. Thinking about governance in *Governance, Growth, and Development Decision-making.* Washington, D.C: World Bank, 2008: 19–20.

Sachs JD, Mellinger, AD & Gallup, JL. 2001. The geography of poverty and wealth. *Scientific American*, 284(3) 70-75.

Sebudubudu, D. 2010. The impact of good governance on development and poverty in Africa: Botswana - a relatively successful African initiative. *African Journal of Political Science and International Relations*. Vol. 4(7) 249-262.

Shekhawat, S. 2009. *Governance crisis and conflict in the Democratic Republic of Congo.* University of Mumbai. *Working Paper No. 6.*

UN. 2013. *Least developed countries.* http://www.un.org/special-rep/ohrlls/ldc/list.htm

UNCTAD. 2009. The least developed countries report 2009: the state and development governance. New York and Geneva: United Nations Conference on Trade and Development, available at < http://www.unctad.org/en/docs/ldc2009_en.pdf >

World Bank. 1989. *Sub-saharan Africa: from crisis to sustainable development.* New York: Oxford University Press.

World Bank: 1991. The Conable Years at the World Bank: Major Policy Addresses of Barber B Conable Jr., Washington, DC: World Bank

World Bank. 2003. *Progress on poverty reduction, 1998-2000.* Washington, DC: World Bank.

World Bank. 2013. Information on poverty. www.worldbank.org/poverty.

Mo Ibrahim Foundation. *2012 Ibrahim index of African governance summary.* Swindon: Mo Ibrahim Foundation.

Annex 2: 2012 IBRAHIM INDEX OF GOVERNANCE

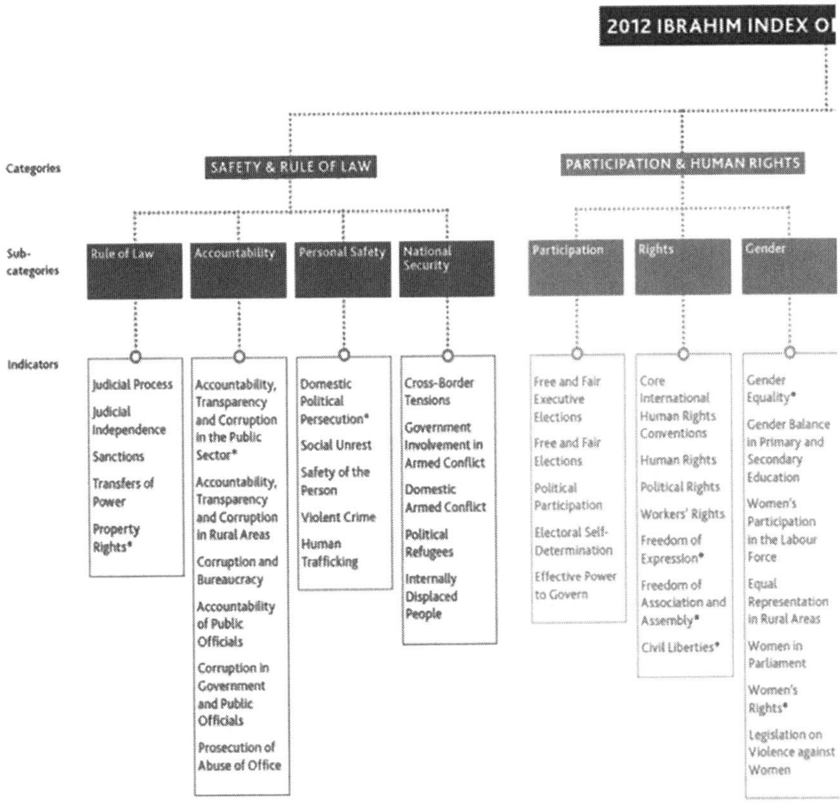

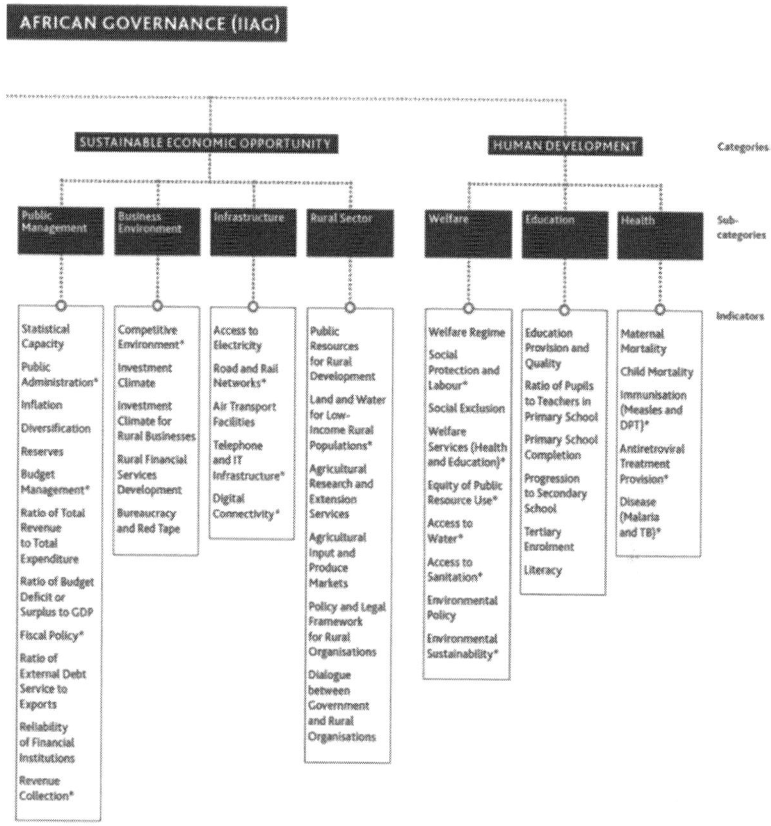
AFRICAN GOVERNANCE (IIAG)
SUSTAINABLE ECONOMIC OPPORTUNITY
HUMAN DEVELOPMENT
Categories
Public Management
Business Environment
Infrastructure
Rural Sector
Welfare
Education
Health
Sub-categories
Indicators
Statistical Capacity
Public Administration*
Inflation
Diversification
Reserves
Budget Management*
Ratio of Total Revenue to Total Expenditure
Ratio of Budget Deficit or Surplus to GDP
Fiscal Policy*
Ratio of External Debt Service to Exports
Reliability of Financial Institutions
Revenue Collection*
Competitive Environment*
Investment Climate
Investment Climate for Rural Businesses
Rural Financial Services Development
Bureaucracy and Red Tape
Access to Electricity
Road and Rail Networks*
Air Transport Facilities
Telephone and IT Infrastructure*
Digital Connectivity*
Public Resources for Rural Development
Land and Water for Low-Income Rural Populations*
Agricultural Research and Extension Services
Agricultural Input and Produce Markets
Policy and Legal Framework for Rural Organisations
Dialogue between Government and Rural Organisations
Welfare Regime
Social Protection and Labour*
Social Exclusion
Welfare Services (Health and Education)*
Equity of Public Resource Use*
Access to Water*
Access to Sanitation*
Environmental Policy
Environmental Sustainability*
Education Provision and Quality
Ratio of Pupils to Teachers in Primary School
Primary School Completion
Progression to Secondary School
Tertiary Enrolment
Literacy
Maternal Mortality
Child Mortality
Immunisation (Measles and DPT)*
Antiretroviral Treatment Provision*
Disease (Malaria and TB)*

Constitutional Democratic Governance in Need of Checks and Balances of Powers in Africa

Joy Alemazung

Introduction

Democratic states are not by nature free states except the state institutions and governmental apparatus is so constituted that no leader can carry out actions which the law does not permit or abstain from actions which the law permits and still go on without the possibility of being called to account for his/her action: for example, by voting him/her out of power. Even in successful western democracies, experience has shown that a human being is apt to abuse the power he/she is invested with, and would carry authority as far as it can go (Montesquieu 1784). The weakness of institutions like the legislative, the judiciary and similar organs to check 'super power and authority', and power misuse in Africa has rendered many governments 'valueless' with regards to serving their people. In other words, ineffective division of power has robbed governments of their normative function to the extent that efforts to make them regain their normative value and reasons for existence require pressure, time and patience (Anyan'g-Nyong'o's 1987). Unfortunately, the resultant struggle to give back power to the people and established governments that serve the people who perform their duties and responsibilities towards their people for the common good in many instances result to conflicts and loss of lives (Shah 2005).

The absence of functional political institutions (notably vibrant independent judiciary and legislative and electoral bodies) in Africa has rendered constitutionalism futile, resulting in strong men versus weak systems. These strong men in the likes of Mobutu Sese Seko of Zaire [now Democratic Republic of Congo (DRC)], Jean Bedel Bokassa of Central

African Republic, Idi Amin Dada of Uganda, Gnassimgbe Eyadema of Togo, Omar Bongo of Gabon, Robert Mugabe of Zimbabwe (the list goes on) have oppressed their people through authoritative rule, despotic actions, arbitrary power, servitude, destructive degrees of corruption, oppression and the forfeiture of liberty and freedom of their people (see Berdal and Malone 2000; Rothe and Mullins 2008; Yeboah 2005). Unfortunately for the people on the continent, these strong men in many countries do not only seize the opportunity of the weak institutions and non-separation of power resulting to lack of constitutionalism to fortify their grip to power but also to amass state wealth at the cost of the people. As a result Africa, despite being one of the richest continents in natural and human resources, remains the economically and socially poorest as well as politically unstable continent on the face of the earth (Africa in Fact 2012). A World Bank report of 1989 traced poverty, conflicts, crises and under-development in Africa back to what it termed as the 'crises of government' and later on bad governance in Africa. The analysis therefore focuses on the impact of non-separation of powers in Africa and examines the role and importance of these democratic institutions (with checks and balances). It considers the kind of political order and institutional arrangements which, according to the argument presented could safeguard functional democratic states and encourage as well as facilitate better governance if established on the continent. It further argues that the right kind of political order and institutional arrangement with effective division of power not only matter but also that the separation of powers in Africa must go beyond the standard judiciary, executive and legislative model to include independent electoral commission and effective constitutional courts. The contribution also asserts that Africa must learn from the failures of the past, that is, from weak or non-existing institutions to check and balance power that resulted to excessive power abuse, as well as consider its African particularities in the area of culture, people, environment and societal and traditional leadership values in the establishment of democratic institutions and states that would preserve the lives, liberty and property of African people: the extent and ends of governments.

The arguments are organised in two parts. The first part analyses the need to learn from the failures of the past. Towards this end, we begin with the origins of the problems of government and leadership based upon the weaknesses or absence of effective institutions with separation of powers - the importance of history. The second part considers and proposes solutions to the political and governance problems. This section presents consensus democracy based on proportional representation as appropriate for segmented societies like those on the continent. It examines the constitutions and institutional arrangement as well as the democratic solution with separation of power, reconstitution of the political order as an appropriate option for a functional democratic solution. The arguments presented in this section are based upon case studies of successful democracies on the continent. The studies show the kind of institutional arrangement necessary for functional government as well as proposals on how these can be achieved in Africa. The third and last part presents the conclusion as well as future perspectives.

Weak institutions and personalised leadership systems in Africa

The establishment of limitless government and authoritarianism in Africa as described in this chapter could be seen and founded upon post-independent leaders and their successor's ability to disempower democratic institutions that could ensure checks and balances through the separation of powers, and thereby curb the abuse of political power. One important political institution that suffered a set back in the disarming of democratic institutions after independence in Africa was opposition parties. The opposition according to the post-independence polity and as colonial masters portrayed them, represented—and in most unsuccessful cases does so to date—represents the 'enemy' of the ruling elites and the West. Nevertheless, following bad governance on the continent and the suffering of the people abandoned by their government, the people sometimes take to resistance. In most cases resistance occurs through institutional and status-wise very weak and 'powerless' opposition. However, these 'resistances' are crushed with utmost brutality on many instances. Some leaders who tolerated no opposition or questioning of their ruling style and instead ruled through oppressing their people and looted state resources include; Idi Amin of Uganda, Mobutu Sese Seko of Zaire (now DRC), Nyassimgbe Eyadema of Togo, Jean Bedel Bokassa of CAR, Colonel Mengistu of Ethiopia and Omar al-Bashir of Sudan (see Meredith 2005). On July 14th 2008 for example, the International Criminal Court (ICC) prosecutor Luis Moreno-Ocampo requested an arrest warrant for Sudanese President Omar al-Bashir due to alleged crimes he is committing against his people/humanity (France TV International News of Monday 14 July 2008). These leaders and their counterparts oppressed the people, conducted arbitrary arrest and killings and looted state resources. Since there is no institutional 'doorway' for them to leave power they only do so as a result of coups like Idi Amin and Bokassa or through their death, like

Eyadema of Togo and Bongo of Gabon, but never through the ballot box. According to Ayittey (1999, 129, 151), rulers of this kind are an "arrogant bunch of oppressive kleptocrats ... worse than the European colonialist" who have hijacked Africa "as gangsters, crooks and scoundrels" and these rulers run governments that do not serve the people. Ayitteh continues by suggesting that the nefarious rule of 'vicious tyrants' like Mobutu and Bokassa is simply an illustration of a greater problem of the 'evil spell' that has been cast on the continent since its leaders have undermined the state with its institutions to regulate and determine the extent and ends of power in order to strengthen their hold on power. Ayittey (1999) categorizies and illustrates these in his book: 'Africa Betrayed' in different forms notably as the march to tyranny (chap. 8) or the repression of freedom of expression (chap. 9) and the looting of Africa (chap. 10).

Consequently, power abuse has gone unchecked in many African countries. This is not only due to the 'disarming' and undermining of opposition parties as explained above but also a consequence of the absence of non-separation of power as well as strong institutions or the abandance of weak institutions under the rulers' control (Le Vine 1986; Ngoh 1987; Yates 1996). The abuse of power, selfish and oppressive leadership in Africa demonstrates and confirms the impact of the absence of checks and balances in the context of the division of powers. This is compounded by excessive control of the executive arms of governments, headed by autocratic heads of states. In order to better comprehend the foundations and perpetuation of authoritative leadership based upon non-separation of powers and the absence of checks and balances a quick look into history is necessary. Thus in this section history's occurrences and development are used as the key to understanding present failures and difficulties faced by African states – the consequences of the 'false start' (Dumont 1966). It also presents the argument that bad governance as it is practiced in many countries on the continent is to a great extent based upon weak institutions that are not able to check selfish and oppressive leadership in these nations.

The origins of weak institutions and bad governments in Africa

Before Europe's first contact with Africa in the 14th century, most African countries on the continent had developed many different societies, empires and kingdoms and even traditional states that had legitimate rulers and traditional laws governing the people (Weber 1978:226-7). These societies had what Max Weber (1978:87) described as traditional leadership. From Weber's (1978:215) definition traditional authority is based on an established belief in the sanctity of immemorial traditions and the legitimacy of those exercising authority under them. Traditional authority, even those that are still very much alive today like the Bamilekes, the Bafut and the Bamoun of Cameroon, to name a few, are almost exclusively transferred from one ruler to the next by inheritance. The people under the authority of the traditional ruler obey him because of his traditional status and this obedience is founded on personal loyalty based on a common upbringing (Erdmann 2001:11). With this leadership form obedience is to the person and not to a set of accepted enacted rules or laws. The personality of the ruler is the cause for loyalty and respect and not some set of laws. The examples of tribes in Cameroon listed above form a few of many such traditional societies and authorities which existed before the colonial period in Africa and are still alive today. They have been incorporated in the present democratic system with correspondingly weak institutions and strong and personalised leadership.

The traditional leadership in Africa demonstrates a vertical power hierarchy contrary to democracy's horizontal power distribution (Albrecht-Heide 1997). Unlike in democracy, traditional rulers may have or may not have an administrative staff. In cases where there is an administrative staff, the staff is either selected on patrimonial–from amongst kinsmen, clients, freedmen etc, or extra-patrimonial grounds, based on the appointee's personal relationship (the relationship may be one through marriage) to the ruler (Weber 1978:228). The type of leadership domination varied from gerontocratic (rule by elders of the group most familiar with the sacred traditions of the people), to patriarchal (rule by a particular individual designated by a definite rule of inheritance) and to patrimonial form of administration (Weber 1978; 231). Sometimes patrimonialism may exist in its extreme, whereby the traditional leader may develop his personal military force for the enforcement of his rule, and by so doing transforms obedience by his people from a group's rights to personal rights (Weber 1978: 231-2). This form exists in the western highlands and in the north of Cameroon amongst the people of Bamoun and Moslem northerners and it is called Sultanism. However, besides the military forces, which Sultans (in the case of North Cameroon the leader with such characteristics bears the title of a 'Lamido') have as their personal administrative instrument. Traditional societies in Africa often had a military apparatus since conflicts were common in such societies.

The powers pertaining to the traditional leaders, such as Emperors, Kings or chiefs were and still are unitary, indivisible and personal (Bayart

1993). These powers in most cases remained within the family and were succeeded or transferred by inheritance. In such a power system the notion of limited government: that is constitutionalism ensured through effective division of power coupled with political competition required in electoral democracy has no room. Thus traditional leadership in this form in Africa would not fulfil the democratic concept of liberalism based on limited government and individual rights. According to this form of traditional leadership, the concept of power is something personal to the leader and this too could not be limited since it is by traditional merits. As leader he is the highest authority and his prerogatives rest primarily on the fact that the obligations of personal obedience tend to be essentially unlimited (Weber 1978:227). The aspect of individual rights and freedoms, also of importance to democracy, contradicts the solidarity value of Africa's collective societies. In family groups extending to villages or chiefdoms where there exists respect for the elderly, from the lowest/youngest to the highest/oldest person, which by tradition is the leader, the elder also has the responsibility of protecting the younger person. This solidarity value also relates to the traditional relationship existing between the leader and his people, whereby the people offer services to the leader to get protections of recognised rights in return, (African Charter on Human and People's Rights, 1981, in Bundeszentrale für Politische Bildung 1999:602-619). Within ethnic groups there is a collective character that forms part of Africa's particularity in terms of its culture. The collective character of African societies is thus endowed with membership responsibility towards one another and the mobilisation of defence against those of different groups, which might be a threat to them. Southall (2003) sees this character of the African society as something positive in the formation of political systems. To Southall (ibid) the acceptance of membership responsibility, the mobilisation of solidarity in defending of basic rights, the closeness within the people, and their participative character and flexibility in defining their priorities provide them with a good foundation for democratic establishment.

This seems to be a far-fetched dream. According to Bayart (1993:228), when the western model of democratic leadership was introduced in Africa, the elite leaders of African nations simply replaced the traditional power stratifications with political vertical stratification of inequality. While Western democracy stresses individual rights and equality, the transformed traditional authority into 'Africanised' western leadership established political networks based on inequality. Furthermore, Western democracies are founded upon institutional distribution of powers into the different branches of executive, legislative and judiciary; these are expected to be independent from one another in order to ensure the protection of the basic individual rights, freedoms and equality of all citizens. On the contrary, the founding fathers of post-independent African nations created these structures by copying from the West but granted them no independence in their function. Thus, the institutions are subjected to the dictates of the head of state. In some African countries the leadership networks are created which allows the leaders in many cases to rule per decree (see Alemazung 2013).

According to Nohlen, Krennerich and Thibaut (1999:3), the systems found in Africa after the departure of the Europeans were systems inherited with institutions similar to those which the Europeans had back home. However, these institutions were politically powerless compared to the European ones. The influences of European masters through exploiting African wealth for European benefits to the detriment of African people continue to dominate local politics even after independence. This is possible because the indigenous elite leaders continue to serve the interest of the West as opposed to the interest of their people. This they do in order to secure Western support to stay in power through suppression of opposition parties and groups and even through the manipulation of multiparty elections. Most post-independence presidents of the new states were educated in the colonising European countries and some served as 'representatives' in the parliaments of the colonisers. For example, Leopold Sedar Senghor and Felix Houphuet Boigny, first Presidents of Senegal and Cote D'Ivoire respectively were 'French Citizens' representing their colonised territories at the French Parliament in France while Amadou Ahidjo, the first President of Cameroon and his successor Paul Biya (since November 1982) were representatives to French Territorial Assembly and students in France respectively. They had either been 'representatives' of their colonised countries to some kind of central administrative organ – the French Constitutional Assembly of 1946 with 586 representatives – or to the French Parliament in France. Senegal followed by Cote d'Ivoire had the majority of African 'French-Citizens'. Despite their African origin and identity these elites still had a superiority complex over their fellow Africans (Meredith 2005:58-59; Shillington 1989:354-5). With this background everything was done to suppress internal challenges or opposition to the governments.

The nationalist leaders took advantage of their popularity, prestige, honour and influence as 'founding' fathers to personify their states and consolidate their powers by the transformation of their countries to one-party states (Meredith 2005:162). One of the reasons the autocratic leaders used against multi-partism was that opposition based upon regional ethnic interests was destructive rather than constructive to national unity, political stability and development in the news states (Shillington 1995:408). In addition, the methods used by the colonial masters to rule their colonies did not instil respect of constitutional government in the indigenous elites. Thus the separation of powers ensuring checks and balances to safeguard constitutionalism, hold governments accountable, ensure effective appropriation of state resources for the common good of the people through effective functional governance was not constituted or regarded as valuable. Opposition parties as 'government on hold' or stand-by alternative for the people in case of failures on the part of the incumbent were de-valued or treated as enemies of the ruling party and leader: in other words, enemies of the nation.

Consequently, leaders like Sekou Toure of Guinea, Hastings Banda of Malawi and Felix Houphouet-Boigny of Côte d'Ivoire all suppressed opposition parties and enforced one-man-one-party-rule and imposed total obedience from their subordinates and the people (Meredith 2005). Houphouet-Boigny for example, took control of Côte d'Ivoire and ran the country under a constitution he designed that vested all state powers upon himself and wiping out checks and balances (Meredith 2005:165). Similarly, his Ghanaian counterpart, Kwame Nkrumah also ruled by decree and rejected parliament (Meredith 2005). These men believed that they had the right vision for their country and needed to do so without any objection especially in the construction of the new nations (Meredith: c.n. 182). Houphouet-Boigny believed that he was the right person to build his country, which was 'not' ripe for democracy. As he put it "Democracy is a system of government for virtuous people. In young countries such as our own, we need a chief who is all-powerful for a specified period of time" (Meredith 2005: 165). Thus nation and state building which was supposed to focus on establishing effective and strong institutions that would steer the right leadership based upon good governance for the good of the people instead focused on fortifying the personality of the president by putting him above all institutions. The head of state rose above the law and the people. The move to one party rule consequently led to the disempowerment of democratic institutions cancelling the effect of checks and balances and limiting of executive power. Many countries moved from multi-party to one-party states and by mid-1960 about half of the democratically elected governments in Africa that won elections after independence had been toppled by military coups, while the rest of the elected regimes gradually degenerated to one party systems by the early 1970s (Mbaku and Takougang 2004; Barkan 2002:72). Those nations which did not transit to authoritarian dictatorship through coups saw their multi-party democratic state transiting gradually to single party state through manipulation by their elites on the pretext that single party means one people and one nation (Mbaku and Takougang 2004:3). These elite leaders used the argument and interpretation of the feeling of one people, one nation as being equivalent to one party under the same leadership. Common national goal was substituted with common party under a 'common leader'. Party politics, thus, lost its meaning of competition whereby the voters have the freedom to choose those who they believe best represents them.

The attitude of the new leaders after independence was one of satisfaction with political power that came with independence. They believed that independence was self-sufficient and by so doing, underestimated and neglected the development of functional and effective state institutions (Dumont 1966:22). These leaders simply sat back enjoying their new privileges and saw opposition as threats to their newly acquired prerogatives. The reverse to one-man-one-party-rule based upon institutions in favour of strong personalised leadership gained stability and durability over the years as leaders learn to rewrite, change or ignore constitutions with impunity (Bratton 1999:25; Mulikita 2003). Based upon missing or disempowered democratic institutions, autocratic rule was consolidated to the detriment of the people's rule and their participation in a government for the common good. The kind of governance by these rulers described by William Easterly (2006:132) as "bad and problem governments" and the decades of their rule as 'the lost decade' by Meredith (2005:368), relied on a deeply rooted patron-client network political structure which hinders the establishment of democracy on the continent.

Thus the personalised leadership established in many African countries after independence ensured that while the elite ruler is in power he can amass as much wealth for himself as possible. Also he can appropriate state resources to his political clients (patronage distribution) in order to secure their loyalty and support (Young 2002:487). This is the character of African politics, which Bayart (1993, chap. 9) defined as the politics of the belly. This goes to the extent that one Nigerian party name and campaign slogan read: 'I chop, you chop' meaning 'I eat and you eat'. This Nigerian Party name and slogan indicates that "if you vote for me and I get to the source of the 'national cake' I will give you a portion to eat when I am eating" (Bayart, chap. 230). This political phenomenon has changed the supposed 'democratic relationship' between leading political actors and the people. The people's adherence or belonging to a party affirms their affiliation to the incumbent rather than to a party's political ideology or programme (Bayart, 235). Africa's political leadership due to its weak and non-functioning institutions is thus short of being 'system-reliable' and is instead 'person-reliable'. The leaders are the dominant 'institutions' and their powers are not limited since they control the system. The existence of 'strongmen' in place of strong political systems results in regular subverting of the law and where there is no law, there is no liberty and therefore no democracy (Foweraker 2001:707).

Authoritarianism, limitless government and power abuse

Authoritarians and those who oppose democracy tend to liken the absence of the ability to oppress as lacking the power/authority to govern (Schulz 1958:210-211). Such thinking is fundamentally wrong and is indicative of a subjective misinterpretation or false understanding of the principles of democracy that require of limiting and restraining power in order to avoid its abuse. Following this line of argument it means that an authoritarian leader who does not come to or retain power through free and fair elections lacks legitimacy. Such a leader's rule depends on his/her potential to oppress and/or use other 'unconstitutionally' persuasive and coercive means to rule. Authoritarian government is thus a limitless government with no institutions to check and regulate the powers of the ruler. Democracy simply requires that with the right institutional division of power a government be limited and checked - constitutionalism. The limitation of government power through separation of powers does not mean a weak government.

The right to rule says Friedrich (1963:233) is founded upon a variety of beliefs and it is possible for autocrats in Africa to feel entitled to their rulership, that is, to be believed and accepted by their people. Since the legitimate authority generally arises from receiving power from the people to serve their interest, the illegitimate use of this power is therefore an abuse of the power itself. In general, when governors take up leadership responsibility it implies that they are accepting the responsibilities of taking care of the welfare of their people, – thus serving the common interest of their nations. According to Boyle (1999) rejecting the responsibility for the welfare of those under one's (something is missing here – does not read right please check) rejecting their responsibility by going as far as using the power they have to pursue personal gains at the detriment of the governed. They fail to provide the necessary and possible public services and instead engage in corruption, oppression, and other tyrannical actions and also allow exploitation or other harm to occur in their societies.

The earmarks of authoritarian government include the absence of accountability to the governed by the autocrat, the negligible value of popular participation in governmental process, the vertical flow of orders in all public places and the absence of the right to remove an autocrat because of dissatisfaction with his rule (Schulz 1958:204-205). Authoritarianism is the abuse of power. In Africa, abuse of power is exercised in many forms and with the introduction of democracy in the continent even many more varieties of abuse now exist. The forms in which power abuse occurs in Africa include corruption, violation of the constitution or ignoring democratic elements in the constitution while enforcing the implementation of autocratic elements, harassment, extortion, excessive tax which rarely enters government coffers, harassment of opposition parties or groups that are critical of the government, rent-seeking, manipulation (for example rigging of election results) and violation of the rights of individuals (Ayittey 1999: chapters 8, 9 and 10).

In the last few decades some authors including Kauzlarich (1995) and Tunnell (1993) have made it clear that states, like individual citizens, can perpetrate crimes. When governments legally or illegally inflict harm on their people it can be regarded as state crime (Ikambana 2007:5). Such crimes that are committed by the state or government which may not be defined as criminal, Ikambana suggests, have significant harmful social consequences. With an Illustration of Mobutu's government as a harmful and dehumanising leadership, Ikambana (2007:2) concludes that, "Mobutu was an African political phenomenon whose regime contributed to the dehumanization of the Zairian people through state crime and the obstruction of democracy." Other examples of harmful governance include Bokassa's cruel rule marked by torture, and prohibition of the use of the words election and democracy in CAR; Idi Amin's mass killings of his suspects and tyranic totalitarian rule in Uganda; Teodoro Obiang Ngeuma of Equitorial Guinea's ordering of unlimited arrest, torture, rape, and murder including the murder of all the former lovers of his mistresses (Meredith 2005: 225-6, 235-7 & 240). As Meredith (chap. 13) noted, Nguema killed thousands even at the hint of any opposition threat. Two-third of his assembly deputies and high ranking civil servants were killed, imprisoned or driven into exile (Meredith, 240). A president like Siaka Stevens of Sierra Leone "systematically reduced human security within Sierra Leone so as to maximise his own personal power" and enforced his control over the country's rents and riches (Rotberg 2004:12).

Crimes by tyrant rulers and governments against their people and against humanity have caused states to collapse, public life to devolve into violence, thuggery, fear, misery and mass murder in many countries in Africa (Mullins and Rothe 2008:1). Mullins and Rothe (p. 3) go back to the colonial rule to trace some of these atrocities committed by governments. African states with this kind of governments are usually characterised by leaders who have amassed fortunes that fill their accounts in foreign countries.

Institutional separation of powers with checks and balances: Africa's solutions?

The constitution and institutional arrangements

The term constitution implies a set of rules and principles that define the nature and extent of government and the rights of citizens. The question of sovereignty in the nation is also regulated in the constitution since the constitution should establish where sovereignty is located in the state - federal, unitary and con-federal. This codified document, in a democratic society usually explicitly divide power between various branches of government, specifying the composition and powers of governmental institutions or branches beginning with Baron de Montesquieu's standard model that includes three main branches: the executive, legislative and the judiciary (Montesquieu 1748). This division of power has the first function of limiting power through checks and balances which is possible when the other powers, say, judiciary and/or legislative can wield sanctions that would restrain the executive from deviating from the laws or norms as put forward in the constitution (Beatie 1967:360-361). Thus the minimal political institutions required must include the judiciary and the legislative branches and an electoral organ for the organisation of democratic elections. All of these must be present and independent from the executive, which is the dominant one with the potential of being oppressive. Constitutions vary depending on the degree of separation of powers between these branches. Most constitutions seek to regulate the relationship between institutions of the state, and in a basic sense they regulate not only the relationship between the executive, legislature and the judiciary, but also the relationship of institutions within those branches. The absence of the rule of law, freedom and the right to free and fair elections as well as 'political choice' in Africa could be blamed on the absence of practical political independence of the judiciary, legislative and electoral bodies.

Due to the human being's greedy nature, the "sweetness and attractiveness" of power and the tendency to exercise unlimited power where and when possible, separation of powers or checks and balances is founded on the deeply held belief that government is best when the potential for power abuse is curbed and when it is held as close to the people as possible (Montesquieu 1748). The extent of any constitutional government depends on the degree to which leaders are deprived by the constitutions and the institutions they set up that have the potential to counter the misuse of the power and authority put in their hands by the people. Limited government thus has effective control over leaders or those in position of power/authority and protects the rights of the individuals or and minorities.

A constitution being such an important legal document needs some mechanism to render it "politically untouchable" by the rulers in order to protect and sustain it – prevent it from becoming flexible according to the leaders taste as is often the case in many African countries (Alemazung 2011). This in turn depends on the efficiency of established institutions (notably the constitutional courts), their structures and arrangements, and their adequacy to preserve and ensure that all actors respect the rules of the game. From the weaknesses or absence of politically non-viable institutions in many African countries and their consequences explained above, it is imperative that African countries with strong personalised leadership urgently need functional and effective institutions that can ensure separation of powers and the independence of these powers from one another. The big question here is how the separation of powers can be achieved in all the countries where the heads of state undermine and control these institutions. According to Goran Hyden (1999) this can most likely be achieved only through a re-constitution of the political order. In line with this view is Samuel Huntington (1993) who suggests three phases for the building of a successful democratic transition: removal of authoritarian rule; installation of a democratic system; and consolidation. Indeed, examples of South Africa, Benin, Ghana and other partly democratically successful countries have shown that the likelihood of establishing democratic institutional arrangements that enforce separation of powers is possible through the making of new constitutions.

Considering the ability and the common practice of elections manipulation by incumbent authoritarian leaders, separation of powers should go beyond the standard Western model of executive, legislative and judiciary to become an African model of executive, legislative, judiciary and an independent election organising body, like the Commission Electorale Nationale Autonome of Benin (Engelbert 2004:68). This would help reduce or free African elections from the danger of rigging and other forms of manipulation by the incumbent.

From the illustrations and cases presented in *figure A* below, it can be noted that a defining step towards a successful transition in the democratisation process is getting rid of autocratic leadership, and constitutions that are autocracy friendly. This presents the chance to start anew by drafting new constitutions which endorse the new system with democratic institutions. The successful cases of Benin, Mali (until the military coup in 2012 which marked the end of Mali as an exemplary democratic nation on the continent) and South Africa clearly demonstrate the value of re-constituting the political order marked by the three phases of Huntington's transition path, pointed to above. These countries, especially South Africa and Benin (Magnusson 1999) have functional and independent state institutions which have, through their independence, been able to safeguard the rule of law as well as the constitution since their establishment in the early 1990s. Both countries have vibrant constitutional courts that are doing a great job to safeguard the democratic components of their constitutions preventing encroachment by the executive branch.

Figure A: The transition route of a democratisation process

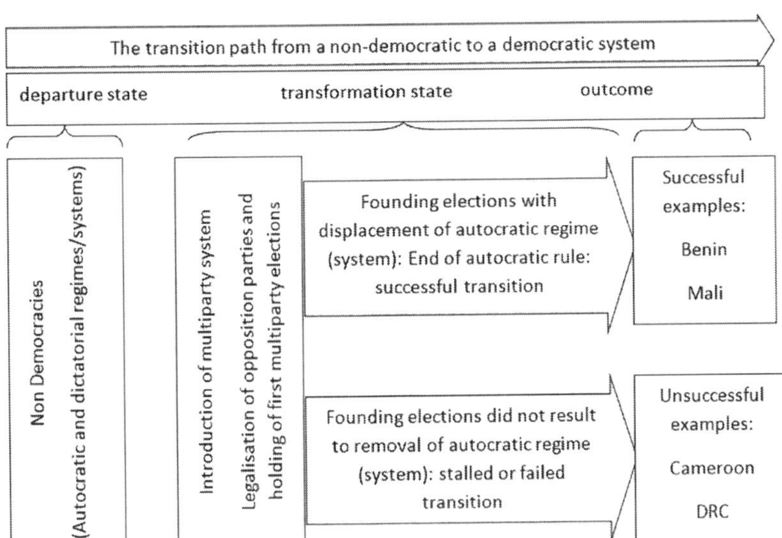

(Source: Alemazung 2013)

In the above figure, the countries that experienced the removal of the autocratic regimes during the first multiparty democratic elections are democracies today including Benin, Mali (until 2012), Ghana and South Africa. These countries are rated by Freedom House, World Bank, Mo Ibrahim Index of African Governance and similar institutions and regarded as free or successful. On the contrary, countries like Cameroon, Gabon or DRC that did not witness the removal of the existing autocratic regime/system are not free and cannot be considered as having experienced a successful transition to democracy (see Freedom House 2007). Thus based on the success of countries that witnessed the removal of the autocratic regimes in their first multiparty elections it can be concluded that the success of transitions to democracy on the continent depends on the 'removal' of existing autocratic system.

In cases where constitution re-writing did not take place and personalised leadership ended, the weak institutions will support consolidation of the power of the incumbent at the expense of new 'democratic institutions', leading to choice-less democracies (Gyimah-Boadi 1999, 34). Choice-less democracies thus reflect countries, where elections do not reflect the people's voice either due to extremely low turnout because of opposition boycott or due to effective manipulation and rigging by the ruling party which is in most cases organised and ran the elections using the compromised electoral bodies: 'voting without choosing' (Mkandawire 1996:2; Ake 1996:136). The absence of institutions that can safeguard free and fair elections and sanction election manipulators leads to compromised election outcomes.

Political actors in elections, especially government and opposition parties, as well as an active and informed civil society and citizens should accept and respect the rules of the game. Borrowing from Larry Diamond (1997: xxxii), "consolidation [of electoral democracy] is a matter of political crafting, the design and maturity of political institutions, and the spread of democratic norms and values". This involves two important aspects: institutions and political education to create and sustain a politically informed citizenry; a people who can play their role in 'checking' the government and holding it accountable. Thus while political education is needed for the understanding, spread, implementation and sustainability of democratic norms and values, effective democratic institutions are needed to oversee, contain and reduce the intensity of conflicts as well as ensuring that actors respect all procedures and rules of the game that safeguards the rights of competitors, especially the opposition parties and other political groups. This could ensure the best end result, which is acceptable and satisfying to the people (Diamandouros 1997:4).

System proposition for a functional democratic order

Democracy as a government for and by the people raises the problem as to what happens in case of divergence in the interests of the people based on high ethnic diversity and divisions, which is a reality in most African countries. Furthermore, how can a people oriented functional democratic system be established and which kind of institutional arrangement can enable better and functional government for the good of the people? According to Lijphart (1999:2), the answer to this dilemma is: majority rule. But again there is the challenge of ethnic allegiance to political parties as well as parties founded on ethnic lines (Nzongola-Ntalaja 1999; Deng 1997.) in Africa already as a persistent political ailment on the continent. Lijphart's (p. 2) answer appears appealing because the choice of the majority or government in accordance with the majority "come closer to the democratic ideal of 'government by and of the people'. But what is majority and which kind of majority in a highly segmental population? An alternative way of reaching a majority government as argued by Lijphart is by consensus: that is, not just majority but the highest level of majority attainable by getting as many votes as possible.

The majoritarian model has an exclusive, competitive and adversarial character as opposed to inclusiveness, bargaining and compromise in the consensus model. Adversarial and exclusive nature of the majoritarian model renders it inappropriate for plural societies due to its potential to lead to conflicts, marginalisation and division that can result from the exclusion of one *or* more 'segments' in the government of the people. Thus besides presidential, parliamentary and hybrid democratic forms, distinction can also be made between majoritarian and consensus model of democracy (Lijphart 1977). Furthermore, Lijphart (1999:32) argues that in non-plural societies—homogenous societies—the competitive, adversarial and exclusive effect of the majoritarian model which may tend to make a system undemocratic due to the exclusion of one or more parties or one or more ethnic groups in terms of the 'government by the people' criterion for democracy may be covered by the 'government of the people' criterion if the voters' interests and preferences of the excluded party/parties are well served by the ruling party. The possibility to fulfil these criteria is uncommon in plural societies in Africa where segmental cleavages result in great divergence in the interests and loyalties of the main parties. Worse still in the absence of division of powers due to powerless judiciaries, legislative branches and electoral bodies and under the conditions of cleavages, majority rule becomes undemocratic and dangerous because minorities are continually denied power: permanent losers. Regardless of which form a people or country chooses, it is important that the basic principle of democracy be preserved. However, from the above explanations and due to the dangers of deviating from the democratic norms, despite having a multi-party system, the best approach should be to seek a political system that can facilitate the achievement of maximum majority and increase participation.

The government, the state and politics in Africa have not failed because they generally cannot work, but due to the many constitutional, institutional and leadership enigma explained earlier, which are common in the continent. In a nut-shell, one can convincingly conclude that: "non-democratic political systems in Africa have failed either to deliver promised benefits of economic (and social) developments and national unity or even to maintain in power the regimes that have espoused them" leaving Africa with the democracy alternative (Clapham and Wiseman 1995:221). Thus despite the absence of checks and balances (constitutionalism) leading to the political system and governance failure explained above, democracy founded upon efficient democratic institutions appears to be the only way out for the continent. Democracy has proven itself as the most successful—though far from being perfect—form of governance in the world. Yet no two of the successful and established democracies in the world practice it in identical forms. Furthermore, it is important to note that democracy has worked in different regions of the world including some African countries (see examples in Fig. A above) and not only in Western industrial nations. From the time of Africa's independence until to date, the difficulties faced by attempts to introduce this form of government in Africa have been basically due to the lack of adaptability to the local African context as well as establishing the right political order with empowered and independent political institutions. In many instances, the constitutions of the colonies were 'virtually a replica' of the constitutions of the home country of the colonial administration (Young 1965:56, 182; Mpozagara 1971:27). This was the first mistake made in the state constitutions of post-independent Africa which has to be corrected in re-constitutions. Unfortunately, this mistake repeated itself with the introduction of democracy as conditions for solving the government crises in the late 1980s (World Bank, 1989). When the World Bank and other Western powers and institutions launched the policy of good governance with conditionality clauses on foreign aid, one disconcerting constituent was the fact that Africa was asked to embrace a 'one-size-fits-all' democracy (Akinrinade 1998:74-75; Chesterman et al. 2005:364).

Furthermore, one of the major problems with political forms in Africa has been the tendency to adopt a majoritarian system based on presidentialism. The majority of these systems are presidential or semi-presidential (Nohlen, Krennerich and Thibaut 1999:25) forms of democracy. This is simply due to the fact that in presidential systems the consolidation of the power of the executive could be more easily achieved through executive domination of the other branches (judiciary, legislative, electoral organ) than in parliamentary systems, in which the head of government is also a member of parliament and can be removed from power even before the end of his office term through a simple vote of non-confidence (Linz 1996:121-122; Riggs 1988). Some African scholars including Osita Afoaku (2005:7-8) emphasise the point that African pre-colonial states/kingdoms were people-centred and this order was distorted by Western political fallacy (also see Anna Diouf 2000:12-36, for more on federal systems in the pre-colonial period). The inheritance of a direct political order of ex-colonial masters with adversarial, instead of coalitional possibility for ethnically divided societies, emplaced these societies in conflicts and instability instead of unity and common purpose. W. Arthur Lewis (1965) logically remarks that the new states in Africa would have fared better if they had American instead of the British or French constitutional heritage (see Lijphart 1977:178). As Lewis (1965:55) suggested: the post-colonial states "would have taken the federal idea for granted, and it would have been the centralisers who were arguing an unpopular case" With its many ethnic groups and ethnic cleavages in multiparty politics on the continent, autonomy for the different regions of these people would supplement coalitions in a consensus democracy is recommended. Thus a federal system would allow the different regions the possibility to be able to 'rule themselves' but at the same time consensus democracy would enable them to form a general will with the majority of majorities in a grand coalition of different parties in a consociational democracy. In addition to consensus democracy this chapter advocates for federal democracy with proportional representation. Democracy calls for popular/maximum participation of the people, facilitated or made possible through elected representatives. Subsequently, for the establishment of democracy in Africa, the first instance of liberal democracy theory, which prescribes the representation of the individual, has to seek ways to maximise the representation of the different peoples (ethnic groups) in public policy debates and processes (Dunn 1986:164). This affirms the logic of the high ethnic diversity, that is, 'nations within nations' (Boulaga 1997:8) in Africa. In other words that a state with each group proportionally represented in the government would most likely be stable and succeed. According to Goran Hyden (1994: 185), Proportional Representation (PR) provides an opportunity for more than one winner in each electoral constituency, thereby mitigating the centrifugal tendencies that are present in plural societies. Hyden (1994:185) further states that: "when this system was first introduced in Europe, it was specifically designed to provide minority representation and thereby set up to counteract potential threats to national unity", a reality which African polities suffer from, due to the plurality of their societies. For reasonable participation in democratic elections some authors have suggested the following: the main political instrument for selecting or sanctioning leaders; and the electoral system should be one that takes into consideration the societal structure of the region as (Reynolds as quoted by Nohlen, Krennerich and Thibaut 1999:18-19, 23) and Bayart (1993, 43). Therefore, PR would be the right system for African countries composing of multiple ethnic groups. PR could work better for African plural societies due to its ability to undermine disunity and non-representation of ethnic groups and the consequential potential for instability and conflicts – a major problem in contemporary African states with presidential system based on majoritarianism.

After settling for a PR electoral design, the next question is that of the political arrangement that would accommodate these proportionally represented configurations in their exercise of power. The PR results of an African polity would reflect the polity's heterogeneous quality (Lijphart 1999 and 1977:189). The heterogeneous character of these societies makes them unfit for a majoritarian model of government. As explained in Patterns of Democracy: Government Forms & Performance in Thirty-six Countries, Lipjhart demonstrated that the majoritarian model works upon the principles of exclusion, a principle which by every indication should be avoided in plural societies of the African nature. In the words of Lijphart (1999:33):—the leading author in consociational democracy—"majority rule spells majority dictatorship and civil strife rather than democracy" Lijphart (1999:33). He concludes that what such societies need is "a democratic regime that emphasises consensus instead of opposition, that includes rather than excludes, that maximises the size of the ruling majority instead of being satisfied with a bare majority: consensus democracy." Subsequently, and based on Lijphart's (1977) consociational model, the question on political power should be considered on two fronts: institutionally and regionally/'segmentally'.

The pluralities in African societies represent segments which, in rural areas, are based on the geographical distribution of the different ethnic and regional diversities present in each nation on the continent. From the institutional point of view, the best arrangement for consensus for such societies then would be what Lijphart (1977:31) describes as 'grand coalition'. The idea behind the grand coalition is that it is not a definite institutional form but a 'prototypal consociational' device that can be replaced by other institutional arrangements so long as they bear the essential characteristic of facilitating "the participation by the leaders of all significant segments in the governing of a plural society." A consociational arrangement with power-sharing also warrants a parliamentary system of government. From the segmental/plurality point of view, the system has to bear in mind that the different regions have different wills and needs. To this effect, considerations have to be made as to the degree of regional autonomy in the distribution of power: that is, there has to be a "guaranteed division of power between central and regional governments"—a federation (Lijphart 1999:186). This makes federalism an ideal form for plural societies in Africa.

Conclusion

Successful democracy and functional governance do not only depend on an established democratic constitution but more importantly, are institutions that determine the outcome of laws and policies of the state as well as checked abusing power. According to Jan-Erik Lane and Svante Ersson (2002:235) "institutions are the rules or norms which are upheld by the means of sanctions". However, Lane and Ersson argue further, that performance does not only depend on compliance with institutionalized norms, but also on how these institutions operate. Support for this argument is provided by the example of different performances that could be displayed by parliament recruited through majoritarian means and that recruited through proportional representation (Lane and Ersson 2002:235-236). The effect of institutions in determining political outcomes is very significant and proves for these, lie in the devastating effects weak institutionalism (powerless judiciary, legislative and electoral branches) has in African political developments.

New institutions in Ghana, for example help strengthen its democracy. There were constitutional provisions made to protect private property which were generally respected (Gyimah-Boadi 1999b:171). As Gyimah-Boadi (1999) explains, constitutional rule opened larger political space for civil societies in the country. As mentioned above, political institutions are not restricted to the *trias politica* of Montesquieu but could include other political arrangements that can ensure the best political outcome according to the need and desire of the societies. This could mean that for a continent like Africa, where election organization and publishing of results is usually characterized by rigging and other forms of manipulations which mars the electoral and democratic process, the institutional arrangement for its countries may go beyond the *trias* in creating a forth power say an Independent Electoral Commission that is completely free and immune to the ruling party's or president's clientelist use of the *allocative* as well as *authoritative* resources placed in their control. In the case of Ghana, there were many institutions devoted to the protections of human rights, sensitization (political and civic education - socialisation) of the people on public issues and promotion of democratic governance like the Institute of Economic Affairs (IEA) and the Ghana Legal Literacy and Resource Foundation (Gyimah-Boadi 1999). The right and required institutions and their divisions and independence from one another are what the new order for successful leadership and governments in African countries still in the state of 'transition' or 'apparent' democracy would have to strive for.

The example of Benin as a true democracy (see Freedom House, World Bank and Mo Ibrahim Governance indicators/rating of African countries) in the country's successful 1990 wind of change transition on the African continent with new political arrangements stemming from the re-constitutio process, steered it into success and the new political arrangement and empowered institutions that resulted from the new constitution continue to play their role in consolidating democracy and good governance in the country (Decalo 1997). After free and fair elections and broad participation resulting from a genuine and successful transition, the responsiveness and accountability of those who receive power from the people come in as two important concepts in determining the working and functioning of the government that the people have entrusted 'power' to. Recalling that in societies people establish a government for their 'common good' (social contract), and that, this in the case of democracy, is done through election mechanisms in which the people make their preferences according to the different choices presented to them by those competing for the people's trust, it is therefore important that the people's preference be translated into policies priorities – responsiveness – and that the parties fulfil their pragmatic promises in terms of policies –

accountability (Keman 2002:63). However, this can only work effectively in a political environment where the rule of law is the order of the day and the rule of law requires empowered and independent political institutions that guarantee and safeguard checks and balances ensuring the respect for the law and effectiveness in performance. These institutions allow the checking, controlling and sanctioning of the misuse of power. In cases where these institutional requirements do not apply, as it is in many African countries, the social contract loses its value; likewise, government becomes weak or non-existent. Leaderships of this kind that have the judiciary, legislative and electoral branches under their control and use powers not provided by the constitution and laws lead to oppression and harm to citizens. These are tyrannies.

The lack of compassion by leaders coupled with the 'privileges' or earmarks of autocracy results in satisfying their personal interests when autocrats put themselves in the unethical position of conflict of interest between their personal interest and the common interest of the nation. According to Boyle (1999) the situation of conflict of interest, where the governors' benefits/gains depends on harming or exploiting others is extremely unethical. Governors who put themselves in such situations are completely ignorant of leadership responsibility and ethics. Statesmanship with qualities of expert knowledge, ethics, compassion, magnanimity lacks in most Africa countries. This is as a result of greed and weakness of institutions of accountability. In the absence of empowered and independent state institutions founded upon the division of powers greedy leadership continue to prevail. True leadership however is still possible if democracy with separation of 'political powers' is allowed to take roots in countries where it has been established. Examples are Benin, Ghana, and South Africa. This end would require committed and informed people and magnanimous leaders, governors who take responsibilities out of a true sense of leadership. The purpose of such leadership must be based on the benefit of the nations. Lastly, there must be the division of powers based upon institutions that are politically empowered and independent from one another in other to ensure proper functioning of a people-centred government that is responsible for the wellbeing of the people and sustainability of good governance.

References

Afoaku, G. O. 2005. *Explaining the Failure of Democracy in the Democractic Republic of Congo.* Lewiston/Queenston/Lampeter: The Edwin Mellen Press.

Africa in Fact, August 2012. Issue 3, www.gga.org retrieved from: http://gga.org/publications/africa-in-fact-august-2012 (15.01.2014).

Ake, C. 1996. *Democracy and Development in Africa*. The Brookings Institution

Ake, C. 2000. *The Feasibility of Democracy in Africa*. Dakar: CODESRIA.

Akinrinade, S. 1998. *The re-democratisation process in Africa: plus ca change, plus c'est la même chose?* In: Sola Akinrinade and Amadu Sesay (Eds): Africa in the Post-Cold War International System: 73-94.

Albrecht-Heide, A. 1997. *Patriarchat*, in: Ulrich Albrecht and Helmut Volger, eds., Lexikon der International Politik.

Alemazung, J. 01/2011. *Leadership flaws and fallibilities impacting democratisation processes, governance and functional statehood in Africa*, in: African Journal of Political Science and International Relations (Academic Journals AJPSIR), Vol. 5(1): 30-41.

Alemazung, J. 09/2010. *Post-Colonial Colonialism: An Analysis of International Factors and Actors Marring African Socio-Economic and Political Development*. The Journal of Pan African Studies, Vol. 3, no. 10: 62-84.

Alemazung, J. 2013: *State constitutions and governments without essence in post-independence Africa: Governance along a failure-success continuum with illustrations from Benin, Cameroon and DRC*. New York, Frankfurt, Zurich: Peter Lang Publishers.

Anyan'g-Nyong'o, P. A. 1987. *Popular struggles for democracy in Africa*. Zed Books.

Barkan, J. D. 2002. The *many faces of Africa: Democracy across varied continent*, in: Harvard International Review. Vol. 24 (2): 72-77.

Bayart, J. F. 1993. *The State in Africa: The Politics of the Belly*. London/New York: Longman.

Beattie, J. 1967. *Checks on the Abuse of Power in Some African States: A Preliminary Framework for Analysis*, in: Ronald Cohen and Middleton John (eds), Comparative Political Systems: Studies in the Politics of Pre-Industrial Societies, Austin/London: University of Texas Press: 355-376.

Berdal, M. and D. M. Malone 2000. *Greed & Grievance: Economic Agendas in Civil Wars*. Boulder/London: Lynne Rienner Publisher.

Boyle, W. A. 1999. *Sibling Rivalry, And Why Everyone Should Care about This Age-Old Problem*, retrieved at: http://www.angelfire.com/md/imsystem/sibriv1.html (15.05.2008).

Bratton, M. 1999. *Second Elections in Africa*, in: Larry Diamond and Marc Plattner, eds., Democratization in Africa. Baltimore and London 1999: The John Hopkins University Press: 18-33.

Bundeszentrale für Politische Bildung 1999. *Menschenrechte: Dokumente und Deklarationen*, Bonn und Berlin: 602-619.

Clapham, C. and J. Wiseman 1995. *Assessing the prospects for the consolidation of democracy in Africa*, in: John Wiseman (ed.): Democracy and Political Change in Sub-Saharan Africa, London/New York: Routledge: 220-232.

Decalo, S. 1997. *Benin: First of the New Democracies, in: John F. Clark and David E. Gardinier (Eds): Political Reforms in Francophone Africa. Oxford: Westview Press: 43 – 61.*

Deng, F. M. 1997. *Ethnicity: An African Predicament*, retrieved from: http://www.brookings.edu/research/articles/1997/06/summer-africa-deng (accessed 27.02.2015).

Diamandouros, P. N. 1997. *Southern Europe: A Third Wave Success Story*, in: Larry Diamond, Marc F. Plattner et al (eds): Consolidating the Third Wave Democracy: Regional Challenges, Baltimore/London: The John Hopkins University Press.

Dumont, R. 1966. *False Start in Africa.* Worcester and London: The Trinity Press.

Dunleavy, P. and B. O'Leary 1987. *Theories of the State: The Politics of Liberal Democracy*. London: The Macmillan Press.

Dunn, J. 1986. *The politics of representation and good government in post-colonial Africa*, in: Patrick Chabal (ed.): Political Domination in Africa: Reflections on the limits of power. London: Cambridge University Press: 158-174.

Easterly, W. 2006. *The Whiteman's Burden: why the West efforts to aid the rest have done so much ill and so little good*. New York: The Penguin Press.

Eboussi Boulaga, F. 1997. *Democracy and Tribalism*, in: Friedrich Ebert Stiftung (ed.): Democracy in the Throes of Tribalism: 7-12.

Elster, J. and R. Slagstad 1993. *Constitutionalism and Democracy*, Cambridge University Press.

Engelbert, P. 2004. *Country Survey, Benin: Recent History*, in: Africa South of the Sahara, Regional Survey of the World: 67-89.

Erdmann, G. 2001. *Vorkoloniale politische Organisationsformen*, in: Bundeszentrale für politische Bildung, eds. Informationen zur politischen Bildung. Afrika I. Bonn: 11.

Friedrich, C J. 1963. *Man and his Government: An Empirical Theory of Politics*. New York: The McGraw-Hill Book Company, Inc.

Giddens, A. 1987. *The Nation-State and Violence: A Contemporary Critique of Historical Materialism*. Volume 2, Cambridge: Polity Press.

Gyimah-Boadi, E. 1999a. *The Rebirth of African Liberalism*, in: Larry Diamond and Marc F. Plattner, (eds), Democratization in Africa. Baltimore/London 1999: The Johns Hopkins University Press: 34-47.

Gyimah-Boadi, E. 1999b. *Ghana's Elections: The Challenges Ahead*, in: Larry Diamond and Marc Plattner (eds), Democratization in Africa. Baltimore/London: The Johns Hopkins University Press: 170-183.

Huntington, S. 1991. *The Third Wave. Democratisation in the late Twentieth Century*, Norman/London: University of Oklahoma Press.

Hyden, G. 1999. *Governance and the Reconstitution of political order*, in: Richard Joseph, ed., State, Conflict and democracy in Africa. Boulder London: 179-198.

Ikambana, P. 2004*: Mobutu's Totalitarian Political System: An Afrocentric Analysis*. New York/Oxon: Routledge.

Kaufmann, Kraay and Mastruzzi 2007. *Governance Matters VII: Aggregate and Individual Governance Indicators, 1996-2007*, World Bank Policy Research Working Paper No. 4654 Available at SSRN: http://ssrn.com/abstract=1148386 (accessed 30.07.2008).

Lane, J. and S. Ersson 2002. *Democratic Performance: Are there Institutional Effects?* in: Hans Keman (ed.): Comparative Democratic Politics, London: Sage Publications: 233-256.

Le Vine, V. T. 1986. *Cameroon, Togo, and the states of formerly French West Africa*, in: Peter Duignan and Robert Jackson (eds), Politics and Governments in African states 1960-1985, Standford/Carlifonia: Hoover Institution Press: 78-119.

Lijphart, A. 1977. *Democracy in Plural Societies*. Yale University Press.

Lijphart, A. 1999. *Patterns of Democracy: Government Forms and Performances in Thirty-Six Countries*. New Haven/London: Yale University Press.

Linz, J. 1996. *The Perils of Presidentialism*, in: Larry Diamond and Marc F. Plattner (Eds): The Global Resurgence of Democracy, Baltimore: The Johns Hopkins University Press: 108-126.

Locke, J. 1689. *Two Treatises of Government*: In the Former, The False Principles and Foundation of Sir Robert Filmer, And His Followers, are Detected and Overthrown. The Latter is an Essay concerning The True Original, Extent, and End of Civil-Government, London.

Magnusson, B. 1999. *Testing Democracy in Benin: Experiments in Institutional Reform*, in: State, Conflict, and Democracy in Africa, edited by Richard Joseph. Boulder, CO: Lynne Rienner.

Mbakum, J. M. and J. Takougang 2004. *The Leadership Challenge in Africa: Cameroon Under Paul Biya*. Africa World Press.

Meredith, M. 2005. *The State of Africa: A History of Fifty Years of Independence*. London/New York: Free Press.

Mkandawire, T. 2004. *Good Governance: Werdegang einer Idee*, retrieved from: http://www.inwent.org/E+Z/content/archiv-ger/10-2004/trib_art1.html (07.01.2006).

Montesquieu, C. L. S. 1748. *The Spirit of the Laws*. Anne Cohler et al. (eds.). Cambridge University Press 1989.

Mpozagara, G. 1971. *La Républic du Burundi*. Paris: Berger-Levrault.

Ngoh, V. J. 1987. *Cameroon 1884 – 1984. A Hundred Years of History*. Navi-Publication Group.

Nohlen, D., M. Krennerich and B. Thibaut (eds) 1999. *Elections and electoral systems in Africa*, in: Elections in Africa: A Data Handbook, London: Oxford University Press.

Nzongola-Ntalaja, Georges 1999. *Ethnicity and State Politics in Africa*. In: African journal of International Aflairs, Vol.2, No I: 31-60.

Riggs, F. W. 1988. *The Survival of Presidentialism in America: Para-constitutional Practices*, in: International Political Science Review, Vol. 9(4): 247-278.

Rothe and Mullin 2001. *State Crimes: Current Perspectives.* New Brunswick-New Jersey-London: Rutgers University Press.

Saxonhouse, A. 2001. *Democratic Origins*, in: Paul Barry Clarke & Joe Foweraker (Eds): Encyclopaedia of Democratic Thought. London and New York: Routledge.

Schulz, E. B. 1958. *Essentials of Government.* Prentice-Hall: University of Virginia.

Shah, A. 2005. *Conflicts in Africa—Introduction*, retrieved from: http://www.globalissues.org/Geopolitics/Africa/Intro.asp#ManyConflictsThroughoutAfrica (12.06.2006).

Shillington, K. 1989/1995. *History of Africa, Revised Edition.* New York: St. Martin's Press.

Southall, R. 2003. *Democracy in Africa: Fragile and uncertain but necessary*, in: Journals of contemporary African Studies, Vol. 21(1).

Talbot, A. 28/01/2008. *Kenya: post-election violence continues*, retrieved from: http://www.wsws.org/en/articles/2008/01/keny-j24.html (11.04.2013).

Vanhanen, T. 1990. *Prospects of Democracy: A Study of 172 states.* Madison: University of Wisconsin Press.

Weber, M. 1978. *Economic and the society.* Berkeley: University of California Press Vol. 1: 226-227.

World Bank 1989. *Sub-Saharan Africa: From Crisis to Sustainable Development.* Washington, DC: World Bank.

Yates, Douglas 1996. *The Rentier State in Africa: Oil Rent Dependency and Neo-colonialism in the Republic of Gabon*, Trenton/NJ: Africa World Press.

Yeboah, A. N. 2005. *Dictator Africa.* USA: Publish America.

Young, C. 1965. *Politics in the Congo.* Princeton: Princeton University Press.

Young, T. 2002. *Democracy in Africa?* In: Africa-London-International African Institute. Vol. 72 (3): 482-495.

Africa's Third Wave of Democracy:

Reform Indispensable to Democratic Consolidation

Westen Shilaho

Introduction

Africa is a complex and diverse continent. This chapter does not by any means seek to reduce Africa into one undifferentiated whole; what it attempts to do is to highlight crosscutting attributes in democratic transitions in sub Saharan Africa since the early 1990s. It underscores antecedents before and in the immediate post-independence period as a setting to the analysis of socio-economic and political issues under the one party state, military dictatorships and the multiparty period. Africa has made milestones with regard to participatory democracy and democratic turnover of leaders. This contribution seeks to argue that in as much as there is no universally agreeable definition of democracy, its tenets are almost universal. Africa's democracy is a mosaic picture. Some countries have made impressive strides towards consolidating democracy while in others there are formidable challenges. Even in countries that seem to have done comparatively better, there are still shortcomings.

The inextricable link between politics and the economy and the influence of 'Big Man' politics are explored. A case is made for entrenchment of the rule of law and constitutionalism to check excesses of informalisation of politics and guarantee credible elections. The chapter highlights the need for reform of the colonial state as a way of addressing poverty and socioeconomic inequalities in Africa. Such evolution would strengthen democracy since the poor lack the capacity and resources to hold governments to account. The focus on a tapestry of Africa's elections since the end of the Cold War brings to the fore mixed outcomes. Overall, the contribution argues for comprehensive reform of African institutions to ensure sustained economic growth, and equitable distribution of its benefits through development to ensure stability and pre-empt conflicts related to contestation over scarce resources.

Transition from Colonialism to Independence

The transition from colonialism into independence held much promise for Africa. The 1960s and 1970s, a period within which most African countries attained internal self-governance and independence, was characterised by euphoria because of what was deemed to be reclamation of dignity by the hitherto dispossessed, demeaned and subjugated people. The period heralded hope for justice, freedom and the rule of law. It was meant to be a break from the brutality and exploitation of colonialism. It amounted to getting rid of the yoke of colonialism. Fundamentally, independence was expected to result in dignity, economic and political emancipation for previously recipients of inferior education and victims of exploitation of natural resources for the benefit of the colonial metropolises. In settler colonies, 'natives', the term the colonialists used, (Mamdani 2001:14) were confined to overcrowded, derelict and unproductive land and were valued only for their labour power. Owing to poor education, they were restricted to menial jobs. Kenya and the then Southern and Northern Rhodesia now Zambia and Zimbabwe respectively had large swathes of fertile land in the hands of settlers (Tordoff 2002). In a word, the 'natives' lost not only their sense of self-worth but also their heritage. Against this background, it was therefore fitting that attainment of self-rule be associated with great hope and promise.

For most people in the continent however, the independence honeymoon was frighteningly short lived. Independence soon led to disillusionment. Ghana's independence in 1957 was inspirational to the fight against colonialism in other African countries and the struggle against apartheid in South Africa. But Ghana was among the first African countries to witness widespread discontent among its citizenry over socioeconomic and political malaise characterised by authoritarianism, economic hardships, and corruption soon after independence. Ghanaian author Kwei Ayi Armah's 1968 book, *The Beautyful Ones Are Not Yet Born,* dramatised the troubled 'political kingdom' under Nkrumah and the quest by Ghanaians for responsive and accountable leadership. The book is a commentary on greed, tardiness, corruption and bad governance by postcolonial leadership not only in Ghana but also in other newly independent African countries. The fictional work is a cry for better governance and an indictment on Africa's postcolonial social malaise in which leaders turned to primitive accumulation through corruption while displaying callous disregard for the welfare of the populace. Postcolonial African leaders seemed to have literally taken Nkrumah's dictum of 'Seek ye first the political kingdom, and all things shall be added unto you' (Mazrui 1993:105). They sought and attained political power to rule but fell short on governance, the critical aspect of leadership. Although they identified disease, poverty and ignorance as cardinal challenges, they did not prioritise them in policies and implementation. Five decades since the independence of many African countries, Africa's development is still hamstrung by these challenges. Most significantly, the first generation African leaders and their successors failed to place emphasis on national identity among disparate groups of people 'at different stages of social and political development' (Tordoff 2002:5). Some African scholars have observed that the Berlin conference arbitrarily carved countries inhabited by people 'with no traditions of shared authority or shared systems of settling disputes' (Mazrui 2010: ii). Politicisation of identity and belonging is one of the contributing factors to postcolonial political instability and conflicts manifest in disputed elections, wars over natural resources such as land, precious stones, water and pasture. Mamdani has identified politicisation of indigeneity as a great crime of colonialism (Mamdani 2001:14). This sad legacy continues.

The tendency by Africa's political elite to exercise power exclusively along oligarchic, ethno-regional and religious fault lines is a hindrance to democracy and thus creates room for unconstitutional power takeovers. The 'politics of autochthony' was exemplified in the infamous *ivorite* (Ivorianess) concept that Henri Konan Bedie devised in Ivory Coast to lock out Alassane Quattara from succeeding Felix Houphouet-Boigny. *Ivorite* demanded that only 'pure' Ivorians had the right to hold jobs and office in Cote d'Ivoire. A 'pure' Ivorian was defined as a person born in the country and whose father had also been born in Cote d' Ivoire. Hutu Power ethnic political ideology in Rwanda in the build up to the genocide in 1994 was another example of the far-reaching consequences of politicised identity (Mamdani 2001: 126-131). Politicians seem to resort to such divisive cynical tactics because of governance shortcomings depicted in and especially seen through appropriation of state resources for personal gain. As such, narrow nationalistic leaders thwart competitive politics by neutralising opposition political parties by use of coercive forces so that they can monopolise patronage opportunities. In turn, factions of the political class excluded from state power respond by politicising group grievances to make claims on the state. When fragmented political groupings compete for control of levers of the state, the poor distance themselves from the leaders and the state. They end up setting up parallel informal channels to meet their daily needs.

Authoritarianism, the hallmark of colonialism, remained intact even after attainment of self governance and independence in most African countries thus vindicating Frantz Fanon's erudite and illuminating thesis about the psyche of the colonised and enslaved mind in his evergreen masterpiece, *Wretched of the Earth* (Fanon 1963). Mamdani captures this situation as one in which 'The bifurcated state that was created with colonialism was deracialised, but it was not democratised' (Mamdani 1996:26). The instruments of state violence such as the police, intelligence, army and gendarme tend to be partisan. This is partly due to skewed recruitment and promotion processes that follow nepotistic and ethno-regional considerations. The security sectors get sucked into patronage politics, which raises stakes in contests over control of the state. So pervasive has been the politicisation of the security sector that 'Many national armies in countries like Liberia, Cote d' Ivoire, Nigeria, and Sudan were turned into ethnic warrior enclaves in which the core consisted of kinsmen of the head of state' (Adebajo 2010:25). Organisation of African Unity (OAU) condoned tyranny within member countries through a clause in the OAU Charter that recognised non interference in the internal affairs of member states (OAU Charter 1963).

The phenomenon had not changed decades into independence in countries such as Kenya, Zimbabwe and Uganda where the security forces lack discipline and professionalism and are beholden to the government of the day. They-take sides during elections and commit atrocities under the guise of maintaining law and order. Hence Mazrui observed that 'In Africa's armed forces, the boundary between the modern and the premodern is ominous. The weapons are of advanced technology; the disciplines are rustic and loose' (Mazrui 2010: xv). In Kenya, this state of affairs had led to calls for security sector reform in order to render multiparty politics competitive. Official reports consistently implicated Kenya's security forces in election related violence since the early 1990s since the country returned to multiparty politics (Republic of Kenya 2008, Republic of Kenya 1999, Human Rights Watch 2008, Kenya National Commission on Human Rights 2008).

Conceptualising Democracy

Democracy tends to evade a precise definition. Regardless of the definition, concepts such as accountability, transparency, the rule of law, and popular mandate undergird the concept of democracy. In Africa's polities, the citizenry exercises little control over leaders owing to a number of factors such as limited levels of formal education, poverty and massive rural populations that make accountability hard to enforce (Bratton & de Walle 1997:11). Not surprisingly therefore African governments could survive in the midst of humanitarian crises such as widespread starvation in rural areas an unlikely scenario in highly urbanised countries (Cheru 2002:45). Due to the link between rural and urban areas, the type of politics exercised in Africa's urban areas do not materially differ from what prevails in the rural areas. Ethnic, religious and regional divisions inform people's political choices rather than cross cutting class interests.

At the core of the notion of democracy are people. But the people must have a consciousness that surpasses sub nationalist loyalties. It is only then that Bratton & de Walle's definition of democracy as a regime whose legitimacy derives from the principle of popular sovereignty would hold true; embedded in this definition is the understanding that ordinary citizens are endowed with the right and ability to govern themselves (Bratton & de Walle 1997:10-1). It is not feasible for people facing a litany of socioeconomic challenges to have agency and effectively contribute to their destiny. Fundamentally they lack access to information that is crucial to making informed political decisions, especially during elections. If they do, it tends to be filtered information mediated by partisan media and political propaganda. Bribery, intimidation, ethno-regional loyalty and voting patterns associated with all these are widespread in Africa.

People govern themselves through participating in credible elections as well as being able to hold those elected accountable through, for instance, the right to recall inefficient and corrupt representatives. Even then, democracy goes beyond competition for power through elections. Political rights and people's liberties could be said to be the linchpin of democracy. Political rights such as leaders picked through elections, equal weighting of votes, the extent of the franchise, the openness of the officeholders, and the timeliness of elections are characteristic of a credible electoral system. Only a democracy guarantees these rights, liberties and freedoms (Bollen 1995:5). The core freedoms include freedom of the media, the freedom of individuals and groups to oppose government policies or officials and absence of political censorship (Bollen 1991:6). Rigged elections, coups, and the recrudescence of the 'life president' syndrome characterise a large number of African countries.

Earlier, Dahl referred to what Bollen called 'political rights and political liberties' as 'institutional guarantees' and proposed eight institutional guarantees that a democracy should have: freedom to join and form organisations, freedom of expression, the right to vote, eligibility for public office, the right of political leaders to compete for support and votes, alternative sources of information, free and fair elections, and institutions that require government policies to depend on votes and other expressions of preference (Dahl 1971). Ultimately the tenets of democracy include competitive elections, held freely and fairly in an atmosphere of civil liberties, and where all contestants 'accept the validity of the election results' (Bratton & de Walle 1997:13). In this context, democracy is understood 'as a form of political regime in which citizens choose, in competitive elections, the occupants of the top political officers of the state' (ibid). Thus the right of the electorate to elect leaders through 'free and fair' elections is supreme. Once people are disenfranchised through mismanaged elections, governments formed out of such elections become illegitimate and cause disputes. If not curbed, such disputes escalate into violence. No meaningful economic activity takes place in an atmosphere of violence, save for what may be regarded as a war economy.

The lingering neo-colonialism: An impediment to Africa's renewal

A few years after independence it started being clear that 'flag independence' without social, economic and political reform meant little to the majority poor in Africa. In the absence of equitable distribution of Africa's natural resources and accountable, transparent and responsive leadership, it would be difficult for the African state to deliver on quality education, healthcare, tackle poverty and provide infrastructure required for economic growth and development. Equitable sharing of Africa's natural resources requires reformation of the post-colonial state.

Although some African countries have tried to overcome the legacy of colonialism through constitutional reform, two features of the colonial state persisted into postcolonial Africa and negatively impact on both development and democracy. First, the colonial state was an oppressive, violent and discriminatory state. Second, it was based on an extractive economy in the sense that its place within the global economic matrix was to supply primary goods to the colonial masters who had curved up the continent into occupied territories at the Berlin conference between 1884 and 1885. The overarching shortcoming of the postcolonial African state is that it remains economically and politically colonial in orientation. Adedeji's description of the postcolonial African state is apt and worth noting. He puts it compellingly as follows:

> Even more inhibitive to the deconstruction and decolonisation of the African economy is the failure to seek and pursue alternative patterns of African development and lifestyles in place of those inherited from European colonial powers. For too long, the impression has been created that African development strategies and lifestyles are an imitation-indeed a poor imitation-of the strategies and lifestyles developed elsewhere for other societies with different historical, cultural, economic, and political backgrounds. Five decades after political independence, not only is the African continent more dependent on the outside world economically than ever before, but its 800 million citizens have also become the 'mimic people', although they often claim to be preparing themselves and their countries for self reliant development as well as for an authentically African lifestyle (Adedeji 2012:86).

The erosion of Africa's sense of 'authenticity' through years of subjugation, have contributed to a lack of agency on the continent. Africa remains a site of scramble. First were colonialists operating under the guise of explorers. Currently we have Africa's leaders working in cahoots with China and other emerging economies and the West in extracting the continent's natural resources, thus maintaining the status of Africa as a site for exploitation. One of the aspects that have negatively impacted on democracy in Africa is that African countries remain producers of primary goods and consumers of value-added products. In the absence of the manufacturing sector, Africa experiences economic growth without development as the proceeds of its natural resources exclusively benefit the local Big Men, their supporters and multinational corporations. This has condemned the populace to abject poverty leading to the 'resource curse' notion cited to explain instability in most natural resources endowed African countries. It should be emphasised that it is not the endowment of resources per se that is the problem but rather the lack of leadership and sound regulatory frameworks in management of these resources. Botswana, for instance, has demonstrated visionary and responsive leadership in the exploitation of natural resources, in this case diamonds, for the betterment of people's living standards. On the other extreme end, we have countries such as Nigeria and the Democratic Republic of the Congo (DRC) in which natural resources have turned into albatrosses around the necks of the citizenry. This is due to a conspiracy between rapacious political elite and multinational corporations.

The cynical exploitation of resources for personal aggrandisement has resulted in atrocities in some parts of the continent. Nigeria's sectarian violence could be attributed to the failure of political leadership throughout the country's post independence period to harness the country's natural resources, specifically oil, for the benefit of the citizens. Warlords such as Foday Sankoh in Sierra Leone, Charles Taylor in Liberia, and a motley group of others in the DRC enlisted idle, illiterate and poorly educated youth into militia groups. The youth had no hope in life due to the lack of economic policies to address educational needs and job opportunities. The consequences of Africa's neglected youth were witnessed during the genocide in Rwanda in 1994. An army of idle and unemployed youth called *interahamwe* (those who work/fight together) were easily brainwashed and mobilised into a lethal militia that carried out horrendous atrocities. Before the genocide, even those in employ of the military had to contend with a precarious existence and feared redundancies during the Arusha Talks that called for downsizing of the Juvenal Habyarimana army to allow integration with the Rwandan Patriotic Front (RPF) rebel forces. The reality confronting them was damning: 'When the army had ballooned into six times its original size in four years of civil war, and when the country was plagued by massive unemployment, this was literally like serving an unemployment notice to young recruits in the army' (Mamdani 2001:210).

African populations grew at a pace faster than economic development. But lack of proper planning by African governments resulted in informal settlements in urban areas, inadequate public amenities, mass joblessness, ecological degradation and crime. The situation in which there were more people competing for scarce opportunities for social mobility and resources did not augur well for security, economic prosperity and consolidation of democracy. The exclusion of large swathes of rural people from the mainstream economy through neglect of rural areas in development policies 'created an aggrieved countryside full of a ready army of unemployed youth who have today become the cannon fodder of Africa's warlords in countries like Liberia, the DRC, and Sierra Leone (Adebajo 2010:25). Decentralisation of power and decision-making could alleviate the plight of the poor in rural areas but for such reform to achieve its objective, a paradigm shift from predatory politics to responsive and accountable leadership is required.

Big Man Politics and Democracy as Polar Opposites

Big Man politics held sway in many African countries during the period immediately after independence. Bratton & de Walle observe that neo-patrimonial rule characterise almost all polities across the world but emblematic of African politics, is antithetical to democracy since it is the polar opposite of the predictable and rule based rational legal authority (Bratton & de Walle 1997:61-89). Neopatrimonial rule manifests itself in different forms. There is the military variety such as Idi Amin in Uganda and Sani Abacha in Nigeria, the civilian variety such as Daniel arap Moi in Kenya and Paul Biya in Cameroon. Then there is a combination of the two such as Mobutu Sese Seko in former Zaire (Barkan 2009:13). Big Man rule has attributes such as leaders with a grandiose sense of themselves seen through numerous self awarded titles and a knack for prestige projects removed from the immediate needs of the populace. Such projects disguised as the brick and mortar evidence of development often turn out to be white elephants and conduits for siphoning money from public coffers (Russell 1999). Kwameh Nkrumah, 'Emperor' Jean Bedel Bokassa of Central African Republic and Idi Amin Dada of Uganda (Martin 1974) typified a bizarre affinity for grandeur. Felix Houphouet Boigny of Cote de' Ivoire built a grand Roman Catholic basilica in his birthplace, Yamoussoukro, modelled on St Peter's Basilica in the Vatican. This was an illustration of pursuit of vanity. Big Men regarded themselves as ordained to rule thus the concept of 'life president', arbitrary rule, dictatorship, patronage, corruption, impunity, and exclusive politics. This was the case in Ghana under Kwameh Nkrumah (Adebajo 2010: 241, Lamb 1983: 286-287), Malawi under Hastings Kamuzu Banda, Kenya under Jomo Kenyatta and later Daniel arap Moi (Meredith 2006, Russell 1999).

Personal rule favours centralisation of power and has no regard for the doctrine of separation of powers so much so that the office of the president is "the virtual monopoly of policy making …without adequate consideration of alternative policies, and elevation of president's own thought into official policy" (Tordoff 2002:7). The judiciary and parliament are emasculated and reduced to appendages of the executive, thus 'centralised despotism' (Mamdani 1996:25). The challenge of setting up strong and independent institutions, constitutional checks and balances against abuse of power after the re-introduction of multiparty politics must be analysed against this background. The caution is that "…just because one-party rule was legally defunct did not, *de facto*, mean that dominant parties would resist using large electoral majorities to revive monopolistic style of rule" (Bratton & de Walle 1997:9). Necephore Soglo, a man who defeated Mathieu Kerekou in Benin during the 1991 elections, lost to his predecessor five years later partly because of the persistence of economic challenges, corruption, arrogance and nepotism (Bratton & de Walle 1997:9).

Political and Economic Liberalisation: The Democratic Mantra

The 1980s were famously described by Adebayo Adedeji, Nigerian scholar cum pan Africanist, as Africa's "lost decade" following a shift in international power equation to the disadvantage of the developing world (Adedeji 2012:90). The 1990s were also described as "the lost decade of development" owing to either stagnation or reversal of gains made earlier in the 1960s and 1970s (Cheru 2002:3). After the end of the Cold War, capitalism triumphed almost all over the world. Democracy, the inextricable component of capitalism, became the US mantra that was promoted in Africa. The 'Washington consensus' that implied 'promoting International Monetary Fund (IMF) policies regarding free capital flows and liberal exchange regimes' came into force (Adedeji 2012:84). These policies included devaluation of currencies, zero tolerance against corruption, the privatisation of non performing state corporations, cutting down on social spending on education, healthcare and effecting redundancies to cut down on bloated wage bills. This prescription was administered through the structural adjustment programmes.

At this stage, democracy was expressed through liberalisation that demanded economic and political reform. The glamour for formation of more political parties increased. It was believed that more political parties would provide avenues for aggregating a multiplicity of views in culturally, religiously, linguistically and ethnically differentiated nations. International donor agencies, primarily the Bretton Woods institutions, viewed political liberalisation as a prerequisite to economic liberalisation. Economic liberalisation implied less government involvement in economic activity and was expected to lead to 'improved economic performance, growth and development' (Cowen and Laakso 2002:12). The idea of 'free and fair' elections and presidential term limits were other salient attributes of political liberalisation. Hitherto economically and politically marginalised groups, dissident politicians, and civil society uncritically embraced this donor prescribed form of democracy.

Some of the dissidents who formed opposition political parties had been part of the incumbent regimes and had either been expelled or decamped opportunistically on the eve of legalisation of alternative political parties. Having been part of the ruling elite, these opposition politicians did not agitate for substantive reform anchored in new constitutions in tune with political pluralism. These opposition politicians were after power but not inspired by a quest for social and economic reform to address poverty through policies responsive to the needs of the people. Incumbent and opposition politicians were not separated by competing policy blue prints. For instance, they were not inspired by the need to rectify the 'urban bias' economic development policies that accounted for inequalities between urban and rural areas (Mills 2010: 15). The overriding objective of most opposition politicians is the removal of the incumbent from power so as to put in place their own patronage networks (Cheru 2002:34-5). On the opposite side, the incumbents were preoccupied with retaining power.

A minimalist understanding of democracy obtains on both sides of the political spectrum. This ensures that wide socioeconomic inequalities will continue to linger on. Per capita income and regional inequalities in African countries form a combustible environment. Upon legalisation of multiple political parties, centrifugal forces came to bear on political activity as factions of political elite competed for state power on the basis of primordial ethno-regional differences. Fanon forewarned about this challenge in chapter three, 'The Pitfalls of National Consciousness' in *The Wretched of the Earth* (Fanon 1963). There has been persistence of corruption, authoritarianism, and impunity under regimes that came into power on a platform of reform in Zambia under Frederick Chiluba in 1991, Malawi under Bakili Muluzi in 1994 and Kenya under Mwai Kibaki in 2002.

Nigeria's Olusegun Obasanjo had a chequered political history as a former military leader who handed over power to a civilian regime in 1979. He was elected into office in 1999 following Nigeria's return to civilian rule and assumed a leading role in African politics as one of the architects of African Union and its strive for a paradigm shift in the continent's affairs. However, under Obasanjo governance did not qualitatively improve in Nigeria. These examples show the futility of change of leadership and political systems without the corresponding institutional reform. Reform must be deep enough to engender democracy:

> For democracy to take root in Africa, there must be significant social reform and reduction of inequalities, as well as the decentralisation of political power and decision-making. This will increase the legitimacy of

> the state; people will make major decisions and feel involved in decision-making and in the promotion of economic reform (Cheru 2002:35).

Integral to political liberalisation are competitive multiparty elections in which people have a genuine say in who governs and how they are governed. Democracy is enhanced in a polity in which the electorate reserves the right to change a regime during elections based on its performance. Furthermore, a confidence inspiring and stable democracy is one in which bipartisanship prevails and the electoral process ensures that today's losers are potential winners tomorrow and vice versa. Prior to the surge of the 'Third Wave'[1] of democracy, what Bratton and de Walle described as 'ritualistic, non competitive elections' were commonplace in Africa. Some modicum of electoral competition took place within the ruling political parties but was more factional than ideological. On the whole, these elections were plebiscitary. It was a foregone conclusion that the ruling party swept all the seats up for grabs with the Big Man's cronies being repeatedly re-elected unopposed (Bratton & van de Walle 1997:6-8; Tordoff 2002:11). This may be an over-exaggeration however in most cases, the 'Founding Father' or 'Father of the Nation' rarely subjected himself to any electoral process. Exceptions to the norm were countries such as Botswana, the Gambia, Mauritius, Senegal, Zimbabwe, Tunisia, Egypt and Mauritius that had varied forms of multiparty systems before 1990. In these countries, opposition parties had some limited political space to organise (Cheru 2002:33; Bratton & van de Walle 1997:6-7). Even among these countries, only Botswana and Mauritius held competitive elections (Cheru 2002:33). The protracted democratisation process in Zimbabwe, the Gambia, Tunisia and Egypt provided two lessons. First, political stability cannot be guaranteed in the absence of social and economic reform. Second, democratic consolidation requires a solid legacy of competitive and plural politics. Even Cote d' Ivoire and Kenya, previously considered bastions of economic advancement and political stability in Africa, plunged into fratricidal conflict following political liberalisation.

Holding of periodic elections is now an established trend in many African countries, although the continent is home to the world's only absolute monarchy, Swaziland. These elections, although flawed in most cases, mark some semblance of democratic development. Few incumbents lost power in Africa between 1960 and 1990 through elections. Only four heads of state voluntarily handed over power. These were: Leopold Senghor of Senegal (1980), Siaka Stevens of Sierra Leone (1986), Julius Nyerere of Tanzania (1985) and Ahmadou Ahidjo of Cameroon (1982). But Ahidjo regretted the decision and unsuccessfully tried to make a comeback in

1983-84 (Adebajo 2012:75; Tordoff 2002:170). Notwithstanding Ahidjo's change of mind, these decisions were at odds with the mentality of 'life president' among their peers. The notion of voluntarily leaving power is still rare in African politics. The 1980s was not only an era of life presidents but also of tin pot despots, and other eccentric leaders. Under Africa's multiparty period, South Africa's Nelson Mandela, out of his volition, relinquished power in 1999 after serving only one five-year term despite stratospheric popularity. Thabo Mbeki, his successor, stepped down in 2008 following recall by the African National Congress (ANC) party over factional politics in the party. In a continent in which leaders would rather have their countries implode into violence than cede power, these gestures were both laudable and surprising.

Africa's Multiparty Elections: A Triumph of Style over Substance?

It is axiomatic that periodic elections per se do not constitute democracy. Respect for the rule of law and a sense of selflessness do count too. It is incumbent upon the African Union to ensure that the principles enshrined in the African Charter on Democracy, Elections and Governance (African Union 2007) find expression in political practices on the continent. But while competitive elections are not the be-all and end-all of democratisation, they are an indispensable first step (Bratton & de Walle 1997:10). The substance but not the form of these elections is relevant to the democratisation process. It is imperative that constitutionalism[2] undergird the organisation and management of elections throughout the entire electoral process right from the registration of voters to the tallying of results and declaration of winners. Unfortunately going by numerous disputes over the credibility of elections, Africa seems to be struggling in this regard. Cowen and Laakso captured the role of elections in the democratisation process as follows:

> While a competitive electoral process cannot in itself be equated with democracy, it is a cardinal precept of liberal democratic theory and practice. According to its own precepts, liberal democracy involves free and fair electoral competition which includes the possibility of criticising government's decision making, of offering alternatives, thereby enabling *choice* to be made between one set of decisions and another and, more generally, holding politicians accountable for their decisions. As such, the actual form and content of the electoral process is one aspect by which one can gauge the extent to which liberal democracy is realised.

> Accordingly, as elsewhere in the world, a detailed analysis of elections is part of an understanding of the possibilities and constraints of democratisation in Africa (Cowen and Laakso 2002:1).

Change of power through elections for its own sake does not add any value to democratisation. That is why democracy recognises the holding of power by a political party uninterruptedly for a long time or with some short interludes as long as it commands the people's mandate through 'free, fair and credible' elections as is the case with Liberal Democratic Party (LDP) in Japan. This contrasts with the notion that once one is elected president, one must serve two terms and even more which seems to be finding foothold in African polities. To an extent this flies in the face of the inalienable right of the electorate to have a say in who governs them. It does not mean that for elections to be credible, the incumbent or the ruling party must lose. In fact, democratic transition envisages the possibility of the incumbent being re-elected following credible elections (Bratton & de Walle 1997). What poses a threat to democracy in Africa is the tendency among some incumbents to secure second terms by hook or by crook and even exploit dominance in parliament to abolish term limits so as to perpetually hold onto power. In 2005 Uganda's Yoweri Museveni marshalled the ruling and dominant former guerrilla movement turned political party, National Revolutionary Movement (NRM) parliamentarians into abolishing presidential term limits. In 2008, Paul Biya in Cameroon took advantage of control of the national assembly to do away with term limits that allowed him to rule for life. Unless this antidemocratic behaviour is checked, it risks reducing elections to "...merely formalistic exercises in the uncontested ratification of incumbents" (Bratton & de Walle 1997:13) thus making it possible for those excluded from power to resort to coups despite the AU outlawing coups and other undemocratic means of assuming power through The AU Constitutive Act (OAU 2000). Of concern too is the abuse of multiparty politics to entrench dynasties. Dynastic power transfers that have taken place in countries such as Togo-Eyadema, Gabon-Bongo, Kenya-Kenyatta, and DRC-Kabila do imperil democracy because they are more about protection of economic and political interests of local and international capital as opposed to transforming these countries into viable modern states.

Zambia and Malawi, two countries whose long serving independence leaders were swept out of power by the groundswell of multiparty politics, are illustrative of the dearth of democratic ideals among incumbents and the opposition politicians alike. Although popularly elected into power from an opposition parties, Bakili Muluzi and Frederick Chiluba of Malawi and Zambia respectively tried to amend constitutions to elongate their stay in power beyond the two fiveyear term limits. Luckily their efforts were thwarted by parliamentarians. Hyden suggests that the dissenting parliamentarians were not driven by democratic norms but impatience at being excluded from state largesse (2006:111). Olusegun Obasanjo reluctantly left office in 2007 after serving the constitutional two four-year terms after his attempt to secure an unconstitutional third term failed after Nigeria's national assembly vetoed his bid. Namibia's founding father, Sam Nujoma's gravitas in the country's politics as a liberation hero helped him amend the Constitution in 1999, which enabled him run for a third term. The amendment applied to him only and not his successors. These forms of political behaviour are characteristic of electoral authoritarian regimes. These are regimes in which institutions are established as a façade to conceal despotic tendencies (Edozie 2009:132). In electoral authoritarian systems:

> Electoral contests are subject to state manipulation so severe, widespread, and systematic that the systems do not qualify as democratic. Elites in EA systems tend to devise discriminatory electoral rules to exclude the opposition parties and candidates from entering the electoral arena. They seek to remain in power by infringing on their opponents' political rights and civil liberties, restrict access to mass media and sources of campaign financing. Wholesale electoral fraud is sometimes used (Edozie 2009:132).

The Western and capitalist form of democracy promoted in Africa has parameters such as freedom of speech and association, multiparty competition and interest group activity, free and fair elections, accountable and transparent governance, social justice, and the rule of law (Tordoff 2002: 19). During the one party authoritarianism, these freedoms were criminalised. Under a multiparty system, access to these rights vary from one African country to another. The mere mention of these rights, even if not upheld, under multiparty politics is a great improvement that some scholars have referred to as a 'democratic break' (Cowen and Laakso 2002: 14). In order for the citizenry to enjoy these rights, there has to be commitment to reform and constitutionalism across the body politic. Weak institutions such as legislatures, local governments, electoral bodies, political parties, the judiciary, the media, and civil society in most African countries cannot act as countervailing forces against the domineering executive (Cheru 2002:34). Crude policing tactics, a carryover of colonial practice of use of crude force and antipathy against dissent, results in egregious human rights violations such as extrajudicial executions, pillage, rape and torture by security forces that is some cases constitute crimes against humanity.

The degree of credibility in Africa's multiparty elections varies. This could be attributed to the need to overcome legacies of one party dictatorship, despotic military regimes and even apartheid while in other cases crude politics based on imperviousness to the rule of law account for sham elections in which the winner is, a priori, decided. The winner is in most instances either the incumbent or his preferred successor. But there are some beacons of hope. South Africa and Ghana are trying to establish a trend of holding elections that, to a large extent, meet international standards. However, in the South African context, the ruling party, the ANC's support by the majority blacks who take part in the elections has ensured its continued dominance of the country's politics since the end of apartheid in 1994, because of strong opposition as well as the dominance of race politics in the country's body politic. This led some scholars to describe the South African democracy as a 'dominant party state' (Southall 2000). In a way, the jury is still out on whether South Africa's democracy is consolidating. A litmus test of the country's democracy lies at the point when a political party emerges that could give the ANC a run for its money.

Democratic Consolidation

It is difficult to point out what constitutes a consolidated democracy, since democracy in Africa tends to be characterised by ebbs and flows, gains and reversals, across and even in the same country. However, successive seamless transfers of power from the incumbent to the opposition especially in tightly contested elections could be regarded as a marker of a consolidating democracy (Beetham 1994). Zambia has had five seamless changes of government during the multiparty period. Ghana has a tortured history defined by coups, counter coups and open execution of some members of the military elite. The country has since distinguished itself as a fledgling model of democracy having had peaceful transitions since entry into multiparty politics. It held five multiparty elections between 1992 and 2008 of varying degrees of credibility. The country also successfully managed a transition in July 2012 following the death of President John Atta Mills. The transition was followed by elections in December 2012 that were relatively credible although the opposition presidential candidate petitioned the results, the case was dismissed in court. Botswana is another distinct democracy on the continent boasting an established tradition of peaceful elections that predate the advent of the popular wave of multiparty politics since 1989. The presence of former presidents enjoying undisturbed retirement is illustrative of democracy finding traction in Africa. During the single party era, there were hardly any retired presidents because incumbents died in office through attrition, got killed during bloody coups or were forced to flee into exile.

The ushering in of multiparty elections[3] in the 1990s saw the defeat of incumbents in almost more than half of the thirty-one party regimes (Bratton & van de Walle 1997:7). However, after leaders such as Matthieu Kerekou and Kenneth Kaunda lost elections in Benin and Zambia respectively, other long serving leaders hardly lost elections. It became virtually impossible for them to be defeated in elections they organised. By 1994, when the first round of multiparty elections ended, neopatrimonial leaders managed to retain power in half of the countries in which multiparty elections had been held (Barkan 2009:16). Initially, a sense of trepidation engulfed despots across sub-Saharan Africa as they feared being swept out of power by the wave of change. Those who survived seemed to have learnt from the 'naivete' of those defeated in participatory elections. These incumbents devised means of 'living with multiparty politics' without it threatening their hold on power (Cowen and Laakso 2002:14). Africa's strongmen, who astutely weathered the political scare, sneered at incumbents who organised elections and still allowed themselves to lose. Although it was difficult for opposition political parties to ascend to power, the greatest pitfall against transition into democracy was that regardless of the party that came into power, reactionary and patronage politics remained prevalent. Therefore, even after regime change in Zambia, Malawi and Benin, reform remained a mirage. Bratton & de Walle captured this situation of old wine in new wine bottles:

> Moreover, even when the faces of top leaders changed, the new rulers were often drawn from the same social and political classes as before, including an aging generation of old-guard politicians who had previously served the postcolonial regime. The election of recycled leaders engendered doubts about whether they would govern differently than the men they replaced (Bratton & de Walle 1997:8).

What is yet to emerge following the 'third wave of democracy' is a trend of credible elections whose results are accepted by all the contesting political parties. Incumbents are inclined to invoke undemocratic means of retaining power while opposition politicians are likely to cry foul even in situations in which elections are relatively credible. This aversion to 'rules of the game'4 across the political spectrum has something to do with the fact that Africa's opposition political parties do not ideologically differ from the ruling parties. Like the ruling political parties, opposition parties do not exhibit internal democracy. Opposition political leaders have 'a pathological fixation on power' and so are after attaining power at whatever means (Ihonvbere 2006:19). One of the distinguishing characteristics of Africa's opposition parties is the fielding of the same presidential candidate repeatedly because party leaders tend to own these parties, command ethno-regional support and as such do not countenance replacement or any challenge. Notable perennial opposition presidential candidates are Morgan Tsvangirai in Zimbabwe, Raila Odinga in Kenya and Etienne Tshisekedi in DRC.

Conclusion

Overall under multiparty politics, Africa offers more freedoms than under single party and military dictatorships. However, the extent to which democracy has spread its benefits differs from country to country. Some countries have experienced democratic gains only to encounter reversals such as Mali and Kenya. Lack of strong institutions to withstand idiosyncrasies of individual politicians, and the absence of a sense of national identity among leaders and their followers smothers democracy, stunts development and condemns people to abject poverty as they nurture deleterious sub national loyalties. Africa needs leadership that is responsive to evidence based policy formulation and implementation. Antipathy against critical intellectualism that is commonplace in Africa's bureaucracies denies evidence based planning and decision making. Thus the propensity for ad hoc policy making approaches, lack of long term planning, misplaced priorities seen through 'prestige', 'grandiose' and vanity projects while the majority of people have no access to the basics of life such clean water, electricity, quality education, healthcare, housing and sanitation.

Elections can be a source of stability or instability depending on the manner in which they are conducted. A trend of conducting credible elections will not only see democracy consolidated across the continent but will also provide germane environments for economic prosperity and development. In this regard AU and regional economic communities (RECs) have to be in the forefront in spreading and defending democracy on the continent. Rogue behaviour that includes electoral fraud must be sanctioned otherwise there is a risk of entrenching 'electoralism' in which elections that do not meet the bare minimum of the tenets of democracy are held, resulting in illegitimate governments, polarised polities and violence. This would cause political instability hence affecting social cohesion and development. Rigged elections with dubious results can lead not only to violence but also to ethnic conflicts. Coups have the capacity to produce similar results as evidenced by ethnic and religious violence in Central Africa Republic.

It is beyond doubt that the postcolonial African state stands in need of reform. It is ideational more than any other kind of reform that is required. Foremost, educational systems have to be redesigned to reflect Africa's social, political, cultural and economic needs. Credibility will be restored when African politicians and the intelligentsia stop wholesale aping of 'best practices' from the West. Failure by Africa to devise its own models of development and political activity has led to experimentation with a hodgepodge of 'foreign' ideas and all manner of exports from other civilisations. Mimicry will not solve the asymmetry between population growth and scarce resources. Instead it will encourage plundering of the continent's resources, breed warlords, enrich a miniscule fraction of Africa's inhabitants while consigning majority of citizens to abject poverty.

Notes and References

1 The first wave of democratic transition in Africa occurred in Benin in 1990 then Zambia the following year. The most recent democtratic waves occurred in Sierra Leone and Cameroon in 2005 and 2006 respectively with the end of civl wars. So 2007 could be said to be the end of the third Wave of democratic transition in Africa (Barkan 2009, 4).

2 The notion of constitutionalism or rule of law 'means the institutionalisation of government, administration and judiciary, as well as of the rights of organisation, expression and property, into regular and predictable forms' (Rudebeck 2002, 105).

3 Referred to as such because the elections marked a shift from authoritarian regimes (Bratton & de Walle 1997, 7).

4 These are political procedures that determine distribution of power, prescribe who may engage in politics and how. 'Rules of the game' 'may be formally codified in constitutions and other legal statutes; or they may be informal, embodying customs and habits to which all participants are attuned' (Bratton & de Walle 1997, 9).

Adebajo, A. 2012. Paradise Lost and Found: The African Union and the European Union. In Adebajo, A and Whiteman, K. eds *The EU and Africa From Eurofrique to Afro-Europa*. Johannesburg: Wits University Press.

________. 2010. *The Curse of Berlin Africa After the Cold War*. South Africa: University of Kwa Zulu Natal.

Adedeji, A. 2012. The Travails of Regional integration in Africa. In Adebajo, A & Whiteman, K. eds *The EU and Africa From Eurofrique to Afro-Europa*. Johannesburg: Wits University Press..

African Union 2007. African Charter on Democracy, Elections and Governance. Online: http://www.ipu.org/idd-E/afr_charter.pdf Accessed April 2011.

Armah. A. K. 1968. *The Beautyful Ones Are Not Yet Born*. Boston: Heinemannton.

Barkan, 2009. African Legislature and the 'Third Wave' of Democratisation. In Barkan, J. ed. *Legislative Power in Emerging African Democracies*. London: Lynne Rienner Publishers.

Beetham, D. 1994. Conditions for Democratic Consolidation. In *Review of African Political Economy*. 21 (60) 157-172.

Bratton, M. & van de Walle, N. 1997. Democratic Experiments in Africa Regime transition. In *Comparative Perspective*; Cambridge: Cambridge University Press.

Bollen, K. 1991. Political Democracy; Conceptual and measurement Traps. In Inkeles A. ed *On Measuring Democracy Its Consequences and Concomitants*. Transaction Publishers: New Brunswick 82-108.

Cheru, F. 2002. *African Renaissance Roadmaps to the challenge of globalization*. London: Zed Books.

Cowen, M. & Laakso, L. 2002. Elections & Election Studies in Africa. In Cowen, M & Laakso, L. eds *Multi-party Elections in Africa*. Oxford: James Currey.

Lamb, D. 1983. *The Africans*; New York: Random house Inc.

Dahl, Robert A. 1971. *Polyarchy: participation and opposition*. Yale: New Haven.

Edozie, R. 2009. Electoral Authoritarianisms and Delegative Democrats: Reconstructing African Democratic Consolidation in Africa. In

Reconstructing the Third Wave of Democracy: Comparative African Democratic Politics. Lanham: University Press of America: 128-154.

Fanon. F. 1963. *The Wretched of the Earth*. London: Penguin Books.

Human Rights Watch (HRW) (2008) *Ballots to Bullets Organised Political Violence and Kenya's Crisis of Governance*. 20 (1) A. Available online https://www.hrw.org/report/2008/03/16/ballots-bullets/organized-political-violence-and-kenyas-crisis-governance (accesses April 2001).

Hyden, G. 2006. *African Politics in Comparative Perspective*. New York: Cambridge University Press.

Ihonvbere, J. 2006. Where is the third wave? Critical Evaluation of Africa's Non-Transition to Democracy. In Mbaku, J and Ihonvebere J. eds. *Multiparty Democracy and Political Change*: Trenton, NJ: Africa World Press.

Kenya National Commission on Human Rights (KNCHR), 2008. On the Brink of the Precipice: A Human Rights Account of Kenya's Post 2007 Election. Available online http://www.knchr.org/portals/0/reports/knchr_report_on_the_brink_of_the_precipe.pdf Accessed retrieved April 2011.

Mamdani, M. 1996. *Citizen and Subject Contemporary Africa and the Legacy of Late Colonialism*. New Jersey: Princeton University Press.

_________2001. *When Victims Become Killers Colonialism, Nativism, and the Genocide in Rwanda*. Kampala: Fountain Publishers.

Martin, D. 1974. General Idi Amin. London: Faber and Faber.

Mazrui, A. 2010. Black Berlin and the Curse of Fragmentation from Bismark to Barack. In Adebajo, A. *The Curse of Berlin Africa After the Cold War*. Durban: University of Kwa Zulu Natal.

_________1993. 'Seek ye first the Political Kingdom.' In Mazrui, A (ed) and Wondji, C. (Asst ed) General History of Africa VIII Africa since 1935. Berkely: University of California.

Meredith, M. 2006. The State of Africa A History of Fifty years of Independence. London: Free Press.

Mills, G. 2010. *Why Africa is Poor and What Africans Can Do about It*. South Africa: Penguin Books:

Republic of Kenya. 2008. Commission of Inquiry into Post-Election Violence (CIPEV) or the 'Waki Commission'. Government Printer:

Nairobi. Online: http://www.dialoguekenya.org/docs/PEV%20 Report.pdf Accessed April 2012.

__________. 1999. Report of the Judicial Commission Appointed to Inquire into Tribal Clashes in Kenya, 'Akiwumi Commission'. Nairobi: Government Printer.

Rudebeck, L. 2002. Multiparty Elections in Guinea Bissau. In Laakso, L. & Cowen, M eds *Multi-party Elections in Africa*. Oxford: James Currey.

Russell, A. 1999. Big Men Little People Encounters in Africa; London: Macmillan.

Southall, R. 2000. The State of Democracy in Africa. In *Comparative Politics*. 38:3. 147-170.

Tordoff, W. 2002. *Government and politics in Africa*: New York: Palgrave Macmillan. Organisation of African Unity (OAU) Charter 1963.

Organisation of African Union (OAU) 2000. Constitutive Act of the African Union. Online: http://www.peaceau.org/uploads/au-act-en.pdf Accessed April, 2012.

Enhancing Governance in Public-Private Partnerships in Africa

Some Lessons Learned from South Africa

Madeleine C Fombad

Introduction

This chapter analyses lessons from Public-Private Partnerships (PPPs) in South Africa and suggests techniques by which governance principles can be incorporated effectively to enhance development through PPPs in Africa. PPPs are sustainable tools for development that may remedy the skewed implementation of infrastructure and improve Africa's socio-economic problems, and enhance cost-effectiveness and service delivery. In effect, since 1999, most African countries have adopted the use of PPPs as an integral strategy in their national and international developmental plans. In order for African governments to realise their developmental objectives through PPPs, effective governance is crucial. Increasingly, the incorporation of governance principles within the designated objectives of PPPs is recognised as an active area of research (Hodge and Greve 2005:6 ; Clifton & Duffield, 2006: 537 Organization for Economic Corporation and Development (OECD) 2007, United Nations Economic Commission for Europe (UNECE 2008); Wilson 2010:15; Brinkerhoff and Brinkerhoff 2011:31). The chapter presents an assessment of the extent to which governance has been achieved in PPPs in South Africa and provides some lessons that may serve as a platform for the possible review of governance in PPPs in other African countries. For a start, taking stock of the fast-growing literature on PPPs, we put forward a working definition of PPPs. In the second section, I shall expound the concepts PPPs and development. The third section provides an overview of the concept of governance in PPPs and the fourth section provides an overview of some governance challenges in PPPs in South Africa. The fifth section examines some lessons for PPPs in Africa the chapter ends with some concluding remarks.

What are public-private partnerships?

The concept of PPPs continues to differ across countries, among scholars and contexts. There are various definitions of PPPs, among them: an institutional arrangement; developmental strategy financial relationship; governance tool; and a language game to a broad concept that accommodates a variety of cooperative arrangements between the government, the private sector and nongovernmental organisations to improve infrastructure networks and enhance service delivery. Brinkerhoff & Brinkerhoff (2011:31) proposes a purpose-based framework that examines the expression of the following five defining features: policy, service delivery, infrastructure, capacity building, and economic development. Two definitions are relevant to the understanding of PPP within the context of this contribution. Firstly, PPP is defined as a partnership between the public and private sector based on a long-term contractual agreement involving high capital costs and risk sharing (Public Accounts Committee New South Wales Parliament 2006).

The second definition considers PPPs as a governance tool. To this end, Bovaird (2004: 70) defines PPPs as working arrangements based on a mutual commitment over and above that implied in any contract between public sector organisations with any other organisations outside the public sector. This definition specifies relationships beyond contractual commitments and includes elements of trust, mutual commitment, and social and community obligations (Fombad 2013: 37). On the basis of these two definitions, PPPs in this chapter are long-term contracts between the government and the private sector based on mutual commitment whereby trust, risks, rewards, resources, skills, expertise and finances are shared. Common models of PPPs are the Design, Finance, Operate (DFO); Design, Finance, Build, Operate, Transfer (DFBOT); Design and Transfer (DT); Build Operate, Transfer (BOT) and equity partnerships (Treasury Regulation 16, 2004)

PPPs as tools for development

Infrastructural deficiencies in roads, water supply, sewers, electrical grids, telecommunications transportation, healthcare and the limited provision of socio-economic and manufacturing services are amongst the common developmental challenges in Africa. These challenges have hindered economic growth, reduced international competitiveness and undermined the poverty reduction efforts of African governments (World Bank 2008; World Bank 2006). It has been estimated that the poor state of Africa's infrastructure has lowered productivity by 40% and have increased the cost of doing business (Escribano et al.2008). World Bank reports, between 2001 and 2009, revealed an infrastructure deficit for sub-Saharan Africa estimated at 93 billion US dollars annually for the next ten years with 40% of this amount required in the energy sector and 20% is for the transport sector (World Bank 2008). Also, the World Bank Private Participation in Infrastructure (PPI) database recorded a continuous drop in investments in infrastructure PPPs in the sub Saharan Africa (Thomson2005). Given these challenges there has been a renewed interest by the African governments to embark on PPPs as a policy option to provide additional resources for the provision of basic services and infrastructure towards delivering basic needs to the majority of the population.

PPPs are significant tools for promoting development (Agere 2000; Paoletto 2000; Fombad 2013a:37). The second democratically elected president of South Africa, President Mbeki in his opening speech to parliament in 1999 specifically said that PPPs were a key part of the government's strategy for service delivery, economic growth and development. This made it an integral part of the state's overall strategy for the provision of public services and infrastructure. Between 1990 and 2004 approximately 14% of Africa's public sector infrastructure in the development of roads, schools, water reclamation, hospitals, and prisons and the provision of health and social services were provided through PPPs (Deloitte & Touche 2006). Notwithstanding, a wide range of governance issues have limited the ability of the PPPs to produce desired outcomes in Africa. Among these are lack of accountability, institutional weaknesses, widespread corruption, lack of transparency, poor regulatory environment, power imbalances between the private sector partners, lack of political commitment and a lack of trust, skills, will and expertise to effectively manage the funds (Sader 2000; Thomsen 2005; Bangura & Larbi 2006; Aaronson 2011:31: Brinkenoff & Brinkenoff 2011:31). There are a large number of existing projects that have either been terminated, classified as distressed or the terms renegotiated under duress (Thomson 2005; Pessoa 2006; Capital 2011).

Given the growing value of commitment to infrastructure through PPPs, an increased attention on issues concerning the effective governance of PPPs as developmental projects have emerged. An analysis by UNECE (2008) on Africa's early experiences with the private financing of infrastructure in the 1990s, revealed that that most advisers tended to ignore the importance of governance. Before examining the governance challenges inherent in PPPs, understanding the concept of governance is crucial.

The concept of governance

The word governance comes from ancient Greek and means 'to steer' or 'to guide' as in a ship. The concept was originally used by Chaucer and Shakespeare in the seventeenth century to mean an act of governing or the method of governing (Clarke 2007). The United Nations Economic and Social Commission for Asia and the Pacific (UNESCAP 2008), defines governance as the process of decision making and process by which decisions are implemented or not implemented. The concept is used in different contexts in literature and includes minimal state, new public management, good governance, corporate governance, project governance, democratic governance, international governance and public governance. It evolved concurrently in 1970s within the fields of public administration, international relations and comparative politics.

From a public administration perspective, governance marks a shift from the formal institutions of the state to a new style of governing through informal networks and nongovernmental actors, increased interdependencies between societal actors from all sectors and the combination of their resources (Angerer and Hammerschmid 2005:5). It focuses on enhancing effectiveness in management by getting things done. It is associated with the New Public Management (NPM), school of thought as an analytical tool for reform in public administration with the prescriptions of constructing out responsibilities to non-state actors (Cleveland 1972, Hyden 2012). Another discourse of governance emerged from the international donor community in 1990s following the end of the Cold War focused on analysing the emergence of global issues on environment, human rights and social development driven by social movements and activist groups. This discourse considers governance as managing principles, norms and decision-making and procedures that facilitate the maintenance of an international order. It places a normative emphasis on creating specific programme interventions and assessing progress towards what is being defined as 'good governance'. This strand of thought is epitomised by open and consensus decision-making, citizen engagement, participation, transparency, responsiveness, accountability, democracy, equality and inclusion, ethical behavior , willingness ability to collaborate, ability to compete , leadership, sustainability, legitimacy, political stability and the rule of law (World Bank 1992; United Nations Development Programme (UNDP 2004), UNECE (2005); United Nations Economic Commission for Africa(UNECA 2005); UN-ESCAP (2008).

In sum, drawing from public administration and international relations the practical space of governance in this chapter is considered as framework through which political, economic, social and administrative authority is exercised at local, national and international level. It entails balancing the roles, responsibilities, accountabilities and capabilities of different levels of governments and different actors in society to manage a country's affairs. It consists of managing principles, norms and decision-making procedures that facilitate the maintenance of an international order.

Project governance extends the principle of governance to the management of individual projects. It is viewed as an intersection of project management and corporate governance (Wilson 2010, 15:3). Corporate governance is considered as a system by which business corporations are directed and controlled through the distribution of rights and responsibilities among different participants in the corporation, such as the board managers, shareholders and other stakeholders, while spelling out the rules and procedures for making decisions (Clarke 2004). An overview of the PPPs South Africa will provide a background to understanding the governance challenges.

PPPs provide a novel approach to delivering goods and services to citizens, based on the mode of managing and governing and are considered as a policy tool for enhancing governance effectiveness (Bovaird 2004:70; Brinkerhoff 2007; Hodge & Greve 2005:5; Khanom 2010 :150). Governance in PPPs includes good governance, project governance and corporate governance. Some of the characteristics attributed to good governance in PPPs are coherent PPP policy, transparency, capacity building, risk sharing, procurement, participatory and consensus oriented, accountability, dispute resolution, responsiveness, effectiveness and efficiency, equitable and inclusiveness, rule of law, clarity of purpose, mutual trust and respect, investment of time and resources, negotiation of roles and responsibilities and long-term sustainability (UNECE 2008:13; UNECA 2005, UNECE 2004 UN-ESCAP 2008, Osborne 2000).

PPPs in South Africa

South Africa is the leading sub-Saharan country in PPPs with robust legislation and policies. The overarching requirement of good governance in the procurement of PPPs is captured in Section 217(1) of the Constitution (Act 108 of 1997). It states that when an organ of state in the national, provincial or local sphere of government or other institution identified in the national legislation contracts for goods or services, it must do so in accordance with a system that is fair, equitable, transparent and cost-effective. Furthermore, the different laws and policies governing PPPs in South Africa emphasise good governance. Among these pieces of legislation are: Treasury Regulation 16, 2004; the Municipal Systems Act of 2000 (MSA); the Municipal Finance Management Act of 2003 (PFMA) and the Promotion of Administrative Justice Act of 2000 (PAJA). The major policy documents that guide the implementation of PPPs at national level are the PPP Manual (2004) and Standardized Public-Private Market Provisions (2004) developed with the PPP unit of the National Treasury.

The country also has a dedicated PPP Unit that is responsible for monitoring and implementing PPP contracts and providing policy guidance, technical support, capacity building, and funding for PPPs projects. The South African government has adopted the use of PPPs as an integral strategy in its national and international developmental plan to solve some of its deeply rooted socioeconomic, political, fiscal and societal problems. Examples of developmental strategies are the Millennium Development Goals (MDGs) [1], The Accelerated and Growth Initiative for South Africa (Asgi-SA) [2] , the Medium Term Strategic Framework (MTSF, 2009–2014) [3] and the National Development Plan (NDP), which charts the planning and progress of the country until 2030 (Fombad 2013b:7). A number of PPP projects have been concluded covering roads, water, hospitals, schools, transport, accommodation, healthcare, ecotourism, education, social development, correctional services, and the railway. Amongst these have been the Inkosi Albert Luthuli Hospital, Free State Social Grants Information, Technology for the Department of Labour, and the Department of Trade and Industry campus concessions. Other operational PPPs worth mentioning are the Gautrain[4] state-of-the-art Rapid Rail link network responsible for the design, construction, operation and maintenance of this public rail transportation system.There is also Fleet Management, the Western Cape Rehabilitation Centre, the Lentegeur Hospital, the renal dialysis service at the Polokwane Hospital, and the Port Alfred and Settlers hospitals. Notwithstanding the existence of these pieces of legislation, and policies, and the numerous PPPs so far concluded, several governance challenges have emerged.

Governance challenges in PPPs in South Africa

If PPPs are to play an important role in enhancing development, understanding of some the governance issues inherent in PPPs is crucial. Amongst these are lack of proper monitoring and implementation mechanisms, lack of consensus community participation, transparency, value for money, risk transfer and political leadership (Fombad 2013b: 7).

Lack of proper monitoring and implementation mechanism

Several indications point to the fact that the monitoring and implementation mechanisms within PPPs are inefficient. Amongst these are inadequate measures to fully implement the different pieces of legislation, out dated policy documents and failure to monitor performance (Fombad 2013a:37).

First with regards to the implementation of the different PPP legislation, there are no visible functional mechanisms in place to ensure that the PPP legislation is properly interpreted, understood and implemented. These laws, that are supposed to put South Africa on the right path towards a coherent regulatory regime, are sometimes contradictory, requiring careful interpretation. An example is the MFMA (2003) and the MSA (2000), both of which require feasibility studies to be undertaken before a municipality forms PPPs. While the period prescribed for feasibility studies in section 78 of the MSA is approximately two years, in the MFMA (2003) an average of six months is stipulated (Fombad 2013a:37). Consequently, a wide variety of partnerships have emerged over time, some adhering strictly to the terms of the law, others established within the law, but outside of the structures prescribed by the different sections of legislation on PPP.

Also, logistics and policy requirements for successful PPP implementation have not been systematically explored. For example, the standardised PPP market provisions that were introduced in 2004 are still currently undergoing revision (Aiello 2010). It may be due to the fact that, this Unit has been experiencing a series of challenges amongst which is lack of capacity.

Furthermore, little thought tends to be given to the management and evaluation phases of PPPs. This may be due to the precontractual focus of the PPP Unit and the legislative vacuum in this area. For example, performance audits on a PPP by the Auditor-General are left to his or her discretion, and there are no provisions for the social and environmental auditing of PPPs or for follow-ups on the Auditor-General's audit report. The Parliamentary Standing Committee on Public Accounts conducted an oversight visit to prison PPPs in the Free State, the Northern Cape and Limpopo revealed that there was a long overdue follow-up on the Auditor-General's three qualified audit opinion reports issued in 2007/2008, 2009/2010 and 2009/2011(Parliamentary Communication Services 2011).

A lack of consensus community participation

The concept of meaningful community participation in decision-making that pervades sections 151(1) (e) and 151 (2) of the South African Constitution and that are further highlighted in the 'developmental' municipal legislation (MSA Act, 2000, White Paper on Local Government 1998, the Municipal Structures Act, 1998, and the MFMA, 2003) and policies such as Batho Pele[5] are missing in the PPP process. Community participation is about giving ordinary people a meaningful opportunity to exercise their voice in processes that shape the outcome of developmental issues that have a direct bearing on their daily lives. Although it may be argued that the involvement of the community may further slowdown the PPP process because the community does not speak with a unified voice and most often tends to be passive receivers of services rather than voluntary participants. Reasonable steps to involve the community in PPPs are crucial.

An example of the absence of consensus community participation in the PPPs is where negotiations between the public and private partners are conducted in private settings with little input by citizens on the grounds of 'commercial confidentiality', 'propriety rights' or data protection. Although 'commercial confidentiality' may be seen in partnerships as a means of protecting trade secrets and negotiating positions (Roberts 2002; TD Economics Special Report 2006) it is important that secrecy should not come at the expense of the public's right to know. Donaldson (2005) observed that there was a lot of opposition that surrounded the viability of the construction of the Gautrain project from the public, the media, politicians, and business since its inception. This could be attributed to the lack of public consultation. The lack of provision for input from citizens and other stakeholders from inception to procurement may be due to the fact that legislation and policies do not protect the legitimate interests of all stakeholders in fostering partnerships.

Transparency

Transparency can be defined as the public's unfettered access to timely and reliable information on decisions and performances in the public sector (Armstrong 2005). The different transparency concerns evident within the PPP processes are procurement irregularities, non-disclosure and corruption.

The increasing demand for sound procurement policies (Venter 2011; Creamer 2012) is indicative of procurement irregularities. For example, a review by the Correctional Services Minister on Prison PPPs highlighted a number of financial and operational problems with the PPP model, resulting in the suspension of four new prisons in order to undertake another review of the model (Venter 2011).

The non-disclosure of PPP contracts to the public raises issues of transparency and could compromise perceptions of the government's integrity. The South African PPP Unit provides a superficial, inconsistent disclosure of PPP information online through the PPP Quarterly. The last quarterly report was published in December 2010 with very superficial information on PPPs. With the impending approval of the so-called secrecy Bill[6] , it is crucial that secrecy must not come at the expense of the proper disclosure of information that is conveniently classified as commercial. It may be argued that the reason for non-disclosure is that PPPs are too technical for ordinary citizens to understand and make judgments. Nonetheless, by virtue of the Promotion of Access to Information (PAIA) (Act 2 of 2000), everyone has the right of access to the records of information held by the state and any information held by another person that is required for the exercise or protection of any rights.

Corruption remains another important transparency issue surrounding PPPs. The PPP Manual (2004) and Treasury Regulation 16 makes provision for accounting officers to sign an anti-corruption policy for PPP projects, and call for forensic audits if fraud or corruption is suspected. However, PPPs still offer considerable latitude for manipulation by companies and government officials that are hard for the public and anti-corruption agencies to spot. In 2009, the South African Finance Minister expressed concern about the number of government tenders that had become tainted by corruption and lamented the pervasive influence of the culture of gifts, wining and dining, and all manner of enticement (Creamer 2011).

A lack of equitable risk allocation

The common types of risk in PPPs are technical risk, design and construction risk, operating and maintenance risk, revenue risk, financial risk, force majeure, legislative risk, political risk, environmental risk, uptake patronage risk and commissioning risk (Grimsey & Lewis 2002; Forerr et al. 2010). Estimating traffic and revenue risk is more of an art than a science, and that it has a tendency to go wrong. For example, the budget of the Gauteng Department of Roads and Transport for 2011/12 included an estimated R259 million in 'patronage guarantee costs' for Gautrain Rapid Rail Link Concessionaires if the train didn't get enough passengers for the subsequent nine months that it was due to be fully operational, and it was expected to rise to R360 million in the subsequent year (Flanagan 2011). Paying this out every year will squeeze out other public transport projects, as it will consume about a third of the Gauteng roads and transport budget (Campbell 2011). Given that the government is bearing the demand risk, the question arises as to whether risks are actually transferred to the private sector, and whether the private sector does bear significant penalties when things go wrong (Fombad 2013b:7).

Value for money

Value for money can be defined in terms of the three Es: Economy, Efficiency and Effectiveness (Glynm 1985). Grimsey and Lewis (2004) define value for money as the optimum combination of whole life cycle, costs, risks, completion time and quality in order to meet public requirements. Value for money is deemed to occur if the discounted cash flows from PPPs are less than those from traditional procurement. South Africa, like the United Kingdom uses a Public Sector Comparator (PSC) theoretical model. The PSC is used in assessing and comparing PPP options with traditional public procurement models after which it is compared with bids from the private sector to evaluate any value for money benefits accruing from the PPP mechanism. The credibility of a cost-benefit analysis to determine value for money in PPPs raises procurement concerns. Firstly, there are no proactive steps to ensure that PPPs meet the criteria of affordability, value for money, substantial technical operational and financial risk transfer. Although the Public Sector Comparator (PSC) is used to determine value for money, it is a hypothetical scheme, and provision is not made for the full publication details of the calculations used. There is no conclusive evidence in South Africa that PPPs actually reduce costs and enhance value for money. This is because of the history of high transaction costs, cost overruns, delays in service delivery, as well as long, complex negotiations surrounding PPPs. For example, it is estimated that the Kimberly prison facility built at a cost of R 300 million would end up costing R 1.5 billion over a 15-year period (Venter 2011).

Political Leadership

The South African government has made significant advances towards creating an enabling environment for a viable PPP market in Africa. Top level policy support for PPPs has been regularly promoted in annual policy and budget speeches. The government's commitment to developing high and predictable standards in respect of PPP was reiterated by the then finance minister, Trevor Manuel's comments at the occasion of the launch of the Standardized Provisions where he said:

> "Too often, in too many countries, in too many projects, weakly specified contracts have led promising partnerships into conflict, contestation, failed services, unmet targets, unpaid bills and court proceedings... we will not go down that route. Those who think that service delivery contracts can be signed off on the basis of casual disregard for procurement procedures do not belong on our government side" (Public-Private Partnership Quarterly 2003).

However, more than eleven years down the line there are several indications to the effect that the government has not lived up to the above rhetoric. The very fact that in spite of the apparent growing government commitment towards PPPs the government is unable to bring the many planned PPP projects to fruition may be a reflection of inadequate PPP political leadership. For example, only 21 PPPs have been procured at the national and provincial level with procurement period for each ranging from 24 –36 months (Burger 2004; Aiello 2010; National Treasury 2011). Also, the fact that transparency, unfair contracts, in adequate supervisory, regulatory and monitoring frameworks are still common within the PPPs as observed in the preceding sections is indicative of crisis of political leadership.

Some Lessons Learned from PPPs in South Africa

In this section some lessons are drawn from the challenges to governance within PPPs examined in the preceding section to suggest some techniques that could serve as a platform for enhancing governance in PPPs in Africa. Amongst the lessons that emerged are: the need for sound procurement procedures, the importance of participatory involvement, firm political will and commitments towards PPPs, frameworks built on transparency techniques, and clarity on risk sharing strategy.

Sound procurement procedures should be emphasized

Sound procurement procedures will enhance PPPs in Africa while complex and cumbersome legislation will slow the roll out of PPPs and contribute to a culture of rule bending and the tendency to use corrupt means to avoid these rules. It is important that all procedures and regulations for PPP procurement be made simpler and clearer with few interpretation possibilities and practical and comprehensive operation manuals available for implementation. Governmental forums on PPPs may be established to deal with issues of alignment, integration and coherence. Adopting a single national PPP legislative framework will enhance consistency, uniformity and procurement in the different spheres of government. Modern PPPs legislation such as Punjab PPP Infrastructure Act 2010 (Act ix of 2010), the Manitoba PPP Transparency and Accountability Act 2012 (Bill 34 of 2012) and the Tanzanian PPP Act 2010 (18 of 2010) are based on a single Act (Fombad 2013a,37:1). Furthermore, the procurement policy should provide opportunities for more competition in the tendering process limit preferred treatment to certain classes of suppliers and make provision for conducting a pre-project analysis.

In addition, PPP legislation should be regularly updated and aligned to operations and strategies of universally accepted principles of governance outlined by international organisations such as UNECHE 2008, OECD 2007, and the ECA 2005. Among these principles are ensuring a coherent PPP policy, capacity-building, risk-sharing, putting people first, transparency, responsiveness, and following the rule of law as well as considering the present and future needs of society.

Participatory involvement

Positive involvement from all stakeholders is vital in all PPP projects. Failure to recognise and secure wider public interest may result in public opposition and project failure (Elgohary et al 2006:594). Stakeholder involvement has moved beyond mere consultation to participation and advocacy. Participatory development in the form of consultation, information sharing, joint formulation and shared responsibility emerged at the dawn of the 21st century as a development concept (OECD 2007; UNECE 2008). As a starting point the concept and need of PPPs should be publicly discussed, defined and communicated to all stakeholders in ways that are sufficiently understood. It may take the form of public education or consultative mechanisms where consortium proposals are explained or various forms of media communication. Furthermore, given that PPPs bring in a variety of stakeholders with varying interests, disparate bargaining powers, competences and resources, the PPP processes should contain mechanisms for conducting stakeholder's analyses that would balance the disparity amongst stakeholders. A thorough stakeholder involvement programme will enable project proponents and stakeholders to communicate effectively. Elgohary et al (2006:594) provide a semantic model for stakeholder involvements in infrastructure process that presents a thorough representation of processes, products, actors, constraints concern resources and mechanisms. In addition, it is crucial for all stakeholders' representatives be co-opted into the governance structure of the PPPs and be actively involved in the planning, designing and construction phases.

Monitoring frameworks are crucial

There is a need for an appropriate monitoring and performance management system and mechanism for their audit to be set out in the contract to ensure that the PPPs process is monitored. One way to enhance the mentoring of PPP is to ensure that the public-sector procuring agencies are established within each PPP to monitor proper implementation, conduct monthly operational review meetings and present quarterly reports on the project. An example may be drawn from the Gautrain Rapid Rail where the Gautrain Management Agency (GMA), the Independent Socio-Economic Monitor (ISEM) and the Independent Certifier. The Gautrain Management Agency (GMA) ensures proper implementation of the contract by the private party on behalf of Government. Also, governments should be able to manage the performance of PPPs systematically and comprehensively over the life of the project rather than relying on once–off reports or enquiries from the auditor-general when an aspect of the PPP goes wrong.

With the exponential growth in the freedom of expression, the critical voice of the mass media, the press and investigative journalism or political commentary is crucial in generating and disseminating information necessary that would hold public officials and agencies accountable. The reality is that the exposure of poor service delivery, inequities, or inefficiencies by citizens, civil society organisations, or the media will not have much impact on increasing accountability unless these actions trigger some sort of legal sanctions.

Also, the parliament, through a PPP parliamentary committee, should carefully examine contracts between the public-sector and private-sector provider from inception to development to ensure that these contracts are delivered according to the terms of the contract. The findings of the parliamentary committee should be tabled in parliament and made available to the public. Furthermore, the parliamentary committee should ensure that the findings of the auditor-general are not reduced to a 'twenty-four hour talking point' after which it is forgotten but rather achieve the desired effect of correcting aberrations and improving operations.

The monitoring of PPP should extend beyond the office of the Auditor-General and the PPP Unit to the ombudsmen and public sector procuring agencies. For example, in Australia, specialised ombudsman such as telecommunication ombudsman are responsible for accountability in PPPs (Watson, 2003). In the UK, the public-sector procuring agency monitors these contracts through monthly operational review meetings and quarterly strategic review meetings (Dimirag, et al 2004:271).

Firm political will and commitments towards PPPs will maintain the momentum of the partnership

Redefining the degree of political support will strengthen governance in PPPs. The United Nations Secretary-General Ban Ki-Moon observed that political will must be mobilised to increase developmental assistance, including capacity building for good governance (UNECE 2008). Similarly, the United Nations Millennium Project (UNMP 2005) report on a practical plan to achieve MDG suggests firm political leadership and strong government commitment in order to realise the goals of improving public investments and capacity building. At the national level the government may achieve a greater political oversight of PPP projects through participatory monitoring and redefining a series of policy directions for PPPs. One example, of participatory monitoring is to ensure that PPP goals are met within the agreed time frame and that those responsible for missing deadlines are held accountable. With regards to policy direction, the government should assume leadership, ethics and genuine legitimacy to ensure the effective implementation, regulation and evaluation of PPPs in ways that best serve the public interest, ensuring that goals are met in agreed time frames, and that those responsible for missing deadlines are held accountable. Furthermore, government should seek to improve capacity and skills development in PPP through on-the-job learning, workshops and seminars. In this way it may enhance the technical ability and willingness of those at the lower levels to be able to take up new roles and adapt to new situations.

At the global level African governments should adopt the different accountability pledges and international accountability standards and be held responsible for implementing these pledges by the community through shadow reports, scorecards and the social media. With regard to pledges, governments should consider signing and implementing the integrity pact tool developed by Transparency International (Nepad Policy Focus 2005; Transparency International 2010). Benin, Nigeria and Bangladesh have formally implemented the principles contained in the integrity pact. Furthermore, the governments should adopt the Extractive Industries Transparency Initiative (EITI) that was launched at the World Summit on Sustainable Development in Johannesburg, South Africa, in September 2002. This is a PPP between governments, international organisations, companies, non-governmental organisations, investors, and business and industrial organisations to increase transparency, avoid corruption and improve governance transactions between governments and companies in the extractive industries (Aaronson 2011,31 50).

A new framework of PPP governance should be built on transparency

There are several ways by which transparency may be enhanced in PPPs in Africa. One way may be to establish a formal public, contractual, communal, managerial accountability processes and mechanisms in the different stages of PPP that will criticise and complement government decisions and private sector actions and keep the public informed. This will be similar to that obtained in the United Kingdom (Sinclair 1995; Demirag & Khadaroo 2011:271). A public accountability structure within PPP is fundamental in Africa given that government draws its authority from the people and is ultimately owned by the people. Besides, the government is the major agent and enforcer of accountability in society and is the body that establishes the contract in the first place. Formal contractual accountability structures that match the standard service specifications with service output with performance indicators, quality standards and penalties expressly included are useful. Community accountability structures will enhance meaningful community participation in decision-making. An internal managerial accountability structure within the contract management clause will enhance the supervision and monitoring of the quality of services of PPPs throughout the life cycle of the project in order to assess the extent to which they are meeting the agreed service standards in the contract.

Another way to enhance transparency in PPPs is to focus on the creation of a people-centered and a people-driven PPPs characterised by equity, quality, accountability and a strong code of ethics. One way is to ensure that citizens as consumers should be able to properly evaluate PPPs and provide valuable feedback to government about the effectiveness of the service provided. For example, in Bangladesh a Community of Concerned Citizens consisting of youths, non-governmental organisations, civil society organisations and other interested parties was formed to monitor and evaluate the quality of service and performance of PPPs and make reports through the press and the media (Transparency International 2010). Citizens may also conduct service delivery surveys through the use of household questionnaires, key informant interviews and community surveillance.

Furthermore, ensuring that anti-corruption initiatives, structures and institutions are reinforced and integrated during the life cycle of PPP project will enhance transparency. It may take the form of signing a PPP integrity pact. The integrity pact provides an agreement between the government department and the bidder wherein they agree to abstain from bribery both during the selection and the implementation of the contract, disclose all commissions and similar expenses paid in connection with the contract and sanctions in case of violation of the contract (Transparency International 2010). In Tanzania, for instance, civil servants publicly make integrity pledges to avoid corrupt practices (Langan & Cooksey 1995). Also, the Bathos Pele eight principles (Batho Pele Handbook 2005) should not only be incorporated and checked within PPPs but measures should be in place to ensure effective implementation of these principles within the PPP life cycle. A simple slogan such as "zero tolerance to corruption in PPPs" may be a warning signal against corruption

Investigating allegations of corruption through a judicial process may deter those who may want to circumvent existing procedures for personal gain. Also, meritocracy should be promoted by ensuring that officials engaged in PPPs have decent wages.

Risk sharing strategy should be clarified at the onset

It is becoming apparent from studies on transportation PPPs such as Juppe's (2011) study on the modernisation and fragmentation of the UK transport infrastructure and the Gautrain that risk transfer argument is not very credible for rail and transportation systems. This is because they are capital intensive systems that do not provide for universal service. Therefore, it should be explicitly recognised that risks are shared and not transferred to the private party. In this way, governments will be conscious that the purpose of PPP is not only to provide some financial cover during concession but that it can also benefit from the expertise and 'best value techniques' of the private sector such as innovation, flexibility, speed, expertise, and efficiency (Watson 2003; Clifton and Duffied 2006:24).

Also, risks should be allocated to the party ready to bear it. In this regard, issues such as the type of risk to be allocated, the party to who risk is allocated, the party who should accept the risk and preventive strategies should be clearly considered (Abednego and Ogunlana 2006:622). The implications are that both the public and private sector partners should be prepared to take calculated risks when entering into PPPs. Alliance contracting techniques may improve long-term service outcomes. Alliance contracting is an agreement between parties to work cooperatively to achieve agreed outcomes on the basis of sharing risks and rewards (Clifton & Duffield, 2006:24). In order for alliance contacting to be effective, partnership needs to move beyond contractual to relational (Wilson 2010). To this end, Boviard (2004: 70) advocates that partnerships should not just involve partners respecting contracts to which they are legally committed but should be genuinely collaborative. Therefore, trust, collaboration, mutual commitment, and social and community obligation are crucial in enhancing risk transfer.

Furthermore, the affordability of a project in terms of the current and the expected future risk should be clearly ascertained. PPPs require proactive expert analysis of the different types of risk. For example, a public agency when entering a partnership should devise a plan to mitigate the impact to the public of an interruption of services as a result of failure by either party to deliver due to forces beyond their control (Forre et al 2010:70). Finally, good project governance inevitable results in achieving proper risk allocation (Abednego and Ogunlana 2006:622). Good project governance involves making the right decision at the right time ensuring that there is contract farness, transparency and responsiveness. It entails continuous project control and monitoring equality, creativeness and efficiency and accountability.

Conclusion

The chapter underscores the importance of PPPs as an integral part of Africa's national and international development plan. It is becoming eminent that in order for PPPs to contribute positively to Africa's developmental goals an increased attention on issues concerning the effective governance PPP is crucial. The key implication of the contribution has been to present an assessment of the extent to which governance has been achieved in PPPs in South Africa given that it is the leading sub–Saharan African country in PPPs, and critically examined the lessons learned for other African countries. It is clear that attaining the promises of development through PPP rests on enhancing the following governance factors: the need for sound procurement procedures, the importance of participatory involvement, firm political will and commitments towards PPPs, frameworks built on transparency techniques, and clarity on risk sharing strategy. It is apparent that poor governance in PPPs will lead to a lack of appeal of PPPs as a new policy alternative for development in Africa. The outcome of a report, on the Africa Public Private Partnership Network (2012) held in Abuja Nigeria suggest that African countries are bound by the same destiny of infrastructural and service delivery deficit and therefore regional collaboration between growing PPP units in Africa may enhance the development of Africa's infrastructure and services.

Notes and References

1 The Millennium Development Goals (MDGs) were drawn up at the United Nations Millennium Summit in 2000 by 193 United Nations member states and several international organizations with a view to achieving eight critical economic and social development priorities by 2015. These eight priorities are: poverty eradication, primary education, gender equality, maternal and child health, the reduction of HIV/AIDS and other diseases, clean water and sanitation, environmental sustainability, and the development of global partnerships.

2 South African strategy for raising economic growth and reducing poverty and unemployment by 2014.

3 The Medium Term Strategic Framework (MTSF, 2009–2014) is state-

ment of government intent. It identifies the development challenges facing South Africa and outlines the medium-term strategy for improving South Africans 'living conditions. The MTSF outlines ten priority areas that are intended to give effect to these strategic objectives.

4 The Gautrain is Africa's first world-class, modern rapid rail and bus service PPP in South Africa.

5 Batho Pele is a Sotho translation for 'People First'. It is an initiative of the South African Department of Public Service and Administration to get public servants to be service orientated, to strive for excellence in service delivery, and to improve their efficiency and accountability to the recipients of public goods and services. The eight principles that allow citizens to hold public servants accountable for the level of services they deliver are: consultation, service standards, access, courtesy, information, openness and transparency, redress and value for money (*Batho Pele Handbook*, 2005).

6 Protection of State Information Bill.

Aaronson, A. 2011. A limited partnership: business, government, civil society, and the public in the extractive industries transparency initiative (EITI). Public Administration and Development, 31, 50–63

Abednego, P. and S. Ogunlana 2006. Good project governance for proper risk allocation in Public private partnerships in Indonesia International Journal of Project Management 24, 622-634

Agere, S. 2000. Promoting good Governance: principles, practices and perspectives London: Commonwealth Secretariat

Aiello, J. 2010. Treasury View on South Africa's PPP. Programme presentation senior project advisor PPP Unit National Treasury. http://wwwCput.Ac.Za/Cgi/Viewcontent.Cgi?Filename=0&Article=1024. (accessed 16 April 2011)

Angerer, D.J and G. Hammerschmid. 2005. Public private partnership between euphoria and disillusionment. Recent experiences from Austria and implications for countries in transformation Romanian Journal of Political Science, 5(1) 129-159.

Armstrong, E. 2005. Integrity, transparency and accountability in public administration: recent trends, regional and international developments and emerging Issues. United Nations Economic and Social Affairs.

http://unpan1.un.org/intradoc/groups/public/documents/un/unpan020955.pdf (accessed 16 April 2011)

Bangura, Y. and G A Larbi. 2006. Fiscal and capacity-building reform, Basingstoke UNRISD/Palgrave.

Batho Pele Handbook. 2005. A service delivery improvement guide: association for public administration and management. http://www.dpsa.gov.za/documents/gics/bphb/BathoPeleHandbook.pd (accessed 16 April 2011)

Bauer, N. 2011. Trevor Manuel's new deal for South Africa. Business Mail, November 15

Bovaird, T. 2004. Public-Private Partnerships: from contested concepts to prevalent practice. International Review of Administrative Sciences, 70 (2) 199–215.

Brinkerhoff, D. and J. Brinkerhoff. 2011. Public–Private Partnerships: perspectives on purposes, public, and good governance. Public Administration and Development, (31) 2–14

Brinkerhoff, J. eds, 2007. Partnership as a means to good governance: toward an evaluation framework. In partnerships, governance and sustainable development: reflections on theory and practice, Glasbergen P, Biermann F, Mol APJ). Cheltenham: Edward Elgar Publishers.

Broadbent, J. 2004b. Finance Initiative in the UK. Critical Perspectives on Accounting 14. (1) 23-48.

Campbel, N. 2011. Democratic alliance Member of Parliament L, June 21 2011 http://www.politicsweb.co.za/politicsweb/view/politicsweb/en/page71619?oid=242040&sn=Marketingweb+detail (accessed 16 April 2011)

Capital, A. 2012. Six factors that will impact growth in Nigeria's property sector in 2012. Frontier market Intelligence. http://www.tradeinvestnigeria.com/feature_articles/1161700.html ((accessed 16 April 2011)

Clarke, T. International Corporate Governance: A Comparative Approach Oxon: Routledge

Cleveland, H. 1972. The future executive: a guide for tomorrow´s managers. New York: Harper&Row.

Clifton, C., & Duffield C. (.2006). Improved PFI/PPP Service Outcomes through the Integration of Alliance Principles. International Journal of Project Management 24(7) 573-586.

Creamer, T. 2011. Tighter tender rules issued in bid to combat fraud, boost transparency Engineering News. (accessed 16 April 2018) from http://www.nwpg.gov.za/Public%20Works/Documents/PressRelease/TenderRegulation.pdf)

Creamer, T. 2012. Future PPP model must balance public, private risk more 'equitably'. Engineering News. 4th May 2012. http:// www.engineeringnews.co.za/.../future-ppp-model-must-balance-public-private-risk-more-equitably-2012-05. (accessed 16 April 2011)

Deloitte and Touche Research 2006. Closing the infrastructure gap: The role of public-private Partnerships. (accessed 16 April 2018 from, http://www.deloitte.com/assets/dcom-shared%20assets/documents/dtt_ps_closinggap061307.Pdf

Demirag, I. and I. Khadaroo, 2011. Accountability and value for money: A theoretical framework for the relationship in public–private partnerships. Journal of manag Gov (15): 271-296

Donaldson, R. 2005. Contesting the proposed rapid rail link in Gauteng. Urban forum 16(1): 55-62

Economic Commission for Africa. 2005. Partnership modalities for enhancing good governance. http://www.uneca.org/eca_resources/publications/dpmd/partnership_modalities_final.pdf. (accessed 25 November 2011)

EL-Gohary M, H. Osman and E. El-Diraby, 2006. Stakeholder management for public private partnerships International Journal of Project Management 24, 595-604

Escribano, A., J L. Guasch, M. de Orte & J. Pena. 2008a: Investment climate assessmentased on Demean Olley and Pakes Decompositions: Methodology and Applications to Turkey's Investment Climate Survey," Working Paper # 08-20 (12), Universidad Carlos III de Madrid.

Flanagan, L. and F. Serrao. 2011. Gautrain hidden millions. 21 June, Pretoria: The Star .

Flanagan, L. 2011. Democratic Alliance fight for transparency in Gautrain's costs. June 22, Pretoria: The Star.

Fombad, M. 2013a. An overview of accountability mechanisms in public-private partnerships in South Africa UFAHAMU: Journal of African Studies 37 (1).32

Fombad, M. 2013b. Challenges to accountability in public-private partnerships from a South African perspective. African Journal of Business Ethics 7 (1) 1-16

Forrer, J., J.E. Kee, K. E. Newcomer, and E. Boyer, 2010. Public–private partnerships and the public accountability question. Public Administration Review, 70(3) 475-484.

Froud, J. and J. Shaoul, 2001. Appraising and evaluating PFI for NHS hospitals. Financial Accountability and Management, 17 (3) 191-297.

Grimsey D. and M. Lewis. 2004. Public-private partnership: The world wide revolution in infrastructure provision and project finance. Cheltenham Edward Elgar.

Grimsey, D. and.M. Lewis, 2002. Evaluating the risk of public-private partnership for infrastructure projects. International Journal of Project Management, (20) 107-118

Hodge, G. and C. Greve 2005. The challenge of public–private partnerships: learning from international Experience. Cheltenham: Edward Elgar

Hyden, G. 2012. The concept of Governance Paper presented at the "IAD Spring Symposium: Elections, Accountability and Democratic Governance in Africa," at the Institute for African Development, Mario Einaudi Centre for International Studies, Cornell University, Ithaca, New York, 19-21 April 2012.

Jupe, R. 2011. The modernization and fragmentation of the UK's transport infrastructure. Financial Accounting and Management 27(1) 44-61

Kelman, S. 2001. Discussion paper on procurement issues in South Africa that affect growth and development Harvard University JFK School of Government http://www.treasury.gov.za/publications/other/growth/06-Procurement%20and%20BEE/01-(accessed 16 April 2011)

Khanom. N A.2010. International Review of Business Research Papers 6. 2. Julep. 150 -163

Langan.P &Cooksey, B. 1995. The national integrity system in Tanzania. Proceedings of a workshop convened by the prevention of corruption bureau, Tanzania. Mount Meru Hotel, Arusha, Taznania, 10-12 August

National Treasury. 2011 Department of National Treasury Republic of South Africa http://oag.treasury.gov.za/Publications/10.%20Practice%20Notes/For%20fin%20year%202011-12/20110531%20Instruction%20Note%2032%20-%20Enhancing%20Compliance%20Monitoring%20SCM.pdf (accessed 16 April 2018)

Nepad Policy Focus Series. 2005. Working together assessing public-private partnership. In South African Institute of International Affairs, (SAII's), Farlam, P. Nepad and Governance Project. Pretoria: Royal Netherlands Embassy

OECD. 2007. Organization for Economic Cooperation and Development: principles for private sector participation in infrastructure. http://www.oecd.org/daf/inv/investment-policy/38309896.pdf. (accessed 16 February 2011)

Osborne, S.P. 2000. Public-private partnerships: Theory and Practice in international perspective). London: Rutledge Teisman.

Paoletto, G. 2000. Public-private partnerships: An Overview of cause and effect, in Wang, Yidan edi, public private partnerships in the social sector, issues and country experiences in Asia and pacific. Tokyo: Adbi press.

Parliamentary Communication Service. 2011. Business of parliament. http://www.parliament.gov.za/live/content.php?Item_ID=1595. Partnerships. http://download.asb.wdev.co.za/download/guideline_on_accountingfor_ppps_1233642022.pdf (accessed 16 April 2018)

Pessoa, A. 2006 Public –private sector partnerships in developing countries prospects and draw backs. Faculdade de Economic do PortoRua Dr. Roberto Frias4200-464 Porto, Portugal, Research works in Progress.

Report of the African Public Private Partnership Network (2012). Promoting Regional Infrastructure as a critical ingredient on achieving greater regional integration. Inaugural meeting www.sadcpppnetwork.org/index.php (accessed 16 April 2018)

Public Accounts Committee NSW Parliament. 2006. Inquiry into public -private partnerships Report No.159 available at www.Parliament Nsw.Gov.Au/Public Accounts. www.Parliamanet .Nsw.Gov.Au / publication (accessed 10 May 2011 from)

Public- private partnership quarterly. 2003. Finance Minister serious about making public-private partnership work. South Africa: Pretoria

Public–private partnership manual. 2004. National Treasury. South Africa: Pretoria.

Public–private partnership manual. 2007. National Treasury. South Africa: Pretoria.

Robert, A. 2002. Closing the window: public service restructuring and the weakening of public of freedom of information law. Salem Papers. http:// www.inpuma.net). (accessed 28 April 2011)

Sader, F. 2000. Attracting foreign direct investment into infrastructure: why is it so difficult? Foreign Investment Advisory Service (FIAS), Washington. https://www.wbginvestmentclimate.org/... (accessed 2 May 2012)

Sinclair, A. 1995. The chameleon of accountability: forms and discourses. Accounting, Organizations and Society, (20): 219-237.

TD economic special report bank financial group (2006). Creating the winning conditions for public-private partnerships (P3s) in Canada. http://www.td.com/economics/special/db0606_p3s.pdf (accessed, 12 June 2011)

The World Bank .2006. Public private partnerships units- what are they, what do they do? By Mark Ditz, Clive Harris, Inderbir Dhingra and Chris Shugart World Bank Occasional Paper. infrastructure.gov.in/pdf/PPP-PROJECT.pdf. (accessed 30 November 30 2011)

Thomsen, S. 2005. Investment for African development: making it happen NEPAD/OECD investment initiative. Imperial Resort Beach Hotel Kama Hal, Entebbe, Uganda. http://www.oecd.org/investment/investmentfordevelopment/34874343.pdf (accessed 16 April 2018)

Transparency International. 2010. The anti-corruption catalyst: realizing the MDGs by 2015 https://www.transparency.org/whatwedo/publication/the_anti_corruption_catalyst_realising_the_mdgs_by_2015 (accessed 16 April 2018)

Treasury Regulation 16. 2004. Public-private partnerships. Issued in terms of the Public Finance Management Act, 1999 Gazette No 25915, 16 January.

UNDP. 2004. United Nation Development Program. Anti-corruption Practice Note http://www.uneca.org/itca/governance/Documents/Anti%20Corruption%20Note%20FINAL%20VERSION%20031704.pdf) (accessed 12 June 2012)

UNECA. 2005. United Nations Economic Commission for Africa. Partnership modalities for enhancing good governance. http://repository.uneca.org/handle/10855/5649 (accessed 16 April, 2018)

UNECE .2004. United Nations Economic Commission for Europe. Governance in public private partnerships for infrastructure development http://www.Unece.Org/Fileadmin/Dam/Ie/Ppp/Documents/Botguidegov.Pdf (accessed 16 April 2011)

UNECE. 2008. United Nations Economic Commission for Europe Guidebook on Promoting Good Governance in public- private partnership. Geneva: United Nations University Press.

UNEESCAP, 2011. United Nations Economic and Social Commission for Asia and the Pacific. A guidebook for public–private partnership in infrastructure. http://www.unescap.org/ttdw/common/TPT/PPP/text/ppp_guidebook.pdf (accessed 10 September 2012)

Venter, I. 2011 Cancelled prison contracts may dampen PPP appetite. http://www.engineeringnews.co.za/article/master-builders-sa-says-cancelled-prison-contracts-may-dampen-industrys-ppp-appetite-. (accessed 12 April 2012)

West, E. 2003. First rand won't duck. Maharaj report. August 1, Business Report

Wilson, D. 2010. A review of Australian PPP governance structures. Journal of Financial Management of Property and Construction. 15, 3, 2010

World Bank.1992. Governance and Development Washington, DC: The World Bank

World Bank. 2008. World Bank Annual Report, Washington D.C.

World Bank. 2005. Infrastructure in Sub-Saharan Africa: The Role of the World Bank and the Donor Community, Washington

PART 3:

African Political Economy, Regional Integration, Trade and Development

Towards Building an Institutional Infrastructure for Africa's Development and Economic Self-Determination

Ogechukwu Ajoku and *Salim Magashi*

Introduction

Africa is in need of a revolution. It is revolution that should traverse the entire spectrum of the continent especially the current socio-economic realities on the ground. The revolution is realizable through the instrumentality of a properly regulated private sector-driven economy to enhance the expansion of economic and regional trade integration. The continent is in need of strong institutions and legal architecture to drive development with the Asian Tigers of China, Singapore, Malaysia, Indonesia, and others as reliable models. African nations are yet to create and fashion out homegrown technological outputs and articulate economic policies that are suitable to their environment. Development models are almost exclusively borrowed, if not dictated from the Western advanced nations. Hence, Africa's economic policies tilt to the conveniences of the advanced economies thereby reflective of their 'vested interests'.

On attaining independence, African nations became plagued with paucity of domestic investment. This was due to lack of huge capital required for such investments, as well as dearth of technical expertise requisite to exploit the vast mineral resources that abound under the belly of the most newly independent Africa nations (Shivji 1989). This is about 50-60 years ago. There was extreme poverty, which has hitherto not ceased to plague these African nations. The compelling alternative became the over reliance on foreign capital in form of either foreign aid from aid agencies, such as the Directorate for International Development (DFID) and United States Agency for International Development (USAID), amongst sundry others, or foreign direct investment (FDI) for economic development programmes, and policies (Salomon 2007; Salomon 2008:121-148). These FDIs came along with the concept of free market economy that later became veritable instruments of dependence by most third world countries. Arguably, the free market economy remains an extension for exacting and consolidating neo-colonialist strategies. The resultant consequence is now what these nations are grappling with high debt burden and fatigue. Following the high debt burden, the multilateral institutions, often under the sponsorship of the capital exporting countries, such as the United States, United Kingdom and their European Union counterparts, began to dictate economic and developmental policies of these nations in order to benefit from the debt burden. These are clearly visible through structural adjustment programmes (SAPs), which left virtually all African countries worse off upon subscription. The developed West deploys all manner of arm-twisting tactics to foist and perpetuate their motives. Such tactics are the various enslaving international investment agreements (IIAs), bilateral investment agreement (BITs) and transnational investments agreements etc. entered into by some powerful transnational corporations (TNCs) with the governments of these African nations. These agreements are largely unbalanced in favour of the capital-exporting countries and to their own beneficial interests. In the midst of extreme poverty in the African countries resulting from budget deficits, and lack of technical know-how to tap into abundant resources, African Countries are compelled, tricked or even conscripted to conclude arrangements that seem like economic development pacts, but which end up being economically exploitative.

To put it emphatically, in over 50 years of TNCs operations and activities in developing nations including Africa, there is absolutely nothing to show in terms of development other than consumerist propensity of its peoples. Unfortunately, also, African nations, despite suffering from the same problem of underdevelopment have not been able to fully unite and chart a formidable, sustainable developmental course. Therefore, the aim of this chapter is to determine how this African tragedy may be corrected. The chapter is divided into five sections. First is a historical narration that also argues why Africa should vigorously pursue the right to economic self-determination. The second section examines the challenges of Africa's unity and development through the concept and principle of economic self-determination. It explores the possibility of regional trade and economic integration. Section three discusses the prospects of a pan-Africanist approach to Africa's regional integration and development challenges. Section four examines the impact and challenges of the transition from OAU to AU as an avenue to solve Africa's problem of development. It addresses the human rights struggle and the challenges that face AU mandate to transform the continent. Section five suggests an architecture towards building an institutional structure for African development. Finally, the chapter is concluded with a recommended solution.

Self-determination as the bane of beleaguered development in Africa

Economic self-determination seeks to reshape the prevailing international legal architecture, thereby serving as the effective tool for reawakening and economic recovery. It is, therefore, obviously not an African invention. What has become so worrisome is why African nations have hitherto ignored to echo this principle louder and clearer. The concept and principle of economic self-determination seeks to broaden the economic power base of African nations by offering a functional interpretation of sovereignty. Sovereignty, in this regard, encompasses both political and economic sovereignty. In other words, this conduces to the inviolable right to freely adopt any preferred economic pleasures and policies for the attainment of economic independence devoid of external interference. This has basis in the UN Charter.[1] It is also the legal basis of several UN General Assembly resolutions, such as "permanent sovereignty over wealth an natural resources",[2] "new international economic order",[3] "the charter of economic rights and duties of states"[4] . In spite of all these, economic sovereignty is yet to be attained in Africa. Is it due to a lack of political will, lack of courage to confront the inimical antics of the western capital exporting nations, or just mere ignorance emanating from the incompetence of those at the helm of governance?

Africa belongs to the group of nations classified as developing nations, third world countries, or underdeveloped (least developed) countries. Certain characteristics consign them to this euphemistic branding. There is widespread poverty and bad governance, with weak institutions. Enterprising Africans are unable to gain access to international credit lines and international markets that are easily available to developed nations and their nationals (AkaaGerger 2001:17). There is a prevailing need to examine the entire legal architecture, institutional and developmental infrastructure so far in place so as to discover the missing link to African home-grown initiatives. It seems that African economic development programmes are externally dictated, perhaps due to the western capitalist strategies and methodologies that smack of implicit colonial linkages. The natural resources that abound in the continent are largely exploited by multinational corporations with huge capital and technical expertise readily available to them. There is yet no proactive positive effort to rid Africa of remaining colonial vestiges. The direct consequence of this has been over dependence on their former colonial masters. This has made it impossible to forge effectively functional regional integration.

What is the formula to be deployed to exit Africa from grinding poverty and strife? How can Africa be self-reliant? What are the institutions and infrastructure that provide an enabling atmosphere for the attainment of economic self-determination? What are the capacity-building measures that are created to enhance growth and advancement, just like the capital-exporting nations? It is worrisome that the African continent relies on foreign aid for socioeconomic development programmes. In this circumstance, the principle of economic self-determination and economic sovereignty has suffered several onslaughts (Uchendu 1981:34). Such onslaughts are traceable to several institutional challenges posed from the Breton Woods institutions represented by the International Monetary Fund (IMF) and the World Bank. It is very obvious that the very Articles of Agreement of these multilateral financial institutions are contradictory and deliberately created for inequality. A direct consequence of the imbalance became the emergence of a consortium of banks that offered syndicated loans to most African countries with unattainable terms. This demonstrates unsavoury efforts of the IMF, mostly for the piecemeal handling of the debt crisis that ravaged many African countries (Frank 1970:55).

The importance of this principle of economic self-determination looms so large that it cannot be underestimated. The essence and value of the principle of self-determination to the African economic sovereignty will not be adequately appreciated without first and foremost addressing the issues and implications of colonialism. This is an unfortunate historical phase that later collapsed in the face of radical economic nationalism (AkaaGerger 2001:11). Sequel to decolonization was the emergence of independent African countries that presently constitute the largest members of the international community. They grouped themselves into several complex relations and blocs.[5] They faced diverse challenges. First and foremost, there was inequality in the basis of their economic capacity as compared with the colonialists' home country, thereby resulting to dependency and underdevelopment. Secondly, the prevailing world order was already dominated by the economically developed powerful nations of Western Europe and North America. These advanced and developed nations view these African countries as existing only to serve their mercantilist interests. This Eurocentric tendency, prejudicial international legal order, devised by these capital exporting countries obviously is a clear endorsement of economic exploitation and thereby consolidates dependence. In order to address this challenge, it is imperative to secure economic self-determination.[6] This has hitherto evolved into a legal regime that has steadily confronted Eurocentric motives. By emphasizing equitable and just economic relations between nations, economic self-determination principle has widened the functional interpretation of sovereignty, thereby seeking to dismantle the edifice of underdevelopment.

The principle of economic self-determination presupposes the inalienable right to freely formulate any laudable and beneficial economic measures and policies for the attainment of economic independence and self-reliance, devoid of external interference. It is pertinent to note that the principle of economic self-determination has its basis in the UN Charter[7]. It is also the legal basis to several UN resolutions, actions of its agencies, as well as economic cooperation programmes like the European Economic Community – African Caribbean and Pacific (EEC-ACP). [8] It is pertinent to further note that the most prominent of the UN resolutions are those that dwell on permanent Sovereignty over Wealth and Natural Resources; the New International Economic order: and Charter on Economic Rights and Duties of States. Additionally, continuous efforts of the UN relevant agencies such as United Nations Industrial Development Organization (UNIDO), United Nations Conference on Trade and Development (UNCTAD) and also, their coordinating agency, the Economic and Social Council (ECOSOC) fully recognizes the economic self-determination principle.

Challenges to economic self-determination

The African continent may be largely poor, but poverty does not necessarily mean lacking in mineral and human resources, but lacking in initiatives, creativity, and brilliance in harnessing these vast resources that abound the continent. It suggests that heavy reliance on FDI for economic development schemes and policies is not a conclusive or a healthy panacea to growth and transformation beneficial to the continent. Attraction of foreign capital should not be the only strategy for economic and industrial growth. In other words, there should be a guided approach to FDI.

Africa is a tourist's haven. There are mountains, grasslands, and the daunting mystery of the largest desert in the world. These provide large aquatic and agrarian vegetation for meaningful livelihood. The African continent offers a diversity of peoples and languages that exceed world's estimate that could take a lifetime to unravel. The continent offers limitless wonder and challenge. Falling in love with the continent is very easy and effortless. On the other hand, there is poverty, famine disease, war, and abuse of the environment. The continent gravitates between dearth and plenty. Africa is always at the cross roads. It has had more military, and dictatorial, regimes in the last decades, and past century than any continent on the planet. Additionally, the spectre of civil war looms large in the collective psyche of those who hope for a new paradigm of progress. The people of the continent are most times implacable and unrelenting. The beauty of Africa is neither pre-packaged nor the product of an uncaring industry. It is a tale that unfolds itself day after day, replenishing itself with each passing phase of hardship and trauma. It is a flower that blooms continually, nourishing the soil in which it grows. Moreover, some parts are richly endowed with vast natural mineral resources. In spite of these, human experiences and livelihood seems a hazardous journey into uncertainty and strife.

Despite its provision in the UN Charter, the economic self-determination principle has suffered several challenges. There are three categories of these challenges. Firstly, the institutional challenge that has its basis in the Breton Woods arrangement (AkaaGerger 2001:19). The Bretton Woods consist of two institutions-the World Bank and International Monetary Funds (IMF). These are instruments of economic dependency. They foisted Structural Adjustment Programme (SAP) on the African continents and worsened the debt crises of many African countries. It is obvious that the very ingredients in the programmes of these multilateral financial institutions are contradictory and deliberate designs of inequality. This laid the foundation for economic inequity, imbalance and dependence to cater for private sector driven economy that is yet to blossom. They came to serve the purposes, inter alia, of rescheduling African countries' debt crisis.

A second challenge to the economic self-determination principle is the emergence of global economic inter-dependence and cooperation for development that de-emphasizes statism and nationalism. The core of this initiative is the changing global policy framework that dwells on the free market concept (i.e. market liberalization). This later culminated to what is now widely regarded as economic globalization, which presupposes the existence of balance of economic capacity of international actors. It is very obvious in this context that while capital exporting countries present marketable assets, such as goods, technology know-how and services, the African continent will trade debts in return. In other words, debt crisis is a deliberate strategy of the capital exporting (developed) countries designed to consolidate dependence. It is pertinent to seriously contend in this regard that the global debt crisis of the African countries should start receiving positive attention. There havc recently been steps already taken in this direction, which is yet a drop in the ocean, but still laudable. Yet it should be stressed that the categorization of some African countries as highly indebted poor countries (HIPC) is grossly unacceptable and unfair, bearing in mind how Europe, serially and consciously under developed Africa (Rodney 1972). Concepts like debt forgiveness, debt remission, conciliation and reparation is a complete travesty and therefore misleading. These have never been helpful due to corruption and policy inconsistency as bane of most African countries such as Nigeria, Mali, Gabon, Zambia, Sudan, among others. Hence, the perceived benefits of the above initiatives are not reaching the governed and most vulnerable population.

One of its cardinal architecture for inclusive development in Africa is the New Partnership for Africa's Development (NEPAD).[9] NEPAD claims to be a home grown economic strategy for Africa's economic development and transformation. However, the current reality is that no entity can develop in isolation. For any realistic development paradigm to be successful, it must be comprehensive and must have the character of promoting cooperation hence, the prevailing cooperation between African countries and other parts of the world. Nevertheless, this chapter doubts the role of FDI in economic self-determination of the African nations. It interrogates how well the transition from OAU to AU fared in extending political independence to economic self-determination, and transformation. There is a prevailing need to inquire whether AU is now in the mould of EU or just an appendage to EU. Is AU the economic and socio-political playground of EU or a collaborative counterpart? Moreover, international law of development recognizes the right to development and self-determination of independent nations, particularly Africa. Suffice to suggest that economic self-determination for sustainable development is a sine qua non to Africa's growth, advancement and transformation. Hence, economic self-determination is a principle of international law, having been provided in the United Nations Charter.[10]

The African integration and the pan Africanism debate

There is a need to automatically transform the way African Societies are integrated into the world economic system. This presupposes the emergence of a supranational authority that shall assume a certain degree of power and authority. This further leads to determining the degree of power and authority to supranational authority, should wield and whether such power and authority are revocable or irrevocable. The debate is still unresolved (Obasanjo 2005).

Pan-Africanism was originated in the Diaspora out of a longing for the African homeland. It was the conditions of slavery which laid the foundation for Pan-Africanism and Black Nationalism in the United States and West-Indies. It is also traceable to the founding of African Association in London in 1897 and the convening, in the same city, of the Pan-African conference three years later by Trinidadian lawyer, H. Sylvester Williams. There were series of other Pan-African congresses in the United States and Europe between 1900 and 1945. Some were under the auspices of Dr. W.E.B Dubois, an American scholar and activist, which brought together peoples of African descent from the Americas, Africa and Europe. Thus, in 1920s (Adogamhe 2008:8), Marcus Garvey began to promote African nationalism and to advocate African self-government with the motto, "Africa for Africans".[11] Moreover, during the I930s, the Pan-Africanist movement was largely influenced by the ideology of Marxism-Lennism and socialism as reflected in the life and works of scholars and activists such as W.E.B. Dubois, C.L Hunton, R. James, George Padmore, and Paul Robeson. The periodic Pan-African congresses served as useful experiences for African nationalist leaders who then assumed the mantle and the historical responsibility of ensuring continental decolonization and integration of Africa. Stimulated by the nationalist struggles for political independence in the aftermath of World War 1I, the newly independent African States adopted a Pan-Africanism in their collective struggle against colonialism and white-dominated territories on the continent. The idea of continental Pan-Africanism can be traceable to an era of African nationalists like Kwame Nkrumah of Ghana, Nnamdi Azikiwe of Nigeria, Ahmed Sekou Toure of Guinea, Modibo Keita of Mali, Julius Nyerere of Tanzania, Jomo Kenyatta of Kenya, among other African Leaders of the early 1960s (Viljoen 2012; Shivji 1989). Nkrumah, on his part, was spearheading the total liberation and unification of Africa under an All-African Socialist Government that will advance the triumph of international Socialist revolution. He also was of the view that Ghana's independence in

1957 was meaningless unless it achieved the total liberation of the African continent (Viljoen 2012).

African states, at independence, shared important history that was to serve as the stimulus for unity. The newly independent states shared the common experience of having been subjected to slavery, colonialism and imperialism. On attaining political independence as sovereign states, they began to contend with an international economic and political system, in which the rules and regulations were not designed by and for them, and were compelled to participate on terms that undermine their progressive development. Shortly after independence, the Pan-African continental movement fractured into two major ideological blocs, namely, the Casablanca progressives led by Ghana and the Monrovia conservatives led by Nigeria. The Casablanca group projected political integration as a prerequisite to economic integration leading to a socialist path to economic development. While the Monrovia group emphasized a functional approach to African cooperation, a view encapsulated by then Prime Minister of Nigeria the Late Sir Abubakar Tafawa Balewa during the inaugural African Summit conference of the OAU in Addis Ababa. The Monrovia bloc considered their political independence to be still very fragile and therefore proposed a gradual approach to the question of African unity over those of the Casablanca bloc that stressed integration based on the institutional framework of a "Federalist model". Despite the deep split between the two groups over the pace and scope of African integration, the two blocs came together in Addis Ababa, Ethiopia to form the Organization of African Unity (OAU) in May 25 1963.

The OAU was an institutional experiment based on the African states system in search of a functional approach to regional cooperation and integration. The OAU provided a body for the African leaders to discuss common African problems and a forum for resolving contentious issues confronting the continent. Although there was no clear unanimity among African states, there was a shared common interest on a number of crucial issues as to constitute an African approach to international affairs. This approach was reflected in the OAU instrumental efforts to destroy the last vestiges of colonialism and apartheid on the continent. For instance, the OAU, pushed for economic and diplomatic sanctions on apartheid, challenged the west and industrialized nations who invested heavily in South Africa's diamond and gold-mining industries. Notwithstanding their economic weakness, the OAU demonstrated to the rest of the world the strength which comes from unity by successfully combating the remaining vestiges of colonialism and apartheid in South Africa.

Further in 1991 there was a move to establish African economic community through successive stages of regional integration over almost three decades as outlined in the Abuja Treaty. The African Economic Community (AEC) was to ensure free movement of people and goods within the continent. There were also experiments with regional economic integration which was to constitute the foundation for AEC. They were to be known as Regional Economic Communities (REC) that would constitute building blocks for AEC. This rather failed because they operated independently. The RECs are Economic Community of West African States formed in 1975 (ECOWAS), Southern African Development Community formed in 1980 (SADC), Union of Arab Magreb formed in 1989 (UAM), Intergovernmental Authority on Development formed in 1986 for North-East (IGA) and Economic Community of Central African States formed 1983 (ECCAS), In other words, the continued dependence of African states on foreign trade taxes, as a source of government revenue has made them reluctant to lower their trade barriers.

A case for an enhanced and guided private sector driven economy

What is the current position of the private sector? This chapter makes for the private sector driven economy, with proper regulation. The private sector is expected to take a more proactive stance in terms of creating jobs and generally improving the quality of life of the people. They should utilize opportunities provided for rapid and sustainable growth of the diversified economy. This can be accomplished with a diversified economy, with a modern agricultural sector, an export driven (manufacturing) industrial sector and competitive services sector in line with the continent's comparative advantage.

The private sector must actively work to expand the export base and be internationally competitive by improving the quality of products and services, deploying the skills and professionalism of local human resources.

It should transform the structure of the regional economy thereby engender the development of strong linkages across the continent, promoting regional integration infrastructure.

It should stimulate the rapid development of local technology thereby proactively implementing the local content policy especially in the manufacturing and service industries sub-sector. This can be accomplished by evolving business partnerships/linkages that engender the learning and transfer of technology processes where the means of production is so complex and intricate.

Government is enjoined to create an enabling environment for increase, but with guided private sector involvement in the economy. Some of such policies and initiatives include reforms in industrial policy and relevant legislation. There is also a need to adopt liberal sectoral policies in consonance with overall economic policy as well as the establishment of institutions that are supportive to the private initiatives.

A boom in the private sector is necessitated by a liberalized environment that has fully democratized, and is open and transparent. The private sector in most African countries, especially Nigeria, has been bedevilled by weaknesses inherent in its skewed structure. This is due to the presence of a few MNCS that are heavily import-dependent. This is worsened by a rent seeking and unproductive culture of over dependence on government patronage and contracts. The SMEs are usually operating at the complex technology due to most of them largely illiterate and rural. They have failed to live up to expectations, despite clarion calls to drive and develop the economy by investing in research and development (R & D). The rapid growth of a resilient and competitive private sector is a key component of a sustainable economic growth. They should aid to diversify the continent's economic base, reduce the relative dominance of the mono-economy and strengthen the linkages between the formal and informal sectors.

The private sector ought to be vibrant so as to easily respond to the rigours of market forces as its engine of growth. There ought to be established technology business incubation centers designed to provide an enabling environment for nurturing of startup and growth of SMEs that would be engaged in value-added and technology related manufacturing. There should be nurturing and growth of science and technology-based SMEs in science and technology parks.

The private sector should utilize the opportunities that abound in the domestic, regional and global markets. There should be respect for the sanctity of contracts and rights of others as well as elimination of bottlenecks and red-tapes, through strengthening the social, legal and regulatory regimes thereto ancillary. Access to financial facility and resources is vital, so as to improve efficiency, productivity and nurturing entrepreneurship. There should be commercialization of results of viable scientific research that shall enhance productivity.

There should be appropriate structures for the regulation of the private sector to develop in a socially and environmentally responsible direction. Moreover, ensuring an investment friendly environment and implementing adequate compensation policies for its employees are the key challenge before the continent at the moment. There is limited access to funds in both money market and capital market. There is a predictable and weak policy framework and governance structure, inadequate and deteriorating infrastructure support.

Why is cost of production cheap in China, and other Southeast Asian countries?

Appropriate government initiatives and infrastructure

Technology is the engine of growth. Within this framework, business and industry are the drivers; government is the catalyst while academia is the fuel. An integrated strategy must link these stake holders in the business of national development. Technology based development can occur only with concerted efforts to revitalize education, develop personnel, and create integrated industries.

There must be appropriate enabling legislation. This legislation would bolster the strategic economic sector, with concomitant positive impact on job creation. There is need for national government to invest in human capital development. A nation will never develop with low and middle level manpower in its labour force.

There must be appropriate jobs for appropriate labour force. Relevant government institutions should ensure they perform the roles which they have been established to perform. There ought to be a sustainable focus on the development and application of technology for transforming the national economy. The education curriculum should be designed to deliver a leadership based on science and technology.

Finally, Africa being endowed with natural resources is still unable to convert its strategic resource endowment into economic growth and sustainable development. Hence, in addition to African unity, Africa needs the technological transformation of its economy and the industrial infrastructure to exploit its natural resources for development. Africa should develop African home-grown institutions that will be slightly different from that of developed nations, in order to gain the benefits of globalization. Additionally, in order to reverse the dire environmental problems, poverty, hunger, health and unemployment that bedevil most African countries, it is necessary to coordinate an integrated investment in the fields of education, science, technology, research and human development.

Conclusion

This chapter seeks to recommend a legal architecture, institutional and developmental infrastructure for Africa's economic self-determination. It attempts to close the lacunae created by poor policy formulation and weak institutions. The chapter explores all those areas which the central governments of African nations have a desired liberalization of the economy and/or the privatization of all state owned institutions, agencies and companies. These measures have been enmeshed in crises of transparency, accountability and probity. Certain precepts that ought to drive growth for a virile economic system and development are therefore suggested. These precepts have been variously ignored owing to ineptitude and gross ignorance. The chapter seeks to review some of the existing international order, and regulatory organs with a view to seeking a plausible framework often obtainable in larger developed economies that share similar fate and history. Africa is replete with raw talents and mineral resources, yet, are very poor, and ignorance pervade with no clue of abating.

The chapter observed that since independence swept the entire continent, the latter had relied on foreign loans and capital. Such foreign capital often comes by way of aid to finance economic development and industrialization. Aside from reliance on aid from donor agencies, the continent contends with deteriorating terms of trade, declining export revenue and heavy debt servicing obligation until recently when IMF and international lenders embarked on expensive debt forgiveness gestures. Lately, commercial lending by foreign creditors and multilateral finance corporations has significantly declined. This chapter seeks for a strong and effective infrastructure to create a very attractive and secure operative atmosphere for growth and economic self- determination. FDI is welcome, but ought to be embraced on the bases of fairness and equity. Africans need to invest regionally, thereby promoting regional integration through acquisition of home grown technology. It is no longer news that a huge percentage of capital, that exits in the African continent, is locally generated to refinance an expansion of the investment of the foreign investor. Suffice it to note that empirical analysis has shown that the aggregate transfer of profit derived from FDI in Africa far exceeds the amount of the funds originally invested (Boss-Sanders 1974:31). Thus, statistics of FDI in Africa reveal the actual source of capital inflow to be un-remitted profit constituting the main source at 76%; trade constitute 50%; while shares and loan capital represent a minimal contribution (Ifeyoti 1984:291). Additionally, frequent policy somersault, poor regulation/

deregulation, interest rates, changes in liquidity ratio, cash reserves and foreign exchange policies have been variously attributed as part of causes of distress in banks that should drive the economy (Business Times, 1995). There are incidences of liquidity shortage for working capital, inflation, low purchasing power, unpredictable tariff, scarcity and high rate of foreign exchange. There is grand corruption that is rife in public and private enterprises. There is also pervading political instability.

There is need for effective regulatory mechanisms that shall pervade sectoral investments that support and encourage intra-regional investments. Such a solution is radical and courageous. Investment capital must be viewed from the perspective of the developmental goals of African Nations, with emphasis being on attaining a sufficient level of self determination. The UN charter stresses interdependence and international cooperation as shared obligations within the comity of Nations. The operations, activities and interests of TNC should seriously recognize the inherent right to the development of host African nations. This shall ultimately foster conditions of global peace and security. FDIs have been acknowledged, over the years, as vectors of development (Morris 1970). Conversely, in the distribution of gains between an investor and the host, the investor usually benefits more (Singer 1974). It is no longer news that FDIs have had negative effects on host African Countries. It is very obvious that they have been the instrument of economic and social dislocations. This chapter draws an analogy from the collapse of otherwise vibrant Asian Tigers and Latin American economies. It seeks, by this analogy, to search for solutions that balance both progressive and socialist perspectives. By progressive, it is meant a radical departure from the prevailing capitalist mantra of the advanced western countries, but embraces a home grown initiative. By progressive perspective also, it portrays a massive developmental programmes, erecting infrastructures that impact lives and socio-economic livelihood. It shall embrace responsible and sustainable investment in infrastructural development for local industry to thrive and blossom. In other words, this chapter advocates a guided nationalization of FDI into national economies. This seeks to increase the number of local investors and technical expertise in the venture. What are the ways and methods to recover national economies from total foreign control? This chapter supports progressive approach to both foreign and local investment, while seeking to promote Africa's economic self-determination. This is not oblivious of the legitimate mercantile interests of the foreign investor and the implicit right to the development of the host country as supported and encouraged by international law of development. Any meaningful discussion of the economic sovereignty of African countries must seriously reflect the principle of self determination. This principle ought not to be ignored, nor underestimated. It is very contemporary that it has shaken the very foundations of dependent economic relations between the developed and developing (under developed) African countries. It serves as a tool for national economic recovery.

Notes and References

1 Article 1(2) OAU Charter.
2 Resolution 1803 (XVII of December 1962.
3 Resolution 3202 (S-VII) of 1 may 1979.
4 Resolution 3171.
5 NAM, ECOWAS, APC, SADC, amongst Sundry others.
6 See Article (2) of United Nations Charter that supports it.
7 Art 1(2) United Nation's Charter.
8 European Economic Commission-Africa, Caribbean and the Pacific.
9 AU NEPAD Declaration 2001.
10 Article – of the UN Charter.
11 Marcus Garvey the head of the Universal Negro Improvement Association (UNIA).

Abdulraheem, T. Taking Pan-Africanism to the people Pamzuka News 24th November 2005 Found: http://pambazuka.org/en/category/panafrican/30541 (accessed 23rd June, 2014).

Adogamhe, P.G. 2008. Pan-Africanism Revisited: Vision and Reality of African Unity and Development. *African Review of Integration* 2(2) 1-34.

AkaaGeer, I. 2001. Legal Perspectives to Transnational Investment Agreements with Special Reference to Developing Nations PhD thesis Ahmadu Bello University Zaria.

Atanesyev V. 1967. *Fundamentals or Scientific Communism*. Motion, progress publishers.

Bos, H.C., Sanders, M. and Secchi C., 1974, *Private Foreign Investment in Developing Countries: A Quantitative Study on the Macroeconomic Effects*", Dardrecht: Reidel.

Clapham, C. 1996. *African and International system. The Politics of the State Survival* Cambridge: Cambridge University Press 1996.

Ifeyoti, I. Ihimodu and Medeupin A: "Foreign investment and Resource Transfer" in Nweke. G.A. (ed) "Nigeria and world Economy", proceedings of the 12th Annual Conference of Nigerian society of International Affairs, University of Ilorin

Elias, T.O. 1988. Africa and Development of International Law 2nd ed. R. Akinjide The Hague: Martins Njoff

Frank, U. 1970 "The Development of Underdevelopment", in Rhodes ed, Imperialism and Underdevelopment: A Reader, Newyork: Monthly Review Press.

Morris, J.H.C. 1970. *Conflict of Laws* 2nd Edition, London: Stevens and Sons.

Naldi, G. 1999. *The Organization of African Unity. An Analysis of Its Role* 2nd ed. London: Mansell.

Murray, M. 2004. Human Rights in Africa from OAU to African Union, Cambridge University Press.

Salomon, M.E. 2007. *Global Responsibility for Human Rights: World Poverty and the Development of International Law* Oxford: OUP

Salomon, M.E. 2008. International Human Rights Obligations in Context: Structural Obstacles and the Demands for Global Justice" in Andreassen B.A. & Marks S.P. *Development as a Human Right: Legal, Political and Economic Dimensions* 2nd ed Antwerp: Intersentia) 121-148

Shivji I.G 1989. The Concept of Human Rights its Africa London: CODESRIA Book Series.

Obasanjo, O. 2005. Obasanjo's Address, Abuja, the Guardian, November 13, 2005.

Onuorah &Oghoho, 2005. The Guardian. November 14 2005

Rodney. W. 1972. *How Europe Underdeveloped Africa.* Washington: DC: *Howard*

Sands P and P Klein, 2001. Bowet's Law of International Law, 5th ed London: Sweet Maxwell,

Singer, H.W. 1974. "The Distribution of Gains Between Investing and Borrowing Countries". Quoted in 13os MC etal (ed). Private foreign investment in Developing countries. Boston— USA, D. Reidel publishing company

Uchendu V.C (ed) (1981) Dependency and under development in West Africa, from Dependent to Development: strategies to overcome underdevelopment and inequality, Boulder Colorado West view Press

Umozurike, U. O. The African Charter on Human and Peoples' Rights. *American Journal of International Law* (1983) 902-912.

Viljoen, F. (2012). *International human rights law in Africa*. Oxford: Oxford University Press.

Wembou M.C.D. 1994. "The OAU and International Law' in Y.E.L.Ayouty (ed), the OAU After thirty Years (Westport, cr: Prager

Yamaawa, I. (ed). 2000. Developing Economics in the 21' century: the challenges of globalization, Japan external Trade organization, The institute of Developing Economies

The Integrative Functions of the African Union Commission:

Reconsidering the Operational Context

Babatunde Fagbayibo

Introduction

The transformation of the Organisation of African Unity (OAU) to the African Union (AU) brought about a new approach to institutional development at the continental level. Established against the backdrop of the inability of the OAU to effectively address integrative issues, the AU was designed to provide the requisite institutional solution to the stunted integration process.

The quest for a strong and assertive continental institution has been the focus of political and academic works in the past five decades. Kwame Nkrumah, the first president of Ghana outlined the imperative of a federal framework for integration in Africa, by calling for the establishment of a 'United States of Africa' (Nkrumah 1963). He recommended that such Union should pursue three key objectives: overall economic planning on a continental basis; unified military and defence strategy; and a unified foreign policy and diplomacy (Ibid, 218-220). Similarly, scholars like Diop and Mazrui advocated practical measures of establishing durable continental institutions. Diop (1987) argued that no serious development can exist outside of the context of a federation of African states. He outlined 15 principles for concrete action, chief of which include effective gender representation, an African-centred constitution, a bicameral legislature, a powerful army, and a strong focus on science and technology (Ibid, 88-89). Mazrui's (1967) theory of *Pax Africana* centred on the imperative of Africans taking the primary responsibility of maintaining peace and security on the continent. As he remarked, *Pax Africana* speaks to an Africa 'that is protected and maintained by Africa herself' (Ibid:203).

The establishment of the AU should thus be seen in the context of the foundational works cited above. Its institutional dimension clearly set it apart from its predecessor, the OAU. Issues of security, promotion of democratic governance, development, and human rights underlined the framework of the institutional development of the new organisation (AU Constitutive Act, articles 3 and 4). Central to this institutional reform was the establishment of the African Union Commission (AUC). Officially designated as the 'Secretariat of the Union' (Ibid, article 20), the Commission is expected to play the role of the 'engine room' of the continental integration process. In the context of the objective of promoting deeper integration, the Commission is broadly tasked with two essential integrative functions: initiation of policy measures and the implementation of measures taken by other organs of the AU (Statutes of the Commission of the AU, article 3(2)).

These two key integrative functions are at the core of any assessment or consideration of whether or not the Commission is in any way relevant in the matrix of the integration process. In other words, it is crucial to ask some serious questions about the extent to which the Commission is able to effectively exercise its incubator role and its relationship with key stakeholders such as the other organs of the AU, member states and the Regional Economic Communities (RECs). This enquiry lies at the heart of understanding the inherent deficiencies of the implementation powers of the Commission. In other words, the issue is about understanding the deficiencies in the implementation terrain of the AUC. The central argument of this article is that the operational context of the Commission is fundamentally deficient, and thus frustrates effectiveness. The existent operational context is largely characterised by issues such as the lack of political will by African leaders to empower the Commission, the lack of legal instrument(s) and policies that clearly define the modus operandi, and limited financial and human resources to exercise some of its critical functions.

This is the backdrop against which this article attempts to propose some politico-legal measures that could redefine and strengthen the operational context of the Commission. It starts with a theoretical overview of the Commission and its roles. This is followed by a discussion of the current operational context of the Commission. It then concludes by looking at some of the feasible measures which are necessary for making the Commission a relevant and effective driver of the integration process.

The African Union Commission: An overview

The AU Commission is the designated 'engine room' cum executive arm of the AU. It is designed to anchor the political and economic objectives of the AU and ultimately be the vehicle for the eventual realisation of a continental government. The policy-making agenda of the Commission cannot function effectively without the cooperation of other institutional players in the integration matrix. These include member states (source of power and authority), AU Assembly (primary decision-making body of the AU), RECs (building blocks of the AU), Pan-African Parliament (control and monitoring of key AU objectives), and the African Court of Justice and Human Rights (judicial body). These institutions are briefly explained below.

The AU currently has 54 member states. Membership is open to all African states, and each member state is mandated to comply with the institutional objectives. Article 23(2) allows for the imposition of sanction on any member state that fails to comply with the decisions and policies of the AU. Also, article 30 of the Constitutive Act empowers the AU to suspend any government that comes to power through unconstitutional means.

Composed of heads of state and government, the Assembly remains the most important organ of the AU. Its functions include the determination of common policies of the AU, monitor implementation of the policies and decisions of the AU, adopt the budget of the AU and make the final decision on reports and recommendations of other organs of the AU (AU Constitutive Act, article 9).

The AU recognises the following eight RECs as the building blocks towards continental integration: Arab Maghreb Union (AMU), Community of Sahel-Saharan States (CENSAD), East African Community (EAC), Economic Community of Central African States (ECCAS), Economic Community of West African States (ECOWAS), Intergovernmental Authority on Development (IGAD) and Southern Africa Development (SADC).

The PAP was established in 2004. Each member state of the AU has 5 representatives at PAP. It, however, remains a consultative body. Its functions include the promotion of human rights, democracy, good governance, peace and security and the effective implementation of AU policies and objectives (Protocol to the Treaty Establishing the African Economic Community Relating to PAP, article 3).

The ACJ&HR is made up of two sections: General Affairs and Human Rights sections. Each of the sections is composed of 8 judges. The Court is competent to hear the following cases: interpretation of the AU Constitutive Act and other AU treaties, any question of international law, decisions and directives of the organs of AU, breach of obligations by member states and the nature and extent of reparation. See generally the Protocol on the Statute of the African Court of Justice and Human Rights (2009). The Court is yet to start operations.

The extent to which the source(s) of real authority (member states and the AU Assembly) are prepared to exercise the requisite political will of transferring powers to the Commission is fundamental (This is discussed later).

At this juncture, it is important to turn to the structure of the AUC. In line with the provision of Article 20(3) of the Constitutive Act, the Statutes of the Commission of the AU (2002) outline the structure and functions of the Commission. Article 2 of the Statutes provides that the Commission shall be headed by a Chairperson, assisted by one deputy Chairperson and eight Commissioners. Article 6(2) of the Statute takes into account the representation of the five regions of Africa in the election of members of the Commission by providing that:

> the region from which the Chairperson and Deputy Chairperson are appointed shall be entitled to (1) Commissioner each. All other region shall be entitled to (2) Commissioners each.

In pursuant of the promotion of gender equality, Article 6(3) stipulates that 'at least 1 Commissioner from each region shall be a woman'.

Each of the Commissioners controls the following portfolios: Peace and Security; Political Affairs; Trade and Industry; Infrastructure and Energy; Social Affairs; Rural Economy and Agriculture; Human Resources, Science and Technology; and Economic Affairs. While the Chairperson remains the head of the Commission, the assignment of portfolio to the Commissioners is a function of the AU Assembly (AU Constitutive Act, article 9(i)).

The functions of the Commission are outlined in Article 3(2) of the Statute. They include:

- Represent the Union and defend its interests under the guidance of and as mandated by the Assembly and the Executive Council;
- Initiate proposals for consideration by other organs;

- Coordinate and monitor the implementation of decisions taken by organs;
- Organise and manage the meetings of the Union;
- Act as the custodian of the Constitutive Act, its protocols, the treaties, legal instruments, decisions adopted by the Union and those inherited from the OAU;
- Assist member states in the implementation of Union programmes and policies;
- Prepare the Union's programme and budget for approval by the policy organs;
- Prepare strategic plans and studies for the consideration of the Executive Council;
- Promote integration and socio-economic development;
- Strengthen cooperation and coordination of activities between member states in fields of common interests.

In broad terms, the integrative functions of the Commission can be classified into two: policy initiation and implementation. In relation of its policy-making role, the Commission can either initiate policy measures for the consideration of AU Assembly and the Executive Council or prepare policy programmes upon the request of these organs. Unlike its policy-making powers, the Commission can only engage in implementation activities if and when the AU Assembly or the Executive mandates it to act or where it is called upon to assist member states.

What can be deduced from the point made above is that while the Commission is regarded as the 'engine room', real powers lie with the member states, through the AU Assembly and the Executive Council. The Commission can independently initiate policies but implementation powers can only be delegated to it by the Assembly or Executive Council. In other words, the Commission only exists at the behest of the Assembly, and the Executive Council (Ibid, article 13). This is the general operational context within which the Commission functions.

Since its inception, the Commission has authored important documents indicating the process and strategy of its transformation and the development of the integration process. These include the 'Strategic Plans', the Programme on Infrastructure Development in Africa (PIDA), and the Continental Free Trade Area (CFTA) and Boosting Intra-African

Trade (BIAT). At the 12th Assembly of Heads of State and Government, the AU Assembly requested the Commission to come up with a programme on continental infrastructure development. PIDA builds on several initiatives on infrastructure development in Africa by providing a strategic plan for the short-medium-long term development of key infrastructure such as energy, transportation network, water, and ICT. PIDA provides a feasibility study of the programme costs, financing strategy and the implementation of continental infrastructure development (African Union Commission 2013: 129-143). Both CFTA and BIAT are seen as twin programmes for enhancing trade and investment across the continent. The 18th Ordinary Session of the AU Assembly in January 2012 adopted the Decision and Declaration indicating 2017 as the year of establishing a CFTA. An action plan for BIAT was also endorsed. The Commission, together with other key stakeholders, is tasked with developing an enabling policy and legal framework for the effective implementation of the CFTA and BIAT (Ibid:155-158).

The 'Strategic Plans' contain an encompassing framework that maps out the general development of regional integration in Africa. Titled 'Strategic Plan of the African Union Commission 2004-2007, 2009-2012, 2014-2017, these documents capture the underlying philosophy and components of African integration, stages of transformation and more importantly, the central role of the Commission in attaining integration objectives.

The first document, 'Strategic Plan 2004-2007', identifies the three components of 'profound' institutional transformation as follows (Strategic Plan 2004:19):

- Institutional strengthening of the AU Commission;
- Rationalisation of the institutional architecture;
- Refinement of AU governance process.

The first point - institutional strengthening of the Commission - adopts an inward looking approach, by stressing the improvement of the overall technical ability of the Commission. As a measure aimed at capacity building within the Commission, the following points are highlighted: the need for structural adjustments of the departments, training of staff members, recruitment of skilled personnel, upgrading the Commission's ICT infrastructure, and improved coordination within the Commission (Ibid:17-24). The process is designed in order to equip the Commission with the necessary skills for coordinating the integration process.

The second point - rationalisation of the institutional architecture - looks at the relationship between the Commission and other stakeholders in the integration process. The recognised stakeholders include member states, RECs, New Partnership for Africa's Development (NEPAD) Planning and Coordinating Agency (NPCA), Specialised Institutions of the AU, AU organs and AU international partners (United Nations Economic Commission for Africa, African Development Bank and international donors) (Ibid:27). The idea is to ensure that there is effective coordination and communication between the Commission and these bodies so as to ensure coherent design and implementation of integration goals (Ibid:27-35). Especially in the relation to the NPCA, the specialised institutions and the RECs, this document points to how the Commission can exert continental leadership in the integration process (Ibid).

An underlying theme of the rationalisation process is the so-called 'Minimum Integration Programme (MIP)', which is:

> [i]ntended to provide greater coherence in the overall movement towards regional integration on a continental level ... [it] includes a set of programmes to deliver on such goals as the establishment of a regional brigade for the African Stand-by Force, coordination of and a common approach to international trade negotiations, trade liberalisation, free movement goals within each REC, regional common policy in various areas, common monetary policy, common policy in various sectors, etc...

In essence, the MIP is a gradualist framework, which provides the stages or process of attaining continental integration. It particularly focuses on the coordination and harmonisation of RECs by putting in place the framework for cooperation and integration of the RECs into a continental programme of action (Ibid:31-32; African Union Commission 2010). The last point - refinement of the governance process - focuses on the need to create an open and transparent management and interaction within the AU (Strategic Plan 2004:38-41).

Building on the 2004-2007 Strategic Plan and realising that the objectives and goals highlighted in this document are yet to be fully realised, the Commission authored the 2009-2012 Strategic Plan (Strategic Plan 2009:17). The report considers the following as the strategic pillars around, which its mandate and functions can be strengthened: peace and security; integration, development and cooperation; shared values; and institution and capacity building.

With regard to the first pillar, peace and security, the Commission aims to stem the tide of conflicts on the continent by coordinating and overseeing the implementation of policies emanating from AU Peace and Security Architecture (APSA), Common African Defense and Security Policy (CADSP) and the Post-Conflict Reconstruction and Development (PCRD) (Ibid, 22).

The second pillar is sub-divided into three: development, integration and cooperation. The programme on development is expected to achieve improved productivity, infrastructure development, agricultural development, youth development, migration policies, social welfare and diffusion of technology (Ibid:23-26). The programme on integration is focused on the implementation of the MIP, free movement of persons, goods, capital and services and the rationalisation and harmonisation of RECs (Ibid:26-27), the programme on cooperation is geared towards the establishment of a common platform for trade negotiations, increased trade and development, enhanced intra-African cooperation and strengthened global strategic partnership (Ibid:27-29).

The third pillar, shared values, focuses on the cultivation and entrenchment of democratic values such as good governance, democracy, human rights, gender equality and cultural values (Ibid, 30-33). In this regard, the Commission will focus the strengthening and full implementation of the APRM, the promotion of cultural diversity, promotion of ratification and entry into force of all outstanding treaties, promotion and protection of African heritage, continental humanitarian policy and the implementation of gender policies (Ibid).

The last pillar, capacity building, aims to refine and develop the internal administration of the Commission. To achieve this, the Commission expects to put in place an effective human resources management reform programme, prioritises gender mainstreaming, improve organisational culture, improve working environment, timely and effective communication, and regular interaction with other AU organs and the RECs (Ibid:34-36).

The third Strategic Plan, 2014-2017, was adopted by the Assembly at the 21st Ordinary Session of the AU on the 26th of May 2013. Like the preceding two plans, it places the Commission at the heart of the policy and strategy planning. It identifies 8 priority areas. These include: Human capacity development focusing on health, education, science, research, technology and innovation; Agriculture and agro processing; Inclusive economic development through industrialisation, infrastructure development, agriculture and trade and investment; Peace, stability and good governance; Mainstreaming women and youth into all our activities; Resource mobilisation; Building a people-centred Union through active communication and branding; and Strengthening the institutional capacity of the Union and all its organs.

These documents speak to the integrative functions of the Commission, by providing a framework that ensures its continued relevance in the intergovernmental matrix of continental integration (this is discussed below). The consideration of the internal reform of the Commission, emphasis on the gradual attainment of continental integration, and the effective cooperation with key stakeholders on achieving the goals of regional integration all point to the exigency of ensuring that policy is translated into practise.

Understanding the existent operational context of the Commission

Having looked at the institutional dimension of the Commission, it is crucial at this point to consider its operational context. In order to understand the limitations of the Commission, special attention should be paid to the variables that inform and shape the exercise of its functions. These interrelated variables can be broadly classified into three categories:

- Intergovernmental nature of the continental integration process;
- Defective institutional capacity of the Commission;
- Lack of a clearly articulated operational framework.

The first category is the intergovernmental nature of the integration process. The primary context within which the Commission operates is the intergovernmental paradigm of the continental integration process. Intergovermentalism is a theory of regional integration that denotes the existence of a framework in which real authority and decision-making powers reside with member states (Schemers and Blokker 1995; Weiler 1999). Schemers and Blokker (1995:40) identify two features of intergovernmentalism as:

(1) The decision-making powers are in fact exercised by representatives of governments. Organs composed of persons independent of the member states, committees of experts or parliamentary assemblies may play an advisory role, but they will generally not have the power to take the final decisions.

(2) In important matters, governments cannot be bound against their will.

> Intergovernmental organisations seek collaboration among governments, and are in no way superior to them. Although intergovernmental organizations can sometimes take binding decisions, this is only possible where the decision in question enjoys unanimous approval by all members. By voting against a draft decision a government can thus prevent its adoption.

Member states are not only the principal players in the integration process; they also remain the principal actors, with transnational institutions merely playing the role of executors.

At the heart of the decision-making structure of the AU are the member states. Through the Assembly and the Executive Council, composed of heads of state and national ministers respectively, the AU is essentially a platform for consensual interaction amongst member states. The determination of common policies, consideration of reports and recommendations of other organs of the AU, monitoring of the implementation of AU policies are powers that are solely exercised by representatives of member states (AU Constitutive Act, article 9). This simply means that both the Assembly and Executive Council exercise the executive and legislative functions of the AU. While there is a provision for the delegation of these powers (Ibid, article 9(2)), the reality on the ground portends otherwise. The lack of political will to engage in any meaningful reform of the AU, by transferring competences to other organs of the AU, is a clear example.

The Assembly is yet to grant full or partial legislative powers to the PAP. Art. 2(3) of the PAP Protocol indicate the possibility of PAP to start exercising meaningful legislative powers after 5 years of existence (which was due in 2009). The conferment of legislative powers is not automatic as it will involve the convening of a conference on the review of the PAP process thus far. Since 2009, no serious effort has been made to deliberate on the need to grant the PAP supranational legislative powers (Lulie 2012). In relation to the Commission, there was an AU Assembly decision in 2009 to transform the Commission into the AU Authority (AU/Dec.206 (XI)). It is important to note that this decision was reversed at the AU Summit in June 2012.

The technocratic competence of the Commission cannot be meaningfully exercised in a milieu that permanently locks it out of the loop of real decision-making process (Fagbayibo 2012:20-22). The rigid intergovernmental structure of the AU is thus a major obstacle that continues to frustrate the efficiency of the Commission. The key is finding effective means through which the Commission can exercise real authority within the intergovernmental structure of the AU.

The second category is Commission's defective institutional capacity. Like any other institution, the efficiency of the Commission, to a large extent, depends on the quality of its human and financial resources. As noted above, the 'Strategic Plans' of the Commission highlights the reform of its internal administration, particularly human resources management, as central to its ability to effectively contribute to the integration process. The 2007 AU Audit Report paints a worrying picture of the internal administration of the Commission. According to the Report, the vaguely articulated delineation of powers and functions within the organisation has resulted in a lack of supervision, failure to delegate functions to Directors and mid-level staff, non-existent internal communication, low morale among staff and consequently, a dysfunctional system (AU Audit Report 2007, 47-48). The Report further noted that an inefficient recruitment process (based on the application of a quota system and inadequate publicity of vacancies) restricts the employment of competent persons and leads to understaffing issues in some of the departments of the Commission (Ibid, 50-51). Similarly, the AU Commission Strategic Plan 2004-2007 (2004:7; Strategic Plan 2009-2012:17) identify the following as some of the critical challenges of the Commission:

> [...] numerical and qualitative staff shortage, ineffective structures resulting in compartmentalisation of the Departments, a highly hierarchical and bureaucratic organisational structure, and systems and procedure that do not enhance modern transparent and results oriented management.

Another factor that limits the efficiency of the Commission is lack of finance for the discharge of some of its critical tasks. Financial contributions from AU member states have been disappointing so far. According to Ncube and Akuna (2012), only five member states contribute two-thirds of the portion from member states, and only two paid up by mid-2012. Only 11 of the 54 member states had made full payments by mid-2012 with 19 countries owing for the current year and 24 having arrears from previous years (Ibid). Further breakdown shows the following (Ibid):

- Donors contribute 56% of the total budget of the AU;
- The total operational cost is covered by member states (which is 96% of their contribution);

- Only 1.9% of the contribution of member states goes to programmes budget;
- External donors finance 97% of the programmes budget;
- The AU functions each year with only 50-60% of its required budget

Limited financial resources have direct impact on the ability of the Commission to effectively discharge its integrative functions. A paltry 1.9% contribution to programmes budget of the AU indicates the levity that is attached to paying attention to integrative issues. Equally worrying is the heavily donarised budget of the programmes budget, a fact that puts into question the control of the policy-making agenda of the AU (Olukoshi 2010:53). As Olukoshi (Ibid) rightly noted:

> Indeed, depending as heavily as many of the institutions of African integration are on donor support, there are justifiable grounds for considering them as increasingly donorised entities whose policy processes are susceptible, as they have been, to hijack by external interests.

Similarly, Mackie and Bossuyt (2010:89) remarked that:

> It is a clear indication of serious governance problem if the AUC, as the main instrument of the Union, has to scramble each year to collect a (largely erratic) budget from its Member States to perform its duties. This undermines the credibility of the Union; it drastically weakens its capacity to deliver and threatens its legitimacy.

The third and last category is the vague articulation of how the Commission is expected to exercise its integrative functions. Both the Constitutive Act and the Statutes of the Commission fall short of defining the specifics of how the Commission should exercise its designated function. In particular, the relationship between the Commission and other organs of the AU and the RECs, especially as it relates to the distribution of powers is not fully elaborated. For example, the Constitutive Act talks about the delegation of the powers of the Assembly, but no clear framework on the outline of such delegation exists. Another example is the lack of a definitive legal framework on the relationship between the Commission and the RECs. The draft Protocol on this relationship is yet to be finalised (EX/CL/158(1X). No further clarification is provided on the Commission's relationship with other organs of the AU and member states.

This lack of clarity fundamentally hampers the operational efficiency of not only the Commission but the entire institutional structure of the AU. The lack of specificity on the operational role of the supposed 'engine room' of the Union is emblematic of the defective state of the continental integration process. It indicates the unwillingness to engage in innovative ways of creating a workable intergovernmental arrangement. An arrangement that not only refers to the importance of the Commission but provides practical means of ensuring that this role is effectively and efficiently fulfilled.

A redefined approach: From 'handmaiden' to the real 'engine room'

What can be deduced from the foregoing analysis is the existence of an operational context that frustrates the effective exercise of the integrative functions of the Commission. It is important to emphasise that this deficient operational context is the result of a culmination of factors, chief of which is the failure of member states to cede authority to the AU. What is then required is to reconsider the intergovernmental framework of the AU, so as to find creative ways of ensuring that the Commission is in practise placed at the locus of integration process. Such measures cannot ignore the politics of continental integration, especially as it relates to its highly state-centric nature. What this means is that a framework that balances the importance of member states (and their representative structures within the AU) with the imperative of empowering the Commission has to be put in place. The key questions that should shape the design of practical solutions for enhancing the integrative functions of the Commission are:

- What should be the nature of the relationship between the Commission and the Assembly, in respect of delegated functions of policy-setting and implementation?
- How should the Commission relate with other key stakeholders, such as the other organs of the AU, RECs and member states?
- How practicable is the implementation of the assigned functions?
- How is realistic is the road-map or timetable set for enhancing the effectiveness of the Commission?
- To what extent is the reform of the internal administration synergised with the acceleration of the integration process?

These questions form the basis of the suggested measures that are offered by this article. This article suggests a SAVE plan for the Commission. The SAVE acronym stands for:

- Specificity of operational context
- Attainability of targets
- Visibility of the Commission
- Evaluation framework

Specificity of operational context

The starting point of any meaningful approach to enhancing the relevance of the Commission is the adoption of a clear and specific framework that details the extent of the powers to be exercised by the Commission and the way in which these function are to be exercised. This directly relates to the integrative functions of the Commission: policy-making/setting and implementation. This will require more elaboration on the provision that allows the Assembly to delegate some of its functions. It will also require the clarification of the relationship between the Commission and the RECs. Such approach should be underlined by a number of factors.

The first is the strengthening of the internal administration or the technocratic competence of the Commission. The recruitment and appointment process of the Commission should not only be transparent but also be geared towards attracting skilled and competent personnel. Beyond the appointment of a capable chair of the Commission, the internal administration process requires increased synergy of efforts by key stakeholders such as the organs of the AU, civil society and the RECs. The implementation of the recommendations of the AU Audit report, especially as it relates to the clear delineation of functions within the Commission, the power of the chair of the Commission to assign portfolios to the Commissioners, and the establishment of an AU Service Commission, to be responsible for recruitment, appointments, promotions and enforcing discipline (AU Audit Report 2007:46-77).

The second is the kind of autonomy in respect of the policy-making/setting agenda of the Commission. An important requirement in this regard is the involvement of the Commission in the determination of common policies together with the Assembly (and the Executive Council). The Commission, through its chairperson, should be actively engaged in the formulation and final determination of the parameters of common policies

(Fagbayibo 2012:27). This is essential as it facilitates the mainstreaming of the Commission, and its institutional processes, into the mechanics of real policy-making activities. The advantage of this is that it moves the policy-making activity of the Commission from the level of abstraction to a concrete plane, where the feasibility of implementation is properly dissected and achieved in the long-run.

Lastly, is the need for a balanced and strategic policy-implementation mechanism. This also requires the full cooperation of the Assembly. As the highest representative body of member states, the Assembly is well positioned to meaningfully engage member states in complying with AU standards. It is, therefore, important to come up with measures through which the Commission can be more effective in the monitoring of the implementation of policies. One such measure is the setting up of an implementation committee - that include the representatives of the Assembly, Commission and other relevant organs of the AU - that will have the power to decide on implementation strategies and also recommend binding disciplinary measures (Ibid; Anyangafac and Mpyisi 2009:4). For example, Anyagafac and Mpyisi suggest a tripartite arrangement, which includes the Assembly, Commission and PAP, for the monitoring of community directives (Anyagafac and Mpyisi 2009:4). Another option is to establish formal structures through which the Commission can participate in deliberations surrounding monitoring and enforcement measures at the RECs level. While the ultimate goal is the adoption of the 'Protocol on the Relationship Between the Regional Economic Communities (REC) and the AU', the AU can in the meantime enter into bilateral arrangements with the different RECs on the facilitation of this process.

Attainability of targets

A major component of enhancing the operational context of the Commission is the understanding of the nexus between effectiveness and the setting of realisable targets. What is intrinsically linked to this is an arrangement that favours variable geometry. Variable geometry implies a framework that takes into account the reality that some member states are more interested in deeper integration than others, and will thus be more interested in proceeding at a different speed (Dashwood et al 2006:112). The general institutional structure remains the same; the difference is that there will be special arrangements that accommodate the interests of member states that are on the same page. This will require a change to the normative framework of the AU. Such framework, either through an amendment of the Constitutive Act or a Protocol, will stipulate the process through which member states can enter into special arrangements for fulfilling critical objectives of the AU.

In this regard, it is crucial to put mechanisms in place that allow the Commission to set targets on thematic issues on the basis of this kind arrangement. On every thematic point, it is important to identify a 'coalition of the willing', that is ready to engage meaningfully on the feasible modalities of policy-making and implementation. These include, but are not limited to, matters of democratic governance (Fagbayibo 2011:209-225), trade, free movement of persons, and sustainable development. The inherent advantage of this process is that it enhances the workability of integrative functions as it limits the possibility of delays and non-compliance.

Visibility of the Commission

The Commission cannot adequately fulfil its integrative functions without enhancing its visibility status at all levels of the regional integration governance process. The multi-level governance structure, that includes the continental, sub-regional and national, should be designed to accommodate the central position of the Commission. This requires the enhancement of the participation of the Commission in policy-making and implementation processes at the continental, sub-regional and national levels. As discussed above, the Commission should be engaged actively in the formulation, determination and implementation of policy measures at the AU level.

At the sub-regional level, the non-finalisation of the Protocol that regulates the relationship between the AU and RECs remain a major obstacle. There are, however, innovative ways of enhancing the visibility of the Commission in the integration processes of the RECs. One such measure is the signing of agreements with the different RECs on the parameters and nature of the Commission's involvement in the pursuant of integration activities. These include the creation of liaison units within the RECs that is responsible for coordinating and synergising activities, active involvement of the Commission in the formulation and implementation of integration policies, and increased joint projects and programmes.

At the national level, it is imperative that the Commission identifies member states that are willing to cooperate in terms of policy implementation of regional integration goals. This will enable a situation that allows the Commission to be involved actively in the formulation of national strategies that align with integration goals. Such process will require that the Commission is represented in national planning structures and is also established as a coordinating hub. As suggested above, a normative framework that stipulates this process should be enacted.

Efforts such as the placing of AU flags alongside national flags, affixing AU symbol to national documents, incorporation of AU studies into national curriculum, explaining national programmes within the context of the Commission's integrative functions, engaging both print and electronic media on strategies of increasing awareness, and partnering with private sector on fulfilling integration goals should be explored. Underlined by its integrative functions, the Commission could for example partner with private sector on issues such as sponsorship of scholarships, provision of loans and grants, internships programmes, youth empowerment projects and, finding feasible means of limiting the reliance on donor funding of the continental integration process.

Evaluation framework

Central to the feasibility of an effective operational context is a framework that not only evaluates critically the phases of the process but also sets realistic time-frames for achieving targets. The measures suggested above have to be evaluated properly within the context of a feasible time-table. A major problem with the integration process is that principal actors set timetables that are in dissonance with the reality on the ground. Many of the goals set for achieving integration goals such as continental free trade area, common market, and the harmonisation of RECs face critical implementation challenges due to the lack of proper consideration of serious impediments and short-comings.

It is, therefore, essential that the process of enhancing the ability of the Commission to perform its integrative functions is considered against this backdrop. The key point here is to ensure that the framework on effective policy-making and implementation are crafted within the context of the following:

- Whether or not the objectives can be achieved with all or only interested member states;
- The level of capacity with regard to implementation of directives by member states;

- The setting of thresholds that are compatible with the political and economic development of member states involved;
- The possibility of working closely with RECs that have achieved relative progress in terms of implementing integration objectives;
- A short to medium term plan on the transfer of powers from the Assembly to the Commission.

The points stipulated above can only be realised effectively if member states are committed strongly to exercising the necessary political will. Such approach has both normative and non-normative angles. An example of a normative angle is the suggested amendment, or enactment of a Protocol, of AU instruments to allow willing member states to set up special arrangements for strengthening the implementation terrain of the AUC. An example of a non-normative approach is the design and implementation of policy frameworks that have no legal underpinning like treaties and protocols but are central to organisational objectives. An example is the APRM process. Although it is not a legal mechanism, effective compliance with the recommendations of the review process can go a long way in entrenching the ethos of good governance. In addition, such compliance could help strengthen the implementation of normative instruments that speak to strict adherence to democracy and good governance.

Conclusion

The general acceptance that deeper regional integration is a panacea to Africa's development problems has not been matched with the desired political will. In five decades, little has been done to create durable and effective regional institutions to drive the integration process. At the continental level, the establishment of the AU was seen as an attempt to change the status quo but events have shown the opposite. A major deficit is the inability to empower the AU Commission with the requisite competence to fulfil effectively its integrative functions. As shown in the foregoing discussion, the integrative functions of policy-making and implementation is curtailed severely by an existent operational context that is intergovernmental in a rigid manner an operational framework that is not articulated clearly and a defective internal administration system in the Commission.

A key element of reforming the institutional architecture of the AU should begin with strong commitment from member states to finding feasible methods of strengthening the Commission. This chapter has proposed some measures that balance the state-centric concerns of member states with the exigency of putting the Commission at the locus of the integration process. Some of the measures considered include the inclusion of the Commission in the implementation structures of the AU and RECs, consideration of flexibility arrangements with respect to some of the functions of the Commission, enhancing the visibility of the Commission in critical aspects of the integration process and a realistic evaluation framework.

The on-going discourse on deepening the continental integration process will benefit a great deal from matching the avalanche of studies and policy frameworks with concomitant action. Until such effort is made, the Commission will remain an obscure and irrelevant player in the regional integration process.

References

African Union, 2007. *Audit report of the African Union*. Addis Ababa: African Union.

African Union Commission, 2010. 'Minimum Integration Programme (2009-2012). Available at http://www.africa-union.org/root/ua/Annonces/2010/EA/MIP/MIP%20Small%20Doc%20English%20Version%20for%20Web.pdf (Accessed 15 April 2013).

African Union Commission, 2013. *Status of integration in Africa (SIA IV)*. Addis Ababa: African Union. Available at http://www.au.int/en/sites/default/files/SIA%202013(latest)_En.pdf (Accessed 15 April 2013).

African Union Commission, 2004. *Strategic Plan of the Commission of the African Union: Volume 2: 2004-2007*. Addis Ababa: African Union

African Union Commission, 2009. *Strategic Plan 2009-2012*, Addis Ababa: African Union

Anyagafac, C and Mpyisi, K. 2009. *The proposed AU Authority: Hybridisation, balancing, intergovermentalism and supranationalism.* (ISS Situation Report), Pretoria: Institute of Security Studies.

Constitutive Act of the African Union (2001)

Dashwood, A, Wyatt, D, Arnull, A, and Ross, M. 2006. *European Union Law.* London: Sweet & Maxwell

Diop, C. 1987. *Black Africa: The economic and cultural basis for a federated state* Trenton NJ: Africa World Press

Draft Protocol on the Relationship between the Regional Economic Communities (REC) and the AU. *EX/CL/158(1X)*

Fagbayibo, B. 2011. Rethinking the African integration process: A critical politico-legal perspective on building the African Union. *South African Yearbook of International Law* 36(1) 209-225.

Fagbayibo, B. 2012. The (ir) relevance of the office of the chair of the African Union Commission: Analysing the prospect for change. *Journal of African Law* 56(1) 15-28.

Lulie, H. 2012. Knocking on a closed door. The African.org Magazine (Issue 18)

Mackie, J and Bossuyt, J. 2010. The role of the EC/EU in supporting the African Union institutional architecture. In *Building the African Union: An assessment of past progress and future prospects for the African Union's institutional architecture,* ed. G Laporte and J Mackie, 83-100. Maastricht: European Centre for Development Policy Management

Mazrui, A. 1967. *Towards a Pax Africana: A study of ideology and ambition*. Chicago, University of Chicago Press.

Ncube, J and Akena, M. 2012. A stream cannot rise above its source: Financing of Africa's regional integration. Available at http://ccpau.org/wp-content/uploads/2012/11/001_Financing_of _the_African_Union2.pdf (Accessed 29 April 2013).

Nkrumah, K. 1963. *Africa must unite.* New York: Praeger

Olukoshi, A. 2010. The African Union and African integration: Retrospect and prospect In *Building the African Union: An assessment of past progress and future prospects for the African Union's institutional architecture,* ed. G Laporte and J Mackie, 36-55. Maastricht: European Centre for Development Policy Management

Protocol on the Statute of the African Court of Justice and Human Rights (2009).

Protocol to the Treaty Establishing the African Economic Community relating to the Pan African Parliament (2003).

Schermers, H & Blokker, N. 1995. *International institutional law: Unity within diversity.* The Hague: Martinus Nijhoff.

Statutes of the Commission of the African Union, ASS/AU/2(1), (2002).

Weiler, J. 1999. *The constitution of Europe: Do the new clothes have an emperor? And other essays on European integration*. Cambridge: Cambridge University Press.

Public-Private Partnerships in Infrastructure Development in Africa

A Magic-Wand for Socio-Economic Growth and Development

Mubarak T. Adekilekun and Ching C. Gan

Introduction

The level of infrastructure development of any nation is directly proportional to the level of its economic development. Infrastructure development is arguably the most important factor for economic development. Infrastructural facilities are the wheels which drive a nation's economy. They provide the enabling environment for sustained and sustainable economic growth, job creation and help in the eradication of poverty.

Roads and highways were considered to be the earliest human demand for infrastructure. The first world's known paved roads were laid in Egypt between 2600 and 2200 BC. Indeed, it could not have been possible to build the pyramids without the roads on which the heavy limestone blocks were dragged. Also, stone paved roads were found in the city of Ur in the modern day Iraq since 4000 BC. Civilization advanced or declined around the qualities of their road networks. The ancient Roman, Persian, Chinese and Indian civilizations built road networks that encouraged and advanced trade and commerce among those empires and also assisted them in the transportation of military equipment (Sawant 2010: 1). The technological advancement in the world today could not have been possible without the invention of electricity and its applications in the eighteen century by the great scientists like Benjamin Franklin, Alessandro Volta, Michael Faraday and many others.

Today, Africa faces huge infrastructure deficits and challenges. The state of infrastructure development in Africa does not meet the requirements for economic development and advancement. A World Bank report stated that for Africa to fill the infrastructure gaps, an annual expenditure of $75 Billion would be required annually for the next ten years. It is therefore apparent that governments alone, even at the best of economic times, lack the capacity to provide for the infrastructure requirements and development of Africa. This underscores clearly the need for the participation of private sector through Public-Private Partnership which has been recognized as a global panacea for infrastructure deficits particularly in developing economies (Avery 2006: 13).

As a result of the growing population and urbanization, citizens demand and require new roads, light rail networks, bridges and tunnels, water and sanitation plants, prisons, hospitals, schools, dams, roads, electricity, modern airport and air control system and other social and economic infrastructure. However, because of the inefficiencies, corruption, lack of skills and technical know-how that have characterized the provisions of public infrastructure through the traditional public procurement model, in the United Kingdom today, for example, the pertinent question which people tend to ask before any investment decision is taken is "Why not use a private finance solution?"

It is, therefore, argued in this chapter that Public Private Parnerships (PPPs) have vast economic and development potentials to supplement Africa's critical infrastructure gaps, where about 587 million people lack access to electricity, almost 300 million people have no access to safe and clean water and about 93% of the population has no access to internet facilities. Public-Private Partnerships will definitely and ultimately boost socio-economic growth and development in the continent and help it to strive for and achieve the Millennium Development Goals.

Meaning, Nature and Basic Concepts of Public-Private Partnerships

Public-Private Partnership (PPP) is a formal collaboration between the government and one or more private companies with the objective of procuring private capital, management, technology and other resources as a means of enhancing infrastructure service delivery. PPPs, through which private companies work with public sector to manage complex infrastructure projects and develop public services, are increasingly being used throughout the world as a solution to provide and speed up major public projects.

The term has also been defined as a legally binding agreement between the government and private sector for the provision of infrastructure assets and efficient delivery of services that allocates responsibilities and business risks among the various partners. According to the World Bank, there is no consensus on the definition of the term Public-Private Partnerships. However, it is referred to as arrangements, ranging from medium to long term, between the public and private sectors whereby part of the services or works that fall under the domain of the public sector are provided by the private partners, with a detailed agreement for the delivery of public infrastructure and/ or services. The term has been defined to exclude privatization of utilities wherein there is a limited role for the public authority to perform.

Public-Private Partnerships occupy a middle position between Privatization and traditional Public Procurement. Privatization and Public-Private Partnerships reflect market principles and the two of them constitute a strategy for improving public management. PPPs are sometimes confused with privatization. Privatization connotes the permanent transfer of the public ownership of an asset to the private sector while in PPPs there is a continuing role to be performed by the public sector as partner in the ongoing relationship with the private sector (Ferguhason, et al 2010: 9). Under the PPPs, accountability for the provision of the service is clearly a responsibility of the public sector that is in a continuing relationship with the private sector, while in Privatization, accountability for providing services will immediately be transferred to the private sector although the citizen would still have the right to complain to the government.

PPP is thus an alternative to the traditional public procurement system by providing the needed facilities to the public sector by using funding generated by the private sector. In PPPs, the government usually sets a target as to the quality and quantity it requires. The designing, financing, building and the operation of the project is left to the innovation of the private sector. This is because if the government carries out the design itself, it would also have to carry the risks resulting from faulty designs.

In most cases on the private sector side, a Special Purpose Vehicle (SPV) which is totally a consortium of financial institutions and private companies will be responsible for all the activities of PPPs including the coordination of the financing and service delivery. Most of the times, this will be a consortium which will have at least two shareholders. The SPV enters into an agreement with the public authority for the building of a new infrastructure or the management or upgrade of existing infrastructure. Under the PPP arrangement, the public authorities or public sector parties are known by different terms such as federal, central and regional, state, municipal, local, governmental institution, public agency or any other entity which is under the public-sector control. While the private sector party is normally a Special-Purpose Company which includes investors, lenders, and companies providing construction and operational services. According to Yescombe, (Yescombe 2007: 17) the relationship between the parties is not really a partnership in the legal sense, but its contractual, being based on the terms of the PPP Contract.

The way in which the infrastructure transactions in PPPs are structured necessitates payment of long term service fees usually over the life of the contract (20-30 years on the average) which is usually on a pre-agreed basis with the intention of repaying the cost expended in financing the project and to also give return to the investors (Yescombe 2007: 3). PPPs allow public authority to retain ownership while engaging the private sector to perform functions such as financing, designing, constructing, maintaining and operating infrastructure like roads or providing basic services like water and electricity. Both parties stand to benefit from the contractual agreement.

Public-Private Partnerships will therefore help African governments in the provision of both social and economic infrastructures which will help to bolster their economies. This may either be in the provision of new infrastructures or in the rehabilitation of the existing ones. The objectives of a typical PPP arrangement in Nigeria is the mission to contribute to the economic integration of the country, accelerate its economic growth and sustainable development, engender and sustain private sector collaboration in traditionally public sector projects and also expand local access to international market thereby ensuring a deeper economic integration with the global world.

History of Public-Private Partnerships

Public-Private Partnerships have been used as concession to finance infrastructure projects in the nineteenth century (Ngwachi et al 2011, 1:2). One of the earliest and best known water projects was the Suez Canal which was managed by the private sector until it was nationalized in the 1950s. Tolling commenced in the United States between 1789 and 1900. Over 2,000 private companies operated turnpikes in Ohio, New York,

Michigan and Albany as a result of inadequate highways that existed at that time. In the 1960s, Spain embarked on its motorways programme which was financed by the private sector because of the inadequacy of the national budget to meet the infrastructure demands of the country at that time.

The energy crises of the 1970s led to the collapse of most of these private companies which necessitated the nationalization of some of these enterprises. Also at that time, the Labour Government in Britain was of the view that the market economy was very unfair and imperfect. Leaving the means of production, distribution and exchange to market forces was considered inequitable and that this would lead to the marginalization and impoverishment of the people.

However, changed economic condition saw the process being reversed in the 1980s when it became clear that governments as entrepreneurs had not succeeded. Most of their investments in commerce had been a colossal waste of government revenue. Interestingly, the philosophical position in the United Kingdom had begun to shift. Then, the Conservative Government of Margaret Thatcher had defeated the Labour government of Sir Harold Wilson. Both Margaret Thatcher and Ronald Reagan of the United States were of the firm view that Government had no business in commerce. The only role of Government was to provide a conducive and an enabling environment for entrepreneurs to flourish.

Also in the 1980s, China under the visionary leadership of Deng Xiaoping radically pursued a policy of private enterprise which changed his country's policy of overdependence on failed state enterprises. This paradigm shift ushered in a new era of positive economic outcomes that continue till today. His famous Chinese saying was "*don't care what colour a cat is as long as it catches mice*" which has unraveled china's economic miracles.

South Africa, Nigeria and Ghana among other African countries have also adopted the PPP initiative. In 1999, the first major legislation on Public Private Partnerships in the country was enacted. These provisions are set out in Treasury Regulation 16 issued by the National Treasury in accordance with the Public Finance Management Act, 1999 (PFMA) which for the first time established a dedicated PPP unit within the treasury in the year 2000. The main objectives of this Act are to enhance sound financial management and maximize service delivery through the effective and efficient utilization of limited resources.

Former President Olusegun Obasanjo in his assessment of the decline in Nigeria's public infrastructures stated that these infrastructures suffer from fundamental problems of defective capital structure, excessive bureaucratic control or intervention in appropriate technology, gross incompetence and mismanagement, blatant corruption and crippling complacency which monopoly engenders. Nigeria has since 2005 adopted the PPP initiative as a solution to its huge infrastructure gap. The Infrastructure Concession and Regulatory Establishment Act of 2005 was enacted to provide the legal and regulatory Frameworks for PPPs to thrive in Nigeria.

In recent times, a worldwide movement has taken place in respect of Public-Private Partnerships (Grimsey 2007: 2). The main aim of this innovation is to introduce the effective functioning principles of the private sector into the public administration (Hammami 2006: 5). This move was necessitated by the need to reduce inefficiencies, wastages in public spending, lack of managerial skills and to attract private capital in the provision of public infrastructure.

The Current State of Infrastructures in Africa

The record of African infrastructure has been both impressive and disappointing. Impressive in the sense that in the 1960s when most African nations got their political independence, infrastructure was almost non-existent. Upon independence, most African leaders swung into action to provide critical infrastructure to their nations. Infrastructure started flourishing because as at that time, most African governments wanted to showcase to their people what is called 'the fruits of independence'. This was made possible by the commitments of those leaders at that time and with the help of the multinational institutions.

However, since the late 1980s, the state of infrastructure has started deteriorating. In spite of urbanization and industrialization, the existing infrastructures were not upgraded or modernized to meet the needs of the growing population. The combination of poor management, poor policies and state monopolies, absence of effective maintenance and lack of re-investment had led to deterioration of infrastructure and had occasioned massive losses. In the process, everyone had become a loser, the consumers, the operators, and the state as well as other sectors of the economy. Within just over two decades, infrastructure in most African countries has now become a hindrance rather than a facilitator to nation's development. It is, therefore, important at this juncture to briefly analyze the current situation of infrastructure in Africa.

Electricity Infrastructure

Power blackout is a regular phenomenon in most African cities, towns and villages with negative impacts on the quality of lives and economic development. Most of the electricity equipment that were erected in the 1950s and 1960s are ageing and operating at a sub-optimal level due to lack of maintenance. Countries in Sub-Sahara Africa are still plagued with electricity crisis due to unreliable supplies, insufficient generating capacity and high tariffs being paid by the consumers.

Electricity generation in the region is the lowest compared to all other regions in the world, whereas the average tariff being paid by the consumers doubles that of other regions in the world. The total electricity generation of 48 countries that make up the Sub-Saharan Africa (with a combined population of about 800 million people) stands at about 68 Gigawatts (GW), which is far lesser than that of Spain alone (with a population of 45 million) which generated about 100 Gigawatts (GW) in 2010 (Anon. 2013: 2). Without South Africa, the total falls to a mere 28 GW, equivalent to the installed capacity of Argentina.

In Sub-Saharan Africa apart from South Africa, power consumption per capital per year is put at 124 kilowatt hours. This is barely enough to power just one 100 Watts bulb for just three hours in a day. Taiwan, Singapore and Malaysia that were almost in the same level with some of these African countries in the 1980s can now boast of 9,502, 7,695 and 3,215 Kilowatt hour per capital respectively.

Nigeria is a country of about 167 Million people with enormous oil and gas reserves, as at year 2014, power generation stood at about 4,000 Megawatts. It is estimated that the country's current electricity demand is well above 15,000 Megawatts which on a per capita basis is still less than one tenth of that of South Africa and two and half times less than Egypt. About $US50 Billion Dollars was disbursed on electricity within Fourteen years leading to generation of only about 1,000 Megawatts from 3000 Megawatts in 1999 to 4000 Megawatts in 2014. Mismanagement and underinvestment in this sector are not unconnected to the fact that since the country's independence in 1960, electricity generation and distribution has been an exclusive preserve of the Federal Government. The same unsatisfactory state of affairs exists in Kenya, Rwanda, Sierra Leone, and Mali and so on. Unreliable and epileptic power supply has been a perennial problem of these Sub-Saharan African countries for decades.

Water and Sanitation

According to the United Nations Environmental report, it is estimated that in Africa, over 300 million people lack access to clean and safe drinking water. Averagely, it is estimated that women and children in Sub-Saharan countries walk for about six kilometers daily in search of drinkable water. The World Health Organization has estimated that not less than 40 billion hours are spent annually in search of safe and drinkable water. That is equivalent to a year of labor for the entire workforce in France. African countries have advanced various reasons for not being able to meet the challenges of providing clean water and sanitary environment and also for not implementing the integrated water management policies. The reason advanced by Sierra Leone, Nigeria and Congo-Brazzaville at the World Water Week held in Stockholm is that they do not have formal water policy. São Tomé and Principe stated that the necessary laws and regulations are not in place, while it was asserted by the representative of Cameroon that the country does not have people who can champion the cause of providing water. About 25 African countries including Rwanda, Swaziland, Mozambique and Namibia among others attribute this problem to inadequate human capacity. Congo-Brazzaville stated that it could not get interested private sector, while to Burundi, incessant changes in administration has been identified as the major cause.

The effects of lack of access to water and sanitation have a macroeconomic impact on the continent and the benefits of improving access to water and sanitation are very enormous. Achieving the water and sanitation Millennium Development Goals would increase the yearly economic benefits of the continent to about $22 billion. This is because it is estimated that every $1dollar judiciously spent on this sector will bring a return of about $8 dollars in saved time, and it will help in reducing health costs and thereby increasing productivity. If the MDG targets on water and sanitation are met by 2015, national governments in sub-Saharan Africa could save about 12% of annual public health expenditures.

ICT infrastructure

Access to internet facilities is low in Africa and far less than any other region in the world. As at 2013, only 7% of the total population has access to internet facilities which amounts to only half of what is obtainable in South East Asia and the Pacific. According to the International Telecommunications Union data, only five countries in the Sub-Saharan Africa have internet penetration rates exceeding 20 percent. The Seychelles has the highest internet penetration per population with 43% than any other sub-Saharan Africa; Nigeria, with 48 million internet users has the highest number of internet users in Africa followed by Egypt, Morocco, Kenya and South Africa in that order. Southern Sudan has the lowest penetration rate of 0%, followed by Ethiopia with 1.1%, and then Congo DR, and Somalia with 1.2% rates.

Although in recent times, the performance of Africa's mobile networks has radically improved, the telecommunications industries all over the world have also evolved. Internet broadband is now considered as central to a long term economic development strategies of a nation. In some countries in Africa, internet broadband is not available and where available, it is highly expensive and far more beyond what the majority of the people can afford (Mark et al 2011: 1). In 2013, the total fixed-broadband penetration rates for developing countries are 6.1% and less than 1% in Sub-Saharan Africa.

Road Infrastructure

The condition of roads in the African continent ranges from fair to poor. There are relatively very few roads that are in a good condition. In Nigeria for example, the existing network of highways in the country is not only inadequate but also largely in a deplorable state. In Kenya, between January and April 2013, over 1,000 deaths have been recorded as a result of road accidents. The situation in most Sub-Saharan countries is not so different. Rural Africa has only 34% of access roads compared to about 90% in the developed world. About 80% of the cargo loads in sub-Saharan Africa are taken through the roads. Good national and regional transportation links are very vital to the governmental policies of reducing poverty and hunger.

Reasons for Private Sector Involvement in Infrastructure Development

There are many reasons why the government needs to collaborate with the private sector in the delivery of public goods and services. It is not in doubt as stated earlier in this work that budgetary constraints and inefficiencies on the part of government are among the reasons. Afeikhena Jerome, listed some of the reasons why government corporations have failed to provide adequate services to the people. He put the reasons succinctly as:

> *"underpricing; low productivity; poor service quality; long queues and large portions of the population without access to basic services; lack of*

transparency; and damaging political interference in the operations of these infrastructure entities."

These reasons have been grouped and discussed under five major sub-headings. They are:

Attracting Private Capital Investment

Governments are attracted by the benefits of mobilizing private capital. The estimated demand for public infrastructure is huge and sometimes above the entire budget projection of a nation. The government alone cannot provide these basic infrastructure because of non- availability of funds. A World Bank report stated that for Africa to fill the infrastructure gaps, an annual expenditure of US$75 Billion (US$38 billion of investment and a further US$37 billion in operations and maintenance) would be required annually within the next ten years. It is obvious that this huge capital deficit cannot be raised through public funds alone.

A typical example of a project financed with the support of the private sector is the R2.6 Billion PPP project for the N3 and N4 toll road linking the South African provinces of Gauteng, Limpopo and Mpumalanga to the port of Maputo in Mozambique. Mozambique lacked the required funds to rehabilitate and maintain its own part of the N4 highway, the railway line and the ports which were long damaged as a result of the civil war that ravaged that country. As at 1997, the total estimation of South Africa's requirement to fix its roads was estimated to be R37 billion, both governments were thus in need of funds to finance and maintain this all important infrastructure. As a result of this, the PPP approach was then resorted to, and with the cooperation of the private sector, the project became a reality.

Therefore, harnessing private capital can help the government to speed up the delivery of public infrastructure without delay. The banking and finance markets have moved in to accommodate the needs of PPP transactions. We have seen extraordinary change in the duration of time for which financial institutions are willing to lend. Loan maturities of 10 to12 years were unusual in the 1980s and 1990s; now we see repayment periods of 30 to 35 years (Avery 2006: 35). In the case of PPPs, there are repayment periods of 25-30 years and even beyond. This is because the manner the infrastructure projects are structured guarantees a high degree of certainty of stable cash flow in these projects. Also, Pension Funds Administrators are also becoming interested in long term fixed-income investment which PPPs provide.

It increases efficiency and the use of resources

Scarce public resources are not being used efficiently by most governments. Also, because of the poor incentives for efficiency, the public sector is not rightly positioned to build efficiently and operate infrastructure. Combining such incentives in the operation and management of the public infrastructure through the private sector is therefore necessary. Typically, private sector operators enter into such transactions with the intention of maximizing profits which are geared majorly by increased efficiency in investment and operations. If the PPPs are designed in such a manner as to allow the operator realize this goal, the efficiency of the infrastructure services will be achieved.

According to Philippe Burger, (Burger 2009: 15) he stated that one major reason why it is better to adopt PPP instead of privatization is where effectiveness, rather than efficiency, is also an aim of the government. A policy becomes effective where the aim of government with respect to which it was conceived is achieved, irrespective of whether the aim is carried out in an efficient manner or not. Achieving the result is the aim, and such aim is carried out effectively.

There is no doubt that the governments have access to more funding than the private sector, the efficiency gains from the private sector participation may in the long run overweight the extra financial cost expended.

The greater efficiency of the private sector can be linked to the following factors:

(i) The private sector's commercial approaches to problem solving with serious focus on cost-effectiveness leads to the rationalization of cost of labour and materials;
(ii) By allowing less politically oriented decision-making will surely lead to better governance and it will improve accountability; and
(iii) Improving competition and transparency will reduce the opportunity greatly for corrupt practices and it will reveal those costs that were hitherto hidden.

Reform of the sectors through a reallocation of roles, incentives, and accountability

Once risks, roles and responsibilities are reallocated, there is a tendency that efficiency and accountability will be assured. Also corruption, which is common in conventional procurement setting will be reduced greatly thereby enhancing greater output.

Technology, Innovation and Know-how

By involving the private sector, access to new technologies and experienced management not currently available through public monopoly could be tapped into and reaped. This will include access to skills and those technologies and know-how, which were otherwise not known to the public sector. These technologies may even be developed for those projects specifically which would not have been developed under the traditional procurement system.

Transparency and Anti-corruption

One of the major challenges facing public procurement in Africa is corruption, which is a major threat to transparency. It does not only threaten but it undermines the legitimacy of the corrupted government (OECD 2007). Unfortunately, in the African countries, there were reported cases of scandals involving major companies and public officials which have been exposed by the media, as a consequence of bribery and other crimes committed during procurement procedures and other government contracts. Corruption in the procurement process in Africa is not insignificant because globalization has brought it across borders.

Openness and good governance will lead to equality in the treatment of the investors and it will promote fair competition. Lack of transparency and good governance, therefore, increases the likelihood of bribery and corruption, increases costs and reduces competition and the quality of the output. PPPs, therefore, provide the opportunity to reduce corruption and promote good governance in the process of implementation.

Achieving Socio-Economic Sustainability through the PPP Initiative

In this day and age, the concept of sustainable development is no longer new (Adeoye et al 2012: 127). Its impacts and usage have traversed all facets of human life. The United Nations has defined the concept as *"Development that meets the needs of the present without compromising the ability of future generations to meet their own needs."*

The African continent lags behind other continents in terms of development. It was noted by Sirleaf and Radelet that the past three decades have been disastrous for Africa because most of her people have been inflicted with poverty (Sirleaf and Radelet 2008: 1). Poverty is said to be caused by lack of access to income and capital assets, lack of political voice and incidence of natural disasters. Of the three, the first two are man-made accounting for the highest challenge of our time. Interestingly, Africa is one of the least continents that are affected by natural disasters. Indeed, it is one of the most naturally endowed continents in the world. Notwithstanding these God–given endowments, we remain the most backward continent as we are unable to put our acts together and harness our resources for the collective good of the citizens.

Harnessing private sector investment, skills and efficiency in the provision of infrastructure will ultimately lead to sustainable development. The Millennium Development Goals and the vision 20:20 may be unrealistic without the involvement of the private sector in development (OECD 2007). For example, achieving safe water and sanitation for all by the year 2015 will require private sector investment and improvement in the technical and managerial performances.

It is important at this juncture to cite a few examples of projects that have been executed through PPPs and how they have alleviated the sufferings of the people and contributed to development. They are:

1. In Gabon for example, PPPs have been used to provide water and electricity to the two main cities of Port-Gentil and Libreville (Ferguharson, Torres and Yescombe 2010: 33). In 1997, the government signed a 20-year concession contract with SEEG, with a capital value of US$135 million. This concession contract has been a success and it was the first real output driven water project in Africa. Through PPP in water project, more than half of the Gabonese population now has access to safe water.

2. In Durban, South Africa, the Inkosi Albert Luthuli Central Hospital was contracted to the private sector for 15 years under the Design, Finance, Build, Operate and transfer (National Treasury 2009). Under the arrangement, the Impilo Consortiun will upgrade and manage the facilities and information technology of an 846-bed state-of the heart referral hospital. The capital value of this project is put at US$746 million. This hospital is well equipped and provides services to the people of Kwa-Zulu Natal and the Eastern Cape Province. The general opinion has been that PPP through which this hospital was built has

delivered a quality service which could not have been achieved by the government alone.

3. In Manila, Philippines, as a result of lack of access to drinkable water, the government engaged the private sector through PPPs to provide access to water in the Eastern Zone of Metro Manila. The contract has a capital value of US$17 million. Since the water project was completed, the company has met all its obligations regarding water supply. In fact, the water project currently serves more than 5.1 million people and the company has increased its coverage of 24hours water supply to about 98 percent of the area.

4. In Lagos Nigeria, in an attempt to eliminate the severe traffic jam along Lekki-Epe Expressway, the Lagos State Government granted a concession contract to the Lekki Concession Company (LCC) to design, construct, finance, and operate the toll road project. The Upgrade and expansion of the 49.36 km road will be maintained by the LCC for a period of 30 years (Lagos PPP Unit 2013). The capital value is estimated to be US$450 million. Since the completion of construction work in 2012, motorists have felt highly relieved because the road is fully operational.

Does Law have any Role to Play in Development?

Where a nation seeks to achieve sustainable development, legal intervention is not only necessary but also inevitable. But the question is intervening to do what? There is no doubt that both the *existence* and *enforcement* of the law are both indispensable (Bondzi-Simpson 2012: 422). Therefore, if a nation has set a developmental target for itself and has not been met, the law must ask itself three (3) questions. The first question is-- "*are there applicable rules and regulations that govern the matter under consideration*?" Where it is found that no rule exists, then there is what is called availability gap. Where there are rules applicable to the subject matter, then the next question goes thus: *"Are the rules adequate to address all conceivable issues touching on the subject matter?"* If the answer is in the affirmative, then there is no problem; but if it is in the negative, then there is an adequacy gap. Thirdly, if there are rules and the rules are adequate, the question is-- "*are they being enforced in such a way that strict compliance is achieved?* If there is enforcement, then no problem, but if they are not, then there is an enforcement gap.

Therefore, the role of law in achieving sustainable development cannot be over emphasized. Legal intervention is not only necessary but indispensable in achieving sustainable development. African governments should therefore adopt a legal intervention that will tackle the availability, adequacy and enforcement gaps that ought to be filled by the law in order to achieve sustainable development in the continent.

Recommendations

The following recommendations are important for African governments to fill the infrastructure challenges confronting the continent through the Public-Private Partnership initiatives:

1. African governments are greatly encouraged to explore the opportunities provided by the private sector which are: the availability of large capital to fund and maintain infrastructure projects; skills and technological know-how; competence in the proper and efficient management of resources as well as the accountability and transparency to drive the continent to achieve sustainable development. Where the necessary infrastructure is provided through the public-private cooperation, definitely, it will boost African economy and promote regional integration. This will also lead to an increase in the standard of living and reduction in the rate of crimes within the continent.
2. African governments should adopt a uniform legal and regulatory regime to address PPPs transactions in the continent. Despite the high level of infrastructure development in Europe, the European Commission, having realized the benefits of having single legal and regulatory regimes for concession contracts, has on 13th day of April, 2011 declared its intention to adopt a uniform legislative framework to govern PPP contracts in the community. This will help the EC in order to further boost growth and strengthens confidence in the investors. Presently, the award of PPP contracts in Africa is subject to a limited number of secondary law provisions which are applicable in the few countries that have legislative framework for PPPs. This gap will limit the access of African business from the international borders and, therefore, lack of access to other markets has led to uneven development within the continent.
3. Governments sometimes find it difficult to establish an effective framework that gives investors sufficient confidence. Investors will

be most concerned if there is uncertainty in the law and lack of political independence of the regulatory agencies. In developing countries, which Africa is part of, successful implementation of private infrastructure investment requires a careful review of the entire business environments and, if necessary, reform of the policy framework underlying it. New institutional structures often need to be designed, legislations need to be enacted or amended and regulatory oversight functions need to be established and strengthened.

4. Political commitment on the part of governments is very important. It is one thing to have sound regulations for PPPs, and it is another thing for the governments and their agencies to be committed to making PPPs work. Unless governments and their agencies are absolutely determined that PPPs succeed, there may be sufficient vested interests in the country against PPPs that would ensure that the government's initiative to promote PPPs fail. In addition to this, the government should also provide political guarantees to investors where appropriate. In Nigeria, for example, despite the fact that there are laws in place to regulate PPP transactions, the Federal Government has not shown enough commitments to support the initiative and that is why no much success has been recorded since the inception of the scheme.

5. The success of Public-Private Partnerships is dependent on mutual trust between government officials and private sector executives. Also, building and maintaining public confidence promotes the integrity of the partnerships. Trusts and confidence are, therefore, the hallmarks of this kind of partnership. Where there is trust and confidence, the private sector will be willing to invest its capital because of the integrity of the partnership programme.

6. Governments should develop the necessary capacity (institutional, negotiating, legal etc.) to handle PPP projects at the national state/provincial and the local government levels. This is because PPP are very complex in nature. Public-Private Partnerships require a host of competent and skilled staff to successfully handle the complex PPP transactions in order to achieve value for money. The required areas of competencies include human resources, project management; financial analysis, legislative and regulatory knowledge, legal matrix of PPPs and insurance. Therefore, the necessary competencies should be deployed in order to achieve the desired goals.

7. Governments should develop laws and policies that are aimed at encouraging private sectors to perform their corporate social responsibilities. The stakeholders in the business communities should now be more concerned with how they are perceived by their host communities and how they project their corporate success image on the scale of social crusade as contributors to social development and economic enhancement partners. They should be more and more concerned with how to contribute their quota to the development of the community.

Conclusion

Economic activities and other social services cannot function effectively in a nation without the modern and adequate infrastructure facilities in place. The present state of infrastructure in Africa does not support the continent's drive for economic development. Africa cannot hope to achieve the Millennium Development Goals and take its rightful place in the global economy without a modern, sound and efficient infrastructure system. As a result of globalization which has removed barriers to a nation's border, it will be increasingly difficult for Africa to remain competitive if its infrastructure development continues to perform at a sub optimal level. More serious and sustained efforts are needed to give more impetus to infrastructure development in Africa in coming years. Development, eradication of poverty and securing peace and prosperity for the people are achievable goals provided that all the stakeholders play their respective roles, seriously and accordingly.

Today, there is a worldwide revolution for infrastructure provision through the Public-Private Partnership initiative. This paradigm shift to PPPs from other procurement methods can help African nations to achieve value for money and sufficient transfer of risks to the private sector. Properly coordinated and well managed partnerships between the private sector and the governments will help African nations to achieve MDGs and sustainable development and therefore can take their rightful place in the global economies. It is in fact a modest and achievable development initiative provided that everything is put in place to make it happen!

References

Adeoye, R A, P.E. Bondzi-Simpson, Egbewole, W.O, Etudaiye M.A and Olatunji, O.A. eds, 2012. *The rights of indigenous People to Sustainable Development in Africa-The Case of Gbagyi People of Nigeria* in *Law and Sustainable Development in Africa.* Surrey: Grosevenor House Publishing.

Anon. 2013. Africa's Energy Situation. Retrieved from www.desertec-africa.org/index.php?option=com_content&view, (accessed 4 May 2013).

Anon. 2012. An Introduction to Public- Private Partnerships http://www.partnershipsbc.ca/pdf/An%20Introduction%20to%20P3%20-une03.pdf.(accessed 8 March 2012.

Anon. 2013. Enabling Private Sector Participation in Electricity Generation. Retrieved from http://www.gsb.uct.ac.za/files/Kenya.pdf(accessed 23 May 2013).

Anon. 2013.Water and Sanitation. http://www.one.org/c/us/issuebrief/99/ (accessed 23 May 2013. Electricity infrastructure in Spain. http://ec.europa.eu/energy/gas_electricity/doc/es_energy_market_2011_en.pdf (accessed 22 May 2013).

Burger, P. 2009. The dedicated PPP unit of the South African treasury. Oxford: Willey Blackwell Publishing Limited.

Eberhard, A, V. Foster, C., Briceño-Garmendia, F. Ouedraogo, D. Camos, and M.Shkaratan. 2008. *Underpowered: the state of the power sector in sub-saharan Africa,* Washington DC: The World Bank.

Energy Statistics: Electricity Production Per Capital. http://www.nationmaster.com/graph/ene_ele_pro_percap-energy-electricity-production-per-capita (accessed 23 May 2013). Fact Sheet: Infrastructure in Sub-Saharan. Africa http://web.worldbank.org/WBSITE/EXTERNAL/COUNTRIES/AFRICAEXT/0,,contentMDK:21951811~pagePK:146736~piPK:146830~theSitePK:258644,00.html (accessed 19 April 2013).

Farquharson, E., C. Torres de Mastle, E.R. Yescombe and Javier, E. 2010. *How to engage with the private sector in public-private partnerships in emerging markets*. Wahington DC: The World Bank.

Grimsey D and Mervyn K.L. 2007. *Public private partnerships: the worldwide revolution in infrastructure provision and project finance.* United Kingdom: Edward Elger Publishing Limited.

Hammami, M. Ruhashyankiko, J and Yehoue, E.B. 2006. *Determinants of public private partnerships in infrastructure.* Washington *DC:* International Monetary Fund.

Jerome A. 2004. Infrastructure privatisation and liberalisation in Africa: The quest for the holy grail or coup de grace?'. http://www.uib.cat/depart/deaweb/smed/pdf/jerome.pdf (accessed 3 Sept 2013).

Mark, D. J. Williams, R.M and Minges, M. 2011. *Africa's ICT infrastructure: building on a mobile revolution.* Washington DC: The World Bank.

Nicholas Avery. 2006. *Public-private partnerships: a practical analysis.* London: Globe Publishing Ltd.

Nyagwachi, J and Smallwood, J. 2011. South African Public Private Partnerships (PPP) Projects. *Journal of Construction Vol. 1, No 2.*

Organisation for Economic Cooperation and Development. 2007. *Integrity in Public Procurement. Good Practice from A-Z.* United Kingdom: OECD Publishers.

Organisation for Economic Cooperation and Development. *Principles for Private Sector Participation in Infrastructure.* http://www.oecd.org/daf/inv/investment-policy/38309896.pdf, (accessed 28 May 2013).

P.E. Bondzi-Simpson. 2012. *Green Jurisprudence: Laws Place in Sustainable Development, in* Law and Sustainable Development in Africa, Bondzi-Simpson P.E, Egbewole W.O, Etudaiye M.A, Olatunji eds Surrey: Grosvenor Publishers.

Public Finance Management Act. http://www.treasury.gov.za/legislation/PFMA/default.aspx, (accessed 21 March 2014).

Public Private Partnerships Quarterly. 2009. *A publication of the PPP Unit, National Treasury South Africa.*

Roads and Highways, Encyclopedia Britannica, Encyclopedia Britannica. http:britannica.com/EBchecked/topic/505109/road/71891/Ancient-roads-of-South-and-East-Asia (accessed May 20 2013.

Sawant, R J. 2010. *Infrastructure investing: managing risks & rewards for pensions, insurance companies & endowments .New* Jersey: John Wiley & Sons.

Shemmy Simuyemba .2000. Linking Africa through regional infrastructure. *Economic Research Paper No 64.* Abidjan: African Development Bank.

Sirleaf E.J and Radelet, S. 2008. *The good news out of Africa: Democracy, Stability and the Renewal of Growth and Development, speech delivered at the* Centre for Global Development.

Stop! The crippling state of Kenya's killer roads reported in The Daily Nation Newspapers of May 27, 2013. Retrieved from Sub-Saharan Africa.Retrieved from https://opennet.net/research/regions/ssafrica. Accessed 23 May, 2013.

Wale Babalakin. 2011. *Legal Dynamics of Privatisation in Nigeria*, http:www.babalakinandco.com (accessed 13 June 2013).

Wildord, J. N. *World's Oldest Paved Road Found in Egypt*. http://www.nytimes.com/1994/05/08/world/world-s-oldest-paved-road-found-in-egypt.html. (accessed 27 April 2013).

William Gilbert. History of Electricity. http://inventors.about.com/cs/inventorsalphabet/a/electricity.htm (accessed 20 May 2013).

World Bank definition of Public-Private Partnerships<http://ppp.worldbank.org/public-private-partnership/overview/what-are-public-private-partnerships>.Accessed8 March, 2012.

Yescombe, E. R. 2007. *Public-Private Partnerships Principles of Policy and Finance*. Oxford: Elsevier Publishing Ltd.

Democratic Governance, The New Aid Architecture and the Future of Human Development in Africa

Dejo Olowu

Introduction

Democracy and good governance occupy an important place in contemporary development discourse. While many observers (Taylor 2007; Bräutigam 2010:8-16; Wamboye and Adekola 2013) regard political regime characteristics such as democracy and the quality of governance as ends in themselves, and inherent features of development, others seem to appreciate them primarily as preconditions for economic growth and integration of developing countries in the global economy. In spite of the variance in motives for emphasising democracy and good governance, most current international aid programmes contain references to aspects of developing countries' political systems that were absent during the era of the Washington Consensus, when the neoliberal emphasis of markets underscored macroeconomic fundamentals and focused on 'structural adjustment'.

One critical challenge for building democracy and good governance concerns the very nature and foundational elements of international development cooperation. Without doubt, national politics matter for society's development and progress. This is a truism which would not be contested in any developed country or established democracy. It is however not reflected in the way international development cooperation works because key political actors such as political parties, parliaments and the civil society essentially remain on the margins of development discourse and practice. Thus continues a vicious cycle in which the legitimacy and effectiveness of these democratic actors is further undermined. Since 2002, the Monterrey Consensus (2002), the Paris Declaration on Aid Effectiveness (2005) (Paris Declaration), and the Accra Agenda for Action (2008) are endeavouring to change the international development architecture to emphasise the importance of national processes. However, much work remains to translate these agendas into concrete strategies which ensure that international development cooperation is supportive of democratic processes and the enhancement of the human quotient of development, not the least in African states.

The challenge even assumes a more profound dimension against the backdrop of new-fangled donor countries, institutions and individuals now joining the fray of aid disbursement to developing countries, outside the framework of established OECD's Development Assistance Committee (DAC) (Kragelund 2008:565; Greenhill et al 2013).

The chapter focuses on Africa as the continent is currently the main target of development assistance, and the performance of African countries on governance indicators is generally perceived as problematic. An urgent need arises for the generation of tangible mechanisms and advocacy for policy change in order to strengthen the democratic dimensions of development cooperation in and for Africa. This chapter thus focuses on the application, effectiveness and viability of various instruments that have been used, in the post-1995 'new international aid architecture' discourse, to assess and improve the functioning of political systems of developing countries, most notably, the level of democratic governance vis-à-vis development aid.

Aid Flows and Human Development: Some Revolving Quandaries

Based on the dominant view of the post-World War II era that newly independent countries should be helped to develop infrastructure and break the trappings of human poverty, Africa has been the showcase of how richer countries have sought to help poorer countries over the past six decades through the instrumentality of aid (Fritz and Menocal 2007). Sub-Saharan Africa (SSA) is cited to be receiving some US$ 20 billion per year, inclusive of relief aid, while SSA countries jointly received nearly one-quarter of the US$ 3 trillion of net Official Development Assistance (ODA) dispensed over the last 50 years (Asiama and Quartey 2009:60-63; United Nations World Economic and Social Survey 2012:83). Although actual monetary figures are difficult to ascertain and empirical statistics from donors, institutions of development and independent analysts often swing between increment and decline in the volume of foreign aid flow – consisting of Overseas Development Assistance (ODA) and Overseas Development Finance (ODF) – into African states, what is unmistakable in reality is the asymmetry in foreign aid and human development indices on the continent, generally.

In the latest *Human Development Report 2013* ('The rise of the South: Human progress in a diverse world'), published by the United Nation Development Programme (UNDP), SSA recorded the lowest indices in health and education, among all world regions (UNDP 2013:14). The human development challenges confronting Africa are indeed overwhelming. With millions of people living on less than US $1 per day in several African countries, the massive human misery in Africa cannot be more graphic than the depictions of the *Human Development Report 2013*. Apart from not only failing to eliminate poverty, but also as experiencing an increase in the number of people living in extreme poverty, SSA registers 37 countries among the 46 listed as "lowest human development" (UNDP 2013:144-147). Whereas the global average human development index value was 0.694, as captured by the UNDP's Report, SSA countries recorded the lowest human development index value of 0.475. The human development index (HDI) is a composite index measuring average achievement in three basic dimensions of human development, namely, a long and healthy life (measured in terms of life expectancy at birth); knowledge (measured in terms of mean years of schooling plus expected years of schooling); and a decent standard of living (measured in terms of gross national income (GNI) per capita) (UNDP 2013:144-147). When compared to other regions of the world, therefore, Africa lags far behind in all three critical measurements of human capabilities and social capital formation.

At the UN Millennium Summit in New York, the international community committed itself to a medium-term development agenda comprising eight goals, now known as the millennium development goals (MDGs). The MDGs consist of commitments (1) to reduce extreme poverty and hunger by half; (2) universal primary education (100% coverage by 2015); (3) gender equality in primary and secondary education (in terms of achieving an equal ratio of boys to girls); (4) to reduce child mortality by two-thirds; 5: improvement of maternal health by reducing mortality by two-thirds; (6) to combat HIV/AIDS, TB and malaria; (7) to reduce the proportion of the population without clean water by half; and (8) to develop a global partnership for development (World Bank 2005). Owing to the peculiar challenges of poorer countries, the MDGs were to be funded through aid (McNair 2012). While estimates of funds required to fulfil the MDGs have varied greatly, the Organisation for Economic Co-operation and Development (OECD) had in 2011 estimated that achieving the first six MDGs globally would require US$ 120bn more to be spent every year (Atisophon et al 2011:12).

While the clamour for more aid has become the mantra of majority of African governments and their sympathisers and/or collaborators (see eg Attaran 2005; Ogunlesi 2013; Kimutai 2013; Development Finance International (DFI) and Oxfam International 2013; Gedolf 2013), hard evidence overwhelmingly demonstrates that aid to Africa has only further impoverished the poor, and rendered human development forlorn. The stealthy aid culture has left African countries more debt-ridden, more inflation-prone, more susceptible to the vicissitudes of the currency markets and more unappealing to higher-quality investment, apart from increasing the threat of civil strife across the continent. Indeed, aid growth has not translated into economic transformation and millions of Africans still live in absolute poverty. What more? The World Bank makes the same point graphically in its latest Global Monitoring Report on the MDGs 2013 with figures displayed prominently that Africa is more off-track than other regions (World Bank 2013).

Empirical data tracked to 1972 demonstrate that aid flow to Sub-Saharan Africa has been higher on average than all other developing regions of world. In the African states of Burkina Faso, Rwanda, Somalia, Mali, Chad, Mauritania and Sierra Leone, from 1970 to 2002, over 70% of total government spending came from foreign aid, according to recent figures (Asiama and Quartey 2009:60-63).

All in all, despite arguments for aid increment over the past decade, those involved in the aid and development debate have been virtually unanimous that global partnerships have not resolved some of the persistent dilemmas surrounding aid effectiveness. These relate to (a) ownership; (b) alignment with country strategies; (c) subsidiarity; (d) accountability; and (e) governance of programmes.

Issues of ownership, pervasive in country assistance programmes, have become more critical because of the proliferation of global development partnership programmes. To ensure accountability the rules and procedures of global programmes tend to reflect the preferences of donors and staff of international agencies largely than do rules of country-focused assistance programmes. There also remains the need to integrate the activities of global programmes and country development agendas as limited global programmes have their goals reflected in the poverty reduction strategy papers (PRSPs) that provide the framework for country-based assistance to poor countries. Another problematic issue relates to subsidiarity – principle whereby matters are handled by the lowest-level competent authority – and aid coordination, because global programmes are often not the best vehicle to organise, finance and coordinate country assistance. Accountability remains about the strongest limitation to global aid programmes, more so with the duplication of donors and new partners resulting in incongruous policy and execution of programmes as well as vague responsibilities for performance and management. A final dilemma is ineffective governance which has been a formidable challenge to global development programmes because they manifest independent governance structures of variable quality and accountability (Linn and Bradford Jr 2006; Lele, Sadik and Simmons 2007).

Multilateral Normative Agenda for Aid Effectiveness and Implications for Africa

Contemporary approach to new aid architecture is built, largely, on changing conceptions of development, which were summarised in the World Bank's Comprehensive Development Framework (CDF). This framework, elaborated during James Wolfensohn's Presidency, is currently the dominant policy theory for development assistance. Other building blocks of the new aid agenda are the UN Millennium Declaration (which led to the formulation of the MDGs), the Monterrey Consensus on financing for development and the Paris Declaration on Aid Effectiveness (OECD 2005).

The new aid agenda displays an awareness of social and political contexts, and does not focus solely on macroeconomic performance. The framework that was adopted during Wolfensohn's tenure at the World Bank included 'the essentials of good governance' (i.e. transparency, participation, free information, anti-corruption policies and a well-qualified civil service), the regulatory framework for a working market economy, social policies focused on health and education, the build-up of infrastructure, and policies for environmental sustainability (Wolfensohn 1998:13-14). The Monterrey Consensus called for "a new partnership between developed and developing countries" and the final declaration of March 2002 contained a commitment to "sound policies, good governance at all levels and the rule of law' as well as to the increase of financial flows to developing countries in the form of aid, investment, trade and debt relief" (UN 2002).

In 2005, the vast wealth of practical knowledge about aid effectiveness was brought together for the first time to shape the Paris Declaration into a single set of succinct ramparts for improving aid governance. The Accra Agenda for Action (2008) later emerged to reaffirm the commitments of the Paris Declaration, marking simultaneously the beginning of a new era in aid relations by insisting on better cooperation among donors, recipients, governments and civil society organisations. Together, these documents form a practical, action-oriented roadmap to improve the quality of aid and its impact on development. The specific implementation measures they put in place are underpinned by a monitoring system to assess progress and ensure that donors and recipients hold each other accountable for their commitments. The Paris Declaration has become the backbone of the new international aid architecture. The declaration contained several principles for aid relationships, among which ownership, alignment and mutual accountability appear to be related directly to issues of governance. The principles of ownership and alignment imply that development policies should be based on developing country initiative and be in line with their policy priorities. Mutual accountability entails that donor and recipient countries should hold each other accountable for the proper implementation of development assistance policies (OECD 2005; OECD 2006).

Endorsed quickly by important actors within the donor community, the new aid paradigm emerging from Monterrey Consensus met with considerable enthusiasm from outsiders, such as international NGOs and the research community. Nonetheless, and inescapably, more than a decade after, questions are being raised. Two major patterns of criticism are emerging. Some question components of the new approach. These critics are not necessarily discrediting the paradigm, but they question some of its operational aspects. Kragelund for instance has questioned whether the new approach reduces transaction costs effectively for recipients (Kragelund 2008:556). Many other examples could be cited. A more sizeable number of critics are sympathetic to the paradigm itself, but fear that donors will not put it to work. Evaluations by both the World Bank (2004) and the IMF (2004) have raised serious concerns about the willingness of donors, including the BWI themselves, to subject themselves to the collective discipline of harmonisation and other aspects of the new aid agenda (Bigsten 2006; Sundberg and Gelb 2006; Bräutigam 2008:14). Critics from the international NGOs and from the academic community have also expressed serious misgivings, for instance, around whether civil society will ever be allowed the depth of participation that the PRSPs architects envisaged. For instance, what kind of rules govern corruption, democracy, and the protection of human rights when it comes to aid and development finance?

The global rules on corruption rest on binding international treaties, particularly the 1997 OECD Convention on Combating Bribery of Foreign Public Officials in International Business Transactions. This convention enjoys the status of a binding law. It made it mandatory for OECD members to make bribery of foreign officials (i.e. kickbacks or corrupt "facilitation payments") a domestic crime in their countries. The United Nations Convention against Corruption, which came into force in 2005, lifts many of the OECD agreements to the level of international law.

In practice, however, it is a challenge to create a framework for detecting these crimes and punishing offenders. For example, as Transparency International (TI) has noted, OECD members have resisted calls for companies receiving officially supported export credits to name agents receiving commissions; to make the size of commissions public; or to bring facilitation payments ("greasing the wheels") into the remit of these conventions (Bräutigam 2010:14). A 2009 analysis by TI also pointed out that only four of the 38 countries that had signed the OECD Convention were actively enforcing it. There was "little or no" enforcement by 21 signatories. Further, the Convention itself focuses on combating specific practices by companies. It does not contain broadly agreed rules or standards for engaging with countries whose governments are thought to be highly corrupt. Individual donors, or even agencies within a donor government, might withhold aid from corrupt countries. In the US, for example, the Millennium Challenge Corporation uses levels of corruption as one of the parameters for assessing whether a country qualifies for assistance or not, but the United States Agency for International Development (USAID) does not have such a specific criterion. Furthermore, practices in areas outside of aid suggest problems with application of the convention. As an obvious example, few export credit agencies, if any, have mandated international competitive bidding for the projects they finance. One other dimension that will be significant for our present purposes is the question of how solid the aid and development finance architecture is in terms of democracy and human rights.

The new aid architecture has undoubtedly resulted in changes relating to the objectives and modalities of assistance and in the conditions that are attached to the provision of aid. In certain important respects, the attention for the quality of governance was the most significant marker of the arrival of the new era in foreign assistance policies. Empirical findings by the World Bank on the centrality of policies and governance mechanisms for the prospects of development and the effectiveness of development aid had led to a departure from policy conditionalities – as it was observed that the promise to allocate aid did not induce sufficient policy change in developing countries – and to a focus on demonstrable improvement of governance and policies (Burnside and Dollar 1997; World Bank 1998).

Over the past decade, multilateral and bilateral aid agencies alike have introduced notions of 'good governance' into their operational assistance policies. 'Good governance' has acquired the status of a new conditionality in the framework of development assistance. It is not, as in the past, a conditionality that is imposed in exchange for promises about future policy change (sometimes referred to as *ex ante* conditionality), but rather a condition related to past performance in terms of certain governance and institutional indicators (*ex post* conditionality).

Various forms of *ex post* conditionality are evident in development assistance policies. At the bilateral level, several donor countries have introduced governance-related selectivity mechanisms to guide their choice of aid recipients (e.g., the Millennium Challenge Account adopted by the US and the Dutch partner country policy) (Hout 2007:49-95). Different innovations have been adopted by multilateral organisations over the past ten years, but two approaches hold particular relevance for Africa, namely,

(a) multilateral development banks (the World Bank's International Development Association and, in its trail, regional banks such as the African Development Bank) have introduced notions of performance-based allocation, leading to annual assessments of borrowing countries' policies and institutional performance, and have implemented instruments aimed at governance reform in borrowing countries, notably to achieve institutional strengthening and combating corruption (Hout 2007:23-48);

(b) NEPAD (the New Partnership for Africa's Development), initiated in 2001, adopted a self-assessment instrument for the assessment of democracy and governance quality: the so-called African Peer Review Mechanism. The idea behind the peer review was that countries that would be judged positively on governance quality would attract more aid and foreign investment through the NEPAD scheme (Taylor 2005:63; Kebonang and Fombad 2006:39-54).

The approach adopted by the African Development Bank (AfDB), focusing on performance-based allocation and institutional reform, is also of considerable importance, as it is both representative of the methods that the multilateral development banks apply generally to their development programmes, and is an example of an organisation that is attuned to specific African realities. The International Development Association

(IDA) is implementing its programmes worldwide, and may be argued to have less intimate knowledge of African situations. The implementation of performance-based allocation and governance reform programmes by AfDB and IDA offers an interesting combination of multilateral policy practices that permit comparisons within the 'family' of multilateral development agencies.

The African Peer Review Mechanism (APRM) is a unique attempt by African countries to implement a self-assessment of governance practices on the continent. Responding to a clear international agenda – one that aimed at attracting development assistance and foreign direct investment to Africa – the APRM is an attempt to get away from purely external judgement of politics and governance, and implement 'home-grown' norms and principles. Although the extent to which the APRM process represents a credible initiative for monitoring aid governance on the continent over the past decade remains debatable and incipient, the APRM's experience provides the opportunity to assess the use and validity of an instrument that is judged by many observers to be more legitimate than others because of the high degree of ownership of the review process by African countries themselves (OSISA 2010:7-22).

The issue of aid effectiveness in Africa is indeed high on the agenda of the governments of the region, the international community as well as other development actors, at least at the formal level (Nsabua, n.d.). Despite this reality, however, foreign aid is widely criticised for not being effective in African countries. Criticisms often arise based on the allegations that the impact of assistance has been limited, that the overall development situation is dwindling, and that funding and resources are either being mismanaged or misappropriated (Love 1999; Wohlgemuth 2008; Alemu 2009; Curott 2010). When development actors, particularly donors, talk about aid effectiveness, they are often referring to the litany of instruments developed since the Monterrey Consensus, including the Paris Declaration; the Accra Agenda for Action, resulting from the Accra High Level Forum (2008); and the Busan Partnership for Effective Development Co-operation, which emerged from the Fourth High Level Forum on Aid Effectiveness (2011), and assessing whether aid to developing countries, including those in Africa, complies with the tenets of these instruments. The Paris Declaration, which is arguably the most elaborate expression of universal consensus on the subject, refers to the effective management of aid at high levels through mechanisms agreed between the donors and the recipient government. The focus of the Paris Declaration is on the effective management of aid rather than its implementation and impact. However, the management of aid and its impact tend to be conflated; although aid is criticised for not having an effective impact, the scale against which its effectiveness is often measured is the management-oriented principles of the Paris Declaration.

Although the ultimate aim of the Paris Declaration is to manage aid effectively to maximise the benefits to the population, its definition of aid effectiveness however differs from what might popularly be understood. For those unfamiliar with the Paris Declaration, aid effectiveness is more likely to be interpreted to mean that aid should meet the needs of the people effectively by having a positive impact during and following project implementation. There are many legitimate challenges to delivering aid on the ground and to the effective management of aid at the national level but these challenges are seldom discussed openly, or addressed systematically. The contextual challenges, which include continued insecurity, lack of national and international capacity, multiple and often incompatible agendas, widespread corruption and lack of coordination, are intricate and interlinked (Dalgaard, Hansen and Tarp 2004; Dunning 2004; Economides, Kalyvitis and Philippopoulos 2008). At the same time, there are international agreements and accepted best practices stipulating how aid should be managed, which hold development actors to mechanisms or processes that may not be the optimum approach given these contextual challenges.

Today's reality is that the dominant approaches to aid and development design and implementation have failed Africa's poorest people and there is now the need for a paradigm shift. The essence of this chapter is therefore to explore the complex factors impeding aid effectiveness in Africa in a holistic manner. Apart from highlighting some of the obstacles to aid effectiveness, this chapter seeks to canvass alternative paths that could strengthen the promise of the Paris Declaration and its subsequent normative frameworks towards an agenda of effectiveness in the management of aid as well as the calibration of opportunities for making aid to positively impact on human development in Africa.

Beyond Normativisation: Rethinking Aid Effectiveness in Africa

International aid architecture is a subset of the global architecture of development finance. It can be defined as the totality of the system of institutions, rules, norms, and practices that govern the transfer of concessional resources for development. It comprises four major areas: (a) institutions and actors; (b) volumes and composition; (c) instruments and modalities, and (d) rules and standards. What, then, counts as foreign aid? OECD defines Official Development Assistance (ODA) as:

Grants or loans to countries and territories on the DAC List of ODA Recipients (developing countries) and to multilateral agencies which are: (a) undertaken by the official sector; (b) with promotion of economic development and welfare as the main objective; (c) at concessional financial terms (if a loan, having a grant element of at least 25%). In addition to financial flows, technical cooperation is included in aid. Grants, loans and credits for military purposes are excluded. Transfer payments to private individuals (e.g. pensions, reparations or insurance payouts) are in general not counted.

It follows that only a small subset of global financial flows qualifies as "foreign aid", classified as private grants (funding from individuals, foundations, Non Governmental Organisations (NGOs), and the new "global funds" such as the Gates Foundation) and official development assistance (bilateral and multilateral donors).

The traditional sources of development finance have rules that discourage corruption in the procurement of aid, but export credits are less well policed. Neither seems to have rules for when or how aid should be restricted when a pattern of corruption characterises an entire recipient government. The global aid regime is not well-institutionalised regarding democracy and human rights. Neither the IMF nor the World Bank applies conditionality in this area. Many bilateral donors do apply such conditions, but relatively inconsistently. Many still lack clear and firm standards.

Compared with regimes that govern international trade (codified in the World Trade Organisation), the rules of the international aid architecture are much less universal. Many were agreed upon by the DAC, founded in 1960 with eight member countries, and since expanded to include 23 members. Others originated in the Bretton Woods Institutions – the World Bank and the International Monetary Fund – while still other rules have come via the informal "Paris Club" of official creditors. Few of these rules have sanctions or other built-in enforcement mechanisms. Most depend on informal practices, expectations, and public opinion for their enforcement. Of these rules and standards, the most codified and concrete involve norms, agreements, or conventions in five areas: (a) transparency; (b) tied aid and export credits; (c) social and environmental protections; (d) corruption and governance, and (e) the management of debt.

The process for allocating development aid has changed markedly over the past decade. The MDGs have provided a greater focus on poverty within aid arrangements, as reflected in the first goal, which aims to halve poverty and hunger by 2015. The new agenda for development aid has placed country-driven and country-owned processes at the core (as emphasised in the Paris Declaration) and attempts to reposition development-assistance strategies to enable national governments and civil society to manage and direct the process. In their consideration of the experience of poverty-reduction policies, for example, some development scholars have found these strategies to be entrenched in living political systems (Hatcher 2006; Akinola 2010; Hout 2007; Hout 2007, 146; Hout 2010). As such, they require a long-term, strategic understanding of the social and political realities of power, which in turn challenges conventional practices by policy makers and aid managers in the design and management of such strategies.

Among commentators, the discourse on aid effectiveness is incipient and largely reflects the predominant ideology of statist leadership over development policies, strategies and the coordination of development-related actions. This chapter considers the dominant approaches in charting new praxis to aid architecture, founded on the philosophy of polycentric planning (Ostrom 2009), and adapted to the control and supervision of polyarchical actors (Dahl 1971). The assumption here is that the emergence of the creation of multiple-centres and multiple layers of decision-making in the design and implementation of aid will engender a relative equilibrium of power among the major competing political blocs of society, and invariably, stimulate a more responsive aid system beyond the dominant approach, such that will yield ultimate dividends for the mass of Africans.

With particular regard to the African experience with donor funding otherwise known as foreign aid, I suggest a further line of criticism. I question whether the dominant aid paradigm is internally consistent. I begin with the observation that while there is a remarkable consensus on the new aid modalities and normative instruments, these are not based on a mutual understanding on how they should be applied. Underlying the patterns of the prevalent aid system are gaping holes. Two critical illustrations suffice here. The first relates to the tensions between the Poverty Reduction Strategy Papers (PRSPs) approach and the MDGs, arguably the two most important components of the new aid agenda of the post-Monterrey era. The second relates to the goals pursued by donors and recipient governments. Although the usual narrative is that donors and recipients pursue similar policy objectives and, therefore, that their mutual relations should be consensual and based on trust, the reality is that they often have sharply different agendas. Allusion to the MDGs now routinely appears in donor documents about poverty reduction strategies, and the MDGs are often presented as the ultimate objectives that must guide actual decision-making in the context of individual country poverty reduction strategies. All through, there is the implicit suggestion that the two approaches are rationally paired. PRSPs are simply the country translation of the MDGs. The donor insistence that recipients use the MDGs as the basis of their poverty strategies does in no way violate the ownership requirement of the PRSPs, as the Millennium Declaration was signed by political leaders from almost 200 countries, including all major aid recipient countries. True, leaders from aid recipient countries may have signed the Millennium Declaration, but it has to be mentioned that seven of the eight MDGs address basic issues of development: poverty, primary education, gender inequality, child mortality, major diseases, and environmental sustainability – which are critical to their very stability and survival.

The eighth and last goal – 'develop a global partnership for development' – is of a different nature, and relates to the ways and means to achieve the first seven goals. Another difference is that the first seven goals are relevant for countries taken individually and thus appropriate for national policy making, whereas the eighth goal in the first place requires action by the rich, developed countries or by rich and poor countries jointly. Is there still any doubt as to why many recipient countries particularly those in Africa pay lip service to the MDGs, if not showing pockets of resistance to the goals? Are the MDGs and targets also owned by aid receivers? Can the MDGs be easily translated in the PRSPs? Are they realistic for countries like Niger or Burundi? (see Renard 2007). As the World Health Organisation remarked: "There is a risk, however, that the MDGs are seen by some developing countries as being of primary concern to donors; they may be perceived to be a new form of conditionality and too restrictive in their scope to cover the multifaceted nature of development" (WHO 2003, 33).

These underemphasised, and yet unresolved, inconsistencies in the aid paradigm considerably weaken the much-heralded promise of increased aid effectiveness under the current normative orthodoxies.

The fundamental principles of aid programmes are well-established. According to the plethora of opinions, aid should be provided (a) in response to need, with a particular focus on the key international target of reducing poverty by half by 2015; (b) on a predictable basis; (c) in the spirit of partnership, involving genuine and reciprocal accountability, from recipients to donors, and from donors to recipients; and (d) in the most efficient way possible (Maxwell 2002; Tavakoli 2013). However, even Maxwell, one of the proponents of these principles agrees that they have not always worked out in every context (Maxwell 2002).

The three major weaknesses limiting the effectiveness of aid in Africa can be surmised as (i) weak alignment of institutional mandates and policies; (ii) Poor top-down performance and bottom-up accountability mechanisms; and (iii) limited scope for local problem-solving and collective action solutions (Maslin 2005; Glennie 2013).

The adoption of a one-size-fits-all approach has had particularly adverse consequences for African states, given their very low level of development and structural weaknesses. There is also a lack of harmony between the existing global systemic regimes and the special international support measures for African states. The design of new international development architecture for developing countries should build on a proper diagnosis of the current international economic architecture. It is obvious that the current architecture is not working effectively to promote development and poverty reduction in Africa and to reduce the marginalisation and vulnerability of African states in the world economy.

Pathways to Aid Effectiveness in Africa

If opinions are indeed crystallising around the failure of aid to achieve its purposes of good governance, development, and not the least, human development (Meredith 2005; Easterly 2007: 330; Erbeznik 2011:880-892), should we not begin to rethink strategies for improving the quality of aid and making it more effective in achieving the goals of *human* development in Africa, seeing the reality that African governments will not end aid receipts any time soon?

A principal aim of recent development initiatives from the Washington-based institutions has been to strengthen country-level aid effectiveness strategies in ways that achieve a high degree of 'ownership' by the countries themselves. This new trend is anchored on heightened participatory roles for ordinary citizens of recipient countries (Farrington 2001).

It is significant to note that some years ago, both the World Bank and the International Monetary Fund (IMF) had recognised the critical role of participatory rights in making aid work. In their review of PRSPs in 2005, these BWIs had asserted that:

> Participation can be a key factor to enable stronger accountability mechanisms. The original emphasis that the PRS approach placed on broad participation of civil society, other national stakeholder

> groups, and elected institutions was based on an expectation that such participation would improve the design and implementation of poverty reduction strategies. In addition, it was expected that civil society could play an important role in monitoring implementation and strengthening accountability (World Bank and International Monetary Fund 2005:26).

From Paris, in 2005 to Busan, in 2011, diverse civil society organisations (CSOs) have been engaged in tracking this agreement, both internationally and in developing countries. CSOs have been raising a range of issues and bringing in different perspectives, trying to ensure that this new framework for aid effectiveness translates into effective and accountable development processes. They have contended that the only true measures of aid's effectiveness are its contribution to the sustained reduction of poverty and inequality; and its support of human rights, democracy, environmental sustainability and gender equality – all integral components of the MDGs. CSOs have also been promoting a deepening of the aid effectiveness agenda, so that it addresses not just the concerns of the donors and recipient governments, but of all stakeholders in the development process. They are concerned particularly about the interests and representation of groups, which are often excluded or marginalised, including women and women's movements (Ngozo 2011).

Although African governments are pronouncing formal commitments to the reinforcement of local capacities as well as ownership and inclusiveness for greater impact and sustainability of aid in Africa (UN ECOSOC 2011), the curious omission in their current proclamation is explicit human rights lexicon that would broaden the latitude for the engagement of ordinary Africans in aid governance on the continent.

While the incursion of several non-DAC donors would lead predictably to an increase in external financial flows to Africa (Kragelund 2008:579; Mawdsley 2010:361), the current and anticipated increases would by no means guarantee enhanced development for human beings in Africa. With rampant graft, wanton profligacy and mind-boggling corruption, inequality, social exclusion and various human rights violations not showing tangible correlation to aid funding on poverty reduction in much of Africa (Mosley et al 2004; Mwenda and Tangri 2006), it strikes the heart of the asymmetry that a fresh approach must be adopted in conditioning aid on the African continent. I contend that if public participation is to play a meaningful role in the future of credible aid governance in Africa, it will be critical to enlarge the rights-based framework and space for public discourse that would enable the autonomous civil society to change the aid landscape on the continent.

Forging a comprehensive aid governance strategy for Africa requires a holistic approach that fosters cross-sectoral, polyarchical collaboration. As the Busan Partnership document (2011) highlights, a fragmented approach is not an effective strategy in tackling aid issues. A rights-based approach to all ramifications of foreign aid in Africa offers veritable possibilities.

What then is a rights-based approach to aid? What is the benefit of a rights-based approach? How can a rights-based approach be translated into a practical tool for planning, monitoring and evaluating projects and programmes aimed at improving aid performance in Africa?

Without highlighting specifically 'human rights', much of current development policy and practice adopts a rights-based approach in terms of focus, emphases and objectives. Among a widely known range of examples are land title issues; poverty reduction; gender disparity; governance; corruption; and judicial reform policies of some major multilateral institutions such as the World Bank (World Bank 2000, 1). Many other international non-governmental organisations and international development agencies have also applied the rights-based approach in their development efforts while the approach has also been canvassed in the writings of many scholars (Schultz 2002; Moser and Norton 2001; Department for International Development (DFID) 2004; Sarelin 2007).

Developing rights-based approaches has been a journey of discovery: exploring new ideas, challenging established beliefs and ways of working and searching for solutions beyond the boundaries of conventional discourses and human rights work. It has been an intensive process of experimentation, questioning and learning. While there is broad consensus on the theoretical foundations of a rights-based approach (Olowu 2005:7-8; Olowu 2009:15-16; Farrington 2001: 2-4), there are yet no practical blueprints on how aid governance should become rights-based. Every intervention therefore has to adopt its own analysis of what a rights-based approach implies for its social, political and cultural contexts.

The distinct mark of a rights-based approach, as against other approaches to social issues, is its contingency upon legal foundations. These foundations are to be located within the relevant international, regional and national arrangements. It has to be conceded however, that asserting these platforms as the basis for a rights-based approach is not as cut-and-dry as it sounds. This is so because the pace of ratification of human rights treaties varies from state to state, and even where states have ratified those instruments, very few take cogent steps at domesticating them (Killander 2009). Similarly, where African governments give formal recognition to human rights, it is often a case of more rhetoric than substance, rhetoric without action. The effect of this scenario is a noticeable limitation in the efficacy of the human rights involved.

Within the UN system, the International Bill of Rights (Drzewicki 1999) provides the cornerstone of the rights-based approach to human development along with all the instruments mentioned in this chapter capable of adding depth and vigour.

In addition, the International Covenant on Economic, Social and Cultural Rights (ICESCR), 1966, makes explicit that national governments should seek international assistance and cooperation to help them meet their obligations to respect, protect and fulfil the rights spelt out in the treaty. When the government is unable to ensure that populations can enjoy their economic, social and cultural rights, the World Bank, the IMF, bilateral, multilateral aid programmes, and world trade negotiators should be engaged explicitly to ensure that their programmes support the full realisation of human rights. The critical goals and targets of Africa's development agenda, if applied properly, therefore, can be assured under a rights-based approach to aid.

Rights-based programming uses a wide range of methods to achieve concrete and sustainable results for people and their rights. This approach works to get duty-bearers to fulfil their obligations, to support people in claiming their rights, to fight discrimination, and to strengthen equality and inclusion. The choice of appropriate action depends on the opportunities in a particular country, on the rights or issues that are being addressed and on the donor's mandate and expertise. To combat child labour in Niger, for example, an aid organisation may advocate for changes in legislation, utilise mass media to educate the public about child labour, train social workers and law enforcement personnel in child protection methods and establish mechanisms for listening to children in schools or in shelters for street and working children.

A rights-based approach to aid will therefore require (a) long- and short-term goals with a clear focus on people and their rights. This further requires analysing problems, causes and responsibilities at local, national and international levels; (b) working together with other governmental and non-governmental agencies towards common rights-based goals; (c) equity and non-discrimination – concentrating on the worst rights violations and paying particular attention to the most marginalised people; (d) accountability – strengthening the accountability of duty bearers for human rights at all levels, in this case, the government concerned. This should be achieved through a combination of direct action, changes in laws, policies and equitable resource allocations, changes in institutional rules and practices and changing attitudes and behaviours; and (e) participation – supporting rights-holders (children, women, adults and civil society institutions, etc) to realise their rights.

The rights-based approach envisages that the effective protection and promotion of human rights can become vital instrumentality in ensuring the accountability of governments, a platform that will in turn support ongoing efforts aimed at promoting socio-economic justice, bedrock for the establishment of truly participatory and democratic economies. In other words, a rights-based approach to aid has the capacity to widen the ambits of existing and emerging liberal democratic regimes around Africa, and thus, allow the interests of marginalised groups like peasants, workers, women, youths, the deprived, people with disabilities, the unemployed, and people living with HIV/AIDS to become relevant issues in mainstream political and socio-economic discourses.

The core of the advocacy here is that when human rights guarantees and concerted mechanisms of social accountability are synergised, the space for positive cooperative action is amplified and incentives for aid failure reduced. Public and local institutions seen as legitimate in multiple domains are therefore crucial in moderating failure risk during rapid social, economic and political transitions such as Africa has witnessed since the 1990s. Establishing credible and transparent mechanisms for popular participation and deliberation in aid management decisions will help build trust and common understanding about alternative courses of action and reduce the likelihood of destructive decline.

Conclusion

It will be apt to close this discussion with the words of Mats Karlsson, then State Secretary of the Swedish Ministry for Foreign Affairs, who had responsibility for Development Cooperation, putting the aid question in Africa so graphically:

> If Africans are again to become the subjects of their destiny, and not the object of somebody else's design, and if we are ever to approach equality in the still unequal relations between Africa and the world, then it is the capacity of African societies, their governments and people, to analyse, choose and shape that must be strengthened...Africa's partners have not yet provided a coherent response on the positive changes unfolding on the continent...This time around, the response cannot come from them alone. This time, the response must build intrinsically on the actions taken and answers given by African societies. More than ever, Africa's

friends need to listen and reflect on what is actually said and done in Africa (quoted in Wohlgemuth 2008:32-33).

This chapter has attempted to discuss the following questions from which a number of conclusions can be drawn: how best aid can achieve development results in a cost-effective manner and how this should be measured in human terms in Africa; how broad-based country ownership can best ensure that these results are sustainable in different country contexts; proposals for a development cooperation accountability framework between recipient governments and their donors, especially in light of planned monitoring and follow-up by autonomous social agents; proposals for improving country-level mutual accountability between developing countries, donors and stakeholders; and measures to enhance accountability for development results produced by aid. The underpinning thrust of this matrix is the rights-based approach vehemently advocated for inclusion in the future of aid in Africa.

Far from being an *ex-cathedra* pronouncement on all the dynamics that should inform the adoption of a new understanding and approach to foreign aid in Africa and scaling up the human development indices of African states beyond the MDGs, this article would have served its purpose if it stimulates further intellectual discourses.

References

Akinola, S. R. 2010. *Institutional crisis, resources governance and economic prosperity in Africa: Crossing the great divide through polycentric development planning. Social Science Research Consultancy Trust*, Midlands State University, Zimbabwe. Monograph Series 1(2), December 2010.

Alemu, G. 2009. *A case study on aid effectiveness in Ethiopia: analysis of the health sector aid architecture.* Working Paper 9, April 2009. Washington, DC: Wolfensohn Centre for Development, 2009.

Asiama, J. P. and P. Quartey. 2009. Foreign aid and the human development indicators in Sub-Saharan Africa. *Journal of Developing Societies*, 25, pp.57-83.

Atisophon, V., J. Bueren, G. De Paepe, C. Garroway and J. Stijns. 2011. *Revisiting MDG cost estimates from a domestic resource mobilisation perspective.* Paris: OECD Development Centre.

Attaran, A. 2005. An immeasurable crisis? A criticism of the millennium development goals and why they cannot be measured. *PLoS Medicine*, 2(10), pp.955-961.

Bigsten, A. 2006. *Aid and economic development in Africa*. Working Papers in Economics No 237. Goteburg University.

Bräutigam, D. 2010. *China, Africa and the international aid architecture*. Working Papers Series No 107. Tunis, Tunisia; African Development Bank.

Burnside, C. and D. Dollar. 1997. *Aid, policies and growth*. World Bank Policy Research Working Paper 1777. Washington, DC: World Bank.

Curott, N. A. 2010. Foreign aid, the rule of law, and economic development in Africa. *University of Botswana Law Journal* 11(2): 3-18.

Dahl, R. A. 1971. *Polyarchy: Participation and opposition*. Princeton: Yale University Press.

Dalgaard, C., H. Hansen and F. Tarp. 2004. On the empirics of foreign aid. *The Economic Journal* 114(496): 191-216.

Department for International Development (DFID). 2004. *Rights-based approaches to social protection*. London: DFID, 2004.

Development Finance International (DFI) and Oxfam International. 2013. *Putting Progress at risk? MDG spending in developing countries*. London: FDI and Oxfam.

Drzewicki, K. 1999. Internationalization and juridization of human rights. In *An introduction to the international protection of human rights: A textbook*, eds. R. Hanski and M. Suski, 33-37. Turku: Institute for Human Rights.

Dunning, T. 2004. Conditioning the effects of aid: Cold War politics, donor credibility, and democracy in Africa. *International Organization* 58(2): 409-423.

Easterly, W. 2007. Was development assistance a mistake? *American Economic Review* 97: 328-332.

Economides, G., S. Kalyvitis and A. Philippopoulos. 2008. Does foreign aid distort incentives and hurt growth? Theory and evidence from 75 recipient countries. *Public Choice* 134(3-4): 463-488.

Erbeznik, K. 2011. Money can't buy you law: The effects of foreign aid on the rule of law in developing countries. *Indiana Journal of Global Legal Studies* 18(2): 873-900.

Farrington, J. 2001. Sustainable livelihoods, rights and the new architecture of aid. *Natural Resource Perspectives* 69: 2-4.

Fritz, V. and A. R. Menocal. 2007. Developmental states in the new millennium: Concepts and challenges for a new aid agenda. *Development Policy Review* 25(5): 531-552.

Gedolf, B. 2013. Why Africa still needs aid. 5 April 2013. http://globalpublicsquare.blogs.cnn.com/2013/04/05/why-africa-still-needs-aid/ (accessed 7 March 2014).

Glennie, J. 2013. We must rethink the role of aid for a new era. 29 May 2013. http://www.undp.org/content/undp/en/home/ourperspective/ourperspectivearticles/2013/05/29/we-must-rethink-the-role-of-aid-for-a-new-era-jonathan-glennie/ (accessed 7 March 2014).

Greenhill, R., A. Prizzon and A. Rogerson. 2013. The age of choice: developing countries in the new aid landscape. ODI Working Papers No 364. January 2013. http://eudevdays.eu/sites/default/files/8188.pdf (accessed 7 March 2014).

Hatcher, P. 2006. Partnership and the International Aid Reform: Challenging Citizenship and Political Representation? In *The World Bank and governance: A decade of reform and reaction*, eds. D. Stone and C. Wright, 189-206. London: Routledge.

Hout, W. 2007. The Netherlands and aid selectivity, 1998-2005: The vicissitudes of a policy concept. In *Netherlands Yearbook on International Cooperation*, ed. P. Hoebink, 146-170. Assen: Van Gorcum.

Hout, W. 2007. *The politics of selectivity: Good governance criteria in U.S., World Bank and Dutch Foreign Assistance*. London: Routledge.

Hout, W. 2010. *Governance and the rhetoric of international development*. Inaugural Address. The Hague: International Institute of Social Studies.

Hout, W. ed. 2007. *EU development policy and poverty reduction: Enhancing effectiveness*. Aldershot: Ashgate.

Kebonang, Z. and C. M. Fombad. 2006. The African Peer Review Mechanism: Challenges and prospects. In *AU, NEPAD and the APRM: Democratisation efforts explored*, eds. H. Melber, 39-54. Uppsala: Nordic Africa Institute.

Killander, M. ed. 2009. *International law and domestic human rights litigation in Africa*. Pretoria: Pretoria University Law Press.

Kimutai, V. 2013. African leaders root for more trade instead of aid at Tokyo meet. 31 May 2013. http://www.standardmedia.co.ke/?articleid=2000084956&story_title=african-leaders-root-for-more-trade-instead-of-aid-at-tokyo-meet (accessed 7 March 2014).

Kinsella, J. and E. Brehony. 2009. Are current aid strategies marginalising the already marginalised? Cases from Tanzania. *Development in Practice* 19(1): 51-60.

Kragelund, P. 2008. The return of non-DAC donors to Africa: New prospects for African development? *Development Policy Review* 26(5): 555-584.

Lele, U., N. Sadik and A. Simmons. 2007. The changing aid architecture: Can global initiatives eradicate poverty? http://www.global-philanthropy.org/pdf/aid_architecture_paper.pdf (accessed 7 March 2014).

Linn, J. and C. Bradford Jr. 2006. *Pragmatic reform of global governance: Creating an L20 Summit Forum*. Washington, DC: The Brookings Institution.

Love, R. 1999. Changing aid patterns in Southern Africa. *Development in Practice* 9(30): 296-309.

Maslin, J. 2005. Africa and its rapacious leaders. *The New York Times* 8 August 2005. http://www.nytimes.com/2005/08/08/books/08masl.html?pagewanted=all&_r=0 (accessed 7 March 2014).

Mawdsley, E. 2010. Non-DAC donors and the changing landscape of foreign aid: the (in)significance of India's development cooperation with Kenya. *Journal of Eastern African Studies* 4(2): 361-379.

Maxwell, S. 2002. More aid? Yes – and use it to reshape aid architecture. *Opinions* February 2002. http://www.odi.org.uk/opinion (accessed 7 March 2014).

McNair, D. 2012. Who's going to pay for the MDGs? *The Guardian* 23 January 2012. http://www.guardian.co.uk/global-development/poverty-matters/2012/jan/23/whos-going-to-pay-for-mdgs (accessed 7 March 2014).

Meredith, M. 2005. *The fate of Africa: a history of fifty years of independence*. New York, NY: Public Affairs.

Moser, C. and A. Norton. 2001. ODI: To claim our rights: Livelihood security, human rights and sustainable development. June 2001. http://www.odi.org.uk/PPPG/activities/concepts_analysis/RightsInAction/Publications/ToClaimOurRights.html (accessed 7 March 2014).

Mosley, P., J. Hudson and A. Verschoor. 2004. Aid, poverty reduction, and the 'new conditionality'. *The Economic Journal* 114(496): 217-243.

Mwenda, A. and R. Tangri. 2006. Politics, donors, and the effectiveness of anti-corruption institutions in Uganda. *The Journal of Modern African Studies* 44: 101-124.

Ngozo, C. 2011. DEVELOPMENT: Time for new approaches says civil society. *International Press Service News Agency* 8 May 2011. http://www.ipsnews.net/2011/05/development-time-for-new-approaches-says-civil-society/ (accessed 7 March 2014).

Nsabua, B. 2011. African leaders agree a common position on aid, development. 30 September 2011. http://www.nepad.org/print/node/2492 (accessed 7 March 2014).

OECD. 2005. *Paris Declaration on Aid Effectiveness, ownership, harmonisation, alignment, results and mutual accountability*. Paris: OECD 2 March 2005. http://www.oecd.org/dac/effectiveness/34428351.pdf (accessed 7 March 2014).

OECD. 2006. Second High Level Forum on Joint Progress toward Enhanced Aid Effectiveness (Harmonisation, Alignment, and Results). Paris: OECD. http://www.oecd.org/dac/effectiveness/34583142.pdf (accessed 7 March 2014).

OECD. n.d. Aid effectiveness: Shaping the agenda. http://www.oecd.org/dac/effectiveness/wpeff.htm (accessed 7 March 2014).

Ogunlesi, T. 2013. Africa: Wanted dead or alive - foreign aid in Africa. *Africa in Fact: Journal of Good Governance in Africa* 10: 29-32.

Olowu, D. 2005. *Conceptualising an integrative rights-based approach to human development in Africa: Reflections on the roles and responsibilities of non-state actors*. Copenhagen: Danish Institute for Human Rights.

Olowu, D. 2009. *An integrative rights-based approach to human development in Africa*. Pretoria: Pretoria University Law Press.

Open Society Initiative for Southern Africa (OSISA). 2010. *The African Peer Review Mechanism: A compilation of studies of the process in nine African countries*. Johannesburg: OSISA.

Ostrom, E. 2009. Beyond markets and states: Polycentric governance of complex economic systems. Nobel Prize Lecture 8 December 2009. http://www.uga.edu/pol-sci/courses/2010/ostrom.pdf (accessed 7 March 2014).

Renard, R. 2007. The cracks in the new aid paradigm. In *Netherlands Yearbook on International Cooperation*, ed. P. Hoebink, 81-98. Assen: Van Gorcum.

Sarelin, A. L. 2007. Human rights-based approaches to development cooperation, HIV/AIDS, and food security. *Human Rights Quarterly* 29: 460-488.

Schultz, J. 2002. ESCR: Promises to keep: Using public budgets as a tool to advance economic, social and cultural rights. May 2002, http://www.internationalbudget.org/themes/ESC/FullReport.pdf (accessed 7 March 2014).

Sundberg, M. and A. Gelb. 2006. Making aid work. *Finance & Development* 43(4): 1-10.

Tavakoli, H. 2013. What do discussions about aid modalities and institutional change have in common? 30 May 2013. http://blogs.worldbank.org/governance/what-do-discussions-about-aid-modalities-and-institutional-change-have-common (accessed 7 March 2014).

Taylor, I. 2005. *Nepad: Toward Africa's development or another false start?* Boulder, CO: Lynne Rienner.

Taylor, I. 2007. Governance in Africa and China-Africa relations: Contradictions or confluence? *Politics* 27(3): 139-146.

Turianskyi, Y. 2013. APRM at 10: Invigorating its leadership. South African Institute of International Affairs. *Opinions & Analysis* 13 June 2013. http://www.saiia.org.za/opinion-analysis/aprm-at-10-invigorating-its-leadership (accessed 7 March 2014).

UN ECOSOC. 2011. Preparing for the 2012 Development Cooperation Forum Report of the Mali High-level Symposium. *Gearing development cooperation towards the MDGs: Effectiveness and results* 5-6 May 2011. http://www.un.org/en/ecosoc/newfunct/dcfmali.shtml (accessed 7 March 2014).

UNDP. 2013. *Human development report 2013 – The rise of the South: Human progress in a diverse world*. New York, NY: UNDP.

United Nations. 2002. Monterrey Consensus of the International Conference on Financing for Development 2002. http://www.un.org/esa/ffd/Monterrey-Consensus-excepts-aconf198_11.pdf (accessed 7 March 2014).

United Nations. 2012. *World Economic and Social Survey 2012: In search of new development finance*. New York, NY: NY.

Wamboye, E. and A. Adekola. 2013. Foreign aid, legal origin, economic growth and Africa's least developed countries. MPRA Paper No. 47846. 26 June 2013. http://mpra.ub.uni-muenchen.de/47846/1/MPRA_paper_47846.pdf (accessed 7 March 2014).

WHO. 2003. *World Health Report 2003: Shaping the future*. Geneva: World Health Organisation.

Wohlgemuth, L. 2008. Can Africa make use of the new aid architecture? *Africa Development* 33(4): 31-41.

Wolfensohn, J. D. 1998. *The other crisis, address to the board of governors of the World Bank Group*. Washington, DC: World Bank.

World Bank and International Monetary Fund. 2005. *2005 Review of the PRS approach: Balancing accountabilities and scaling up results*. Washington, DC: The World Bank.

World Bank. 1998. *Assessing aid: What works, what doesn't and why*. New York, NY: Oxford University Press.

World Bank. 2000. *Focus on voice, empowerment, participation, transparency, accountability*. Washington, DC: World Bank.

World Bank. 2005. *Global monitoring report 2005 – Millennium Development Goals: From consensus to momentum*. Washington DC: World Bank.

World Bank. 2013. *Global monitoring report 2013 – Rural-urban dynamics and the millennium development goals*. Washington DC: World Bank.

Analysis of the Potential Impact of Economic Partnerships Agreements (EPAs) with Europe on Africa's Development

Victoria Qhobosheane

Introduction

In 2000 the European Union introduced a system of economic Partnership Agreements as a new framework to focus official development assistance but mainly trade relations with the African Caribbean and Pacific (ACP) countries. The EPAs are essentially free trade agreements being negotiated with the ACP in order to replace the Lome Conventions, which characterised trade and development cooperation between the EU and some developing countries between 1975 and 2000. The Lome Conventions agreements were non-reciprocal afforded by the EU to ACP countries. However, under the Cotonou agreement (2000), which guides negotiations for EPAs, agreements negotiated with the ACP were to be reciprocal, ending the preferential trade agreements regime. The justification by the EU is that the agreements must be World Trade Organisation compatible, development oriented, build upon ACP regional integration as well as improve upon the Lome regarding access to the EU markets for these countries.

The EPAs are being negotiated under the six regions of the ACP; West Africa (WA), Central Africa (CA), Eastern and Southern Africa (ESA), Southern African Development Community (SADC) and the Caribbean and Pacific. Further within the regional EPAs, countries are classified into Least Developed Countries (LDCs) and non-LDCs. LDCs benefit from the

Everything But Arms agreement, (i.e. all products but arms benefit from EU preferential market access) none-LDCs are eligible to the Generalized Systems of Preferences (GSP), thus creating two different markets within the same EPA or regional grouping. This chapter assesses the extent to which the proposed EPA framework within the context of reciprocity will impact on trade facilitation, economic development and growth in developing countries in general and particularly in the Sub-Sahara region.

The chapter is divided into seven sections; section 1 is the introduction, section 2 gives a brief background on the previous performance of the ACP countries under non-reciprocal trade arrangements. Section 3 analyses the effects of market liberalisation on the general economy, industry, welfare and the revenues of the ACP countries. Section 4 examines the impact on regional integration with a focus of the Sub-Sahara countries while section 5 discusses the potential opportunities available in intra-Africa regional trade and the emerging economies, section 6 is a summary of the findings from the analysis of the paper and section 7 gives a conclusion with recommendations.

Overview of trade performance under previous preferential trade agreements

As indicated above, under the Lome Conventions, the ACP countries benefited from a range of preference schemes in developed country markets including the Generalised Systems of Preferences (GSP); the EU Cotonou agreement for African Caribbean and Pacific countries and 'Everything-But-Arms' for least developed countries only, and the USA's African Growth and Opportunity Act (AGOA) for African countries only. However, the evidence is that despite these preferences, these countries have not improved their terms of trade in the global markets. In particular, Kaggwa's (2012) sample of trade performance of 20 countries in Africa under the EU Preferential Trade Agreements (PTAs) found that out of the countries, except for the three countries, Nigeria, Congo and Cameroon, the rest of the countries recorded increasing trade deficit. Those that maintained trade surplus were exporting natural resources with no value addition like oil (in Nigeria) and mineral resources (in the case of Congo and Cameroon), which have uncontrolled high demand in developed countries. Trade deficit with the EU alone increased from 20 billion pounds in 2001 to 40 billion British pounds in 2008.

One of the main reasons attributed to non-performance in previous cooperation arrangements is the asymmetries that exist between the LDCs and the EU as trading partners. Firstly, most of these countries, particularly in the Sub Sahara Africa (SSA), are still undeveloped with a GDP ranging between US$5-1billion (Hartzenberg 2011) stemming mainly from low productive capacities, which makes them uncompetitive in the global markets. Secondly, and most importantly, persistent protectionism in developed countries, which not only continues to undermine agricultural development and food security concerns undermines industrial development. CAIT02E (2012) lists some of these protection mechanisms, which include (a) high tariffs for protection of sensitive sectors - often concentrated on agricultural products such as fisheries; tobacco; food industry products with high sugar content, and clothing and foot ware. (b) Non-tariff barriers (NTBs) such as costly sanitary and phytosanitary standards for health and safety requirements, which African exporters must comply with. c) Billions of subsidies per year to support agricultural sectors, which continue to threaten millions of agricultural jobs and livelihoods of West African countries' cotton farmers. (d) 'Tariff escalation' involving a tariff structure whereby tariffs increase with the level of processing of raw commodities such as cocoa or coffee-Tariff escalations still remain where products deemed 'sensitive' are excluded from the preferences (e.g. soya bean, oil, groundnuts, sugar, cocoa, tobacco and cotton).

These practices effectively impede access of the developing countries to the EU markets particularly in their areas of competitiveness as agriculture is the mainstay of most of these countries. While the African least developed countries benefited from trade preferences from the EU, these did not translate into significant economic gains; thus, protection policies of the EU effectively stifled development and export diversification in Africa.

The next section analyses the impact of market liberalisation based on two studies by the European Union Commission and the United Nations Economic Commission for Africa (UNECA).

Liberalisation of ACP Markets to the EU through reciprocity requirement

The EPA requires that ACP countries reduce tariffs to 80% of the EU imports while the EU will reciprocate through 90% reduction for the ACP goods. The central issue raised by the African countries is that this will allow for the penetration and erosion of the African domestic markets leading to unemployment and general economic decline. This point is also raised by Collier (2012) that in fact by opening their markets to the

EU, the ACP countries will be handing over the terms of trade to the EU since their tariffs are high. The Council for the Development of Social Science Research in Africa (CODESRIA) (22 September 2010) further expands on this: "opening up African economies to highly competitive EU producers and exporters will place enormous pressures on African producers and traders within their own national markets as has been evident under the current levels of external trade liberalisation though the International Monitory Fund (IMF) and the World Bank structural adjustment programmes (SAPs), as well as under the World Trdae Organisation (WTO) tariff reduction rules." Such external pressures on national traders and producers will also apply to their possibilities within the markets of their countries in the same African region of those that open up under EPAs. They give an example of SADC traders, where this would erode their preferential access to the nearby larger and richer South African market. In this way, EPA trade liberalisation will undermine one of the main aims of regional integration, which is to create combined and enlarged markets to encourage local, national and regional producers and expansion of intra-regional trade.

In their study, Fontagne, Laborde and Mitaritonna (2009) analysed the perceived impact of trade related aspects of the negotiations using different indicators including changes in exports and imports, changes in income from tariffs reduction and countries' current accounts.

Looking at the whole of the ACP regions, Fontagne, et al analyse the trade impacts of the Economic Partnership Agreement (EPAs) are as follows, (sub-section 3.1 to 3.3 below):

Exports from the ACP

Using a base year of 2009 (that no EPAs have been signed in the case where the Everything But Arms (EBA) is applied to LDCs and GSP is applied for non-LDCs), the loss of preferences associated with the lapse of the Cotonou scheme will result in a fall of 4.9% of ACP exports to the EU. The reduction will even be greater for the Pacific counties (-8.4%), Caribbean (-9%) and (Common Market for Eastern & Southern Africa) COMESA (-12.1) because these countries have high tariffs.

Overall, EPAs are expected to bring 10.7 % increase in the volume of ACP exports to the EU than under GSP/ EBA in 2022. See table 1 below.

Table 1

Trade Trade consequences for ACP regions through Volume changes, (Percent).
Implementation of EPAs

Regions	Exports to the EU	Imports from EU	Imports
All ACP	10.7	17.7	13.1
ECOWAS	4.0	15.1	10.3
CEMAC	7.3	17.2	12.6
COMESA	25.5	20.7	16.0
SADC	6.6	10.6	6.6
CARIFORUM	25.2	27.1	22.5
Pacific	37.1	-02	1.0

Source: Simulation results. Fontagne et al (2009,36)

This gain is the result of improved market access compared to the benchmark under GSP/ EBA, which the countries are eligible for without EPA. In percentage terms, the largest increases in the exports were expected to occur in the livestock sector, which was forecast to at least double in the EPA scenario. Exports of agricultural products (excluding meat and cotton) and textiles were forecast to increase by 40%. The sectoral cost of not signing an EPA agreement is concentrated in products associated with specific protocols – sugar and bananas (with a drop of 54%) explaining the situation of the Caribbean region. The consequent fall in sugar prices in the EU market were expected to reduce the preferential margins granted to ACP countries. Other products that were strongly affected include livestock (30% drop in exports) and textiles (-27%).

Distribution of gains by sectors and countries indicates that only a few countries were expected to benefit from exports and few exported products mostly in agricultural products textiles and apparel were the only manufacturing sector registering sizeable changes in value in Mauritius.

Table 2 – ACP Changes in export values towards the EU

Products (gains value (Mios of 2004 Euro)	15-25	25-50	50-100	100-150	>150
Raw sugar-170111				Zimb. 145	Guyana 178.6 Fiji 180.6 Swaz. 397.6 Maur.51111
Bananas- 080300	Jamaica 16.9	St Lucia-25.1 Belize 36.9	Domin Rep		C,d'voire 245. 9 Cameroon 309.8
Rice brown 100620		Surin.26.4 Domin Republic 35.9			Guyana 259.3
Rice, semi or wholly milled – 100630		Surin 28			
Rice, broken – 1000640		Guyana-36			
Tuna-160414		Ghana-27.8 Maur.28.1	C,d'voire 54 Seychelles 68.7		
Fish fillets, frozen - 030420		Namibia 28.2			
Bovine meat, fresh or chilled - 020130		Botsw. 29.5 Namib. 40.8			
Bovine meat, prepared - 160250		Zimb28.3			
Poultry, fresh or chilled - 02o714	Nigeria 16.6				
Pineapples - 200820	Kenya 15.5				
Flowers - 060310		Kenys 47.7			

Tobacco - 240120		Zimb41.1	
0live oil - 151000	Ghana16.4		
Corn flour - 110200	Ghana18.8		
Cocoa butter - 180400	C,d'voire 17		
Aluminium - 7601100	Ghana 15		
	Cameroon, 23.1		
T-shirts - v610910			Maur 108
Men overcoats knitted - 610100	Maur 22.47		
Men shirts knitted - 610110	Maur 16.06		
Men overcoats	Maur 23.01		
Men shirts - 620520	Maur 19.84		

Source: Simulation results. Fontagne et al (2009,38)

Imports from the EU

The authors, Fontagne et al, projected an average of 17.7% increase in the flow of imports from the EU by 2009time horizon at full liberalisation, with 7.9% in 2015 implying a transitory gain for ACP countries' trade balances over this period. (Table 1 above). The sectoral composition of these import increases points to concentration in industrial goods, mirroring traditional trade specialisation in the EU and ACP. ACP countries tend to specialize in a few key products, mainly agriculture while the EU concentration is highly industrial and processed products. The exception is the textiles sector where both exports and imports increases are explained by the vertical division of labour with the ACP countries importing intermediate products from the EU and the EU exporting finished products.

The product exclusion of sensitive products, which is the major contention in the EPA negotiations contributes to reduction in the flow of imports from the EU. If this is not applied, imports from the EU would increase to 23% by 2022 instead of 17%. High priority was given to exclusion of agricultural products in order to alleviate the shock faced by the agricultural sector in the ACP countries.

The highest imports flow of 27% will go to the Caribbean and the lowest to Southern African Development Community (SADC) at 11%.

Analysis and interpretation of the results of the study

What is emerging out of this analysis is that although figures show an increase in exports from the ACP, EU imports grow faster than ACP exports to the EU, this means unfavourable balance of trade for the ACP countries, resulting in current account deficit and general economic decline to the ACP countries. Collier (2012) argues that "by opening up markets access to EU the SSA will be handing over the terms of trade to the EU because by nature the tariffs in these countries are naturally high."

Secondly, because of the low production base in these countries, which was further eroded through deindustrialisation due to the IMF SAPs, means that ACP need to build capacity for exports so as to gain competitiveness in the global markets. This is evidenced by the concentration of a few products that are being exported. The decline in the meat and cotton exports further explains the protection policies applied by the EU on the agricultural sector (discussed under section 1 above), which prohibits the entry of agricultural products from developing countries to enter their markets. In terms of the EPAs, the EU will liberate all industrial products except for agriculture.

The third issue of importance from the import side is the role of *sensitive* products, which can be used as an instrument by developing countries to reverse the terms of trade in their favour. According to the authors, Fontagne et al, application of sensitive sectors, reduced the EU imports flow to ACP to 17%; otherwise, the volume would be 23% without sensitive sectors. As explained in Busse (2004: 47) the Economic Community of West African States (ECOWAS) countries have to decide on the coverage of the proposed free-trade agreement with the EU in line with their individual comparative advantages and disadvantages. This requires the targeting of goods and services where temporary or indefinite protection of ECOWAS industries would still be needed for them to either become internationally competitive (infant industry protection) or, for example, maintain national autarchy in certain areas. In particular, areas have to be identified where the EU inhibits the utilisation of comparative advantages of ECOWAS countries by protectionistic trade practices both in international and ECOWAS markets.

Price Water House Coopers (2004:10-11) identified a range of sensitive products in light industries such as agro-industry and textiles that should be exclusions to the six regions under EPAs in the ECOWAS including the wheat and meslin as well as the poultry industry which should be protected from the EU imports. This is for economic reasons, as well as stabilizing and growing the industries, protecting employment and ensuring food security.

The poultry industry in Western Africa is a viable industry that provides employment in the urban areas. In the EU poultry benefits from high levels of subsidy support, which makes it cheaper to import than to raise domestically in Western Africa. If tariffs are lowered in the region, EU exports of poultry could expand further, which could threaten the domestic poultry industry in West Africa, which has implications for employment, and expansion of the domestic production for regional market and for food security. The poultry sector is also linked closely to the maize sector in light of the importance of maize in poultry feed while maize is also a staple food.

This section has argued that the issue of reciprocity in the EPAs, which requires zero tariffs by ACP countries to 80% of imports from the EU will negatively impact local industries in ACP countries as they will be under pressure from cheap imports from the EU industries leading to unemployment and general economic decline. The ACP countries should be given policy space to develop its industrial base to build competitiveness for gains in trade. The issue of sensitive products has been identified as critical for Africa's expansion of its exports, which is needed to improve its terms of trade, as such should be pursued within the EPA negotiations.

The UNECA study by K Karingi, Lang, Oulmane, Perez, Sadni and Hammouda (2005, 2008) also looked at the effects of trade within EPAs on GDP, employment, revenue and overall effect on welfare. Their analysis looked at the three scenarios of the EPAs in Sub Sahara Africa: (1) reciprocation of EU preferential tariffs, the SSA, is currently receiving - this scenario addresses the question of whether full reciprocity is feasible under the EPAs; (2) deeper integration without reciprocity - the rational of this scenario is that most of the SSA countries were not able to exploit the preferences under the Lomé Convection agreements because of lack of supply capacity, so they need sufficient time to build capacity so that they can compete with the EU producers and exporters (3) and Free Trade Area - in this scenario, a free trade area addressing all trade barriers in the EU is exploited. The following is the summary of the findings of analysis of the SSA scenarios:

Overall the results of the analysis points to the following:

Full reciprocity, at least in the short-term stand to lead to losses both in terms of economic and welfare outcomes for SSA; *based on the volume of the GDP, other than the EU, all other regions stand to lose from full reciprocity*. SSA income marginally declines, SSA imports grow faster than exports accompanied by a deterioration of terms of trade, its balance of trade worsens by US$1,868 million, and this result in poor welfare of the people due to poor performance of GDP and worsening of the terms trade and balance of payments.

Table 3: Income, trade and welfare effects of EPAs

Scenario 1: Full reciprocity	GDP	Imports%	Exports%	ToT%	BoT(USSmin)	EV(US$)
EU15	0.0044	0.0095	0.05	0.0565	52.7352	1748.8019
CEEC	0.0019	-0.01	0.0211	-0.0058	23.4368	-2.5357
NAAM	-0.0001	-0.0317	0.0207	-0.0103	529.9121	-83.1632
Japan	-0.0005	-0.0574	0.0493	-0.0214	366.1649	-45.8012
SSA	-0.0129	4.4775	2.3152	-0.5477	-1868.361	-563.9485
China	-0.0018	-0.6671	-0.0115	-0.0282	45.5154	-57.3101
ROW	-0.003	-0.003	-0.0406	-0.0406	850.6011	-921.4965
Scenario 2 :Deeper intra-Africa Integration						
EU15	0.0044	-0.0082	0.0045	-0.0048	191.6676	-150.4622
CEEC	0.0005	-0.0043	0.0049	-0.0018	11.8501	-5.3033
NAAM	0	-0.0078	0.0902	-0.0042	150.7274	-58.1692
Japan	-0.0001	-0.0106	0.0186	-0.0083	98.9025	-45.1652
SSA	-0.4916	2.4112	1.2906	-0.2996	-629.7655	-1204.2651
China	-0.0002	-0.0113	0.0016	-0.0056	16.5255	-16.4879
ROW	-0.0002	-0.0045	0.0014	-0.0024	161.0926	27.1114
Scenario 3 :EU-SSA Free Trade Area						
EU15	0.0079	0.2245	0.2331	0.0194	934.9118	1116.3458
CEEC	0.0030	-0.0696	0.1245	-0.0829	169.0720	-131.7854
NAAM	-0.0003	-0.0780	0.0751	-0.0349	1437.1685	-438.9070
Japan	-0.0013	-0.1163	0.1579	-0.0693	928.5612	-313.1068
SSA	3.3890	18.2476	8.8278	1.8336	-5484.2998	8028.7661
China	-0.0032	-0.1236	0.0051	-0.0557	144.5395	-144,1505
ROW	-0.0040	-0.1205	0.0072	-0.0327	1870.0596	-883.5765

Source: Karingi et al (2013, 52)

Overall, the EPAs that take the form of the FTAs and address all trade barriers, inclusive of sensitive products, would be beneficial to the SSA with a GDP growth of 3.4% and would improve the terms of trade in the region. This suggests that unless EPAs aim to include the *sensitive sectors* in the EU, the African economies are unlikely to benefit. Unrestricted market access into the EU even with reciprocation by SSA countries can derive benefits in the long term. This further suggests that the exports that are of interest to Africa should also be allowed access to the EU markets in the EPA agreements. Thus, UNECA study by Karingi et al confirms the analysis and findings by Fontagne et al above on the outcomes of EPAs regarding the unbalanced terms of trade and the importance and role of sensitive sectors in ensuring trade gains for the SSA countries. The interpretation of the results by the author above confirms this.

The lesson emerging from the analysis is the findings that deeper regional integration should occur before implementation of EPAs to allow necessary economic adjustments in the SSA, and most important, that the role of sensitive sectors is vital for ensuring SSA counties to gain from trade with the EU.

EPAs and regional integration in Africa: Reciprocity and its impact on intra Africa integration

This section looks at the implications and the impact of the EPAs and the changes to the industrial structure of the SSA economies. It examines the factors that drive structural changes necessary for improved SSA competitiveness in the global markets, as presented by the EPAs.

A contentious issue in the EPA agreements remains that of regional integration. While the EU insists that the EPA will deepen regional integration through the FTAs ultimate elimination of tariffs, the African countries insist that developmental integration should first take place for the objectives of the EPAs to happen. The major reason why Africa and other developing countries have not achieved positive results in global trade and in particular in the Lomé Conventions is lack of supply capacities of these counties to compete effectively in the markets. This view is supported by ADB/OECD/UNDP/UNECA (2012) that indicates the concern that a hasty conclusion of the EPA agreements might impede Africa's regional integration agenda. The risk of an unfavorable impact of such a process on fostering the deeper integration of African economies calls for further reflection, as it is only through boosting intra-African trade, that the continent can unlock its potential and competitively situate itself in a strong position in the global economy.

Another point of contention within the context of the EPAs is with regard to the structure of the EPAs. By clustering the SSA countries into LDCs and Non-LDCs effectively imposes different market access arrangements on the same region. This means that efforts to consolidate the region's customs union will be impossible. Coordination of sensitive products will also be a challenge. This will further lead to requirements for rigorous border controls to prevent transshipment of cheap EU goods which prohibits intra-regional trade which is the SSA priority.

Patel (2007) for example cites the Western African situation, where (except for Ghana, Nigeria and Cote d'Ivoire), already have duty-free access into the EU market without having to provide reciprocity, under the 'Everything But Arms' Agreement. If these African LDC countries choose not to enter an EPA and still remained part of the ECOWAS-FTA (and scheduled customs union) in practical terms they would only be able to prevent the *de facto* liberalization of their markets if they erected border controls and costly rules of origin checks between them and non-LDC West African countries. This would further increase barriers to intra-regional trade. If these weaknesses are not addressed, the risks further exacerbate the problem of the 'hub and spoke' regional integration. African countries would become increasingly dependent on the EU imports at the expense of supporting the development of regional markets.

Changes in industrial structure

This section focuses on the scenario in which there is deeper regional integration without reciprocity. The main objective is to look at the changes to the industrial structure in SSA, whether industrial upgrading concomitantly with intra-region trade will be achieved and under what conditions.

The overall results from this analysis are that, SSA countries have potential to develop an industrial base under regional integration.

Table 4: Industry outputs in Sub-Sahara (percent change in output from the base)

	Full reciprocity	Deeper integration	Free trade area
Cereals	0.0213	0.5554	7.7333
Vegetables	-0.2063	0.2536	4.8533
Oilseeds	-0.0199	0.2588	5.0238
Sugar	0-0423	0.0423	12.8798
Cotton	0-6788	0.4369	-3.2957
Other Crops	0.5084	0.0293	0.9048
Livestock	-0.2478	-0.0616	5.5269

Animal products	-0.0189	0.4614	4.9162
Fishing	-0.1151	0.4063	3.4621
Energy	-0.1458	0.2612	-1.9289
Other natural resources	0.2248	-0.2934	-17175
Agro-processing	0.0885	-0.1383	12.482
Textiles	-0.6989	1.3384	2.3047
Clothing	-2.6639	2.7493	9.1321
Low tech industries	-4.8511	1.2875	-50218
Medium tech industries	-3.0865	1.0426	-2.9961
Heavy industries	-3.2136	1.2986	-10.7966

Source: Karingi et al (2013,55)

However, if there is full reciprocity without the exports of interest to SSA countries being considered in the liberalization, then SSA will stand to lose its existing industries. On the other hand, the capacity for the current industries in SSA to withstand competition can be strengthened through enlarged African markets if the intra-African trade barriers were to be eliminated. Therefore, the industrial base that appears possible under the FTA scenario with the EU is realisable if the sequencing of the implementations of the EPA was such that the SSA countries have room to build competitiveness, broaden supply capacities and diversify their industries. The implications on the industrial structure of SSA countries then suggest that the best way to configure the EPAs is by first undertaking deep integration within the African market and thereafter have unrestricted market access to the EU market with reciprocity.

This confirms the argument already made that it is important before liberalising the markets through the EPAs that production processes and industrialisation should occur in order to diversify the African economies in the exports sector. Otherwise the current trend whereby Africa exports are concentrated in few commodities in primary products and raw materials will persists while receiving high volumes of cheap imports. This results in the balance of payments deficit and puts pressure on the fiscus.

Liberalisation should be measured and managed to allow for industrial process to grow.

Impacts on government revenue

The impact of liberalization on government revenue is likely to be significant given that African countries are heavily dependent on import taxes.

Fontagne et al (2008) estimated a shortfall of 70% loss in revenue collections in the ACP countries due to elimination of tariffs under the EPA agreement.

The authors in turn recommend that the affected governments should restructure their fiscal base through other broad based taxes such as the VAT. What is being overlooked here is that these countries are already under the strain of taxes including the VAT; secondly, taking into consideration the levels of poverty and unemployment in the LDCs, further imposition of financial strain will hit the poor and may lead to upheavals of civil unrest and political instability while the poor people will be the most squeezed. Another option recommended is donor funding of the shortfall. The question that arises is sustainability of these measures since donors impose terms on the recipient.

An analysis by Karingi et al confirms the revenue losses but differs with Fontange et al in that they see this as one of the major adjustment costs that EPA will impose on the economies of the countries concerned.

Patel (2007) argues that Ghana's import duties account for 15.5% of total government revenue and if the Ghanaian Government is unable to offset these financial losses, this could lead to possible cuts in public expenditure in important areas such as health and education. The potential loss in revenue is estimated at US$900 million.

To conclude on the effects of EPAs and the pressure by the EU to have ACP African countries commit to the programme, most commentators are of the view that the EU intension is to block out the possibility of the South-South cooperation so as to avoid competition. CODESRIA, 22 September 2010 argues that any terms agreed between counties / regions of the South be extended also to the EU. Brussels is actively intervening to prevent the diversification of their international relations and emergence of alternative inter-regional development arrangements.

Potential for intra Africa trade and the emerging economics

The stalling in the negotiations opens a window for pursuing the strategic integration of the African agenda. Intra-regional trade in Africa remains the most important tool for upgrading industrialisation in Africa, and therefore overall development. The African Development Bank (2011) indicates that intra-Africa trade increased from US$ 11.6 billion in 2000 to US 29.3 billion in 2008. The increase was driven by the region's shift in the source of imports from Europe to South Africa following the end of apartheid and the implementation of the SADC Trade Protocol; however, the intra-regional share of total trade remains low compared to other developing regions. On the other hand, the scrutiny of intra-African trade data reveals that goods traded internally are more sophisticated than those traded with partners outside the continent.

See table 5 below.

Table 5: Signs of Export Sophistication in Intra-African Trade

Ghana top 5 exports to the world	**Ghana top 5 exports to Africa**
Gold, semi-manufactured forms	Gold, semi-manufactured forms
Cocoa beans, whole or broken, raw or roasted	Machinery parts, non-electrical
Cashew nuts, fresh or dried	Plywood, all softwood
Gold in unwrought forms	Panels, laminated woods
Lumber, non-coniferous	Aluminium alloy plate, sheet, strips
Kenya top 5 exports to the world	Kenya top 5 exports to Africa
Tea, black in packages	Tea, black in packages
Cut flowers and flower buds, fresh	Oils, petroleum, bituminous distillates
Vegetables, fresh or chilled	Portland cement, other than white cement
Cut flowers and flower buds, dried	Cigarettes containing tobacco
Coffee, not roasted not decaffeinated	Medicaments, in dosage

Source: United Nations 2011

Table 5 presents the evidence for Kenya and Ghana's largest exports, showing that exports destined for African markets contain more value add than those exported elsewhere. This evidence of mutually reinforcing relationship between regional integration and export sophistication adds further impetus to the case for expanding intra-Africa trade.

Another window of opportunity for Africa's diversification and investments is to cement its South–South co-operation aimed at advancing Africa's diversification and investment by devising a long term strategy as to how to frame its engagement with its southern partners into a mutually reinforcing affiliation. ADB (2011) suggests a strategy include the following:

- That while strategic engagements should focus on channelling FDIs towards enhancing productive capabilities in upgrading infrastructure;
- Upgrading and processing of agricultural products;
- Resources for the infrastructure should also be targeted to incorporate upgrading of domestic skills, local content requirements and technological requirements;
- The ability for Africa to innovate is depended on its technological capabilities and lack thereof has negatively impacted on its competitiveness constraining growth.

Summary of findings

The main conclusion that can be drawn from the above analysis is that the EPAs through full reciprocity will be detrimental to Africa's economic advancement, both through loss of the revenue and loss of industrial development.

However, the region has the potential to develop an industrial base with the focus on deep regional integration with a view to enhancing intra-regional trade. The role of sensitive sectors is very important for EPAs to benefit Africa – in particular the region should use product exclusions to strategically position themselves according to their different comparative advantages in a manner that will allow for industrialisation and encourage agricultural expansion, considering that agriculture caters for the rural population which is about 90% of the Africa's population.

The EU Protection measures and related policies including the sanitary and phytosanitary requirements are central to negative trade gains for Africa. It is in the scenario where there is full access to the EU market that, even with reciprocity, that Africa can benefit from the EPAs.

Conclusion and Recommendations for an African Agenda

1) The central issue is that it would be premature for SSA countries to implement EPAs as proposed. In section 4 it is pointed out that the major reason why SSA countries have not achieved positive results in global trade and in particular the Lome Conventions is lack of the supply capacities of these countries to complete effectively in these markets. Hence SSA priority should be to build necessary industrial base and diversify its export base to build necessary competitiveness that will enable it to withstand competition in the EU and other global markets. As argued by the ECA report for the AU Ministers of Trade October 2013, besides the establishment of a Continental Free Trade Area, in other fundamental drivers of trade are development of productive capacity and industrial sophistication because a country cannot trade effectively unless it can produce and add value to its raw material endowments. This then suggests that:

   The EPAs should focus on deepening regional integration with a view to boosting intra-Africa trade. This should be given sufficient lead time to allow the African countries to build requisite competitiveness accompanied with significant developmental and industrial programmes to complement the larger markets with increased supply and diversified capacities.

   Regional integration aims to increase the density of economic ties among African countries so that producers can find regional markets for their goods. It means linking Africa's productive capacity into regional value chains that lead to taking advantage of local specialisation and building economies of scale so as to compete more effectively in the global marketplace. It also involves linking the continent's economically marginal areas to its regional growth poles, so that the benefits of growth are shared more equitably (AFDB 2012:11).

   Dismantling of tariffs to open markets for the EU goods should be gradual and implemented over a longer period of time to allow industrial upgrading and export diversification in the continent. This should also be made conditional to removing restrictions to the continent's goods to the EU markets.

2) Building industrial complementary for the continent's competitiveness. Brenton, Isik, (May 2012) highlighted the following from the recently launched World Bank report that;

   a. Given the rising incomes in Africa, there are emerging opportunities for cross border trade in basic manufactures, including metal and plastic products that are costly to import from the global market. The potential for regional production chains to drive global exports of manufacturing, such as that of East Asia, has to be exploited.

   b. The testimony for the potential of intra Africa trade is reflected in the cross border trade currently embedded in the informal sector. This informal trade usually involves women and youth buying and selling goods across the borders to generate income and provide food for their families and as such it is an important factor of poverty alleviation. It is therefore important to use the cross border informal sector model as a formality to building industrial complementary across the continent.

3) Modernizing Agriculture to increase production and value addition

   As argued by Amoako (May 2012) although liberalized trade can be one of the solutions to food insecurity in Africa as some countries are net food importers, it can also reduce agricultural employment and shift African countries' incentives away from self-sufficiency. So the first step to food security is to modernize agriculture in order to raise production capacity, ease distribution and prevent wastage. Agriculture can also boost transformation by becoming a stepping stone for agricultural marketing, agro-processing, other forms of manufacturing, and services.

4) Addressing barriers to intra-Africa Trade

   In order for the continent to achieve optimal results from the opportunities presented by regional integration and intra-Africa trade, it is imperative to address impediments to intra-regional trade. The following issues should be given prominence:

   a. Following from the issues of informal and formal cross border trade raised in the World Bank report discussed above, it is evident that the barriers and non-barriers to intra trade in the continent should be addressed. According to the ECA report to the AU Ministers of Trade conference, October 2013, 46) intra-African trade that stands at 10% is significantly lower than the level of intra-regional trade of other developing regions. The major reason cited being that two thirds of African countries are either more protectionist, in particular intra African trade in agriculture faces a higher rate of protection than non-agricultural sectors. Almost all African countries and sub-regions impose higher tariffs on agriculture imports from other African countries. Addressing these barriers through the Common Free Trade Area provides the opportunity for Africa to maintain food security and boost trade in agricultural products.

b. In her address to the recent ADB African Economic Conference on 28-30 October 2013, the Chairperson of the African Union Commission, Dr Nkosazana Zuma stressed that the soft issues challenges such as harmonizing policy and movements of goods and services are the primary challenges that must be addressed to tackle impediments to achieving regional integration and intra Africa Trade.

c. In addition, the ECA report to AU Ministers of Trade cited above identifies the problem of power imbalances within the African states as one of the major impediments to integration. Some countries are skeptical of regional integration fearing domination by richer or more powerful states. The economically powerful states should support weak states to industrialize so that they can also share the benefits of intra Africa trade.

References

ADB/OECD/UNDP/UNECA. 2012. *African Economic Outlook Report. Trade policies and regional integration in Africa.* Abidjan.

ADB African Economic Conference. 2013. www.adb.org

African Development Bank Group. 2012. *Development Effectiveness Review*. Abidjan.

Borrmann, B. and Großmann . 2004. *The impact of ACP/EU Economic Partnership Agreements on ECOWAS countries: An empirical analysis of the trade and budget*. Hamburg Institute of International Economics. Germany.

CAIT02E. 2012. *Africa and the politics of international trade.* Thabo Mbeki African Leader ship Institute.

Collier, P. 2012. A European trade paradigm for African trade. *Bridges Africa.* Vol 1 Issue 1. International Centre for Trade and Sustainable Development (ICTSD).

Conference of AU Ministers. 2013. Action Plan for boosting intra –African trade ECA report. http://ti.au.int/en/content/8th-ordinary-session-conference-au-ministers...

Fontagne, L., Laborde, D and Mitaritonna, C. 2008. *An impact study of the EU-ACP Economic Partnerships in six ACP regions:* Paris School of Economics, Universite´ Paris 1 and CEPII Paris.

Karingi, S. Lan, Oulmane, N. Perez, R. Jallab, S. and Hammouda, H. 2005, 2008. *Economic and Welfare Impacts of the EU- Africa Economic Partnership Agreements.* UNECA

Amoako, K.Y. 2012. Future of African trade. Bridges Africa Review. Vol 1. Issue 1. International Centre for Trade and Sustainable Development (ICTSD)

Kaggwa, K. 2012. The European Union's Economic Partnership Agreements with Africa and the scramble for the African Market. *The Africana World, Africa Institute of Southern Africa, Pretoria.*

Patel, M. 2007. Economic Partnership Agreements between the EU and African Countries: potential implications for Ghana. Global Economic Governance (GEG) Programme. Oxford University.

Price Water House Coopers. 2004. *Sustainability impact assessment of the EU- ACP Economic Partnership Agreements.* Paris. France

Brenton, P. and Isik, C. 2012. Defragmenting Africa: delivering benefits from regional trade integration to ordinary traders. Bridges Africa, Vol 1 Issue 1. Washington, DC. The World Bank. De-Fragmenting Africa.

Hartzenberg, T. 2011. Regional integration in Africa. Trade Law Southern Africa, (Tralac)

African Resources and Markets:

The Mortar for Brazil, Russia, India, China and South Africa (BRICS)

Amos Saurombe

Introduction

The hosting of the fifth BRICS Summit in Durban, South Africa was a momentous occasion not just for South Africa but for the whole continent of Africa. For the first time in the history of BRICS, Africa was well represented by the African Union (AU) as well as Africa's regional economic communities (RECS). The theme of the Summit spoke volumes of the intent of the BRICS in its expression that 'BRICS and Africa: Partnerships for integration and Industrialisation'. This theme was meant to paint a picture that the BRICS partners consider Africa as an equal partner in the relations under consideration. This has been argued as a clear indication of how important the continent of Africa is on the BRICS agenda. The BRICS are not only influential on the African continent but are forces to be reckoned within the global arena from an economic and political perspective where consciousness is rife on this group's influence in shaping global balance of power. This chapter seeks to establish the existence of the opportunities and calls for Africa to seize them to enhance cooperation with other developing countries, playing a significant role in the economic and social development of the continent. Each of the BRICS countries and its relations with Africa will be discussed before a summary of the opportunities offered by the whole group. While foreign direct investment opportunities created by BRICS is positive thing for Africa as a strong catalyst for economic growth and development, there are serious concerns over the BRIC countries' appetite for the continent's natural resources (Kimenyi and Lewis 2011)

What are the BRICS?

In 2001, Goldman Sachs's Chief Economist, Jim O' Neill coined the term 'Bric' and predicted that by 2041; Brazil, Russia, India and China would be superpowers of the world economy. However, before long, these countries started talking and signalled an intention to join hands and BRIC was formed. Thus, the BRICS are a group of leading emerging economies that consists of Brazil, Russia, India, China and South Africa. Before South Africa joined, the group was known as the BRIC (Brazil, Russia, India and China). This group of countries are now well known for playing a key role in the world economy to the extent that each of them is now referred to using a name or terminology that expresses their economic muscle. China is considered 'the world's factory', India as the 'world's office'. Russia has come to be known as the 'world's gas station' because of its vast gas natural resources. Brazil's huge farming enterprise has earned it the title of 'the world's farm'. South Africa is known as the 'gateway to Africa' because of its strategic position on the African continent as well as its vast natural resources. The combined population of BRICS represent 42% of the world population and 18% of its gross domestic product (GDP) (Fundira 2012) The BRICS economies have risen above expectation to become novel major economies to be reckoned with.

It is important to ask, what have these characteristics of BRICS got to do with Africa? These countries are ideally placed to make a valuable impact on Africa especially within the context of 'South to South partnerships' that presents an opportunity for cooperation among developing countries especially in economic and social development of the African continent. Africa is seen as the fertile ground for natural resources and readymade markets for processed goods. South Africa is therefore seen as a gateway to Africa and its natural resources (Van den Bosch 2011) African countries have a vast amount of natural resources and this attracts foreign direct investment related to these sectors (Marafa 2009:10). In the words of Collins Chabane, Minister in the South African Presidency; the BRICS wish to align its interests in supporting the integration agenda in Africa. South Africa's influence in BRICS is about a willingness to extend geopolitical influence in the region and the world. However, a number of questions regarding the extent of benefits for Africa still need to be addressed.

The African continent considers a relationship with the BRICS as of mutual benefit. Africa expects the opportunity of a BRICS partnership to improve its levels of infrastructure development, poverty reduction, improve production capacity and transfer of technology, improve food security, ease energy and financial problems. These opportunities are realistic but African countries need to be cautioned that by emphasising that such opportunities are not automatic. As recipients of foreign direct investment (FDI), Africa needs to create the conducive environment for benefits to accrue. Africa needs to take stock and make an account of what it is putting in the BRICS relations and how such investment is paying dividends.

Historically, Africa has been regarded as underdeveloped and poor, but this perception is fast changing with many seeing the potential and opportunities that are available especially for the future. These opportunities are directly created through the economic boom in China and India where the demand for raw materials is generating valuable new opportunities. This in itself gives Africa a leeway to control how the relationship develops with the BRICS. The African and Chinese populations combined constitute an estimated one fourth of the global community, thus aspects of this relationship have a major impact on global sustainable development. Africa will need to be strategic in formulating checks and balances so that the colonial mindset in which Africa was previously colonised for the sake of its resources cannot be repeated. It is therefore vital for Africa to have policies, laws and regulations that can effectively promote development and give protection against overuse, abuse especially of its non-renewable natural resources by foreign investors (Susswein 2003). This chapter will now discuss and analyse each of the BRICS interests in Africa as well as Africa's opportunities these interests offer.

Brazil

Preliminary remarks

Brazil has the largest population in Latin America and ranks 5th in the world. Brazil has become the kingmaker in world trade, having wielded its strong hand in leading the developing countries to demand reforms at the WTO Doha Round Trade negotiations. The incoming WTO Director General is from Brazil. Brazil's rise to power has been influenced by a combination of a strong domestic demand that has been complemented by a favourable external environment that has resulted in steady growth and averaged between 6 - 7.5 % between 2008 and 2010. These positive results were achieved despite the global economic crisis. By 2010 Brazil had reached a GDP of US$2 trillion. Brazil is now ranked third among the BRICS countries (Richardson 2011) A number of factors have led these achievements. Ranking high among them is Brazil's willingness to undertake reforms that have shifted its focus from domestic and inward looking orientedness to become a global player whose focus on economic growth that is being driven by export promotion. This strategy has led the Brazilian government to seek foreign market access through trade negotiations and expert promotion measures (Fundira 2013)

Brazil's relations with Africa dates back to the 18th century slavery era when African labour was sought after to drive the agricultural enterprise in the Americas. However, as noted above, recent developments indicate a relationship of equals where interests of the South drive the common agenda. For instance, ten years ago in 2003, Brazil's then President, Lula da Silva started a new era in Brazil-Africa relations by presenting a combination of a new stance towards the global engagement and social domestic reform. Three years later, an African continent wide engagement Summit was held in 2006 to cement Brazil's serious consideration of Africa as an important and strategic partner. This initiative has been supported by strong economic and political ties that have led to the establishment of about 31 formal diplomatic posts in Africa. Areas of bilateral and trilateral cooperation include 'education, health as well as investment cooperation agreements in energy, manufacturing and services'. Besides being involved in the BRICS arrangement, Brazil also engages Africa in the IBSA (India, Brazil and South Africa) initiative where similar discussions and promotions of the 'South-South' partnerships are discussed.

Brazil's investments in Africa and opportunities for Africa

Brazils' principal interest on the African continent is access to natural resources. Brazil has invested in mining, construction, agriculture, bio-diesel, energy and pharmaceutical industries. Brazil's mining giant Vale is in the process of investing $15-20 billion in Africa for the next 5 years with most of the money being spent in Mozambique, Zambia, Guinea and Liberia. This is not at the same levels of China and India. However, Brazil's resource driven goal mirrors those of China and India and at times collides with interests of host African States (Lewis 2011) Brazil's main investments go to formerly Portuguese colonies of Angola and Mozambique. In SADC Brazil has already signed a number of strategic partnership agreements with the Secretariat, for example to provide funding to translate all official documents into Portuguese.

Brazil's National Development Bank (BNDES) provides important funding for FDIs but is limited its stringent conditions that prohibit it from financing in risky and unstable markets. This is in direct contrast with China's non strings attached approach.

The Brazilian mining giant, Vale's investments have the potential of making it the third biggest copper producer on the continent. There is even potential for significant increase in investment since most of the projects are in the exploration phase. Brazilian investments in Africa are also accompanied by infrastructural development. The Brazilian firm 'Odebrecht' operates in Angola, Libya, Liberia and Mozambique and Ghana and has also completed projects in Congo, Botswana, South Africa, Gabon and Djibouti. In 2009, Africa accounted for $2.427 billion in revenues for the group, or about 10% of its earnings (Fundira 2013)

The oil company Petrobras is investing heavily in Africa especially in Angola and Nigeria. In agriculture, through the state agricultural research institute, Brazil provides technical assistance to the cotton sector in Benin, Burkina Faso, Chad and Mali. This is part of Brazil's commitment to facilitate the transfer of agricultural technology from Brazil to Africa.

Although Brazil has a considerable influence on Africa, the impact is still very small. However, the most worrying fact is that Africa is not benefiting as much from this relationship. In 2012 trade data revealed that over US$26 billion worth of goods was traded between Brazil and Africa. Imports from Africa accounted to about US$14 billion while exports were a less, amounting to approximately $12 billion. This is a far cry considering that these figures accounts for the whole continent of Africa against one country, Brazil.

Areas of comparative advantage where Africa should have been strongly involved are in agriculture but indications are that Brazil actually exports sugar (33%) and meat (15%) which is a combination that amounts to 50% of total exports. African countries should do better in Agriculture and tilt the scares so that the continent can start to have a significant impact on their domestic markets and start exporting agricultural products to Brazil. The majority of Africa's exports to Brazil are mineral fuels which account for 83% of total exports' and 8% that is made up of fertilisers.

Russia

Preliminary remarks

After the collapse of the Soviet Union, Russia has been transformed into a more globally integrated market based economy. Russia went through a very bad financial crisis in 1998 but has bounced back to record an average growth of 7% annually. Russia has also implemented key economic reforms. Russia is rich in oil reserves and it is expected that the prevailing high oil prices will continue to bolster Russian growth and help reduce the budget deficit. However, Russia has many challenges that include a shrinking workforce, a high level of corruption, difficulty in accessing capital for smaller, non-energy companies and poor infrastructure. The country's need of large investments remain a threat to its economic performance. Russia faces enormous disparities between prices in Russia and world market prices. Russia had to use domestic subsidies to protect the domestic market during the transition to a globally integrated economy. In addition, Russia's manufactured products were not of sufficient quality to be exported to Western markets.

According to Tarr, the Russian government took the position to apply, export quotas, export taxes and foreign exchange surrender requirements as opposed to import restrictions (Tarr 2009) In trying to be part of the global trading economy, Russia has been involved with accession to the WTO and membership was finalised at the end of 2011. Accordingly, Russia has been reforming and harmonising its trade rules and policies to be compliant and compatible with WTO rules to make it more transparent and predictable for the global trading world.

Russia's investment in Africa and opportunities for Africa

Russia's involvement in Africa dates back to the time the continent was struggling against imperialism. Russia offered assistance to a number of

African countries in their fight against colonialism. However, once Russia started experiencing a financial crisis in the 1990s, ties with Africa became neglected. A further financial crisis during 2008/09 period saw the value of total trade between Russia and Africa decreasing by 23%. However, before the start of BRICS, Russia sought to revive its relations with Africa. African leaders have visited Russia and Russian leaders also reciprocated by visiting Africa. One of the highlights was Russia's President Dmitry Medvedev's visit to Africa in 2009. In 2013, before the BRICS Summit in South Africa, the current Russian President Putin started with a number of visits on the African continent before the start of the Summit. These visits have produced high level bilateral agreements with African states. Thus, Russia's foreign policy strategy to Africa is to work on strengthening the traditionally friendly relations with the states of the African continent by developing bilateral and plurateral cooperation arrangements with them. Areas of cooperation include strategic geo political arrangements that include but not limited to developing common positions on key aspects of the international agenda, including the issues of promoting strategic stability, strengthening the central United Nation's role, and countering new challenges and threats, primarily terrorism and extremism.

Russia has become one of the leading FDI exporters in Africa. Its expansion has targeted the Commonwealth of Independent states (CIS) and is part of the initiative to industrialise Africa. In line with its domestic strength, Russia is investing heavily in oil, gas and other natural resources sectors for its outward investment. In addition, Russia has also intensified its effort to compete in the financial, telecom and retail trade. Russian companies' expansion abroad is exposing Africa to new technologies, know-how and resources (Nestmann and Orlova 2008) In the process higher revenues and lower funding costs achieved by investing abroad support the build up of the capital stock and infrastructure investment within Russia (Fundira 2013)

Figures show that Russia's investments in Africa in 2011 had reached US$20 billion (Barka and Mlambo 2011). A ten year (2001-2012) analysis by Fundira shows there has been steady growth of Russia's total trade with Africa's share increased by 20%. The growing demand for securing energy resources amongst global players investing in Africa puts Russia at a competitive advantage, being the only oil and gas exporter in BRICS as it seeks partnerships that go beyond extracting resources and also ensuring technology transfer in the process (Natufe 2011) Russia has also turned to Africa for resources since it has become clear that its domestic resources are depleted. Fundira notes that 'the absence of new discoveries and technological advancement, which are weakening Russia's domestic energy, together with the lack of easy access to the remaining underground mineral deposits in Russia' are some of the factors attracting Russia to Africa's considerable natural resources.

India

India is ranked the second most populous country with a diverse and rich cultural heritage (CIA World Factbook 2013). It is also the second fastest growing economy in the world. Like the other BRICS countries discussed earlier, India embarked on economic reforms that began in the 1990s with the objective of accelerating the country's growth into an open-market economy with a modern industrial sector. Reforms included economic liberalisation, industrial deregulation, privatisation of state owned enterprises and reduction of controls on foreign trade and investment. India has a strong domestic demand that contributes to positive economic performance. India's services and manufacturing sectors contribute over 80% of GDP. India also focuses on export promotion as part of its trade and investment policy. Like the whole global economy, India has been affected by the global recession.

India's investment in Africa and opportunities for Africa

India-Africa bilateral trade has grown from $1billion in 2001 to around $50billion in 2011-12. At the same time, India's investments in Africa are estimated to be over $50billion now. (Confederation of Indian Industry). The India-Africa Forum is the official platform for the African-Indian relations. It was first held in 2008 in New Delhi, India and became the first of such meetings where African leaders meet their Indian counterpart to discuss how they can cooperate and coordinate their political and economic issues for mutual benefit. This initiative was started after it became clear that the future growth of Indian companies will be substantially driven by the share they have in global market. Indian foreign presents is characterised by the acquisitions of overseas assets as a measure strategy to upgrade its competitive strength (IBER 2011)

Fundira's research and analysis indicates that India has invested more than US$33 billion in Africa to date. These investments are mostly in Kenya, Nigeria, Uganda but recent records show that India is doing business in more than 20 countries in Africa (Dickerson-Nyema: 2011). According to Gelb, the entry into Africa by Indian businesses is mostly driven by market seeking and has been driven by the liberalisation of regulations and lowering of entry barriers in the host countries (Gelb 2005) The areas of speciality for Indian FDI investment in Africa include mining, pharmaceuticals, machinery and equipment, chemicals, textiles, paper and paper products, financial services, software, refinery and printing.

Countries that have benefited from India's investment in Africa include the traditional recipients identified above. In addition, countries in the region that have benefited include Mauritius, especially in software. India has invested heavily in Sudan where most concessions are in the oil and gas sectors. India has also established a very good presence in automobile and light engineering goods. A number of Indian companies such as Arcelor Mittal Steel, Tata Steel, Mahindra are making headway in Africa. India's prominence is also felt in the pharmaceutical industry where it is providing Africa with cheap and reliable alternative to the expensive Western patented medicines. India also has a competitive edge in the area of services. India is involved in agro processing and cold chains, tourism, hotel, retail and financial sectors.

During the 10 years (2001-2011), the total compounded growth of India's total trade with Africa increased by 29% with imports and exports increasing by 32% and 24% respectively. After the recession, 2010 figures showed a recovery where total trade increased by an estimated 44% and annual growth reached US$47 billion. However, this trade with India is not well spread on the African continent, it is concentrated among a few countries both for imports and exports. The major Indian trading partners from Africa include Nigeria (34%), South Africa (23%) and Angola (15%) account for about 72% of total import trade, while in terms of exports, South Africa (18%), Nigeria (11%), Egypt (10%) and Kenya (9%) account to about 48% share (Fundira 2013)

China

China has often been described as the Africa of 50 years ago. China has a population of over 1.3 billion and registers an annual growth rate of

10%. Its GDP for 2012 was US$8.25 trillion. This impressive economic performance over a period of two decades has given China the title of the next global economic superpower and is expected to overtake the United States in the process. This growth has been influenced by China's export growth. China remains the largest exporter and second largest importer in the word. Like the other BRICS countries, China's growth was preceded by reforms that took shape since the 1970s. These reforms included among other initiatives, the phasing out of collective farming, the gradual liberalisation of process; fiscal decentralisation; increased autonomy of state enterprises; a diversified baking system and trade liberalisation. (CIA World Factbook 2013) Trade and investment liberalisation played an important role in extending China's reform programme to the manufacturing sector (World Trade Policy Review 2010)

China's reform programme is unique in that it does not comprise of a fully privatised industry. It still has support for state owned enterprises (SOE) in sectors it considers important to 'economic security'. The agricultural sector is fully privatised but some of the heavy industry sector remains in the hands of the state. The state is still dominant in sectors like finance, telecommunications, petroleum and other important sectors of the economy.

Reform is an ongoing process in China where the government's emphasis is on increasing domestic consummation and less dependence on exports for GDP growth. In doing this China is trying to curb the effects of the global recession which left it vulnerable when exports declined by 16%, thus affecting its export-led growth (World trade policy review 2010)

China's investment in Africa and opportunities for Africa

The Forum on China-Africa Cooperation (FOCAC) is the platform for China-Africa relations. In 2006, 40 African Heads of State and government met in Beijing to start a new chapter in China-Africa relations. From that Summit, African leaders went back home with a number of concessions and commitments from the Chinese government. These included cancellation of debts, preferential loans and donations. This was a signal that China is serious about long term diplomatic relations with African countries. Post 2003 it became clear that China's outward FDI outflows to Africa increased by US$5 billion. Besides having a continent wide agenda for Africa, China maintains a country to country based relationship that is based on mutual benefit. Examples can be drawn from the China-Angola joint venture (Liaonign Huajin Tongda Chemicals and Sonagol) an Angolan petroleum parastatal. This deal is worth $US2.1 billion. In Mozambique, China is leading the rehabilitation of existing road infrastructure, jointly funded by the Mozambican government and the World Bank to the value of $US35 million. The Chinese Henan Internationl Cooperation Group is leading the project that includes the upgrades of the road built between Gazza and Inhambane.

The Chinese investments in Africa are not coincidental but are a clear strategic move. China requires abundant resources to satisfy its rapid growth. All sectors of the Chinese economy require huge raw materials be it in industry where gas, metals and minerals are needed. There have been fears that China's involvement in Africa will erode efforts to promote transparency and accountability in trying to fight corruption and the promotion of democracy. In addition, China has often been criticised for ignoring African governments' disrespect for human rights. China's no strings attached strategy has produced a good diplomatic climate in Africa where some governments prefer non interference in the way they conduct their business. This is a direct opposite to other Western investors in Africa that demand good governance and the respect of human right before going into business.

Africa stands to benefit from China's imports of raw materials as well as African-manufactured value-added goods such as processed foods and household consumer goods. This is paying dividends by helping to integrate the African continent further into the global economy. It is not a secret that since China became interested in investing in Africa; other global investors came scrambling to get a share. This environment has created a healthy completion for African raw materials and products. They have a number of competitors to choose from. African countries should therefore make sure that they maximise the competition and get the most of the situation, for example by reaping better prices and good terms of business.

South Africa

South Africa is strategically situated at the base of the African continent and has the most developed economy on the continent. With a population of over 48 million and an estimated GDP on US$579 in 2012, the country deserves to be recognised as an economic powerhouse in Africa. The end of apartheid also signalled a new growth path in the early 1990s only to hit a snag after the global economic crisis hit in 2008 and the country went into a recession for the first time in 18 years. Evidence of this crisis became apparent with the introduction of higher interest rates, power shortages and weakening commodity prices. However South Africa has managed to keep inflation within the target range of between 3% to 6% per annum.

South Africa still battles to create jobs and address the inequalities caused by apartheid. Its trade policy has been guided by three interrelated strategies, namely; import substituting industrialisation, the development of strategic industries and the development of minerals- related exports. The government has thus incentivised these industries to perform (Lewis 2011) South Africa also plays an important role in global trade and policy especially after it acceded to the WTO and started with a drive for trade policy reform that saw a robust tariff reform that started in 1995. Tariffs were reduced from 15% to below 7% by 2011. Now the focus has shifted towards market-led supply-side support measures that are compatible with WTO rules to facilitate industrial restructuring, technology upgrading, investment and export promotion as well as supporting small, medium and micro enterprises (SMMEs) (Fundira 2013)

South Africa's investment in Africa and opportunities for Africa

South Africa's presence in Africa dates more than a century especially in Southern Africa where the country is a cornerstone to both the Southern African Customs Union (SACU) and the Southern African Development Community (SADC). For example, more than 22% of FDI flows received by SADC from 1994 to 2004 were from South Africa (UNCTAD 2004). These FDI flows at times exceeded 40% (UNCTAD 2004) Thus, the impact of South Africa's presence in Africa as part of BRICS has both positive and negative connotations. It can be said in some circles that South Africa never required the BRICS to improve its relations with Africa. South Africa was already there both physically and long established relations. In character, South Africa's presence in Africa is in the form of joint ventures, mergers and acquisitions. South Africa uses a number of government backed initiatives to promote its agenda in Africa, for example through the use of entities like the Industrial Development Corporation (IDC) and the Development Bank of Southern Africa (DBSA) as funding conduits that share the risk of investors by taking a direct stake in some projects. Key project areas include mining, construction, manufacturing, financial services, telecommunication, tourism and retail.

The presence of BRICS in Africa will therefore intensify South Africa's efforts in increasing their political and economic influence on the continent. South Africa companies have continued to increase their footprint in Africa as shown by figures that indicate an increase from US$3 billion to US$13 billion between 2005 and 2009 (UNCTAD 2011) South Africa has established a huge footprint in Angola, Botswana, DRC, Namibia, Mozambique, Swaziland, Tanzania, Zambia and Zimbabwe. These are all SADC countries. However, South Africa has spread its wings to the rest of the continent in both West and East Africa. Companies that have risen to prominence in these regions include Absa, Standard Bank, MTN, Vodacom, Eskom, Sasol, Shoprite and Multi choice.

General findings

Now that each of the BRICS countries interest in Africa have been analysed, it is important that a general overview of the impact of BRICS on Africa is discussed before concluding remarks. Firstly, it is clear from this presentation that the BRICS offer Africa a number of opportunities. It is however important to establish how Africa will use these opportunities to its advantage. A number of question marks surround the long-term impact of the BRICS grouping on Africa as a whole. Differing economic interests among both BRICS and between South Africa and other African countries could stifle the possibility of coordinated action.

The 2013 BRICS Summit in South Africa was significant in that further steps were taken to establish the BRICS Development Bank. The bank will be ideal in helping members deal with short-term liquidity problems, and to fund development and infrastructure projects. This is ideal for Africa where infrastructural problems continue to hamper economic growth. The Summit also established a Business Council to strengthen trade and investment between members. The South African representatives in the Council have been earmarked to strongly represent the African voices.

They are ideally placed to help the BRIC countries' understand how to operate in Africa and helping negotiate bilateral agreements.

The BRICS countries also still have a number of challenges amongst themselves, for example, there have been numerous disputes. Just after the BRICS conference, Brazil declared a trade dispute with South Africa and India over supposed dumping of polypropylene (UNCTAD 2011).

Conclusion

The fact that the BRICS countries are running to Africa because of its vast raw materials and the depletion of such resources in their countries should ring alarm bells to Africa to consider how it spends its natural resources. In future, Africa will face similar challenges and there will be nowhere to run. What BRICS means for Africa will depend on a combination of the strength of the BRICS itself, South Africa's influence within the group, and how South Africa chooses to represent Africa's broader interests, if at all? All BRICS players see potential benefits for themselves in Africa, and all engage there independent of each other. Thus Africa should be open minded and engage the BRICS more as individual countries and less as a group. African policymakers must work to shift Africa's relationship with the BRICS from one based primarily on natural resources to one that advances the continent's long-term economic growth and development trajectories (Kimenyi and Lewis 2011). Besides China and to some extent India, not much is known about the intention and behaviour of the other BRICS on the continent.

References

Barka, H.B and Mlambo, K., 2011. Russia's Economic Engagement with Africa. Africa Economic Brief 7 (2). [e-book]. Available at: http://www.afdb.org/fileadmin/uploads/afdb/Documents/Publications/Russia%27s_Economic_Engagement_with_Africa.pdf [accessed on 13 Dec 2013].

CIA 2013. World Factbook. India. Washington, D.C.: Central Intelligence Agency. [e-book]. Available at: https://www.cia.gov/library/publications/the-world-factbook/geos/br.html: [accessed 15 June 2013].

CIA, 2013. World Factbook. China. Washington, D.C.: Central Intelligence Agency. [e-book]. Available at: https://www.cia.gov/library/publications/the-world-factbook/geos/br.html [accessed 15 June 2013].

Confederation of Indian Industry. [e-book]. Available at: http://www.cii.in/ [accessed on 20 Nov 2013].

Dickerson-Nyema, A.E., 2011. Investment in Africa. The Diaspora Voice. [e-book]. Available at: http://www.thediasporavoice.com/index.php?option=com_content&view=article&id=141:investment-in-africa [accessed 22 June 2013].

Fundira, T., 2013. The BRICS engagement with Africa. In BRICS: South Africa's way ahead. [e-book]. Available at:http://www.namc.co.za/upload/other_trade_publications/SA%20Agric%20exports%20to%20BRICs%2020130222.pdf [accessed on 20 June 2013].

Fundira, T., 2012. Trade at a glance: the BRICS and Japan's engagement with Africa. Stellenbosch: tralac [e-book]. Available at: http://www.tralac.org/files/2012/01/S12WP012012-TradeAtGlance-BRICSJapanAfrica-20120125fin.pdf [accessed on 26 Jan 2014].

Gelb, S., 2005. South to South Investment: The case of Africa.[e-book]. Available at: www.fondad.org [accessed 12 June 2013].

IBER, 2011. India Trade at a Glance. India Brand Equity Foundation. [e-book]. Available at: http://www.ibef.org [accessed 21 June 2013].

Kimenyi, S.M. and Lewis, Z., (2011). Foresight Africa: The Continent's Greatest Challenges and Opportunities. [e-book]. Available at: http://www.brookings.edu/~/media/research/files/reports/2011/1/africa%20economy%20agi/01_africa_economy_agi.pdf#page=21 [accessed 20 June 2013].

Lewis, D., 2011 Special Report. In Africa, Brazil takes a different track. Thompson Reuters. [e-book]. Available at: http://graphics.thomsonreuters.com/specials/Brazil%20in%20Africa.pdf: [accessed on 01 February 2014].

Marafa, (2009:10). Africa's Business and Development Relationship with China Seeking Moral and Capital Values of the Last Economic Frontier. [e-book]. Available at: http://nai.diva-portal.org/smash/get/diva2:272966/FULLTEXT02 [accessed 28 June 2013].

Natufe, I.O., 2011. A Review of Russia-Africa relations. New challenges and new opportunities. Geopolitics. [e-book]. Available at: http://www.trcw.ru/en/articles/detail.php?ID=2791 [accessed 20 June 2013].

Nestmann, T and Orlova, D., 2008. Russia's outward investment. Deutsche Bank Research. [e-book]. Available at: http://www.dbresearch.eu/PROD/DBR_INTERNET_DE-PROD/PROD0000000000224964.PDF [accessed 15 June 2013].

Richardson, H., 2011. Brazil economy achieves highest growth in 25 years. [e-book]. Available at https://itdecs.com/2011/03/brazil economy-achieves-highest-growth-in-25-years/ [accessed 20 June 2013].

Susswein, (2003). Environmental Law and policy in Africa; Towards making Africa the tree of life. [e-book]. Available at: http://www.environment-namibia.net/tl_files/pdf_documents/publication/Environmental%20Law%20and%20Policy%20in%20Namibia%20-%20Towards%20making%20Africa%20the%20Tree%20of%20Life_2013.pdf [accessed 21 June 2013].

Tarr, D.G., 2009. Political Economy of Russia's trade: PolicyEarly Transition, Customs Unions, WTO Accession and Protection for Industrial Diversification. Tulane. [e-book]. Available at: http://www.tulane.edu/~dnelson/PEBricsConf/Tarr%20Russia.pdf [accessed on 23 Jan 2014].

The term 'South to South' is generally used to characterize the relationship that exists among the countries of the developing world. The South is also used to refer to the third world of countries that are not developed. However, such distinct characterization is no longer very relevant considering that some of the countries belonging to the 'South' are now having better economies than those of the 'North', the developed.

UNCTAD 2004. World Investment Report The Shifting Towards Services. Geneva. United Nations Conference on Trade and Development (UNCTAD).

UNCTAD. 2011. World Investment Report Non- Equity Modes of International Production and Development. Geneva. United Nations Conference on Trade and Development (UNCTAD).

Van den Bosch, S., 2011. African LDCs won't benefit much from BRICS arrival. IBSA News [e-book]. Available at www.ibsanews.com/

development-africanldcs-wont-benefit-much-from-bricsarrival/ [accessed on 20 June 2013].

World trade policy review 2010. China Trade Policy Review. Secretariat Report. Geneva. World Trade Organisation.

PART 4:

Land, Human Rights and Justice for Africa's Development

The Link Between Governance and Land Grabs in Sub-Saharan Africa

Menzi Sithuli Dlamini

Introduction

In recent years there has been a noticeable increase in the "purchase or lease of vast tracts of land by wealthier food-insecure nations and private investors from mostly poor, developing countries in order to produce crops for export" (Daniel and Mittal: 2009). The lack of transparency surrounding a majority of these deals and the speed with which they take place coupled with the negative implications on the general welfare and food security of the indigenous people who occupy the land, has resulted in these deals to be dubbed 'land grabs' (De Schutter 2011; Zoomers 2010). The deals have been heightened by the convergence of the financial and food crises of 2008. Even though food prices have since stabilised to normal levels post the 2007/08 upsurges, multinational interests in large scale acquisitions in Sub Saharan Africa have persisted. For example, evidence suggests that between 2005 and 2009, large scale deals reached 20 million hectares (Grain 2008; Cotula et al. 2009). However, given that information surrounding the deals is often vague and closely guarded, these figures cannot be pronounced with certainty (Colutal et al. 2009). Besides Sub Sharan Africa, other countries mainly targeted for these deals are in developing nations of Latin America and Asia, which currently have the most abundant arable and un-explored land. It is estimated that the world currently has approximately 1.5 billion hectares already under cultivation with a remainder of 445 million hectares of virgin land available for farming (Deininger et al 2011). An estimated 201 million hectares of this land is in sub-Saharan Africa, Latin America has 123 million hectares and Eastern Europe has a meagre 52 million hectares (Deininger et al 2011), these figures clearly show that sub-Saharan Africa has the biggest amount of uncultivated land, which explains why it may be a target for these deals.

'Land grabs' have had their fair share of controversy and as a consequence, analysts and activists have also labelled them 'the second scramble for Africa '(Carmody 2012). Noteworthy is that other observers and analysts see these as an opportunity for foreign direct investment (FDI) in Africa. The argument is that foreign investors could potentially bring with them the much needed new technologies which could lead to increased productivity in host countries (van der Werf 2012). Considering the nature of sub-Saharan African countries, which are characterised by poor agricultural productivity and limited use of technology in agriculture, this could be a valid argument. However, it is the secret that surrounds these deals that is a cause of concern for policy making. Information regarding these deals is scarce and highly unreliable, thus information is often based on media reports and civic organisations.

The Main Drivers

Judging from the figures available, it is clear that sub-Saharan Africa is at the centre stage of 'land grabs' and the predominant expert argument by large-scale land investments promoters is that land is unoccupied and available for investors (Cotula et al 2009). According to the World Bank (2009) land in sub-Saharan Africa is not being used to maximum capacity and is ready for intensive agricultural production. The World Bank (2009) goes on to argue that Africa will play a pivotal role in the world's endeavour to feed its growing population, which is expected to reach an astounding nine billion by 2050.

There are three main drivers that are attributed to 'land grabs', namely; food, fuel and investment (Hall 2011). Firstly, the food price hikes of 2008 coincided with the financial crisis. These formed the perfect ingredients for exposing the vulnerability of nations that are net food importers. As consequent of volatile global food commodity prices, a large number of these countries were forced to turn to other countries to produce food for their own nation's food security. This is done through multinational companies or directly by the governments of the countries involved and civil servants in their own capacities. The major food commodities being promoted by foreign investors and their governments in the sub-Saharan region for example are rice, maize and wheat (Ibid).

Secondly, the volatile oil prices that sky rocketed around the same period as the 2008 food crises made the world to realise that depending on oil alone for fuel is a risk. This created incentives for multinational companies to procure land in order to produce biofuel crops which would substitute for oil (Cotula et al 2009). This initiative is being driven in part by companies seeking to meet the European Union's demand for renewable fuel stocks to meet its target of 10% by 2020, despite the evident cost this might have on food production (Oxfam 2011). The major crops used for the production of biofuels are maize, soybean, jatropha, and palm oil for biodiesel whilst sugarcane is produced for bioethanol. The International Land Coalition's (ILC) estimates that 44 percent of 'land grabs' in 2009 were meant for biofuel production (ILC 2010). Interestingly over the same period the World Bank (2009) found that only 21 percent of land deals were for biofuel production, highlighting the secrecy surrounding these deals and inaccuracy of information on "land grabs' (Hall 2011).

Thirdly, owing to the financial crisis and subsequent global financial meltdown of 2008, there was a sudden upsurge in investors seeking to invest in more tangible and safer investment vehicles such as farmland. Logically, investors were banking on the increasing demand for food due to exponential population growth and increase in demand for biofuels due to concerted efforts to limit the world's dependence on crude oil, perceived land to be a safe haven for investment given a volatile global investment environment. The consequent outcome of this, as Richardson (2010) notes was a boom in private equity investors establishing 'farmland funds' which were used to acquire land in numerous countries especially sub-Saharan and Asia.

Lastly, an increase in carbon markets, which mainly relies in controlling farmland activities may have also contributed to 'land grabs'. Hall (2011) contends that since sub-Saharan Africa has large tracts of land covered in savannah, which can be counted as natural forests for the purpose of carbon markets, it became the obvious target for such deals. Thus in as much as investors acquire land to cultivate crops for food and fiber, they are also exploring ways of acquiring land with forests not to cultivate, but to enable them to earn carbon credits (Ibid).

Land grabs and governance

Numerous studies have explored 'land grabs' in sub-Saharan Africa within the context of the injustices they cause to communities affected and the uses of land acquired. There is a limited body of literature exploring the causal relationship between 'land grabs' and governance in the host countries. The core argument of this chapter is that there is a link between governance and land grabs. The chapter identifies countries with weak governance and high corruption as likely to have high incidence of 'land grabs'. The focus of the chapter is on sub-Saharan Africa with closer analyses on the countries with high incidences of land grabs. The chapter also suggests possible ways in which exploitive large scale land acquisitions can be prevented.

In this chapter, the Pearson's Correlation Coefficient Model is employed to establish a link between governance and land grabs in sub-Saharan Africa. Although it is possible to extend the research further to analyse causal effect and conduct socio-institutional analysis of land, this is beyond the scope of this chapter. Similarly, even though there are countries that have low governance scores who have recorded a low number of large-scale land acquisition deals, such countries are not considered in this analysis primarily because they are regarded as outliers. Rather, it is concerned with those who have thus far attracted the highest numbers of large-scale land acquisitions deals.

The Dynamics of Land Grabbing

This chapter's concern with 'land grabs' has to do with the secrecy and corruption that surrounds large-scale land acquisitions which are a main feature in sub Saharan Africa (Cotula et al. 2009); De Schutter (2011). There is no available comprehensive information on major transnational large scale land acquisitions in sub-Saharan Africa. Information about these acquisitions is often brought to the fore as a result of local resistance or investigative journalism; however, this information is often incomplete (Hall, 2011). Extensive research on 'land grabs' is mainly published on two blogs: the GRAIN website and the International Land Coalition (ILC) website, which source most of their information from media articles. These deals are characterised with secretiveness where details on the identities of the investors, the terms of the deals and the distribution of rents from them are never provided to the public (AldenWily 2010).

Withstanding the challenges that surrounds the availability and accuracy of data Friis and Reenberg (2010) attempted to quantify the magnitude of large-scale land acquisitions in Africa based on media reports that were posted on the ILC forum. The authors argue that this information is highly dependent on which deals are reported by the media in the first place and, secondly, on the reliability of the sources used by the media. There is evidence that a large number of projects or land grabs are not reported in the media and even fewer are posted on the major land studies blogs i.e. ILC blog. This suggests the scale at which large land investment are taking place might be far greater than those being reported in the media. By contrast, Cotula (2011) claims that figures reported in the media are substantially higher than those based on actual field research. These divergences suggest that caution should be taken when assessing figures on large-scale land investments.

Table 1 shows the current picture of land grabs in the major affected sub-Saharan African countries (exceeding 1 million hectares)

Table1. Main host African countries of large-scale foreign land investment

Country	Number of deals	Land Grabbed (ha)	Rating Score (%)
DR Congo	7	2 964 532	33
Ethiopia	77	2 514 481	47
Ghana	30	2 320 203	66
Guinea	3	1 607 215	43
Liberia	16	2 016 885	47
Madagascar	41	3 626 721	46
Mali	28	1 318 274	55
Mozambique	112	3 887 813	55
Sudan	29	5 580 585	33
South Sudan	21	5 219 763	33
Sierra Leone	23	2 007 779	48
Tanzania	37	1 218 026	59
Uganda	11	1 037 763	55
Zambia	18	1 063 628	58

Source: *Author's Calculations from the Land Matrix Database* (www.landmatrix.org)

Historical context of governance in the African continent

In the late 1950s and 1960s the African continent experienced independence euphoria filled with jubilation and hope for the future, as one after the other African countries gained their political independence. There was a new dawn where African nations could rewrite history and decide their destinies without their colonial masters. Ambitious nation building programs got off the ground with remarkable success in earlier years (World Bank 1994). The honeymoon was short lived; soon multiparty states became one-party states, states began to fall successively as leaders became despots and military coups ushered in dictators (Meredith 1985). By the 1980s, the African continent was engulfed by bitter civil wars and civil strife was rampant. Africa was in a political and economic crisis. These failings were enough proof to indicate the incapability of Africans to govern themselves in the absence of their colonial masters (Obadina 2000).

Internal pressures and the collapse of the USSR gave a boost for the rally for re-democratization; the people of the continent took resolute steps to demand participatory and democratic systems of governance (UNECA 1999). Since the pro-democracy wave swept through the continent in the 1990s there has been significant strides made towards improving governance on the continent, from dictators and one-party states, elections have become a common feature in the continents political landscape (Lal, Gaumer and Manhica 1999: Mule 2000). This improvement in the political landscape, discovery of natural resource deposits together with other factors such as, improvement in the policy environment and has led to significant improvements in the continent's economic performance. Economic growth rates are improving (AFDB 1999). Notwithstanding the significant gains brought about by political and economic reforms, by and large the continent still has unresolved challenges that led to the pressures for participatory democracy and good governance.

A broader perspective on governance

Governance is defined in both political and economic contexts. Political governance defines how a country is governed and it comprises but is not limited to; governance of citizens, institutions, and businesses, exercising of rights and obligations. Thus political governance entails political process that defines how decisions are taken, how much participation citizens are given in decision-making and in the management of public affairs (Decalo 1994). Economic governance defines mainly how resources are managed and the role of governments in the process of socioeconomic development. Economic governance provides a context in which corporate governance takes place, it sets out the laws under which corporations are established and the regulatory framework for conducting corporate affairs.

A large body of research suggests that the cornerstone of successful economies is good governance and public sector management. Africans and African leaders seem to have also realized that good governance is central to development as they try to rectify past errors and making governance apparatus operate better and more efficiently (UNECA 1999). In the presence of good governance abundance of a natural resource can be a catalyst to foster poverty reduction and economic growth (Mehlum, Moene, and Torvik 2006). In the lack of proper governance discoveries of natural resources give rise to what is referred to as a 'resource curse', which shows itself through social polarization and corruption instead of economic development.

De Crombrugghe et al. (2009) argue that indeed as measured by the Institutional Profiles Database countries with weak governance are the ones that are most attractive to investors as measured by the amount of large scale land investments. The fact that it would be easier to obtain land, where land rights are weak and protection of property rights is limited is a possible explanation to this anomaly. Since it is normally expected that if land rights are weak investors will be sceptical since their investment is not secure. But under these circumstances, investors would have their own resources to defend their property rights given that public protection may not be enough (Fuentes-Nieva and Nicholls (2013). This also poses a huge risk, since the sustainability of investments can become compromised in the long-run, when host governments change. It can also pose as a threat for the investors if the affected locals decide to revolt (Oxfarm 2011).

In a recent study by Fuentes-Nieva and Nicholls (2013) on the link between poor governance and land grabs, using data from the Land Matrix, which gathers data on land deals and World Bank's Worldwide Governance Indicators (WGI), they conclude that countries that had significant 'land grabs' between the years 2000 and 2011 had lower WGI scores than those who had non or insignificant number of 'land grabs'. The study concluded that countries with weak governance are actively being targeted by investors in their quest to maximise profits. This is possible since investors can sidestep costly and time consuming rules and regulations under weak governance. They further argue that in countries where public participation is low and governance institutions are weak or where corruption is rife an environment where investors can create investment conditions suitable for them but not to the interest of the host country is possible.

In other studies, (Anseew et al (2012); Deininger et. al (2011); Arezki et al (2011)) on large scale land deals it was found that weak governance facilitates an environment where investors have easy access to large tracts of land. The studies also argue that often the large-scale land deals are designed in such a way that they benefit the investors rather than the countries involved or affected communities. This therefore means that a legal framework to enforce rights should be in place, because even when the right institutions governing property rights are present, they are often not adhered to, since the capacity to enforce is not there. Secure property rights, transparent processes and sound institutions with proper legal frameworks to facilitate enforcement of property rights should be prerequisites for investment under normal circumstances (Fuentes-Nieva and Nicholls 2013).

A majority of these studies have used data from the Land Matrix and the World Bank's Worldwide Governance Indicators (WGI). However, none of these studies used data based on African governance indexes, such as the Ibrahim Index of African Governance (IIAG), which is what these papers sought to do.

Methodological approach

This chapter uses the 2012 Ibrahim Index of African Governance (IIAG) and the Land Matrix to analyse the link between national governance and 'land grabs'. This method is in a sense similar to the methodology used by Fuentes-Nieva and Nicholls (2013) who combined data from the Land Matrix and the World Governance Indicator (WGI) Project to perform their analysis. The usage of the IIAG was done with knowledge of its limitations and other models from other schools of thought such as co-operative and agri-estate models.

The Land Matrix Database is a global online database that includes indicative information on land deals covering 200 hectares or more as reported in the media which were conducted in 2000-2013. It is composed by a partnership of the Centre de Coopération Internationale en Recherche Agronomique pour le Développement (CIRAD), Centre for Development and Environment (CDE), German Institute of Global and Area Studies (GIGA), Deutsche Gesellschaft für Internationale Zusammenarbeit (GIZ) and the International Land Coalition (ILC).

The Ibrahim Index of African Governance is a composite index, constructed by combining underlying indicators in a standardised way to provide a statistical measure of governance performance in the African countries1. The Board of the Mo Ibrahim Foundation defines governance as perceived from the citizen's viewpoint. The definition of governance is broad in this case and can be summarised into four over-arching categories: Safety & Rule of Law, Participation & Human Rights, Sustainable Economic Opportunity, and Human Development[1].

Aggregated data on the total number of deals in each country from the Land Matrix data based on the 38 sub-Saharan African countries where 'land grabs' had been registered at the time of the study was used and overall governance scores from the IIAG were also used. The IIAG defines the rule of law as "Having a firmly embedded judicial system that is just, effective, accessible to all, administered by competent and impartial judges who work independently of political influences and in a corruption-free environment and make decisions according to merit, is a major prerequisite for ensuring Safety & Rule of Law".

In assessing the entrenchment of the rule of law within a state, it is important to take into consideration not only the performance of judicial systems but also matters of accountability, personal safety and national security. The exercise should take into account the actions of public officials as well as the prevention, control and elimination of corruption in the country.

Transparency and public accountability are of critical importance in determining governance outcomes. Experience has demonstrated that a legal system can easily be subverted if its enforcers are not accountable to those they serve and if they are prone to influence through financial and other considerations.

To ensure maximum progress in the efforts to promote good governance in Africa, the imperatives of rule of law and individual safety must be pursued in equal measure.

These two databases were merged and the link between the countries where 'land grabs' were concluded or were not concluded and the safety and law governance indicator (Rule of law, Accountability, Personal Safety and National Security) score for the period 2011 – 2012, were analysed.

We used the safety and law scores which ranks the extent to which countries' legal and regulatory environment is able to protect the rights of investors. Low scores characterize countries with poor governance. Given the long time horizon of any agricultural investment, security of property rights is likely to be a key determinant of long-term investment decisions as investors will not tie up large amounts of resources in a country where weak or unclear rights create a danger of opportunistic government behaviour and creeping expropriation (Schnitzer 1999) once investments are sunk. The opposite could, however, also be true, i.e. large investors may find it easier to establish and defend property rights if governance and the state's law enforcement capacity and presence are weak. Some investors unfamiliar with customary tenure systems may indeed believe that it will be easier and more 'secure' to acquire land directly from governments rather than by engaging in a dialogue with local rural populations. Others are quite outspoken about the perceived need and desire to enforce property rights through private militias--despite the problematic historical precedents (Hall 2011).

The hypothesis is that investors are targeting countries with less regard for local property rights. This hypothesis has been proven in an empirical study by Arezki, et al (2011) using the GRAIN database of land deals that weak governance is targeted by large scale land investors. However, the study also cautioned that too much emphasis should be put on the finding because this could also be a primary case of correlation rather than causation.

The main reason for (Ibid) to be cautious is that conventional wisdom suggests that investors are risk averse enough to avoid countries where property rights are weak or uncertain. If it is so easy for investors to collude with corrupt government officials to expropriate local land, it should be equally easy for these same government officials to renege on their promises and take back the land at any point in time.

Arezki et al (2011) also rightly points out that the negative correlation between land governance and investment suggests that these concerns are not at play, neither does it guarantee that investors are actively seeking out poorly-governed countries. If we imagined a very simple world where investors chose countries at random to target, it is inevitable that countries with governments that show little concern for local property rights are going to be the first ones to secure a deal.

Pearson's Correlation Coefficient Model

H_0: There is no linear correlation between governance and large scale land acquisitions.
H_1: There is a linear correlation between governance and large sale land acquisitions.

Thus:
H_1 $\rho \neq 0$
H_0: $\rho = 0$

To calculate the statistic value of the correlation coefficient (r), we use the following equation:

(1)

where (n) is the number of pairs of data.

Let (x) represent a rating score and (y) represent the amount of land acquired. The sample of paired (x,y) data was purposely chosen to target

$$r = \frac{n(\sum xy)-(\sum x)(\sum y)}{\sqrt{n(\sum x^2)-(\sum \text{AkaaGeer}}\sqrt{n(\sum y^2)-(\sum y)^2}} \quad (1)$$

tions. Any outliners were

1. RESULTS AND DISCUSSIONS

Figure: 1 Land acquisitions by country, and number of projects

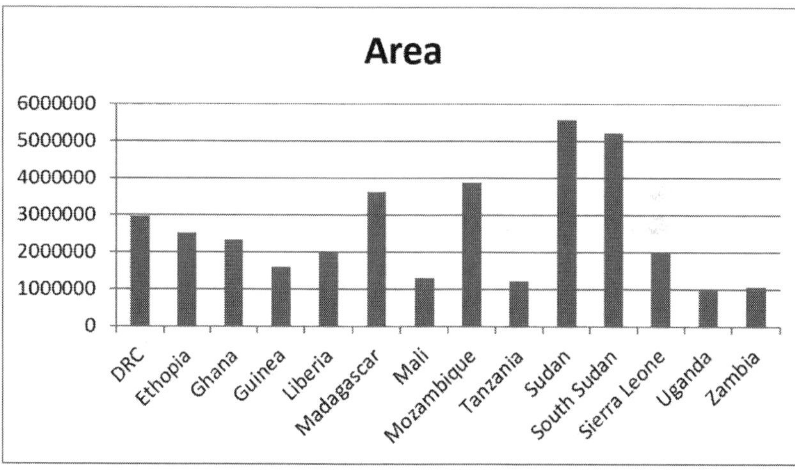

Source: Author's calculations

The results show that countries such as Mozambique, Madagascar, Tanzania, Ethiopia, Democratic Republic of Congo, Sudan and South Sudan have the highest area of land under 'land grabs'. Interestingly is that in most of these countries there has been recent unstable political climate which often goes hand in hand with poor governance.

Figure: 2: Land acquisitions by country and size

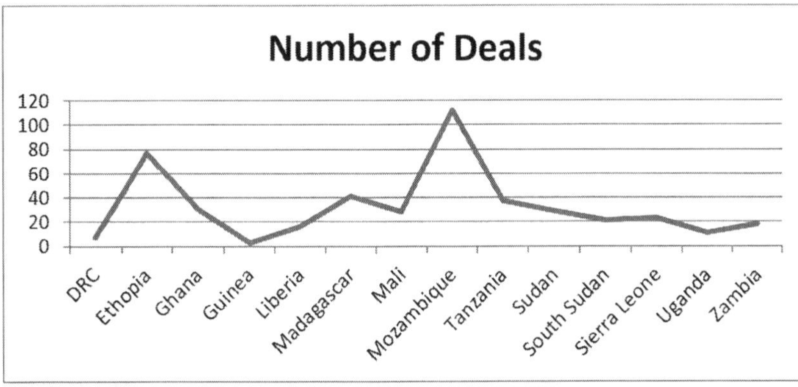

Source: Authors own calculations.

According to reported observations (Anseew et al (2012), sub-Saharan African countries also represent a significant chuck of the number of the most targeted countries for 'land grabs'. Our results show that countries such as Mozambique, Madagascar, Tanzania, Ethiopia, Sudan and South Sudan are recipients of the large part of the demand for land by foreign investors, both in terms of cumulative size and number of projects. It is worth noting that observations by various researchers often vary, however a majority of these countries are always coming up as the most targeted. These validate the accuracy of the data that was used for this analysis (Hall 2011).

Table 2. Correlation

Correlation	
Overall Score and Land Grabbed	
Pearson Coefficient of Correlation	-0.4157
t Stat	-2.7421
df	36
P(T<=t) one tail	0.0047
t Critical one tail	1.6883
P(T<=t) two tail	0.0094
t Critical two tail	2.0281

Source: Owners own calculations

The computed r = - 0.416 and the value of the test statistic is t= -2.742, which has a p-value of 0.009. At 95% confidence there is enough evidence to infer that there is a linear relationship between overall governance score and land grabs, thus we reject H_0. Furthermore, the negative sign of the statistic value (- 0.416) implies that the relationship between overall governance score and land grabs is negative, i.e. when the overall governance score increases, the amount of land grabs decreases or when the overall governance score goes down, the amount of land grabs goes up.

These is a strange anomaly since instead of land acquisition projects being contingent on good land governance and the associated strong protection of rights, we find that weak land governance makes a country more attractive for large scale land-related investment. Although more detailed work at country level would be required to establish a causal link, a correlation along these lines suggests that, for much of the investment demand considered here, long-term security of tenure has been less of a concern for investors. Taken at face value, this coefficient of correlation means that expressed concerns of civil society about the interests at play being mostly extractive with little concern about long-term benefits to local populations may not be entirely misplaced. However, in countries with weak land governance or weak recognition of local land rights, successful implementation of projects is expected to be difficult for a number of reasons, including resistance by local people at various stages of implementation. Alternatively, it could imply that the phenomenon is too new to be observed in operations or that much of the interest evident in press reports may be speculative.

To this point, the chapter has confirmed the case made by other researchers in this area that weak governance and land grabs often go hand in hand. In the case of this study, we considered governance to entail; Rule of Law, Accountability, Personal Safety and National Security as measures of governance and land grabs as any large-scale land deal exceeding 200 hectares.

Conclusion

Notwithstanding the need for further work at project level to establish a causal link, the correlation link does suggest that for a majority of the large-scale land investments demand considered here, the security of long-term tenure was not regarded a priority by investors. Land grabs certainly deserve our attention and concern, as it is clear that large scale investors are actively targeting countries with poor governance institutions. Extensive on-the-ground work still needs to be done in this area to conclude these findings concretely.

Of immediate concern, is secrecy of thesedeals and negative impact they often have on the indigenous people who are affected. In as much as large scale land investments are welcomed in Africa, under the current configuration they tend to be non-beneficial to host countries' governments and citizens. If there are any benefits, it is possible that these end up being corrupt government officials and lawmakers including the local elite who ensure that these deals are concluded. Regardless of all the negative perceptions surrounding large-scale land acquisitions in sub-Saharan Africa, they however have potential opportunities including technological transfer and job creation. However, the fact that host countries with weak governance are clearly being targeted regardless of the risks associated with such deals highlights the need for host countries to review policy and regulatory frameworks in such a way that host countries reap the potential opportunities that come with large scale land deals.

Concerted efforts should be put on improving governance specifically land governance and administration by institutionalizing / formalising local land rights and creating awareness amongst indigenous people about their land rights, and ways to exercise those rights, this can help in avoiding foreigners using nationals as intermediaries. The terms of land transactions must be transparent and should respect the social and environmental rights of host countries, compliance should further be monitored by host countries. One way of doing this is to make land transactions public and allow public participation to minimise the corruption risk. (Arezki et al 2012)

Positive strides towards responsible land investments have been made through the development of the Voluntary Guidelines on the Responsible Governance of Land Tenure, however efforts should be made to make this an internationally accepted norm on good land governance.

References

African Development Bank, African Development Report 1999 (Abidjan, African Development Bank.

Alden, W. L.2010. *Whose land are you giving away, Mr President?* Paper presented at The World Bank Conference on Land Administration, Washington, DC.

Anseeuw, W., M.Boche, T.Breu, M.Giger, J. Lay, P.Messerli, and K, Nolteet,. 2012. *Transnational Land Deals for Agriculture in the Global*

South. Analytical Report based on the Land Matrix Database", CDE/ CIRAD/GIGA, Bern/Montpellier/Hamburg, http://landportal.info/ landmatrix/media/img/analytical-report.pdf (Assessed 2 April 2013).

Arezki, R., K.Deininger, and H. Selod,. 2012. *Global Land Rush: Finance & Development*, Vol. 49, No. 1 International Monetary Fund: www. imf.org/external/pubs/ft/fandd/2012/03/arezki.htm (Assessed 30 March 2013).

Arezki, R., K.Deininger, and H.Selod,. 2011. *What drives the global land rush?",* International Monitory Fund Working Paper, Washington D.C.: International Monetary Fund Institute, www.imf.org/external/ pubs/ft/wp/2011/wp11251.pdf (Accessed 28 February 2013)

Carmody, P. 2012. *A global enclosure: the geo-logics of Indian agro-investments in Africa*. Dublin: Trinity College, Department of Geography.

Cotula, L. 2011. *Land deals in Africa: What is in the contracts*? International Institute for Environment and Development, London.

Cotula L, S. Vermeulen, R. Leonard and J. Keeley,. 2009. *Land grab or development opportunity? Agricultural investment and international land deals in Africa*. International Institute for Environmental and Development, Food and Agricultural Organisation, International Fund for Agricultural Development, London/Rome.

Decalo, S. 1994. *"The Future of Participatory Democracy in Africa,"* Futures, Volume 26, Number 9 .London, Butterworth-Heinemann.

de Crombrugghe, D., K.Farla, N. Meisel, C. de Neubourg A.J. Ould and A. Szirmai,. 2009. *"Institutional Profiles Database III"*, presentation of the Institutional Profiles Database, Agence Française de Développement (AFD) Working Paper No. 89, Paris

Daniel, S. and A.Mittal,. 2009. *The Great Land Grab Rush for World's Farmland Threatens Food Security for the Poor*. The Oakland Institute, Oakland, CA 94619, USA

De Schutter, O. 2011. *How not to think of land grabbing: three critiques of large-scale investment in farmland*. Peasant. Stud. 38: 249-279.

Deininger, K., D.Byerlee, J. Lindsay, A. Norton, H.Selod and M. Stickler. 2011a. *Rising global interest in farmland: Can it yield sustainable and equitable benefits?* Washington, D.C.: World Bank.

Deininger, K. and D. Byerlee. 2011. "*Rising global interest in farmland: can it yield sustainable and equitable benefits?*", Washington D.C.: World Bank.

Friis, C. and A. Reenberg. 2010. Land grab in Africa: Emerging land system drivers in a tele-connected world. Copenhagen: GLP International Project Office, University of Copenhagen.

Fuentes-Nieva, R and M.Nicholl. 2013. *Bad governance leads to bad land deals: The link between politics and land grabbing*, Oxfam International, available from http://www.oxfamblogs.org/fp2p/?p=13636 (Accessed 22 June 2013).

GRAIN, 2008. '*Seized: The 2008 Land Grab for Food and Financial Security*'. Barcelona: GRAIN.GRAIN, www.grain.org; Food Crisis and the Global Land Grab. Available at www .farmlandgrab.org (Assessed 3 April 2013).

Hall, R. 2011. Land Grabbing in Africa and the New Politics of Food, Future Agricultures, Policy Brief.

Ibrahim Index of African Governance, 2012: available from http:// www.moibrahimfoundation.org (Assessed 22 June 2013.

ILC (International Land Coalition), 2010. '*Commercial pressures on land*', PowerPoint presentation at the Conference on Global Land Grabbing hosted by the Land Deal Politics Initiative at the Institute of Development Studies, University of Sussex, UK, 6-8 April 2011.

Lal, B., Gaumer, G. and Manhica, S. 1999. "*Information and Communication Technologies for Improved Governance in Africa*", E/ECA/ADF/99/6, Theme paper for ADF September 1999 (Addis Ababa, United Nations Economic Commission for Africa).

Meredith, M.1985. *The First Dance of Freedom: Black Africa in the Post War Era* (London, Abacus, 1985).

Mehlum, H., K.Moene, and R.Torvik. 2006. "*Institutions and the resource curse*", The Economic Journal, 116, 1-20

Mule, H.2000. "*Challenges to African Governance and Civil Society,*" Africa Notes, May 2000, page 8.

Tunde Obadina, "Africa's Crisis of Governance," (Africa Economic Analysis, 2000), http://www.afbis.com/analysis/crisis.htm

Oxfam.2011. "*Land and Power: The Growing Scandal Surrounding the new wave of Investments in Land*", Oxfam, http://policy-practice.

oxfam.org.uk/publications/land-and-power-the-growing-scandal-surrounding-the-new-wave-of-investments-in-l-142858 (Assessed 28 June 2013)

Richardson B, 2010. *'Big Sugar in southern Africa: rural development and the perverted potential of sugar/ ethanol exports'*, Journal of Peasant Studies, Vol 37, No 4, , pp. 917-938.

Schnitzer, M. 1999. *"Expropriation and control rights: A dynamic model of foreign direct investment."* International Journal of Industrial Organization 17 (8): 1113-37.

UNECA, 1999. *Progress in Good Governance since the Social Summit* (Addis Ababa, United Nations Economic Commission for Africa), www.un.org/Depts/eca/summit/govkenya.htm (Assessed 11 June 2013)

Van der Werf, W.2012. Large-scale foreign land investments in Africa, with particular attention to the case of Zambia. Unpublished MA dissertation, University of the Witwatersrand, Johannesburg.

World Bank, 1994. Adjustment in Africa: Reforms, Results and the Road Ahead (Washington, DC, The World Bank, 1994), page 21.

World Bank, 2009. *Awakening Africa's Sleeping Giant: Prospects for Commercial Agriculture in the Guinea Savannah Zone and Beyond*, Washington DC: World Bank

Zoomers A (2010). *Globalisation and the foreignisation of space: seven processes driving the current global land grab*. Peasant. Stud. 37:429-447.

Indexes

Data on land deals

Country	**Number of deals**	**Land Grabbed (ha)**	**Rating Score (%)**
Angola	14	333 500	44
Benin	6	342 800	58
Burkina Faso	2	400 000	55
Cote d'Ivoire	8	581 423	39
Cameroon	9	823 183	45

Central Africa Republic	29	632 317	34
Congo Brazzaville	5	680 000	43
DR Congo	7	2 964 532	33
Egypt	6	119 552	58
Ethiopia	77	2 514 481	47
Gabon	5	722 826	54
Gambia	1	200 000	52
Ghana	30	2 320 203	66
Guinea	3	1 607 215	43
Kenya	17	776 179	53
Liberia	16	2 016 885	47
Libya	1	40 000	44
Madagascar	41	3 626 721	46
Malawi	4	277 500	56
Mali	28	1 318 274	55
Mauritius	1	500	83
Mauritania	2	52 000	48
Morocco	3	714 400	57
Mozambique	112	3 887 813	55
Namibia	5	68 000	70
Niger	3	29 513	50
Nigeria	29	632 317	42
Rwanda	2	20 000	53
Senegal	19	675 035	56
Sudan	29	5 580 585	33
South Sudan	21	5 219 763	33
South Africa	2	29 000	71
Swaziland	5	104 919	52
Sierra Leone	23	2 007 779	48
Tanzania	37	1 218 026	59
Uganda	11	1 037 763	55
Zambia	18	1 063 628	58
Zimbabwe	4	536 000	34

Source: Authors own calculations from the land matrix

Leadership for Land Governance in Africa

Robert Home

Introduction

Land is essential for shelter and for getting a living. Without the rule of law and some system for land governance, land-grabbing and power struggles within and between states can proliferate, as Africa has experienced all too often. A great transition has dominated the history of the poor in every continent: from land-rich poverty, where labour is scarce and the poor are generally those who lack access to labour, to land-scarce poverty, where the poor lack viable land-holdings, cannot sell their labour, and increasingly migrate to the towns in search of a livelihood. Sub-Saharan Africa's particular colonial history created land shortage in various ways: the confiscation of land and mineral resources by white settlers and foreign capital; state control of urban and unused land; and exclusionary rules of land tenure and use (Iliffe 1987).

Land governance offers a convenient term for the legal and bureaucratic system for managing social relationships in land, and is receiving increasing attention from the international development community. In the modern nation-state it involves a wide array of agencies, professions and bureaucracies, requiring significant resources. The tasks undertaken include the following: confirming ownership and use rights, surveying and subdividing, processing plans and documents, valuing and managing property, handling appeals and disputes, and reviewing laws and regulations. State or public lands need managing in their various forms, such as local government estates, national parks, heritage areas and defence/security estates. Valuers (public and private) appraise property for taxation, securitisation and development purposes. Environmental agencies seek to protect and manage the natural environment and resources, including wild-life habitats that earn revenues from tourism. The state may have extended control over land use and ownership through local authorities and parastatal bodies (such as utilities), while recent neo-liberal policies have facilitated the large-scale privatization of land to foreign individuals and companies, justified in the interests of open markets and international capital.

Unfortunately, the capability of land governance in Africa and elsewhere is often inadequate to the tasks demanded of it, increasing rather than reducing tenure insecurity and conflicts over land, and seeming remote and irrelevant to the everyday lives of the poor. In the words of the late Patrick McAuslan (2003, 3), writing of Tanzania, the practical reality has been that:

> The peasants were pushed about by high-handed petty bureaucrats, their land was seized without compensation, the urban poor were by a legal sleight of hand deprived of the land on which they might have lived for years, they received no or derisory compensation and no alternative land on which to build another house.

This complex subject is now approached by examining the context for land governance in Africa, tracing the history of colonial land laws and subsequent reforms. It then addresses the issue of leadership in land governance, with particular attention to the professions concerned with land (especially lawyers, planners and land surveyors), and to the rise of local civil society.

Africa's development challenges

The United Nation's World Development Report has identified three specific 'continentwide' challenges for African development: 'the triple disadvantages of low density, long distance and deep division' (United Nations 2008, 121). Firstly, its average human population density is still among the lowest of any continent, notwithstanding rapid population growth over the last two centuries. Secondly, Africa's large land mass makes it physically separated from other continents by large oceans, while internal transport has to move over great distances. Thirdly, it is divided by its peoples' linguistic diversity: over a thousand distinct languages are spoken, and many of its countries contain twenty or more different ethnic groups within their borders. The European 'scramble for Africa' after the Berlin Treaty of 1885 created deep political and social divisions which postcolonial national boundaries have generally continued. The continent now has over fifty countries (some still struggling for full international recognition), which represents the most countries in relation to land area of any continent.

Apart from these basic geo-political challenges, Africa's recent and unprecedented demographic surge poses a further challenge for land governance in national and local jurisdictions that are ill-equipped to meet. During the 20th century, and particularly after decolonization, the continent's population rose hugely, as a result of falling mortality and rising birth rates, as well as improved food production. The combined populations of South Africa, Zimbabwe and Zambia, for example, are now 75 million, but were only a tenth of that eighty years ago, while the population of Kenya has grown by five times since independence in 1965, adding a million people a year in the first decade of the 21st century.

Such rapid population growth creates the potential for destabilization and civil conflict. Population Action International has identified much of sub-Saharan Africa at particularly high risk of conflict because of certain demographic stress factors (Cincotta 2003). It considers the so-called 'youth bulge', when young adults (particularly young men) comprise 40% or more of the adult population, as a reliable predictor of social unrest, war and terrorism, when associated with poverty and mass unemployment. Other stress factors include rapid urban growth, decline in available cropland and fresh water, and high levels of disease.

Africa's combination of great land and mineral resources with weak political entities has attracted outside exploitation for centuries. Its human population was seen as a pool of potential slave labour, and once the railways and motor vehicles had facilitated access to the interior its minerals could be extracted, while low population densities led to often violent land grabbing for foreign-managed estates. European colonizers took the best land into their control, and the land laws and regulations they introduced continue to influence postcolonial realities long after they surrendered political control.

The legal framework inherited from past colonialism

> AkaaGeer Europe is in Africa for the mutual benefit of her own industrial classes, and of the native races in their progress to a higher plane...[I]t is the aim and desire of civilised administration to fulfil this dual mandate... [I]n Africa to-day we are ... bringing to the dark places of the earth, the abode of barbarism and cruelty, the torch of culture of

> progress, while ministering to the material needs of our own civilization (Lugard 1922).

This mandate was reinforced between the two world wars when the League of Nations placed a 'trusteeship' duty upon colonial administrations towards the subject peoples they governed, who were perceived as peculiarly 'backward' and vulnerable (Lindley 1926).

In Africa the dual mandate - and its associated policy of indirect rule - led to dual land tenure systems. On one side were the plantation estates and townships of the European colonisers, protected by the legal concept of absolute and exclusive private property, a philosophy of possessive individualism deriving from John Locke (Macpherson 1962). On the other side were the tribal areas, where Africans continued under their customary land tenure and individual land-holding was denied. A dual system was instituted when British colonial administrations claimed, effectively without consulting the actual occupiers, rights over land, which was termed as crown, public or state land, arguing that there was ample surplus land in the new territories that was not obviously in beneficial use. This was supported by the legal concept of *terra nullius* (empty land), and colonial administrations then felt free to transfer such 'crown land' through grant, sale or lease to new settlers or public bodies (such as the railways).

The essentials of African customary land tenure were strikingly described by the American social anthropologist Paul Bohannan, writing about the Tiv tribe of Nigeria. He described it as 'geometry on a rubber sheet':

> '[I]nstead of seeing their maps primarily in terms of 'property', Africans see something like a map in terms of social relationships in space. They emphasize the spatial aspect of their social groups and provide themselves with a social map...they were usually imprecise, because group membership was the valued quality. Westerners, on the other hand, think about their map in terms of property and values, and see the social system which results as fundamentally a series of contracts...'[W] hereas the Western map is rigid and precise, the Tiv map is constantly changing both with reference to itself and its correlation with the earth. The land may be fixed, but the people, their compounds and farms, shift around on it (Bohannan 1973).'

In the often-quoted words of a Nigerian chief:

> 'I conceive that land belongs to a vast family of which many are dead, few are living and countless are yet unborn' (quoted in Meek 1949, preface).

Land was thus not merely a possession and a means of production, but an intrinsic part of Africans' social, economic, political and spiritual being, something to be cherished and responsibly enjoyed by present and future generations. Land thus belonged not to individuals but to the wider community, family or lineage. This kind of land law has been called variously tribal, customary, indigenous, aboriginal, or native (Glenn 2004).

The 'colonial masters' rejected indigenous peoples' use rights if they did not change the character of the land. Hunting and gathering, even farming if land was unfenced, were regarded as reflecting only an ephemeral attachment to land, not enough to claim ownership, and the British Privy Council cases in the 1920s held that customary land tenure did not confer ownership and private property rights upon the 'native' occupiers. In recent years customary land rights have achieved greater recognition as indigenous groups assert their claims to land, emboldened by the Australian Mabo case and the (admittedly rather ineffective) United Nations Declaration on Indigenous Peoples (Russell 2005; United Nations 2007).

The dual mandate approach to land tenure put Africans and their customary land rights into so-called native reserves or tribal trust lands (Hailey 1956:759-771). In South Africa the 1913 Natives Land Act (later the Black Land Act, called the 'first pillar of apartheid') provided for the creation of scheduled 'native' reserves, outside which Africans were generally prohibited from acquiring land. A systematic reserves policy quickly spread across Southern, Central and East Africa, although the land areas allocated to reserves fluctuated. African 'native reserves' or 'trust land' were managed by colonial officials and local leaders, who handled disputes in 'native courts', from which western-educated lawyers and judges were largely excluded as a matter of policy (Chanock 1985).

The evolutionary theory of land rights saw customary tenure as a vestige of the past, heading for extinction through an inevitable historical process 'towards a greater concentration of rights in the individual and a corresponding loss of control by the community as a whole' (Simpson 1976:225; Platteau 1996). Tribal or customary law was increasingly involved with competing claims to land, and by the 1940s Lord Hailey's *African Survey* was noting the growth of individualistic tendencies in customary land tenure. Subsequently conversion of reserve lands for African individual ownership was allowed under a new policy to accommodate progressive African farmers. In Kenya the British responded to the so called Mau-Mau armed liberation movement with a policy of encouraging individual African ownership in the trust lands, an 'ambitious programme of social engineering, aimed at the total extinction of customary land law' (Coldham 1978).

The dual mandate policy also had particular implications for the rapidly growing towns in Africa, which the colonialists were regarded as largely exclusive European areas, to be kept segregated from the local population (Home 2013). In the settler colonies, where Africans were prevented from legally owning land in urban areas, local authorities were empowered to build housing in so-called 'locations' for Africans not housed by their employers, usually outside the urban area, while mining townships maintained separate highly controlled regimes separate from the wider community. In South Africa a distinctive urban morphology resulted - the *apartheid* city (Smith 1992). African town-dwellers were also subjected to the so-called 'Durban system', which became a general model for labour control in British central and southern Africa: the proceeds of a municipal monopoly of beer-halls were paid into a 'Native Revenue' account to pay for African services, kept separate from other municipal finances. As Africans justifiably complained: 'How much beer must I drink before my children can drink water? Do other countries make poor people drink beer to collect money for water?' (quoted in Hall 1964:135). Tribal or communal lands lying near urban areas became places where Africans could live free from pass laws and other restrictions, in unregulated, unserviced settlements. Often called slums, these proliferating peri-urban informal settlements are now reluctantly accepted as permanent features of the urban landscape, designated for upgrading rather than clearance - 'here to stay' (Hindson and McCarthy 1994). This division between urban and peri-urban forms has marked the African urban landscape ever since.

Unscrambling colonial land laws

It is now over half a century since most African countries achieved independence, and they have been reworking their complex inherited land laws (Manji 2012). Ambitious and complex land tenure reform has extended ownership to a wider range of tenure forms, and given easier access to title deeds for occupiers in certain circumstances. Examples of such law reforms include the following: the military government of Nigeria nationalising land in its 1977 Land Use Decree; Uganda reforming its feudal *mailo* land tenure with its 1998 Land Act; Botswana passing a Tribal Land Act in 1968; and Tanzania's new land laws in 1990-93. Perhaps the most comprehensive approach was in South Africa, where various new land laws after 1994 dismantled apartheid and attempted a transformative approach, embedded in its new constitution.

Moving towards a more equitable distribution of land rights was frustrated by guarantees of private property rights written into the new constitutions of the independent states (Allen 2000:83). These guarantees were limited by the usual provisions for compulsory acquisition by the state in the public interest, subject to appropriate compensation being paid, and regulation of land use through the planning system. Thus land redistribution in southern Africa moved slowly: The South African government adopted a target in 1994 of transferring 30% of commercial farming land to 600 000 smallholders, but a decade later only 3% of land had been transferred, a situation which reflected both institutional weakness and owner reluctance to sell. The Namibian Government bought out white-owned ranches (by 2004 120 of them, totaling 700 000 hectares), converting freeholds into 99-year leases, but was handicapped by the gap between a high open market price and the low government grant that could be afforded. Zimbabwe's Land Acquisition Act 2000 removed the requirement that land redistribution should only take place through the market (the often-quoted principle of 'willing buyer, willing seller'), and empowered the state to take land for fast-track resettlement, following which a programme of eviction (the so-called third *chimurenga* or revolution) has reduced the number of white farmers from four thousand to a few hundred, and transferred a quarter of the land area to the government's accelerated land programme (Ntsebeza and Hall 2007).

Sub-Saharan Africa has, when compared with other regions of the world, a high proportion of community land, legally controlled neither by the state nor by private individuals, and in a postcolonial and pluralist world customary or communal land practices are now being revived and reconstituted. If land tenure can be reduced to three basic types (private, public and community land), communal land can fulfil an important welfare function, as a reservoir of cheap, unserviced land in peri-urban areas, an important common property resource, and a community defence against the penetrative forces of globalization and capitalism. The protection of communal land tenure is being reinforced, with new legal forms to accommodate communal value systems; examples include co-operative land in South Africa, the social tenure domain model, and common pool resource management. Communal land tenure has been reinforced internationally as indigenous groups pursue legal challenges and human rights arguments to reassert claims to ancestral lands, emboldened by the Australian Mabo case and the United Nations Declaration on the

Rights of Indigenous Peoples. With ever-increasing exploitation of natural resources, and the establishment of protected areas for wildlife, indigenous peoples have found themselves often displaced from their land without compensation or even the offer of alternative land, and are asserting their rights through the courts. In South Africa one such case was brought by the Richtersfeld San community, and in Cameroon the Bakweri tribal group have long pursued their claim (Chan 2004; Njoh 2011). While such claims are still few in number, and can be frustrated by national governments' reluctance to comply with court judgments, they can be expected to increase.

Meanwhile private land tenure continues to make inroads into communal land areas, with both communities and individuals taking advantage of the stronger legal status it confers. In Kenya the Land Adjudication Act 1968 provided for the 'ascertainment and recording of rights and interests in Trust land' through a process of systematic adjudication of boundaries, consolidation of holdings, and registration of individual ownership. The process has resulted in much corrupt land allocation through legal manipulations, such that a leading Kenyan property lawyer has claimed that:

> 'The land owning ethic has now become a national mania whereby everyone dreams of owning land.' (Wanjala 2000: 177).

The complex tapestry of African land governance continues to evolve. A mix of state constitutions, statute and customary law is sometimes framed in a unified land code, with a complex web of secondary laws and regulations, and new policy approaches often originate from international development agencies and promoted by the African Union. Globalizing forces of foreign inward investment and market capitalism are in tension with the internal pressures of relentless population growth, urbanization, and environmental sustainability. Three particular ideas gaining strength in the international circulation of policy ideas are discussed next: the rule of law, human rights, and pro-poor strategies.

The rule of law is increasingly seen as vital for economic, political and social development. The underpinning theory is still subject to debate, particularly the extent to which the legal order could or should respond to the aspirations of the poor, while protecting established property rights. Both the UN and World Bank are committed to rule of law activities in nation states such as strengthening constitutions and the institutions of justice and governance (United Nations 2008). In sub-Saharan Africa, however, the rule of law is complicated by legal pluralism: 'a fixture of the colonial experience...characterizing at the present day the larger part of all of the world's national legal systems' (Fitzpatrick 1992:9). The colonial powers imported their own systems, leaving some African nation states with a legacy of two or more overlaid colonial legal orders, while multiple attachments and identities are inevitable attributes of complex modern cultures, which legal systems reflect.

To complicate matters further, land governance is influenced by an array of international and regional agencies, with their many programmes, initiatives and associated networks. Increasingly these international agencies co-ordinate their efforts, such as the UN-HABITAT (concerned with human settlements), FIG (representing the surveying profession internationally) and the International Fund for Agricultural Development (an off-shoot of FAO). The importance of land governance is now recognised in most sub-Saharan African countries, as well as by regional bodies such as SADC and the African Union, which have each produced, after much consultation and effort, land policy guidance in recent years (SADC 2007).

As well as the rule of law agenda, the scope of two other powerful ideas, human rights and pro-poor law, has grown in recent years. The expansion of human rights law from individual to collective responsibilities for economic, social and cultural rights is attracting a broader and more grassroots constituency, and it may yet become a framework to hold institutions (both state and non-state) accountable for their role in creating and sustaining poverty. A 'pro-poor' state is encouraged to develop effective relationships with poor people: assessing the poverty impact of public policies, strengthening poor people's assets and capabilities, correcting gender inequity and children's vulnerability, and protecting poor people's rights (Department for International Development 2008). Improving security of tenure for the world's poor, for example through such UN-driven initiatives as the Global Campaign on Secure Tenure and the Global Land Tools Network, is linked to Target 11 of MDG 7 (improving the lives of slum dwellers).

What might a pro-poor approach to land governance mean? A universal right to adequate housing was affirmed by the UN Committee on Economic, Social and Cultural Rights in 1992, and has subsequently been included in the African Charter on Human and Peoples' Rights. If poverty means not being able to meet such basic human needs as land for shelter and a livelihood, then a pro-poor approach to land governance would seek especially to guarantee legal access to land for the poor. But where would such land come from? Land will have to be redistributed, which means from the 'haves' (either the state or private individuals) to the 'have-nots', but the 'haves' can hardly be expected to welcome such a redistribution, and they are generally those who control the law-making process. This is the paradox inherent in the very idea of a pro-poor land law and governance, making it highly political and difficult, and requiring leadership if progress is to be made.

The current discourse on land and property rights is strongly influenced by Hernando de Soto's best-selling book *The Mystery of Capital (*2000). He asserted that, unless recognised by a formal legal system, the property of the world's poor is merely so much 'dead capital', which locks them in the "grubby basement of the pre-capitalist world". His main remedy would be to integrate all property rights into one unified formal record system, which would confer rights and responsibilities upon property-owners both rich and poor, and provide them with a sense of identity, dignity, and belonging. Private property rights, particularly the right to exclude others, create a form of monopoly over the basic and finite resource of land. He has, however, been criticised for reinforcing a narrative of inferiority in the South by treating poverty as a specific phenomenon of those societies. People derive much of their sense of personal, communal and even religious identity from their relationship with the land (Abramson and Theodossopoulos 2000). Identification with land can be a vital component in retaining cultural identity, and the deliberate with-holding of land from state land-titling processes may be a means of preserving family and community cohesion and continuity.

The 'land question' or 'land issue' remains persistent and politically sensitive. To quote Kenya's national land policy:

> The land question has manifested itself in many ways such as fragmentation, breakdown in land administration, disparities in land ownership and poverty. This has resulted in environmental, social, economic and political problems including deterioration in land quality, squatting and landlessness, disinheritance of some groups and individuals, urban squalor, under-utilization and abandonment of agricultural land, tenure insecurity and conflict (Kenya Government 2011).

Land governance that is able to address such complexities indeed creates a challenge for leadership in Africa.

Leadership in land governance?

Land governance might not seem at first glance a suitable forum for leadership, since it is largely a technical, bureaucratic and professional exercise. Theories of leadership, concerned with organizing a group of people to achieve a common goal, have usually been concerned with specific leader attributes. With the complex and shifting agenda for law and policy on land governance, leadership is certainly needed, and good leaders "develop through a never ending process of self-study, education, training and experience" (Jago 1982:315). A transforming or transformative leader (Nelson Mandela inevitably comes to mind) can offer a moral exemplar with an inspiring mission and vision, while relationship-oriented leadership focusses more upon the relationships within the group and the overall effectiveness, well-being and satisfaction of its members. This chapter focuses now upon the role of professions and civil society organisations for collective leadership in land governance, and particular issues of education, training and knowledge transfer.

Collective leadership in land governance is needed, both from politicians and from the so-called professions of the land - lawyers, land surveyors, planners and valuers. Yet these groups have been deeply compromised by their associations with past colonial structures of power and knowledge. Unfortunately, the technical complexities of their work can be used to obscure issues, hide the power relationships underlying law, and confuse the public. Furthermore, as the management writer Donald Schon has claimed, research has been largely ineffectual in addressing major societal problems, since the 'high ground wherein practitioners make effective use of research-based theory and technique' can mean little to those who have to operate in the figurative 'swampy lowland where situations are confusing messes incapable of technical solution'. It is in the 'swamp where we find the problems of greatest human concern', the basic issues of shelter and survival (Schon 1983).

Lawyers and the rule of law

Law is increasingly realised as having a vital role in development generally and land reform in particular, by international financial institutions, aid agencies and academics. Since the decline of the 'law and development' movement, issues of poverty and land were researched by other disciplines within the social sciences, hence the title of Patrick McAuslan's 2003 book on the role of law in development - *Bringing the law back.* For de Soto lawyers and legal culture are a problem because of their in-built conservatism: 'their knee-jerk reaction to extralegal behaviour and to large-scale change is generally hostile' (De Soto 2000:210). Others have criticized the legal culture in developing countries:

> 'Generations of South lawyering elites (which provide a common law South archetype of excellence in lawyering) acquire specialist legal knowledges through Anglo-American circuits of 'higher' legal education. Versatile in dominant North common law discourse, they bring their formative, and formidable, knowledges of comparative precedent in the course of argumentation at home. They thus remain the carriers of contemporary metropolitan common law to South legislation and adjudication (Baxi 2003).'

> 'The blind and hegemonic push for uniformity around a non-African standard simply increases resentments which have been simmering since colonial times. We are dealing with a people who have grown suspicious of the purveyors of 'modernisation', which in their minds translates into 'Westernisation', a process not characterised in the past by too much respect for the African viewpoint.' (Ajibola and van Zyl 1988).

The very concept of a pro-poor land governance offers a challenge to legal culture. The existence of a pro-poor constitution in post-apartheid South Africa did not guarantee pro-poor judgments in its constitutional court (Dugard and Roux 2006). In Zambia land law reforms in 1995, while ostensibly designed to create more secure forms of land tenure for the poor, actually resulted in unprecedented dispossession and worsened economic inequality, by concentrating land titles in the hands of local Zambian elites and foreigners. The formal legal system in Africa still only reaches only a small section of the population, and has little relevance to the everyday lives of the poor majority.

According to AkaaGeer a transformation in legal thinking about land is needed, perhaps contributing to the shaping of a distinctive African jurisprudence. The concept of transformative constitutionalism in post-1994 South Africa has been advocated as an approach to social transformation through law-grounded processes (Klare 1998). The post-Mabo recognition that pre-existing indigenous land rights have not been extinguished by the colonial process, and can be revived, has led Zimbabwean academics to argue that land redistribution can be justified through a *humwe* doctrine of consent, sanctioning a 'rejection of private property rights that were forcibly or immorally instituted under the shield of colonialism' (Chigara 2004: 31). The rise of human rights as a framework for holding states more accountable to their citizens has yet to be better absorbed within the legal culture, leaving plenty of scope for leadership in this complex area of law.

Land surveyors

Land surveyors have a key role in the organisation of land for development, and in the past were associated with the taking of land from indigenous occupiers through the 'power of the map'. It was the colonialists' land surveying profession that demarcated the precise boundaries of landed property. A Ndebele chief in Southern Rhodesia as early as 1887 expressed the conflict between African and European concepts of land in these words:

> 'In olden times ...we never talked about boundary lines... It is only now they [the colonisers] talk about boundaries' (quoted in Hughes 2006:7).

The Dutch at the Cape after 1653 introduced Roman-Dutch legal concepts of private property, conferring absolute right of ownership (*dominium*), and title transfer deeds were officially registered in a public deeds registry, offering minimal opportunity for legal challenge. British colonial surveyors, setting out to map and divide up its new colonies and protectorates in Africa, imported their so-called 'systematic survey' methods through the Torrens system of survey and registration, with its origins in the settler colony of South Australia (Stone and Stein 1991). A systematic central record of land rights, locating fixed boundaries on a map base, seemed to offer the promise (or illusion) of the 'continuous finality of the register'. Such documentation builds a public memory that permits society to engage in activities such as: identifying and gaining access to information about individuals, their assets, their titles, rights, charges and obligations; establishing the limits of liability for businesses; knowing an asset's previous economic situation; assuring protection of third parties; and quantifying and valuing assets and rights.

Under the neo-liberal market-based approach, the state protects the security of private property title as a source of capital, supported by land surveyors and valuers who define property parcels and appraise their value for mortgage or hypothecation purposes. Transnational capital flows allow large tracts of land to be transferred to absentee legal entities, a process which started in the colonial period and continues today with large-scale land acquisitions (called 'land grabbing' by their opponents). World Bank land titling programmes in Africa have attempted comprehensive land titling, but governments have come to recognise the costs and difficulties, preferring state land registration on demand as land parcels come forward (sometimes called 'sporadic registration'). Recent innovatory approaches have attempted to combine effective land records with local community control, bringing land registration closer to the people on the ground. An alternative to formal registration of individual rights is the registration of collective or common property rights, potentially a simpler, cheaper and more equitable process. Practices of 'counter-mapping' have emerged as attempts to reclaim communal value systems hitherto disavowed by state institutions, and can be used as a basis of local negotiations with the state (Durand-Lasserve and Royston 2002). These require new working methods for the land surveying profession, which fortunately can be facilitated by advances in surveying technology.

The planners

Town planning, the planning and regulation of land use, was a relatively late arrival as an activity for land governance activity, being about a century old, and it was responsible for applying on the ground the racial segregation and separate development policies most notoriously articulated in South Africa under *apartheid*. The early advocates of town planning believed that it offered a modern approach to colonial management, and British design concepts of the garden city – low-density, self-contained residential neighbourhoods, with most houses on their own plots with gardens - were used in much African urban planning. Town planning legislation proved, however, to be an inadequate technical response to massive pressure for social and political change, and was recognized by its law-makers even at the time as a policy of expediency. Its legacies still survive in the physical landscape of African cities, right down to the level of the individual land parcel and building structures.

The profession of planning has undergone much change. While still involved in the detail of regulating development and use of land, a wider framework for future spatial development is now expected which incorporates such aspects as environmental sustainability. Lack of capacity means that probably most new development in Africa takes place without permission, especially in the unplanned peri-urban areas, which makes the owners vulnerable to bribery and extortion. Town planning seems stuck in the traditions and techniques of colonial planning, existing to assist with government land development, but with little public involvement, or even interest by local politicians. It needs to decolonise its thinking - 'unlearning privilege' - and adapt to the new pressures on land and land use. The reform of planning law and regulations, and changes to the remit of the planning profession, that address the realities of African urban development are overdue, although comprehensive, reform may be less desirable or achievable than incremental approaches (Berrisford 2011).

Bottom up land governance?

In the 1990s what has been called the 'NGO revolution' saw new social movements emerging on a global scale, as weak state institutions and pressures for states to shrink expanded the role for alternative civil society institutions (Keck and Sikkink 1998). The advent of the Millennium Development Goals after 2000, and the subsequent Millennium Campaign, have provided a new platform for NGOs to press their governments for greater accountability, transparency and the legal empowerment of the poor.

While even the expanded approach to human rights does not confer any express right of access to land, the state can do much to help its citizens, by providing plots on state land for home-ownership by the poor, offering low-interest loans, and withholding from summary forced evictions (UN-HABITAT 2009). Where land remains a primary means of generating a livelihood, and the main element in household wealth, the way land rights are defined and structured has far-reaching social and economic effects. The UN-Habitat Global Campaign for Secure Tenure encourages the progressive regularisation of unauthorised and informal settlements through changes in legal frameworks, policies and standards. With full land titling seen as too complex and expensive, incremental tenure regularisation can be linked to the physical upgrading of plots and infrastructure.

Women are often particularly disadvantaged and vulnerable in land matters, holding fewer assets and less access to resources. In many African countries the proportion of female-headed households has grown, as a result of such factors as male migration, male deaths in conflicts, unpartnered adolescent fertility and family disruption (IFAD 2008). Notwithstanding constitutional guarantees of women's property rights in many countries, property settlements often disinherit and impoverish women, for example after divorce or death of spouse. International bodies, such as the Huairou Commission, the Housing and Land Rights Network, and the GLTN, are promoting women's property rights, but there is little systematic information on better legal instruments (the so-called 'gendered land tools') other than a general support for flexible tenure types (Munyoni 2003).

For most of the poor, the state is either irrelevant or an unwelcome interference with their daily life. It creates illegality, and may only refrain from harassing them because of its inertia and inefficiency, but they remain at risk of eviction if they are settled on land without permission from the state or private landowners. Their temporary structures reflect not just their poverty and limited access to building materials, but also the ever-present threat of demolition and eviction. Official disapproval and harassment of the poor, problematised as squatters and slum-dwellers, has deep roots in the colonial experience, and has only begun to moderate in recent years. A so-called 'cadastral politics' is emerging through practices of 'counter-mapping', which attempt to record uses of land by groups that have not been recognised by state institutions. One achievement of the new thinking about tenure security has been to soften official hostility to 'squatter' settlements, and to acknowledge the rights of the poor to secure tenure. Governments have come to recognise the political costs of squatter eviction, and are more willing to respond to pressure exerted by the poor. Tenure reform allows a formalising of customary or community land arrangements, and the status of such land, with its traditional social importance, needs protecting if it is not to be eroded and converted into a tradable commodity.

New styles of land rights advocacy and dispute resolution have emerged, with community-based organisations trying to keep control of land use and allocation outside the planning and property system offered by the state. Informal property rules devised in squatter settlements may provide the poor with practical recourse to protect their possessory title. Generally, however, the poor are understandably pre-occupied with day-to-day existence, rather than engaging in time-consuming solidarity activity, and outside elites can manipulate processes for their own advantage.

Land law reform needs to be applied on the ground, recognising the complexities of local situations. Special courts and tribunals, hybrid forms of judicial administration, can be created alongside the main court system to deal with the intricacies and factual evidence involved in land disputes. Such transplanted forms of bureaucracy, usually held close to where the disputes arise, may be quicker and cheaper than the courts, addressing factual rather than legal issues, with determinations made by professionals in land matters. They have potential to innovate, help protect the poor from arbitrary eviction, and allow the recognition of local communal rights, but have also been criticized for arbitrary decisions, even (in one author's view) absurdity (Werbner 1982: 131).

Land for housing may be provided through community self-help movements, who buy and subdivide land for sale to their members, using collective funds raised through subscription. Incremental tenure upgrading can include such measures as: registering all plots and occupiers, providing basic services, resolving land disputes, and allocating property rights to recognised claimants. A community may keep its own registers of rights, applying hybrid law through some form of local court or tribunal, and indeed maintain its boundaries against outside forces by such practices as beating the bounds, where the whole community turns out to re-assert boundaries and break down any unsanctioned land enclosure.

The challenges for land governance in Africa today require a re-envisioning of professional roles, especially a greater recognition of the importance of local community-based organisations. The practicalities include building stakeholder relationships, dispute resolution methods and record-keeping systems. The traditional professional and technical skills of surveyors, planners and lawyers need to be supplemented by more political skills of mediation, dispute resolution and local coalition-building. Such new approaches develop through reflective practice, but also through education and capacity-building measures. The academic community has a responsibility for review and revision of its educational programmes for professional training, and teaching materials need designing for new approaches, such as the World Bank's Rule of Law in Africa publishing project (Home 2012). The continued growth of professional doctorate programmes as alternatives to the traditional PhD can offer a model linking academic to professional practice which is particularly relevant to development issues. Cross-disciplinary collaborative research in universities can offer new perspectives. For instance, the inclusion of law within the social sciences in universities has stimulated new areas of academic investigation, and traditional legal scholarship (jurisprudence and 'black letter law') can be enriched by other approaches such as socio-legal studies, empirical legal studies, critical legal geography, legal history and legal anthropology. Thus one finds pluralism existing not only within legal systems, but also within the academy.

The networks of knowledge - academic and professional, national and international - are important arenas for new thinking to develop and circulate. Worth mentioning are the International Federation of Surveyors (FIG), the African Real Estate Society (AFRES), the Association of African Planning Schools (AAPS), the various Commonwealth Associations such as the Commonwealth Association of Planners (CAP) and Commonwealth Association of Surveyors and Land Economists (CASLE), as well as networks associated with the United Nations such as UN-Habitat's Global Land Tools Network. Among the international networks of NGOs one can mention the Habitat International Coalition, Housing and Land Rights Network, Cities Alliance (with its Cities Without Slums action plan), and the emerging coalition against land grabbing. In Africa the 'tyranny of distance' and the costs involved have hindered opportunities for networks to get together, but ever-easier electronic communication and social networking are transforming the situation.

Another important source of new approaches is the diaspora of African academics and professionals, both within Africa and beyond, who can contribute new approaches from outside yet within a shared professional perspective. Africa has lost many skilled professionals to the diaspora, but often they still wish to contribute their knowledge and expertise in their places of origin, provided that facilitating mechanisms can be found. Examples of such mechanisms include the initiatives of the African Community Development Foundation and Voluntary Service Overseas in piloting a Diaspora Development Volunteer programme in Kenya; individual higher education institutions have created travel scholarships to allow visits by diaspora professionals; organisations like the Malawi Women's Association seek to connect diaspora professionals and entrepreneurs with their countries of origin.

Conclusion

Although many sub-Saharan African countries since independence have undertaken land law reform, high aspirations have been frustrated by poor achievements. A modernizing state needs to promote better relations between poor people and the state, assessing the poverty impact of public policies, strengthening poor people's assets and capabilities, and combating gender inequity and children's vulnerability. The idea of a pro-poor land governance should mean easier access to land for the landless, and protection against arbitrary forced eviction.

Delivery of land to the poor may come from land held in private, state or communal ownership, typically through confirmation of effective occupation or possessory title, legal recognition through adjudication processes, and protection from arbitrary forced eviction. State and society are thus involved in a continuing struggle over their respective roles and entitlements. Attempts to unscramble complex and discriminatory laws often only replace them with yet more complex ones, while resource and capacity constraints hold back much-needed improvements.

Achieving better land governance is a long process, and requires a national conversation. Without more participatory local strategies, the management of land, that most basic resource of the modern territorial nation-state, will not meet the needs of 'the poor'.

References

Abramson, A. & Theodossopoulos, D. eds. 2000. *Land, Law and Environment.* London: Pluto Press.

Ajibola, B & van Zyl, D. eds. 1988. *The Judiciary in Africa.* Johannesburg: Juta Press.

Allen, T. 2000. *The Right to Property in Commonwealth Jurisdictions.* Cambridge: University Press 83.

Baxi, U. 2003. Global Development and Impoverishment. In P. Cane and M.Tushnet, (eds), *Oxford Handbook of Legal Studies.* Oxford: University Press.

Berrisford, S. 2011. Revising Spatial Planning Legislation in Zambia: A Case Study. *Urban Forum,* 22:229–245.

Bohannan, P. 1973. *'Land', 'Tenure' and Land-Tenure.* Madison: Land Institute.

Chan, T.M. 2004. The Richtersveld Challenge: South Africa Finally Adopts Aboriginal Title. In R. Hitchcock & D.Vinding, (eds), *Indigenous People's Rights in Southern Africa.* Copenhagen: International Work Group for Indigenous Affairs.

Chanock, M.J. 1985. *Law, Custom and Social Order.* Cambridge: University Press

Chigara, B. 2004. *Land Reform Policy.* Aldershot: Ashgate.

Cincotta, R. 2003. *The Security Demographic.* New York: *Population Action.*

Coldham, S. 1978. The effect of registration of title upon customary land rights in Kenya *Journal of African Law 22.*

De Soto, H. 2000. *The Mystery of Capital.* London: Black Swan.

Home, R.K. & Lim, H. eds, 2004. *Demystifying the Mystery of Capital: Land Titling and Peri-Urban Development in Africa and the Caribbean.* London: Cavendish.

Department for International Development and Swiss Agency for Development and Cooperation. 2008. *Operational Guide for the Making Markets Work for the Poor Approach.* London: DFID.

Dugard, J. & Roux, T. 2006. The Record of the South African Constitutional Court in Providing An Institutional Voice for the Poor. In R. Gargarella (ed.), *Courts and Social Transformation in the new Democracies.* Aldershot: Ashgate. 107

Durand-Lasserve, A. & Royston, L. eds. 2002. *Holding their ground.* London: Earthscan.

Fitzpatrick, P. 1992. *The mythology of modern law*. London: Routledge

Glenn, H.P. 2004. *Legal Traditions of the World: Sustainable Diversity in Law.* Oxford: University Press.

Home, R.K. 2013. *Of Planting and Planning: The making of British colonial cities,* 2nd edition. London: Routledge.

Home, R.K., ed. 2012. *Essays in African Land Law* and *Local Case studies in African Land Law.* Pretoria: University Law Press.

IFAD. 2008. The issue of poverty among female-headed households in Africa. Online: www.ifad.org/gender/learning/challenges/women

Hailey, L. 1956. *African Survey.* London: HMSO, pp.759-771.

Hall, B. 1964 *Tell Me, Josephine*, London: Andre Deutsch, p.135.

Swanson, M.W. 1976. The Durban System: Roots of Urban Apartheid in Colonial Natal. *African Studies,* 2: 159-76.

Hindson, D. & McCarthy, J. eds. 1994. *Here To Stay*. Daldridge, South Africa: Indicator Press.

Hughes, D. 2006. *From Enslavement to Environmentalism: Politics on a Southern African Frontier.* Seattle: University of Washington Press.

Iliffe, J. 1987. *The African Poor: A History.* Cambridge: University Press.

Jago, A.G. 1982. Leadership: Perspectives in theory and research. *Management Science,* 28(3): 315-336.

Keck, M. & Sikkink, K. eds. 1998. *Beyond Borders.* Ithaca: Cornell.

Kenya Government. 2011. *Land Policy.* Nairobi: Government Press.

Klare, K. 1998. Legal culture and Transformative Constitutionalism. *South African Journal of Human Rights,* 14: 146 – 188.

Lindley, M.F. 1926. *The Acquisition and Government of Backward Territory in International Law.*London: Longman Green.

Lugard, L. 1922. *The Dual Mandate in British Tropical Africa.* London: Frank Cass (reprint).

McAuslan, P. 2003. *Bringing the Law Back In: Essays in Land, Law and Development*. Aldershot: Ashgate.

Macpherson, C.B. 1962. *The Theory of Possessive Individualism.* Oxford University Press.

Manji, A. 2012. *The Politics of Land Reform in Africa: From Communal Tenure to Free Markets*. London: Zed Books.

Meek, C.K. 1949. *Land Law and Custom in the Colonies.* New York: Oxford University Press.

Munyoni. L.M, ed. 2003. *Women and Land in Africa.* London: Zed Books.

Njoh, A. 2011. Indigenous peoples and ancestral lands: Implications of the Bakweri case in Cameroon. In R. Home (ed), *Themes in African Land Law.* Pretoria: University Law Press: 69-90.

Ntsebeza, L. & Hall, R. eds. 2007. *The Land Question in South Africa: The Challenge of Transformation and Redistribution.* Cape Town: HSRC Press.

Platteau, JP. 1996. The evolutionary theory of land rights as applied to Sub-Saharan Africa. *Development and Change,* 27.

Russell, P.H. 2005. *Recognizing Aboriginal Title*. Toronto: University Press.

United Nations 2007. *Declaration on Rights of Indigenous People.* New York: UN.

SADC 2010. *Framework and Guidelines on land policy in Africa.* Banjul, Gambia: AU.

Schon, D. 1983. *The Reflective Practitioner*. New York: Basic Books.

Simpson, J.R. 1976. *Land Registration.* Cambridge: University Press.

Smith, D.M. ed. 1992. *The Apartheid City and Beyond: urbanization and social change in South Africa* London: Routledge & Witwatersrand University Press.

Stone, M.A. & Stein, R. 1991. *Torrens title.* London: Butterworths.

Toulmin, C. & Quan, J. eds. 2000. *Evolving land rights, policy and tenure in Africa* London: IIED & NRI.

United Nations 2008. *UN Approach to Rule of Law Assistance.* New York: UN.

UN-HABITAT 2009. *The Rights to Adequate Housing.* Nairobi: UN-Habitat.

UN-HABITAT 2007. *Forced Evictions: Towards Solutions?* Nairobi: UN-Habitat.

Wanjala, S.C. 2000. *Essays on land law: the reform debate in Kenya.* Nairobi: Oxford University Press.

Werbner, R.P. ed. 1982. *Land Reform in the Making.* London: International Institute.

Economic and Institutional Determinants of Foreign Land Acquisition in Africa

An empirical analysis

Ayodele Odusola

Introduction

Foreign land acquisition in Africa is receiving an increasing attention among policymakers, the public and media. This is due to the unprecedentedly rising wave and intensity of agricultural land investment over the past decade. For instance, as at 2012, out of the 1,217 publicly reported deals, 62 per cent took place in the continent. This translates to 56.2 million hectares for Africa, 17.7 million for Asia and 7 million hectares for Latin America. This corresponds to 4.8 percent of Africa's total agricultural areas compared to 1.1 per cent and 1.2 percent for Asia and Latin America respectively. The volume of foreign land acquired in Africa is almost equivalent to landmass of Madagascar or Kenya or Botswana. Out of 11 countries accounting for 70 percent of the targeted lands, 7 are from Africa. Besides, out of 32 countries (each with more than 3 million ha of arable land available) that account for more than 90 per cent of available land - 16 are from Africa, 8 in Latin America, 3 in Eastern Europe and Central Asia, and 5 in the rest of the world (Bruinsma 2009; Anseeuw et al 2012 and Nkonya et al 2012).

The unequal global distribution of arable land plays an important role in shaping this trend. While possibility of agricultural land expansion is very limited in developed countries, about 90 percent of the remaining 1.8 billion ha of arable land is in developing countries – mostly in Sub-

Saharan Africa and Latin America. Particularly, 60 per cent of arable land remains unused in Africa. In contrast, regions such as South Asia and Near East and North Africa have virtually run out of arable land and it is rare in developed regions.

Several factors account for the surge in African land from both foreign and domestic dimensions. Economic, institutional and political stakes are at play. From the external side, the recent recurring food and fuel price hikes are important drivers. To address this, countries want to reduce import cost of food and fuel and ensure future security of these commodities. Outsourcing of food and fuel production has become an important investment policy and national food strategy in many developed and emerging economies facing serious challenges in expanding their arable land and the associated water requirement. The growing reserves of some sovereign wealth funds make speculative investment in land rife while other use land as an alternative investment to avoid the global financial crisis. From the African side, abundant under-utilised arable land and water resources for irrigation, low input cost, low productivity, unclear land titles, and weak governance and related institutional challenges are key factors making land grab very attractive in the continent. A few of the countries have large arable land resources which cannot be utilised because of size relative to what is needed, production capacity and financial constraints to provide the needed agricultural infrastructure and services.

The rising trend and intensity of large scale land acquisition in Africa has been well documented. Most of the discussion has been based on qualitative analysis. However, there has been limited quantitative analysis of the determinants of land deal in Africa. The knowledge about the socio-economic and institutional determinants of land grabs in Africa is scanty and is not yet fully understood. This chapter aims at bridging this knowledge gap by providing greater clarity on the factors driving large scale land investment in Africa. To achieve the objective, the chapter has been structured into five parts. Following the introduction is section two that examines the overview of large scale land acquisition in Africa. Some reflections on economic and institutional determinants of land grab are examined in part three while section four delves into modeling economic and institutional determinants of land grab demand an analysis of results. Section five concludes the chapter.

Overview of land grab in Africa

Over the last four decades, land area used for agricultural production has been rising globally. For instance, the global area used for crops increased by 187 million ha between 1967 and 2005. The increase occurred mainly in developing countries (227 million ha) while it decreased by 40 million ha in developed countries. The decrease in developed countries was as result of the continuous growth of yields and the deceleration of agricultural commodity demand (Gorgen *et al* 2009). The recent food crisis and growing demand for biofuel appear to have changed the trend of demand for agricultural products in the past decade.

A quick review of the existing literature on this issue confirms the unprecedented volume and intensity of land acquisition in Africa. For instance, Friis and Reenberg (2010) provide a snapshot of the media reports on Africa over the period 2008–2010 and conclude that between 51 and 63 million hectares (ha) were involved in land acquisition in the continent. The documentation by Deininger *et al* (2011) over 2008 and 2009 puts the global acquisition at about 56.6 million ha with about 40 million ha in Africa (Friis and Reenberg 2010). The findings from Oxfam (2011) using a combination of media and triangulation sources put it 227 million ha globally over the period 2001–2010 - about 67 million ha have been cross-checked with respective governments and other actors. Several factors explain the differences in figures, including time of coverage, method of inventory and level of coverage[1] As articulated in Odusola (2012), irrespective of the various methods used by the numerous authors for such countries as Ethiopia, Madagascar and Mozambique, the media figures are substantially higher than the research-based values. This, however, does not invalidate the intensity of land grab in the continent.

Evidence from Land Matrix Database[2], which has gone through an error-checking process of triangulation and covers 200 million ha with 2,200 deals between 2000 and early 2012, provides some illumination on the issue. Unlike most other sources that do not consider any deal less than 1000 hectares, this covers 200 hectares and above per deal. An important aspect of land deal is land concentration - the size of single land acquisitions approved to individual investor. Based on the five countries studied by Cotula *et al* (2009), it ranges from 452,000 ha in Madagascar to 100,000 ha in Mali (Table 1). Cotula (2012) also reveals that the average sizes of projects above 1,000 ha are much smaller than what is suggested by media reports. Contrary to a mean ranging between 111,000 ha and 135,000 ha for Ethiopia and of about 186,000 ha for Mali from the media reports, the research based findings put it at 7,500 ha for Ethiopia[3] and 22,000 ha for Mali. Evidence from the top targeted countries also reveals that the average land deal ranges from 40,951 ha in India to 217, 968 ha (Sudan), 252,601 ha (Zambia) and 805,187 ha (DRC) (Anseeuw, *et al* 2012). Other countries with high average land deals include Indonesia and Malaysia.

The rising trend of land acquisition at the provincial levels (e.g. Mozambique and Ethiopia) is another issue. The number of approved land leases in Manica Province of Mozambique alone rose from just 562 ha in 2007 to 21,334 ha in 2008, 58,880 ha in 2009 and by January 2010 applications for 367,165 ha were pending (Cotula 2012). Land, being the major asset of rural dwellers and core of their likelihoods, calls for caution for this phenomenon not to lead to intense vulnerability, poverty and inequality.

When land acquisition for only agriculture is considered, a similar trend is also observed. For instance, the evidence from above is further supported by the finding from Anseeuw *et al* (2012), which concludes that Africa appears to be the main target of the land rush because of the 1,217 publicly reported deals, 62 percent of the projects took place in the continent. This translates to 56.2 million hectares for Africa, 17.7 million for Asia and 7 million hectares for Latin America (Figure 1). It represents 4.8 percent of Africa's total agricultural areas compared to 1.2 percent and 1.1 percent for Latin America and Asia respectively (Ibid).

Odusola (2014 a) provides a detailed analysis of the relative share of land grab to each of the African countries. For instance, he posits that this corresponds to about a quarter of DRC landmass or almost the size of Botswana or Kenya or Madagascar landmass. It is twice the size of Burkina Faso, ten times that of Togo and twenty times that of Guinea Bissau or Equatorial Guinea. Interestingly, the size of land acquisition between 2008 and 2010 is almost equivalent to the combined size of some 18 African countries in terms of surface land area.[4]

Figure 1: Regional distribution of acquired agricultural land (2000 - early 2012) in million hectares

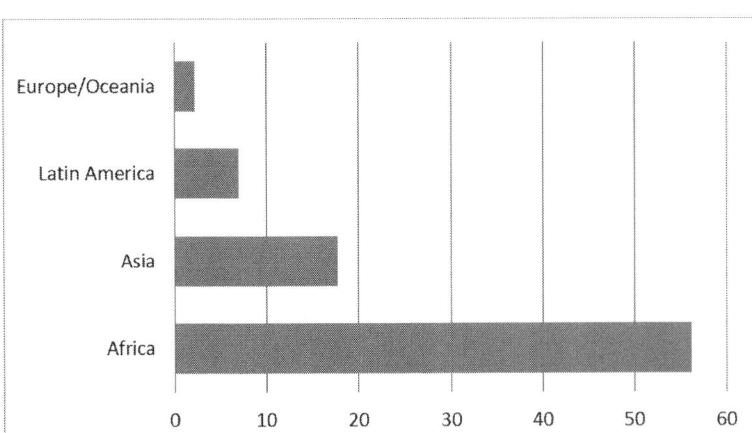

By Source: Compiled and computed by the author from Anseeuw *et al* (2012).

Although a large number of countries (84) are targeted by foreign investors for agricultural purposes, only 11 of them account for 70 percent of the targeted surface. Among the 11, countries 7 are from African (Sudan, Mozambique, Tanzania, Ethiopia, Madagascar, Zambia and DRC). Other countries are Philippines, Brazil, Pakistan and Indonesia[5]. The lands of these African countries, among others, are in hot demand and therefore experienced largest pressures both in terms of volume of hectares and number of deals. Figure 2 provides a graphical view of the most targeted twenty countries in Africa. Countries where over one million hectares of land had been acquired are Sudan, Ethiopia, Madagascar, Mozambique, Tanzania, Sierra Leone and Benin.

Several factors explain the intensity of land grab in Africa. The most important factor is availability of unused arable land. Based on estimation from Fischer *et al* (2002), out of 2.8 billion ha potential arable land in developing countries, only 970 million ha was being utilized. The literature is replete with the evidence that South America and Sub-Saharan Africa account for 90 per cent of the potential available land for crop production globally with seven countries (Brazil, Democratic Republic of the Congo, Angola, Sudan, Argentina, Colombia and Bolivia) accounting for 50 per cent of the potential arable land, which is estimated to be 1.8 billion ha (Gorgen *et al* 2009). Given the concentration of the un-utilised arable land in these two regions, the urge for food and fuel security, with associated price incentives for agricultural commodities, could play an important role in the rising demand for land in Africa.

Figure 2: Most targeted twenty African countries as at 2012

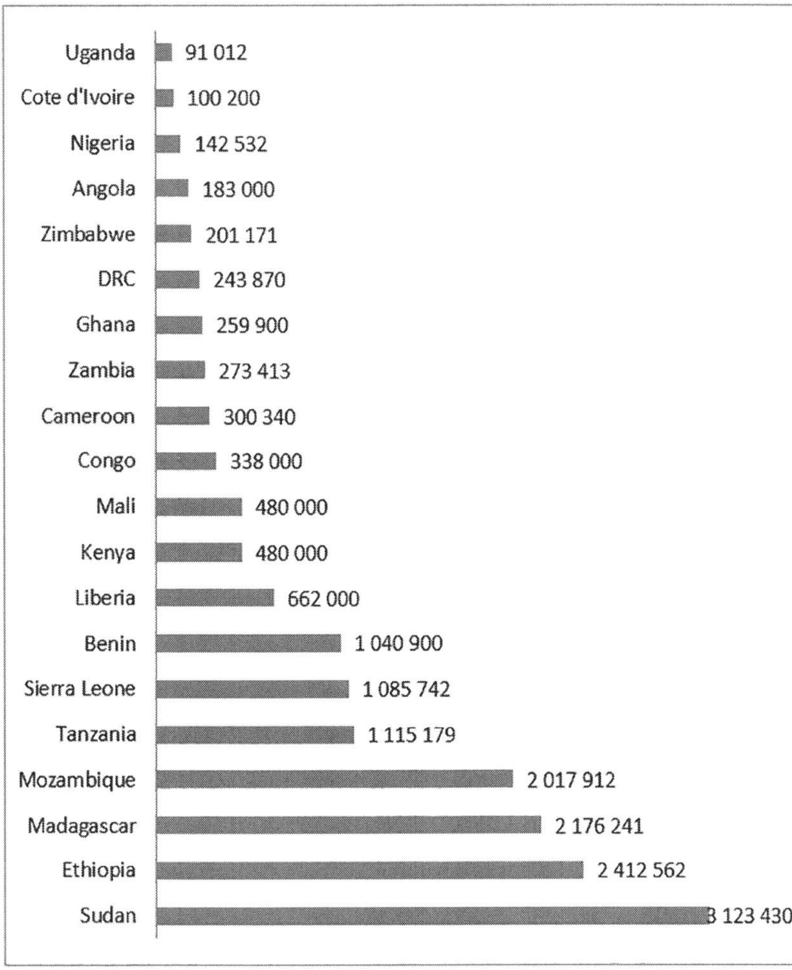

Source: Author's computation and compilation from Anseeuw *et al* (2012).

Analysis of the top ten land acquirers (including food production, agri-fuel production, mineral extraction, conservation and tourism) reveals USA, Malaysia, India and UK as the largest acquirers (Figure 3). About 10 percent of investors account for 68 percent of the acquired lands (Land Matrix 2012). However, when only agricultural land is considered, the role of China became more pronounced as the lead actor. Countries such as USA, UK, Malaysia, South Korea, Saudi Arabia, Sweden, South Africa, Qatar,

Norway and Singapore are among the leading thirteen acquiring nations (Anseeuw *et al* 2012). While the dominance of the North still holds sways, the role of emerging countries is becoming more entrenched especially some of the BRICS countries (China, India and South Africa). This, to a large extent, confirms the pronounced agitation about the dominance of China and the Gulf State (especially Saudi Arabia and Qatar) in formal land acquisition in Africa.

An important feature of land grab is the heterogeneity of investors, which if well managed could be an opportunity for the continent. A copious review of the Land Matrix data brings to the fore four different types of investors, namely, private companies, public or state owned enterprises; investment funds and private-public partnerships. Private companies are dominant with 442 deals and 30.3 million ha – representing two-thirds of the cumulative land acquired. The state-owned agencies comprise 172 deals and 11.5 million ha – representing a quarter of the affected land. Investment funds have 32 deals and 3.3 ha while the private-public partnerships record 12 deals and 0.6 million ha. Analysis from Anseeuw *et al* (2012) reveals that investors from North America, Europe, Asia and the Gulf States are almost exclusively private companies.

Perhaps due to the heated debate about land grab globally, large scale land acquisition is taking a new dimension. For instance, two African countries have emerged as strategic transit countries - South Africa and Mauritius (IIED 2012). Foreign investors are leveraging South Africa's proximity, knowledge and experience in African agriculture and commercial farming. Many South African companies have facilitated commercial farming on behalf of foreign investors (e.g. those with UK origin; partnership with Chinese origin is emerging) in countries such as Mozambique, Swaziland, Malawi, Tanzania and Zambia. As a result of good tax system and the existence of several bilateral investment treaties with many African countries which could protect foreigners' investments, some foreign investors (especially from Australian, UK and Singaporean origins) (Cotula 2012) prefer to reach out to other countries through Mauritius.

Most databases and studies focus on direct land acquisition for greenfield investments with limited attention on activities such as taking over the management of existing farms previously or currently run by government establishments; including rehabilitation of existing irrigation and related infrastructure as well as equity participation in existing agribusinesses. Richardson (2010) reviews the strategy of a South African sugar company in the takeover of many existing ventures and equity participation in a number of Southern African countries over the past two decades. In addition, many foreign investors now operate through nationally incorporated subsidiaries – a phenomenon that blurs the borderline between national and foreign investments.

Figure 3: Top 10 land acquirers (2000-April 2012) by million hectares

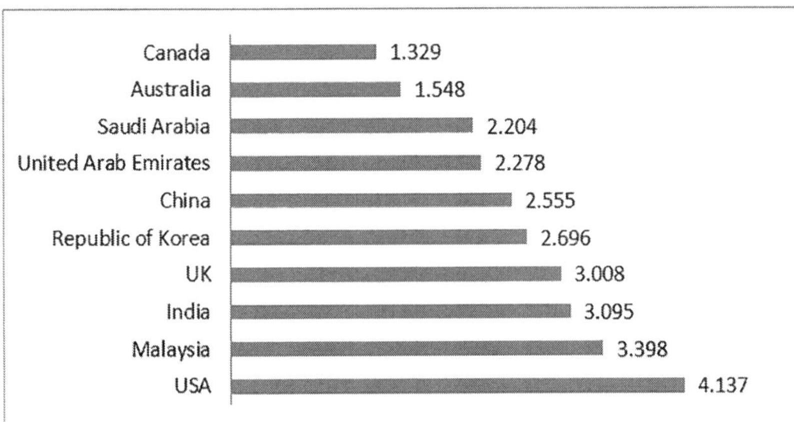

Source: Author's computation and compilation from Anseeuw *et al* (2012).

Table 1: Approved land for investors' claim (2004 to early 2009)

	Ethiopia	Ghana	Madagascar	Mali	Sudan	Total
Total Land allocated (ha)	602,760*	452,000*	803,414*	162,850*	471,660*	2,492,684*
No of projects approved (over 1000 ha)	157	3*	6*	7*	11*	184*
Largest land allocation (ha)	150,000	400,000	452,000	100,000	109,200	
Total investment commitments (US$)	78,563,023*	30,000,000*	79,829,524*	291,988,688*	439,600,000*	919,981,235*

Source: Cotula, Vermeulen, Leonard and Keeley (2009).

Note: * indicates incomplete data.

Large-scale lands acquired are used for multidimensional purposes. Of the projects with commodity data, 37 percent focus on food crops, 21 percent on industrial or cash crops, and 21 percent on biofuels, with the rest distributed among conservation or game reserves, livestock, and plantation forestry. The scale of investors' ambition is huge, with a median project size of 40,000 ha (Deininger 2011). It is important to note that foreign investors target land with high yield gaps, good accessibility and considerable population densities. Other drivers, from the African side, which will be discussed in the subsequent section of this chapter, are access to water and some institutional factors such as property rights.

From the acquirers' side, important factors boosting demand for large scale land acquisition include a shortage of fertile land due to unfavourable climate conditions or population growth on the one hand and sufficient financial status of land acquirers. Good examples of countries with substantial land deals are Saudi Arabia, Qatar, UAE (Gulf States) and China, South Korea, and India (Asia). In the analysis of Europe's global land demand, Lugschitz, *et al* (2011) explain that Europe's lifestyle is dependent on how foreign land resources can be assessed for outsourcing of production processes. It concludes that land demand is a function of countries' high level of consumption (e.g. the EU-15, Russia and CIS, and USA) and countries with elevated population (e.g. China and India). The authors conclude that outsourcing agricultural production (or demand for foreign land) is pronounced in countries with very low land productivity dominated by grassy landscapes and savannahs which are often being farmed very extensively (e.g. USA, EU-27, Japan, China and India). In addition to the price incentives associated with outsourcing of production in the context of rising prices of agricultural commodities, there is also the demand for natural resources especially in Sub-Saharan Africa, Latin America and the Caribbean (Gorgen *et al* 2009).

Some reflections on economic and institutional determinants of land grab in Africa

The demand for land is a derived one. People demand for land for what comes from it in terms of food, raw materials for industrial production and residential needs. To some extent, it is held as a portfolio asset and also to hedge against inflation. As these needs become intense, the demand for land also builds up. For instance, the recent recurring food price hikes are a manifestation of an excess demand for food over its supply. The world population is expected to rise from 7.2 billion in 2013 by 1.0 billion over the next 12 years and reach 9.6 billion by 2050 (UN 2013). If the current consumption pattern of industrialized countries is maintained, the 9.6 billion people in 2050 will be consuming at the rate of 12.0 billion people (IFPRI *et al* 2012:3) – a phenomenon that will lead to a substantial rise in the demand for food. The food and nutritional requirements of the world population have been projected by FAO to raise global current food production by 70 per cent and that of the developing countries by 100 per cent (Bruinsma 2009).

The use of land intensification of land use, through biotechnology, which has enhanced agricultural yields over the past decades have started to lose ground to public opposition to genetically modified food production. The growing use of biofuel as a substitute to fossil fuel has also added industrial demand in agricultural markets. Woodhouse and Ganho (2011) explain the rising demand for foreign land to be driven by the rising insecurity of energy and food supply and concomitant volatility in energy and food commodity prices. FAO (2009) sees the combination of environmental and security concerns which have diverted agricultural outputs from food to biofuel production as the principal driving force for land acquisition in Africa. Meeting the food security concern is an important factor in explaining land demand in foreign countries. For instance, the Saudi Arabia's 'Agro Globe 7x7' scheme which is targeting 7 million tons of rice in Africa has designated 70 per cent of the products for export to the investing country (GRAIN 2010).

Some other economic factors play a significant role in the demand for agricultural land. A decomposition of the global growth in crop production between 1961 and 2005 shows yield growth and crop intensification outweigh arable land expansion. For instance, the decomposition reveals that 77 per cent of the growth came from yield growth, 9 per cent from crop intensification, and 14 per cent from the expansion of arable land area (Bruinsma, 2009). Over this period in Sub-Sahara Africa, crop yield accounted for 38 percent of output growth and this is expected to rise to 69 per cent in the future. Licker *et al* (2010) also finds that although yield gap varies considerably by crops: yield gap for maize (63 percent), rice (65 percent) and wheat (52 percent), it is extremely larger in Africa relative to North America (15 percent, 12 percent and 39 percent) and Western Europe (32 percent, 24 percent and 12 percent). Countries pushing for agricultural outsourcing are therefore competing to take advantage of this yield gap in Africa.

Deininger and Byerlee (2011) also provide some illumination on the role of yield gaps in the establishment of large farms in land abundant countries. Of all the sub-regions of the world, only Oceania is close to realising its potential, followed closely by North America (0.89), Europe (0.81), and South America (0.65). Sub-Saharan Africa, however, is quite far from its potential – it realizes only 20 percent of potential yields. The authors also examined the non-forested uncultivated area suitable for rain fed cultivation and found 446, 306 and 198 million ha for population density cut-offs of 25, 10, and 5 persons per km^2 respectively. The total non-cultivated area suitable for rain fed cultivation is highest in Africa (202, 128, and 68 million ha) corresponding to 45, 42, and 34 percent of the total, respectively. This is followed by Latin America. Also of the 32 countries (each with more than 3 million ha of arable land available) that account for more than 90 per cent of total global available land, 50 per cent are from Africa. Only 25 per cent is from Latin America, 9.4 per cent from Eastern Europe and Central Asia, and 15.3 per cent from the rest of the world. Availability of yield gap and uncultivated arable land is one of the drivers of foreign demand for agricultural land in Africa. Nkonya *et al* (2012) also emphasize land suitability for foreign countries' crops of interest and specie abundance as one of the significant factors for land demand. The findings from Arezki *et al* (2011), using gravity a model, also underscore the role of agro-ecological suitability in explaining both demand and actual implementation of land deals.

Figure 4 provides additional insight into the yield gap. In spite of abundant fertile arable land, Sub-Saharan Africa recorded the least cereal yield across all the regions. This is a clear indication of very high yield gap in Sub-Sahara Africa relative to other regions. Regions with large yield gaps often experience substantial pressures for land demand. This, to a large extent, explains the unprecedented demand for the continent's land from foreign investors.

Figure 4: Cereal yield (kg per hectare) across world regions, 1961-2011

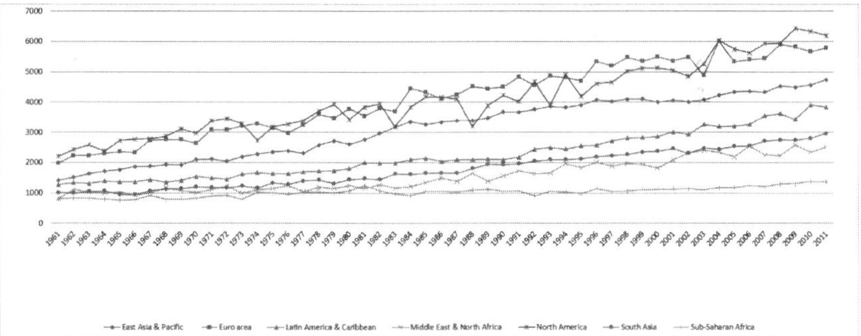

Source: Author's computation from http://data.worldbank.org/indicator/AG.YLD.CREL.KG [Accessed, July 2013].

Fertilizer is an important input into yield expansion by adding to soil nutrients, which have been a limiting factor over the years. In spite of the importance of fertilizer consumption in agricultural yield, many regions of the world still consume very low rate of it. As pointed out by Potter *et al* (2010), more than 50 percent of global cropland applied just 2.5kg per ha while only 8.5 per cent applied fertilizer in excess of 36 kg per ha. Many countries with arable land limitation are therefore looking for countries with low fertilizer consumption for large scale land acquisition with a view to taking advantage of land and crop intensification. As opposed to the astronomical improvement in East Asia and the Pacific, fertilizer consumption is extremely low in Sub-Saharan Africa and Latin America and the Caribbean (Figure 5). While rate of fertilizer application has been rising in other regions of the world especially since 2008, it actually declined in these two regions. This could contribute to why foreign pressure on Sub-Saharan Africa and Latin American lands has been intense in recent times. This is premised on the assumption that enhanced fertilizer utilization will bring about rapid productivity improvement.

Water is an essential input for agricultural production as availability of adequate moisture is an important requirement of agricultural use of land productivity. As argued by Hertel (2010), the rapidly diminishing rate of water availability in many parts of the world coupled with increasing wave of soils degradation are putting more pressure on land demand for agricultural production. Water is therefore an important economic determinant of foreign land acquisition. Water and irrigation facility availability constitutes an important factor in land demand. Mann and Smaller (2010) and Cotula (2011) consider virtual demand for water as the critical element of land deal in recent times. The negotiation between a Libyan company (Malibya) and the Government of Mali on priority water allocation to the company's farm during off season, when water supply is low from river Niger (GRAIN, 2009), is an important example of the centrality of water in land deal.

Countries with large volume of water for agriculture, mostly not fully utilized, are often the target for large scale land acquisition. Bruinsma (2009), Neumann *et al* (2010) and Hertel (2010) have argued that absence of irrigation is a major impediment to wheat, maize and rice potential yields in many countries. As shown by UNDP (2006) and Neumann *et al* (2010) agriculture alone accounts for between 70 and 80 percent of water withdrawals in less industrialized countries. Evidence from Bruinsma (2009) also observes that pressure on water resources is highest in Near East and North Africa and lowest in Sub-Saharan Africa and Latin America. A juxtaposition of topmost land acquirers and targeted countries, as indicated in Figure 6, reveals most acquirers (India, China, USA, Egypt, Brazil and Canada) are under pressure of water withdrawer as opposed to the targeted countries such as Benin, Liberia, Sierra Leone, DRC, Mozambique and Burkina Faso. While water pressure from India, China and USA was over 470 billion cubic meters, it was less than 1 billion cubic meters in most targeted countries listed above – see figure 6. Incidentally, few countries with medium size water withdrawal (e.g. Sudan and Madagascar) are among the heavily targeted. This could suggest the rising impact of land deals on water in these countries. The low level of water withdrawal in many Africa countries explains the rising wavc for land demand from countries experiencing high water pressure. An interesting part of demand for land in Africa is the water paradox.

Figure 5: Fertilizer consumption (kilograms per hectare of arable land), 2002-2010

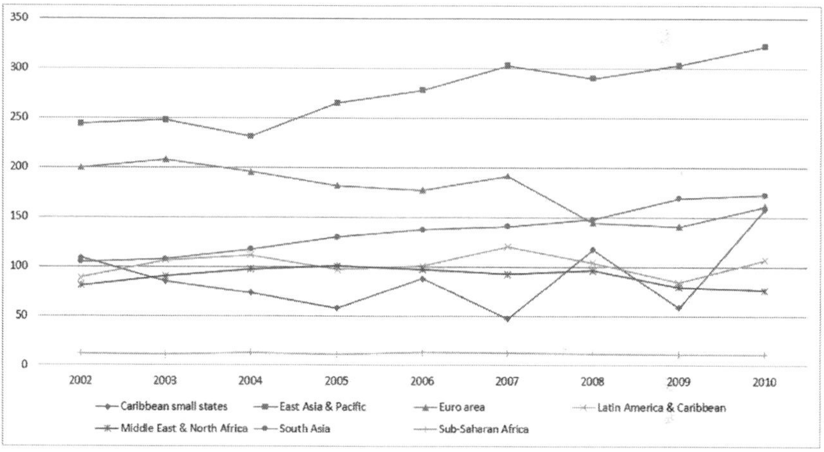

Source: Author's computation from http://data.worldbank.org/indicator/AG.YLD.CREL.KG [Accessed, July 2013].

While the current pressure on water is higher in Sudan and Madagascar than those of such land acquirers as Saudi Arabia, United Kingdom, Malaysia and UAE, the future water requirement of food security in the latter countries is making them to pass the burden to the former (Sudan and Madagascar). This could weaken most African countries' capacity to make water available for non-agricultural use especially for domestic consumption – a development that could make water more expensive in the future. Woodhouse and Ganho (2011) provide some useful examples from the Sahel. They point out that in spite of the commercial desirability of irrigation in the region (e.g. Senegal and Mali), past and present foreign investments in agriculture have been focused on the major river floodplains and the production of crops with higher water requirements. They therefore conclude that the impact on water use may constitute a significant 'hidden agenda' of foreign land acquisition. The relatively high level of under-utilisation of irrigation infrastructure in most African countries (73 percent utilized in Senegal, 43 per cent in Sudan and 11 per cent in Congo (FAO 2005)) makes the continent a primary target for agricultural land[6]. However, the lack of regular maintenance and low operational budget account for low utilization of irrigation infrastructure in many sub-Saharan African countries.

The structural adjustment programmes embarked upon in the early 1980s and further consolidated in the 1990s is also another factor for turning agricultural facilities and investment previously managed by public institutions into commercial ventures. The urge to reduce government budget deficit through privatization and foreign direct investment in many African countries led to foreign acquisition of rich agricultural lands including irrigation facilities. As part of the market–based 1984 Agricultural Policy of Senegal, the existing irrigation facilities (including Manantali and Diama dams) were transferred to farmers' associations while new investments were to come from commercial investors. The rising cost of production (including removal of fertilizer subsidy) associated with the market-based strategy in the Sahel (Woodhouse and Ganho 2011) and the rising water fees (Aw and Diemer, 2005) especially for the farmers cultivating on the Office du Niger, are important causes of under-utilization of irrigation facilities. The investment proclamations and regulations of 2002, 2003 and 2008 in Ethiopia provided for tax exceptions and export facilitations also created incentives for foreign investments (IS Academie 2012).

Figure 6: Water withdrawal (billion cubic meters) from topmost land acquirers and targeted countries, 1997-2011

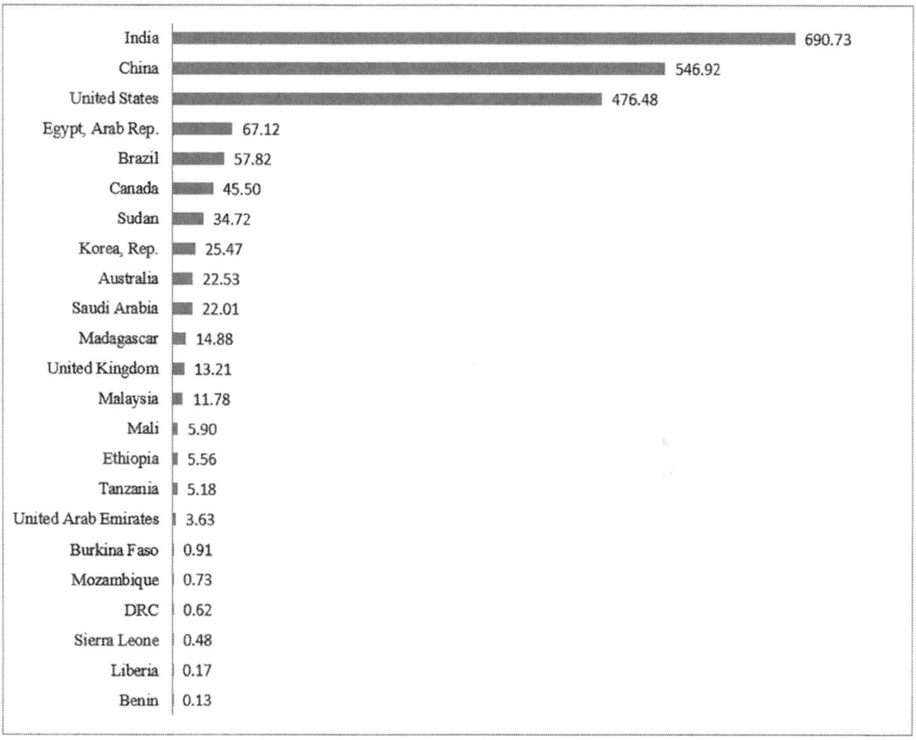

Source: Author's computation from http://data.worldbank.org/indicator/ER.H2O.FWTL.K3/countries [Accessed, July 2013].

The African government divestment in agricultural infrastructure was also influenced by declining multilateral lending to agriculture. Official development assistance to agriculture declined from 15 per cent in the 1970s to about 5 per cent in 2007 (GTZ 2009) while the World Bank loan to this sector declined from 30 per cent in 1980 to 7 percent in 2000 but rose to 12 percent in 2010 due to the need to proactively address the recurring food price hike (IPS 2013). A similar institutional change, which accelerated land-use and land cover change as well as shifting the land-use in the new mode, was experienced in Eastern Europe after the collapse of socialism and the transition from state-command to market-driven economies in the early 1990s. This development has been linked to land use and abandonment in several Eastern Europe countries (Prishchepov *et al* 2011).

Urbanisation Evidence from several studies reveals that demand for land is more intense in countries with very weak formal land rights (Cotula 2011). Results from Deininger (2011) show a high likelihood of a country with weak institutional arrangement for land management being subjected to intense land demand by foreign investors. Several institutional issues have also been raised on land deals. The emphasis placed on large scale land acquisition in Africa, for instance, constitutes a major change in international economic relationships. Anecdotal evidence from several authors, including World Bank (2009) and World Bank *et al* (2009) reveal that heavy agricultural land investment is happening in many African countries where regulatory and legal frameworks are ill-equipped to defend the interests of existing land users or the wider public interest. Most of the targeted countries are characterised by weak regulations, absence of property rights and limited land titling. In most African countries, especially rural areas, land rights are insecure. There are ambiguities within and between the customary and statutory systems, partly due to inaccurate and incomplete records (Garvelink 2012). The weak, confusing and contradictory formal and customary laws provide opportunities for the elite, especially those with financial standing and people with political connections, to acquire land held by rural and indigenous people without any protection. In most countries, agreements for large scale land acquisition are not fair and regulatory frameworks are always not in place to prevent negative externalities, provide benefits to land owners and local communities in a way that safeguard people's livelihoods (Odusola 2012, 2014a and b).

Property rights index is quite low in Africa. When countries are ranked between 1 and 100 points, only three African countries scored 70 points (Mauritius, Cape Verde and Botswana). Another three scored 50 points (South Africa, Seychelles and Ghana). Furthermore, nine countries scored between 35 and 40 points (e.g. Senegal, Malawi and Madagascar) while 22 countries recorded between 20 and 30 points (e.g. Benin, Burkina Faso and Ethiopia). Thirteen countries scored between 10 and 20 points – categorized as very low scores (Table 2). Particularly, countries such as DRC, Congo, Eritrea, Sierra Leone, and Zimbabwe scored 10 points. Interestingly, of the thirteen most targeted African countries on land deals only one of them had 40 points while others scored between 10 and 30 points[7]. Also, out of 24 countries whose property rights scores declined between 2012 and 2013, almost all the targeted countries are included

– excepting Mali, Liberia and Zambia (which all belong to the low scores category). In fact, highly targeted countries such as Ethiopia and Mozambique are among those with highest rate of decline in property rights. As indicated in Table 2, none of the highly targeted countries is among those with high property rights index.

How does rapid urbanisation and conversion of peri urban/rural land impact on this subject?

Arising from growing debates on land administration in Africa, some progress has been recorded in recent times. This includes decentralizing land management and rationalizing customary and statutory laws in such countries as Burkina Faso, Kenya, Malawi, Mozambique, Rwanda, and Zambia; the establishment of Customary Land Secretariats that trains people in land record keeping and dispute resolution (e.g. Ghana); and the creation of regional and community land management administrations (e.g. Tanzania and Uganda) (Garvelink 2012). This also includes the innovative local approach to land registration and certification in Ethiopia, which has culminated into over 15 million households holding land titles between 1995 and 2012 (IS Academie 2012). It is expected that this will enhance rural people's benefit in large scale land acquisition in these countries.

Ordinarily, the law provides the foundation for rights and accountability. In several countries, however, laws legitimize abuses of power against the powerless. In the case of effective land laws, legal frameworks provide some opportunities to protect the land rights of people (especially the rural dwellers) and for holding decision-makers to account for land they administer. As argued by Polack *et al* (2013), when land becomes of interest to commercial investors, the legal options available to local groups are few and the effectiveness of public accountability framework becomes compromised. In many African countries, most governments arrogate the right to allocate land to rich individuals or business entities, often with minimal or no consultation with land users, and with meager or no compensation to rural people. Using the indicators of political space as a measure of accountability, Ghana provides a sharp contrast of Ethiopia (a targeted country) in terms of freedom of association, participation and human rights and press freedom. Madagascar, another targeted country, was rated very low on participation and human rights as well as freedom of association. Cameroon and Mozambique are also low on freedom of association while Uganda was rated low on freedom of the press.

Accountability is not only in the formal setting. Weak accountability on the part of traditional landlords in DRC is an important institutional factor. The local land tenure system where local chiefs arrogate substantial power to themselves and behave as landlords rather being trustees complicates the already weak public institutions[8]. Weak transparent and accountability framework attract large scale investors to most targeted African countries.

Ambiguity in land ownership is another issue. For instance, in Madagascar, foreigners are not allowed to own land but they could have access to land via a company, which has the right to lease the purchased land. The legal situation about foreign ownership of land is not clearly defined (Gorgen *et al*, 2009). Other institutional considerations in land demand in developing countries with low world market integration include limited information about land market, unclear land titles, weak governance and high prevalence of corrupt practices.

Table 2: Level and change in property rights among African countries, 2012 and 2013

Countries with low property rights index			Countries with medium property rights index			Countries with high property rights index		
Countries	Property rights index (2013)	Change in property rights index from 2012	Countries	Property rights index (2013)	Change in property rights index from 2012	Countries	Property rights index (2013)	Change in property rights index from 2012
DRC	10	-1.5	Algeria	30	-1.4	Ghana	50	0.6
Congo, Republic.	10	-0.3	Benin	30	1.9	Seychelles	50	1.9
Eritrea	10	0.1	Burkina Faso	30	-0.7	South Africa	50	-0.9
Sierra Leone	10	-0.8	Cameroon	30	0.5	Botswana	70	1
Zimbabwe	10	2.3	Comoros	30	1.8	Cape Verde	70	0.2
Angola	15	0.6	Djibouti	30	0	Mauritius	70	-0.1
Equatorial Guinea	15	-0.5	Ethiopia	30	-2.6			
Burundi	20	0.9	Gambia, The	30	0			
CAR	20	0.1	Kenya	30	-1.6			
Chad	20	0.4	Liberia	30	0.7			

Guinea	20	0.4	Mali	30	0.6			
Guinea-Bissau	20	1	Mozambique	30	-2.1			
STP	20	-2.2	Namibia	30	-1.6			
Cote d'Ivoire	25	-0.2	Niger	30	-0.4			
Mauritania	25	-0.7	Nigeria	30	-1.2			
			Rwanda	30	-0.8			
			Tanzania	30	0.9			
			Togo	30	0.5			
			Uganda	30	-0.8			
			Zambia	30	0.4			
			Egypt	35	-3.1			
			Gabon	40	1.4			
			Lesotho	40	1.3			
			Madagascar	40	-0.4			
			Malawi	40	-1.1			
			Morocco	40	-0.6			
			Senegal	40	0.1			
			Swaziland	40	0			
			Tunisia	40	-1.6			

Note: DRC is Democratic Republic of Congo, CAR is Central African Republic, and STP is Sao Tome and Principe.

Source: Author's computation and compilation from Heritage Foundation's Index of Economic Freedom http://www.heritage.org/index/explore[Accessed July 2013].

Overview of the model and analysis of results

The data

Data for land grab is sourced from the Land Matrix Database, managed by international partnership initiated by International Land Coalition (ILC). The partnership adopts a crowd sourcing approach to identify land deals and subsequently subject them to data triangulation (checked and confirmed). The land matrix initiative emerged from a coalition of research and funding organizations that have worked over time to improve accuracy, crosschecking and verification of land acquisition data[9]

The economic variables such as cereal yield, fertilizer consumption, food production index, gross national income (GNI) per capita and fresh water withdrawal were sourced from the World Development Indicators.[10] They are therefore as defined in the World Development Indicators. For instance, cereal yield, is measured as kilogrammes per hectare of harvested land, includes wheat, rice, maize, barley, oats, rye, millet, sorghum, buckwheat, and mixed grains. The inland water per 1000 ha was obtained from the FAO Statistical database[11]

The institutional variables (property rights, corruption index and accountability index) were also derived from the World Development Indicators. They are based on the public sector management and institution cluster averages as defined in the World Bank database. Property rights and rule-based *governance, for instance,* assess the extent to which private economic activity is facilitated by an effective legal system and rule-based *governance* structure in which property and contract rights are reliably respected and enforced.

To normalize the cross section constants, most variables were measured as averages over period where data is available. For instance, the institutional variables were averaged 2005 -2011. On the other hand, the economic variables are based on data availability: fresh water withdrawals (1997-2011), fertilizer consumption (2002 - 2009) and GNI per capita (1980 - 2011).

Overview of the Model

The concentration of un-utilised arable land in Sub-Saharan Africa and the penchant urge to address food and fuel security challenges, and the associated price incentives for agricultural commodities have been identified as outstanding factors driving the demand for agricultural land in Africa. The shortage of fertile land due to unfavourable climate conditions and the buoyant financial status of such countries as those in Gulf States (e.g. Saudi Arabia, Qatar and UAE) and some in Asia (e.g. China, South Korea and India) contribute to foreign land acquisition (Gorgen *et al* 2009). The latter is an income effect emphasized in Ando and Shah (2009) particularly from investing countries. Attempt is also made to examine the income effect of targeted countries on large scale foreign land acquisition.

Land productivity plays an important role in land demand for agricultural purpose. Fertility of land promotes crop intensification, thereby reducing demand on land (actual or derived). This is a practical case in Brazil and Japan (Lugschitz, *et al* 2011). This informs the use of three important variables in the model for demand for land grab in Africa: yield gaps, freshwater water requirement and level of fertilizer utilization. For instance, the role of yield gaps has been emphasised in Hertel (2010), Licker *et al* (2010) and Bruinsma (2009) while Woodhouse and Ganho (2011) conclude that the impact of meeting food and bio fuel security on water constitutes an important hidden agenda of land deals in Sub-Saharan Africa. Rulli *et al* 2013 examine the extent of water resources appropriated through large scale land acquisition. Potter *et al* (2010) and Hertel (2010) underscore the contribution of potential production intensification in driving demand for large scale land in many developing countries (e.g. fertilizer utilisation).

This chapter employs the ordinary least squares estimation technique to a set of panel data from 28 African countries[12] - based on data availability in the land matrix database. To be able to do this, some vectors of economic and institutional variables are regressed on the log[13] of land acquired by foreign entities in recipient countries in Africa. The model is presented in equation 1 below:

$$lgit = b0 + \beta Ait + \emptyset Bit + \mu it \quad .....(1)$$

where $_{it}$ stands for a country *i* in year *t*, *lg* is the land grab variable, *A* is a vector of economic variables, and B is a vector of institutional variables that are considered to be important determinants of foreign demand for land in Africa. Because the data is used as a point variable (average over some period of time), the issue of fixed effect was not examined. To this end, t is equal to 1. μ is a random error term.

A vector of five economic variables were used, namely, inland water per 1000 per ha, crop production index, cereal yield per hectare (log), gross national income per capita (log) and level of fertilizer utilization per hectare. The three-vector of institutional variables are: property right index, corruption perception index and index of accountability.

When the vector of economic and institutional variables is substituted into equation 1, the following equation is derived:

$$lg_{it} = b_0 + \beta_1 crppi_{it} + \beta_2 fert_{it} + \beta_3 ypc_{it} + \beta_4 yd_{it} + \beta_5 wid_{it} + \emptyset_1 cpi_{it} + \emptyset_2 aci_{it} + \emptyset_3 pri_{it} + \mu_{it} \quad .....(2)$$

where *crppi* stands for crop production index, *fert* is fertilizer consumption. GNI per capita income (*ypc),* yield per hectare (*yd*), inland water (wid), corruption perception index (cpi), accountability index (aci), and property rights index (pri).

A semi-log function was applied to the model. Land grab, GNI per capita and yield per hectare were logged while the others were not. To deal with disturbances associated with omitted variables, misspecification and systemic errors in measurement that could bias the estimation technique, the second order iterative procedure of Cochrane-Orcutt framework was used. This enhances the robustness of the results from the panel. The results of the econometric analysis are presented below.

Analysis of the results

Evidence from bivariate analysis

To deepen the analysis of determinants of large scale land acquisition in Africa, a combination of bivariate and multivariate analyzes were applied. Evidence from Table 3 and figures 7, 8 and 9 shows the correlation between land grab on one hand, and economic and institutional variables on the other hand.

Table 3: Results of correlation analysis

	Land grab (lg)	Crop production index (crppi)	GNI per capita (ypc)	Cereal yield (yd)	Fresh water withdrawal (fw)	Property rights index (pri)	Accountability index (aci)	Corruption index (cpi)
Land grab	1.000							
Crop production index	-0.084	1.000						
GNI per capita	-0.230	-0.097	1.000					
Cereal yield	0.071	-0.208	0.325	1.000				
Fresh water withdrawal	0.432	-0.166	-0.216	-0.130	1.000			
Property rights index	-0.196	0.209	0.249	0.418	-0.112	1.000		
Accountability index	-0.162	0.192	0.318	0.397	-0.317	0.882	1.000	
Corruption index	-0.295	0.202	0.202	0.455	-0.319	0.765	0.844	1.000

Results from correlation analysis reveal an inverse relationship between large scale foreign land acquisition and the three institutional factors (corruption index, accountability index and property rights index). The correlation index varies from -0.162 for accountability index to -0.295 for the corruption index. This tends to suggest that land grab would be more intense where corruption, transparency and property rights indexes are very weak. Figures 7a to 7c provide more illumination on these inverse relationships. Countries highly targeted by foreign land investors such as Sudan, Ethiopia and Madagascar scored less than 3.0 points on property rights index[13]. About 70 percent of the countries scored 3.0 points and below. The Kernel density function from Figure 7a shows most (about 90 per cent) of the targeted countries clustered between 2.0 and 3.5 points for property rights.

A similar relationship is established in Figures 7b and 7c. On the accountability index, majority of the countries clustered between 2.4 and 3.6 points. The four most targeted countries scored less than 3.2 points on accountability index. All the highly targeted countries scored less than 40 points (out of 100 points) on corruption index. In fact, only 3 out of the 28 countries experiencing land grab in the continent scored less than 40 points. As shown by the Kernel density function (Figure 7c), 23 of them scored between 20 and 40 points. Rwanda, Ghana and Sierra Leone are the only countries with more than 40 points.

Figure 7a: Land grab and property rights index

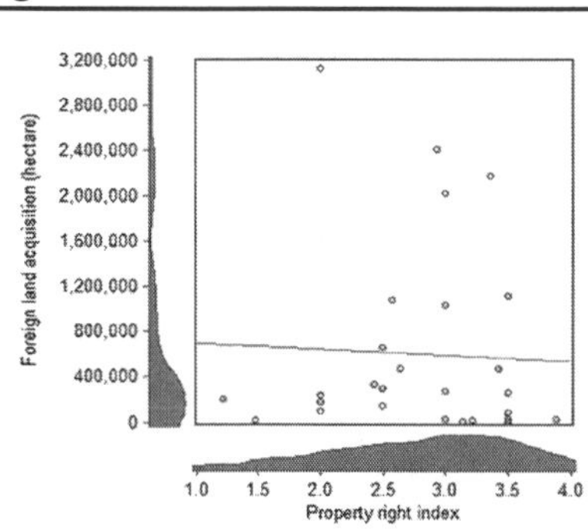

Figure 7b: Land grab and accountability index

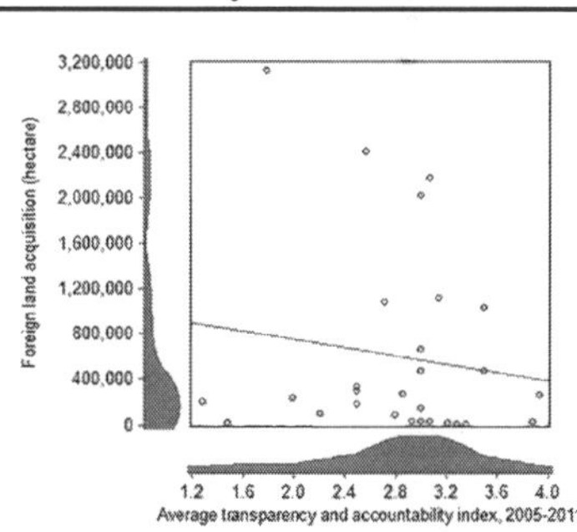

Figure 7c: Land grab and corruption index

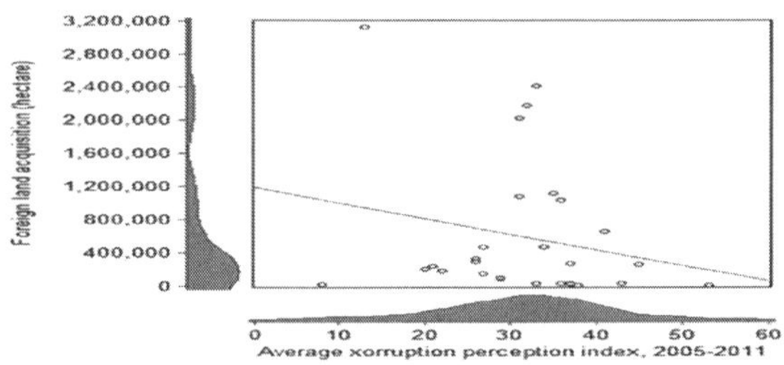

Evidence from the correlation between land grab and economic indexes is quite revealing. The inverse correlation between large scale land acquisition and targeted countries' level of per capita income is relatively strong. The majority of the targeted countries are those with per capita income of about $1,000.00 and below (Figure 8c). The implication of this is that investing countries are targeting countries with limited capacity to meet the investment requirements of large scale agricultural production (e.g. Ethiopia, DRC, Burkina Faso, Liberia, Madagascar and Mozambique).

The production index also exhibits some inverse correlation with land grab. The Kernel density function shows land acquisition is more intense in countries with low production index in recent times relative to the 2004-2006 average production index. Fertilizer utilization is used as an index of crop intensification. This index is always very low in Africa. The negative correlation is quite pronounced (figure 8b). For instance, land acquisition is much more pronounced in countries experiencing very low fertilizer consumption. Land grab clustered more in countries with less than 20kg of fertilizer per hectare (e.g. Sudan, DRC, Niger, Congo, Angola, Uganda and Madagascar).

As earlier presented, water is very critical to agricultural land demand. There is a high correlation between inland water availability (per 1000 ha) and large scale land acquisition. Land acquisition tends to be low in countries with less than 2000 cubic feet of inland water availability (excepting Sierra Leone, Madagascar, and Mozambique) (Figure 8d). Land grab is highest in countries with tremendous inland water resources especially those with over 10,000 cubic feet of inland water (e.g. Sudan and Ethiopia). A similar positive trend is also observed for fresh water withdrawal (see Figure 9a). Demand for land is low where fresh water withdrawal is very low and tends to be high when the converse holds.

Figure 8a: Land grab and production index

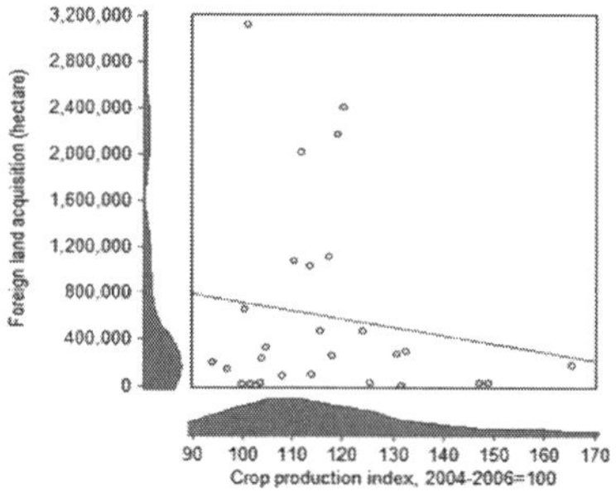

Figure 8b: Land grab and fertilizer consumption

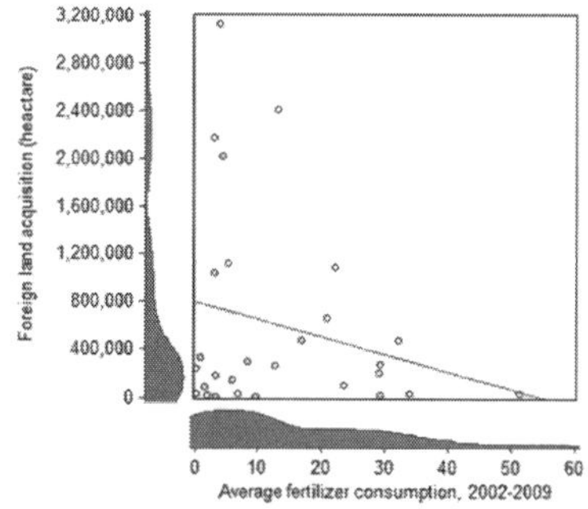

Figure 8c: Land grab and per capita income

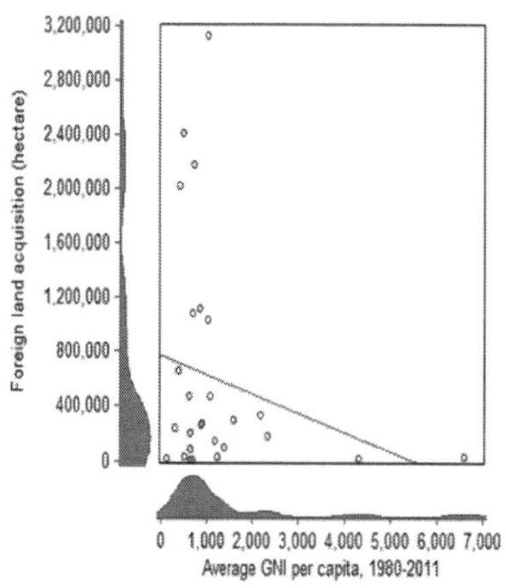

Figure 8d: Land grab and inland water availability

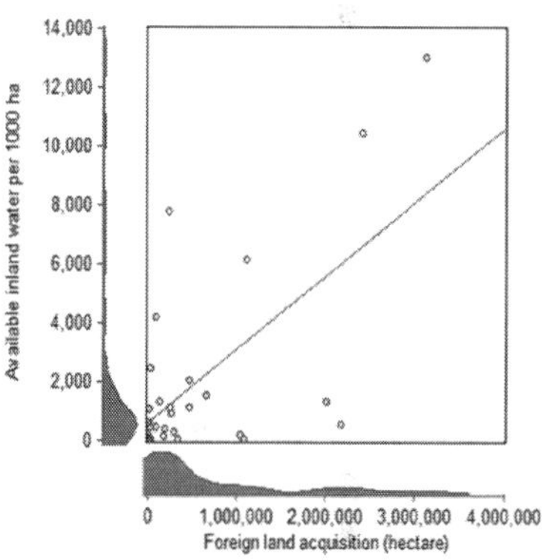

As evident in Figure 9b, there is a negative relationship between foreign demand for agricultural land and cereal yield per hectare. Given high yield potential in Africa, which Deininger and Byerlee (2011) currently put at only one-fifth of the targeted potential, this tends to suggest that yield gap plays an important role in land demand in Africa. The relationship between the two variables shows a bimodal Kernel density function and the series clustered between 400 and 1,600 kg per hectare.

Figure 9a: Land grab and fresh water withdrawal	Figure 9b: Land grab and cereal yield per ha
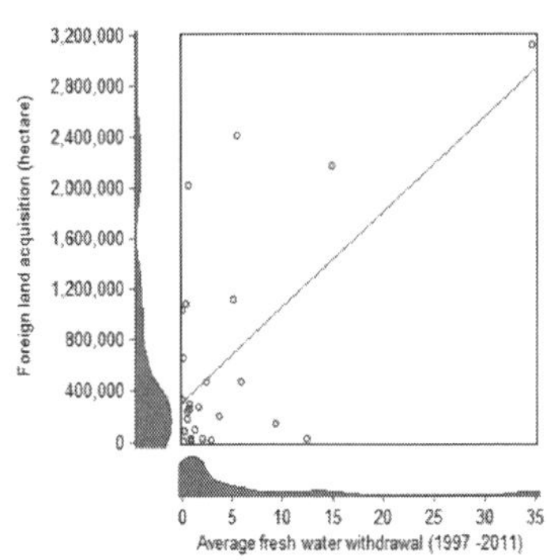	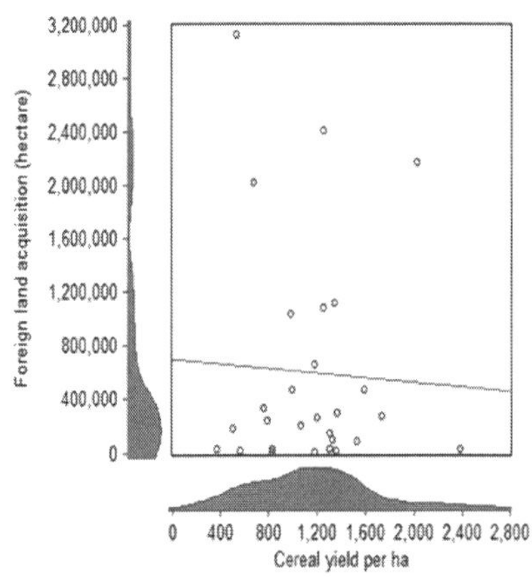

Evidence from multivariate analysis

Results from multivariate analysis also reinforce the evidence from foregoing correlation exploration. An important message from the literature of global food security is premised on the need to increase agricultural productivity in low income countries where the yield gap is quite large (Nkonya *et al* 2012). The findings from this study tend to support this conclusion. For instance, there is an inverse relationship between demand for agricultural land by foreigners and level of per capita income. One percentage increase in per capita income reduces propensity for foreign demand for land by 1.02 per cent. This relationship is statistically established at 5 per cent level of significance. This, to a large extent, explains why large scale land acquisition is dominant in low income countries such as Sudan, Ethiopia, Madagascar, Tanzania, Benin and Sierra Leone (See note 15)[15] Providing the needed capital to small farm holders, medium and large scale agro-businesses in these countries, targeted towards agricultural productivity, could reduce the incentives for foreign demand for land.

Many studies have confirmed the wide gap between the actual and potential yields in Africa. As computed by Deininger *et al* (2011), Africa is only at 20 percent, 32 per cent and 54 per cent of its maize, soyabean and sugarcane potential as opposed to 65 per cent, 67 per cent and 93 per cent in South America. The finding from this chapter tends to support that because of high potential of yield expansion, many foreign investors demand for African arable land. For instance, 1 per cent increase in cereal yield raises foreign demand for land by 3.8 per cent. This is established at 99 per cent confidence interval. The relationship with crop production index is also positive but not statistically established. An important way of reducing the rising intensity of land grab is for Africans to bridge the yield gap substantially. One way of doing this is for African governments and their private sector counterparts to invest in improved seedlings, increased access to inputs and capital, and promote technology acquisition.

Agricultural productivity has been linked to fertilizer consumption rate globally and has contributed to varying level of productivity across different regions. Demand for land grab in Africa is concentrated in countries with low fertilizer consumption. For instance, a one percentage point change in fertilizer utilisation between 2002 and 2009 tends to reduce demand for land in such countries by about 0.03 per cent. However, this relationship is not statistically established. As such, it is not considered to be an important factor in explaining the rush for agricultural land in Africa.

Many studies have mentioned, though not quantified, the role of water resources in demand for agricultural land (e.g. Nkonya *et al* 2012), and Woodhouse and Ganho (2011)). Given the large scale orientation of such farming system, it requires a combination of 'green' water (e.g. rainfall and plant transpiration) and 'blue' water resources (e.g. rivers, lakes and aquifers). This chapter examines the role of inland water resources (i.e. blue water) play in demand for land in Africa. Evidence from this chapter reveals that countries with substantial inland water resources are more likely to experience intense land demand from foreigners. For instance, a 1.00 percentage point increase in the volumes of inland water resources raises demand for land by about 0.0003 per cent. Although the coefficient is very small, the statistical evidence is quite strong (1.00 per cent level of significance). This finding tends to support the arguments that most land grabs are located in the major rivers floodplains in many countries (e.g. Ethiopia, Liberia, Mali, Madagascar, Niger, Senegal, Sierra Leone and Sudan).

Government needs to invest heavily in water resources management. This includes developing the water resources management capacity (underground water, rainwater, and run-off water). This requires promoting water harvesting technologies, utilisation and management, building capacity in rainwater harvesting among professionals, technicians, artisans, farmers and communities. Effort to develop medium and large scale irrigation system to support commercial farming among local and elite farmers is equally important to reduce incentives for land grab.

Table 4: Regression results with land grab (lg) as the dependent variable

Variables	Coefficient	t-statistics	Probability
Constant	-11.211	1.968	0.067
cpi	-0.164	-3.489	0.003
aci	4.062	3.739	0.002
pri	-2.229	-2.434	0.027
crppi	0.026	1.458	0.164
fert	-0.025	-1.039	0.313
lypc	-1.022	-2.850	0.011
lyd	3.815	5.367	0.000
wid	0.0003	4.686	0.002
$Coct^2$	-0.785	-4.666	0.000
Equation statistics Adjusted R^2 0.56 F-statistics 4.481 Probability 0.004 DW Statistics 1.80			

Note: $Coct^2$ stands for the 2nd order Cochrane Orcutt procedure while other variables are as defined above.

The inverse relationship between property rights and land grab is a clear confirmation that the weak and low rate of land titling, registration and certification crates incentives for land grab. One percentage point improvement in property rights in Africa reduces foreign demand for African land by more than two percent. This is clear evidence that the current practice where more than 90 percent of Africa's rural land is undocumented, makes it highly vulnerable to land grabbing and expropriation with poor compensation. This confirms findings from Arezki *et al* (2011), which observed that weak land governance and tenure security for current users make countries more attractive for investors. This tends to confirm the main message from Byamugishe (2013) that modernizing the complex governance procedures on land ownership and management, including documenting rural land is vital to reducing land grab in the continent. This includes championing reforms and investments to document all communal lands and prime lands that are individually owned. The innovation in communal land registration and certification is making land titling accessible to the poor people in several countries. For instance, the cost of the certification was estimated to be as low as $1.00 per plot and $3.50 per farm household (Deininger *et al* 2008) compared to the cost of S150.00 in Madagascar which is still relied on demand based land titling (Jacoby and Minten 2007). Compared to very prohibitive price when it was based on individual basis, it is an average cost of about US$500 per village in Tanzania and it ranged between US$500 and S$700 per kilometer in Ghana. It is still relatively expensive in Mozambique - the unit cost of delimiting and certifying a community land ranges between US$2,000 and US$10,000 (Byamugisha 2013). Innovations on land titling and registration are also taking place in several countries including Malawi and Uganda. All these point to the fact that with strong commitment from the political leaders to build on current efforts, improved land governance and management is achievable in Africa.

Land administration has been acknowledged as a major source of rent seeking and corrupt practices in developing countries (e.g. Van der Molen and Tuladhar (2007), and Byamugishe (2013)). In addition to the findings from the bivariate analysis, the results from the regression show an inverse relationship between corruption and land grab. It reveals that one percentage point improvement in corruption reduces foreign demand for land by 0.16 per cent. Therefore, tackling the weak governance and corruption associated with land governance and administration in Africa will not only reduce incentives for land grab but will make large scale agricultural investments more beneficial to the rural dwellers whose livelihoods are tied to the land. In-depth study of the major sources of corruption in land management should be undertaken for appropriate policy actions to be determined.

In contrast with the negative relationship between accountability index and land grab, the regression result shows a positive association. This is contrary to the extant literature (e.g. Zoomers 2010), it tends to suggest demand for land rises when the land governance system is accountable. Perhaps, based on the rising wave of conflicts associated to many of land deals in the continent, foreign land investors now see accountability as an important factor for land security and use. This notwithstanding, local landowners must be fully involved in the negotiations of such land deals while adequate compensation is also a prerequisite.

The model's goodness of fit, as measured the adjusted R^2, is 0.56 and the F-statistics for the model is statistically established at 99 per cent confidence interval. To this end, the reliability of the model estimates is good.

Conclusions

There is a clear evidence of unprecedented demand for large scale agricultural land in Africa. Apart from accounting for over 60 percent of land deals globally, seven of the 11 most targeted countries are from the continent. This chapter bridges some knowledge gap by adding to the empirical evidence on demand for arable land in Africa. The chapter shows that both economic and institutional factors play some vital role in intensifying the scrambling for African arable land. Countries with large unused arable land as well as those countries experiencing high yield gap with per capita income of about $1,000.00 and below are the primary target due to limited capacity to meet the investment requirements of large scale agricultural production. Strategies that promote income capacity of small farm holders and agro-businesses, through access to low-interest bearing or subsidised credits, are vital in providing the required investments to improve local utilisation of such arable lands.

Evidence from the analysis also reveals that availability of inland water resources is a major determinant. While most of the leading land acquirers are under serious water pressure, the converse holds for most of the targeted countries. The rising and higher pressure on water in Sudan and Madagascar relative to such acquirers as Saudi Arabia, United Kingdom, Malaysia and UAE, tends to suggest that the later countries have started to pass the burden to the former (Sudan and Madagascar). Reversing this trend is vital in countries that have started to experience this water burden. Government of targeted countries need to invest heavily in ground water, rainwater and run-off water management and develop national stakeholders' capacity to better manage integrated water resources for agricultural transformation. Appropriate policies should be put in place to ensure foreign land acquisition does not compromise water use for domestic and industrial purposes.

Weak governance and related institutional challenges also come out very strongly as key determinants. Both property rights and corruption appear to have inverse relationship with land grab. The current weak property rights and endemic corruption create incentives for demand for arable land in the continent. Africa needs to modernise and simplify the complex land management and procedures in a way that involves people and communities in land governance. The political class and the

CSOs should champion land reforms and serve as vanguard of the poor. Government, on the other hand, should invest heavily in documenting (titling, registration and certification) all communal lands and lands owned by individuals to enhance property rights. The innovations already in place in countries like Ethiopia, Ghana, Malawi, Mozambique, Tanzania, and Uganda should be strengthened and replicated in other African countries. A continent-wide strategy is vital in accelerating progress on this. To avoid the inherent risks associated with large-scale land acquisition, African governments should promote other forms of investment such as joint ventures or contract farming and out-grower schemes or investments. These are vital to promoting livelihoods and security of supply to investors without dislodging people of their cherished landed asset.

There seems to be some emerging lessons from the rising wave of conflicts, production disruption and uncertainty associated with many land deals in the continent. It appears foreign land investors now see accountability as an avenue of land security and use. This reality should be deepened by ensuring local chiefs and landlords fully involve local people in the negotiations of land deals, their consent sought and adequate compensation provided when their land is acquired.

Notes and References

1. Friis and Reenberg (2010) use the blog from the International Land Coalition blogs while Deininger et al use the GRAIN blogs.
2. Several factors explain the differences in land grab figures. For instance, the Oxfam's study is longer in time coverage and it covers agriculture, mining and timber concessions while the previous two inventories are restricted to only agriculture. In addition to difference in sources, there are also differences in method of inventory. For instance, only projects above 1,000 ha were considered by Cotula et al (2009) while Gorgen *et al* (2009) capture land 'demanded' but not necessarily approved deals. Variation also occurs through coverage. Using Ethiopia as an example, Deininger *et al* (2011) include land allocations by regional government agencies, while Cotula *et al* (2009) only include allocations by federal government agencies and by Oromia regional government.
3. The Land Matrix monitors land transactions in rural areas that are made for agricultural production (for food or agro-fuel production), timber extraction, carbon trading, mineral extraction, conservation, and tourism (see http://landportal.info/landmatrix/media/img/get-the-idea/top-10-target-countries.pdf).
4. Computations from the Ethiopian Ministry of Agriculture portal reveal an average of 14.6 ha when Ethiopians and Ethiopians in Diaspora acquisitions are included. The average for only foreign acquisition is 28.5 ha.

5. Eritrea, Liberia, Malawi, Sierra Leone, Togo, Lesotho, Guinea Bissau, Equatorial Guinea, Burundi, Rwanda, Djibouti, Swaziland, Gambia, Cape Verde, Comoros, Mauritania, Sao Tome and Principe and Seychelles (Odusola, 2014a).
6. See Cotula (2012) for this type of partnership.
7. Nkonya *et al* (2012) provide some illustrations on how local chiefs have sown limited sense of accountability on land management in DRC.
8. See http://www.landmatrix.org.
9. See http://data.worldbank.org/indicator. [Accessed, July 2013].
10. See http://faostat.fao.org.
11. Angola, Benin, Burkina Faso, Cameroon, Congo, Cote d'Ivoire, DRC, Ethiopia, Ghana, Kenya, Liberia, Madagascar, Malawi, Mali, Mozambique, Niger, Nigeria, Rwanda, Senegal, Sierra Leone, Somalia, South Africa, Sudan, Swaziland, Tanzania, Uganda, Zambia and Zimbabwe.
12. The use of logarithmic (log) transformation allows for the measure of elasticity (changes in land demand as a result of changes in economic and institutional variables).
13. The World Development Indicators rate countries on property rights from 1.0 (very low) to 6.0 (very high). See http://search.worldbank.org/data?qterm=Governance%20indicator&language=EN

Ando, A.W. and P. Shah, 2009. Demand for factors in optimal land choice, paper presented at the Agricultural Economics Association 2009 and the ACCI Joint Annual Meeting, Milwaukee, Wisconsin, July 26-29, 2009.

Anseeuw, W., M. Boche, T. Breu, M. Giger, J. Lay, P. Messerli and K. Nolte, 2012. Transnational Land Deals for Agriculture in the Global South, *Analytical Report based on the Land Matrix Database Number 1*: April 2012. Available from: http://farmlandgrab.org. [Accessed May 2012].

Arezki, R., K. Deininger and H. Selod, 2011. What drives the global land rush?, *IMF Working Paper (WP/11/251)*, The International Monetary Fund, 2011.

Aw, D. and G. Diemer, 2005. Making a Large Irrigation Scheme Work. A Case Study from Mali. *Directions in Development*. Washington, DC: The World Bank.

Bruinsma, J., 2009. The resource outlook to 2050. By how much do land, water use and crop yields need to increase by 2050? In *Session 2: The resource base to 2050: Will there be enough land, water and genetic potential to meet future food and biofuel demands?* Rome, Italy, June 24.

Byamugishe, F.F.K., 2013. *Securing Africa's land for shared prosperity: A programme to scale up reform and investments*. Washington, D.C.: The World Bank.

Cotula, L., S. Vermeulen, R. Leonard and J. Keeley, 2009. *Land grab or development opportunity? Agricultural development and international land deals in Africa*. London: International Institute for Environment and Development, Rome; Food and Agricultural Organization, Rome: International Fund for Agricultural Development.

Cotula, L., 2011. *Land deals in Africa: What is in the contracts?* London: International Institute for Environment and Development (IIED). Available from: http://pubs.iied.org/12568IIED.html [Accessed July 2013].

Cotula, L., 2012. The International Political Economy of the Global Land Rush: A critical appraisal of trends, scale, geography and drivers, *The Journal of Peasant Studies*, Vol. 39, Nos. 3–4, July–October 2012, 649–680.

Deininger, K. and D. Byerlee, with J. Lindsay, A. Norton, H. Selod and M. Stickler, 2011. *Rising global interest in farmland: can it yield sustainable and equitable benefits?* Washington, DC: The World Bank.

Deininger, K., 2011. Challenges posed by the new wave of farmland investment, *Journal of Peasant Studies*, http://www.tandfonline.com/loi/fjps20

Deininger, K. and D. Byerlee, 2011. The Rise of Large Farms in Land Abundant Countries: Do They Have A Future?, *Policy Research Working Paper 5588*, March 2011.

Deininger, K., D. A. Ali, S. T. Holden and J. Zevenbergen, 2008. Rural land certification in

Ethiopia: Process, initial impact, and implications for other African countries. *World*

Development 36, pp. 1786-1812.

Food and Agricultural Organization (FAO), 2009. The *State of Agricultural Commodity Markets 2009*. Rome: United Nations Food and Agriculture Organization.

FAO 2005. Irrigation in Africa in figures, *Aquastat Survey (2005)*. Rome: The United Nations Food and Agriculture Organisation.

Fischer, G., van Velthuizen, H., Shah, M. and F. Nachtergaele, 2002. *Global Agro-ecological Assessment for Agriculture in the 21st Century: Methodology and results*, RR-02-002, Laxenburg: International Institute for Applied Systems Analysis (IIASA).

Food and Agricultural Organization (FAO), International Fund for Agricultural Development (IFAD), United Nations Conference on Trade and Development (UNCTAD) and The World Bank, 2010. Principles for Responsible Agricultural Investment that Protect Rights, Livelihoods and Resources. *Discussion Note 25 January 2010.* Rome: FAO, IFAD, UNCTAD and the World Bank Group. Available from http://siteresources.worldbank.org/INTARD/214574-1111383886611/22453321/Principles_Extended.pdf. [Accessed June 2012].

Friis, C. and A. Reenberg, 2010. Land Grab in Africa: Emerging land system drivers in a teleconnected world. GLP Report No.1. Copenhagen: GLP-IPO, University of Copenhagen.

Garvelink, W.J., 2012. "Land Tenure, Property Rights, and Rural Economic Development in Africa", Centre for Strategic and International Studies, February 2012. Available from http://csis.org/publication/land-tenure-property-rights-and-rural-economic-development-africa. [Accessed June 2013].

Gorgen, M., B. Rudloff, J. Simons, A. Ullengerg, S. Vath and L. Wimmer, 2009. Foreign direct investment (FDI) in land in developing countries. Eschborn: GTZ Division 45 – Agriculture, Fisheries and Food, GTZ.

GRAIN, 2008. Seized! The 2008 land grab for food and financial security. *Briefing October 2008*. Barcelona: GRAIN.

GRAIN, 2009. The new farm owners: corporate investors lead the rush for control over overseas farmland[online]. GRAIN: Barcelona: GRAIN, 20 October 2009. Available from: http://www.grain.org/article/entries/194-the-new-farm-owners. [Accessed June 2013].

GRAIN, 2010. Saudi investors poised to take control of rice production in Senegal and Mali [online].

29 November 2010. Available from: http://www.grain.org/article/entries/3997-saudi-investorspoised-to-take-control-of-rice-production-in-Senegal-and-Mali. [Accessed July 2013].

GTZ,2009. *Foreign direct investment (FDI) in land in developing countries*. Eschborn: Work of division 45, Agriculture, fisheries and food, GTZ.

Hall, R.,2011. "Land Grabbing in Southern Africa: The Many Faces of the Investor Rush", Paper for STIAS Colloquium on Land reform, agrarian change and rural poverty in Southern Africa Venue: Wallenberg Conference centre, Stellenbosch, 8-9 March 2011.

Hertel, T., 2010. The global supply and demand for agricultural land in 2050: A perfect storm in the making, *GTAP Working Paper No 63*.

Haralambous, S., H. Liversage and M. Romano, 2009. The growing demand for land: Risks and opportunities for smallholder farmers. *Discussion Paper for Round Table 2, Governing Council*, 18-19 February 2009, IFAD.

International Food Policy Research Institute (IFPRI), Welt Hunger Hilfe and Concern Worldwide and Green Scenery, 2012. *2012 Global Hunger Index: The Challenge of hunger: ensuring Sustainable Food Security under land, water and energy stress.* Bonn, Washington, DC, and Dublin: IFPRI Concern Worldwide, Welthungerhilfe and Green Scenery.

International Institute for Environment and Development (IIED), 2012. The Global Land rush: What the evidence reveals about scale and geography? *IIED Briefing on the Global Land Rush. Available from IIED: http://pubs.iied.org/pdfs/17124IIED.pdf.* [Accessed June 2013].

Inter Press Service (IPS), 2013. World Bank boosts agricultural lending ahead of MDG Meet.

http://ipsnews.net/news.asp?idnews=52815. [Accessed July 2013].

IS Academie, 2012.Ethiopia: Food security and land governance factsheet. Land Governance for Equitable and Sustainable Development. Available from: http://www.landgovernance.org/system/files/Ethiopia%20Factsheet%20-%202012.pdf.

Land Matrix, 2012. Land Matrix data (April 2012). Available from: http://landportal.info/landmatrix/media/img/get-the-idea/top-10-target-countries.pdf. [Accessed May 2012].

Jacoby, H. G. and Minten, B.,2007. Is Land Titling in Sub-Saharan Africa Cost-Effective?

Evidence from Madagascar. *The World Bank Economic Review 21(3)*, pp. 461-485.

Licker, R., M. Johnston, C. Barford, J. A. Foley, C. J. Kucharik, C. Monfreda, and N. Ramankutty, 2010. Mind the Gap: How do climate and agricultural management explain the "yield gap" of croplands around the world? *Global Ecology and Biogeography*, Volume 19, Issue 6, pp. 769-782.

Lugschitz, B., Bruckner, M. and S. Giljum, 2011. Europe global land demand: A study on the actual land embodied in European imports and exports of agricultural products. Final Report, Sustainable Europe Research Institute (SERI). Vienna: SERI.

Mann, H. and Smaller, C., 2010. Foreign Land Purchases for Agriculture: what impact on sustainable development? *Sustainable Development Innovation Brief No 8.*. New York: United Nations *Department of Economic and Social Affairs.*

Miller, T., K.R. Holmes, E.J. Fueler, A.B. Kim, B. Riley and J.M. Roberts, 2013. *2013 Index of Economic Freedom.* Washington DC: The Heritage Foundation.

Neumann, K., P. H. Verburg, E. Stehfest, and C. Müller, 2010. The yield gap of global grain production: A spatial analysis, Agricultural Systems, *2010, vol. 103, issue 5*, pp. 316-326.

Nkonya, E., A. Karsenty, S. Msangi, C. Souza Jr, M. Shah, J. von Braun, G. Galford, and S. Park, 2012."Sustainable land use for the 21st century", United Nations Department of Economic and Social Affairs Division's Project on Sustainable Development in the 21st Century (SD21), May 2012

Odusola, Ayodele (2012): Land Grab in Africa: An Overview of Emerging Issues and Policy Options. *Mimeograph.* UNDP Regional Bureau for Africa, New York.

Odusola, A.F., 2014a. Land grab in Africa: A review of emerging issues and implications for policy options. *International Policy Centre for Inclusive Growth Working Paper 124*, April 2014.

Odusola, A.F., 2014b. Land grab in Africa: A review of emerging issues and implications for policy options. *International Policy Centre for Inclusive Growth One Pager No. 248*, April 2014.

Oxfam, 2010. Addressing land grabbing in Africa: why governments should stand up for marginalized communities. Oxford: Oxfam.

Oxfam, 2011. Land and power: the growing scandal surrounding the new wave of investments in land. *Oxfam International Briefing Paper 51*. Oxford: Oxfam.

Polack, E., L. Cotula and M. Cote, 2013. Accountability in African Land Rush: What role for local empowerment? London: International Institute of Environment and Development and International Development Research Centre (IDRC).

Potter, P., N. Ramankutty, E. M Bennett, and S. D. Donner, 2010. Characterizing the Spatial Patterns of Global Fertilizer Application and Manure Production. *Earth Interactions* 14, no. 2, pp. 1-22.

Prishchepov, A.V., Radeloff, V.C., Muller, D., Dubinin M. and Baumann, M., 2011. Determinants of agricultural land abandonment in post-soviet European Russia. *No.1 No 1, IAMO Forum 2011: Will the "BRICs Decade" Continue? – Prospects for Trade and Growth from Leibniz Institute of Agricultural Development in Central and Eastern Europe (IAMO).*

Richardson, B., 2010. Big sugar in Southern Africa: rural development and the perverted potential of sugar/ethanol exports. *Journal of Peasant Studies*, 37(4), pp.917–938.

Robertson, B. and P. Pinstrup-Andersen, 2010. Global Land Acquisition: Neo-colonialism or development opportunity? *Food Security (2010)* 2, pp. 271-283.

Rulli, M.C., A. Saviori and P. D'Odorico, 2013. Global land and water grabbing. Proceedings of the

Scoones, Ian, Ruth Hall, Saturnino M. Borras Jr, Ben White and Wendy Wolford (2013): "The Politics of Evidence: Methodologies for understanding the global land rush", *The Journal of Peasant Studies*, volume 40, no 3, pp. 469-483.

United Nations Development Programme (UNDP), 2006. Beyond Scarcity: Power, poverty and the global water crisis Human Development Report 2006. New York: United Nations Development Programme.

United Nations (2013): World Population Prospects: The 2012 Revision – Key findings and advanced tables. New York: UN Department of Economic and Social Affairs, 2013.

United Nations Development Programme (UNDP), 2012. African Human Development Report 2012: Towards a food secure future. New York: UNDP.

Van der Molen, P. and A. Tuladhar, 2007. Corruption and Land Administration, *International Federation of Surveyors, Article of the Month*, March 2007, The Netherlands, http://www.fig.net/pub/monthly_articles/march_2007/march_2007_vandermolen_tuladhar.pdf

Woodhouse, P. A and S. Ganho, 2011. "Is water the hidden agenda of agricultural land acquisition in Sub-Saharan Africa?" Paper presented at the International Conference on Global Land Grabbing, 6-8 April 2011. Organized by the Land Deals Politics Initiative (LDPI) in collaboration with the Journal of Peasant Studies and hosted by the Future Agriculture Consortium at the Institute of Development Studies, University of Sussex. Available from: http://www.iss.nl/fileadmin/ASSETS/iss/Documents/Conference_papers/LDPI/12_P_Woodhouse_and_A_S_Ganho.pdf. [Accessed June 2013].

World Bank, 2010. *Rising Global Interest in Farmland: Can it yield sustainable and equitable benefits?* Washington DC: The World Bank.

World Bank, FAO and Agricultural Rural Development (2009): Awakening Africa's Sleeping Giant: Prospects for Commercial Agriculture in the Guinea Savannah Zone and Beyond, *Agriculture and Rural Development Notes, Issue 48, June 2009*. Washington, DC: The World Bank.

Zoomers, A., 2010. "Globalization and the foreignisation of space: Seven processes driving the current global land grab", Journal of Peasant Studies, 37:2, pp. 429-447.

Land Reforms and Development:

Meta-narrative in Botswana

Chadzimula Otsetswe Molebatsi

Introduction

Access to land is increasingly becoming a topical subject in Botswana. In 2011, with a land mass of 582 000 km2 and a population of just over two million, the country's average population density was estimated at 3.8 persons per km2. The low average population density is deceptive in that population distribution is skewed with higher concentrations in the south-eastern parts of the country where most urban centres are located. Access to residential land is the most prevalent challenge in the country's urban areas while in the sparsely populated rural areas, particularly the western parts of the country, problematic access to land is largely a result of conflicting land use demands and the increasing *de facto* privatization of communal land.

Since the beginning of 2013 a series of events surrounding land dominated the country's media. In February, the leader of the Botswana Congress Party (BCP) tabled a motion in parliament calling for a national land audit (Moeng 2013:a). Despite widespread support for the motion outside parliament, the motion was defeated largely due to the numerical dominance of the ruling party - the Botswana Democratic Party (BDP) in parliament (Modise 2013). In yet another incident, residents of Tlokweng a peri-urban settlement to the east of Gaborone challenged a decision by the local land authority - the Tlokweng Land Board to allocate land on a first come first served basis as per the provisions of the Tribal Land Act. Instead, the residents called for preferential allocation in favour of indigenous residents of Tlokweng (Shabani 2013). It does appear that sentiments expressed by the residents of Tlokweng found favour with the ruling Botswana Democratic Party and resulted in the amendment of the Land Policy such that 70% of the available land in peri-urban areas is allocated to indigenous population.

In a widely publicised case, residents of Ranyane a San settlement in the western part of the country took the Botswana Government to Court over a decision to relocate them from what residents considered their ancestral home (Moeng 2013:b). In June 2013, street vendors in the tourist town of Maun woke up to find their stalls uprooted from the street by the Council byelaw enforcement agents who claimed that they were acting on instructions from the Government (http://www.the voicebw.com/2013/06.21). This claim was refuted by the Assistant Minister in the Ministry of Local Government. A phone-in programme for one of the private radio station -Gabz FM - heavily criticized the move as insensitive to the plight of the low income groups who draw their sustenance from the informal sector.

The argument presented in this chapter is twofold: first, the land question and its manifestations as noted above is viewed as emanating from the development practice orchestrated by the state in Botswana. Through a review of land reforms that the country has undertaken, it is argued that the development project in Botswana has been accompanied by systematic land dispossession and marginalization of the poor particularly San communities. Secondly, drawing on the post-development critique of development, the chapter identifies sites of resistance effected by local communities in relation to the development interventions. It is argued that these sites of resistance are important pointers towards more inclusive social transformation.

To develop the argument the chapter uses a combination of archival material and commentaries on land tenure reforms and local community responses. These are drawn from both published and unpublished sources. The chapter is divided into four sections: following the introduction in section 1, section 2 provides a conceptual framework around which the chapter seeks to understand the land question and responses from the grassroots. This is followed by a review of the land tenure system reforms under the country's development project. Section 4 provides case examples showing attempts by groups and Non-Governmental Organisations to address land related problems. The case examples are viewed as having some affinities with the post-development thinking and could possibly lead to more than just land distribution and diversified land uses in Botswana.

Post-development debate

Post-development thinking is considered important not only in providing a perspective from which the land question in Botswana could be understood but also in charting innovative ways of addressing them. It is widely believed that the emergence of the post-development discourse brought about significant shift in development theory (Ziai 2007). Escobar (2007) places the origins of post-development in the post-structuralist critique of development that 'questioned the ways in which Asia, Africa and Latin America came to be defined as underdeveloped.' For Gibson-Graham (2007), post-development voices expressed disillusionment with the one-size-fits all model of development. To some analysts, post-development calls not for alternative development but alternative to development and an era in which development would no longer be the central organizing principle of social life (Escober 2007:20). According to some observers, post-development proponents perceive development as rooted in meta-narrative which reflects the interest of the practitioners (Rapley 2004:350). Viewed as such, development does not aim for human improvement but human control and thus, building hegemony as it consolidates power of the modernizing elites (Rapley 2004:351). Post-development proponents reject the notion that there can or should be one model of development. In the place of the one-size-fits all model of development post-development 'brings an awareness that reality can be redefined in terms of other than those of development and that consequently, people and social groups can act otherwise on the basis of those definitions' (Escober 2007:40).

Furthermore, Escobar (2007:20-21) identifies the following as central to the idea of post development:

i) the possibility of creating different discourses and representations that are not so mediated by the construct (ideologies, metaphors, language, premises etc) of development

ii) the need to change the practices of knowing and doing and the political economy of truth that define the development regime

iii) the need to multiply the centres and agents of knowledge production - in particular, to give salience to the forms of knowledge produced by those who are supposed to be the objects of development so that they can become subjects of their own right.

Escobar (ibid:21) posits that the above could be effected through two major ways: focusing on adaptations, subversions and resistance that local peoples effect in relation to development...and by highlighting the alternative strategies produced by social movements as they encounter development (ibid). Of interest is the approach's support for popular initiatives and what Escober refers to as 'sensitivity to difference and unwillingness to accept without question the authority of the expert' (Escober (1995) quoted in Matthews 2007). The contention is that alternatives to development lie mainly in grassroots resistance to dominant interventions from mainstream development practice. The argument here is that social movements and NGOs come up with strategies through which they address the challenges accompanying the development project. Some of the strategies used include the utilization of what has been dubbed 'sites of resistance" which could be in the form of spaces for participation.

Cornwall and Caelho (2007:1) assert that such spaces may be provided for by the state, and they may also be viewed as spaces conquered by civil society demands for inclusion. Spaces for participation are conceived as a continuum which includes invited spaces and created spaces (Gaventa 2004:35). Invited spaces are defined as those into which people as users, citizens or beneficiaries are invited to participate by various kinds of authorities (Cornwall 2002:24). The contention is that such spaces could be innovatively used by the marginalized to call for meaningful changes in policy formulation. It has been argued that counter-hegemonic planning practices could be effected through 'sanctioned spaces for participation' (Miraftab 2009:34). The contention is that while such spaces might be created by the state, they can be innovatively used as sites for mobilisation for social transformation. Drawing on the Foulcauldian concept of 'strategic revesibility" of power, it is opined that "government invitations to participation are in themselves always already sites of resistance" and that such ''sites are productive of possibilities of subversion, appropriation and reconstitution" (Corrnwall 2002:9). Thus, according to Cornwall (2009), particular spaces may be produced by the powerful, but filled with those whose alternative visions transform their possibilities. Spaces may be created with one purpose in mind, but used by those who come to fill them for something quite different (ibid). For their part created spaces or invented spaces are defined by John Gaventa as 'spaces claimed by less powerful actors from or against the power holders or created more autonomously by them' (Gaventa 2004:35). Miraftab (2009:39) defines invented spaces as collective actions by the poor that directly confront the authorities and challenge the status quo. As shown later in this chapter, marginalized communities in Botswana have attempted to use both invited and invented spaces of participation in a bid to access land.

Land tenure systems in Botswana

The evolution of land tenure system in Botswana demonstrates how mainstream development practice in the country has been accompanied by systematic land dispossession and marginalisation of the poor. In this section, we provide a historicized account of land tenure reforms in Botswana. In the account we try to understand factors or justification for the changes instituted by policy makers. It is argued that at each stage, the rationale for land reforms was always lodged in what was perceived as the inefficiencies of the indigenous tenure systems. Land reforms undertaken in Botswana are informed by rationalistic development models that denigrate 'other forms of being, knowing and acting'. This is evident for example in the manner in which all the major land reform systematically undermined communal land and projected it as counter-productive.

Land tenure is understood to mean the land holding systems pertaining to a given community. Such systems are sanctioned by the laws and cultural practices of the community in question. FAO define land tenure as ''rules invented by societies to regulate how property rights to land are to be allocated within society (http://www.fao.org,1). Prior to colonisation in 1885, the ethnic groups that later constituted Botswana lived as autonomous entities consisting of Bantu and non-Bantu groups. The Bantu groups included the predominant Tswana stock namely Bangwato, Batlokwa, Balete, Bakwena, Bangwaketse, Bakgatla and Barolong. Other ethnic groups of Bantu stock included Bakalanga, Basubiya, Bayeyi and others.

Land tenure systems between the Bantu and non-Bantu groups differed significantly. Amongst the Bantu groups land was communally owned and administered on behalf of the tribe by the chief (Schapera 1943). A tripartite land use system was common amongst the Bantu groups particularly those of Tswana stock and each member of the community had access to land for residential, arable and livestock grazing purposes (Kalabamu 2000; Schapera 1943). Land rights for the above uses were inheritable and perpetual (Kalabamu 2012). An important attribute of indigenous tenure system which was to change later in the post-colonial period was that every member of the tribe had access to natural resources in unallocated land and land that was fallow (Schapera 1943).

The land tenure system among the San groups differed significantly from that of the Bantu groups described above. Schapera, (Ibid) contends that land was commonly owned and there was equal access to land and land resources among members of the band. According to Nthomang

(2002) members of the band had the right to exploit the resources within a specific territory. Such land could not be bought, sold or used as collateral for a loan. Studies on San have shown for example that communities had highly developed concepts of territoriality which in turn regulated access to local resources. For example, outsiders could only harvest natural resources within a given area only with the express permission of the resident or local community. As shown later in this chapter, the San land tenure system and accompanying land use as described were never recognized but instead were ignored and discarded under the development project resulting in their socio-economic marginalization.

Botswana's land tenure system is largely a creation of the colonial period and was retained at independence. Colonial land tenure aimed primarily at furthering the economic and political objective of colonisation. A three tier land tenure system was introduced during this period namely native reserve (communal land), freehold and crown land (Malatsi and Finnstrom 2011; Kalabamu 2012). Crown land was reserved mainly for game and nature reserves as well as some of the emerging urban centres. Freehold land was created specifically for the settler communities engaged in pastoral farming. The creation of both Crown land and freehold was accompanied by eviction of local communities. In the case of the present day North East District for example, activities of the Tati Company led to the eviction of local communities to give way to farms for settler farmers. Similar evictions and relocations took place in the Tuli Block and Gantsi Block Farms were the indefatigable Cecil John Rhodes's British South African Company was active in settling European farming communities (Molebatsi 1994). Freehold land was curved out of the country's most fertile areas and once evicted from these areas, the native population either enlisted in labour migration system for South African mining economy or became labourers in the European owned farms. In the case of the Gantsi Block Farms, for example, displaced San communities became labourers in the freehold farms where they worked under extreme exploitative conditions (see for example Mogalakwe 1986). The post-colonial period saw the retention of the colonial land tenure system with changes mainly in the nomenclature. While the category freehold was retained, native reserves and crown land became tribal land and state land respectively (Malatsi and Finnstrom 2011). It is estimated that tribal land constitute 71% of the total land in Botswana with Freehold and State land taking up the remaining 23 % and 6 % respectively (see Fig.1).

Figure 1: Land Tenure (Source: DTRP, 1998)

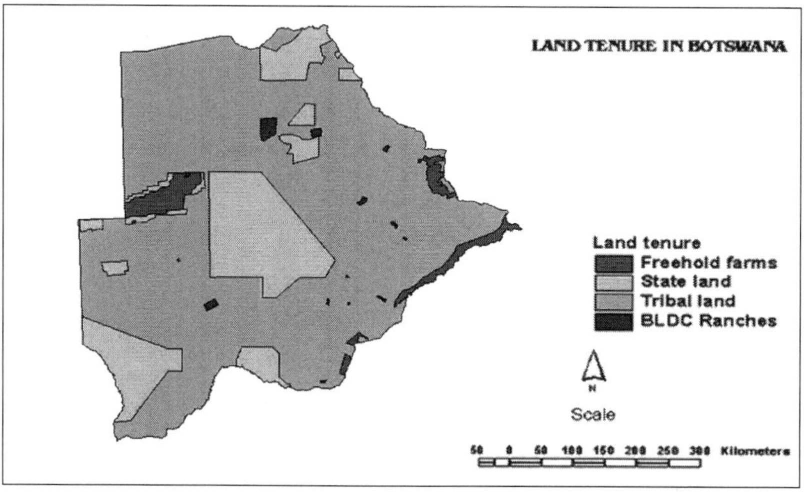

Table 1 shows that the proportion of land falling under each category has changed over time. While there has been an increase in the proportion of tribal land and freehold, state land has significantly declined. This has led Adams *et.al.* (2003) to conclude that the policy in Botswana has been to increase the area of tribal land at the expense of both state land and freehold. While the above observation is true, it should be stated that, through issuance of leasehold and various land management practices, a significant proportion of tribal land is held under *de facto* privatization. This is the case with leasehold farms allocated under the Tribal Grazing Land Policy (TGLP) (1975) and its successor – the fencing component of the National Policy on Agricultural Development (NPAD) that was introduced in 1991.

Table 1 Land Tenure Categories in Botswana, 1966-1998

Year	Tribal land		Stateland		Freehold	
	Area	%	Area	%	Area	%
1966	278,535	48.8	270,761	47.4	21,356	3.7
1979	403,730	69.4	145,040	24.9	32,960	5.7
1998	411,349	70.9	144,588	24.9	24,572	4.2

Source: White 1999 as cited in Adams et.al. 2003

Land held under the three tenure systems is administered differently. Tribal land is administered by the Tribal Land Boards and ideally, citizens of

Botswana have access to tribal / communal land for residential, arable and grazing purposes. Tribal land is allocated under customary or common law grant basis and cannot be sold. Holders of tribal land tenure can however sell developments on their land. The above notwithstanding, tribal land holders have found ways through which tribal land is sold.

The administration of State land is the responsibility of the Department of Lands on behalf of Government. Ownership of state land rests with Government and allocation is made on leasehold basis as either Fixed Period State Grant (FPSG) or in the case of Self-Help Housing schemes Certificate of Right (COR). Included under state land are some of the country's game reserves and national parks - such as CKGR. Some of the settlements in Botswana that fall under state land tenure include Lobatse, Gaborone, Francistown, Jwaneng, Gantsi, Kasane and Selibe Phikwe. Generally, there is an acute shortage of land within state land areas, particularly around the main urban centres.

What is of significance to the present chapter are the reasons or justification for the changes in land tenure systems in particular the introduction of freehold, state land and leaseholds in the customary land, which as argued above were introduced in the colonial period and retained at independence. According to Cullis and Watson (2005), the changes in land policy were founded on Garret Hardin's 'tragedy of the commons' thesis, which projects a negative view of the commons. Communal land was viewed as implying open access and as such lacking in control mechanisms. In the post-colonial period, communal land tenure was viewed as highly susceptible to degradation due to lack of control mechanisms on the number of animals that could be allowed into such areas. Individuals within the communal areas were viewed as pursuing personal interest with minimal regard for consequences on the environment. The contention was that rangeland degradation could be addressed by replacing communal ownership with individual allocation of land.

The rationale for changes in land tenure is also found in conceptions of colonization as a capitalist expansion project. Armstrong and McGee, (1985) employ the concepts of dissolution and conservation to describe how capitalist expansion takes place. The concept of conservation / dissolution is used to describe the interaction between market-based economic formations and indigenous / non-market based formations. The argument is that there exist cases in which despite being linked to international economy, the capitalist sectors in a given society would at the same time be interacting with non-capitalist formations. Mechanisms of conservation describe the tendency of the capitalist sector not to act immediately to dissolve this other system. There are, however, cases in which the capitalist formations will immediately move in to dissolve the non-capitalist formation. Conservation occurs when the non-capitalist formation poses little danger to the capitalist formations. Dissolution is effected in those cases where non-capitalist formations pose a danger to capitalist formations (Ibid).

When applied to the case of Botswana, it can be argued that communal land ownership as practiced in pre-colonial period is not conducive to the market based economies where land is treated as a commodity. Private ownership of land was instead promoted as the desirable tenure system which allowed individual owners to improve the productivity of land. The denigration of communal land ownership continued into the post-colonial Botswana where various land reforms were introduced. Communal land ownership is portrayed as inappropriate and in its place *de facto* privatisation of land is promoted through the introduction of leaseholds and land management practices that promote individualistic ownership of land. In the discussion that follows we focus on how land dispossession and marginalization of the poor was realised through two processes- first, *de facto* privatization through fencing and secondly, the non-recognition of gathering as a *bona fide* land use.

De-facto privatisation of land through fencing in rural areas

The fencing of grazing areas in Botswana can be traced back to the introduction of freehold tenure system in the colonial period. This was largely facilitated by the policies of the colonial government and the activities of the British South African Company. Fencing was particularly common in areas such as the Gantsi Block, Lobatse Blocks, Gaborone Block, the Tuli Block and the Tati District. Quite often the process was accompanied by the eviction of local communities as was the case in the Tuli Blocks and the Tati Districts (Tapela 1982). The above notwithstanding, the farms were well managed and to an extent provided range management practices to be emulated (see Chambers and Feldman 1972; Tsimako 1991).

In the post independence period two land reform policies promoted fencing of communal areas. These were the Tribal Grazing Land Policy (TGLP) introduced in 1975 and the 1991 National Policy on Agricultural Development (NPAD). Several authorities have discussed the circumstances surrounding the formulation of the Tribal Grazing Land Policy (cf Sandford 1980; Republic of Botswana 1975; Parson 1981;

Tsimako 1991). The policy sought to address the perceived overgrazing in the country's rangelands by creating commercial leaseholds ranches. It was envisaged that this would enable large livestock owners to move out of the overstocked and overgrazed communal areas. Furthermore, the new ranches each measuring 8km x 8km would also provide an opportunity for the farmers to adopt improved livestock management system. The shift of livestock by large cattle owners from communal areas to leasehold ranches was also viewed as promoting social equity in that it would create room for expansion for small farmers. Between the two land reform policies a total of 1028 ranches were demarcated for allocation to individuals. It is important to note that once fenced, these former communal areas become semi-private areas that could only be accessed with express permission from the leaseholders.

Non-Recognition of gathering as a *bona fide* land use

The collection of veldt products or gathering forms an important component of livelihoods for the rural poor in Botswana. Despite public sector pronouncements on the significance of gathering to rural communities, gathering is not yet a recognised activity for which land has to be set aside. Recognised land uses for which land is often set aside are depicted in Figure 2 and include arable, pastural, settlement, wildlife and forest reserves.

Map 1: Botswana Land Use

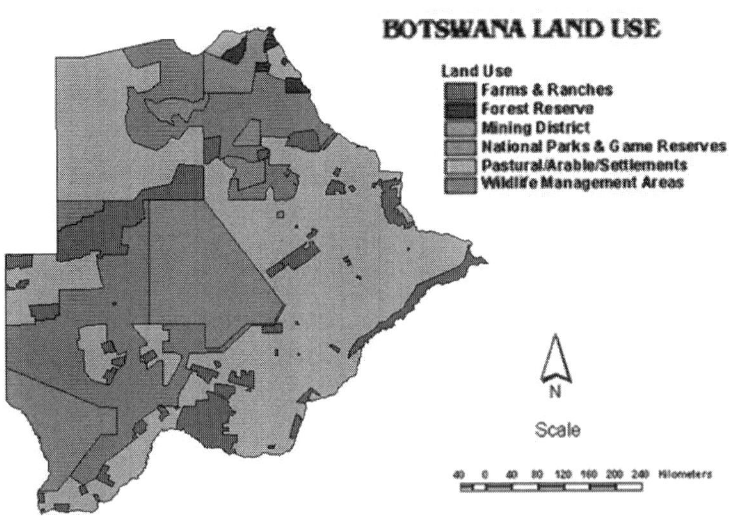

Source: Botswana Atlas 2001

The non-recognition of gathering as a land use in its own right is closely linked to the socio-political and economic marginalization of groups historically associated with hunting and gathering - the San communities. Arable and pastoral farming are the main economic activities of the Tswana / Bantu groups living in Botswana. Land use practices of the Tswana groups are captured in the tripartite settlement pattern comprising village, lands and cattle-post. This settlement pattern is often projected as typical of Botswana society. The tripartite classification informs land use planning and policies in Botswana and as shown in Figure 2, gathering as a land use is conspicuous by its absence. Failure to recognize gathering as a land use in its own right means that expansion of arable and pastoral farming is often at the expense of land on which gathering of veld products as a source of livelihood takes place.

Marginalisation of gathering is demonstrated in the thinking that informs the Tribal Grazing Land Policy and the National Policy on Agricultural Development introduced above. Under the both policies communal range lands were largely viewed as farming areas hence the classification as either commercial farming or communal grazing areas. A common attribute found in both policies is the failure to recognize the multiple use nature of range lands (Ramphete 1996; GoB 2003, Cullis and Watson 2005). In the process, those who use these areas for purposes of gathering or foraging often lose their land use rights to cattle owners.

Non-recognition of gathering as a land use is also evident in those cases where arable agricultural land uses expand over veldt product rich areas. Areas that are known to be rich in 'mo*phane* worms (*Gonimbrasea belina)* – are often under threat to pave way for arable agriculture. Thus despite the low output from the agricultural sector, there is still an increase in size of the land put under arable agriculture. The introduction of programmes like the National Master Plan for Arable Agriculture and Dairy Development (NAMPAADD) will accelerate the increase in arable land and inevitably, reduce areas available for the gathering of veldt products. Under the existing set-up, expansion of agricultural land - be it grazing or arable farming cannot be curbed or halted on grounds that such expansion threatens the availability of veldt products in a given area.

Non-recognition of gathering as a *bona fide* land use is deemed to have rendered the San landless. Moeletsi (1993) traces the landless status of the San to failure by the Tribal Land Act to recognise their land uses. The Tribal Land Act recognises residential, arable, grazing and commercial use. Gathering and hunting the two primary land uses associated with the San are thus not recognised as land uses in their own right.

The promulgation and subsequent implementation of the Tribal Grazing Land Policy and the National Agricultural Development Policy are often cited as clear indications of the non-recognition of San land rights. The two policies are thus viewed as a continuation of San land dispossession, a process that can be traced back to the colonial period (Moeletsi and N'gong'ola, 1996; Ditshwanelo 2007:3) Quoting the work of Campbell, Main and Associates, Good, (2001: 22) concludes that in the case of the Western Sand Veldt, the demarcation of ranches proceeded without regard for the San who could be told to move by anyone who had been awarded land rights by the land board.

Commentators have raised equity issues in relation to the fencing component of the 1991 Agricultural Policy. For example, Perkins (1996) refers to 'fencing out of the equity issue' - an attempt to describe the de facto privatisation of communal land under the NPAD. A study of the Kaka area by the Central District Technical Committee (on the Fencing Component of the NPAD) in 1995 demonstrates the limited access to land accorded the San under the NADP. The study followed a decision to use Kaka as a pilot area for the fencing of communal rangelands. Extensive socio-economic studies carried out revealed the presence of San communities in the area. Most of these people were settled around boreholes and were regarded by the borehole owners as squatters. The Technical Committee recommended that at least some of the ranches should be reserved for the local San communities. It does appear that the recommendation was never implemented as ranches have been demarcated and allocated to individuals and in the process entrenched landlessness among San communities. In the next section we examine attempts by San communities to address the land question. It is in these attempts by the San that we see elements of post-development practices, which could possibly bring about more equitable land distribution practices that recognise pluralism in land uses.

Grassroots attempts at improving access to land

Post-development theorists view social movements and NGOs activities as offering possibilities for more inclusive transformation than is currently the case under mainstream development practice. In this section, we examine attempts by NGOs working mainly with San communities to address the land problems identified above. Such attempts or sites of resistance have been in two related forms - namely sanctioned spaces of participation as well as invented or created spaces of participation. For invited spaces of participation, San groups have used the provisions of the Tribal Land Act. As for invented spaces of participation, there have been attempts by San groups to address displacement from their traditional lands through innovative strategies such as participatory Geographical Information Systems mapping.

Utilising sanctioned spaces of participation

Working within the provisions of the TLA entails following the provisions of the Tribal Land Act, which theoretically guarantees equitable access to land to all citizens of Botswana. Ideally anyone can collect application forms for land, fill them in and submit to the land board. This approach requires mobilisation and awareness raising to help San communities to apply for residential and also acquire the necessary documentation showing proof of ownership.

NGOs that have successfully used this approach include Tqii Xu Yani (TXY), TOCaDI and Komku. TXY was formed in 1996 as a syndicate for purposes of supporting the process of San self-determination in their socio-economic and political development. It is a fully registered organisation through which Basarwa communities in Kang and its environs are mobilized for self-development. Further, through community mobilization efforts, Basarwa living in and around Kang have been assisted to apply for residential plots and arable land of their own. Many people have now applied for residential plots in Kang and are waiting for allocation by the Kgalagadi Land Board.

TOCaDi and Komku are some of the eight San organizations that constitute the Kuru Family of Organisations (KFO). Like in the case of TXY, the two organisations used existing structures to facilitate land acquisition by San groups. One of the strategies employed to assist the San to acquire land was through the establishment and registration of syndicates. An evaluation exercise of KFO activities revealed that TOCaDI has managed to assist 10 groups to register borehole syndicates. Komku increased the registration of cattle syndicates from 5-10 between 2009 and 2010. This is a major achievement given the role that boreholes play in facilitating or limiting access to grazing land in Botswana. Water rights conferred on individuals or groups automatically gives them de facto grazing rights over an area ranging from 36 000 ha to 64 000 ha. Ownership of a borehole or water rights is important in terms of control over of the grazing areas in which the borehole is located.

Perhaps the greatest success in using sanctioned spaces of participation by San communities has been recourse to existing legislation and structures for purposes of accessing land. San communities successfully challenged the Government of Botswana decision to relocate them from the Central Kalahari Game Reserve. In a similar case the Government of Botswana lost a case in which residents of Ranyane were to be relocated from their ancestral land (Open Society Initiative 18th June 2013 http://allafrica.com/stories/201306181724.html).

Created / invented spaces of participation

San communities have also embarked upon activities aimed at reclaiming land that they have lost to other groups in Botswana. These efforts are at the heart of Participatory Geographical Information System mapping exercises facilitated by the Kuru Family of Organisations (KFO). According to Taylor et. al. 2006, PGIS has been used in Community Based Natural Resource Management (CBNRM) projects in southern Africa to empower local communities to 'articulate their spatial thinking'. Nuulimba (2003) emphatically asserts that the process is aimed at helping the San peoples to regain control over traditional lands. The above view is corroborated by Hitchcock et al.(2006:23) who argued that 'mapping of traditional and contemporary land use and tenure patterns are an important strategy in the effort to gain more secure access to land and to help promote land conservation and development efforts among the San."

Early examples of mapping used for purposes of protecting San land rights include the First People of the Kalahari (FPK)'s Show the Land Pilot Project. The project was formulated in response to the increasing land use pressure on traditional N/oakwe areas and the continued displacement of the people from their resource areas'. The project was planned to take place inside the CKGR. It does appear that the project was curtailed in the 2001 as the Central Kalahari Game Reserve controversy intensified.

One of the organisations that have actively used PGIS mapping among the San people in Botswana is the Kuru Familiy of Organisations. KFO is described as an affiliated group of NGOs working in Botswana and South Africa with the common goal of empowering the San people through a holistic approach to development" http:/wiser.org/. According to Job Morris KFO membership is made up of independent San-owned organizations (Morris 2008). These include Letloa, Trust for Okavango Cultural and Development Initiatives (TOCaRDI) Bokamoso, Kumku Trust, Kuru D'Kar Trust. Gantsi Craft, and, San Art and Craft. Each of the Trust has an area of focus and which include issues of land, income generation and natural resource and cultural heritage.

KFO has worked relentlessly on increasing San's access to land and land resources in the Gantsi District and Okavango sub-districts. With the support of the Canadian based company Strata 360, the KFO trained San people in PGIS mapping. As described by Nuulimba, (2005:1) the exercise involves a team of trained community members who carry out the mapping accompanied by elders who provide a detailed description of the landscape. This is followed by geo-referencing of salient features and the production of a resource map. Resource inventory maps produced under this exercise include those for Shaikarawe, a small settlement of less than 500 people located about 20km south-west of Shakawe. The Shaikarawe community was faced with resource depletion due to unsustainable harvesting from neighbouring communities. On the basis of the resource map, the community initiated a dialogue with the Government of Botswana to start a community forestry project.

Conclusion

Perhaps the question that could be posed is how successful PGIS mapping has been in improving access to land for San communities. For now, the greatest potential lies in that PGIS mapping has become the basis for San land and land use advocacy and calls for the type of development that takes on board San knowledge. This is evident in the KFO 2009 Annual report that calls for integration of San values into the development process (KFO 2009). The values are viewed as "*a gift to the world*" (KFO 2008) in that the world could learn a different approach towards bringing about change to communities. Similar sentiments on the importance of the San values to the wider development process were expressed in the Norwegian Council of Churches Evaluation report of KFO. The Report emphatically argued "As we move into the new millennium, these first people who preceded us, and their future development, hold keys for our own development, as we do to their" (Davidoff and Kaplan 2006:2). This seems to be a clear recognition of other forms of "knowing and doing" and is very much against the dominant thinking that informs the development project in Botswana. This resonates well with what Sandercock (1998,184) dubbed 'a literacy about another culture'. According to Sandercock, there is need for ...honoring of a different way of life and of a desire to preserve that difference (ibid). There is no doubt that in the case of the San, state-led development does not only denigrate San concept of land and access to land, but has set out to completely obliterate it. Efforts such as those by KFO where PGIS is used as a tool for reclaiming land bring a glimmer of hope and real possibilities for a more just plural society.

The attempt in this chapter was to show how conventional development practice in Botswana entrenched marginalisation and land dispossession among the rural poor, in particular San communities. Post independence land reforms continually failed to recognize land tenure and land use practices unique to San communities. The chapter has also shown that working through local NGOs San communities in Botswana are utilizing both invited and invented spaces for participation in a search for meaningful social transformation. Perhaps in Botswana the challenge is how those concerned with a just society could lend support to such initiatives by San communities.

References

Ando, A.W. and P. Shah, 2009. Demand for factors in optimal land choice, paper presented at the Agricultural Economics Association 2009 and the ACCI Joint Annual Meeting, Milwaukee, Wisconsin, July 26-29, 2009.

Anseeuw, W., M. Boche, T. Breu, M. Giger, J. Lay, P. Messerli and K. Nolte, 2012. Transnational Land Deals for Agriculture in the Global South, *Analytical Report based on the Land Matrix Database Number 1*: April 2012. Available from: http://farmlandgrab.org. [Accessed May 2012].

Arezki, R., K. Deininger and H. Selod, 2011. What drives the global land rush?, *IMF Working Paper (WP/11/251)*, The International Monetary Fund, 2011.

Aw, D. and G. Diemer, 2005. Making a Large Irrigation Scheme Work. A Case Study from Mali. *Directions in Development*. Washington, DC: The World Bank.

Bruinsma, J.,2009. The resource outlook to 2050. By how much do land, water use and crop yields need to increase by 2050? In *Session 2: The resource base to 2050: Will there be enough land, water and genetic potential to meet future food and biofuel demands?* Rome, Italy, June 24.

Byamugishe, F.F.K.,2013. *Securing Africa's land for shared prosperity: A programme to scale up reform and investments*. Washington, D.C.: The World Bank.

Cotula, L., S. Vermeulen, R. Leonard and J. Keeley, 2009. *Land grab or development opportunity? Agricultural development and international land deals in Africa*. London: International Institute for Environment and Development, Rome; Food and Agricultural Organization, Rome: International Fund for Agricultural Development.

Cotula, L., 2011. *Land deals in Africa: What is in the contracts?* London: International Institute for Environment and Development (IIED). Available from: http://pubs.iied.org/12568IIED.html [Accessed July 2013].

Cotula, L., 2012. The International Political Economy of the Global Land Rush: A critical appraisal of trends, scale, geography and drivers, *The Journal of Peasant Studies*, Vol. 39, Nos. 3–4, July–October 2012, 649–680.

Deininger, K. and D. Byerlee, with J. Lindsay, A. Norton, H. Selod and M. Stickler, 2011. *Rising global interest in farmland: can it yield sustainable and equitable benefits?* Washington, DC: The World Bank.

Deininger, K., 2011. Challenges posed by the new wave of farmland investment, *Journal of Peasant Studies*, http://www.tandfonline.com/loi/fjps20

Deininger, K. and D. Byerlee, 2011. The Rise of Large Farms in Land Abundant Countries: Do They Have A Future?, *Policy Research Working Paper 5588*, March 2011.

Deininger, K., D. A. Ali, S. T. Holden and J. Zevenbergen, 2008. Rural land certification in

Ethiopia: Process, initial impact, and implications for other African countries. *World Development 36*, pp. 1786-1812.

Food and Agricultural Organization (FAO), 2009. The *State of Agricultural Commodity Markets 2009*. Rome: United Nations Food and Agriculture Organization.

FAO 2005. Irrigation in Africa in figures, *Aquastat Survey (2005)*. Rome: The United Nations Food and Agriculture Organisation.

Fischer, G., van Velthuizen, H., Shah, M. and F. Nachtergaele, 2002. *Global Agro-ecological Assessment for Agriculture in the 21st Century:*

Methodology and results, RR-02-002, Laxenburg: International Institute for Applied Systems Analysis (IIASA).

Food and Agricultural Organization (FAO), International Fund for Agricultural Development (IFAD), United Nations Conference on Trade and Development (UNCTAD) and The World Bank, 2010. Principles for Responsible Agricultural Investment that Protect Rights, Livelihoods and Resources. *Discussion Note 25 January 2010.* Rome: FAO, IFAD, UNCTAD and the World Bank Group. Available from http://siteresources.worldbank.org/INTARD/214574-1111383886l/22453321/Principles_Extended.pdf. [Accessed June 2012].

Friis, C. and A. Reenberg, 2010. Land Grab in Africa: Emerging land system drivers in a teleconnected world. GLP Report No.1. Copenhagen: GLP-IPO, University of Copenhagen.

Garvelink, W.J., 2012. "Land Tenure, Property Rights, and Rural Economic Development in Africa", Centre for Strategic and International Studies, February 2012. Available from http://csis.org/publication/land-tenure-property-rights-and-rural-economic-development-africa. [Accessed June 2013].

Gorgen, M., B. Rudloff, J. Simons, A. Ullengerg, S. Vath and L. Wimmer, 2009. Foreign direct investment (FDI) in land in developing countries. Eschborn: GTZ Division 45 – Agriculture, Fisheries and Food, GTZ.

GRAIN, 2008. Seized! The 2008 land grab for food and financial security. *Briefing October 2008*. Barcelona: GRAIN.

GRAIN, 2009. The new farm owners: corporate investors lead the rush for control over overseas farmland[online]. GRAIN: Barcelona: GRAIN, 20 October 2009. Available from: http://www.grain.org/article/entries/194-the-new-farm-owners. [Accessed June 2013].

GRAIN, 2010. Saudi investors poised to take control of rice production in Senegal and Mali [online]. 29 November 2010. Available from: http://www.grain.org/article/entries/3997-saudi-investorspoised-to-take-control-of-rice-production-in-Senegal-and-Mali. [Accessed July 2013].

GTZ,2009. *Foreign direct investment (FDI) in land in developing countries*. Eschborn: Work of division 45, Agriculture, fisheries and food, GTZ.

Hall, R.,2011. "Land Grabbing in Southern Africa: The Many Faces of the Investor Rush", Paper for STIAS Colloquium on Land reform, agrarian change and rural poverty in Southern Africa Venue: Wallenberg Conference centre, Stellenbosch, 8-9 March 2011.

Hertel, T., 2010. The global supply and demand for agricultural land in 2050: A perfect storm in the making, *GTAP Working Paper No 63*.

Haralambous, S., H. Liversage and M. Romano, 2009. The growing demand for land: Risks and opportunities for smallholder farmers. *Discussion Paper for Round Table 2, Governing Council*, 18-19 February 2009, IFAD.

International Food Policy Research Institute (IFPRI), Welt Hunger Hilfe and Concern Worldwide and Green Scenery, 2012. *2012 Global Hunger Index: The Challenge of hunger: ensuring Sustainable Food Security under land, water and energy stress.* Bonn, Washington, DC, and Dublin: IFPRI Concern Worldwide, Welthungerhilfe and Green Scenery.

International Institute for Environment and Development (IIED), 2012. The Global Land rush: What the evidence reveals about scale and geography? *IIED Briefing on the Global Land Rush. Available from IIED: http://pubs.iied.org/pdfs/17124IIED.pdf.* [Accessed June 2013].

Inter Press Service (IPS), 2013. World Bank boosts agricultural lending ahead of MDG Meet.

http://ipsnews.net/news.asp?idnews=52815. [Accessed July 2013].

IS Academie, 2012.Ethiopia: Food security and land governance factsheet. Land Governance for Equitable and Sustainable Development. Available from: http://www.landgovernance.org/system/files/Ethiopia%20Factsheet%20-%202012.pdf.

Land Matrix, 2012. Land Matrix data (April 2012). Available from: http://landportal.info/landmatrix/media/img/get-the-idea/top-10-target-countries.pdf. [Accessed May 2012].

Jacoby, H. G. and Minten, B.,2007. Is Land Titling in Sub-Saharan Africa Cost-Effective?

Evidence from Madagascar. *The World Bank Economic Review 21(3)*, pp. 461-485.

Licker, R., M. Johnston, C. Barford, J. A. Foley, C. J. Kucharik, C. Monfreda, and N. Ramankutty, 2010. Mind the Gap: How do climate and agricultural management explain the 'yield gap' of croplands around the world? *Global Ecology and Biogeography*, Volume 19, Issue 6, pp. 769-782.

Lugschitz, B., Bruckner, M. and S. Giljum, 2011. Europe global land demand: A study on the actual land embodied in European imports and exports of agricultural products. Final Report, Sustainable Europe Research Institute (SERI). Vienna: SERI.

Mann, H. and Smaller, C., 2010. Foreign Land Purchases for Agriculture: what impact on sustainable development? *Sustainable Development Innovation Brief No 8.* New York: United Nations *Department of Economic and Social Affairs.*

Miller, T., K.R. Holmes, E.J. Fueler, A.B. Kim, B. Riley and J.M. Roberts, 2013. *2013 Index of Economic Freedom.* Washington DC: The Heritage Foundation.

Neumann, K. , P. H. Verburg, E. Stehfest, and C. Müller, 2010. The yield gap of global grain production: A spatial analysis, Agricultural Systems, *2010, vol. 103, issue 5*, pp. 316-326.

Nkonya, E., A. Karsenty, S. Msangi, C. Souza Jr, M. Shah, J. von Braun, G. Galford, and S. Park, 2012."Sustainable land use for the 21st century", United Nations Department of Economic and Social Affairs Division's Project on Sustainable Development in the 21st Century (SD21), May 2012

Odusola, Ayodele (2012): Land Grab in Africa: An Overview of Emerging Issues and Policy Options. *Mimeograph.* UNDP Regional Bureau for Africa, New York.

Odusola, A.F., 2014a. Land grab in Africa: A review of emerging issues and implications for policy options. *International Policy Centre for Inclusive Growth Working Paper 124*, April 2014.

Odusola, A.F., 2014b. Land grab in Africa: A review of emerging issues and implications for policy options. *International Policy Centre for Inclusive Growth One Pager No. 248*, April 2014.

Oxfam, 2010. Addressing land grabbing in Africa: why governments should stand up for marginalized communities. Oxford: Oxfam.

Oxfam, 2011. Land and power: the growing scandal surrounding the new wave of investments in land. *Oxfam International Briefing Paper 51.* Oxford: Oxfam.

Polack, E., L. Cotula and M. Cote, 2013. Accountability in African Land Rush: What role for local empowerment? London: International Institute of Environment and Development and International Development Research Centre (IDRC).

Potter, P., N. Ramankutty, E. M Bennett, and S. D. Donner, 2010. Characterizing the Spatial Patterns of Global Fertilizer Application and Manure Production. *Earth Interactions* 14, no. 2, pp. 1-22.

Prishchepov, A.V., Radeloff, V.C., Muller, D., Dubinin M. and Baumann, M., 2011. Determinants of agricultural land abandonment in post-soviet European Russia. *No.1 No 1, IAMO Forum 2011: Will the "BRICs Decade" Continue? – Prospects for Trade and Growth from Leibniz Institute of Agricultural Development in Central and Eastern Europe (IAMO).*

Richardson, B., 2010. Big sugar in Southern Africa: rural development and the perverted potential of sugar/ethanol exports. *Journal of Peasant Studies*, 37(4), pp.917–938.

Robertson, B. and P. Pinstrup-Andersen, 2010. Global Land Acquisition: Neo-colonialism or development opportunity? *Food Security (2010)* 2, pp. 271-283.

Rulli, M.C., A. Saviori and P. D'Odorico, 2013. Global land and water grabbing. Proceedings of the Proceedings of the National Academy of Sciences.

Scoones, Ian, Ruth Hall, Saturnino M. Borras Jr, Ben White and Wendy Wolford (2013): "The Politics of Evidence: Methodologies for understanding the global land rush", *The Journal of Peasant Studies*, volume 40, no 3, pp. 469-483.

United Nations Development Programme (UNDP), 2006. Beyond Scarcity: Power, poverty and the global water crisis Human Development Report 2006. New York: United Nations Development Programme.

United Nations (2013): World Population Prospects: The 2012 Revision – Key findings and advanced tables. New York: UN Department of Economic and Social Affairs, 2013.

United Nations Development Programme (UNDP), 2012. African Human Development Report 2012: Towards a food secure future. New York: UNDP.

Van der Molen, P. and A. Tuladhar, 2007. Corruption and Land Administration, *International Federation of Surveyors, Article of the Month*, March 2007, The Netherlands, http://www.fig.net/pub/monthly_articles/march_2007/march_2007_vandermolen_tuladhar.pdf

Woodhouse, P. A and S. Ganho, 2011. "Is water the hidden agenda of agricultural land acquisition in Sub-Saharan Africa?" Paper presented at the International Conference on Global Land Grabbing, 6-8 April 2011. Organized by the Land Deals Politics Initiative (LDPI) in collaboration with the Journal of Peasant Studies and hosted by the Future Agriculture Consortium at the Institute of Development Studies, University of Sussex. Available from: http://www.iss.nl/fileadmin/ASSETS/iss/Documents/Conference_papers/LDPI/12_P_Woodhouse_and_A_S_Ganho.pdf . [Accessed June 2013].

World Bank, 2010. *Rising Global Interest in Farmland: Can it yield sustainable and equitable benefits?* Washington DC: The World Bank.

World Bank, FAO and Agricultural Rural Development (2009): Awakening Africa's Sleeping Giant: Prospects for Commercial Agriculture in the Guinea Savannah Zone and Beyond, *Agriculture and Rural Development Notes, Issue 48, June 2009*. Washington, DC: The World Bank.

Zoomers, A., 2010. "Globalization and the foreignisation of space: Seven processes driving the current global land grab", Journal of Peasant Studies, 37:2, pp. 429-447.

The Impact of Climate Change in Africa
Constructing Human Rights as a Regional Response

Ademola Oluborode Jegede

Introduction

The neo-liberal notion of economic development has become a global faith (Woods 2010:3; Rist 2009:21-24).[1] A theory that promotes the notion of an economy independent of government control, minimisation of government ownership or provision of goods in order to maximise profit, neo-liberal economic agenda has thrived in the context of the human right to self determination and natural resources (Woods 2010:4). Often engaged as a ground to dispose of environmental resources within a given territory, (Woods 2010:7), the neo-liberal economic model is supported by developed nations including the United States of America, which are acclaimed for projecting human rights, Donelly (1998: 74-1, 1-24), as 'standard of civilisation'.

In the context of the foregoing paradigm has emerged activities including large scale agriculture, and unsustainable mining, construction and logging, which as researches have demonstrated are a substantial driver of climate change (Gorte and Sheik 2010; Quan and Dyer 2008; Helmut and Lambin 2001). This is not surprising as this development model has left its carbon print on earth, thus driving evidence of climate change and its negative implications for society beyond debate (Toulmin 2009; Wold, Hunter and Powers 2009; Collier, Conway et al 2008: 24:2, 337; Reid and Huq 2007). With an economy largely dependent on agriculture, limited adaptation capacity and repercussions of mitigation strategies adopted by the rest of the world, Africa is, and will be, affected seriously by climate change (Toulmin, 2009:15-87; Wold, Hunter and Powers 2009:1-47; Collier, Conway and Venables 2008: 24,337). This is despite contributing very little to its cause (Collier, Conway and Venables 2008:24,2, 337; limit references to the absolute minimum High Level Panel for the African Development Bank 2008:45). There is no African-wide climate homogenous effect (Collier, Conway and Venables 2008:24:2, 338). However, in general terms, established vulnerability assessment of climate change impact for Africa, actual and projected, are documented as involving sectors such as water resources, food security, natural resource management and biodiversity, human health, settlements and infrastructure, and desertification (Toulmin 2009: 15-87; Boko et al. 2007:433-467).

While there logically exists a close link between the above impact assessment and human rights, this is only little reflected in the international climate change policy. Rather, as exemplified in the climate policy making trend, more attention has been devoted globally to addressing climate change as an environmental concern. As authors including Humphreys (2010:1) and International Council on Human Rights Policy (2008:3-6) have argued, this is because climate change emerged from the meteorological field, before being rooted in the physical sciences, and is only recently connecting with the social sciences. Yet, while there is little doubt about the environmental dimension of climate change, an uncritical acceptance of this conception is unhelpful. This is not least because it may deflate the application of human rights to climate repeating points already made about related human wrongs and particularly deny vulnerable populations in Africa of appropriate attention in difficult climate situations.

Thus far, the rare literature on the subject in relation to Africa, has linked the implication of climate change to a number of human rights guaranteed under international human rights instruments. [2] However, little attention has been devoted to the basis and how human rights can be engaged as a regional response to climate change impact in Africa. Accordingly, this chapter explores the basis and how human rights can operate as a regional response to climate to the impact of climate change in Africa. In doing this, the chapter demonstrates how climate change implicates a range of human rights guaranteed under the African Charter on Human and Peoples' Rights (African Charter 1981) and the prospects in the functions of the African Commission on Human and Peoples' Rights (the African Commission) as a response to threats posed by climate change in Africa.

The chapter begins with a definition of climate change and an overview of the conceptual tension around the application of human rights, stressing the human source and vulnerability to climate change as a basis for constructing the impact of climate change as a human right issue in Africa. It demonstrates the implication of this impact on a range of human rights guaranteed under the African Charter. It then explores the potentials in the functions of the African Commission to serve as a regional human rights response to climate related impact. This is followed with conclusion.

Conceptualising climate change

Although, change in climate has been denied for long,[3] the contributions of Working Group 1 to the Assessment Reports of the Intergovernmental Panel on Climate Change (IPCC) in 1990 (Watson et al. 1990), 1995 (Houghton et al. 1995), 2001 (Baede et al. 2005) and 2007 (Le Treut et al. 2007) explain the scientific and factual basis of climate change. According to these contributions, human activities are substantially increasing the concentration of greenhouse gases in the atmosphere, thus enhancing greenhouse effect, which has in turn led to increased warming of the earth surface resulting in climate change (Le Treut et al. 2007; Baede et al. 2005, Houghton et al. 1995; Watson et al. 1990). Hence, section 1(2) of the United Nations Framework Convention on Climate Change (UNFCCC 1992) defines climate change as 'a change of climate which is attributed directly or indirectly to human activity that alters the composition of the global atmosphere and which is in addition to natural climate variability observed over comparable time periods'.

The subject of climate change is not, however, devoid of conceptual tension. At the heart of this controversy is the competing claim as to whether climate change is an environmental and not a human rights concern. Evidence of this tension is visible in the divergent focus of scholarship relating to the global need for urgent action in addressing climate change.

Climate change as an environmental concern

Scholarship which perspectives that climate change is an environmental challenge by projecting the environmental or ecological dimension of climate change impact, that is, its effects on the physical environment have been advanced. For instance, Rajamani (2000:9:2, 120) posits that climate change is 'the most significant environmental problem of our time.' To Suckling (2007), the 'polar bears are the icon for climate change'. According to Cloutier (2006), the arctic is the 'world's barometer of climate change', while McKibben (2003:48) notes that in increasing the amount of carbon dioxides in the atmosphere, human beings may well be 'ending nature.' Similarly, in the debate leading to the adoption in 2009 of the United Nations Resolution 10/4 on the link between climate change and human rights (UNHRC Resolution 10/4 2009), key stakeholders in the climate change negotiations, particularly, the United States of America projected the environment-impact image of climate change. This is by consistently arguing that climate change is a complex environmental issue and that the shifting of its discourse toward human rights is 'unrealistic' and 'unwise' (United States Submission 2008, para. 17).

The negotiation and outcome of international climate change instruments are patterned along international environmental law making processes. This began with the adoption of a framework convention establishing basic issues and followed by a more regulatory instrument in the form of a protocol (Bodansky and Rajamani 2013:2). To that end, rather than a binding instrument, what was established in 1992 was a framework, that is, the UNFCCC 1992, which merely set out the basic structure for addressing climate change. This was followed by a regulatory and binding instrument of the Kyoto Protocol (1995), while in between, and afterward, there has been a number of Conference of Parties (COP) decisions that have emerged from international climate change negotiations (Bodansky and Rajamani 2013:4). This approach follows a rulemaking tradition for which the international environmental law making process has for long been known (Bodansky and Rajamani 2013:2).

Also, strong evidence of the conception of climate change as an environmental concern is discernible in the language used in the two pillar instruments, that is, the UNFCCC and Kyoto Protocol. Suggesting that climate change is an environmental concern, article 2 of the UNFCCC demonstrates a strong inclination toward environmental protection. This is discernible from its objective, which is to ensure the 'stabilization of greenhouse gas concentrations in the atmosphere at a level that would prevent dangerous anthropogenic interference with the climate system'. Furthermore, article 3(1) of the UNFCCC, enjoins parties to protect the climate system for the benefit of present and future generations. The environmental dimension of climate change is similarly expressed in the commitment of the global community toward the mitigation of climate change under the UNFCCC. The UNFCCC requires parties to embark upon activities aimed at mitigating climate change (art 4(1)(b)).

Indeed, if there is any doubt that the climate regulatory instruments are generally environmental in their core focus, this is removed by the Kyoto Protocol. The instrument requires developed states, listed under Annex 1 of the UNFCCC to 'implement and/or further elaborate policies and measures in accordance with its national circumstances.'[4] These policies include the promotion of energy efficiency, protection and enhancement of sinks and reservoirs of greenhouse gases not under the Montreal Protocol, the promotion of sustainable forest management practices, afforestation and reforestation (art 2(1)(a)).

However, the foregoing approach is not without its weaknesses. One weakness is that too much detail, condenses these paragraphs and sticks to key point commitments under article 4 of the UNFCCC and the prescriptions for developed states under article 3 of the Kyoto Protocol are not conceived in terms of rights holders and duty bearers. Another is that, similar to what obtains under international environmental law, the dispute resolution mechanism is essentially non-adversarial. Although, provided necessary conditions are complied with, parties may have recourse to the International Court of Justice for Settlement of Disputes arising under the UNFCCC (art 14(2)), this is limited. The option only operates in the shadow of article 14(1), which stipulates for negotiation and peaceful settlement of disputes as the preferred and first option. This conception differs largely from the human rights' notion of dispute resolution which is generally adversarial. Again, the sentiment that international cooperation and not contestation is necessary in fixing the climate crisis was shown by the United States which argues that:

> The process of pursuing human rights claims would be adversarial and require affixing blame to particular entities; this contrasts with the efforts to achieve international cooperation that have thus far been pursued through the international climate change negotiations (United States Submission 2008, para 26).

The above position was merely reiterating by the consensual nature of the compliance mechanism, which exists under the Kyoto Protocol (Decision 24/CP.7 2001). This arrangement involves a Compliance Committee of 20 members functioning in two main branches: a Facilitative Branch and an Enforcement Branch (Decision 24/CP.7 2001, paras. 1, 2 and 3). The Committee does not address individual cases of non-compliance, but only reports on its activities to the Conference of Parties (Decision 24/CP.7 2001, sec. III; Ulfstein and Werksman 2005:39-62). Hence, the pertinent question is what are the basis and prospects for constructing human rights as a regional response to the impact of climate change in Africa?

Climate change as a human rights concern: Exploring the basis

Human source of climate change

Climate change is justifiably a 'human wrong' concern considering the human responsibility and vulnerability which define its reality. There are scholarly works, which arguably reflect that the human responsibility for its cause and human vulnerability in the face of its impact, as a strong basis for regarding climate change as a human rights issue. For instance, Mckibben (2003: 46) views that climate change is a consequence of the 'way of life' chosen by one part of the world, an argument which Robinson (2010) takes further in pointing out that the 'human source' of climate change is a strong force for involving human rights framework in the climate change discourse.

The human source of climate change is also visible in the climate change regulatory framework. Article 3 of the UNFCCC on the objective of the Convention reiterates that it is meant to address the human cause (anthropogenic) of climate change. Also, the fact that the populations in developed nations of the world contribute more to climate crisis is not hidden from the key instruments on climate change, that is, the UNFCCC and the Kyoto Protocol. The preamble to the UNFCCC, for instance, notes that emission of green house gases has largely and historically originated from developed countries. This is in fact the basis behind the principle of common but differentiated responsibility, which is entrenched under articles 3(1) and 4 (1) of the UNFCCC and article 10 of the Kyoto Protocol.

Human vulnerability to climate change

Scholarly writings have focused on human vulnerability in the face of climate change. For instance, drawing attention on this, Aminzadeh (2007:234), urges that 'human beings are the icon of climate change'. In terms of human impact of climate change, particularly on the indigenous peoples, Cloutier (2006) describes the indigenous peoples as 'the mercury in the barometer' of climate change in the Arctic. This signifies that the plight of vulnerable groups is the appropriate indicator of global climate impact and the failing efforts in addressing a global crisis. Also, in an article referring to a research commissioned by the Christian Aid in Northern Kenya, Beaumont (2006) reported pastoralists as 'climate canaries', who are fated to become the first victims of world climate change as a result of its impact on their land.

The foregoing trend in human vulnerability is particularly reflected in most parts of Africa. No doubt, the change in weather variation may be positive for economic benefits of some regions of Africa. However, generally, established areas of climate change impact and vulnerability for Africa, actual and projected, are of negative implication (Collier, Conway and Venables 2008, 338; Toulmin 2009:15-109). To illustrate different aspects of this vulnerability, a review of situations of populations in Africa who particularly depend on land resources for survival merits some consideration. According to IWGIA and African Commission (2005:18), in West Africa, there are the Bororo, and Tuareg communities, mainly pastoralists. These peoples experience the impact of climate change ranging from destruction of grazing lands, drought, access to safe water, destruction of plants and animals, traditional fishing activities, displacement and conflict (IPACC Web; Bals, Harmeling and Windfuhr 2008:84-99). Similarly, pastoralists as well as hunters and gatherers in East Africa, among whom are the Maasai, Ogiek, Endorois, and Yaaku in Kenya, suffer severe conditions including drought, flood, famine, displacement, and loss of lives, due to climate change (IWGIA 2011:410). This generally affirms the finding of the IPCC that the cumulative impact of climate change on livestock farming will, among other things, lead to the decline of large livestock by 22 per cent in Africa (Boko et al. 2007:448).

Besides, the implementation of global climate change response initiatives aimed at adjusting to (adapting) and avoiding (mitigating) climate change have actual and potential peculiar impact on populations in Africa, particularly where the initiatives are situated. For instance, of relevance to Africa are projects under the Clean Development Mechanism (CDM) and the United Nations Reduced Emissions from Deforestation and forest Degradation (UN-REDD) program. The CDM is established under the Kyoto Protocol (1998, arts. 6, 12 and 17), and seeks to promote sustainable developments such as reforestation and alternative use of energies in developing states including Africa (Kyoto Protocol 1998, art.12). In Africa, evidence on the implementation of CDM projects is in Nigeria, [5] Uganda, [6] and Kenya. [7] Similarly, launched in 2008, the UN-REDD which supports nationally-led REDD+ is central to climate change adaptation and mitigation under the Kyoto Protocol (Robledo, Blaser and

Bryne 2010:354-76; Griffiths 2007:8). States in Africa involved with UN-REDD+ program of implications to forest dependent indigenous peoples include DRC, Tanzania, Zambia, South Sudan and Nigeria (UNREDD Web).

No doubt, these initiatives have potential benefits for Africa. The CDM is a potential avenue, generally for Africa to access finance and sustainable projects (Toulmin 2009:128). Under the REDD+, participating nations will benefit from payment for controlling deforestation, thereby reducing emissions associated with clearing land (Toulmin 2009:130). However, there are documented general concerns on the actual and potential impact, particularly on the forest dependent populations, which inhabit sites of projects (UNPFII 2008, paras.42-56). With respect to CDM, these include displacement and deprivation of traditional land (Milan Declaration 2003, principle 3). CDM has been discussed as capable of negatively impacting human rights (Orellana, Kothari and Chaudhry 2010:6). In relation to REDD+, Toulmin (2009:130) and Griffiths (2007:26) note that there are concerns that projects will reinforce the status quo in the forest sector in many countries and largely benefit forest departments and commercial interests, and not the populations who are forest dependent. Principally, REDD programmes for reforestation and protection of forests as carbon sinks can reduce traditional access of peoples to forest resources (OHCHR Report 2009:22-23). In all, it has been projected that projects under the CDM and REDD+ will require changes in use of land, compromise tenure, displacement and ultimately exclude them from benefit sharing (Crippa 2013:143; Robledo, Blaser and Bryne 2010:366; Toulmin 2009:83).

In light of the above, the application of human rights can address the wrong behind the impact of climate change. For instance, Olivier De Schutter (2012) argues that issues such as deforestation, mining and ocean degradation should be considered in terms of their impacts on human life. Scholars have also argued that human rights can be interpreted to include environmental protection, protect human rights, and place pressure on their governments to act more proactively on climate change (Peart 2012:24,2, 77-78; Anton and Shelton 2011; Sinden 2007:255). The next question then is how does climate change implicate human rights in Africa?

'Source' and 'Vulnerability to climate change are a threat to human rights in Africa

The human source of climate change and vulnerability of population in the light of its challenge are a threat to human rights. The foregoing regional scenarios are a threat to a number of rights including the right to food, water, housing, peace, health and environment for which states in Africa have the obligation to safeguard under the African Charter on Human and Peoples' Rights (African Charter 1981).

Right to food

In Africa, agriculture is the backbone of the economy of most states (Toulmin 2009:50). Destruction of grazing land, low yields in farm produce, and drop or loss of fishing activities constitutes a threat to the right to food in its entire ramification. This may challenge the availability, accessibility, acceptability and safety of food (General Comment No.12 1999, paras 10-13). While the African Charter does not expressly guarantee the right to food, it can be implied from the right to enjoy the best attainable state of physical and mental health under article 16 of the African Charter, as well as its jurisprudence. In *Sudan Human Rights Organisation & Centre on Housing Rights and Evictions (COHRE) v Sudan,* 2005 (Darfur's case), the complainant argued that the prevention of Darfurians by militias from farming land, collection of fireweed for cooking, and grass to feed livestock, constitute a violation of their right to adequate food (para. 124). The African Commission agreed with this argument but, having considered that the right is implicit in the rights to health, it grounded the violation on the right to enjoy the best attainable state of physical and mental health under article 16 of the African Charter (1981, paras. 209-212).

Right to water

Water is of great importance to the economies of African states, particularly those which heavily rely on it directly for agricultural products (Toulmin 2009:32). According to United Nations World Water Development Report (2009:11), 'about 340 million Africans lack access to safe drinking water, and almost 500 million lack access to adequate sanitation' (Toulmin 2009:32). Drought, flood and displacement of populations will worsen the scarcity of water in Africa (Toulmin 2009:33), and threaten the right to water. Although not expressly in the African Charter, the right to water has been a subject for consideration in the jurisprudence of the African Commission. In the *Darfur's case,* it agreed with the complainant's contention that the right to water is implicit in article 16 of the African Charter and that state connivance in 'poisoning wells and denying access to water sources in the Darfur region' constitutes a violation of it (para. 126). Also, in *Free Legal Assistance Group and Others v Zaire* (1993), the

African Commission held that the failure of the Government to provide basic services such as safe drinking water constitutes a violation of article 16 of the African Charter (1981, para. 1).

Right to housing

Climate change mitigation measures can affect human settlement and constitute a threat to right to housing. This is particularly so in Africa, where, notwithstanding a low adaptive capacity global warming will generate problems including heatwaves, flooding, pollution and rising in sea level (Toulmin 2009:87). This has the potential to displace population and devastate human shelter. Also, mitigation measures which essentially involve Africa, as explained earlier, can cause the displacement of a population. This development, no doubt, poses a challenge to the right to adequate housing, which principally aims at providing and setting standards for adequate shelter. General Comment No. 4 of the International Covenant on Economic Social and Cultural Rights (ICESCR) enunciates the seven elements constituting the normative content of the right to adequate housing (General Comment No.4 1991). These are legal security of tenure, availability of services, materials, facilities and infrastructure, accessibility, location, affordability, habitability, and cultural adequacy (para. 8).

General Comment No.4 is further strengthened by a subsequent General Comment 7 (1997) on the right to housing, which deals with the issue of forced evictions. This is defined as the 'permanent or temporary removal against their will of individuals, families and/or communities from the homes and/or land which they occupy, without the provision of, and access to, appropriate forms of legal or other protection' (para. 3). Forced evictions do not only interfere with the right to housing, but also with other rights of the ICESCR, and with rights enshrined in the International Covenant on Civil and Political Rights (ICCPR), such as the right to life, the right to security of person, the right to non-interference with privacy, family and home as well as the right to the peaceful enjoyment of possessions (para. 4).

Considering that climate change, and the implementation of mitigation measures can lead to displacement and forced evictions in Africa, these effectively will undermine the right to adequate housing of populations in Africa. All the elements in the right to adequate housing, namely, legal security of tenure, availability of services, materials, facilities and infrastructure, accessibility, location, affordability, habitability, and cultural adequacy are disturbed when populations are displaced or forcefully evicted from their shelter in the event of climate change and implementation of mitigation initiatives without alternative provisions that meet with their rights. Although the right to housing is not expressly guaranteed under the African Charter, it is of little doubt that it can be construed as implicit in the right to property under article 14. In the *Darfur's case,* it was the argument of the complainant that the forced evictions and destruction of housing and property in the Darfur region violated the right to property guaranteed under article 14 of the African Charter (para. 15). In agreeing with this contention, the African Commission held that the right to property is breached whether the Complainant had legal title or not. This is considering that the complainant has lived in the territory for generations and State has failed to show that it refrained from the eviction, or demolition of victims' houses and other property. Also, it did not take steps to protect the victims from abuse of non-state actors (para. 205).

Right to peace

Where scarcity of natural resources such as water and displacement result from climate change, it is capable of leading to conflict. Climate induced displacees may be constrained to look for resources elsewhere and thus clash with other populations. For instance, incidence of conflicts in the Darfur has been connected with drought and famine, which led to dislocation from social and economic life and the loss of herding and farming families (Toulmin 2009:111; Hammill and Mcleman 2007:83,6, 1141-1154). Further reiterating such possibility is the evidence found in West African states including Ghana and Burkina Faso (Brown and Crawford 2008:9-39). Also, in the Eastern part of Africa, competition for resource among the pastoralists has significant impact on the risk of conflict between diverse groups of land users (Oxfam 2008:21). In undermining peace, conflict implicates the right to national peace guaranteed under article 23 of the African Charter. Hence, the potential in climate change to result into conflict in Africa is a threat to peace of populations in Africa.

Right to health

Different scenarios of climate change challenge in Africa also have health consequences which may threaten the right to health and life of populations (Mwebaza 2009:240). For instance, warmer weather, according to the IPCC, in regions of Africa which are previously free of malaria such as Ethiopia, Kenya, Rwanda and Burundi are likely to occur along with intrusion of malaria by 2050 (Boko et al. 2007:446). Similar experience is projected for central Somalia and the Angolan highlands (Boko et al. 2007:446). This development will worsen the malaria mortality in Africa, which according to the World Health Organisation World Malaria Report (2012:1) stands at about 90% of all global malaria deaths. There are other health risks of climate change which may be associated with the implementation of adaptation and mitigation measures particularly when they result into displacement of populations. This will certainly undermine the right to health which is guaranteed under article 16 of the African Charter. In *Social and Economic Rights Action Center (SERAC) and Center for Economic and Social Rights (CESR) v Nigeria*, 2001 (Ogoniland case), the Complainants alleged that by failing to protect the Ogoni population from the harm caused by the NNPC and Shell Consortium, the government of Nigeria was in breach of the right to health under article 16 of the African Charter (para 56).

Right to healthy environment

Issues related to climate change such as pollution arising from gas flaring or environmental despoliation arising from oil exploration are a potential threat to the right to environment. A unique provision which nowhere exists in other regional instruments, the right to 'a generally satisfactory environment' is guaranteed under article 24 of the African Charter. The right to satisfactory environment is linked with other rights such as life, water, food, and health. Reference is made to environmental conditions in the provisions of the United Nations General Comments on the right to water (General Comment 15, paras. 6, 8, 22, 48 and 53), right to health (General Comment No 14 2000, paras. 4, 11 and 15), right to food (General Comment No 12, paras. 4, 10 and 20), and right to housing (General Comment No.4 1991). More particularly, the General Comment on the right to health (2000), acknowledges that the right to health embraces a wide range of socio-economic factors that promote conditions in which people can lead a healthy life, and extends to the underlying determinants of health, such as…a healthy environment.' (para. 4).

The expansive nature of the right suggests that it is able to help address the reality that the impact of climate change may threaten a range of rights. At the domestic level, this may arise where a particular government runs afoul of its obligations under the African Charter in failing to address the impact of climate change in its state. Although, climate change has a global causation, it is unlikely that this can be used as an excuse by a state to deflate its obligations to safeguard the rights of the inhabitants of its state being challenged by climate change impact. In *Ogoniland case*, the African Commission expatiated the obligations required of states in relation to article 24 of the African Charter. It interpreted the right to environment as imposing 'clear obligations upon a government[...]to take reasonable and other measures to prevent pollution and ecological degradation, to promote conservation, and to secure an ecologically sustainable development and use of natural resources' (para. 52).

Having explained the implication of climate change for a range of human rights guaranteed under the African Charter, the next section explores the potential in the functions of the African Commission as a regional response to the impact of climate change. While this chapter focuses on the African Commission, it should be noted that at the regional level, the human rights architecture is still evolving (Viljoen 2012:410-446). Aside from the African Commission, there exists the African Court on Human and Peoples' Rights (African Court), which was established pursuant to article 1 of the Protocol to the African Charter on Human and Peoples' Rights on the Establishment of an African Court on Human and Peoples' Rights (Protocol to the African Charter 2004). There has been further development to merge the African Court with the existing African Court of Justice under a new mechanism reffered to as the African Court of Justice and Human Rights (Protocol on the Statute of the African Court of Justice and Human Rights 2008). The establishment of the African Court strenghtens the protective mandate of the African Commission in that the decisions of the African Court enjoy a binding force (Protocol to the African Charter 2004, arts. 27 and 30).

Potential in the functions of the African Commission

Generally, accountability for the impact of climate change on human rights is difficult as a result of the extraterritorial causation (Posner 2007, 155, 1925-1945; Gupta 2007, 16:1, 76-83; Allen 2003, 891-892). This is because every nation, developed or developing, contributes to the causation of climate change as a result of quest for development (Adelman 2010, 159-180). Also, its impact is extraterritorial, involving both the developed and developing world. While these features justify the resort to global negotiation, this does not exclude activities at the regional level where states, as earlier shown are duty bearers with obligation towards their citizens, as rights holders (McInerney-Lankford 2009:33, 431; Koch 2005:81-103).

State Reporting

Regarded as the 'core' of the African Commission's promotional mandate (Viljoen 2012:349), state reporting aims at reviewing at the regional level the extent to which states have complied with their obligations under the charter in their territory. Hence, this serves the dual purposes of 'introspection' and 'inspection' (Viljoen 2012:350). As the author further explains, state reporting serves the purpose of introspection in that it allows the state to 'take the stock of its achievements and failures in making the guarantees under the charter a reality'. The inspection aspect of state reporting comes into play in that it takes place before an independent or external body, which is able to engage the state in an objective dialogue in relation to the delivery of their obligations under the African Charter (Viljoen 2012:350). According to article 62 of the African Charter, each party to the Charter is enjoined to file the state report every two years on the legislative or other measures being taken to realise the rights guaranteed under the African Charter. While states do not have the general practice of submitting this Report as at when due (Viljoen 2012:355) there is little doubt that it serves a useful tool for addressing human rights implication of climate change impact on the vulnerable populations in Africa. This is particularly possible if the exercise is not treated as a mere formalism but conceived by states as a mechanism which can assist in generating solutions or best practices on the crisis of climate change. Among other things, to guard against formalism, the African Commission can begin with raising questions about compliance by states with previous concluding remarks made in previous state reports of a given state. The civil society at the regional and national levels can also hold states accountable for commitments imposed in the remarks by the African Commission (Viljoen 2012:367).

In respect of climate change impact, each state in Africa can be required to retrospect by including climate change as part of the issues to report on. To realise this, states can include organisations and institutions which focus on climate or environmental related issues in the compilation of the report. Also, when documenting the realities of climate change impact, states may be required to cast this in the sense of what human rights are being threatened by the climate change impact and steps taken as safeguard measures. Once this is done, the inspection of the report by the African Commission offers the state and other participants in the process the opportunity, not only to share their challenges, but more importantly to invite concrete comments as well as concluding remarks on how these challenges can be managed. When concluding remarks are eventually made public, it will serve the purpose of empowering the civil society which may use such remarks in holding states accountable to its obligations in the face of climate change challenge. Publicity around state reporting may also be helpful in attracting global attention to human right dimension to climate change.

Special mechanisms

In practice, the African Commission has developed special mechanisms which are greatly complementing its promotional role in engaging with states for the realisation of human rights in Africa (Viljoen 2012:369). These are the Special Rapporteur and Working Groups. Functionally these mechanisms are the same as they serve the purpose of advancing human rights issues around a given mandate (Viljoen 2012:369; Killander 2012:241). The only difference between the Special Rapporteur and Working Groups lies in the composition of the former, which is occupied by a single individual who is a commissioner within the African Commissioner while the latter is made of Commissioners and experts selected outside the African Commission (Viljoen 2012:369).

While, there is no express provision of the Charter which serves as legal basis provides for these mechanisms, the African Commission has adopted a progressive approach to create space for these mechanisms in the operationalizing of mandate (Viljoen 2012:371; Harrington 2001:247). Dating back to 1994, the African Commission has been establishing Special Rapporteur to address a number of substantive provisions of human rights under the African Charter (Viljoen 2012:371). As a mark of its endorsement of the relevance of these mechanisms in the African human rights system, guidelines have been adopted for their functioning (Viljoen 2012:371). Examples of Special Rapporteurs established thus far include the 'Special Rapporteur on Extrajudicial, Summary or Arbitrary Execution in Africa, Special Rapporteur on Prisons and Conditions of Detention in Africa, Special Rapporteur on the Rights of Women in Africa, Special Rapporteur on Human Rights Defender in Africa, Special Rapporteur on Refugees, Asylum Seekers, and Internally Displaced Persons in Africa, and Special Rapporteur on Freedom of Expression in Africa (ACHPR Web).

So far, none has been appointed in relation to environmental protection, let alone climate change impact. Two reasons can be conjectured for this gap. One reason perhaps lies in the conception that climate change is a pervasive phenomenon with consequences perceived not as tangible enough or at par with established basis for appointing Special Rapporteur. The peculiar validity of this comes home, for instance, in the sense that it is easier to conceive the emotive and logical necessity for a Special Rapporteur on Extrajudicial, Summary or Arbitrary Execution in Africa. This is on the account that there is immediate and visible evidence of human losses and harm done to victims when peoples are extrajudicially executed or detained in prisons illegally.

Another possible reason for this worrying gap is that climate change has engaged less attention of non-governmental organisations with observer status before the African Commission. When Special Rapporteurs are established, it is often linked with consistent advocacy of NGOs, which pique interest in a particular issue at the regional level. For instance, such overbearing role of NGOs is at least crucial in the creation of Special Rapporteur on Extrajudicial, Summary or Arbitrary Execution in Africa, Special Rapporteur on Prisons and Conditions of Detention in Africa, Special Rapporteur on Prisons and Conditions of Detention in Africa and Special Rapporteur on the Rights of Women in Africa. It has been reported that the establishment of the Special Rapporteur on Extrajudicial, Summary or Arbitrary Execution in Africa was proposed by Amnesty International in 1993, an NGO which has maintained an observer status with the African Commission since 1988 (Viljoen 2012;371; Harrington 2001;251). Also, the initiative to create the position for the Special Rapporteur on Prisons and Conditions of Detention in Africa came from Penal Reform International (Viljoen 2012:371; Viljoen 2003:27, 125), while NGOs such as Women in Law and Development in Africa (WILDAF) consistently advocated for the establishment of the Special Rapporteur on the Rights of Women in Africa (Viljoen 2012:375). However, even if present, such dedicated activities are not yet visible in relation to environmental protection, notwithstanding that NGOs such as SERAC with special interest in environmental rights enjoy observer status with the African Commission. Certainly, it has not crystalized into the establishment of a Special Rapporteur on climate related violation of rights, in spite of the anecdotal and disproportionate impact of climate change on populations in Africa.

While establishing a new special rapporteur for this purpose may be necessary, there is potential in the mandate of the existing holders which offers a platform at least for seeking and receiving information on the plights of populations in the light of climate change challenge. This can be achieved if climate change is mainstreamed into existing the mandate of Special Rapporteurs which are more directly linked with climate change. For instance, the mandate of the Special Rapporteur on Refugees, Asylum

Seekers, and Internally Displaced Persons in Africa (Viljoen 2012:376), include to 'act upon information', to undertake fact finding missions to refugee and IDP camps, to assist states in developing appropriate legal and policy framework, to raise awareness about the plight of these vulnerable groups and to promote the implementation of the relevant standards (Ibid). This mandate can accommodate climate related displacement or migration, more so as researches have shown that environmental crisis may underlie internal displacement and result into migrating out of national boundaries (Warmer 2011:1-19).

This possibility is indeed reinforced in the African Union Convention for the Protection and Assistance of Internally Displaced Persons in Africa (Kampala Convention 2009). Article 5(4) of Kampala Convention, for instance, enjoins state parties to take 'measures to protect and assist persons who have been internally displaced due to natural or human made disasters, including climate change'. Hence, adding a dimension of climate change to the tasks of the Special Rapporteur on Refugees, Asylum Seekers, and Internally Displaced Persons in Africa will help in bringing out the special circumstances of peoples experiencing climate crisis. It will also assist the government, perhaps in formulating appropriate legal and policy response, which may help in safeguarding the human rights of such vulnerable groups in the light of climate change challenge. Also, climate change can be accommodated in the activities of the Special Rapporteur on the Rights of Women in Africa as the office holder embarks on visits and reporting on the situation of women. The special circumstances of women in the light of climate change will avail states with necessary evidence to tackle the gender effects of climate change. Additionally, it seems that there is nothing in the mandate of Special Rapporteur on Human Rights Defender in Africa that is inconsistent with an inclusion of environmental rights activists who face challenges while advocating environmental cause. This may serve the useful purpose of encouraging such individual or organisations to sustain the few voices being raised in connection with issues such as gas flaring, environmental pollution in Africa which have implications for global warming and climate change (Orunoye 2012:2,14, 152-156).

The African Commission has also established a number of working groups, which can be useful in addressing the vulnerability of populations in the face of climate change. A distinguishing feature of the mandate of working groups is that unlike that of the Special Rapporteur, is more exploratory and research related focusing on emerging issues or matters (Viljoen 2012:377). Since 2000 when the Working Group dealing with the rights of 'indigenous or ethnic communities in Africa' was established, there have been no less than seven working groups. These include the Working Group on Economic, Social and Cultural Rights in Africa, [8] and the Working Group on Extractive Industries, Environment and Human Rights Violations (2009). [9]

Climate change or and climate related issues have featured particularly in the activities of the Working Group on the Rights of Indigenous or Ethnic Communities in Africa. This is at least evidenced in its visits to African states including Congo, (DRC Report 2010:37) Rwanda (Rwanda Report 2010:30), and Kenya (Kenya Report 2010:37). During its visit to Kenya, the Working Group reported that environmental degradation and deforestation have been a result of poor land use. According to the Working Group, this is because over the years the government of Kenya has discouraged pastoralism or hunting and gathering as a viable way of life but has instead been pressurising indigenous peoples to become sedentary farmer (Kenya Report 2010: 37). In fact, as documented by the Kenya Report (2010), it is the argument of the indigenous peoples that 'had pastoralism and hunting-gathering been recognized as viable livelihood systems in the traditional sector, such a situation would not have prevailed' (para. 37).

Arguably, even though the foregoing - were submitted in the context of indigenous peoples' rights, it demonstrates that working group activities are an important channel of investigating a human rights angle to climate change impact. Hence, the possibility of including climate change in the agenda of working groups cannot be ignored. For instance, it is not impossible to mainstream the issue of climate change in the mandate of working groups such as the Working Group on Economic, Social and Cultural Rights. In implementing its mandate to undertake 'studies and research on specific social, economic and cultural rights', the working group may for instance explore the implications of climate change on the realisation on social economic and cultural rights. It may also, in doing so, come up with helpful policies to ensure the realisation of vulnerable groups living in the reality of climate change. Similarly, the mandate of the Working Group on Extractive Industries, Environment and Human Rights Violations (Extractive Working Group 2009) 'to undertake research on the violations of human and peoples' rights by non-state actors in Africa', is also relevant to climate change. This is in the sense that non-state actors are involved in the implementation of climate related projects such as CDM and REDD+ as earlier mentioned (Decision 3/CMP.1 2005, paras. 27, 35-52). Hence, the Working Group offers an opportunity to promote sustainable implementation of projects under these initiatives and receive human rights concerns arising in the process.

'Promotional visits', Seminars and Conferences', 'Publication and Information Dissemination'

Promotional visits are an important anchor on which other 'promotional activities' of the African Commission rests. This is embarked upon by commissioners among whom the states in Africa are shared (Viljoen 2012:379). Through these visits, commissioners are able to sensitise high ranking officials about the importance of the African Charter, persuading them to ratify outstanding treaties and urging them to submit state reports and comply with resolutions (Viljoen 2012:379). In an atmosphere where political elite still live in denial of climate change and consider the right of states in Africa to the development as urgent (UNFCCC 1992, preamble), promotional visits are helpful in sensitising states in debunking the myth around the reality of climate change and sensitising political leadership to the importance of embarking on eco-friendly development. This is necessary, particularly considering that in different parts of Africa where exploration takes place, it seldom occurs with conscious regard for the protection of the environment. In Nigeria, as shown by the *Ogoniland case*, the environmental degradation which has resulted from the exploration oil in Nigeria by Shell in collaboration with the Nigerian National Petroleum Company has been a subject of decision by the African Commission. Hence, promotional visits can be helpful in drawing the attention of government to the plight on of such activity on the populations residing in the areas of operations. It is also significant in challenging activities which are ultimately harmful on the global environment. Additionally, it is useful in urging state parties which have yet not done so, to reflect on the need to guarantee the right to a healthy environment under the African Charter in their bill of rights. This will, in turn, strengthen the activities of advocacy groups, both as whistle blowers and litigants in relation to actions which aggravate the climate and threatens the rights of populations.

The agendas of the African Commission and activity reports contain several references to its aspiration of hosting seminars on a variety of topics (Viljoen 2012:382). More than 'talk shops', as Viljoen observes, workshops and seminars are often organised by NGOs along with the African Commission as 'nominal co-organiser' (Viljoen 2012:382). Examples of such workshops and seminars include seminars on refugees and contemporary forms of slavery. A seminar on socio-economic rights was held in September, which spearheaded the process leading to the adoption of 'a general comment' on socio-economic rights and guidelines on state reporting pertaining to these rights (Viljoen 2012:382; Khoza 2005:5, 334). In collaboration with NGOs which focus on the environmental rights, workshops and seminars can be engaged, for instance, in further elaborating on article 24 of the African Charter on the right to environment. This may lead to the adoption of a general comment on the right to a healthy environment. Workshops and seminars may also be useful as a tool to generate appropriate guidelines on state reporting pertaining to the rights to healthy environment.

'Publication and Information Dissemination' (PID) as a promotional activity is done with the aim of educating and ensuring greater visibility for the promotional mandate of the African Commission (Viljoen 2012:383). This is achieved through information supplied in its functioning website and the distribution of information through electronic means to NGOs enjoying observer status with the African Commission (Viljoen 2012:382). There are possibilities that through publication and information dissemination, a lot can be realised in addressing the vulnerability of populations to the impact of climate change. First, PID is useful in carrying along NGOs on African position on a number of climate specific issues in the continuing international negotiation of the issues. Also, through this, necessary input of this critical community can be fed into future negotiation of climate change as relates to Africa.

NGOs and National Human Rights Institutions

Since 1988, the African Commission has been granting consultative status which has now grown to 455. [10] The participation of NGO has been critical in its growth and consolidation (Viljoen 2012:383). According to Viljoen, they have participated in the drafting of the African Charter and the development of communication procedures, drawn attention to human rights problems, proposed resolutions, facilitated missions and lobbied governments to comply with obligations (Viljoen 2012:384). While it is almost impossible to investigate the mandate of 455 NGOs for the purpose of an environmental audit, if the name of an organisation is anything to run with, only 5 representing less than one per cent of these NGOs have 'environment'[11] or related words such as 'land' and 'forestry' in their name. If a name offers an insight to the mandate of an NGO, it means that there are few of these organisations with observer status that have a specific mandate on environmental protection. This leaves much to be deserved in the light of increasing vulnerability of Africa to climate change impact.

The paucity of organisations with observer status which have an interest in the protection of the environment will affect the level of engagement of states while presenting their reports. It will undermine a range of activities including, the bringing of climate related issues to the attention of the African Commission, proposal of relevant resolutions, lobbying of government to comply with obligations toward environmental issues as they affect climate change. Conversely, an increasing presence of NGOs with environmental mandate offers vulnerable populations some hope that the delicate connection between climate change and their human rights will be highlighted and discussed at an independent forum where government is likely to be named and shamed for non-compliance with human rights obligations.

Considering their affiliate status, the National Human Rights Institutions (NHR1s) are required to assist the African Commission 'in the promotion and protection of human rights at national level (NHRI Observer Status Resolution 1998, para 4(a)). The affiliate status also entitles the NHRIs to be invited, be present at and to participate 'without voting rights' in the African Commission sessions (Viljoen 2012:389). If properly constituted as 'protectors' and not 'pretenders' (Human Rights Watch 2001) the NHRIs can offer an objective report on the vulnerability of populations to the impact of climate change. Also, at the national level, particularly in African states where environmental protection belongs to the fundamental objectives section, the NHRIs can consistently draw the attention of states to the link between environmental degradation and climate change and urge legislative reform to accommodate such a link.

Resolutions

In elaborating on the substantive provisions of the African Charter, resolutions play a similar role to that of the 'General Comments' adopted UN human rights treaty bodies (Viljoen 2012: 379). Resolutions inform the obligations of states as well as the promotional and protective mandates of the African Commission. Resolutions can be thematic dealing with a specific issue in view. It can also be directed against states where reports of human rights abuse are rampant (Viljoen 2012:380). In 2009, with the adoption of Resolution 153 titled 'Resolution on Climate Change and Human Rights and the Need to Study its Impact in Africa' (Resolution 153

2009) the African Commission demonstrated how this normative tool can be used in elaborating the link between climate change and human rights.

Resolution 153 expresses the concern that human rights standard are lacking in 'various draft texts of the conventions under negotiation' and that this could jeopardize 'the life, physical integrity and livelihood of the most vulnerable members of society notably isolated indigenous and local communities, women, and other vulnerable social groups' (Resolution 153 2009, preamble). It notes that the 'African regional standards for the protection of the environment, management of natural resources and human rights are consistent with provisions of the Convention on Biological Diversity ….' (Resolution 153 2009, preamble). Arguably, based on this position, it can be stated that the African Commission appears to have set the stage for the application of human rights to climate change in the region.

The reference to the 'African regional standards for the protection of the environment… and human rights' presupposes that there are the prospects that some of its key provisions can be engaged in addressing the plight of a population or an individual facing the impact of climate change. Reinforcing the position that the reference to human rights in this Resolution is far from being casual, the African Commission went further to make significant decisions. Among others, it urged the Assembly of Heads of State and Government of the African Union (AU) to ensure the following:

> [1] That human rights standards safeguard, such as the principle of free, prior and informed consent, be included into any adopted legal text on climate change as preventive measures against forced relocation, unfair dispossession of properties, loss of livelihoods and similar human rights violations… (2) that special measure of protection for vulnerable groups such as children, women, the elderly, indigenous communities and victims of natural disasters and conflicts are included in any international agreement or instruments on climate change (Resolution 153 2009)

However, this resolution could have been more clearly articulated by taking into consideration the existing works in other AU institutions on this matter. For instance, there is no reference to the joint report of United Nations Economic and Social Council Economic Commission for Africa and the African Union Commission on Climate Change and development (UNESCEC and AU Commission Report 2010). Similarly, it neither makes reference to *Declaration on Climate Change and Development* (AU Declaration 2007) nor the *Decision on Climate Change and Development in Africa* (AU Decision 2009). Yet, the two instruments respectively implicate the human rights focus of the African Commission in calling for cooperation between regional institutions in climate change matter and its integration into 'national decision-making so as to reduce its negative effects on resources, livelihoods and the wider economy' (AU Decision 2009, para. 2; AU Declaration 2007). If harmonised with the activities of other institutions in the region, resolutions can increase the publicity of the activities of the African Commission on climate change and human rights and shape compliance at the state level. This is in the sense that it offers the civil society an important tool in engaging the government on the implications of climate change for human rights.

Protective Mandate

The protective mandate of the African Commission is exercisable through the consideration of inter-sate and individual communications. Generally, such communications are based on allegations of violations of rights under the African Charter, but may not necessarily be limited to it. This is considering that the African Charter allows the African Commission to draw inspiration from international law and the provisions of other human rights instruments (African Charter 1981, art. 60). Communications alleging violations of human rights of populations in Africa resulting from climate related wrongs, states in Africa, may therefore be brought before the African Commission.

There are concerns which may be argued as constituting challenges to the effectiveness of the exercise of protective mandate. Viljoen (2012:339) identifies some of these challenges as including the question as to the binding or otherwise nature of the decisions of the African Commission and extent of compliance. Other issues include the 'resources' argument, which according to Hansungule (2009, 235), has characterized the historical evolution of the African Commission. Addressing these issues is just as important for the effectiveness of the African Commission in redressing claims based on impact of climate change in Africa. As Viljoen (2012: 339) has argued, the findings of the African Commission become binding once included in the Commission's Activity Report and endorsed by the Assembly or Executive Council of the AU. Even if this argument is helpful, ultimately, what counts for compliance is the ability of complainants or their agents to engage government on implementation, an end that can still be achieved even where decisions are not binding. Similarly, with a level of creativity in allocation of time, improvement of processes and responses, this may be reduced.

Given the foregoing therefore, it can be reasonably expected that the inter-state and individual communications of the African Commission can serve as in important tool in engaging the government on the implications of climate change for human rights.

Inter-state communications

Article 69 of the African Charter provides that a state party which believes that another member state has infringed in the rights guaranteed under the African Charter may submit the matter to the African Commission after an unsuccessful attempt to resolve it bilaterally or through amicable settlement procedure (African Charter 1981, arts. 47-50, 51-53). These victims may extend from individuals to groups or the entire nation. While the cause of climate change is global (Posner 2007), inter-state communications on climate related wrongs may arise for instance, where cross-border pollution occurring within an African state affects the populations in another. This may or may not be traceable to an inadequate policy of the state where such pollution originates.

How a policy decision in one state or states in Africa may affect the rights of populations in another is illustrated by the facts of *Association pour la sauvegarde de la paix au Burundi v Kenya, Uganda, Rwanda, Tanzania, Zaire (DRC), Zambia* (1996). In that case, following the unconstitutional change of government in Burundi, the governments of Tanzania, Kenya, Uganda, Rwanda, Democratic Republic of Congo, Ethiopia, and Zambia adopted a resolution the purport of which imposed an embargo on Burundi. It was the case of the complainant that the embargo violates articles 4, 17(1) and 22 of the African Charter, in that it prevented the importation of essential goods such as fuel and the exportation of tea and coffee, which are the country's only sources of revenue.

The complainant further alleged that the embargo is in contravention of articles 3(1), (2) and (3) of the 'OAU Charter' which respectively guarantees sovereign equality of states, non-interference in internal affairs and respect for territorial integrity of member states (para. 4). In dismissing this case, the African Commission noted that economic sanctions and embargoes in so far as they are not excessive and disproportionate are legitimate interventions in international law and such interference with internal affairs is legitimate (paras. 76-78). While this is one matter where no case was made for environmental damage, let alone climate related impact, it at least suggests that an excessive and disproportionate act which gives rise to violation of rights in another may be considered as a breach of relevant provisions of the African Charter. As Bhulto (2011:29, 4, 21) argues, the position of the African Commission has significance for its jurisprudence on extraterritoriality of human rights in that it shows the willingness to find states responsible for disproportionate actions which violate the rights of populations in foreign states.

Individual communications

The provisions of articles 55-57 of the African Charter particularly relating to the mandate of the African Commission to consider 'communications other than those of states parties' have been correctly interpreted as including complaints brought by individuals (Yeshanew 2011:153; Odinkalu 1998:8, 372-374). As discussed earlier, climate change implicates a range of human rights which are guaranteed under the African Charter and enforceable as shown in the jurisprudence of African Commission on individually lodged communications. Individual communications are a potential tool for climate related human rights alleged violation considering the possibilities it offers.

One is that, unlike most domestic jurisdictions where only a 'victim' or person affected by a violation can sue, individual communications before the African Commission do not require for one to be a victim (Viljoen 2012:304). In relation to climate change and effect, the deviation from victim requirement particularly means a lot to communities which may have become too powerless to institute actions by themselves. Also, it is to the advantage of individuals or peoples who may have been silenced and prevented from raising their voices against the activities of gas flaring, deforestation, which in addition to negative impact on the global climate also leave their communities environmentally degraded.

Another is that, while exhaustion of local remedy is required as a rule (Viljoen, 2012, 316), the admissibility practice of the African Commission can excuse this requirement if remedies are not available, or effective or inadequate. A remedy is unavailable if it cannot be used without hindrance; ineffective if it offers no prospect of success and inadequate if it cannot redress an alleged wrong (Viljoen 2012:317). In situations where national laws do not guarantee the right to environment, but criminalize the activities and deny access to court to those who wish to question activities which contribute to climate change and compromise rights, as was decided in the *Ogoniland case* (para. 41), it is difficult to imagine that domestic remedies will be available. Hence, individual communications offer complainants an opportunity to have a cause heard and make their cause visible to regional public opinion far from legislative and political suppressions at home.

Interpretive function

While the interpretation of every provision of the charter may be fulfilled during the consideration of inter-states and individual communications, it does not seem to end there. In line with article 45(3) of the African Charter, the function of the African Commission in relation to interpretation of provisions under the African Charter may extend to where no complaint has emerged. It has in fact done so in the case of the indigenous peoples in the process of the negotiation of the UN declaration on indigenous peoples' rights (Advisory Opinion 2007). In the same vein, the discussion that are taking place under the UNFCCC have implications for the work of the Commission in that it implicates on the realisation of human rights in Africa, as has been shown. Hence, on climate change issues, it should be possible for an advisory opinion to be sought by an NGO enjoying observer status at the AU, at least on the extent of extra-territorial obligations of states in relation to an article 24 of the African Charter.

Assembly entrusted tasks

According to article 45(4) of the African Charter, the Commission may perform 'any other tasks which may be entrusted to it by the Assembly of Heads of State and Government'. As the 'supreme organ' of the AU (Viljoen 2012:171), the AU Assembly of Heads of State and Government (AU Assembly) involves in championing the common position of Africa in climate change negotiation. For this purpose, it established the Committee of African Heads of State and Government on Climate Change (CAHOSCC) in 2009 which worked with COP 15 in Copenhagen (2009) to ensure that Africa speaks with one voice in global climate change negotiations. The Copenhagen Accord which is the singular outcome of the event at COP 15, (Decision 2/CP.15 2009), made progress in relation to issues including its scope, guiding principles and safeguards of REDD+. Signed by 114 nations amidst much disagreement regarding other matters on the agenda, the Copenhagen Accord set the stage for REDD+ as a global initiative to decelerate the alarming rate of deforestation (Decision 2/CP.15 2009). It has worked closely with the African Ministerial Conference on the Environment (AMCEN), which was established in December 1985, following a conference of African ministers of environment held in Cairo,

Egypt (AMCEN Resolution para. 3). Among others, the mandate of AMCEN includes the provision of advocacy for environmental protection in Africa and observance of the implementation of environmental conventions including the UNFCCC and the Kyoto Protocol (AMCEN Resolution).

To foster the link between CAHOSCC and AMCEN in connection with climate change negotiations, the Assembly has taken some measures. For instance, in preparation for 2014 COP 19 in Poland, the Assembly endorsed that country of host for the presidency of AMCEN should serve as coordinator of CAHOSCC in such a way that secures the link between the two institutions.

The Assembly is however yet to link with the African Commission in its activities on climate change. This is evidenced in the request made by the African Commission in Resolution 153, calling for its inclusion by the Assembly in the African Union's negotiating team on climate change. While this is yet to be effected, it can be argued that, if invited, the participation of the African Commission will pass for an Assembly mandated task. It will offer the African Commission an important platform in introducing human rights dimension to the climate change discourse. More importantly, this may begin the all-important process of harmonising the environmental activities of AMCEN and CAHOSCC with the African Commission mandate on human rights protection.

Conclusion

Despite Africa's limited contribution to global climate change, the negative implications of climate change for Africa are beyond dispute. Vulnerability assessment of climate change impact, actual and projected, are documented as water resources, food security, natural resource management and biodiversity, human health, settlements and infrastructure, and desertification. While there exists a link between these impact scenarios and human rights, as noticeable in the international climate policy making trend, more attention has been devoted to addressing climate change as an environmental concern. In Africa, an uncritical acceptance of this position is inferable in the sense that human source and vulnerability define and exemplify climate change and constitute a threat to a range of human rights such as rights to food, water, housing, peace, health and environment which are guaranteed either expressly or impliedly under the African Charter. Also, there is potential in the promotional, protective, interpretive and assembly-entrusted functions of the Commission in addressing threats posed by climate change impact to human rights in Africa.

Notes and References

1 This position is generally true except for autocratic nations such as China which is achieving economic development certainly not within the neo-liberal paradigm, see Tisdell, C. 2009. Economic Reform and Openness in China: China's Development Policies in the Last 30 Years. *Economic Analysis & Policy*. 39(2) 271-294.

2 An example is Uganda Nile Basin Reforestation Projects 1-4. https://cdm.unfccc.int/Projects/DB/JACO1200649370.95/view (accessed 27 October2013)

3 An example is Project 3207: Aberdare Range / Mt. Kenya Small Scale Reforestation Initiative Kirimara-Kithithina Small Scale A/R Project. http://cdm.unfccc.int/Projects/DB/JACO1260322919.16/view> (accessed 27 October 2013).

4 The Working Group on Economic, Social and Cultural Rights', established by the African Commission on Human and Peoples' Rights with the adoption of Resolution 73 at the 36th Ordinary Session held in Dakar, Senegal from 23rd November to 7th December 2004

5 'The Working Group on Extractive Industries, Environment and Human Rights Violations', established by the African Commission on Human and Peoples' Rights with the adoption of Resolution 148 at the 46th Ordinary Session held in Banjul, The Gambia from 11th-25th November 2009

6 'NGO with Observer Status' http://www.achpr.org/network/ngo/by-name/ (accessed 26 June 2013)

7 Cameroon Environmental Protection Association' http://www.achpr.org/network/ngo/362/(accessed 26 June 2013); 'Citizens for a Better Environment' http://www.achpr.org/network/ngo/365/ (accessed 26 June 2013)

8 'Arid Lands Institute'http://www.achpr.org/network/ngo/399/ (accessed 26 June 2013)

9 'Forest Peoples Programme' http://www.achpr.org/network/ngo/347/(accessed 26 June 2013);'Institute of Wildlife, Forestry and Human Development Studies' http://www.achpr.org/network/ngo/371/ (accessed 26 June 2013)

10 Committee of African Heads of State and Government on Climate Change (CAHOSCC) meeting' http://www.nepad.org/climatechangeandsustainabledevelopment/news/2570/committee-african-heads-state-and-government-climat (accessed 26 June 2013)

11 Summit Ends with Strong Decisions and Declarations by AU Heads of States on Crucial and Topical Issues on the Continent' http://summits.au.int/en/20thsummit/events/summit-ends-strong-decisions-and-declarations-au-heads-states-crucial-and-topical (accessed 26 June 2013).

ACHPR Web *see* African Commission on Human & Peoples' Rights 'Special Mechanisms'. http://www.achpr.org/mechanisms/ (accessed 25 June 2013)

Adelman, S. 2010. Rethinking human rights: The impact of climate change on the dominant discourse. In *Human rights and climate change*, ed. S. Humphreys 159-180. Cambridge: Cambridge University Press.

Advisory Opinion *see* Advisory opinion of the Afircan Commission on Human and Peoples' Rights on the United Nations Declarations on the Rights of Indigenous Peoples. Adopted by the African Commission on Human and Peoples' Rights at its 41st Ordinary Session held in May in Accra, Ghana.

Allen, M. 2003. Liability for climate change: Will it ever be possible to sue anyone for damaging the climate? *Commentary in Nature* 891-892.

Aminzadeh, S.C. 2007. A moral imperative: The human rights implications of climate change. *Hastings International and Comparative Law Review* 231-265.

Anton, D.K. and D. L. Shelton. 2011. *Environmental protection and human rights*. Cambridge: Cambridge University Press.

Bals, C.H., S. Harmeling and M. Windfuhr. 2008. *Climate change, food security and the right to adequate food.* Stuttgart: Germanwatch.

Beaumont, P. November 12, 2006. Kenya's herdsmen are facing extinction as global warming destroys their lands. *The Observer*.

Bodansky, D. and L. Rajamani. 2013. The evolution and governance architecture of the climate change regime. In *International relations and global climate change*, 2nd ed., eds. D. Sprinz and U. Luterbacher, 1-45. MIT Press.

Boko, M.I. *et al.* 2007. Africa. In *Climate Change 2007: Impacts, Adaptation and Vulnerability. Contribution of Working Group II to the Fourth Assessment Report of the Intergovernmental Panel on Climate Change,* eds. M. L. Parry et al, 433-467. Cambridge: Cambridge University Press.

Brown, O., A. Hammill and R. Mcleman.2007. Climate change as the 'new' security threat: Implications for Africa. *International Affairs* 83(6) 1141–1154.

Brown, O., and A. Crawford. 2008. *Assessing the security implications of climate change for West Africa' country case studies of Ghana and Burkina Faso.* IISD.

Bulto, T.S. 2011. Towards rights-duties congruence: Extraterritorial application of thehuman right to water in the African Human Rights System. *Netherlands Quarterly Human Rights* 29(4) 1-40.

Collier, P., G. Conway, and T. Venables. 2008. Climate change and Africa. *Oxford Review of Economic Policy* 24(2) 337-353.

Crippa, L.A. 2013. REDD+: Its potential to melt glacial resistance to recognise human rights and indigenous peoples' rights at the World Bank. In *Climate change and indigenous peoples: The search for legal remedies, eds.* R. S. Abate and E. A. Kronk, 123-150. United Kingdom: Edward Elgar Publishing Limited.

De Schutter, O. 2012. Climate change is a human rights issue – and that's how we can solve it. Tuesday 24 April. *The Guardian* http://www.guardian.co.uk/environment/2012/apr/24/climate-change-human-rights-issue (accessed 15 June 2013).

Donelly, J. 1998. Human rights: A new standard of civilisation. *International Affairs* 74(1) 1-24. DRC Report see Report of the Country visit of the Working Group on Indigenous Populations/Communities to the Republic of Congo. 2010. 15 – 24 March.

Extractive Working Group, see The Working Group on Extractive Industries, Environment and Human Rights Violations. 2009. Established by the African Commission on Human and Peoples' Rights with the adoption of Resolution 148 at the 46th Ordinary Session held in Banjul, The Gambia from 11th-25th November.

Gorte, R.W. and A.M. Sheikh, March 2010. *Deforestation and climate change.* USA: Congressional Reserve Service.

Griffiths, T. 2007. *Seeing 'RED'? 'Avoided deforestation' and the rights of indigenous peoples and local communities.* Forest Peoples Programme.

Gupta, J. 2007. Legal steps outside the climate convention: Litigation as a tool to address climate change. *Review of European Community & International Environmental Law* 16(1) 76-86.

Hansungule, M. 2009. African courts and the African Commission on Human and Peoples Rights. In *Human rights in Africa: Legal perspectives on their protection and promotion,* eds. A. Bosl and J.Diescho 233-217. Namibia: Macmillan Education.

Harrington, J. 2001. Special Rapporteurs of the African Commission on Human and Peoples' Rights. *African Human Rights Law Journal* 1(2) 247-267.

Helmut, J. and E. F. Lambin. 2001. *What drives tropical deforestation: A meta-analysis of proximate and underlying causes of deforestation based on subnational case study evidence.* LUCC Report Series No. 4.

High Level Panel for the African Development Bank. 2008. African Development Bank. 2008. *Investing in Africa's Future: ADB of the 21st Century.* High Level Panel for the African Development Bank.

Human Rights Watch. 2001. *Protectors or Pretenders- Government Human Rights Commission in Africa.* http://www.hrw.org/legacy/reports/2001/africa/ (accessed 13 March 2014).

Humphreys, S. 2010. Introduction: Human rights and climate change. In *Human rights and climate change*, ed. S. Humphreys, 1-34. Cambridge: Cambridge University Press.

International Council on Human Rights Policy. 2008. *Climate change and human rights: A rough guide.* Switzerland: International Council on Human Rights Policy.

IPACC Web *see* Indigenous Peoples of Africa Coordinating Committee. West Africa. http://www.ipacc.org.za/eng/regional_westafrica.asp (accessed 11 October2013).

IWGIA *see* International Working Group on Indigenous Affairs. 2011. *The world indigenous report.* IWGIA.

IWGIA & African Commission, *see* International Working Group on Indigenous Affairs and African Commission on Human and Peoples' Rights. 2005. Report of The African Commission's Working Group of Experts on Indigenous Populations/Communities. Adopted by The African Commission at its 28th Ordinary Session.

Kenya Report *see* Report of the Working Group on Indigenous Populations/Communities Research and Information Visit to Kenya. 1-19 March 2010. Adopted by the Commission at its 50th ordinary session, 24 October - 5 November 2001.

Khoza, S. 2005. Statement on social, economic and cultural rights. *African Human Rights Law Journal* 5 182-193.

Killander, M. 2012. The African Commission on Human and Peoples' Rights. In *The African Regional Human Rights System: 30 years after the African Charter on Human and Peoples' Rights* ed. M Ssenyonjo 235-248. Leiden-Boston: Martinus Nijhoff Publishers

Koch, I. E. 2005. Dichotomies, trichotomies or waves of duties? *Human Rights Law Review* 81-103.

McInerney-Lankford, S. 2009. Climate change and human rights: An Introduction to legal issues. *Harvard Environmental Law Review* 33 431-437.

Mckibben, B. 2006. The end of nature: Humanity, climate change and the natural world. NewYork: Random House Trade Paper Back.

Mwebaza, R. 2009. Climate change and the international human rights framework in Africa. In *Environmental governance and climate change in Africa: Legal perspectives,* eds. R. Mwebaza, and L. J. Kotze, 227-253. Institute for Security Studies Monograph 167.

NHRI Observer Status Resolution *see* Resolution on Granting Observer [Affiliate] Status to National Human Rights Institutions on Africa. 1998. Adopted at the Commission's 24th session, Banjul, the Gambia, 22-31 October 1998.

Odinkalu, C.A. 1998.The individual complaints procedure of the African Commission on Human and Peoples' Rights: A preliminary assessment. *Transnational Law and Contemporary Problems* 8 359-405.

OHCHR Report *see Report of the Office of the United Nations High Commissioner for Human Rights on the Relationship Between Climate Change and Human Rights.*2009. UN Document A/HRC/10/61, 15 January.

Orellana, M.A., M. Kothari and S. Chaudhry. 2010. *Climate change in the Work of the Committee on Economic, Social and Cultural Rights.* Centre for International Environmental Law.

Oruonye, E.D. 2012. Multinational oil corporations in Sub Sahara Africa: An assessment of the impacts of globalisation. *International Journal of Humanities and Social Science* 2(14) 152- 156.

Oxfam. 2008. *Survival of the fittest pastoralism and climate change in East Africa.* Oxfam.

Peart, N. 2012. Human rights-based climate change litigation - a radical solution? *Environmental Law & Management* 24 (2) 77-78.

Posner, E.A. 2007. Climate change and international human rights litigation: A Critical Appraisal. *University of Pennsylvania Law Review* 155 1925- 1945.

Quan, J. and N. Dyer, 2008. *Climate change and land tenure: The implications of climate change for land tenure and land policy.* International Institute for Environment and Development: FAO.

Rajamani, L. 2000. The principle of common but differentiated responsibility and the balance of commitments under the climate regime. *Review of European Community & International Environmental Law* 9(2) 120-131.

Reid, H., and S. Huq. 2007. *How we are set to cope with the impacts.* International Institute of Environment and Development 1-4.

Rist, G.2008. *The history of development: From western origins to global faith* 3rd ed. Trans. P. Camiller, London: Zedbooks.

Robinson, M. 2010. Foreword. In *Human rights and climate change*, ed. S. Humphreys. Cambridge: Cambridge University Press.

Robledo, C., J. Blaser and S. Bryne. 2010. Climate change: What are its implications for forest governance. In *Governing Africa's forests in a globalised world,* eds. L. A. German, A. Kersenty and Anne-Marie Tiani, 354-76. London: Earthscan.

Rwanda Report see Report of the Working Group on Indigenous Populations/Communities Mission to the Republic of Rwanda.1 – 5 December 2008. Adopted by the Commission at its 47th Ordinary Session, 12-26 May 2010.

Sinden, A. 2007. Climate change and human rights. *Journal of Land Resources & Environmental Law* 27, 255-271.

Suckling, K. 2007. An icon for climate change: The polar bear. Indian Country Today Mediation Network. http://indiancountrytodaymedianetwork.com/ictarchives/2007/01/04/suckling-an-icon-for-climate-change-the-polar-bear-90193 (accessed 20 June 2013).

Tebtebba Foundation. 2010. *Indigenous peoples, forests & REDD plus: State of forests, policy environment & ways forward.* Tebtebba Foundation.

Tisdell, C. 2009. Economic Reform and Openness in China: China's Development Policies in the Last 30 Years. *Economic Analysis & Policy*. 39(2) 271-294

Toulmin, C. 2009. *Climate change in Africa*. Zed Books.

Ulfstein, G. and J. Werksman. 2005. The Kyoto compliance system: Towards hard enforcement. In *Implementing the climate regime: International compliance,* eds. O. S. Stooke, J. Hovi and G. Ulfstein, 39-62. London: Earthscan.

UNEP Web. AMCEN at a glance.http://www.unep.org/roa/amcen/About_AMCEN/default.asp (accessed 26 June 2013)

United States Submission *see* Submission of United States to the Office of High Commissioner for Human Rights. 2008. Observations by the United States of America on the relationship between climate change and human rights. http://www.ohchr.org/Documents/Issues/ClimateChange/Submissions/USA.pdf.(accessed 13 January 2014).

UNPFII *see* United Nations Permanent Forum on Indigenous Issues. 2008. *Report on the impacts of climate change mitigation measures on indigenous peoples on their territories and lands.* E/C 19/2008/10.

UNREDD Web *see* The United Nations Collaborative Programme on Reducing Emissions from Deforestation and Forest Degradation in Developing Countries. UN-REDD Programme Partner Countries. http://www.un-redd.org/Partner_Countries/tabid/102663/Default.aspx ((accessed 26 September 2013).

Viljoen, F. 2005. The Special Rapporteur on prisons and conditions of detention in Africa: Achievements and possibilities. *Human Rights Quarterly* 27(1) 125-171.

Viljoen, F. 2012. *International human rights law in Africa.* Oxford University Press.

Watt Cloutier, S. 15 January 2005. Our land is changing - soon yours will too. The Guardian. http://www.theguardian.com/environment/2005/jan/15/science.climatechange (accessed 20 January 2014).

WHO *see* World Health Organisation. 2012. *World Malaria Report Fact Sheet.* WHO.

Wold, C., D. Hunter, and M. Powers. 2009. *Climate change and the law.* LexisNexis Matthew Bender: Mathew and Bender.

Woods, K. 2010. *Human rights and environmental sustainability.* Cheltenham, UK: Edward Elgar

Yeshanew, S.A. 2011. *The justiciability of economic, social and cultural rights in the African Regional System.* Finland: Abo Akademi University Press

Instruments

African Charter *see* African Union African Charter on Human and Peoples' Rights. 1981. Adopted June 27, OAU Doc. CAB/LEG/67/3 Rev. 5, 21 I.L.M. 58 (1982). Entered into force 21 October 1986.

AMCEN Resolution *see* The African Ministerial Conference on the Environment. Environmental co-operation in Africa.Resolution adopted by the Conference at its first session. UNEP/AEC.

AU Decision *see* Decision on Climate Change and Development in Africa. 3 July 2009. Adopted by the Thirteenth Ordinary Session of the Assembly in Sirte, Great Socialist People's Libyan Arab Jamahiriya.

AU Declaration *see* Declaration on Climate Change and Development in Africa. 29-30 January 2007. 3Assembly/AU/Decl.4 (VIII) the 8th Ordinary Session of our Assembly in Addis Ababa.

Decision 2/CP.15. 2009. Copenhagen Accord. FCCC/CP/2009/11/Add.1.

Decision 24/CP.7 2001. Procedures and mechanisms relating to compliance under the KyotoProtocol. 8th plenary meeting 10 November. FCCC/CP/2001/13/Add.3.

Decision 3/CMP.1. 2005. Modalities and Procedures for a Clean Development Mechanism as defined in article 12 of the Kyoto Protocol. FCCC/KP/CMP/2005/8/Add.1.

General Comment No 14 see United Nations General Comment No 14: The Right to the Highest Attainable Standard of Health. 2000. E/C.12/2000/4.

General Comment No 7 see United Nations *General Comment No 7: The Right to Adequate Housing, art 11 (1) of the Covenant: Forced Evictions.* 1997. Sixteenth Session.

General Comment No. 12 see United Nations *Committee on Economic, Social and Cultural General Comment No 12: The Right to Adequate Food art 1.* 1999. 12/05/99.E/C.12/1999/5.

General Comment No.4 see United Nations *General Comment No 4: The Right to Adequate Housing, art 11 (1) of the Covenant.* 1991. Sixth Session.

Kyoto Protocol *see* Kyoto Protocol to the United Nations Framework Convention on Climate Change.1998. Entered into force 16 February, 2005.

Milan Declaration *see* Milan Declaration of the Sixth International Indigenous Peoples Forum on Climate Change. 2003. At COP 9 UNFCCC, Milan, Italy, November 29 – 30 http://www.tebtebba.org/index.php/all-resources/category/80-ipfccc-meetings-2000-2004?download=374:milan-declaration-of-the-sixth-international-indigenous-peoples-forum-on-climate-change (accessed 11 October2013).

Protocol to the African Charter see Protocol to the African Charter on Human and Peoples' Rights on the Establishment of an African Court on Human and Peoples' Rights. 1998/2004. African Union.

Protocol on the Statute of the African Court of Justice and Human Rights. 2008.

Resolution 153 *see* African Commission of Human and Peoples' Rights Resolution on Climate Change and Human Rights and the Need to Study its Impact in Africa. Nov. 25, 2009. ACHPR/Res153(XLVI)09.

UNESCEC and AU Commission *see* United Nations Economic and Social Council Economic Commission for Africa & African Union Commission. 2010. Report on Climate Change and Development in Africa. 2 March. E/ECA/COE/29/5 AU/CAMEF/EXP/5/(V).

UNFCCC *see* The United Nations Framework on Climate Change Convention. 1992. Adopted at World Conference on Environment and Development at Rio de Janeiro, 3-14 June.

UNHCR Resolution 10/4 *see* United Nations Human Rights Council. March 20, 2009. *Resolution 10/4 Human rights and climate change.* UN Doc. A/HRC/10/29.

United Nations World Water Development Report 3. 2009. *Water in a Changing World.* United Nations.

Case law

Communication 155/96 Social and Economic Rights Action Center (SERAC) and Center for Economic and Social Rights (CESR) v Nigeria 15th Activity Report: 2001 – 2002 27 October 2001.

Communication 157/96 Association Pour La Sauvegarde De La Paix Au Burundi v Kenya, Uganda, Rwanda, Tanzania, Zaire (DRC), Zambia.

Communication No 279/03-296/05 *Sudan Human Rights Organisation & Centre on Housing Rights and Evictions (COHRE) v Sudan.*

Communications 25/89, 47/90, 56/91 and 100/93. Free Legal Assistance Group and Others v. Zaire

Developing a Positive Attitude for the Reduction of Xenophobia and the Realisation of Human Rights in Migrants and Refugees' Communities

A South African Perspective

Serges Djoyou Kamga

Introduction

Political conflict, wars and economic instability are key reasons why foreigners leave their home countries. For those who fall into the refugee/asylum seeker category, violence usually underpins and influences their decisions to leave. However, for many of these the grass is not always greener away from home. They are generally confronted with xenophobia and economic hardship in foreign lands.

Originally the word xenophobia comes from the Greek words *xénos,* meaning 'the stranger' and 'the guest' and *phóbos*, meaning 'fear'. Thus, xenophobia stands for 'fear of the stranger', but usually the term is taken to mean 'hatred of strangers'(Smelser & Baltes:2001). In this globalisation era, migration is part of life and a social phenomenon. People have to move to different places and are likely to encounter xenophobia. Therefore, the question arises: what can be done to tackle xenophobia and improve sustainable development of all parties involved? To answer this question, this chapter will first examine the scale of the problem, expose its causes, provide recommendations and finally examine the effects of these recommendations on the development of all the parties.

The scale of the problem

In many parts of the world, migrants and refugees are harassed, discriminated against, victimised, and economically exploited.

Harassment and violence against foreigners

Xenophobic attitudes have indeed translated into violent attacks on foreigners. Recently in South Africa, a wave of violent attacks against Somali-run businesses around Cape Town have exposed tension between poor South Africans and the millions of refugees who have flocked to the country in the hope of a better life (IRIN: 2006). As observed during the Xenophobic attacks of 2008, incidents of violence against foreigners in South Africa are not scarce.

Discrimination against foreigners

The International Convention on The Elimination of All Forms of Racial Discrimination (1965, art 1) defines racial discrimination as:

> "... any distinction, exclusion, restriction or preference based on race, colour, descent or national or ethnic origin which has the effect of nullifying or impairing the recognition, enjoyment or exercise, on an equal footing, of human rights and fundamental freedoms."

However, this very important treaty has no specific provision that tackles the specific issues of discrimination against migrants. Consequently, migrants including, refugees and asylum seekers feel unsupported and unprotected in their host countries. They ascribe their circumstances largely to the host country, which, they suggest, does not fulfill its international and legal obligations towards them.

Reports show that people are apprehended for being 'too dark' or "walking like a black foreigner". These people are actively targeted by the police for their (real or imagined) foreignness. In this regard, the mechanisms of identification are arbitrary and racist (Human Rights Watch 1998. Williams:2008). On a daily basis, migrants encounter institutional discrimination, verbal abuse and public hostility. Furthermore, the unemployment rate is very high in the immigrant communities.

Refugees face the following major problems in accessing HIV-related health services: non-recognition of the red refugee ID book or refugee permit; insecure refugee livelihoods; the slow pace of the public sector (antiretroviral) ARV roll-out and the poor level of assistance provided by different refugee service-provider NGOs (Mandisa & Baruti:2005).

The perception of refugees as criminal

Refugees are frequently perceived as inherently criminals, fueled by war reports from their countries of origin and the construction of inaccurate stereotypes around the character of those who tend to flee (Human Rights 1St: 2001). A commonly held belief is that 'illegal immigrants' are primarily responsible for crime, and/or the increase of crime, a belief that contains the potential to inflame vigilante violence against foreigners. In the West, foreigners, especially Muslims, are considered terrorists by some people. People with long beards can be attacked in the streets or arrested (UNCHR: 2007).

Economic exploitation of foreigners

Without money, there is no service for many seeking to attain and maintain legal status in host countries. Money and corruption are central to staying in the country. The guise of checking status (more than any concern with status *per se*) also creates a space for ongoing economic exploitation. Even those who hold valid, legal documentation are not exempt from corruption and extortion. In many cases, authorities threaten to, and do, tear up documents unless they are paid a certain amount of money. In these cases, foreigners - whether legal or not - are often arrested and sent to detention centers where they face repatriation, unless they are able to buy their way out of the system.

The host countries increasingly blame foreigners for corrupting officials, thereby shifting responsibility from the officials to foreigners. Although the institutional system renders foreigners vulnerable to corruption and abuse, many foreigners play an active role in the corruption. Their role is therefore not exclusively that of 'victim' because they are also perpetrators as they pay for documents (e.g. undocumented migrants).

Aliens work in conditions which are inferior to citizens of the host countries. In most countries including South Africa, they are underpaid, work long hours, and have no benefits like medical aid. For example, a survey of manufacturing firms in Korea undertaken by the International Labour Office (ILO) and the Korea Labour Institute Found that foreign workers received less than half the wages earned by nationals (International Labour Office (ILO), International Organisation for Migration (IOM) and

Office of the UN High Commissioner for Human Rights (OHCHR): 2001, 12)). They fill the 'three-D' jobs, dirty, dangerous and difficult. Moreover, migrants, including refugees are unable to open bank accounts in their host countries. This increases their vulnerability to theft and violence because foreigners are known to personally hold their money outside safe banking environments (Harris:2001).

Causes of xenophobia

Xenophobia is generally caused by the competition between citizens and foreigners in the host country, the competition between states due to globalization, the negative description of foreign nationals by the media, the negative political statement, and the excessive power of the police over migrants.

Competition between citizens and foreigners

In the receiving countries, social groups in poorer positions consider refugees as competitors for jobs and public services. In reality severe inequality in South Africa leads to frustration of the marginalized who perceive migrants as competing for the limited resources. This creates resentment amongst the South Africans have not who end up believing their poverty is informed by foreign nationals who take away their jobs. This cultivates a social and political climate that generates xenophobia and racism (i.e. defensive reactions against migrants), as well as nationalism (i.e. demands that the state provides better protection against foreigners for its own population) (UNCR:2006).

Competition between states due to globalisation

Globalisation has increased competition between states and has led states to reduce their services in areas of social welfare, education and healthcare. This reduction has influenced those people who are less privileged. They are often in direct competition with migrants for welfare services and are the main breeding ground for xenophobic and racist ideologies. Research has shown that severe economic inequalities and the marginalisation of persons from access to basic economic and social conditions give rise to tensions and manifestations of racism and xenophobia (ILO, IOM and OHCHR:2001).

Media portrayal of foreigners

The media presents migrants as illegal people involved in criminal deeds. According to Harris, (2001) some of the issues raised are:

- 'Illegal immigrants are infiltrating the cities, suburbs, townships and squatter camps and taking away the available housing;
- The growing numbers of illegal aliens add to the decay of inner cities;
- Illegals take away jobs
- Illegals are prepared to work for very low wages and are thus destroying the workers' struggle for better pay and working conditions, and
- Illegals are a threat to the Reconstruction and Development Programme'

Migrants are commonly presented in news media coverage as associated with crime, trafficking, drugs, diseases and other social ills. Even though in some cases, some migrants could be criminal or dishonest, they are presented by media as uniquely criminal and their migrant status is more represented than the crime committed itself. It is almost like migration is synonymous with crime even though there are many honest migrants in the country.

Political statements

A number of public figures and politicians have made hostile, xenophobic statements about foreigners. For example, in South Africa in his introductory speech to parliament, Mangosuthu Buthelezi, then Minister of Home Affairs, stated (Human Rights Watch, 1998:20).

> 'if we as South Africans are going to compete for scarce resources with millions of aliens who are pouring into South Africa, then we can bid goodbye to our Reconstruction and Development Programme'.

In South Africa, the Refugee Act states that all refugees are entitled to health care, employment and education in the same way as host citizens. It also states that all people in the country are entitled to the rights enshrined in Chapter 2 of the constitution (Bill of Rights) with the exception of right to vote. Legal immigrants and refugees should, therefore, be entitled to services offered at municipal level such as safety, housing, clinic services, libraries etc. Not only is there a lack of awareness at local government level of the rights of refugees, but there appears to be no plans for ensuring that services are extended to refugees. Indeed, in some instances, non-nationals are actively denied these services. Local government officials interviewed for this research felt that provision of services for refugees should be the responsibility of the Department of Home Affairs at national level. As one city official stated (Harris:2001):

> 'There is no land for these immigrants ... They're taking every piece of land they can get and occupying it ... If you go to town on the N1, there's a piece we call the Valley where we have about 50 to 60 immigrants living there, under cardboard boxes, in the open, making fires against the bridges and all that ... They occupy city-owned land illegally. So we take action against them. We're trying to get central government to take full responsibility for this Because the city does not have the resources or the manpower to deal with this. Tonight I've got to go again, go deal with the immigrants'.

Home Affairs is becoming increasingly hard-lined about foreigners. In some countries, In South Africa legislation also locates responsibility for surveillance and control of foreigners within the hands of Home Affairs Officers and some of them may be xenophobic themselves. The latter work hard and even enlist public participation in the 'detection, apprehension and removal of 'illegal aliens" (William:1999,2-3). In the context of high levels of xenophobia and intolerance towards foreigners, it is likely that the actions of citizens of the host country will not be limited to mere reporting. There is the danger of citizens taking the law into their own hands, even considering it their patriotic duty to take action against 'illegal aliens' (assuming they can distinguish between various categories of foreigners in the country)'. The envisaged role of the public in controlling and reporting 'illegal aliens' is thus one that seems likely to fuel and encourage xenophobia and related acts of violence in the host country.

Excessive power of the police towards migrants

If any immigration officer or police officer suspects on reasonable grounds that a person is an alien he may require such person to provide him with proof that he is entitled to be in the Republic. If such a person fails to satisfy such officer that he is so entitled, such officer may take him into custody without a warrant and if such officer deems it necessary detain such person in a manner and at a place determined by the Director-General, and such person shall as soon as possible be dealt with (South African Human Rights Commission: 1999a). For example, during the week-long launch (mid-March 2000) of 'Operation Crackdown' in Hillbrow in Johannesburg over 1 000 police and military personal were deployed to search 22 568 vehicles, 293 buildings and over 205 324 people (Pelser 2000:7-10). Some 7 068 people were arrested on the suspicion that they were illegal immigrants (2000:8; Harris:2001). In contrast, only 14 individuals were arrested for serious crimes such as murder, rape and robbery (Pelser:2000). More broadly, in a 2 month period of Operation Crackdown, 10 000 suspected 'illegal aliens' were arrested, 7 000 of whom were taken to Lindela (detention centre in South Africa) (Harris:2001) This is not exclusive to Africa. In many Europeans countries, whenever a foreigner is arrested on the street without his papers, he is not given a chance to explain or get them from his house. He or she is taken immediately to the deportation centre. Moreover, in European airports, all young Africans have their passports checked at the exit of the planes before they get to the immigration counter and this is victimisation.

Strategies to reduce xenophobia

The reduction of xenophobia can be done through education, protecting refugees and migrant's rights and securing their cultural integration.

Education

Schools, colleges and work places should promote respect for differences and highlights the benefits of cultural diversity.

Immigration officers and the police must receive training to bring their actions in line with international law, so as to protect the rights of immigrants and refugees. A 'Know your rights' training and awareness raising are similarly recommended for foreigners themselves (Harris:2001). For example, community leaders should distribute educational pamphlets/posters (in the foreign languages most commonly spoken) to frontline workstations and border posts. It is also recommended that victims of xenophobia are included as a constituency within wider victim empowerment initiatives and that remedial alternatives, such as complaints desks and/or toll-free telephone lines are implemented to tackle incidents of secondary victimisation.

There is also the need for inter-agency communication, co-ordination and protocol with regard to the few service providers that are working in the field. A co-ordinated national strategy is recommended to raise awareness and share information about cross-border migration as well as to create interventions for tackling violence in a sensitive manner that avoids generating stereotypes. In this regard, the city of Johannesburg launched a migrants help-desk in April 2007 after consultation with migrants' service providers Harris:2001).

Policy makers and government should take more responsibility for ensuring accurate and balanced public information on refugee and other migrant issues. Governments should identify and counteract misinformation in particular where it incites fear and mistrust of refugees, and explain clearly that refugees are people in need of protection.

A human rights- based approach to international migration

Human rights must be at the centre of any analysis of migration and xenophobia because they recognize that certain principles are true and valid for all people, in all societies, under all conditions of economic, political, ethnic and cultural life (ILO, IOM, UNHCR: 2001,3). Human rights approach will lead to the protection of refugees and migrants' rights. This entails addressing civil and political as well as socio-economic rights of migrants without forgetting their cultural integration.

Civil and political rights

As far as civil rights are concerned, discrimination against migrants including refugees and asylum seekers is a contemporary form of racism and should be criminalized (Human Rights 1[st:] :2001). Where an asylum procedure is in place, the way that the system is accessed and administered can minimize or exacerbate discrimination against refugees seeking protection. The guarantee of non-refoulement is the foundation stone of refugee protection.

Similarly abuse of power (eg. corruption and violation of the principle of non-refoulement) must be criminalised and punished by the criminal justice system in order to eradicate the culture of impunity that prevails along the countries' borders where immigrants usually enter. In the European Union for example, inciting racism and xenophobia constitutes a crime and everyone can be imprisoned for one to three years prison terms for incitement to violence or hatred "against a group of persons or a member of such a group defined by reference to race, colour, religion, descent or national or ethnic origin".[1] However, this disposition should not hamper the freedom of expression.

States must make sure refugees are aware of their rights. They should be given the right to vote at least at the local level to allow them to raise their issues and make politicians more responsive and aware of them. In Ireland for example, where refugees and asylum seekers were allowed to vote in local elections in June 2004, the political debate was changed, refugee-related issues were debated and members of the immigrants and refugee community were successfully elected (European council on refugees and exiles nd).

Securing refugees and other migrants' economic and social rights

To secure migrants access to economic and social rights, it is important to establish systems to monitor their access to the labour and housing market as well as health social education and other community services. Because housing provision impacts on a number of other integration outcomes such as education, health and employment, refugees and other migrants should be allowed to choose their areas of residence.

Vocational training, recognition of qualification education, education and language factors are capital in helping refugees in achieving gainful employment, empowerment and integration (Harris:2001). Study grants should also be made available for those who want to further their studies.

Many refugees arrive in the host country with physical and mental trauma that need to addressed. Integration related policy should target the vulnerable such as children, women the elderly and persons with disabilities.

Cultural integration of refugees and other migrants

To ensure cultural integration, every migrant should be allowed to practice his/her religion, culture and beliefs in the host country. It is fundamental to establish platforms to strengthen the knowledge of other religions and cultures among the government staff and the public in general as it will facilitate cultural integration. The role of religious organisations in promoting respect and understanding and providing essential services should be recognised by policy makers. All migrants also need to be aware of the values of the host countries and respect them.

Municipal actions such as the 'Rotterdam Multicoloured City' should be encouraged. In the municipality of Rotterdam in the Netherlands, diversity is set to be the normative basis for all municipal policies. These policies include: proportional participation by all immigrants in Rotterdam, in particular, proportional representation of immigrants in executive committees and personnel; strengthening immigrant entrepreneurship and encouraging initiatives by immigrants and above all making cultural diversity apparent in Rotterdam (International Labour Office (ILO), International Organisation for Migration (IMO) & The Office of the UN High Commissioner for Human Rights (OHCHR):2001,11).

To close this section, there is a need to have more initiatives like ISOP "human rights integration" in Austria. It is an organization providing training courses, which combine social, educational legal and political elements with vocational training and advice on labour market opportunities to migrants. It also works to develop intercultural understanding by raising public awareness on anti-discrimination and anti-racism issues (ILO, IMO & OHCHR: 2001,8).

Results of establishing a wellcoming society

Migrant integration is a dynamic two-way process in which migrants or refugees, government and society work together to establish a coherent society with positive results as outlined below.

Improvement of sustainable development among refugees

Creating a welcoming society will allow migrants including refugees to have all benefits the citizens of the host country have. They will access social economic and cultural rights and even political rights (for refugees), which will empower them and lead to their sustainable development. Their integration into the local market will combat crime since they will be able to provide for themselves and their families. While resources are limited and their scarcity is behind xenophobia, the Ubuntu philosophy that can be summarised as carry for one another should inform the relation between alien and nationals.

Improvement of sustainable development in the host country

Migrants including refugees are a fundamental work force and their participation in the local economy adds more resources to the country. If refugees and other migrants are given a chance to be educated, to trade, to work and participate in society, the end result is that the host country will have more human capital. It is commonly agreed that the USA is what it is today because of migrants. It is a country where individuals like the former President Barak Obama, who is a descendant of immigrants, have made a mark.

Improvement of sustainable development beyond the borders of the host country

Empowered migrants including refugees will benefit their home countries. Refugees who work abroad send some money home to support their families. Some build schools and other infrastructure in their home country. These investments will bring sustainable development back home and hinder other departures or migrations because conditions will be improved for others in the community. In reality, the Africa diaspora is playing a significant role in the development of the continent (Douglas:2012). However, the remittances sent home should not be used to fuel conflicts through acquisition of weapons and other deathly gadgets.

Conclusion

Improving the protection of migrants and refugees in the face of xenophobic hostility, discrimination and violation of human rights calls for common approaches, strategies, coordination, and the aptitude to mobilise human and material resources. Officials and institutions of governments, international organisations and migrant groups all have roles to play and contributions to make.

A rights-based approach to protecting migrants and refugees from xenophobia needs to be more incorporated in national policies. Though this chapter is not the solution to xenophobia, it is hoped that it might lead to further thought, reflection and then definitive action. Political will or the lack of it is a capital question that can make the difference between effective interventions to tackle xenophobia or the continued exposure of migrants and refugees to its effects.

End note

1. Article 27 of the EU Convention.

References

Douglas K. 2012. 'How the African diaspora is contributing to the continent's growth story' https://www.howwemadeitinafrica.com/how-the-african-diaspora-is-contributing-to-the-continent%E2%80%99s-growth-story/23044/

European council on refugees and exiles' Towards the Integration of Refugees in Europe' at http://www.fmreview.org/FMRpdfs/FMR23/FMR2308.pdf. (accessed 01-5-2007)

Harris B .2001. 'A Foreign experience: violence, Crime and Xenophobia during South Africa's Transition,' *Violence and transition* series. v5 available at http://www.csvr.org.za/docs/racism/aforeignexperience.pdf

Human Rights Watch World Report 1998 - South Africa, https://www.hrw.org/news/1997/12/03/human-rights-watch-world-report-1998

International Labour Office, International Organisation for Migration and Office of the UN High Commissioner for Human Rights 2001. 'International migration, Racism, Discrimination and Xenophobia' A discussion paper available at http://publications.iom.int/system/files/pdf/international_migration_racism.pdf

IRIN. 2006. 'SOUTH AFRICA: Attacks on Somalis expose xenophobia', 31 August 2006

Mandisa M and Amisi, Baruti A.2005. A Report on Refugee's access to HIV-related health services' Centre for Civil Society

Pelser E (2000) 'Operation Crackdown: the new policing strategy'. *Nedbank ISS crime index, 2 (4)*, 7-10. Pretoria: Institute for Security Studies.

Smelser, N. J.and Baltes, P. B. (eds.) 2001. International Encyclopedia of the Social and Behavioural Sciences. Elsevier. Oxford Science Ltd.

The International Convention on the Elimination of All Forms of Racial Discrimination, adopted by UN General Assembly resolution 2106 A (XX) ON 21 December 1965 and entering into force on 4 January 1969.

UNHCR 'State of World Refugees 2006-Chapter 3 addressing refugee's security' http://www.unhcr.org/publications/sowr/4444afc80/state-worlds-refugees-2006-human-displacement-new-millennium-chapter-3.html

Williams V, 2008. "Xenophobic attacks in South Africa: Not a completely new phenomenon" https://www.boell.de/en/navigation/foreign-affairs-security-3460.html

William V .1999. 'Spot the Alien' *crossings* 3(2).2-3.

Conclusion

Africa's development:

Way Forward

Alinah K. Segobye

The task of finding solutions for Africa's development problems would seem to be a fairly obvious preoccupation of African leaders. However, as the chapters of this book have demonstrated, it is not always a given that Africa's development challenges will be a priority for African leaders nor that they will be addressed from within the continent. Many African states remain dependent on donor funding for most sectors of their economies and overall development planning. What this book has done is highlight how this scenario continues to be the reality of the continent despite Africa being one of the most resources-endowed continent. Some have argued that Africa lacks leaders (Mo Ibrahim 2013) while others have accused African academics of laziness in framing issues about Africa's development agenda (Lopes 2015). Other thought leaders have challenged African intellectuals to be more daring in imagining Africa's future and to take responsibility for this lest others do this (Sall 2015). What has emerged from this book is a general consensus that a multiplicity of actors are needed to take leadership and ownership of Africa's development agenda. These include leaders across the board, African intellectuals, state and non-state actors and more importantly civic society. In contextualising their discussions, authors have drawn attention to the need for a historical context in not only finding Africa's development problems but also in highlighting their complexity. In this regard there is no magic bullet which will provide solutions nor is it a given that such solutions if coming from Africans would work. The book highlights the need for African thought leadership and engagement at all levels from within and from outside of Africa for sustainable solutions to Africa's development challenges. What has emerged from the various thematic strands covered in the book is the need for open and sustained conversations and action to remedy the wrongs of the past, address current issues and boldly take ownership of a shared vision for the future.

What many authors and indeed participants of the symposium highlighted was the need for commitment at all levels to sustainable solutions and a deeper understanding of Africa's position in the global geopolitical landscape which is in constant flux. To this end, solutions that are relevant today may be obsolete tomorrow in the same way that development challenges which seem fairly simple may be insurmountable tomorrow. One of the factors which a number of authors raised and which has subsequently been the subject of a thought leadership symposium hosted by the University of Johannesburg and the Concerned Africans Forum in November 2015 has been inextricable linkage of Africa's future with that of the rest of the world. To this end, inasmuch as Africa can take charge of its destiny, as Africans we must be mindful of the dynamics of the global world order particularly ways in which more powerful actors exert influence on Africa's futures. Thabo Mbeki spoke to this in his keynote presentation at the symposium highlighting the dangers of a unipolar world for Africa (Mbeki 2015). Former president Mbeki noted the opportunities in the post 2008 economic meltdown which opened possibilities for new partnerships for Africa to mitigate overdependence on the global North. A key development has been the continent's forging of stronger ties with China, India and Latin American.

An area of interest which has gained global priority is the area of illicit financial flows. Former president Mbeki's report on the illicit financial flows commissioned by the UNECA and the AU has also brought into sharp relief one of the major sources of impoverishment for Africa's citizenry. The subject of the impact of illicit financial flows on global relations and Africa in particular have been trending in the news and other platforms as they highlight the linkages between African leaders, elites and international corporates, particularly those in the financial services sector. What has been revealed so far suggests that the state in Africa has predatory tendencies, which are associated with poor governance and looting of Africa's resources. This has exacerbated poverty, insecurity and the fragility of Africa's economies. Leaders fell short of their commitments to citizenry by plundering resources meant for development. This practice, which has been going on with impunity for decades has drawn attention to the corruption nature of power holders and global capital. Several chapters highlight the above dilemmas for Africa's development and go further to urge greater transparency and accountability on the part of leaders. They call for paradigm shifts particularly in the operation of state oversight institutions including the Courts and other agencies. In South Africa, The Constitutional Court, and Chapter 9 institutions such as the Public Protector have been at the forefront of promoting accountable leadership and championing citizen participation in building a more democratic developmental state.

This volume has also raised questions about the capacity of African countries to lead their own development agendas. In the last two years we witnessed the transition from the Millennium Development Goals to Sustainable Development Goals. What emerged in discourses of these global development goals was that Africa had not met the MDGs and would also be challenged to finance and implement the SDGs. Further, as the AU Commission was advancing Agenda 2063 as the continent's development goals the question arises as to which goals will get priority attention for the continent? Be it as it may, the continent took part in the sign off of the SDGs and efforts are under way to align these with Agenda 2063. Other initiatives to explore how to fund these processes saw the convening of meetings such as the Financing for Development (FFD3) in Addis in 2015 (Kabukuru 2015). As noted by several of the volume's authors, Africa is not resource-poor. Therefore, the question of affordability ought not to be the challenge. The big challenge remains how to leverage the continent's resource rich status and transform this into meaningful domestic financing capability. The ambivalence of leaders to African talent whether on the continent or in the Diaspora was highlighted. One of the problems noted is leadership unease with their own citizenry with skills particularly vocal voices. These are often seen as potential threats to leaders stay in power and some have encountered a painful fate facing incarceration, exile or worse, death. Coupled with weak institutional infrastructure such as exists in education sectors, human capability development is hardly ever based on foresighted or visionary frameworks so there remains a huge deficit of critical skills to drive industrialization and knowledge economies in Africa.

On the subject of democracy and governance, a recent edition of *New African* highlighted the challenge facing deepening democracy through electoral processes on the continent. As at 2015, almost a third of African Heads of state were in power for over two terms with several having been in power for more than three decades. Leaders have changed the constitutions of their countries to favour additional terms whilst others have used the power of their office to ensure elections favored their parties (Kalombo 2015). Even in countries where elections were declared free and fair there were cries of foul play from opposition parties and civic organizations. Some chapters allude to this problem of the 'Big Man' in Africa's political landscape and highlight how this stymies human freedoms and human rights. The litany of violations of basic human rights in countries supposedly enjoying stabile government has not escaped scrutiny and or criticism. Several authors present case study evidence of how leaders undermine the rule of law in their countries. The AU Commission could play a more engaged leadership role through its organs.

A more enhanced leadership role of the AU has taken place as evidenced by the Peace and Security Commission, which has shown greater visibility in recent conflicts across the continent. Concern has been raised about the capacity of the AU to finance its own peace keeping initiatives. The fact that initiatives for peace keeping and peace-building are finally being considered by leaders of the continent provides hope for the future. Lessons learnt from the Libyan crisis (Pahad 2015; Sall 2015) suggests that the continent's leaders and AU Commission need to work together to address conflict and security issues on the continent, particularly with the increasing activities of militia and other forms of insurgency following the Libyan crisis. The volume probably could have featured more chapters in the thematic area of peace and security as this significantly undermines human development for African citizenry.

A number of authors have chosen to adopt an Afro-pragmatic stance in respect to Africa's future opportunities in the arena of economic development. An international conference on *The Emergence of Africa* hosted by the government of Cote d'Ivoire and several development partners in 2015 suggested that several countries could potentially realize significant growth and could become key players in regional and continental growth and integration. Whilst some chapters in this volume noted this opportunity, they also highlighted the challenges facing Africa's emergence. A leadership deficit facing many African institutions was cited as a key problem. Further, the tension between national or state-centric development agendas versus regionalism created weak systems for promoting intra-Africa trade and integration. Conflicting policy messages and priorities negatively impacted citizen-led initiatives to do business in Africa by Africans. Some of the examples cited are the often stringent policies targeting African citizenry by Home Affairs/Immigration services. These, coupled with bureaucratic impediments for trade and 'doing business' have dissuaded many African investors from intra-Africa trade (c.f. Saunders et. al. 2012 *passim*). These are often in contrast to very open and often aggressive policies targeting non-African partners to invest in Africa.

A few chapters highlight the link between the phenomena of poor intra-country/region trade opportunities and corruption. Seemingly preference for external investors, particularly foreign corporates is often driven by self-interest for elites and politicians who directly benefit from such investments. Unfortunately, the effects are often more widespread and long term as such practices filter to other public institutions including law enforcement agencies. To this end, greater transparency for Africa's culture of doing business and policies to protect public institutions such as state owned enterprises are essential if African states are to realize true emergence. The need for capacity building to ensure effective institutions and to develop better monitoring and evaluation systems in Africa is key. This may especially hold true for new partnerships such as China where protecting workers' rights and compliance with environmental management have been found wanting at times.

In advocating for African solutions for Africa's development challenges, it is important to highlight that the continent remains rich with possibilities not least because it remains a rich repository of diversity. Given its rich endowment with natural resources, diverse cultures and population the continent is indeed in a good space to direct its future. The ambivalent message often made about Africa's youth as a potential keg waiting to explode should be cast in a more forward looking light to use Africa's youthful population as a developmental dividend rather than a negative factor in Africa's future outlook. The continent's youth have demonstrated passion and energy particularly in embracing new technologies and innovating for entrepreneurship in most cases without state support. The contributions of youth in the informal sectors have led to globally lauded tech-startups which have benefited the poor in areas such as finance and security.

Perhaps what is critical at this juncture is to go beyond identifying problems and their possible solutions but to critically engage on how a shared and Africa-centric vision of the continent's development can be owned by citizens and leaders. Agenda 2063 is a good start and probably begins this journey. Developed by the AU Commission as a successor to the Lagos Plan of Action, Agenda 2063 provides a framework for Africa's future development. The slogan "The Africa we want" suggests inclusivity for African citizenry which some view as deceptive as the vision is still very much a leadership project. Several international forums have interrogated the framework including exploring how it can garner more citizen ownership. How to translate it into a 100% citizen-centric and owned platform will be an important task for the AU and all its partners including member states. A commendable effort on the part of the AU Commission has been the leadership and championship to promote Agenda 2063 including facilitating the first 10-year plan of action and ECOSOCC buy in. Whether the regional economic communities can facilitate and champion more support for the vision including ensuring that countries develop and or align their development plans to the pillars of the Vision document remains to be seen (see Ewusi and Butera 2014 *passim*).

A major challenge facing the AU Commission's vision of making Agenda 2063 the blueprint for Africa's development is funding. The failure to raise resources internally for projects led by the African Union has meant heavy dependence on donor support, which no doubt comes with constraints. As observed during the Symposium's discussions, Africa can ill-afford the illusion that donor support, no matter how well intentioned, comes with no conditions (c.f. Moyo 2010). To this end, a good deal of effort needs to be spent revisiting the idea of domestic financing and ensuring member states pay their dues and contribute to financing the implementation of Agenda 2063. Further, developing more rigorous financing plans including engaging the private sector in Africa should be on the priority of the AU's to do list. Given the sums hemorrhaging from the continent through illicit routes an important step would be to review and improve financial regulatory systems across the continent.

Though the land issue has been a cross cutting theme in this volume, it is a subject that could probably have had greater coverage and more in-depth analysis from the authors. Across the continent, land has been at the core of many disputes and conflicts some of which have led to the displacement of millions of people. Conflict over land resources and some of the conflicts over borders between countries fuel the insecurity experienced by many African citizenry from the time of independence. An area for future research which should be high on Africa's research agenda is the impact of climate change on land resources. Over the last few years, global platforms to discuss climate change particularly COP meetings have highlighted the adverse impacts of climate change on human security including food security. The encroachment of desert in the Sahelian region and loss of land to coastal erosion are some of the examples of problems affecting communities and leading to extreme vulnerability including hunger. Coupled with conflict, poverty, and hunger, climate induced migration has resulted with millions of internally displaced persons across the continent some of whom have little hope of returning to their homelands. It is therefore critical for land to be at the heart of finding solutions for Africa's development problems. In particular, addressing the challenges of Africa's rural-urban migration patterns and urban development should be key. With some of the fastest growing urban zones the continent needs a more strategic approach to urbanisation and development. This subject was highlighted at the Africities Conference held in South Africa at the end of 2015. Further, addressing access to land resources by vulnerable groups including the youth should also be a priority of the continent's leadership. It goes without saying that the majority of the urban poor Africa's youth are disenfranchised and locked in vicious cycles of poverty which can and should be broken. Moreover, the solutions to Africa's development ills also go through building welcoming societies or communities where xenophobia has no place. For this to happen it is imperative to educate host countries on the need to respect migrants' dignity, or to rely on a human rights based approach to migration which promotes sustainable development in the host as well as home country.

In conclusion, this volume has highlighted some of the gaps in research on Africa's development. The AU Commission designated 2015 as the *Year of Women's empowerment and development towards Africa's Agenda 2063*. As a development issue, the situation of women in Africa and more broadly the discourse on gender and development has not gained as much traction as it should across Africa's development agenda. The World Bank, UNWomen and other development agencies have released reports demonstrating the disparities in areas such as access to information, inequalities in paid work and lack of remuneration for care work as some of the main issues driving gender inequalities. This is despite concerted efforts to address the issue of gender inequality across many sectors. This problem is not only facing the African continent, but is a global challenge where data from the EU has also reflected persistent inequalities in paid work and disproportionate representation of women in politics, the private sector and other areas of public life. Similar observations were made in 2015 at the Gender Summit and the World Social Science Forum which were both held in South Africa. As a continent that has endured multi-facetted forms of oppression, the total liberation of Africa's people including fighting gender-based inequalities should be at the core of Africa's development agenda. More urgently, gender–based violence particularly in conflict and post-conflict settings needs greater leadership attention than is currently the case. Failure to do this completely undermines the basic tenets of Agenda

2063 and limits any opportunity of realizing the healthy developmental states Africa aspires to. Until the nearly 50% of Africa's peoples (female) enjoy equal access to development opportunities such as education, jobs, security and peace then the continent will struggle to determine and realize its futures. It is disheartening that the African academy has witnessed lack of support and indeed cuts in funding for gender research and in particular women's studies programs. Given the rise of gender based violence in emerging conflicts and new insurgencies such as those experienced in East and West Africa, it is imperative that resourcing research on gender and social dynamics particularly in the areas of women in peace building is enhanced rather than reduced. The role of CODESRIA in promoting gender research is laudable and exemplary.

The African academy's role in developing Africa-centric globally relevant development knowledge products cannot be overemphasized. Given the low levels of Africa's contribution to global scientific research, researchers need to forge stronger, sustainable partnerships to ensure that research on Africa by Africa-based think tanks and practitioners has global impact and translates into policy informing products. Given the multiplicity of out-of-Africa based research institutes, think tanks and academy, it is apparent that Africa does not lack research material or knowledge fields to be researched. Perhaps what is critical to unlock these opportunities are the basic ingredients of leadership, funding and innovation to optimize the scholarship capabilities of the African academy. Partnerships and collaboration in research and knowledge production are important ventures to strengthen capacity for researchers on the continent particularly where lack of investment and conflict have depleted institutional resources. Finally, the migration of academics from the continent to pursue opportunities elsewhere should be treated in a more positive light to enhance knowledge transfer and exchange as academics by their nature are migratory. The tendency of penalising and or ignoring academic skills and talent when academics seek opportunities elsewhere does not augur well for African academies and in the age of technology and enhanced communications undermines Africa's efforts to develop knowledge economies. Hopefully this volume will encourage further dialogue on these and other issues currently faced by African academics and policy makers. For the student and reader for general reference, this volume provides a guide to some of the topical issues emerging in Africa's post-independence research landscape through the lens of scholars working in African institutions who are also development practitioners par excellence in their daily quest to balance academic jobs and an ever changing sociopolitical and economic landscape.

References

S. K. Ewusi S. K. and J. B. Butera (eds.) 2014 *Beyond state-building Confronting Africa's governance and socio-economic challenges in the 21st Century* Addis Ababa, UPEACE Africa Programme.

Ibrahim M. 2015 Invited Speaker, 11th Annual Nelson Mandela Lecture, Pretoria

Kabukuru W. 2015 'Post-2015 'In whose hands is Africa's future?' *New African* August/September No 553 pp10-16.

Kalombo B. 2015 'Who's who in Africa's roll-call of long-term leaders' *New African* June 2015 No 551 pp40 - 43.

Lopes C. 2015 'It is Africa's time' *New African* October 2015 No 554 pp8 - 10

Mbeki T. 2015 'Order or Disorder? Exploring the implications for Africa' *The Thinker* Q1 Vol. 67 pp10-15.

Moyo D. 2010 *Dead Aid: Why aid is not working and how there is another way for Africa*, London, Penguin

Sall A. 2015. Panel Discussion on the occasion of book launch University of Johannesburg, Pahad A, G. Le Pere G. & M. Strydom M. (eds.) 2015 *Promoting progressive thought leadership*, Pretoria, AISA

New African 2015 *Buying Democracy The fate of elections in Africa* No 549 April 2015

New African 2015 *To go or not to go: The drama over African presidential terms* No 551 June 2015

New African 2015 *Debating the post-2015 Development goals Africa's future in whose hands?* No 553 August/September 2015

Saunders, C. G. A. Dzinesa and D. Nagar (eds.) 2012 *Region-building in Southern Africa Progress, problems and prospects* London, Zed Books.

Notes about the Authors and Editors

Vusi Gumede is a professor at the University of South Africa and Director of the Thabo Mbeki African Leadership Institute. He was previously an associate professor at the University of Johannesburg, he has also lectured public policy at the University of Witwatersrand and lectured economics at the University of Durban-Westville and facilitated research workshops at the University of Mpumalanga. He worked for the South African government, in various capacities, for about twelve years. He serves on various boards and committees, including as Deputy President of the National Council of the South African Association of Political Studies. He has been Distinguished Africanist Scholar at Cornell University and Yale World Fellow at Yale University, among other fellowships. He currently also holds an Honorary Professorship at the University of Cape Town where he lectures economics at the Graduate School of Business. He has published two books on South Africa and edited 9 books focusing on Africa's political economy of development as well as numerous journal articles and book chapters. He is also Editor-in-Chief for *Africanus* (Journal of Development Studies) and for *Africa Insight* as well as member of various Editorial Boards/Committees.

Alinah Kelo Segobye is the Dean of Faculty of Human Sciences at the Namibia University of Science and Technology. She holds an honorary professorship at the Thabo Mbeki African Leadership Institute at the University of South Africa and is a Research Scholar at the African Futures Institute and at the Institute of Economic Research on Innovation at the Tshwane University of Technology. She was a Visiting Scholar at the Rotary Peace Centre at the University of Bradford, served as Deputy Executive Director at the Human Sciences Research Council of South Africa and taught at the University of Botswana. Professor Segobye has extensive teaching, research and consultancy experience in African studies, HIV/AIDS, gender and development. She has authored and co-authored many essays and book chapters on African heritage, culture and development.

Shadrack Gutto is a seasoned professor who was the founding Director of the Institute for African Renaissance Studies at the University of South Africa. He is an expert in constitutional law, international law, Human and People's Rights, Property and Land Rights, and political economy. He was associate professor of Law at the University of the Witwatersrand, Chairperson of the Society of University Law Teachers of Southern Africa, Chairperson of the Rural Legal Trust, Trustee of Black Lawyers Association, among other things. Has published many books and academic/scholarly articles, chapters in books and presented many conference papers and written several commissioned research reports, ad-hoc advisory opinions and policy research. He is a member of various editorial boards of journals such as the *South African Yearbook of International Law and is the editor of International Journal of African Renaissance Studies: Multi-, Inter- and Transdisciplinarity.*

Serges Djoyou Kamga is an associate professor at the Thabo Mbeki African Leadership Institute at the University of South Africa. He previously worked as a Researcher at the Centre for Human Rights at the University of Pretoria, and the South African Institute for Advanced Constitutional, Public, Human Rights and International Law at the University of Johannesburg. He is a member of the Cross-cultural Human Rights Centre. His areas of interest include Leadership and African renaissance, Development and human rights, human rights from a cross-cultural perspective, and disability rights. He has published many journal articles and book chapters as well as two books and he is a co-editor of the *African Disability Rights Yearbook.*

Sabelo J. Ndlovu-Gatsheni is Professor and Director: Scholarship in the Change Management Unit (CMU) in the Vice-Chancellor's Office at the University of South Africa (UNISA). He is the former Head of Archie Mafeje Research Institute for Applied Social Policy (AMRI) based at the University of South Africa. His has published more than ten books and over a hundred articles and book chapters.

Tendayi Sithole is Associate Professor at the Department of Political Sciences. He is the author of *Steve Biko: Decolonial Meditation of Black Consciousness* (New York: Lexington Books, 2016).

Siphamandla Zondi was the Head of the Institute for Global Dialogue at University of South Africa and a faculty member at Thabo Mbeki African Leadership Institute, now Professor of and Head of the Department of Political Sciences at the University of Pretoria.

William Mpofu holds a Doctorate from UNISA. His research interests are in African Literature, Political Communication in the field of semiotics, and the Philosophy of Liberation, in the categories of Coloniality of Power, Coloniality of Knowledge and Coloniality of Being as part of the broad planetary movement of Decoloniality studies.

Akhona Nkenekana is an emerging decolonial scholar whose research interest is on Decoloniality, Decolonial feminism, pan-Africanism and African Renaissance. These are the areas of Research she has written and presented in various international conferences on. Ms Nkenkana also works for Statistics South Africa as a Survey Statistician. She forms part of the alumni of World Economic Forum Global Shapers of Tshwane Hub.

Asanda Fotoyi is a researcher at the Trade and Industrial Policies Strategy. She holds a Master of Commerce in Economics from the Nelson Mandela Metropolitan University. She has a BComm Honours in Economics, and a double major undergraduate degree, BComm Accounting and Economics.

Paul Kwengwere is a researcher based in Malawi with a particular interest in work that pertains to Africa's development, particularly in governance, trade, food security and health. He has worked in banking and investment, public and NGO sectors during his 20-year career. During the time he was doing research for this chapter, Paul was affiliated to Harvard Kennedy School's Ash Center for Democratic Governance and Innovation in Cambridge, Massachusetts, USA (Aug 2012 – July 2013).

Joy Alemazung is a Senior Analyst in the Peace and Security Section of the Global Governance Institute in Brussels, focusing on state transformation and on good governance in Sub-Saharan Africa. He holds a double MA in Political Science and Sociology from the University of Erlangen-Nuremberg and a PhD in Political Science from the University of Kiel. He is currently the Project Manager for political education, development cooperation as well as municipal development program under the German Federal Ministry of Economic Cooperation and Development in the federal states of Bavaria and Baden-Württemberg, Germany.

Westen K Shilaho is a National Research Foundation (NRF) Scarce Skills Post-Doctoral Research Fellow, South African Research Chair (SARChI): African Diplomacy and Foreign Policy, University of Johannesburg. He holds a doctorate in Politics from the University of the Witwatersrand, Johannesburg. The financial assistance of the NRF towards this research is acknowledged. The views expressed are the author's own.

Madeleine C. Fombad is currently a Senior Lecturer at the Department of Information Science at UNISA. She completed a postdoctoral fellowship on Collaborative Governance & Partnerships at the Institute for Corporate Citizenship at UNISA. Her research focus is in knowledge management; information communication technologies accountability and good governance in public-private partnerships (PPPs).

Ogechukwu Ojimaduekwu Ajoku is a lawyer and a consultant. He is a 1997 graduate of law from Abia State University Uturu, Abia state Southeast Nigeria. He obtained his masters degree in 2007 from Ahmadu Bello University Zaria, Kaduna State, Northwest Nigeria. He particularly has interests that border on international trade and investment, developmental law, corporate governance and best practices, human rights, socioeconomic rights crusade, corporate criminal liability.

Salim Bashir Magashi holds an LLB (Abuja) LLM (Nottingham) LLD (Stellenbosch) BL(Lagos) is a Senior Lecturer at the Department of Public Law, Ahmadu Hello University, Zaria. His interests are in international Human rights and Development Law and Constitutional Law in Nigeria.

Babatunde Fagbayibo is currently an Associate Professor in Law at the University of South Africa. His research interests include supranational regionalism, African Union, transnational policy development, and governance and democratisation in Africa. His writings have been published in a number of academic journals, as chapters in books, online platforms, and also serves as a commentator on African issues for print and broadcast media. He is a South African National Research Foundation (NRF) rated researcher. In 2014, he was recognised by the Young People in International Affairs (YPIA) as one of the top 35 Africans under the age of 35, for his research on supranational integration in Africa. He currently serves as the assistant editor of the Southern African Public Law journal and also a member of the editorial board of the African Journal of Democracy and Governance (RADG).

Dejo Olowu is Research Professor of Law (Public Law and Legal Philosophy), Faculty of Law, North-West University, Mafikeng Campus, South Africa.

Mubarak Tijani Adekilekun is a Lecturer in the Department of Business Law, Faculty of Law, University of Ilorin, Nigeria. He is a member of the Procurement Law Academic Network (PLAN), UK; Member, Law Teachers Association of Nigeria and also member of the Nigeria Bar Association (NBA). He is an alumnus of the University of Malaya, Malaysia. His area of teaching and research include Company law and legal aspect of Public-Private Partnerships (PPPs).

Ching Chuan Gan is a distinguished academic and expert in Administrative Law. He is an Associate Professor in the Faculty of Business, Curtin University, Sarawak Malaysia. He is an alumnus of the University of Malaya and University of London (Queen Mary). He is a member of the Procurement Law Academic Network (PLAN), UK. His area of teaching and research include advanced administrative law and law of marine insurance.

Victoria T. Qhobosheane is a Research Coordinator at the Thabo Mbeki institute of Africa Leadership at Unisa. She is a researcher and policy analyst and holds an MBA.

Amos Saurombe serves as the Head of Graduate Studies, Research and Innovation in the College of Law. He is a 'Y' NRF rated researcher, a member of the Southern African Academy of Science (SAYAS) and Chair of the SADC/SAPOA Universities Research Board. He writes and presents widely on issues of regional integration, international trade law and Intellectual Property Rights.

Menzi Dlamini is a Phd Candidate in Agricultural Economics with the University of KwaZulu Natal. Mr Dlamini is an agricultural economist with over 10yrs experience in the agricultural sector. He has experience in agri business development, farm project management and investment facilitation within the agriculture sector. As a researcher, he has an interest in rural livehoods, rural and agricultural finance as well as large scale land acquisitions.

Ayodel Odusola is a Chief Economist and Head of Strategy and Analysis, UNDP Regional Bureau for Africa, New York.

Robert Home is Professor in Land Management at Anglia Ruskin University (UK). He has undertaken research and consultancy in many African countries, and his published books include 'Demystifing the Mystery of Capital' (on land titling in Botswana, Trinidad and Zambia), 'Of Planting and Planning' (on British colonial town planning) and two edited books on African land law (through Pretoria University Law Press and the World Bank.

Chadzimula O. Molebatsi teaches in the Department of Architecture and Planning, University of Botswana. His most recent research is on the democratisation of the urban planning process. He has published widely in the areas of settlement planning and environment. Dr Molebatsi is actively involved in community development initiatives in various parts of Botswana.

Oluborode Jegede holds an LLD (Human Rights), Centre for Human Rights, Faculty of Law, and University of Pretoria.

Index

O

P

R

S

T

U

V

W

X